Also by Gordon Bowker

Inside George Orwell: A Biography

Through the Dark Labyrinth: A Biography of Lawrence Durrell

Pursued by Furies: A Life of Malcolm Lowry

James Joyce

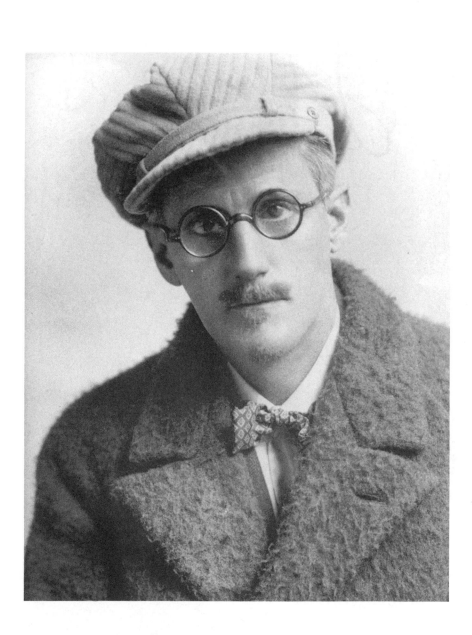

James Joyce

A NEW BIOGRAPHY

Gordon Bowker

FARRAR, STRAUS AND GIROUX   NEW YORK

Farrar, Straus and Giroux
18 West 18th Street, New York 10011

Copyright © 2011 by Gordon Bowker
All rights reserved
Printed in the United States of America
Originally published in 2011 by Weidenfeld & Nicolson, Great Britain
Published in the United States by Farrar, Straus and Giroux
First American edition, 2012

Library of Congress Cataloging-in-Publication Data
Bowker, Gordon.
  James Joyce : a biography / Gordon Bowker. — 1st American ed.
    p. cm.
  Includes bibliographical references and index.
  ISBN 978-0-374-17872-7 (alk. paper)
    1. Joyce, James, 1882–1941. 2. Authors, Irish—20th century—Biography.
  I. Title.

PR6019.O9 Z52616
823'.912—dc23
[B]

2011045954

www.fsgbooks.com

1   3   5   7   9   10   8   6   4   2

Frontispiece: Joyce holidaying at Bognor in 1923. The author of Ulysses, *suddenly absurdly wealthy thanks to the generosity of his eccentric patron Harriet Weaver, is here sporting a suitably eccentric hat to celebrate his newly bestowed riches.*

To Rhoda, who was there
at every step

Contents

Illustrations

1. Joyce as a child (Poetry Collection, NYU at Buffalo)
2. The Joyce family, 1888 (Poetry Collection, NYU at Buffalo)
3. Graduation photograph, October 1902 (Poetry Collection, NYU at Buffalo)
4. At University College, Dublin, 1902 (Poetry Collection, NYU at Buffalo)
5. Postcard to Byrne from Paris, 1902 (Beinecke Library, Yale University)
6. Oliver St John Gogarty
7. The Martello Tower, Sandycove (Courtesy of the *Irish Times*)
8. Joyce in his friend Curran's garden, 1904 (Poetry Collection, NYU at Buffalo)
9. W. B. Yeats
10. No. 7 Eccles Street, Dublin
11. Nora, c. 1904
12. Alessandro Francini Bruni
13. Svevo family
14. Amalia Popper
15. Giorgio and Lucia at window (Poetry Collection, NYU at Buffalo)
16. Roberto Prezioso
17. Stanislaus Joyce, c. 1906
18. Schaureks' wedding
19. Nora as Cathleen in Synge's *Riders to the Sea* (Beinecke Library, Yale University)
20. Nora, Giorgio and Lucia, Zurich, 1918
21. Joyce in Trieste, 1914, author of *Chamber Music* (Poetry Collection, NYU at Buffalo)
22. Frank Budgen

Acknowledgements

Almost all biographers stand on the shoulders of their predecessors, and the biographers of Joyce and the Joyce family I have benefited from reading are Richard Ellmann, Herbert Gorman, Peter Costello, John McCourt, Brenda Maddox, Carol Loeb Shloss and Edna O'Brien. I also owe a debt to the many friends and acquaintances of Joyce who left behind reminiscences of him, as well as the scholars whose work has informed the writing of this book.

Along the way, I have also received help from Dr Thomas Staley (Harry Ransom Center, University of Texas at Austin) and Professor Robert Spoo (University of Tulsa), who kindly read the manuscript and offered advice and encouragement. Dione Venables, Michael Beasley and Anna Pollard also read the book in earlier drafts and made valuable suggestions. Others who were helpful at various stages were Cecily Mackworth, Desmond Hawkins, Jan Gabrial Lowry, Gordon and Sheila Robinson, Brian and Doris Southam, Sue Huitt, Phyllis Corr and Peter Mulligan.

In getting this project started and finished, I owe special thanks to Anthony Goff, my agent, his colleagues Georgia Glover, Marigold Atkey and Nann du Sautoy, to Alan Samson, my publisher, who commissioned the book and offered unfailing support throughout its long gestation, to Bea Hemming, my patient editor, and to Jane Birkett and Dr Anthony Hippisley for meticulously correcting the proofs.

In researching this book I am in debt to the following: Ciara McDonnell and Tom Desmond of the National Library of Ireland, Gill Furlong at the University College (London) Library Manuscripts Collection, Helen Monaghan and the staff of the James Joyce Centre, Dublin, Lori Curtis and Melissa Burkhardt of the University of Tulsa, Dr Fritz Senn of the James Joyce Foundation, Zurich, Professor Dr Christoph Eggenberger, Director of the Zentralbibliothek, Zürich, Sigrid Krause of the Staatsbibliothek zu Berlin, Edda Tasiemka of the Tasiemka Newspaper Cutting library, London, Sarah Brown of the Brotherton Library, Leeds, and staff at the British Library, the London Library, the National Archives, Kew, the BBC Written Archives, Princeton University Library, Trinity College Library, Dublin, the Joyce Centre, Trieste, the Bibliotheque Jacques Ducet, Paris, the Irish Registry Office, the UK General Register Office, Cambridge University Law Library, Reading University Library, Bognor Regis Local History Library, Worthing Local History Library, Torquay Public Library, Kensington & Chelsea Local History Library, the Library of St Mary's College, Strawberry Hill, Cornell University Library, the University of Wisconsin Library, The Huntington Library, the Harry Ransom Center, Austin, Texas, Marquette University Library, the Library of Congress, Washington, Glasgow University Library, Sussex University Library, Moira Fitzgerald at the Beinecke Library, Yale University, Pamela Hackbart of the Morris Library, Southern Illinois University at Carbondale, Andreas Weigel, Dr Michael Basinki and Dr James Maynard at the Poetry Collection, New York University at Buffalo, and the following helpful and informative individuals: Ronan Kelly, Caitríona Cullen, Dr Paul Vanderham, Madame Fourny of Pornichet, and the Mayor of Saint-Gérand-de-Puy.

Finally, I would like to thank my editors, Jonathan Galassi and Miranda Popkey of Farrar, Straus and Giroux, and my agent, Phyllis Westberg of Harold Ober Associates, for their help and enthusiasm in bringing the book out in the United States.

James
Joyce

Epiphanies

Late one night in the second week of August 1898, a college boy of sixteen left a Dublin theatre (the Gaiety) with his father and a friend. They had just seen a play called *Sweet Briar*. He was a pious boy, but the play had left him strangely aroused, and on the way home he parted from the others to walk alone, to contemplate and pray. The religious life, the priestly vocation, had a powerful attraction for him, but recently he had been assailed by temptations of the flesh, thoughts that he had banished only by revealing them to his Jesuit confessor. He had much to dwell upon as he strode off into the night. Coming to a canal, he decided to follow the tow-path. He had not gone far before a shadowy figure approached him – a woman. She had a cigarette in her hand and asked for a light. He apologized, explaining that he carried no matches. His youthful voice seemed to animate her, and she suddenly pressed herself against him, asking whether he liked girls. The boy felt overwhelmed and confused. Her hands were exploring his body and before he knew what had happened he was pulled to the ground and deftly seduced. From that moment onward his life would be changed for ever. Darkness would no longer be the haunt of the wicked, but an enshrouding milieu, exciting beyond all imagination. His Jesuitical conscience now had something serious with which to contend. He did not, on this occasion, confess what had happened to the college priest but took his guilt to a church where he was unknown. Thereafter he began to skip confession, to neglect his biblical studies and embrace art as passionately as he had previously embraced religion. Gradually the vocation of artist would displace that of the Jesuit priesthood.

It was 10 June 1904. A young man was sauntering along Nassau Street in Dublin when he spotted a head of luxurious red hair. He turned and, as if drawn by a powerful magnet, sidled up to the girl and doffed the yachting cap which sat at a rakish angle over his left eyebrow. They immediately struck up a flirtatious conversation, and he was soon aware that he had captured not just her attention but also her interest. Despite her playful pretence of rebuffing him, a glint of coquettish amusement in the girl's eyes encouraged him enough to try coaxing her to meet him again a few days later. She tossed her head and laughed – the deep, knowing laugh of an enchantress – and, in a voice which sang of the Irish west, quickly agreed, then skipped off along the pavement, smiling at the thought of her unexpected conquest and the prospect of adventure to come. The young man gazed after her, his eyes squinting, trying to keep her in focus, but the redhead finally disappeared from view along the busy pavement running beside the high walls of Trinity College. This brief encounter was to change not just the course of her life and the life of the young man in the yachting cap but the whole course of twentieth-century literature. A master had just stumbled into his Irish muse.

On Sunday 17 April 1932, the weather in Paris was sunny and mild, though showers from the east were forecast. The platform for the Calais-bound boat train at the Gare du Nord was more than usually crowded. One party struggled through the crowd towards its reserved compartment, accompanied by a trunk and a variety of other much-labelled baggage. Their belongings were taken aboard and the porters returned to wrestle the heavy trunk up the steps to the luggage compartment at the end of the coach. A tall thin man in dark glasses who stood supervising all this finally seemed satisfied. The well-dressed, matronly figure beside him looked on coolly and the somewhat distracted young woman who moved about, nervously tugging and tweaking at the hat in her hand, grew ever more agitated.

The man turned and held out a hand, beckoning the others to board the train. The matron turned towards the younger woman and gestured impatiently. Suddenly a piercing shriek rent the air, bringing the bustling platform to a breathtaking halt. The distracted young woman had erupted with a great howl, flinging her arms out as if fighting off an invisible monster. In this catatonic position she froze, but the shrieks continued as a great never-ending wail of anguish. People turned and converged on the girl, fearing that she had been attacked or had been struck with sudden pain. The man in dark glasses, her father, it transpired, took hold of her and tried in vain to hush her up and urge her aboard the waiting train. The matron, her mother, joined in but all to no avail. People crowded round offering advice, but the man in dark glasses shrank from the crush as if fearing any kind of contact with the gaping onlookers. In a moment he had summoned a porter and issued an order. The porter in turn summoned a colleague and together they began unloading the baggage they had carefully and laboriously stowed away a few minutes earlier. The man and woman now held the girl, whose shrieks had subsided to a whimper. She had, it seemed, got her way and this family would not, after all, be leaving on the boat train for England that day.

The tall thin man behind the shades was, of course, James Joyce, the mother was Nora Barnacle Joyce and the distraught daughter was Lucia, a strange, impulsive young woman, wilful and talented and only too aware of her father's reputation as a genius of modern literature. After this traumatic event, Joyce's great labyrinthine *Work in Progress* (later unveiled as *Finnegans Wake*), the nocturnal offspring of his earlier novel, *Ulysses*, ground to a halt. When it restarted, disturbing personal themes would begin to weave themselves into it, leaving him open to dark and prurient suspicions.

Preface

The past exudes legend: one can't make pure clay of time's mud.
There is no life that can be recaptured wholly; as it was. Which is to
say that all biography is ultimately fiction.

Bernard Malamud, *Dubin's Lives* (1979)

In almost every poll taken in recent years, *Ulysses* has been acclaimed the
greatest novel of the twentieth century. Among critics and intellectuals it
is generally regarded as one of the outstanding landmarks of literary
modernism, as important, say, as T. S. Eliot's *The Waste Land*, in expressing
the experimental and international spirit of post-war Europe in the 1920s.
From any point of view, of all the 'modernists', James Joyce has had
probably the most lasting effect on serious fiction. Even so, his impact
was not immediate, and *Ulysses* was still not widely available in unexpurgated form until shortly before his death. However, the slow but
certain impact of that book on the wider consciousness is mirrored in the
gradual but inexorable progress towards permissiveness in the West. Eliot
said Joyce had 'killed the nineteenth century' and Edmund Wilson called
him 'the great poet of a new phase of the human consciousness'.

The 'riverrun' of Joyce's life was a never-ending escape route into exile
of the sort often taken by creative writers in search of a broader vision.
His fight against Irish parochial prejudices and Anglo-Irish censoriousness
casts him in a heroic light. Under the influence mainly of Ibsen, Zola
and Maupassant, he embraced realism, writing fearlessly about the more
squalid aspects of human life. And yet his considerable poetic and comic
gifts enabled him to lend an aspect of beauty and humour to what many
regard as repugnant.

Joyce's religious dedication to authorship also picks him out as a writer
in the romantic tradition of total commitment, suffering near poverty
and financial dependency for much of his life in his determination simply
to write. He was fortunate in his sponsors. Certain women (Dora Marsden,
Edith McCormick, Harriet Shaw Weaver, Jane Heap, Margaret Anderson,
Sylvia Beach and Adrienne Monnier in particular) ensured that he was
able to concentrate fully on his great works, *Ulysses* and *Finnegans Wake*,
and see them published.

From a fading middle-class background, James Joyce, born a Dubliner, became riveted and possessed, even in exile, by the Dublin of his youth. But he needed to escape the suffocating atmosphere of British Ireland and the paralysing grip of Irish Catholicism to find in Europe a milieu in which his art might flourish. That experience fed into his writing a stream of important influences and ideas, but as his reputation grew, he retreated further – into a tight circle of friends and admirers and the strange world of his fiction. This withdrawal, however, only added to his mystery and fame. As war approached or the intellectual climate changed, he moved on – to Paris, Trieste, Zurich, and back to Paris. He escaped one final time – from Vichy France to neutral Switzerland in 1940 – and died shortly afterwards, far removed from most of his friends and remote from his Dublin family, in the obscurity of a Zurich hospital.

Following his death, critics and scholars set out to explore and anatomize the remains of a great life – the progress, the work, and the extraordinary mental landscape. Apart from Shakespeare and the Bible, Joyce has probably spawned one of the most extensive bodies of analytical and interpretive scholarship of all time. Since his death, editions of his work, some well annotated, have continued to appear, the flood of critical tomes and articles has never abated, literary journals have been devoted exclusively to him, and numerous film adaptations, radio and television programmes have featured his life and work.

Joyce's fiction is highly autobiographical, but it is also fiction and therefore shaped by the author into a form that served his many purposes in writing and presenting himself to the world as an artist. *Dubliners*, his first book of fiction, reflects the world in which he grew up – turn-of-the-century Ireland – and many of the characters, whose identities he hardly bothered to disguise, were people known to him. But what his more perceptive early critics noticed was its revolutionary narrative technique, and the unusual economy and bite of his prose. *A Portrait of the Artist as a Young Man* is both an extended confession and a droll commentary on the young life of Stephen Dedalus, a Catholic schoolboy with intimations of immortality, which, together with *Dubliners*, can be regarded as portents of the greater works to come.

Ulysses takes the reader for a whole day and night's jaunt seen through the eyes and imagination of an older Stephen and the Jewish Everyman, Leopold Bloom, around the streets of Dublin on 16 June 1904. En route, they encounter a multifarious cast of Joyce's acquaintances in a literary free-for-all satirizing a series of styles and genres, closely mimicking the form and spirit of Homer's *Odyssey*[1] and the form and spirit of an old society confronting modernity. 'With *Ulysses*,' declared Edmund Wilson, 'Joyce has brought into literature a new and unknown beauty.'

Finnegans Wake, his final work, is a tidal wave of teasing verbal conjuration – a dream-like play of voices, the meaning of which is as slippery as the multitude of allusions milling around and interpenetrating the prose. As Joyce himself explained, while *Ulysses* deals with day and the conscious mind, *Finnegans Wake* deals with night and the unconscious mind – the single night's sleep of a single if polymorphous character. Although it seems formless and chaotic, it has a strange coherence, a mysterious music, and tells its own hidden story, enriched by great myths and legends. Joyce was, as Wilson has pointed out, 'the great poet of a new phase of the human consciousness', whose influence has gone deeper than literature. Like D.H. Lawrence, he was aware of the fluidity of human identity, the malleability and unreliability of perceived reality and representations of reality.

To his innovative use of the *monologue intérieur* (or 'stream-of-consciousness'), Joyce brought a curiosity about the working of his own mind and the minds of those around him. This coincided with the growing interest in Freud's explorations of the human unconscious. And, even though he rejected psychoanalysis, *Ulysses* in its own way followed the same path, drawing deeply on traditional sources while using the imagination rather than reason as his guide.

But Joyce was not simply a serious-minded experimenter who took the modernist novel to its ultimate conclusion. He was a great and playful satirist with a highly developed comic imagination. Once, asked about *Ulysses*, he replied, 'I've put in so many enigmas and puzzles that it'll keep the professors busy for centuries arguing over what I meant.' *Finnegans Wake*, he said, no doubt with a hint of irony, was intended as nothing less than 'a history of the world'.

His life was not without its problems, dogged as it was for many years by near poverty, failing eyesight, and the mental illness of his daughter, Lucia. He suffered also the slings and arrows of uncomprehending critics, including some fellow modernists, among them Gertrude Stein and Virginia Woolf, while Lawrence complained that *Ulysses* was 'more disgusting than Casanova'. Lawrence's disdain was reciprocated, and in 1929, given the opportunity to meet the author of *The Rainbow*, Joyce refused, calling him 'a propagandist and a very bad writer'.

Any survey of modern literature reveals how widespread and profound the impact of *Ulysses* has been. Those who have been clearly influenced by Joyce include Virginia Woolf, John Dos Passos, Eugene O'Neill, William Faulkner, Samuel Beckett, Djuna Barnes, Anthony Burgess, Jorge Luis Borges, Umberto Eco, Salman Rushdie, and just about every modern writer who has chosen to experiment with the novel form rather than remain confined within its traditional limitations.

The importance of Joyce has grown, and his greatest work has come to stand as a touchstone of perfection with fiction writers, ever more conscious of their craft. Anthony Burgess said that whenever he sat down to write a novel it was with a sense of despair because he knew he could never match *Ulysses*. George Orwell, who found the novel inspiring, came to regret having read it because it made him feel inadequate. Eliot and Thornton Wilder said much the same while Virginia Woolf regretted having read it for other reasons.

The first full biography of Joyce, by Herbert Gorman, published in 1939, was shaped and edited in significant ways by Joyce himself. Richard Ellmann's biography, written after Joyce's death but influenced by some of his friends, was first published in 1959, and regarded as a milestone in literary biography. A revised edition appeared in 1982, and since then, Peter Costello's *James Joyce: The Years of Growth, 1882–1915* and John McCourt's *The Years of Bloom: Joyce in Trieste, 1904–1920*, have added freshly unearthed detail to the story. The same goes for John Wyse Jackson and Peter Costello's biography of Joyce's father, John Stanislaus Joyce, Brenda Maddox's life of his wife Nora, and that of his daughter Lucia, by Carol Loeb Shloss.[2] Drawing on these accounts and on more recently discovered material this biography will attempt to go beyond the mere facts and tap into Joyce's elusive consciousness. Furthermore, the work is informed by the belief that it is enlightening to view the work of a highly autobiographical writer like Joyce in the context of his life.

A character with many facets, he was very conscious of his image and often 'on stage' – certainly as a teacher and always as 'the great writer'. In these roles we can glimpse Joyce from revealing moments (epiphanies) in his fiction or reflected in the memories of others. There was, therefore, the Joyce of wide repute – the reclusive, near-blind genius trapped in a world of darkness, a remote and superior eminence who chose 'silence, exile and cunning', a merry toper who would dance a jig as the spirit took him, the pornographer obsessed with scatological fantasies, and the very correct gentleman with an aversion to obscenity. There are also the complex series of self-created alter egos – Stephen Dedalus (in *A Portrait of the Artist*), Leopold Bloom (in *Ulysses*), Giacomo (in *Giacomo Joyce*), Humphrey Chimpden Earwicker and Shem the Penman (in *Finnegans Wake*). Beyond that there is Joyce the letter-writer in confessional mood, lifting the mask to allow us glimpses of the inner being.

Like most writers of genius, Joyce was a man of contradictions. He loved his father yet reacted against his tyranny; he loved his mother but spurned her intense Catholicism; he loved Ireland but not its romanticization; he grew up an Irish nationalist but rejected the Ireland that nationalism created; he loved the English language yet attempted to reshape and reinvent it; he grew up hostile to Britain but had a lingering attachment to it. This pattern of ambivalence lies at the heart of the man and goes some way towards explaining the many facets, contradictions and convolutions of a tortuous mind. As a child, because of his placid temperament, he was known as 'Sunny Jim'; as an adult he was dubbed 'Herr Satan'. He was an unflinching realist yet was deeply superstitious and steeped himself in myth and legend. He was immersed in the past yet set the future course of serious modern fiction.

Certain attitudes and sentiments dominated Joyce's personality. He had a fascination for, and understanding of, women, yet he could also be misogynistic (though rarely after the early stressful years of his marriage), and a woman very close to him, his own daughter, baffled him utterly. He was intensely curious about Jews and Jewish life (the 'Bloom' side of him), and although some of his family (his wife in particular) sometimes expressed anti-Semitic prejudice, Joyce himself never did.[3] At the end of his life he was so moved by the plight of European Jewry that he directly aided individual Jews and Jewish families to escape the Nazis.

Writers draw on their lives for fictional purposes, but it is considered a mistake to draw on fiction for biographical purposes, even on highly autobiographical novels like *Stephen Hero* and its revised version, *A Portrait of the Artist as a Young Man*. After all, while based on real lives such fictions are created retrospectively, and shaped by unfettered imagination. Added to that, Joyce was adept at cultivating and projecting an image – a further source of unreality. When he did allow a biography of himself to be written, he was careful to ensure that it remained under his control.

However, although autobiographical fiction must always be suspect biography, this cannot mean that it is of no value whatever to biographers, especially where their purpose is to explore the inner lives of their subjects. Novels and stories are, after all, traces and reflections of mental effort and have some place in the history of their author's consciousness – the movement of a mind and imagination through time. Writers do reveal themselves in some fashion through their creative work, and sometimes it should be possible to say that a passage in an autobiographical novel chimes with known facts or thoughts expressed in other forms, or offers a motivation for this or that course of action. Biographies, too, require a creative effort if we are to get beyond the mere exteriority of a life.

Joyce presents the biographer with a set of particular problems. His letters and manuscripts are widely dispersed throughout Europe and America. There are gaps in the story due to correspondence having been destroyed (many of his letters to his wife Nora, to his brother Charlie and sister Margaret, for example). Some influential accounts of Joyce's life appear to reflect the controlling hand of Joyce himself (Herbert Gorman's biography, and Frank Budgen's story of the writing of *Ulysses*) or of significant figures in his life, such as his brother Stanislaus and Maria Jolas (Richard Ellmann's biography). Fortunately, new material and the work of various scholars have helped clarify some of the resulting distortions, though no doubt others persist. In attempting to tap into the flow of Joyce's consciousness it is possible to glimpse a figure both fraught with contradictions and beset by deep feelings of guilt and self-doubt, even teetering on the edge of madness. But his many faults cannot blind one to the undoubted genius that shines through and manifests itself in his great achievements.

Sorting through the relics of a life is not unlike sorting through the tangled wreckage of a deserted house – windows shattered, rooms in chaos, bits of broken furniture, smashed china, books and papers torn and scattered, smithereens of mirrors bouncing back flashes of fractured sunlight and fragmented images. Amid the chaos we may catch a fleeting impression of what the place once was like when occupied, a presumption of lives lived, of memories stored and passions spent. Salvaging all the scattered pieces and reassembling them can only produce an approximation of the original, and the drama of ghostly existences will depend on efforts of imagination as much as accumulations of fact.

1

Past Imperfect

(1800–1882)

'The past is not past. It is present here and now.' Joyce, *Exiles*

In a class-conscious society like British Ireland at the turn of the twentieth century, family origin was the main determinant of social status. For John Stanislaus Joyce and his son James, identity was inseparable from family – its historical line and ramifications. The ancestral presence reminded them of who they were and reinforced their sense of social distinction. As James's father began to squander his inheritance and the family descended into poverty, asserting claims to a distinguished ancestry became ever more important to him. Family associations, escutcheons and portraits became more meaningful, and the family legend passed on to his children became increasingly colourful and inventive.

Two ideas were very important to James Joyce – that the Joyce family had distant Scandinavian origins, and that Daniel O'Connell, the Liberator, was a paternal ancestor. From his father he inherited portraits of various ghostly forebears, to which he added family portraits of his own. He had a close relationship with his mother and his bond with his father was strong and formative enough for many of the old man's eccentricities to shape his own personality. But he had very little time for his siblings, except Stanislaus, his next-eldest brother, George who died young, and Mabel who suffered the same fate. Consequently for him, as time went by, the past was more immediate than the present, and became the chosen playground of his fiction.

His family had its Irish roots, he claimed, somewhere in the so-called Joyce country of County Galway, in the far west of Ireland, whence, it is said, come *all* Irish Joyces. They had migrated from Normandy to Wales following William's conquest of England, and thence to Galway following Cromwell's conquest of Ireland. For any imagination haunted by ghosts, here was a rich legendary past to inhabit and explore – as Joyce did in *Finnegans Wake*.[1] But his immediate branch of the family, the historically present Joyces, had by the very late eighteenth century gravitated southwards to County Cork, 'a southern offshoot of the tribe', or so he claimed.[2]

The Joyces' recorded history originates with a certain George Joyce of Fermoy who begat the author's great-grandfather, James, born in Cork and married to Anne McCann, an Ulsterwoman. Great-Grandfather Joyce, a lime burner by trade, was by repute 'a fierce old fire-eater' and probably a member of the Whiteboys, a secret terrorist group operating in Munster during the 1820s, attacking the larger landed properties and acting to defend tenant farmers. He was said to have been arrested, tried, and barely escaped hanging, living on to establish himself as a successful building contractor.

According to Peter Costello, unlike his strong-willed forebears, the son of James and Anne Joyce, James Augustine Joyce (1827–66), another Corkman, was 'little more than a feckless charmer; a typical man of the third generation only too happy to spend what his father and grandfather had won.'[3] He was a horse-trader and reckless gambler who lost a great deal of money. Perhaps in the hope of stemming his excesses, his family married him off to a woman ten years his senior, Ellen O'Connell, an ex-nun. She was a member of the extensive O'Connell clan which included the great Daniel, MP for Clare and a dominant force in Irish politics during the first half of the nineteenth century. When James Augustine's business eventually failed, his father-in-law, Alderman John O'Connell, secured him a sinecure as Inspector of Hackney Coaches (or 'jingles'), with an office in the City Hall. Here, it has been suggested, is where the idea that the world owed the Joyces a living, which the author's father evidently inherited, first took root.[4]

John Stanislaus Joyce, James's only offspring, was born in Cork city on 4 July 1849. James proved an affable father, but Ellen a sour and censorious mother. Although John was coached by a pious aunt, who later took the veil, he eventually became anticlerical, possibly influenced by his grandfather, old James Joyce, who believed that religion was only for women.

Intent on transforming his son into a gentleman able to move in the highest circles of Irish society, on St Patrick's Day, 1859, John's father entered him at the newly established St Colman's College in Fermoy, but he was to remain under priestly eyes for barely a year. The youngest boy in the college, he was said to have been spoiled, and although not much of a scholar, acquired a ready wit and gained a familiarity with the priesthood which later he came to despise. He began to imbibe ideas of Fenianism from these men of the cloth and other boys at the college, as well as from those of his relatives prominent in Irish politics. Music and singing, a significant part of college life, became a significant part of John's life. He had 'a good treble voice', it was said, and 'sang at concerts at an early age',[5] acquiring a passion for operatic arias and old Irish ballads, a passion communicated to James, the son who took after him most. Some of his favourite songs, such as 'Blarney Castle', formed part of young James's repertoire, and 'The Last Rose of Summer' became Mina Kennedy's favourite song in the 'Sirens' episode of *Ulysses*. John's stay at St Colman's was curtailed when he was withdrawn on 19 February 1860, either because his fees were unpaid, or after a severe attack of rheumatic fever rendered almost lethal by typhoid.[6] After that, most likely he completed his education under private tuition.

After St Colman's, John's parents resolved to build him up, and he began a programme of cold baths, exercise, rowing and athletics, which he claimed accounted for his relative longevity. There are allusions to this Spartan lifestyle in James's story 'The Sisters', and in *Ulysses* in Bloom's interest in the exercises of the German strongman, Eugen Sandow.[7] As part of this regime, John's father arranged for him to work aboard a Cork Harbour pilot boat. There he acquired a stomach for sea travel and what his biographers call a 'vocabulary of abuse that for years was the delight of his bar-room cronies',[8] able to draw upon a whole lexicon of inventive expletives. Favourites included 'Shite and onions!', 'I'll make you smell hell!' and, when things went badly for him later, 'Curse your bloody blatant soul ... Ye dirty pissabed, ye bloody-looking crooked-eyed son of a bitch. Ye dirty bloody corner-boy, you've a mouth like a bloody nigger.'[9] The story of the seaman (D.B. Murphy) encountered by Bloom and Stephen at the cabman's shelter in the 'Eumeus' episode of *Ulysses*, full of hair-raising stories of treacherous foreigners, has the smack of John Stanislaus, the young salt, knocking around Cork Harbour. And the songs of Italian sailors, alluded to in the 'Sirens' episode, must have passed through John's musical memory into the creative imagination of his son.

Later in life he followed the hounds, a love of the chase caught presumably from his father's love of horses. 'Begor, hunting was the game for me,' he told a journalist in old age.[10] This passion is given voice in *Ulysses*, when, in 'Circe', the hunting cries 'Holà! Hillyho!' and 'Bulblul Burblblburblb! Hai, boy!' echo between Bloom and Stephen amid the surrealistic anarchy of Bella Cohen's whorehouse. And John's habit of regular long walks around Dublin and environs, caught by his children, foreshadows the wandering narrative line which snakes through most of his son's fiction.

Politics was a running theme throughout John's life. As well as the Fenianism imbibed as a schoolboy, two O'Connell uncles became town councillors in Cork, and one of his cousins, Peter Paul McSwiney, became Lord Mayor of Dublin. The 1860s saw the resurgence of a Fenian movement prepared to take up arms to liberate Ireland. Under their leader, James Stephens, they led an abortive uprising in February 1867, resulting in imprisonment for the rebels. The movement's conspiratorial air appealed to John, and while the extent of his involvement with it is unknown, escaping to university might have saved him from a stint behind bars.

Although he gained entry to Queen's College, Cork, in October 1866, the death of John's father, who was barely forty, delayed his starting there until the following year. He chose to study medicine and found life as a medical student highly congenial – the conviviality, the drinking, the swapping of obscene anecdotes. Cherished memories of those carefree days were passed to his son who fed them into *A Portrait of the Artist*. John is said to have had 'stage presence', and the demands of student life did not prevent him from acting, singing comic songs at college concerts (including the then-popular 'Tim Finnegan's Wake'), and throwing himself into college sports. He was especially keen on field athletics and cricket, a passion his literary son inherited. In the 'Lotus-Eaters' chapter of *Ulysses*, Joyce recalls one celebrated Dublin cricketing hero:

Heavenly weather really [muses Bloom] … Cricket weather. Sit around under sunshades. Over after over. Out … Duck for six wickets. Still Captain Buller broke a window in the Kildare street club with a slog to square leg.[11]

John failed his second-year exams, and returned to college for a further year before leaving without a degree.

In July 1870, at the age of twenty-one, he came into part of his inheritance, including properties in Cork yielding an annual income of some £500 from rents. Almost simultaneously the Franco-Prussian War broke out. It caused a sensation in Cork, with demonstrations and Irish volunteers rushing to the aid of the embattled Catholic French. John decided to join the fray, only to be intercepted in London by his mother and shipped straight back home. She was also alert to any female entanglements she considered unsuitable, and John's affairs were often cut short by maternal intervention. However, he was not deterred. As a young man, according to James, his father was 'a conqueror of women'. This reckless pursuit of the female once led, it seems, to a venereal infection, though his claim to have cured himself of a syphilitic chancre seems exaggerated. The idea that inherited syphilis led to his favourite son's later near-blindness has been argued and discounted, John never having shown any of the advanced symptoms of the disease. Nevertheless, that James may himself have contracted some sexual infection leading to rheumatic and ocular afflictions is not entirely improbable.[12]

Following university, John's life began to progress. After a few years as an accountant he took a job, for £300 a year and a £500 shareholding, as secretary of a distillery established by Henry Alleyn, a Cork businessman, at Chapelizod (meaning 'the Chapel of Isolde'). This Dublin suburb with legendary associations would capture the imagination of his son, the author, who made it the home of James Duffy in his short story 'A Painful Case', and is the setting of Joseph Sheridan Le Fanu's 1861 novel, *The House by the Churchyard*, which features in *Finnegans Wake*. Robert Broadbent of Chapelizod, a friend of John's, owned the Mullingar Hotel which became in the novel the home of landlord Humphrey Chimpden Earwicker, him of the ambiguously recurrent initials. H.C.E. (Here Comes Everybody; Haveth Childers Everywhere) owed something to Hugh C. E. Childers, Gladstone's Chancellor and Secretary of State for War, an Irish Home Ruler, whom John met at Dublin's United Liberal Club in 1880.[13]

To his various pastimes John now added yachting around the mouth of the River Liffey and into Dublin Bay, and serious opera-going. He delighted in the great singers who visited Dublin during that period. John himself had developed a fine tenor voice, and sang occasionally in concerts at Dublin's Antient Concert Rooms. He was thrilled on being told that he had been declared 'the best tenor in Ireland' by Barton McGuckin, a celebrated singer with the Carl Rosa Opera Company – a story he never tired of repeating to anyone who cared or did not care to listen.

At that time, Dublin musical culture was suffused with a passion for opera. As Joyce told Stuart Gilbert:

> One of the most remarkable features of Dublin life in the heyday of Mr Bloom [and John Joyce] was the boundless enthusiasm of all classes of citizens for music, especially of the vocal and operatic varieties ... and their cult of the divo, carried to a degree unknown even in Italy.[14]

The lasting and profound influence of this enthusiasm on James has been well noted, and Peter Costello underlines the point by asking, 'What after all is *Finnegans Wake* but a species of operatic chorus?'[15]

Nor had John lost his penchant for acting, especially when tipsy and telling colourful stories. One which spun itself into *Finnegans Wake* was the Crimean War story of Buckley the Irish soldier, who once had a Russian general in his sights, but, in awe of his uniform and decorations, was unable to fire. Then, reminding himself of his duty, he took aim again, at which moment the general dropped his pants to relieve himself, again prompting the soldier, unable to shoot so vulnerable a target, to lower his gun. However, when the man then proceeded to wipe himself with a piece of turf, Buckley could no longer respect the man and shot him. How he might use this story did not dawn on Joyce until, in the late twenties, he told it to Samuel Beckett, who commented, 'Another insult to Ireland.' 'Now,' said Joyce delightedly, 'now I can use it.'[16]

At the distillery, fate suddenly took an unfortunate turn. The manager, Alleyn, was misappropriating the firm's funds, and, when challenged by John, disappeared with the spoils. The company later went into liquidation and John lost not just his job but his £500 investment. Alleyn barely survived to enjoy his ill-gotten gains, dying just two years later in January 1880. Unsurprisingly, perhaps, he became Joyce's model for the irritable, curmudgeonly boss in his story 'Counterparts'.

John worked for a time in an accountant's office in Westland Row in central Dublin, and became a familiar figure in various city bars and hostelries where his congeniality, scathing wit and fondness for drinking became legendary. He was something of a dandy, sporting a monocle, a carefully waxed moustache, and sometimes a colourful waistcoat later memorialized in his son's short story 'The Dead' – 'a waistcoat of purple tabinet, with little foxes' heads upon it, lined with brown satin and having round mulberry buttons', made for him by his mother as a birthday present.[17] In keeping with the image, he was also very charming – a 'character' – convivial, amusing, full of 'blarney' with a sharp line in repartee. Asked if he knew anything about the quality of Liffey water, he replied, 'Not a damn bit because I never drank it without whiskey in it.'[18]

Through O'Connell contacts John was appointed secretary of Dublin's United Liberal Club, catering for members of the party which represented the independence-minded rising middle class against the Conservative pro-British Establishment. It was that section of Irish society which produced James Joyce and upon which he would focus his creative intelligence. For John, here was an opportunity to enjoy the social life, the parties and balls at the Mansion House.

At around this time he became romantically involved with nineteen-year-old Mary Jane Murray (known as May), the beautiful, blonde, blue-eyed daughter of John and Margaret Murray (née Flynn) who ran a tavern in what is now Terenure, a suburb in the west of Dublin, and he patronized the distillery. May's father disapproved of the small, handsome but rakish John Joyce pursuing his beautiful daughter (someone dubbed them 'Beauty and the Beast'), and his mother, reproachful as ever, objected to her only son's marrying into the family of a mere innkeeper. But John ignored his mother for once, and his ardent pursuit of May first charmed and finally won the young girl's heart.

Mary Jane was born in the county town of Longford on 15 May 1859, the third child of a Leitrim Murray and a Dublin Flynn. John Murray's family, it was said, included a priest with literary talent; Margaret Theresa

Flynn's family were musical and, claimed Joyce, she and her sisters had studied singing with Michael Balfe, the Dublin composer of *The Bohemian Girl*. May had two older brothers, John and William, who did not get on, a family situation, as Costello points out, replicated in *Finnegans Wake* – a pub landlord, his wife, a beautiful daughter and two quarrelsome brothers. Brother John, a journalist with the *Freeman's Journal*, was forced into marriage when he impregnated the sixteen-year-old daughter of his lodging-house landlady, something John Joyce, who disdained his brother-in-law, never allowed to go unmentioned. John Murray's plight – a young man inveigled into marriage – became the basis for his nephew's story 'The Boarding House'.[19] William, the younger of the brothers, a self-employed cost accountant, married the convent-educated Josephine Giltrap, who became James's favourite aunt. Kind and empathetic though *she* was, William was a martinet who bullied his children, providing James with yet more material for a story – 'Counterparts' – in which a browbeaten clerk in turn browbeats his own son.

May was schooled mostly by the musical Misses Flynn at their finishing school for young ladies at 15 Usher's Island (on the south bank of the Liffey in the heart of Dublin). There she learned deportment, how to dance, play the piano and sing, and, as John also sang, James would grow up in a world of music and song – from Irish ballads to operatic arias. This was the background evoked in 'The Dead', in which the Flynn sisters become the Misses Morkan, who also feature *en passant* in *Ulysses*.[20]

As secretary of the United Liberal Club, John played a key role in helping Maurice Brooks, a Home Ruler, and Robert Lyons, a Liberal, triumph over the Conservatives James Stirling and Sir Arthur Guinness (later Lord Ardilaun, doyen of the Dublin brewing family) in the election of March 1880. Afterwards, so he alleged, he had the pleasure of informing Sir Arthur that he was no longer an MP. It was a triumph for the energetic secretary who liked to boast that he had received 100 guineas for his services from each of the grateful candidates. 'I won that election,' he would claim, and from this success he acquired a reputation for organizing election campaigns which would find him employment in harder and less friendly times. A month after that election, in May 1880, Charles Stewart Parnell became leader of the Home Rule League, of which John was to become an ardent supporter. (Parnell's close associates Michael Davitt and Timothy Healy, also among the Joyce family's heroes, would play a key role both in Irish politics and in the lives of John and his impressionable son James.) As it was, with his reputation riding high, there was talk of John being offered a parliamentary seat. The future looked assured for this young man on the rise.

By the beginning of 1881, as Irish opinion, with Parnell in the vanguard, turned against Gladstone, the United Liberal Club was losing its purpose, the secretaryship was dispensed with and John was looking for a job. He got his break when the post of rate collector at the Collector General's Office in Dublin became vacant. This pensionable Civil Service post (in the gift of the Lord Lieutenant) was worth over £400 per annum (comparable to that of an experienced Irish doctor) – with additions for administering jury lists and checking electoral registers, John's friend Alf Bergan put it at £800.[21] With support from various political contacts, and after having to re-sit the Civil Service entrance examination (failed first time), he was duly offered the post by W. E. Forster, the Chief Secretary for Ireland.

John and May were married on 5 May 1880, ten days short of her twentieth birthday, at Rathmines Church. May afterwards liked to say, 'I was born in May, am known as May and was married in May.' The newly-weds honeymooned in London and Windsor before setting up home at 15 Clanbrassil Street, a few doors from the Murray family home. In *Ulysses*, drawing as ever on his personal past, Joyce made this street the home of Rudolph Virag, father of its wandering anti-hero Bloom, pictured as 'precociously manly, walking on a nipping morning from the old house in Clanbrassil street to the high school, his booksatchel on him bandolierwise, and in it a goodly hunk of wheaten loaf, a mother's thought'.[22]

But living close to his in-laws did not suit John. Like his mother, who, outraged by the marriage, had now cut him out of her life, he thought the Murrays beneath him, and the bad blood between him and that family would persist. He always referred to May's twice-married father as 'the old fornicator', and on hearing William refer to one of his children as 'Daddy's little lump of love', John quickly rendered it into 'Daddy's little lump of dung'. They soon moved to Ontario Drive, Rathmines, just a brisk walk from the United Liberal Club on Dawson Street.

May Joyce, a pious Catholic, would endure seventeen pregnancies from which came thirteen survivors, two of whom died in infancy. The first child, John Augustine Joyce, was born three months prematurely on 23 November 1880 and died after eight weeks. His father, unlike his mother, found little consolation in religion and was known to call Irish bishops and priests 'sons of bitches' – as does Simon Dedalus, his fictional incarnation.[23] But John could forget his troubles in the company of his many congenial friends.

For May, the sad loss of her firstborn was compounded in February 1881 by the death of her mother Margaret (the only Murray John liked), and her life was further disturbed when her restless husband moved twice more within the next twelve months. Less mourned was the death in

June that year of John's mother, Ellen, who had not communicated with him since his marriage.

Coming from a strong male line, the loss of his first son affected John profoundly, and probably explains why he focused almost all his affection and pinned all his hopes on the next son to come along. James ('Jim' to his family) was born at 6 a.m. on Thursday 2 February 1882 at 41 Brighton Square West, in Rathgar. That day, reported London's Meteorological Office, the barometer was falling, south-easterly winds turning to gales were forecast, with fog, dull mists and rain over all Ireland. The outlook, said the report, was gloomy.

The new arrival was baptized three days later by the Rev. John O'Mulloy at St Joseph's Chapel of Ease at Terenure. A distant relative of John, Philip McCann (ship's chandler on Burgh Quay), and his wife Helen were godparents, undertaking to pray for him regularly, set a Christian example, and encourage him in the faith. In the case of the newly christened 'James Augustine Joyce' that would prove a somewhat thankless task.

The date of Joyce's birth coincided with the religious festival of Candlemas and the pagan Groundhog Day, an appropriate birthday for a writer who would combine a religious (if impious) cast of mind with a fascination for myth and legend. He had emerged into a solid, predictable Victorian world dominated and enshrouded by tradition, in a country which stood in the shadow of another, and whose indigenous language and culture had been supplanted. He was not only destined to shake the world of modern letters, but eventually, by taking and subverting the intrusive English language, would help put Ireland firmly on the literary map.

2

The Dawn of Consciousness
(1882–1888)

'Once upon a time and a very good time it was.'
Joyce, *A Portrait of the Artist as a Young Man*

Not surprisingly, echoes, fleeting memories and epiphanies are all that remain of James Joyce's 'once-upon-a-time' years. Moving through and around them we may try to comprehend and re-weave the threads of an evolving consciousness.

Emerging from the fog of half-forgotten childhood, young James's awareness of the world seems to have focused most fixedly on the jovial John Stanislaus, the proud father playfully absorbed with his new son. Little Jim (if the imaginative memory of his alter ego Stephen can be trusted) was 'a nicens little boy named baby tuckoo', his father, 'a hairy face' looking at him, as he later recalled, 'through a glass'. He seemed to know he was the focus of this man's attention and his amusing fancies – the 'nicens little baby tuckoo' encountering 'a moocow' remained a defining memory of a blissful beginning. His mother was a more fragrant, musical presence, playing sailor's hornpipes on the piano for him to dance to. These are the glimpses of a recollected past filtered through imagination to personify in print an idyllic but ultimately disrupted childhood.[1]

His father recalled them as 'the happiest moments of my life'.[2] James, thinking back, agreed with Aristotle that childhood is a time of both wonder and confusion, and from this wondrous confusion he was able to fish a few lingering fragments of memory – that 'nicens boy' and that 'moocow' – and, a song learned from his crooning father, 'O, the wild rose blossoms/On the little green place', of which he managed only 'O, the green wothe botheth'.[3]

Much later, contemplating an early photograph of himself (a young Fauntleroy in lace collar and velvet dress carefully posed on a piano stool), James thought himself 'fierce-looking' – perhaps a child already taking issue with the world or frowning in imitation of some implacably dis-approving priest or relative.[4] He was in fact wan-looking and slight, with pale steely-blue eyes affording him an air of self-possession and detachment rather than ferocity. As the detail of his childhood faded from consciousness, he would ask his Aunt Josephine to refresh his memory, so that he could conjure up what he called his 'youthful soul capable of simple joys'.[5]

His young world would gradually widen to encompass a long and colourful cast of characters, all destined to achieve immortality in the pages of three of the most important works of twentieth-century fiction. Simon Dedalus in *A Portrait of the Artist* and in *Ulysses* was a likeness of his father; his mother, until her untimely death, would appear first as a steady then as a haunting presence; and John's many friends from hustings and bar room, would dance across all his pages (including *Finnegans Wake*) like characters in a pantomime, while relatives, fellow students and drinking companions only swelled the boisterous throng.

His mother's piety meant that there were priestly presences in James's early life, as well as all the paraphernalia and iconography of the religious life with which she surrounded herself – rosaries, crucifixes, madonnas and breviaries. This atmosphere would suffuse the Dublin fiction which harked back to his childhood, such as his story 'The Sisters', and early chapters of *A Portrait*. Eva Joyce, a younger sister, remembered him as 'a very religious boy'. 'He wrote a lot of very beautiful verse, holy verse; things to the Blessed Virgin, and things that his mother thought a lot about.'[6] But in *Stephen Hero*, Joyce's doppelgänger, Stephen, remarks with Joycean irony, 'I was sold to Rome before my birth.'[7]

Forty-one Brighton Square was a newly built red-brick two-storey terraced house on a tree-lined square (more a triangle), an appropriately respectable middle-class area for a man like John who, on James's birth certificate, now styled himself 'Government Clerk'. When the birth was registered, the registrar got his name wrong – 'James Augusta' instead of 'James Augustine' – as if attributing a feminine side to him which he in turn attributed to Bloom; and in *Finnegans Wake*, Shem (one of Joyce's alter egos) refers to his childhood as his 'augustan days'.[8]

He had been born into a musical home. Love of music was probably what bound John to his wife, at least initially – he sang at concerts and both belonged to choirs. Their singing solo, in duet, and as a family, provided young James with a fund of memories – songs from opera (like the popular '*M'appari tutt' amor*' from Flotow's *Martha*), songs brought in from Dublin hostelries (like 'Finnegan's Wake'), sentimental songs for the drawing room (like 'Silver Threads Among the Gold'), old Irish ballads (such as 'The Boys of Wexford') and much sacred music too. John loved especially patriotic ballads and sentimental recitations such as 'The Arab's Farewell to his Steed'. May would also dance and John would caper and jig as the mood and moment took them, or would read aloud for the benefit of the boy. But perhaps even more influential was his father's partiality for storytelling, elaborated with his own very distinctively colourful Irish vernacular – modified at its extremities no doubt for the Brighton Square drawing room.

For the British Empire, as 1882 dawned, it was business as usual. Queen Victoria, Defender of the [Protestant] Faith, had ruled her domain for forty-five years and would reign for a further nineteen. Ireland was just another imperial outpost, and while British authority was based at Dublin Castle, the country was ruled ultimately from London.

Despite the air of political stability and social stagnation, the old order was under challenge. Gladstone's Liberals had Home Rule for Ireland on its agenda, but its progress had stalled. And so it was also business as usual for opponents of British rule. There was Whiteboy activity in County Laois, and in County Clare armed and masked 'Moonlight' marauders were reportedly terrorizing local households (mostly small farmers thought to have taken over the land of those dispossessed by British landlords). Parnell was incarcerated in Kilmainham Jail for 'seditious conspiracy' in opposing Gladstone's 1881 Land Act, denying Irish tenant farmers freehold. The impetus towards Home Rule was gaining wider support, and that February the American House of Representatives was calling for information about American Fenians in British prisons.

More dramatically, in Dublin on 6 May 1882, the newly appointed Chief Secretary for Ireland, Lord Frederick Cavendish, and his Undersecretary, Thomas Henry Burke, were stabbed (gruesomely with surgical instruments) while walking through Phoenix Park on their way to the Viceroy's Lodge. Those responsible, the so-called 'Invincibles' ('Ignorant invincibles, innocents immutant!'),[9] were caught and hanged, except for three, including John FitzHarris, their jarvey (coachman), known as 'Skin-the-goat', who would later materialize in the 'Eumeus' episode of *Ulysses* as keeper of a cabman's shelter, and later still (September 1910) earn himself an obituary in the *New York Times*.

In August, tragedy came a little closer to home when a family called Joyce was massacred near Maamtrasna in Galway. A number of relatives, including seventy-year-old Myles Joyce, were tried for murder in English, though they spoke only Irish. Myles and two others, whom the British took to be Fenian terrorists, were crudely hanged, hardly knowing what was said at the trial. Many thought it a grave miscarriage of justice. A friend of John, Tim Harrington, later Lord Mayor of Dublin, was involved in the case which was much discussed in the Joyce household. James would write about the affair in a newspaper article twenty-five years later, and in the 'Circe' episode of *Ulysses* the hanging of the Croppy Boy echoes the barbarity of the botched execution.[10]

The end of a literary epoch was signalled that year by the deaths of Longfellow, Rossetti, Darwin, Emerson and Trollope. Meanwhile, the heralds of a modern age of literature, Virginia Woolf, Lytton Strachey, Wyndham Lewis, D. H. Lawrence, Ezra Pound and T. S. Eliot were either just born or about to be, Ibsen was fifty-four and W. B. Yeats not yet seventeen. In 1882, also, Puccini composed his first opera, *Le Villi*, Wagner finished *Parsifal*, and Nietzsche announced that 'God is dead!'

Since the Act of Union in 1800, Ireland had been incorporated into the United Kingdom. Not only did its politicians lose control of their own affairs but slowly, over time, its ancient tongue had been usurped by the alien English. The future author of *Ulysses* and *Finnegans Wake*, however, would master French, Italian, Norwegian and German, and become familiar with half a dozen other languages, which, in the circumstances of his birth, was a remarkable achievement.

The Joyces had survived the great Potato Famine of the 1840s, which had decimated the Irish population, and through shrewd investment maintained their social status. At the time of James's birth, migrant-ships were still leaving fully laden. The country seemed to hold few prospects for the bright and imaginative: 'When the soul of a man is born in this country there are nets flung at it to hold it back from flight,' he wrote – an image reiterated in *Finnegans Wake*.[11] Those who remained were destined to die – either by the bullet or by spiritual decomposition.

With little hope of moving beyond the class into which one was born, an air of fatalism and claustrophobia hung over the lower and middle classes, an atmosphere which Joyce captured brilliantly in *Dubliners*. One way out of this quagmire, university education, was only slowly becoming available. Dublin's Trinity College was predominantly for Protestants, but a Catholic university had been established in 1851 (under the Rectorship of Cardinal Newman), one of whose first students was the grandson of Daniel O'Connell. In 1880, Newman's establishment became University College, Dublin, able to award degrees of the newly founded Royal University. For those of Joyce's generation, therefore, there was at last some hope of breaking free from the old shackles of social inertia.

By 1884 John was not only enjoying his new official status but satisfying somewhat his search for respectability. However, he had a greater dream beyond mere respect – gentility. To this end he had on display an etching of the coat of arms of the Galway Joyces with its motto: '*Mors aut honorabilis vita*', and, of course, those family portraits, maliciously rumoured to be a bogus collection acquired from various sources.

Just prior to James's birth, John had mortgaged the first of his inherited properties in Cork. In 1884, he mortgaged three more and moved his family to a bigger house at a better address – 23 Castlewood Avenue, Rathmines – a step up the property ladder. John's appetite for social advancement was matched only by his appetite to spend, so that gradually he acquired a reputation for profligacy driven by a strong desire to be thought a good fellow. That swagger is captured in *A Portrait* when Stephen reflects that his father 'always gave him a shilling when he asked for sixpence'.[12]

At Castlewood Avenue there were spare rooms, and taking in lodgers meant extra income. And so, the dancing, singing boy soon found an audience, not just in his prideful father and sweet-smelling mother but with older presences in the Joyce ménage – his Uncle William O'Connell and 'Dante' Elizabeth Conway[13] ('Uncle Charles' and 'Dante Riordan' in *A Portrait*)[14] – distant relatives of John. On 18 January 1884, the first of James's sisters, Margaret (known as 'Poppie'), was born, followed on 17 December by the first of his brothers, Stanislaus (or 'Stannie'). The house would not remain spacious for long.

Uncle William, a bankrupt draper, was a hearty, rugged old man with white sidewhiskers, who sported an antique tall top-hat which he wore even in the outhouse while smoking a pipe of black twist and singing 'O Twine me a Bower all, of Woodbine and Roses' or 'The Groves of Blarney', one of John's favourites.[15] Dante – 'unlovely ... very stout, baleful and terrifyingly devout'[16] (who moved in as governess to the children) – apart from sitting in judgement on the world at large, collected tissue paper for wrapping parcels, and gave Baby Tuckoo a cachou for every piece he brought her. Equally strangely, she kept two brushes in her wardrobe – her totems, a brush with a maroon velvet back representing Michael Davitt and one with a green velvet back standing for Parnell.[17] This red-green colour coding recurs throughout *A Portrait*, symbolizing opposites in Stephen's mind. When Dante arrived at Castlewood Avenue she was a keen Parnellite, which must have commended her to John, himself a passionate supporter of the charismatic Home Ruler.

Dante's nationalism was so intense that she once belaboured an elderly gent with her parasol for standing to attention for 'God Save the Queen' at some public function. James began to learn a great deal from Dante, and, despite the menace of her unbending religiosity, in his first novel, as young Stephen he represents her not unsympathetically.

Dante knew a lot of things. She had taught him where the Mozambique Channel was and what was the longest river in America and what was the name of the highest mountain in the moon ... both his father and uncle Charles said that Dante was a clever woman and a wellread woman. And when Dante made that noise after dinner and then put up her hand to her mouth: that was heartburn.[18]

Stanislaus's memory of her was more jaundiced, recalling that, while teaching reading, writing and the elements of arithmetic and geography, 'she inculcated a good deal of very bigoted Catholicism and bitterly anti-English patriotism'.[19] But even he credited her with giving Jim a good start in life – and by the same token probably himself, too.

Dante, a one-time Sister of Mercy in America, had left the Order after inheriting £48,000 from two brothers who died almost simultaneously. Back in Ireland she married a Dublin solicitor, Patrick Henry Conway, who shortly afterwards decamped with her fortune to South America. The bereft Dante now became attached to John Joyce's emergent clan, and in the spirit of her old Order set out to secure for Eternity the soul of young James Augustine and his siblings.

Throughout the day, Dante exerted her daunting influence, religiously presiding over their spiritual welfare. Every evening she had them reciting the Rosary and the Litany of the Blessed Virgin, something which the well-behaved James seemed to accept, but the more surly Stanislaus found increasingly oppressive. Her teaching always carried an underlying moral threat. An excursion to Inchicore, just south of Phoenix Park, was no mere outing but an occasion to view a waxwork representation of the Holy Family at the birth of Christ; a visit to Dublin's National Gallery in Merrion Square meant having to contemplate a painting by Francis Danby depicting the opening of the seventh seal, the Day of Judgement, with sinners being struck down by thunderbolts and hurled to damnation.[20] Dante, a terrorist of Apocalypse, warned them that thunderbolts were an instrument of God for the destruction of the wicked, and, observing an infant's funeral, declared that those who died unbaptized would surely go to hell. The cynical Stanislaus considered all this ridiculous (or so he recalled), but James took it deeply to heart and, although he later scorned baptism, throughout his life he reacted with unconcealed terror to the sound of thunder. It was, claimed Stanislaus, 'the only real weakness my brother showed as a boy.'[21] That fear of thunder rumbles and rips through his most obscure but revealing last work, *Finnegans Wake*, in which the voice of 'Him Which Thundereth From On High'[22] is heard at the outset.

Because the influence of Dante was so overwhelming, that of Joyce's parents was probably more muted. While musical, John and May were not especially literary. John's reading was patchy, limited to Sheridan Le Fanu's *The House by the Churchyard*, and a few other favourite novels such as Frank E. Smedley's *Frank Fairleigh: or, Scenes from the Life of a Private*

Pupil. John, it is suggested, had a taste for books of a saucy kind – much like Leopold and Molly Bloom, and James and Nora Joyce.[23] He did, however, use public libraries so the house cannot have been entirely book-free.[24] His papers of choice were the pro-Parnell *Freeman's Journal*, the more radical *United Irishman*, and the less controversial *Modern Society* and *Licensed Victuallers' Gazette*. His eclectic taste also included *Tit-Bits*, a popular weekly full of curious and sensational trivia, and *Answers*, a paper which included competitions with cash prizes irresistible to the ambitious spendthrift. James once gave his father's occupation as 'Going in for competitions', and having Leopold Bloom utilize a copy of *Tit-Bits* for private purposes in the outside privy, he passed the ultimate critical judgement on his father's choice of popular reading.[25]

May knew her religious texts and was something of a reader, even later reading Ibsen at her son's behest. Uncle William would read aloud to entertain the children, as Stanislaus recalled. '[He] read us fairy stories, working his way steadily through Grimm and Andersen, and when the story was of the misadventures of some beautiful princess, he would interpolate pathetic asides, which escaped us, but were intended for my mother sewing in another part of the room.'[26] Children's stories greatly affected many aspects of Joyce's fiction,[27] as did Lewis Carroll's *Alice* books, read much later.

On 24 July 1886, a fourth child was born to the Joyces – Charles Patrick ('Charlie' to his family). And another move was pending as John sought to distance himself even further from his wife's family. Wishing for an ever-larger house, he rented No. 1 Martello Terrace at Bray, an affluent resort known as 'the Brighton of Ireland', in County Wicklow overlooking Dublin Bay. By the time they moved there in May 1887, May Joyce was again pregnant.

Bray had an air of fashionable gentility – gents in blazers and straw hats, ladies in white tennis dresses, a boat club and all the usual summer seaside entertainments. Number 1 Martello Terrace, sitting adjacent to the broad-sweeping strand, had thirteen rooms, a sea-view, and although it was cheaper than their Castlewood Avenue house, John had raised two more mortgages on his Cork properties to prepare himself financially for the move. There was money enough to employ more than one servant for his growing family, including a nursemaid called Brigid.[28] On John's thirty-eighth birthday, 4 July 1887, another boy was born. He was christened George Alfred, after George Washington and his great-great-grandfather Joyce.

Conveniently for John, Bray was just a short train journey from the city, close enough for his old Dublin pals to travel down for convivial weekends. All would find themselves in James's cast of characters. There was Alf Bergan, a man with a taste for excremental jokes, whom Stanislaus 'disliked', his boss, the tall Dublin sub-Sheriff, John Clancy ('Long John Fanning' of *Ulysses* and himself in *Finnegans Wake*), whom he 'disliked very much', and Tom Devin ('Mr Power' in 'Grace' and himself in *Ulysses*). Bergan remembered how John would be at Bray station every Sunday morning to meet any friends who cared to visit. James he recalled as 'very handsome ... very sensible and extremely well-behaved for a boy of his age' with a slight lisp and who asked amusingly childish questions.[29] This was the charmingly amiable face of the young boy they called 'Sunny Jim'.[30] The visitors would be taken for lunch, then for a stroll and finally back home for an evening of musical entertainment. John would sing to May's accompaniment, and there was many a jolly chorus for all to join in. Jim, he remembered, was always attentive, keen to participate – keen and attentive enough for such evenings to resurface in *A Portrait*.

Another and probably more glamorous visitor to Bray was John Kelly, an active and much-imprisoned Fenian, who, after the passing of a new Crimes Act in July 1887, was in constant danger of re-arrest. John had invited him to stay at Martello Terrace to recuperate following his last prison sentence, and was ever ready to help him avoid capture. On one occasion he escaped fractionally ahead of the law thanks to the warning of a sympathetic local policeman. Kelly duly found his place in *A Portrait* and *Ulysses* as John Casey, who taught Stephen to sing songs in Irish and to say 'Sinn Fein' instead of 'Good Health' when raising a glass. Jim would learn to say 'Good Health' in many other fashions and languages before his time was up, but the conviviality and taste for Irish gossip that went with alcohol never left him.

Aged five, James was sent to a local nursery school run by a Miss Raynor. There he met a neighbour's young daughter, Eileen Vance, whose father, James, was the local chemist and a Protestant. Joyce picks up a thread from his past as his alter ego Stephen Dedalus recalls the Vance family in his novel:

> The Vances lived in number seven. They had a different father and mother. They were Eileen's father and mother. When they were grown up he was going to marry Eileen. He hid under the table. His mother said:
> —O, Stephen will apologise.
> Dante said:
> —O, if not, the eagles will come and pull out his eyes.[31]

This savage remark from this emissary of a vengeful God set up in the mind of the embryonic poet a chanted refrain, the lines repeated over and over, round and around in the mind of the haunted young boy: *'Pull out his eyes/Apologise/Apologise/Pull out his eyes.'*[32] If his eyes were weak, which they were, the threat, associating blindness with guilt, must have been only too terrifyingly real.

The Vances and the Joyces became quite close. According to Eileen, 'We ran in and out of each other's home all the time.' Her father and John Joyce were, she said, 'both great sinners' who indulged in a great deal of drinking and singing together, raising the roof with their Irish 'Come-all-ye' songs. Vance's bass voice would blend well with John's tenor in 'The Moon has Raised her Lamp Above', a duet from *The Lily of Killarney*, an opera based on Dion Boucicault's play, *The Colleen Bawn* (which crops up in *Stephen Hero*, in *Ulysses* and in *Finnegans Wake* as 'colleenbawl'), in which a youth sets out to charm a girl, but is trapped into marriage by a wily seductress.

There were also parties with the Vances where the children donned fancy dress, played games, sang and performed little skits. At one party Jim sprinkled salt in everybody's drink, which Eileen thought very clever of him. Sometimes, donning a red cap, he played the Devil, condemning some of them to hell which he decided was under a wheelbarrow. But the children were mostly well-behaved, and at Miss Raynor's kindergarten Jim, with whom Eileen was frequently paired, stood out as leader. Playing together at home, the imaginative Jim also took charge, persuading them that if they misbehaved at the Joyce house, his mother would hold them head-down in the toilet and pull the chain. However, despite the reputation her son had given her, Eileen found May delightful and welcoming. Uncle William, she thought 'very pompous', a figure from Dickens; Dante, on the other hand, was an enemy, who regarded close contact with Protestants a threat to the immortal soul. If James continued to play with Eileen, she warned, he would undoubtedly go to hell. But on this occasion his attraction to the girl next door overcame his fear of Dante's inferno.[33] Anti-Protestant bigotry was quite alien even to the young impressionable boy.

James would sometimes take Stannie for walks along the beach. Living and walking beside the sea became a lifelong pleasure for him. It gave him his liking for seaside entertainment and the setting for the 'Proteus' and 'Nausicaa' episodes of *Ulysses*. It also gave him a lifelong phobia, when one day, out along the beach with Stannie, they came across a dog, an Irish terrier, at which they began to throw stones. Taking exception to this, the dog attacked and bit the terrified James on the chin. He carried a scar thereafter, and dogs, like thunderstorms, would drive him into a frenzy of fear, astonishing those who witnessed it.

In February 1888, May Joyce suffered a miscarriage. The luck of the Joyces seemed to be deserting them. That same month saw John under suspicion at the Collector General's office and his position there endangered. He was suspected of 'borrowing' from his takings, an accusation cooked up, according to his friends, by anti-Parnellites out to destroy him. Perhaps hoping to restore his reputation, he claimed to have fought off robbers who attacked him for his collector's bag in Phoenix Park, but it did little to lift the impending cloud. He was moved from collecting rates in rural areas to collecting in and around central Dublin. Whether this amounted to punishment or promotion is unclear but it brought him closer to the pubs and clubs haunted by his cronies. To give himself more time to play, he farmed out some of the clerical work he found irksome. Back at Bray he joined the Boat Club, and in June he and May took part in a concert there, with James singing along with them. It was his first public performance; it would not be his last.

However, the boy was about to move into a wider world and on to a bigger stage. In September, aged a mere 'six and a half', he fulfilled the first part of his father's ambition of transforming his favourite son into a gentleman by way of a Jesuit education. If his pious mother shared the dream, it was that he became both a gentleman *and* a priest.

3
Willingly to School
(1888–1893)

'Above all things, Jesuits are "confessors".'
John Daniel, *The Grand Design Exposed* (1999)

Not yet seven, James Joyce was a slight, pale, bright, attentive but not very communicative child, and small for his age. John's choice of school for him was Clongowes Wood College, generally considered the best school for Catholic youngsters in Ireland. It was situated at Sallins, partway along the road between Dublin and Kildare, forty miles from Bray. Close to Sallins, the River Liffey, which washes one side of the town, enters the Bog of Allen, a river and a bog which were to loom large in the imagination of James Augustine Joyce. The sorrowful Liffey flows in and out of *A Portrait* and *Ulysses*, and it runs and eddies and pitches drunkenly throughout *Finnegans Wake*. The Bog of Allen is conjured up as part of the magnificent image of Ireland under snow at the conclusion of 'The Dead'.

In September 1888 James was five months short of the usual age of entry to the college. His early admission indicates just how precocious he was considered. Dante and Miss Raynor had done their work well. He was eager to start school, showing, even at that age, a taste for travel and new experiences. But – a sign of things to come – having trouble with his eyes he was tested and fitted with spectacles.

Clongowes Wood College, a medieval castle in 500 acres of wooded grounds with a mile-long, elm-lined driveway, had been purchased by the Jesuits in 1814 from an old landed family called Browne. Because of James's tender age, for his first two years there, John was charged £25, half the usual fee. Apart from its wider prestige, Clongowes carried other associations important for him. Daniel O'Connell had assisted in founding the college together with the grandfather of Charles Stewart Parnell.

May Joyce was more concerned to protect him from bad influences, as his fictional doppelgänger, Stephen, reflects:

His mother had told him not to speak with the rough boys in the college. Nice mother! The first day in the hall of the castle when she had said goodbye she had put up her veil double to her nose to kiss him: and her nose and eyes were red. But he had pretended not to see that she was going to cry ... And his father had given him two five shilling pieces for pocket money [and] told him if he wanted anything to write home to him and, whatever he did, never to peach on a fellow. Then at the door of the castle the Rector had shaken hands with his father and mother, his soutane fluttering in the breeze, and the car had driven off with his father and mother on it. They had cried to him from the car, waving their hands:

— Goodbye, Stephen, goodbye![1]

The Rector in the fluttering soutane was the distinguished, humane and charismatic Father John Conmee, who would flutter into both *A Portrait* and *Ulysses*, just as other images of childhood are evoked and re-invoked throughout Joyce's fiction. Being the smallest and youngest boy, James was lodged in the infirmary in the care of the matron, Nanny Galvin, and the kindly Brother Hanly (the odd and 'sorrowful' Brother Michael in *A Portrait*).[2] Asked his age, he is said to have replied, 'Half-past-six', which soon became his schoolboy nickname.

Not all the Jesuit Fathers at Clongowes were as fair and liberal as Father Conmee. There was the harsh Director of Studies, Father James Daly ('Baldyhead' Father Dolan in *A Portrait*, the Squeers-like martinet who unjustly punishes young Stephen). Daly had been brought to the college to instil discipline into the boys' studies, and (solely *'pour encourager les autres'*) he would thrash them with his 'pandybat' for simply not knowing their Latin texts or, in Joyce/Stephen's case, not reading.

Daly's programme of studies, a variant of the Jesuits' *Ratio Atque Institutio Studiorum Societatis Iesu* ('The Official Plan for Jesuit Education'), specified the teaching of rhetoric, ancient poets such as Virgil and Horace, the speeches of Caesar, Sallust and Livy, and the philosophy of Cicero, all of which required rudimentary Latin and Greek. Young Joyce joined what was called 'The Elements', the beginners' class, where the elements of the Catholic religion were taught, under the colourful, eccentric and somewhat childish Father William Power – Father Arnall, who 'got into waxes', according to Stephen Dedalus in *A Portrait*. And, in the guise of Stephen D., James was quick to locate himself – as schoolboys always do – in relation to the rest of creation, scrawling in a geography book, 'Class of Elements/Clongowes Wood College/Sallins/County Kildare/Ireland/Europe/The World/The Universe'. Symbolically and prophetically in

Joyce's case, the camera zooms from sharply focused close-up to all-embracing wide angle.

The pedagogic method employed at Clongowes was rote-learning, pre-scribed questions and answers (fourteen chapters of the Maynooth and three hundred pages of Deharbe's *Catechism*, and 150 pages of Old Testament history), feats which came easily to a boy with a highly retentive memory like Joyce's. A copy of the Maynooth Catechism 'sewn into the cloth cover of a notebook' sits at the end of James Duffy's top bookshelf in 'A Painful Case', and Maynooth College, where the Catechism originated, is called a place of 'holy boys, priests and bishops of Ireland' by Joe Hynes in the 'Cyclops' episode of *Ulysses*, while the 'Ithaca' episode adopts the Catechism's quizzical form.

It is not very clear how young James took to college life. Although Stanislaus thought him quite happy and at home in the company of his schoolfellows, Patrick Butler (later a World War II hero), recalled him as 'a thin, pale boy who never said very much to anyone'.[3] The experience of Stephen Dedalus in *A Portrait* seems to confirm that impression – of a boy anxious (at least at the outset) to follow his mother's advice to avoid the rough boys around him:

> The wide playgrounds were swarming with boys. All were shouting and the prefects urged them on with strong cries ... He kept on the fringe of his line, out of sight of his prefect, out of the reach of the rude feet, feigning to run now and then. He felt his body small and weak amid the throng of players and his eyes were weak and watery.[4]

And, like Stephen, Joyce was remembered by some at Clongowes as 'more delicate than brilliant'.[5]

Most of the other pupils came from upper-middle-class backgrounds, the sons of government officials, professionals, successful tradesmen, and the odd member of Ireland's Catholic upper crust. They were said to be snobbish and looked down on Dubliners. The son of a Dublin rate collector attending the school on half-fees, therefore, must have felt socially somewhat insignificant even in such youthful company, and probably indulged in a little creative self-gentrification, like Stephen, who reflected how he had told the young gentry of Clongowes that he had a judge and an army general as uncles.[6] If true of Joyce, it was probably his first attempt seriously to disguise his true identity.

Among the boys who swarmed and shouted and milled around the playground, there were those he would immortalize in *A Portrait* – the 'decent' Roddy Kickham, the snobbish, cocoa-drinking 'stink', 'Nasty' Roche, and Saurin, all sons of magistrates, the know-all Cecil Thunder, and the bullying Wells who teased Stephen about kissing his mother at bedtime and shouldered him into the slimy, foul 'Square Ditch' cesspit in the college grounds. Then, reaching back into the mind of his younger self, he conjures up a scene of misery and yearning – 'All the boys seemed to him very strange ... He longed to be at home and lay his head on his mother's lap. But he could not: and so he longed for the play and study and prayers to be over and to be in bed.'[7]

The college routine was designed more for the salvation of the soul than the comfort of the body. Sleep would end abruptly at 6.30 a.m. for a wash, early mass and then breakfast. Morning study was followed by two hours of class-teaching, a midday break, two afternoon classes, playtime (sometimes including time in the library), then a further wash before dinner at 3.30 p.m. Beads were told in the chapel at 5.15, then came evening study, with supper at seven and night prayers before bedtime.

In January 1889, another sister, Eileen Isabel Mary Xavier Brigid Joyce, was born. On 2 February 1889, his seventh birthday, James attained the age of reason and soon afterwards, on 21 April, attended his first communion. 'Give me the child until he is seven', goes the Jesuit motto, 'and I will give you the man.' The Jesuits of Clongowes Wood must have been eager to capture not just the soul but also the prospective brilliance of James Augustine Joyce for their Order.

In *A Portrait* he has Stephen overwhelmed by the sense of sin at his first touch of the communion cup and the smell of the wine. The only other hint of what the occasion meant to him is captured in a typical passage of sensually aware prose from *Stephen Hero*, in which his alter ego recalled some poor countryfolk present at the occasion, peasants exuding 'the odour of debasing humanity'.[8] Even at his first communion he considered himself among the elect, and marked the occasion by adopting as his saint's name, Aloysius, the noble patron saint of youth and of Clongowes, who abandoned all worldly trappings for his faith.

In the care of the pious and disciplined Jesuits, young Joyce would learn to observe their religious devotions, rites and practices. At his first communion, being small gave him a special role for once, and, like Stephen Dedalus, he carried the boat of incense beside the thurifer who bore the censer at the Benediction of the Blessed Sacrament.[9] The intricacies and paraphernalia of Catholic liturgy became an essential part of his symbolic vocabulary, running not just through *A Portrait* but through *Ulysses* and *Finnegans Wake* too, and some of the feast days and routine services which marked out his days at the college became habitual observances throughout his life.

In addition to a brotherhood of scholarship, discipline and devotion, Joyce had entered a world of Irish myth and legend. The burial mound of

Mesgedra, the legendary King of Leinster, stood at nearby Clane; the grave of Wolfe Tone, the so-called father of Irish nationalism, lay some four miles to the south; and Anna Livia, goddess and spirit of the River Liffey, haunted waters nearby. The Ulster poet Samuel Ferguson celebrates the 'limpid Liffey fresh from wood and wold,/Bridgeless and fordless', and invests it with shades of Tristan and Isolde, the tragic Cornish knight and Irish princess whose legend would impress itself upon Joyce as what he called one of the few 'original themes in world literature', and insert itself into the warp and woof of *Finnegans Wake*. The college also had its supernatural presences; a bloody ghost haunted a staircase in the castle, as did that of an old patriot pursued by British soldiers whose bullet marks still scarred the college's main doors. Both spectres would entrance the receptive mind of young 'Stephen Dedalus'.

Soon after his seventh birthday, Joyce was punished for not bringing his books to class, which seems quite out of character since books were already important to him. He consumed not just the set books but books that simply caught his interest – Peter Parley's *Tales of Greece and Rome* and Richmal Mangnall's *Historical and Miscellaneous Questions for the Use of Young People*, a history primer which also adopted the catechistical method. From the former he learned of the gods and heroes of the Ancient World, including Ulysses; in the latter he met 'great men ... whose heads were in the books of history'.[10] In the college library he found a collection of Byron's poems, 'a ragged translation' of *The Count of Monte Cristo*, and a book which truly captivated him – a book about Holland, full of exotic names and images of faraway places which gave him a warm glow.[11] History, both ancient and Irish, and anything pertaining to the Greek myths would be devoured hungrily throughout his life, and the prospect of faraway places would never cease to entice him.

There were also essays to write, with such titles as 'Zeal without prudence is like a ship adrift',[12] the paper always headed with the initials AMDG (*Ad Majorem Dei Gloria*, the Jesuit motto) and signed off with L.D.S. (*Laus Deo Semper*). Apart from his fiction and letters, the essay was Joyce's major form of self-expression, in which he was able to develop his critical and journalistic skills. Poetry would also engage him early on, though his poetic powers would only blossom as a vehicle for his most intensely absorbing prose fiction. His initial experiences of verse at Clongowes, however, were not particularly auspicious. Peter Butler remembered him being forced to recite a mawkish ditty, 'Little Jim, the Collier's Son', in which an impoverished miner and his wife sit at the bedside of their dying child. The last stanza has the bereaved couple kneeling beside Little Jim's deathbed:

With hearts bowed down with sadness
They humbly ask of Him,
In heaven, once more to meet again,
Their own poor Little Jim.

During this recital, 'Little Jim' Joyce had to endure the scornful smirks of his classmates, especially at the final line.

In spite of his apparent contentment at Clongowes, the pious young scholar had a streak of contrariness, and he was already revealing to others a complex persona. He was 'pandied' on occasions (like his hero Stephen), once, in March 1889, for using vulgar language – inspired no doubt by his father's unique command of the vernacular. As a youngster, he was assertive with his peers and playmates, but scared of dogs and thunderstorms; he was brilliantly precocious yet ready to accept religious instruction unquestioningly; he was pious yet prone to using vulgar language. That confusion of incompatibles must have made him someone difficult to fathom, marked by an enigmatic aura which persisted and came also to characterize his fiction.

Beyond the school gates national history was about to mark Joyce almost as profoundly as his Jesuit education. In 1889, events turned against Parnell. In an attempt to damage his reputation, one Richard Pigott published letters purporting to show that the Home Ruler supported the Phoenix Park murders and was even acquainted with the Invincibles. The letters were found to be forgeries and 'the Chief', as Parnell was known, was vindicated. The forger, who later committed suicide, had sons at Clongowes at the time, and ironically enough it was in order to pay their fees that he had sold the fake letters.

But worse was to come for the Chief. On 17 November 1889, following an uncontested divorce case, a jury found him guilty of adultery with Kitty O'Shea. The shock of the verdict overtook many of those around young Joyce – not just his father and his Parnellite friends, but some of his school-friends and even some of his Jesuit teachers. But then, under pressure from the Catholic Church and from Gladstone, previously close associates, notably Timothy Healy and Michael Davitt, voted him out of the leadership of the Irish Party. The Chief's downfall made a deep and lasting impression on the Joyce family, especially John, and changed the course of Irish history. The part played by Timothy Healy and Michael Davitt, an erstwhile friend of John, would never be forgotten.

In the wake of the Parnell affair, John began drinking more heavily[13] and muttering to himself about 'finishing it',[14] so that May, who was normally very self-assured, became fearful of him enough to consider leaving him.[15] The outraged Dante ripped the green velvet for Parnell

from the back of her hairbrush. Young James was more and more aware
of arguments and a sense of disharmony at home. 'That,' said young
Stephen Dedalus, 'was called politics.'[16] After a solemn and probably
uncomfortable Christmas, Joyce was back at Clongowes. On 18 January
1890 Mary Kathleen, known as 'May', was born. Now he had three
brothers and three sisters.

James's relationship with Eileen Vance, the girl next door in Martello
Terrace, had blossomed in a childish way, notwithstanding Dante's
warning of hellfire. His Stephen remembers her placing her hand inside
his pocket, and, recalling in a captured memory-fragment that hand's soft
whiteness, he muses:

—She too wants me to catch hold of her, he thought. That's why she
came with me to the tram. I could easily catch hold of her when she
comes up to my step: nobody is looking. I could hold her and kiss her.[17]

And she, too, had feelings for 'Sunny Jim'. On 14 February (shortly after
his ninth birthday), he received a Valentine's Day card from her reading:

O Jimmie Joyce you are my darling
You are my looking glass from night till morning . . .

Joyce, however, was more embarrassed than seduced by this flattering
overture. The lines were later written into Leopold Bloom's incestuous
musings about his daughter Milly.

That autumn of 1891, he returned for the last time to Clongowes. He
was there when on 26 October, his mother gave birth to yet another
daughter, Eva Mary, who would become especially attached to him. At
the college he found the place convulsed by scandal. Five boys, two
from his class, had run away after being caught *in flagrante delicto* while
'smugging' (slang for 'mutually masturbating') in the closets on the
College Square. Reflecting on events, his Stephen Dedalus remembers that
one of the Moonan boys wore fine clothes and the other, 'Lady' Boyle,
was forever paring his fingernails. (The college records note the abscond-
ing, but give no further details.) 'Smugging' became a word James stored
and savoured, slipping it not only into *A Portrait* but also into *Finnegans
Wake*, where he refers to 'hugging and smugging' and 'swap sweetened
smugs, six of one for half a dozen of the other'; and the coined term
'homosodalism' suggests the 'smugging' sin committed behind monastic
walls.

Early that term Joyce caught a fever and was taken to the college
infirmary. There he has Stephen, stricken and homesick, writing to ask

his mother to bring him home and, recalling another boy's death at the school, he lies terrified in his bed, taking us into the feverish consciousness of the ailing child.

> He might die before his mother came. Then he would have a dead mass in the chapel like the way the fellows had told him it was when Little had died. All the fellows would be at the mass, dressed in black, all with sad faces. Wells too would be there but no fellow would look at him. The Rector would be there in a cope of black and gold and there would be tall yellow candles on the altar and round the catafalque. And they would carry the coffin out of the chapel slowly and he would be buried in the little graveyard of the community off the main avenue of limes. And Wells would be sorry then for what he had done. And the bell would toll slowly.[18]

Premature death would be a recurring motif in Joyce's work, most notably that of Michael Furey in 'The Dead' and of Rudy Bloom in *Ulysses*. While in the infirmary Stephen hears, as no doubt Joyce himself heard, the devastating news from a tearful Brother Michael that Parnell was dead. The memory became part of his personal folklore.

The tragedy of Parnell did not improve John Joyce's outlook and temper. With a character as volatile and splenetic as his, there had to be a dramatic and explosive climax to these events. The crisis came to a head over Christmas dinner that year at 1 Martello Terrace, all bedecked with holly and ivy – an outward display of conviviality masking a less-than-convivial family atmosphere. The events are conjured up from memory and lent a brilliantly dramatic flavour in *A Portrait*. It all begins amiably enough. Before dinner, Simon (John) and his friend Casey (John Kelly) return after a brisk walk around Bray, to join the rest of the Dedalus family (including Uncle Charles and Dante) minus the younger children, with Stephen (James) for the first time allowed to join the family for dinner. Simon, as usual, is bursting with bonhomie and, as all are seated around the table, is more than ready to start on the whiskey and get to work on the turkey which the servants set before him. But Parnell's betrayal by the Church in cahoots with Gladstone, and his death just two months earlier, are still too fresh in the minds of the two friends for the matter to go unmentioned. The morose Dante sits hunched over her meal, seething with self-righteous indignation as Simon and John Casey begin cursing the priests and bishops who preached against Parnell from the pulpit. Dante snarls at them and defends the Church and her religion, driving Simon to denounce the bishops as 'sons of bitches' and 'lowlived dogs'.[19] Mrs

Dedalus tries in vain to pacify the old woman and shame the men into silence, but finally Casey explodes, shouting that Ireland has had enough of religion and would be better off without God. The enraged Dante denounces the two Parnellites as 'blasphemers' and 'devils', and flounces out in high dudgeon.

She later wreaked her vengeance on the sacrilegious John Joyce. Framed photographs of his old girlfriends stood on the piano, something May had tolerated for the sake of peace and quiet. One day he came home to discover them gone. 'Where are they?' he demanded. 'Burnt,' said May. 'Who burnt them?' 'I did.' 'No, you didn't,' shouted John. 'It was that old bitch upstairs.' The discreet Dante had retired for the night.[20] Shortly afterwards (on 29 December, says *Ulysses*) she left the Joyce ménage, and died alone five years later. Ironically, shortly thereafter, her truant husband resurfaced to claim her remaining £40.[21]

Although he would get involved in electioneering, John lost his earlier commitment to politics. He was now intensely anticlerical, and never forgave those in the Irish Party who had turned against Parnell. His son captured the mood and moment well and turned his own literary guns against the Chief's main betrayer, composing a poem about Parnell on the back of one of his father's old legal notices.[22] The poem called 'Et Tu Healy', probably the very first he ever wrote, so delighted John that he had thirty or forty copies printed and distributed among his friends. Although it is lost, Stanislaus recalled some fragments envisaging Parnell as an eagle, looking down disdainfully upon the spineless mediocrities who had betrayed him, but now above their petty manoeuvring.

> His quaint-perched aerie on the crags of Time
> Where the rude din of this ... century
> Can trouble him no more.[23]

The image of the lofty writer standing alone against critics became part of James's own self-image, and the allusion to Parnell as an eagle, which has Shakespearean resonances, suggests that drawing of literary parallels was a pattern established early in his creative conscience.

The Parnell affair left bitter traces on Joyce's life and work. But such feelings, he discovered, could always be alleviated by music. In his third year he had piano lessons from one of the Clongowes Fathers, and took small parts in plays and burlesques. As an adult, he would sing and play the piano with alacrity, mostly improvising rather than reading from a score, and his ability to capture the rhythms and turns of vernacular phraseology in his fiction owes much to music and the theatrical flourish of his father's gestures and conversation. He would also turn burlesque to his own use, transforming grotesque exaggeration into an art form, most notably in the 'Circe' episode of *Ulysses*, and in more cerebral fashion in *Finnegans Wake*.

Cycling had become a craze at the college, and one day some boys cycle-racing around the school's cinder path collided with the diminutive 'Stephen' and broke his glasses. On being told about the accident, Father Arnall (Power), his class master, excused him from work until his father sent him new glasses. But then he was pandied in front of the class during Lent, for not reading, by the hard-hearted Father Daly/Dolan (portrayed in the novel through suitably stark and colourless imagery) – 'whitegrey face and the nocoloured eyes behind the steelrimmed spectacles'[24] – a bully on the rampage in search of 'idle, lazy loafers' to punish.

Although the college punishment book does not record the incident, Joyce told Herbert Gorman, his first biographer, that it had occurred and went on to tell how he had gone to Father Conmee, the Rector, 'a remote and awesome figure in the college',[25] to complain about the cruel unfairness of being punished for something he had not done. Conmee commiserated with the aggrieved child, and promised to speak to Father Daly. Some have thought this story was invented to fit Joyce's self-image as 'Stephen Hero', a story lying somewhere between history and fiction. But clearly his sense of betrayal (by Father Power's not rescuing him) was acute. Throughout his life Joyce suffered a heightened fear of treachery bordering on paranoia, and this tale of childhood injustice suggests how it originated. Later, when John Joyce raised the matter of the unjust punishment with Father Conmee, the priest said that he had spoken to Daly and they had both laughed about it. The boy's courage had provoked their amusement if not their admiration. But to his schoolmates (at least in his novel) he was 'Stephen Hero', and some of those who had previously bullied him now came to apologize. However, he did not remain to enjoy his new celebrity for long. Possibly due to another illness or because his father could not afford the full fees, in June 1891 he was removed from Clongowes leaving the bill for his final term at the college unpaid. He also left behind a high opinion of his intellectual capabilities, especially with Father Conmee. The young scholar was now allowed to study at home with the help of his mother.

John's fortunes were about to change for the worse. The City Corporation, having taken over the Rates Office from the government at Dublin Castle, announced that it planned to pension off almost all the collecting staff, including John. But, with the sale of his properties in Cork, for the moment John felt secure enough to contemplate another move. He did not go far – to Blackrock, seven miles north of Bray. The new house was even more impressive than the last, sustaining the myth of a man continuing to prosper. It was semi-detached with a stucco facade and porticoed front door, four bedrooms, two thirty-foot drawing rooms and a large garden at the rear. A stone lion crowning the portico gave No. 23 Carysfort Avenue its name of 'Leoville'. Stained-glass windows at the front door represented the story of Dante and Beatrice.

Leaving Bray for Blackrock meant leaving Eileen Vance. But at least at Blackrock they were still only a short walk from the seafront. Joyce's love of seaside life must have been born during these early years living close to the promenade where holidaymakers strolled, minstrel troupes and *pierrots* entertained the crowds, and Punch and Judy enraptured the youngsters. Even through the mesh of memory and language which is *Finnegans Wake*, those images resurface. 'Punch may be pottleproud but his Judy's a wife's wit better,' says Glugg in his lamentation to the girls in the classroom scene in Book II.[26]

From 'Leoville' with its fine views of Blackrock seafront and of Howth Head across Dublin Bay, Stephen Dedalus made forays into the town with his 'Uncle Charles', to shops and to the park, stopping sometimes at a church for a sprinkling of holy water and a prayer. His father likewise would be off on those long walks he loved, taking along the elderly uncle, stopping often at pubs for more than a sprinkle of not-so-holy water. The real 'Charles', Uncle William O'Connell, soon left the household, returning to Cork where he died at the end of August 1892. John took James to the funeral, to show him his birthplace and introduce him to old friends. He also introduced him to the pleasures of yachting, and took him to what he later called 'an incomprehensible regatta' at Clontarf,[27] a memory which later resurfaced in *Finnegans Wake* – 'the plage au Clontarf to feale the gay aire of my salt troublin bay and the race of the saywint up me ambushure.'[28] However, he never took to the water and never overcame his fear of storms at sea.

Despite his apparent advancement in moving to 'Leoville', the outlook for John was darkening, and he was facing a disastrous future. His situation at work was becoming increasingly insecure. The children may have sensed this and Stanislaus recalled returning home to see his father in the street outside the house, drunkenly playing a hurdy-gurdy while the bemused hurdy-gurdy man looked on.

Because of his heavy spending, by the following year John was again in trouble, borrowing £130, using his furniture as collateral. The cloud that had been hovering menacingly over John's head finally burst. He was beset by creditors, and on 2nd November 1892 he was published as a debtor and suspended from his job. On the 8th, May Joyce gave birth to Florence Elizabeth, her fifth daughter, an added expense for a family facing financial collapse. In December John had to raise a further loan, this time mortgaging one of his last Cork properties to Reuben J. Dodd, a Dublin lawyer, for £400, in order to help make up some deficiency in his accounts.

But now he faced the future with no job in prospect. At first he was considered by officials at the Collector General's Office for a half-salary pension of £264 per annum, a respectable sum in those days, but instead, because of his 'questionable record', they seemed intent on quashing it altogether. May is said to have petitioned on his behalf,[29] and finally, after four agonizing months, the authorities relented and agreed grudgingly to half the original sum. John and his already large family were now expected to exist on £132 a year, out of which he would have to repay various loans taken out in more affluent times. He never held a salaried position again.

Even in this precarious situation, John still harboured hopes of betterment. Aided by his loan from Dodd, in the summer of 1893, he again moved his family, first, to a gloomy house at 29 Hardwicke Street, then to a far grander, four-storey end-of-terrace property at 12 Fitzgibbon Street close to Mountjoy Square. It was a bigger house than any they had occupied before, with three drawing rooms and seven bedrooms. But the north side of the Liffey was an area in decline; and this apparent advancement did not betoken any sudden improvement in his finances but rather the grand, almost final, flourish of a man teetering on the edge of a social abyss.

Thus began the gypsy life of John Joyce and his family which had them flitting from one address to another, often pursued by angry landlords waving unpaid bills. As John found more and more solace in drink, and his rake's progress continued, the Joyces' goods and possessions diminished. What had once taken two furniture vans and a float to move, eventually took just a float. Stanislaus calculated that they passed through nine addresses in eleven years.

Liberated from the schoolroom, James and Stanislaus were free to wander the streets of Dublin, taking in the various distinctive features – streets, pubs, cafés, railway stations, hotels, hospitals, churches and bookstalls. The statues especially fascinated James and he enjoyed putting amusing words into their mouths. Above all there was the Liffey and its tributaries (river images permeated his later fiction) – the Dodder and the less-than-sanitary Poddle, which, according to *Ulysses*, 'From its sluice in Wood quay Wall . . . hung out in fealty a tongue of liquid sewage.'[30] Samuel Ferguson's 'limpid', 'murmuring' Liffey which washed by Mesgedra's grave at Clane, was here washing by distilleries, the Customs House and docked freighters, before emptying itself and Dublin's waste-matter into Dublin Bay.

James was absorbing the intricate layout of the city he was to immortalize in literature – College Green, St Stephen's Green, Kildare Street, Nassau Street, O'Connell Bridge, Dame Street, Grafton Street, the Quays along the Liffey – landmarks not just on the map of Joyce's Dublin but also on the map of his creative consciousness. And through those streets of that Victorian city, past shops, cafés, bars and newspaper offices, moved and jostled the Dubliners (tradesmen, Irish gentry, students, servant girls, jarveys, drunks, beggars, British soldiers and police) who would people his fictions.

John sometimes joined in his sons' sightseeing perambulations, regaling them with tales of Dublin life and characters and pointing out places of interest – the house of Swift ('Ireland's Rabelais'), the birthplace of Oscar Wilde, and the haunts of the essayist Joseph Addison. It was a leisurely city with an air of languor, not subject to the dictates of business or industry.[31] The sights, sounds, smells and texture of Dublin introduced James to a world he would transform into the focus and playground of his imagination. The spirit of the place would permeate his thoughts and writing, wherever he happened to be in the world, and would supply the dream-like setting for the great rumbustious *Finnegans Wake*.

Dublin also meant more access to plays, operas, pantomimes and music-halls, memories and images of which would become woven into the texture of his fiction. These offered Joyce magical worlds into which to escape from an increasingly wretched present, and his father's passion for Italian opera and the theatre would also colour his imagination. Even as John's job was about to disappear, on 26 December (St Stephen's Day) he took the whole family to the pantomime of *Sinbad the Sailor*. The memory was so vivid that in the 'Ithaca' episode of *Ulysses* Joyce was able to list the star, producer, lyricist, scenery and costume designers, and then ring his own characteristic verbal changes on the title.

> Sinbad the Sailor and Tinbad the Tailor and Jinbad the Jailer and Whinbad the Whaler and Ninbad the Nailer and Finbad the Failer ... Vinbad the Quailer and Linbad the Yailer and Xinbad the Phthailer.[32]

The lure of the theatre never left him; nor did the delight in having witnessed some of the great performers of the Victorian stage in action. The British music-hall, with its comedic anarchy, its leers and innuendos, provided a sideways glimpse of Saturnalia which would form the basis for the 'Circe' episode in *Ulysses* and parts of *Finnegans Wake*.

Despite the colour and excitement of the passing show, Joyce would gradually come to see 'dear dirty Dublin' as Ireland's 'centre of paralysis', and that combination of expectation and inertia would characterize his own sad and moving tribute to the city, *Dubliners*. Its stories would be based on events and characters and moments of epiphany he thought it the duty of writers to capture. These stored recollections would together embody the spirit of the city of his childhood and youth which was to haunt his mind and imagination ever afterwards.

The Joyces' new location brought May closer to her family, and her children's favourite aunt, Josephine. And there were occasional visits to the Flynns at Usher's Island, such as is glimpsed in a fleeting memory of a dark old house, an old woman busying herself about the place talking of 'the old days' and gossips with the priest and doctor, and James/Stephen wandering through the house, exploring, and in a doorway coming with a shock upon the skull of a monkey. That encounter and the boy's shock later inserted themselves into *A Portrait*.[33] These impressions suggest that young Joyce already enjoyed a rich inner life, a world already peopled by many of the characters who would find their way into his adult fiction.

Facing his own nightmare of failure, John's dream of social advancement now depended heavily on his eldest son, and he was beginning to worry about his education. Finally, in January 1893, and very much against their parents' wishes, Jim and Stannie were sent to the O'Connell School in nearby North Richmond Street, run by the Christian Brothers. The Brothers were laymen and their school was dedicated to educating the children of the disadvantaged. What James thought about this we may guess from his assuring Herbert Gorman that he had never been there, a version of events also written into *A Portrait*. There, Stephen's father, Simon, says, 'Christian brothers be damned! ... Is it with Paddy Stink and Micky Mud? No, let him stick to the jesuits in God's name since he began with them ... Those are the fellows that can get you a position.'[34]

James and Stanislaus attended the O'Connell School for a few months, until rescued by a stroke of good fortune. One day, crossing Mountjoy Square, John encountered Father Conmee, now Prefect of Studies at the Jesuit Belvedere College in Great Denmark Street. Conmee remembered James, the brave youngster who had come to him to plead the injustice of Father Daly/Dolan's pandying. He must have thought very highly of him, because on being told that he and his brother were having to attend the Christian Brothers' school, he saw to it that both were taken on at Belvedere free of fees, an arrangement from which around a quarter of the pupils then benefited. He probably also saw the bright and dedicated James as a potential candidate for the priesthood.[35] John was delighted. His Jim would be back where he deserved to be, among the Jesuits. Later, when referred to as a Catholic, Joyce could say by way of correction, 'You allude to me as a Catholic. Now for the sake of precision and to get the correct contour on me, you ought to allude to me as a Jesuit.'[36]

At this stage in the evolution of Joyce's consciousness, religiosity was already deeply embedded. He had been thoroughly seduced into the ecstasy of religion by the efforts of Dante, his mother and the subtle Jesuits, and as yet there was nothing much to disabuse him of his faith, nothing to disturb the sense of rapture – except perhaps his father's sudden turning against the Irish bishops and their acolytes. However, the Jesuits, as even his father would continue to believe, were different – 'clever men' who held the key to the advancement and gentrification of equally 'clever boys' like James Joyce.

4
Belvedere: In the Arms of the Jesuits
(1893–1898)

The spirit burning but unbent,
May writhe, rebel – the weak alone repent!
Byron, 'The Giaour'

Part of the reason why James's schooldays made such a lasting impression
on him, said Stanislaus, was that 'he suddenly found himself among boys
bigger and older but less intelligent than himself'.[1] It must have fed that
sense of intellectual snobbery that led him to despise what he called 'the
rabblement'.

When James started at Belvedere College in 1893 it was just sixty years
old, a younger and less prestigious establishment than Clongowes. It was
a day school drawing pupils from a different class – aspiring middle class
rather than established upper class and Catholic gentry. Moving from
Clongowes to Belvedere was generally considered a comedown, and its
lesser status only emphasized John Joyce's decline in fortune, something
for which James blamed a paralytic Irish society rather than his father's
prodigality.[2] However, the college was still an important avenue of
advancement for young Irish Catholics wishing to enter university,
medical college, or the professions. Furthermore, being taught by Jesuits
still carried kudos, and for the chosen few there was the prospect of the
priesthood.

The college occupied Belvedere House, at 5 Great Denmark Street, a
fine mansion built in 1775 by George Rochfort, the rakish 2nd Earl
of Belvedere. The Rochfort family saga involved tales of promiscuous
debauchery, with the young Countess, Mary Molesworth, incarcerated for
life in a County Westmeath mansion accused of adultery by the jealous
Earl. Later, in *Ulysses*, Joyce roguishly has Father Conmee contemplating
a book on the subject, *Old Times in the Barony*, and meditating on incest
and adultery.[3] Joyce's own obsession with cuckoldry played itself out in
Exiles, in *Giacomo Joyce*, and in *Ulysses*, while mistresses pervade *Finnegans
Wake*.

James, now eleven, entered Belvedere on 2 April 1893; the nine-year-
old Stanislaus enrolled a day later. The Rector was Father Thomas Wheeler,

and the teaching staff consisted of both Jesuit Fathers and laymen. At that time the student body stood at around 150, some ninety of these in the top three classes. Joyce was considered clever enough to go directly into III Grammar, and would move into II Grammar the following year.

Belvedere brought a return to the familiar rituals and sacred texts, to the Jesuitical cast of mind, the philosophical mode of thought derived from Aristotle and Aquinas, the scholarly disciplines of the Jesuitical *Ratio*, and to writing 'AMDG.' at the top of his essays. New requirements of a government-approved curriculum meant greater attention to mathematics and science, and in the study of literature emphasis shifted towards etymology and grammar. But, while taking on some of the new emphases, the conservative Jesuits were able to retain the liberal traditions of the *Ratio*. Translation, for example, did not focus solely on accuracy but also on trying to capture the spirit of the original. Kevin Sullivan, in his study of Joyce's college education, argues that it was classic Jesuit pedagogy ('The five steps in the process – reading, translation, explication, analysis of poetic or rhetorical structure, and *eruditio* [knowledge or learning]') that supplied Joyce with the mental discipline he always attributed to the Order.[4] Probably this is where he first developed his fascination with words, an interest bordering on obsession. If *Stephen Hero* is any guide, he read everything as if reading a thesaurus, and studied Skeat's *Etymological Dictionary* 'by the hour'.[5] The future author of *Ulysses* and *Finnegans Wake* was learning the value of language, its roots and ambiguities.

Now he was studying not just the fundamentals of his religion, English, and Latin, but also three foreign languages, arithmetic, Euclid and algebra. English, Joyce's best subject, was taught by his favourite teacher, George Dempsey, a lay master, a tall thin man of around fifty with the manner and bearing of a retired military officer, who in *A Portrait* appears as Mr Tate. Although he had a fine line in sarcastic comments, which the boys dreaded, they probably feared it less than the usual pandying handed out by other masters.[6] Dempsey, whose critical judgement was widely respected, was reader for a Dublin publisher and had literary contacts in England. Each week he would ask certain boys to read out their essays, on the usual schoolboy topics (such as 'My Favourite Hero'), and Joyce, whom he called 'Gussie', was often afforded this honour. A fine performer, he would frequently reduce Dempsey to appreciative laughter, though his signature, 'James A. Joyce', he regarded with amused irony. Pleasing so easily someone he admired must have given a great boost to young Joyce's confidence and urge to write.

Dempsey's opinion of the schoolboy writer was well-founded. Joyce's flair for English composition would win honours for himself and the college. One of his early essays, entitled 'Trust Not Appearances', has survived. Although it can be dismissed as a piece of immature schoolboy prose, florid and overblown, it is strangely revealing. He writes of 'the fickleness of appearances' and that 'the cringing, servile look, the high and haughty mien alike conceal the worthlessness of character', and ends with a flourish: The hypocrite is the worst kind of villain yet under the appearance of virtue he conceals the worst of vices.[7] Significantly, the vices he chose to castigate – 'treachery', 'hypocrisy' and 'financial and political corruption' – were all charges levelled at the betrayers of Parnell.

He read voraciously. By the time he got to Belvedere he already had some knowledge of the Classics – from his Latin texts, from Lamb's *Adventures of Ulysses* ('Odysseus' in Greek), and from certain poetry anthologies. He was now more than familiar with Byron, his favourite poet, and had discovered Cardinal Newman whose style he admired and sought to emulate. On one occasion after Dempsey had claimed (probably humorously) to have detected a 'heresy' in a composition referring to Byron, Joyce was assaulted by self-righteous bullies (led by the intimidating Albrecht Connolly – 'Heron' in *A Portrait*) who thought Byron 'a bad man'. It was an experience which aroused not only the artistic martyr in him but also the budding poet, and bound him even more closely to such 'bad men' of poetry. In fact he would later become increasingly attracted to sin, and rarely forgave his enemies. As his counterpart Stephen says, 'He became a poet with malice aforethought.'[8]

During his first summer holiday from Belvedere, John took James to Cork to revisit scenes of his youth and arrange for the sale of the last of his properties there – a sale forced on him by Reuben J. Dodd's refusal to postpone repayment of his £400 loan. But, with his son beside him, he treated the occasion as a holiday, meeting old friends and reliving old times. The clever, ever-observant James memorized all for later use in *A Portrait* where Stephen recalls his father, standing at the dressing-table at the Victoria Hotel, on their first morning in Cork, singing, 'with quaint accent and phrasing', 'Tis youth and folly/Makes young men marry.' He learns from one past acquaintance that in 'the old days' Simon (John) was 'the boldest flirt' in town, and in the lecture rooms of the Queen's Medical School, searching for his father's carved initials, something else caught his eye. Cut several times into the dark wood of the desktop, he reads the word *Foetus*.[9] This discovery brings to Stephen a sudden awareness of student life of those days in a way that his father's words failed to do, a sense of something racy and secretive. The word recurs in capital letters in the scene of brilliant stylistic variation and ingenious wordplay among cynical, bantering medical students at the Hollis Street Lying-in Hospital in the 'Oxen of the Sun' episode of *Ulysses*.

While in Cork John diverted to Crosshaven, ostensibly to visit an O'Connell relative, but, it is thought, probably to try to persuade the Mother Superior of the Presentation Convent there to take two of his daughters off his hands. On the return journey, by chance they encountered James's godfather, Philip McCann. As John revealed to him the dire state of his affairs, the reproachful look in McCann's eyes stayed with the boy long enough to be recorded in his notes for *Stephen Hero*. It made him aware of how the respectable world regarded his father, and although he portrayed him relatively sympathetically as 'Simon Dedalus', in his story 'Grace' John is depicted with cold remorselessness as a legless drunk.

If John thought he had a surplus of daughters, he would gain another on 27 November that year (1893) when Mabel Josephine Anne ('Baby') was born. Joyce now had six sisters and three brothers. All would grow into distinctive personalities – Stannie solemn, square and direct, a little in awe of his big brother but never afraid to disagree with him; Charlie less intelligent and less predictable; George as bright and funny as James. Among the girls, Margaret was much like her mother, Eileen more volatile, Mary, Eva and Florence more reserved and Baby (who became John's favourite daughter) more inclined to be jolly.

The loss of his Cork inheritance signalled John's impending doom. Stanislaus, who loathed his dissolute father, described him as a failed medic, actor, singer and commercial secretary.[10] By 14 December his Cork properties had been auctioned and he became a failed property owner. One house fetched £499, the other £1,400. Most of the money was taken in fees and repayment by Reuben J. Dodd, who thus earned for himself the everlasting hatred of the Joyces. In the 'Circe' episode of *Ulysses*, Dodd, whose son had almost drowned in the Liffey, becomes 'blackbearded Iscariot, bad shepherd, bearing on his shoulders the drowned corpse of his son' – a suitably demonic image for the 'treacherous' lawyer.[11]

Not long after his twelfth birthday, James was advised by the Belvedere school doctor, Dr Thomas O'Connell Redmond, to dispense with his glasses for the next ten years. The consequence was that for a decade thereafter he lived, so Costello argues, with restricted sight in a world in which he came to rely more than ever on the written word, sounds and smells. The very literary texture of his writing, the odours he describes in evoking character and place, and the keen ear he demonstrates for odd turns of phrase, habits of speech and strange verbal constructions, seem to bear this out.

The sweet smell of his mother and the foul stench of the 'Square Ditch' represented an olfactory heaven and hell for Joyce. Odours permeate his work – the 'warm humid smell' and 'perfumed bodies' of ladies of the Paris streets (*Epiphanies*), 'the warm heavy smell of turkey and ham and celery' at Christmas dinner (*A Portrait*), and Bloom's detecting 'Smells on all sides bunched together, each street different smell. Each person too. Then the spring, the summer: smells' (*Ulysses*).[12] To Arthur Power, an Irish writer friend, Joyce said later, 'What is the first thing you notice about a country when you arrive in it? Its odour, which is the gauge of its civilization, and it is that odour which percolates into its literature. Just as Rabelais smells of France in the Middle Ages and Don Quixote smells of the Spain of his time, so *Ulysses* smells of the Dublin of my day.'[13] Sounds echo through Joyce's work, too, from the silent house in 'Araby', to the fog-horn at the Pigeon House in 'An Encounter', the 'soft and mellow' notes of a piano in *Stephen Hero*, the deluge of sound in the 'Sirens' episode of *Ulysses* and the thunderous crack of doom in *Finnegans Wake*.

Events which Joyce later turned into fiction were very often ones which would have passed unnoticed by most people but to which he ascribed a deeper significance. For six days from 14 May 1894 a spectacular charity bazaar, a 'Grande Oriental Fête' called 'Araby', visited Dublin to raise funds for the city's Jervis Street Hospital. Admission was a shilling and meant a train journey out to Ballsbridge where the fête was held. His story 'Araby' suggests that he had waited all day for the money to get there, almost missing the event. When he arrived, most of the stalls had packed up and others were about to close. It afforded him a story which, by having his young hero anxious to buy a special present to impress the girl next door, adds poignancy to the incident. The location is recognizable; the girl remains obscure.[14]

In early June, Jim and Stannie went 'miching' – bunking off – to Ringsend and Irishtown, as far as the Pigeon House on the spit of land which points a finger eastwards into Dublin Bay at the mouth of the Liffey just beyond that of the Dodder. Out on this wasteland they encountered 'a queer old josser' who enticed the boys with licentious and mildly sadistic banter before satisfying himself at a distance. Joyce built on this in his story 'An Encounter'.

In the summer of 1894, James sat his first Intermediate Examination in which high-flyers stood to win exhibitions. His marks were outstanding enough to win him £20. John took the prizewinner and his money off to Glasgow and back as guests of a ferry skipper acquaintance. It rained continuously and the trip was a wash-out. On the return journey a drunken John got into a violent argument with the Captain over Parnell. Later, a sober John reflected on a lucky escape, saying, 'By God, man, if he had been drinking he would have thrown me overboard.'[15] James began lending small sums to family members, carefully recording all transactions. Like his father among his bar-room cronies, he was discovering the pleasure of his own liberality.

That summer, the Joyces moved to 2 Millbourne Avenue, Drumcondra, a newly built, comfortable house standing in an impoverished rural setting, where the Joyce children found local youth hostile. It was a decided come-down for John, the moment when his pretensions to middle-class respectability began to look hollow. In the autumn of 1894, with bills and rent unpaid, the family decamped yet again, this time back into the city, to 13 North Richmond Street, a cul-de-sac off the North Circular Road close to the Christian Brothers school. It was a fine-looking three-storey Georgian property with two reception rooms and four bedrooms, but cold and empty, strewn with the debris left behind by previous occupants. It provided James with the setting of 'Araby', and passing locations in *Stephen Hero* and *Ulysses*.[16] Other families in the street made enough of an impression to be woven into his future fictions – the Boardman children at No. 1 gave him Edy Boardman and the cycling brother so admired by Gerty MacDowell in *Ulysses*; Long John Clancy at No. 7 appeared as Long John Fanning in both *Dubliners* and *Ulysses*; Ned Thornton, a tea-taster living opposite, served as a model for Mr Kernan in 'Grace' and is numbered among the mourners at Dignam's funeral in the 'Hades' episode. Finally, the Gallahers' son gave his name to the returned exile who so excites the narrator in 'A Little Cloud'.[17]

That year John worked briefly on commission as a freelance advertising salesman for the Parnellite *Evening Telegraph*. The work suited him, and later he did similar work for the *Freeman's Journal*, where James, visiting him, imbibed the atmosphere and commotion of a newspaper office, and found a job – advertisement canvasser – for Leopold Bloom. Eyeglass screwed in and looking dapper, the proud father would take his two eldest sons for Sunday-afternoon strolls around Dublin, imparting more of his city folklore. James also took occasional long hikes with Alf Bergan, once as far as the Clontarf estate of Lord Ardilaun who inserts himself into both *Ulysses* and *Finnegans Wake*. Sometimes Aunt Josephine and their mother would take all their children for a day to the Bull Wall, a stone sea wall projecting into Dublin Bay at the mouth of the River Tolka – a favourite bathing place for Dubliners. Jim would invariably take a book to read or an essay to write; John would take a bottle which he called his 'medicine'.[18]

At the beginning of the new school year, the benign Father Wheeler was replaced by the stern Father William Henry, an English convert, who injected a new element of personal zealotry into Belvedere. He was feared and disliked by most of the boys, and, although he could be tolerant and good-humoured with certain pupils, he could also be both sinister and devious. He was a man with many mannerisms and expressions, the sort that delight schoolboy mimics, but, where his pupils' morals were concerned, he had an unhealthily suspicious mind.

Henry's stiff religiosity and his increasingly restrictive regime appealed to the very devout students, including Joyce, who found the new Rector more amusing than fearful. Beyond his ecclesiastical responsibilities, Henry taught the boys Latin, which, with French, all were required to study plus an optional third language. For this, Joyce chose Italian over Greek (his father's preference) and German (his mother's). He later came to regret his lack of Greek but Italian stood him in very good stead during his eventual exile, and gave him entry into a wider world of European literature.

During his first years at Belvedere, however, James was still enthralled by his religion and noted for his piety. His Catholic devotion was sufficiently well regarded by Father Henry and his colleagues for him to be admitted to membership of the Sodality of the Blessed Virgin at the end of 1895, of which, by the spring of '96, he had been made Head Prefect. This meant having to lunch with the Rector, giving rise to the rumour that he was receiving free meals because of poverty.[19]

Stanislaus, meantime, was progressing well – both a diligent reader and a worshipful shadow of his brilliant sibling. One day the devious Rector summoned him and began asking about his work. Gradually he turned the conversation towards matters spiritual and James's morals in particular, warning him against the worst of all sins, 'the sin of telling a lie to the Holy Ghost'. The bemused Stanislaus thrashed around in his mind for something to say and finally mentioned an occasion at home when his brother and a 'hoydenish' young housemaid had indulged in a little horseplay – what Stanislaus called 'a kind of catch-as-catch-can spanking match'. That was enough to excite the prurient Rector who immediately called in May Joyce to alert her to some unspecified moral defect in her eldest son. May, a little shocked and bewildered, returned to North Richmond Street, got the story out of Stanislaus, and promptly dismissed the servant girl. John, who had been kept in the dark but suspected that something was up, questioned Jim, and on being told, 'I am under a cloud at school,' paid a visit to Father Henry. The Rector told him solemnly that 'that boy' would give him trouble. 'No he won't,' came the reply, 'because I won't let him.'[20] If he did grasp the import of Henry's suspicions, John was probably pleased enough to think that his son and heir was nothing but a chip off the old block. According to Stanislaus, Jim considered it a great joke.

The extent of his devotion to both scholarship and religion is reflected in his reading at this time. Books assigned by teachers included selections from Ovid, Alvarez's *Grammar of Latin Verse*, Newman's *Apologia Pro Vita Sua*, Defoe's *Robinson Crusoe*, and Lyster's *Selected Poetry for Students*. But Joyce began to stray from the set texts and follow his own literary inclinations, forever haunting Dublin's second-hand bookshops in search of something new. He turned to Thomas à Kempis's *The Imitation of Christ*, highly suitable for so deeply devout a young man, Ovid's *Metamorphoses*, some opera scores, and – influences on his first novel – George Meredith's *The Ordeal of Richard Feverel* and *The Tragic Comedians*.

When the class was assigned an essay on Lamb's *Tales from Shakespeare*, Joyce wrote about his *Essays of Elia*; asked to write about Pope's *Essay on Man*, Joyce tackled his translation of the *Odyssey*. Of the French syllabus he devoured the works of Erckmann-Chatrian, including the play *Le Juif Polonais*. For Italian he read Machiavelli's *History of Florence* which introduced him not just to that great Italian city state but to Dante, Savonarola, and the Medicis. Costello argues[21] convincingly that Joyce came to see the Italian city state as something like the perfect social unit, which only confirmed in his mind and imagination the special nature and cultural richness of his own native city, Dublin.

His straying into less orthodox realms of literature led him into trouble with the librarian at the local public library. Stanislaus tells how, after he had borrowed Hardy's *Tess of the d'Urbervilles*, the keeper of books decided to warn John of the dangerous literature his son was reading. James, however, was able to reassure his father, deriding the librarian as 'an ignorant old clod-hopper'. But when he sent Stanislaus back to borrow *Jude the Obscure*, the boy misread the title and innocently asked for *Jude the Obscene*, much to the confusion of the prudish librarian. On hearing the story James hooted with laughter, sorry he had not been there to witness the scene.[22] John's attitude towards his son's reading was that if Jim thought it suitable to read then he should be free to read it.

By his fourteenth year, the intense devotion to religion which had marked Joyce's first two years at Belvedere was under threat from the onset of puberty and its fleshly temptations. He told Stanislaus that his first sexual experience had occurred at around this time. It involved a nursemaid, who, out walking with him, had retired behind a hedge to relieve herself. The sounds of the girl urinating had excited him to the extent that he had an erection leading to orgasm. Now, having discovered his 'sincorrupting flesh', he was amazed that one of Dante's thunderbolts had not struck him dead. But it left him in an agony of remorse to which he later referred by its Middle English name, 'agenbite of inwit'. If he did not confess his unmentionable sins to a priest he certainly did to himself in the guise of his self-reflective, guilt-ridden doppelgänger Stephen locked in his private confessional – the conscience of Stephen/Joyce the penitent speaking through the consciousness of Stephen/Joyce the confessor, one *monologue intérieur* filtered through that of the other.

> Yes, he had done them, secretly, filthily, time after time, and, hardened in sinful impenitence, he had dared to wear the mask of holiness before the tabernacle itself while his soul within was a living mass of corruption ... The leprous company of his sins closed about him, breathing upon him, bending over him from all sides.[23]

Haunted by sexual guilt, at the end of November Joyce went on a four-day retreat based on 'The First Week of the Spiritual Exercises' of Ignatius Loyola, founder of the Jesuit Order. It probably strengthened his religious commitment but was also an experience he would savour as a writer, building it up later and using it to powerful effect in *A Portrait*. The scarifying hellfire sermon appears to have been preached by Father James Cullen (Father Arnall in the novel) or perhaps by the rather more terrifying Father James Jeffcott,[24] who, in the words of Stanislaus, stirred up 'a brainstorm of terror and remorse' in both him and his brother. Joyce may have acquired a copy of Jeffcott's sermon, taken, it seems, from the meditations on hell of the seventeenth-century Italian divine Alphonsus Liguori.[25]

After defaulting on his rent, late that year John moved his ménage yet again, this time to 29 Windsor Avenue in Fairview. He had developed the midnight flit to a fine art, and delighted in outsmarting his dunning landlords. Somehow or other he had persuaded yet another gullible lessor (this time a man of the cloth called Love) to accept him as a reliable tenant. The new house stood, wrote Stanislaus, 'near the road that winds round the wide shallow mouth of the Liffey to Clontarf'.[26] The family remained there for the next three years, years which would see the waning of James's religiosity and his faltering yet inexorable conversion to Ibsenite atheism. In *A Portrait* he depicts the trauma of this transformation as a resurrection of the soul, a divesting of the grave-clothes of fear, guilt and incertitude, a rebirth which saw him emerge for the first time as an adult.[27]

As a budding writer he cannot have been unaware of the literary renaissance stirring in Ireland since the end of the 1880s with the appearance of W. B. Yeats's *The Wanderings of Oisin* and *The Celtic Twilight*. Yeats had been greatly influenced by the mysticism of George Russell (AE) and in 1886 had formed a Dublin branch of the Hermetic Society. Joyce was both attracted by and then scornful of the siren call of the cultural

nationalists, increasingly torn, as he told Gorman, between a variety
of competing claims – his father's expectation that he should act the
gentleman, the Jesuit injunction to become a good Catholic, the patriotic
demand to work for a new Ireland, and that of his peers to be what they
called 'a decent chap'.[28] The tug of his sexuality only added to this state
of confusion, though, if this were so, the cool face he presented to his
contemporaries would have largely concealed his turbulent state of mind.

James had his head permanently in books. Since living in Blackrock he
had made some early stabs at writing fiction. Now, in his fourteenth year,
he began a set of sketches called *Silhouettes*, the title story based on the
shadow-play of figures behind drawn blinds observed one night strolling
the city streets.[29] But his creative impulse also had another focus. The
inspiration of Byron, Ferguson and Yeats led him to continue what he
had begun with 'Et Tu Healy' and produce a series of poems entitled
Moods. These early efforts did not survive, except fleetingly in the memory
of his brother, though a few are to be found in what he called *Epiphanies*,[30]
copied down carefully on green ovals of leaves.

This notion of epiphany has a classical and religious origin and significance (referring in Greek drama to the climactic moment and in
Christianity to the moment of Christ's manifestation). Wordsworth, De
Quincey and the great Jesuit poet Gerard Manley Hopkins embodied
epiphanies in poetry as did his Italian hero, Gabriele D'Annunzio. Joyce's
revelations are not, like those of Hopkins, revelations of the divine mysteries, but of our somewhat less divine human natures. Much of his
writing afforded glimpses of his own hidden life and so is as much
confessional as revealing. This drawing on epiphanies from his own life,
using himself as a guinea-pig as he so often did, Stanislaus called 'a
peculiar form of self-exploitation for artistic purposes'.[31] But observation
also afforded him glimpses into the souls of others, giving him the sense
that behind respectable appearances there often lie sordid, even debased
realities. Such moments of insight formed the basis of his short stories in
Dubliners, as well as many scenes and incidents which make up his novels.

Pressures at home were intensifying. On 18 July 1895 another boy,
Frederick, was born, but within twelve days he sickened and died. As
Stanislaus tells it, his drunken father, faced with yet another disaster,
suddenly cracked, seized his wife by the throat, and yelled, 'Now, by God,
is the time to finish it.'[32] The children all screamed as James wrestled his
father to the floor, pinning him down while May escaped next door with
her two youngest. Some days later a policeman came and spoke to the
couple. James appeared unaffected by all this, but for Stannie it was just
a new level of degradation to which his father's dissolution had brought
the family.

James managed to avoid the tensions at home by attending open-house parties given on the second Sunday of every month at the Belvedere Place home of his classmates Richard and Eugene Sheehy, usually with Stannie and occasionally with his mother. The family name fascinated Joyce because it was epicene – comprising both feminine and masculine pronouns. David Sheehy was a Westminster MP (once famously arrested by a policeman inside the Houses of Parliament) who had sided against Parnell at the time of the Irish Parliamentary Party split, though this does not seem to have spoilt such occasions for James. As well as the two boys there were four daughters, Margaret, Hanna, Mary and Kathleen, of whom Mary became the special object of his undeclared passion, and Kathleen became the model for the nationalist Miss Ivors in 'The Dead'. Entertainment consisted mostly of singing, burlesques and charades, all of which brought out the best in the otherwise reticent young epiphanist. His repertoire included ballads such as 'Blarney Castle' or 'Turpin Hero', and music-hall songs like 'The Man Who Broke the Bank at Monte Carlo' – a swaggering performance, by all accounts. Eugene Sheehy recalled that whenever his mother played for the singers, James would conduct her to the piano 'with Old World courtesy'.[33] There was a gentlemanly formality about Joyce on such occasions.

He was well aware that economically and socially his family was on the slide and even made self-deprecating jokes about being poor, leaving the other students in no doubt about it. But not everyone saw the wry side of failure. Eileen Vance who visited him during the summer holidays, was shocked by the Joyces' new-found poverty and quickly lost interest in the boy who was once her Valentine. However, in a school which valued scholarship, James's evident intellectual ability guaranteed him high regard among the Jesuits. Whatever else they thought of Joyce, those who have left memories of him always acknowledge his brilliance, his wit and his amusing streak of contrariness. One fellow Belvederean who thought otherwise was Reuben J. Dodd Jnr, whose father had ruined John Joyce. He and James regarded one another with mutual contempt. Once in class, Dempsey asked, 'What is a pedestrian?' An arm shot up./'Well, Reuben, what is a pedestrian?'/'A pedestrian is a Roman soldier, Sir.'/Joyce's laugh at this was described as 'more like a howl of agony, as if his little frame were being torn apart'.[34] James would lampoon the Dodds unmercifully in *Ulysses* and Junior would sue for libel.[35]

As he matured, Joyce took on more of the characteristics which marked him out when be became an adult. Eugene Sheehy provided a snapshot of the youthful Joyce: 'He was a tall, slight stripling, with flashing teeth – white as a hound's – pale blue eyes that sometimes had an icy look, and a mobile sensitive mouth. He was fond of throwing back his head as he walked, and his mood alternated between cold, slightly haughty, aloofness and sudden boisterous merriment.'[36] His merry comedic spirit which led him into baiting his masters and fellow students, and later in trying to outwit his professors, went towards producing yet another great Irish satirist in the tradition of Swift, Sheridan, Shaw and Wilde.

Joyce's final college year began in September 1897. Having successfully concealed his guilt about unclean thoughts and actions, he was again elected Prefect of the Sodality. Father Henry's suspicions had been laid to rest, so much so that he invited him seriously to consider the priesthood. The previous summer he had again won an exhibition, this time one of £30 to be paid for two years, plus an essay prize of £3. His progress in French had been excellent and in English he had covered literature from Chaucer to Goldsmith. Now his talent for mimicry extended easily to an ability to reproduce the styles of past writers, a skill which began to reveal itself during that year. But he was neglecting the college curriculum in hot pursuit of his own literary interests and ambitions. This ferocious course of self-prescribed reading culminated in his discovery of Ibsen, and of Shaw's *The Quintessence of Ibsenism*. Father Henry's advances were rebuffed. There was no question of his donning the Jesuit habit, and his devout mother must have been sorely disappointed. His father had hoped he would go in for law, but literature and languages had now claimed his devotion.

Joyce's attitude towards authority had turned to open disdain. A gymnasium had been installed in the college theatre and a certain Sergeant Major Wright attempted to enthuse the boys about exercise using Indian clubs, the dumb-bell and horizontal bars. Joyce is remembered as performing at them all with exaggerated comic gusto, teasing the worthy sergeant by tying himself into knots around the exercise bars and loudly feigning injury.[37] His self-mockery also extended to swimming. William Fallon, a fellow student, recalled him out at the Bull Wall at Dollymount, standing on a rock looking frail in bathing trunks, posing as 'Poverty'.

At the beginning of 1898 James's godfather, Philip McCann died and left some money in trust for his education. Now flush, he took his parents to the theatre. He was hooked on drama, and, according to Stanislaus, saw performances by most of the great actors of the day – the comedian Edward Terry, the tragedians Henry Irving and Herbert Beerbohm Tree, and the great actresses Mrs Patrick Campbell and Eleanora Duse.[38] May Joyce might have preferred him taking her to church, but Jim now preferred thespians to priests.

With his departure from Belvedere approaching, the college's Whitsun play gave Joyce an opportunity to demonstrate his talent for burlesque. The play was F. Anstey's *Vice Versa*, with Joyce decked out in gown and mortarboard as the tyrannical, cane-wielding schoolmaster, Dr Grimstone. Egged on by Albrecht Connolly, he decided to send up the unsuspecting Father Henry.[39] Eugene Sheehy recalled how he took gleeful aim at Henry, mimicking his favourite catchphrases and mannerisms to great hilarity all round. The play was brought to a halt as the rest of the cast forgot their lines and missed their cues. 'Father Henry, who was sitting in one of the front rows . . . showed what a sportsman he was by laughing loudly at this joke against himself and Joyce received no word of reprimand for his impudence.'[40]

But he did finally push his luck too far. Tolerant of a bit of end-of-term lampoonery, Father Henry was not amused when Joyce and Connolly absented themselves from the final catechistic examination set by himself. They claimed they had spent the time preparing for their final Inter-mediate Examinations (Stanislaus hinted that it was a deliberate snubbing of the over-zealous priest). The angry Rector rejected their excuse and decided to ban them from taking *any* exams. Luckily for the truants, the young French master, Father Andrew McErlean, whose best student was Joyce, managed to talk him round. Whether this experience unnerved Joyce or whether he had just strayed too far from the syllabus, his results were poor compared with earlier years. He won no exhibition but did take the first prize of £4 for composition. One of the examiners, Belfast-born William Magennis, Professor of Philosophy at the college, pronounced Joyce's essay worthy of publication.[41]

Having rejected the priesthood, he persuaded his father that he should proceed in September to Dublin's University College, grandly housed on St Stephen's Green. His education would still be in the care of the Society of Jesus, but this more adult setting would afford him the freedom he now needed to forge and fashion his own intellectual and creative per-sonality. As part of the Royal University the college curriculum was for-mally secular, even though the Jesuitical presence was evident in both the staff and students, something Joyce would find not only amusing but challenging to his new spirit of critical independence.

Before he had quite shaken off his adolescent sense of melancholy, still suspended between innocence and experience, he underwent an epiphany which sparked in him 'an outburst of profane joy'. Wandering alone on the Dollymount Strand, he came across a solitary figure, a girl standing in a rivulet cutting through the sand down to the water's edge, gazing out to sea. The moment is recaptured in the mind of young Stephen Dedalus, his consciouness hovering metaphorically between the sacred and the sacrilegious.

She seemed like one whom magic had changed into the likeness of a strange and beautiful seabird. Her long slender bare legs were delicate as a crane's and pure save where an emerald trail of seaweed had fashioned itself as a sign upon the flesh. Her thighs, fuller and softhued as ivory, were bared almost to the hips, where the white fringes of her drawers were like feathering of soft white down. Her slateblue skirts were kilted boldly about her waist and dovetailed behind her. Her bosom was as a bird's, soft and slight, slight and soft as the breast of some darkplumaged dove. But her long fair hair was girlish: and girlish, and touched with the wonder of mortal beauty, her face.

They exchanged glances and she blushed. It was enough to pitch him, cheeks aflame, into 'a holy silence of ecstasy', and 'Her image had passed into his soul for ever.'[42] It would linger in the pages of A Portrait, resurface in his adult fantasies and supply Leopold Bloom with voyeuristic sexual self-satisfaction in the form of the enchanting Gerty MacDowell (also bare-legged on a beach).

He made his final farewell to innocence and piety that summer, a turning point on the road to becoming James Joyce. He later spoke of the event to Stannie – that encounter on the canal bank with a prostitute after having seen Sweet Briar, a play about an aristocratic girl and a costermonger who wins her love despite the class divide – where at each performance perfume was handed out to the ladies in the audience, drenching the air with alluring odours. The starting-point of this adventure is alluded to in Ulysses (appropriately enough in the Nighttown episode and in Nighttown imagery) as 'the dark sexsmelling theatre ... [which] ... unbridles vice'.[43] Years afterwards he told his patroness, Harriet Weaver, that he attributed what talent he might have to the 'extravagant licentious disposition' inherited from his father.[44] Exactly when he began his clandestine visits to 'Monto', Dublin's old brothel quarter (the area between Talbot Street and Montgomery Street – today's Foley Street), is unclear, but some amount of Philip McCann's money probably trickled away down those streets over the next few years. Four decades later he recalled a song his father's friend Tom Devin sang – 'O boys, keep away from the girls I say'. In his case, he reflected ruefully, the moral had most certainly fallen on deaf ears.[45]

By the time he left Belvedere, Joyce had already evolved into a more polymorphous personality. The devout youth had begun to slough off the crust of religious superstition which home and school had laid upon him, while leaving behind it a deposit of entrenched sentiment – an unbeliever's fascination with, and attachment to, church liturgy and holy days – which formed a permanent part of his make-up. In the process he had learned well the protean trick of presenting various faces to the world, firstly in his personal life, more profoundly later in his fiction.

5

Cultivating 'the Enigma of a Manner'
(1898–1899)

'Who makes up the majority in any given country? Is it the wise
men or the fools? I think we must agree that the fools are in a terrible
overwhelming majority, all the wide world over.'

Ibsen, *An Enemy of the People*

Escaping the nets of his religion was painfully difficult for Joyce. Jesuitical
Catholicism had cast a spell over him, a spell from which he had to break
free if he was to become the writer he had it in him to become. In the
process he underwent the profound metamorphosis from pious believer
to free spirit, regarding life no longer as a struggle between God and the
Devil but as a human comedy – not the *Divine* Comedy of Dante but the
essentially *carnal* one of Rabelais. Devotion to high art replaced blind
faith as the supreme virtue, bad art became the greatest of sins, and
imagination supplanted prayerful mantra as the means to salvation. Aesthetics became his new theology. Reason would enable him to discard old
muddled beliefs and suffocating customs, and logic to break free from the
constraining ignorance of the Lilliputian rabblement.

University College, presided over by Father William Delany, was housed
in three large eighteenth-century town houses situated on the south side
of St Stephen's Green. Numbers 85–86, once the home of the Dublin rake
Thomas 'Buck' Whaley, was where Cardinal Newman – no doubt having
first exorcised the libidinous spirit of Mr Whaley – chose to open his
Catholic University in 1854. In 1880, with the addition of two adjoining
properties, Newman's foundation became University College. Five years
later, in 1885, the Jesuits took over. Many of the college's brightest students
were drawn from either Clongowes or Belvedere, and not a few from the
Christian Brothers' school so despised by John Joyce. According to Joyce's
dissolute and witty friend Oliver St John Gogarty, their generation of
students were 'young men ... in a rebellious condition ... getting away
from parents and also getting away from the accepted canons'.[1] That
certainly applied to James Augustine Aloysius Joyce.

The college Dean of Studies and Fellow in English, Father Joseph
Darlington, was a Shakespeare scholar, who earlier that year, 1898, had
published a celebrated paper in the *New Ireland Review* on 'The Catholicity

of Shakespeare's Plays'. In it he took issue with Edward Dowden, Professor of English at Trinity College, who argued that Shakespeare's sympathies were Protestant. The struggle for the soul of the Warwickshire bard fascinated Joyce, and would surface in the 'Scylla and Charybdis' episode in *Ulysses* in Stephen's discussion of *Hamlet* at the National Library with 'John Eglinton' (W. K. Magee), Richard Best, George Russell ('Dublin's Socrates'), and Gogarty. 'Your dean of studies,' says Eglinton mockingly, 'holds he was a holy Roman.'[2]

At college, however, Joyce's engagement with Shakespeare was more direct because his discovery of European drama had convinced him that playwriting was his métier. Even his epiphanies were revealing a keen ear for dialogue. His essay on 'Drama and Life' would draw teasing comparisons between *Macbeth* and Ibsen's *The Master Builder*, and he would slip amusing references to 'The Scottish Play' into *A Portrait*, *Ulysses* and *Finnegans Wake*. Joyce's early passions were rarely discarded or outgrown.

Gradually his attendance at English lectures diminished, but his reading gathered pace and grew in range. In that first university year, Joyce read Carlyle, Newman, Macaulay, De Quincey, Ruskin, Sudermann, D'Annunzio, Dante, Zola, Turgenev, Pater, Yeats, Blake, Maeterlinck, Arthur Symons's *The Symbolist Movement in Literature*, and most of Ibsen, complemented by Shaw's *The Quintessence of Ibsenism*. He could identify closely with the playwright whose country was still struggling against Danish–Swedish domination, claiming that because of early Scandinavian invasions, Dublin was a Norwegian city and he himself of Norwegian descent. Then, importantly for him, Ibsen, like few others, had managed to resolve the tension between realism and symbolism, to both of which Joyce was powerfully attracted.

Joyce also found Ibsen's stand against Victorian philistinism exhilarating, as he wrote to him three years later. 'Your battles inspired me – not the obvious material battles but those that were fought and won behind your forehead, how your wilful resolution to wrest the secret from life gave me heart and how in your absolute indifference to public canons of art, friends and shibboleths you walked in the light of your inward heroism.'[3] The Ibsenite vision offered heroic opportunities even to someone physically frail – the intrepid life of the liberated mind. Ibsen was, for Joyce's shadow, Stephen Dedalus, the true successor of 'Europe's first poet', Dante: 'a human personality had been found united with an artistic manner'.[4] He provided him with a brave identity with which to face a world full of hypocrisy and corruption. Because few had heard of Ibsen, this identification also set Joyce apart, assisting him in his design of 'constructing the enigma of a manner', a principle he also gradually extended to his work.[5] Having divested himself of the devout and monkish role he had adopted at Clongowes and Belvedere ('that fever-fit of holiness' he called it),[6] he was now set upon constructing for himself the persona of secular priest devoted to the cause of high art.

At university he found some familiar faces from Belvedere. One was John Francis Byrne, son of a Wicklow farmer, omnivorous reader, tireless conversationalist and wit. Stanislaus had his own take on Byrne, seeing him as 'a rather idle but very solemn-looking student' with a 'monastic manner' and the face of a Cistercian abbot.[7] He was a keen chess-player, hence his nickname, 'The White Bishop'. In *A Portrait*, Joyce would call him 'Cranly' after a medieval Bishop of Dublin, also known as 'The White Bishop'.[8] Even in the simple matter of finding a fictional name for a friend, Joyce's mind would conjure up these kinds of tenuous associations. In the same vein, calling himself Stephen Dedalus implies both creator and aviator – Dedalus after the designer of the Labyrinth of Minos and the wings to escape it. Stephen, of course, was the first Christian martyred for his beliefs. Other names he chose were more obvious and not always especially friendly, such as 'Maurice' for the character based on Stanislaus – Maurice was the patron saint of infantrymen, possibly a sly indication of the company to which he thought his unimaginatively plodding brother and faithful follower belonged.

His search for material carried on well beyond the classroom and the library. Partying at the Sheehys, he would often divest himself of his protective mask to reveal a talent for playful exuberance, adding memorable stories to Joycean folklore. There was Joyce playing 'to the life' the upper-class English Colonel Hawtree in a family production of T. W. Robertson's *Caste*, Joyce sending up Queen Gertrude in *Hamlet*, wailing over a comic Ophelia (William Fallon in drag), like 'a woman "keening" at an Irish wake in the very ecstasy of grief'.[9] And there was his witty repartee, comic improvisations and clever mimicry in charades.

But this uninhibited manner did not commend itself to everyone. Some found Joyce almost irresistible, but others found him rude and rough. Mary Sheehy recalled how a Limerick cousin of hers, Kathleen Sheehy, a rather eccentric girl, would sit beside him, and whenever he made a witty remark would throw her arms around him and shout with laughter, which always left Joyce frozen with embarrassment.[10] And on meeting him in the street she would slap him heartily on the back and leave him cringing. In fact, most of the time Joyce was reserved and formal and even disliked being addressed by his Christian name, except by members of his family. Often he was so reserved as to appear cold and indifferent, shaking hands with what a friend called 'the frozen mitt'.[11]

More than once, his lack of couth showed through the dignified poise. At one of the occasional 'hops' at Belvedere Place, when they rolled back the carpet and danced, Joyce asked Mary for a waltz. He was a good dancer, she thought, but had no idea how to hold a girl. He held her very slackly, and whispered, 'Hold my thumb,' which she misheard as 'Hold my tongue.' 'How can I do that?' she asked, and when he repeated the invitation, said, 'Oh! I thought you said your tongue.' At this Joyce let out one of his whoops of delight and just carried on dancing.[12] There were, however, women to be found in Dublin who enjoyed this uninhibited side of him, or pretended to for a suitable fee, in that part of town which woke after nightfall. Intimations of his nocturnal wanderings may have filtered back to his respectable friends. Jokingly, Richard Sheehy called him 'James Disgustin' Joyce'.

It was not only at night that he wandered the Dublin backstreets and along the Liffey, a nocturnal *flâneur*, the novelist observing and absorbing. His doppelgänger Stephen haunts the city's slums by day, taking in 'the sordid lives of the inhabitants'.

These wanderings filled him with deep-seated anger and whenever he encountered a burly black-vested priest taking a stroll of pleasant inspection through these warrens full of swarming and cringing believers he cursed the farce of Irish Catholicism: an island the inhabitants of which entrust their wills and minds to others that they may ensure for themselves a life of spiritual paralysis, an island in which all the power and riches are in the keeping of those whose kingdom is not of this world . . . [who] . . . wax fat upon a starveling rabblement which is bidden ironically to take to itself this consolation – in hardship 'The Kingdom of God is within you'.[13]

This was the hellish part of the city his characters in *Dubliners* and *Ulysses* feared – the abyss into which they could so easily plunge – rendered through the premeditated cast of Stephen's consciousness.

Joyce saw the underside of Dublin life at close quarters in another way, when Samuel Childs went on trial in October 1899 for the murder of his brother. Knowing a member of the jury, he attended the trial and doubtless took notes. Although Childs was found not guilty the question of fratricide fascinated Joyce. There is reference to the case in *Ulysses* and the Cain and Abel story underlies the conflict between the brothers Shem and Shaun in *Finnegans Wake*. The following summer, another murder case attracted his attention. Henry Flower, a policeman, was charged with killing a housemaid, Brigid Gannon, whose body was found floating in the Dodder. After a lengthy trial, Flower was cleared, leaving the country but also leaving behind a legend. 'Henry Flower' became the name under which Leopold Bloom writes secretly and salaciously to Martha Clifford.

*

Joyce launched himself into his matriculation-year studies in preparation for entrance to a degree in Modern Languages and Literature, a course then considered more suitable for women than men.[14] But for Joyce, henceforth, literature and languages rather than sacred texts and theology would be the royal road to self-realization. These passions and his interest in philosophy encouraged him to think deeply about words and their meanings. Two essays written during that first year, one on 'Force', the other on 'The Study of Languages', survive in fragmentary form. In the former, he argues that while force may successfully crush men's spirits and aspirations, it can also be 'productive of ill-will and rebellion'.[15] Evidently he had the Irish situation in mind even though his arguments were pitched at a relatively abstract level. His style, however, still lacks the inventive fluency that came later, and his reasoning suggests he had not yet been won over completely to Ibsenite rationality.[16]

Possibly from reading Wilde, who had left Reading Gaol in May the previous year, Joyce developed an interest in Walter Pater and John Ruskin, whose *Mornings in Florence* he bought that September. His essay on 'The Study of Languages' includes a critical appreciation of a fresco in the Florentine Church of Santa Maria Novella in which the artist attempts, as he puts it, to show the gradual progress from science through grammar to rhetoric and music and on to arithmetic, a progression which mirrors both his Jesuitical education and his new-found passion for the old Italian city state. His ruminations about languages, his growing fascination with other tongues and alternative modes of expression, afford a further glimpse into his evolving mindscape. Above all, he acknowledges both the beauty of the rules of language and the attractions of escaping those constraints into the more figurative world of literature.

Stanislaus, meanwhile, was undergoing his own crisis of conscience which led him eventually to reject religion even more vehemently than his brother. But he remained, as he had been since childhood, somewhat in awe of James's brilliance, a confidant and critical devotee. 'I was,' he claimed, 'my brother's first believer.'[17] He was also his most honest critic and – at least for the early part of his life – his Boswell. Two important ways in which they differed were in their attitudes towards religion and their father. Stanislaus hated both without reservation; James rejected both, but with a degree of lingering affection.

His father, whom he saw increasingly less often, he rarely criticized. In *Ulysses*, Stephen merely refers to Simon as 'a necessary evil'.[18] Stanislaus wrote that his brother's two great passions were love of his country and city – a love that was rejected – and love of his father, 'who was like a mill-stone round his neck'.[19] His mother he also loved, pitying her for her life of relentless childbearing and increasing poverty endured so stoically, but he found himself ever more alienated from her devout Catholicism. His sister May thought that in rejecting the Church and turning atheist he had broken the poor woman's heart,[20] and in *A Portrait* he hints that she blamed the university for having undermined his faith.[21] But, according to Stanislaus, 'My mother had become for my brother the type of the woman who fears and, with weak insistence and disapproval, tries to hinder the adventures of the spirit.'[22] Her sin, from James's point of view, was to want to confine his imagination inside the nets of her beliefs. Family sentiment would never constrain his sheer determination to pursue his new vocation.

His attitude towards the rest of his family and religion is cruelly spelled out in a letter he wrote two years after graduating: 'My brothers and sisters are nothing to me. One brother alone is capable of understanding me.'[23] But his dismissive attitude towards his siblings was not exactly reciprocated, as they later remembered regarding him as their idol. So while his sister Eileen recalled their father giving Jim 'absolutely everything' and depriving the rest of the family to do so,[24] Eva claimed that 'all the brothers and sisters seemed to be quite happy that he was the one that got the most attention. He was a very gentle child, indeed I never remember seeing him in a temper about anything – in fact, he always laughed at everything.'[25] In March, he took his parents to the Gaiety Theatre to see Mrs Patrick Campbell as the eponymous heroine of *Magda*, a dramatization of Hermann Sudermann's novel *Heimat*. Afterwards he told them, 'The subject of the play is genius breaking out in the home and against the home ... It's going to happen in your own house.'[26]

Although Joyce's hostility towards the Church was angrily reciprocated by those who felt he had betrayed the faith, for him apostasy was a deeply personal matter. His natural impulses, he later told Nora Barnacle, made it impossible for him to return to the Church which he had left at sixteen, hating it passionately. 'By [leaving it] I made myself a beggar but I retained my pride. Now I make open war upon it by what I write and say and do. I cannot enter the social order except as a vagabond.'[27]Here he reveals one of the prime intentions motivating and infusing his fiction.

Vagabondage would take him first into alienation and then into exile. At university he cultivated the air of the enigmatic deviant – sphinx-like at one moment, cuttingly witty the next, and a fount of unorthodox ideas. 'Critical superiority' was how one of his contemporaries described it.[28] This critical superiority found its natural outlet in the college Literary and Historical Society whose debates took place in the Physics Theatre at 86 St Stephen's Green. In January 1899 he and Thomas Kettle, a brilliant wit and fine debater (regarded by some as a future Parnell), opposed and defeated a motion before the Society, 'That in the last decade of the nineteenth century English literature reached a very low ebb'.

The following month Joyce took on Hugh Boyle Kennedy who, because he would brighten up with blushes on occasions, was nicknamed Hugh 'Boilin' Kennedy. This, it is said, gave Joyce the name 'Hugh Boylan' for Molly Bloom's lover in *Ulysses*. Kennedy was a prude who disapproved of Joyce – so making him, even by association, an adulterer, was the sort of mischievous lampoonery Joyce always relished. Kennedy read a paper entitled 'The War Machine, A State Necessity' and Joyce's reply was a satirical, military-style parody of the beatitudes to discomfort his pious opponent. John, who had gone along to watch the fun, squinting through his eyeglass, is reported saying, 'My God, he [Jim] spoke for half an hour and left Kennedy in a condition that he was not fit to be washed.'[29]

Joyce's oddly controversial and unpredictable disposition was giving him the reputation of an eccentric. Arthur Clery, the Society's Auditor, who wrote a column for the college magazine *St Stephen's*, dubbed him 'The Mad Hatter', forever going on about Sudermann, Ibsen, Bjornson and Giacosa and challenging received opinion. Joyce didn't care. He had replaced the carapace of invulnerable faith with one of disdainful irony. It was as if mentally he had withdrawn into exile, returning only to discomfort with badinage or disconcert with mockery.

On 11 March,[30] Arthur Clery delivered a paper on 'The Theatre – Its Educational Value'. Clery (who became Davin in *A Portrait*), a witty and urbane character, said to have had a 'cultured eighteenth-century style', took a strictly Aristotelian view of theatre – that drama should be 'elevating'. He praised the traditional canon of Greek drama and Shakespeare, especially *Macbeth*, and condemned the new European drama, denouncing the effect of Ibsen as 'evil'. Joyce spoke against the paper, and, now a passionate devotee of modern European theatre, proposed a paper of his own to be entitled 'Drama and Life'.

Another event further added to Joyce's reputation as a singular personality. In Dublin on 8 May 1899, Yeats, aided by Lady Augusta Gregory, George Moore and Edward Martyn had founded the Irish Literary Theatre (forerunner of the Abbey), and was to perform his verse play *Countess Cathleen* (partly inspired by his unrequited passion for the actress Maud Gonne) at the city's Antient Concert Rooms. Yeats's play was meant both as a call to arms for cultural nationalism and an allegorical mixture of religious belief, Irish superstition and myth in which the Countess sells her soul to devils (merchants from the east) for the salvation of her starving people. However, on rumours alone, a Cardinal of the Church had denounced the play as 'heretical', and some of the more nationalistic students who had also pre-judged it, turned up on the first night to make their feelings known. Having taken exception to Yeats's portrayal of Ireland and its peasantry, they heckled loudly, attempting to disrupt the performance. Joyce, however, who found the Faustian theme and its libertarian attack on the poverty of ignorance appealing, was in the other camp, perched up in the 'gods' applauding and cheering vigorously throughout. The next day's Dublin *Daily Express* reported that above the hissing a voice from the gallery cried, 'Don't mind them, Mr Yeats, they're only Tim Healy's curates.'[31] It can only have been Joyce, identifying the poet's accusers with those who had betrayed Parnell.

The day following the performance, a letter to the *Freeman's Journal* by Francis Skeffington, protesting about the play, was left at the college for students to sign. Joyce declined, boasting that he was 'the only student who refused his signature', which probably owes more to the symbolic importance he attached to his contrariness than to historical accuracy. Skeffington was a genuine eccentric – a bearded vegetarian, anti-vivisectionist and feminist, whose breeches earned him the sobriquet 'Knickerbockers' ('Hairy Jaysus' to Joyce). (He eventually married Hanna Sheehy, and from a sense of sexual equality adopted the name Sheehy-Skeffington.)

Joyce had been particularly moved during the play by the singing by Florence Farr (playing Aileel) of Yeats's poem, 'Who Goes with Fergus?', struck by its dream-like quality and assertion of the liberating power of nature.

> Who will go drive with Fergus now,
> And pierce the deep wood's woven shade,
> And dance upon the level shore?
> Young man, lift up your russet brow,
> And lift your tender eyelids, maid,
> And brood on hopes and fear no more ... [32]

It was a song not only to be added to his repertoire, but also to incorporate into his personal metaphysic. It would become a leitmotif in *Ulysses* when a snatch is teasingly sung by Buck Mulligan in the 'Telemachus' episode, and returns to haunt Stephen later on in the stews of Nighttown. It also came to possess his mind for very personal reasons as an evocation of a sadness that would soon overcome him.

By June 1899 Joyce had passed his matriculation examinations, achieving, at least in Latin, a creditable second-class honours mark, and was free in September to proceed with his main degree. It meant far less pressure of work for students, more freedom in which to develop their intellectual personalities. To this end, the college regime was relatively liberal, as

Eugene Sheehy recalled: 'The lectures which I had to attend were few, and afforded me ample time to browse elsewhere.'[33] 'Elsewhere', for Joyce and his University College contemporaries, was primarily the National Library in Kildare Street. This, claimed Sheehy, was his generation's 'real Alma Mater', serving effectively as the college library, and Thomas Lyster, the director, encouraged the idea. Constantine Curran remembered Joyce as an irregular visitor to Kildare Street, rarely studying books relevant to his university courses but pursuing his own literary interests. And although he had his favourite table, he rarely took part in the discussions in which others engaged on the portico outside after closing time. Curran believed that Joyce had made up his mind on most live issues and did not think debating his views worth the effort.

The college Dean, Father Darlington, was an English convert to Catholicism – recalled by another student, Felix Hackett, as a 'wooden-minded Aristotelian', but by Curran as 'a kind, harmless and pitiable soul' with a quick and responsive mind. Darlington taught English to the matriculated freshmen, and Curran, newly arrived at the college, recalled his first English Literature lecture from Father Darlington.

> His opening words were from Aristotle's Poetics. [He] made some passing allusion to Stephen Phillips who had just published his Paolo and Francesca. 'Have any of you gentlemen read Paolo and Francesca?' he inquired, and then immediately: 'Have you read it, Mr Joyce?' A voice behind me replied indifferently: 'Yes.' I looked round and saw my first poet.[34]

Curran, a year younger than Joyce, was very much struck by this unusual character and his distinctive appearance:

> ... tall, slim, and elegant; an erect yet loose carriage; an uptilted, long, narrow head, and a strong chin that jutted out arrogantly; firm, tight-shut mouth; light-blue eyes which I found could stare with indignant wonder and which were uncommonly like Lord Rosebery's as described by [his biographer], 'at times altogether expressionless like the eyes of a bird. They gave an air of inscrutability and sometimes of lack of interest in the surroundings of the moment.'[35]

Darlington's interest in aesthetics based on Aristotle and Aquinas gripped Joyce's imagination and he plunged into their work and absorbed it with an almost feverish intensity.

Joyce had opted to read French and Italian. Undergraduate French was taught by Professor Edouard Cadic, a patriotic Breton and survivor of the Franco-Prussian War. His Italian teacher was Father Charles Ghezzi, an easy-going Italian Jesuit who had spent time in India. Ghezzi was less rigid than his Jesuit colleagues and he and Joyce would converse in Italian for long periods, leaving the only other student, Eugene Sheehy, a lone spectator. Joyce and Ghezzi forged a bond which would last beyond the university, and the Italian's portrayal in *A Portrait* is more sympathetic than those of Joyce's other teachers, such as Darlington. It was no doubt under Ghezzi's tutelage that the aspiring writer came to rate Dante above Milton and Homer and acquired an enthusiasm for D'Annunzio. But Joyce did not confine himself to languages taught in the college; he set himself to master other European languages, notably Norwegian to enable him to read Ibsen in the original, and German in order to read Hauptmann and Sudermann. There was, however, another advantage in this – it made him appear extraordinary.

His mastery of foreign languages only enhanced his command of English, but the rise of Irish cultural nationalism, committed to revive the Irish language, posed a dilemma for Joyce. He relished old languages and felt a deep affinity for Irish, but English was a bridge to the wider world in which he felt his destiny lay. His attachment to English would bring him into conflict with nationalists scornful of so-called 'West Britons' who refused to renounce the imposed alien culture, a charge levelled at Gabriel Conroy in 'The Dead'.

The sphinx-like, critically superior Joyce was ever alert for epiphanies – any glimpse of character, or incident, however commonplace, which he believed pointed to some hidden secret. But behind the detached observer lurked the comic, mercurial Joyce. The watchful monologist expounding matters philosophical, could in an instant be overcome by what Curran called 'sustained bouts of hilarious drollery'.[36] Even in class Joyce could suddenly turn jester. Once he and a fellow student, George Clancy, feigned a dispute in Cadic's class and challenged each other to a duel in Phoenix Park, much to the bewilderment and horror of the humourless Cadic. It took the efforts of the rest of the class (in on the joke) to smooth 'ruffled feathers' and have the bout called off. On another occasion, in the library, he found Byrne reading a paper on 'Diseases of the Ox' and was so convulsed with laughter at the title that Lyster asked him to leave the building. Byrne and Curran became two of his closest companions, walking the streets of Dublin discoursing principally on matters that most concerned Joyce – religion and aesthetics, discussions he recaptured with some fidelity in both *Stephen Hero* and *A Portrait*.

What Byrne called Joyce's 'undeniable egoism', and a burgeoning interest in the modern drama, led him to take a bold step into a wider public arena. Encouraged by his old English master, George Dempsey, he wrote to the editor of the *Fortnightly Review* in London, W. J. Courtney, proposing an essay on Ibsen's latest play, *When We Dead Awaken*, which he had read in French. Courtney was encouraging and by the end of the year Joyce had sent him a manuscript. Its reception in London would prove to be a transformational moment in his life and career.

6
Making a Reputation
(1900–1902)

'One of the things I could never get accustomed to in my youth was
the difference I found between life and literature.'

Joyce to Arthur Power

The turn of century saw Joyce celebrate his eighteenth birthday and the
pace of his life quicken. On 20 January 1900 he delivered his long-
pondered talk on 'Drama and Life' to the college's Literary and Historical
Society. It was to be an important event in Joyce's artistic evolution. It
confirmed his reputation for eccentric brilliance, and provided him with
a springboard to a new literary future.

An eager audience packed the Physics Theatre to hear 'The Mad Hatter'
in full flow. The chair was taken by William Magennis, who had so
admired Joyce's final examination essay at Belvedere. Out of courtesy,
Joyce had sent the paper in advance to the college president, who was
unhappy about references to Ibsen and the paper's ethical neutrality, and
pencilled in some suggested changes. Joyce, however, refused to read a
censored paper, and argued with Father Delany, producing copies of the
plays mentioned for him to look at. Beauty, he maintained, following
Aquinas, was that which is seen to be pleasing. In the event, Joyce and
Aquinas won the day and the paper was delivered as written,[1] in a flat,
even tone 'of low innocuous melody', according to *Stephen Hero*, and
concluded 'in a tone of metallic clearness'.[2]

His argument, read and discussed at length with Stanislaus, revealed
the extent of his thoughts on Greek drama and the Elizabethan theatre.
Shakespeare's rich talents, he began, lifted his work above 'mere drama'
into 'the realm of literature'. But the unchanging laws of drama were also
embodied in the controversial 'New School' in which playwrights had
demonstrated their superiority in showing how drama – 'strife, evolution,
movement' – was independent of its setting, compared to which literature
was 'a comparatively low form of art'. Theatre was both communal and
classless and so the 'fittest vehicle' for conveying truth. In its highest
form – as with Ibsen's *The Wild Duck* – it was almost beyond criticism.
The demands of the religious, 'that the drama should ... instruct, elevate,

and amuse' were chains to encumber it. The truth was more real than the
beauty demanded by those aesthetes who never looked beyond form. 'Art
is true to itself when it deals with truth.' Belief in idealism had often
meant escapism – the babyish desire to hide under the blankets. The
philistines merely offered medicine against the dreariness of life.

He then launched into his peroration, displaying a nice touch of dash
and drama:

> Out of the dreary sameness of existence, a measure of dramatic life may
> be drawn. Even the most commonplace, the deadest among the living,
> may play a part in a great drama ... Life we must accept as we see it
> before our eyes, men and women as we meet them in the real world, not
> as we apprehend them in the world of faery. The great human comedy
> in which each has a share, gives limitless scope to the true artist, to-day
> as yesterday and as in years gone ... The sooner we understand our true
> position, the better.

He concluded with the last two lines from Act One of Ibsen's *Pillars of
Society*. 'What will you do in our Society, Miss Hessel?' asks Rörlund/'I will
let in fresh air, Pastor,' answers Lona.[3]

Having taken swipes at the *littérateurs*, conventional aesthetics, cultural
nationalists and religion, and having dared commend a play about
syphilis (*Ghosts*), it is not surprising that Joyce was fiercely attacked from
all sides, all angles and at length, by the speakers who followed him, until
a bell announced the end of the session. Unusually, he was permitted to
reply and turned in a bravura extempore performance, thereby demonstrating at first hand one of his main points – the essential spontaneity
of drama. One by one he took apart his critics, receiving rounds of
applause as he did so from 'the back benches' of the Physics Theatre. At
the end, one of his student admirers, Seamus Clandillon, clapped him on
the back saying, 'Joyce, that was magnificent, but you're raving mad!' He
judged his own performance as measured and to the point. As he wrote
to Ibsen later, 'I enforced attention by no futile ranting.'[4] Felix Hackett
likened him to Disraeli promising that one day he would be heard.[5]
Stanislaus commented that his brother had taken the care he had in
preparing it because he was 'defining his position to himself and others –
contra Gentiles' – and clarifying his claims as an artist.[6]

The impetus gained from delivering this talk would carry him on to
higher things. The day before he delivered it, Courtney had written saying
that while he had no space in February's *Fortnightly Review* for an article
on Ibsen, there might be in the following issue. Two weeks later he wrote
inviting Joyce to revise and resubmit his review for the April number. On

1 April, 'Ibsen's New Drama' duly appeared in Courtney's *Review*. In college circles the impact was considerable. For a youth of eighteen to appear in so prestigious a periodical was an unbelievable distinction and he was regarded with both awe and respect from then on. For Joyce it was undoubted confirmation of his own capabilities and gave him a self-assurance bordering on arrogance. 'I started at the top,' he would say proudly.[7] Shortly afterwards he received a fee of twelve guineas. The slip accompanying the cheque survived him, suggesting that he held on to it not simply as a memento but as a talisman.[8]

He was now convinced that his future did not lie with Yeats's Irish cultural movement. He would become the lone wolf, keeping himself apart from the pack and seemingly not much wanted by them. In fact, his friend Byrne saw him as seriously isolated by his success. 'After his Ibsen article had been published,' he wrote, 'Joyce's relationship with his few associates became impaired by either their jealousy or sycophancy.'[9] This turned him inward, away from drama and aesthetics towards composing short lyrical poems which he rewrote and retouched until they were ready to be copied in a neat stylish hand on to separate sheets of paper. His alter ego, Stephen Dedalus, thought that 'the beauty of verse consisted as much in the concealment as in the revelation of construction'.[10] 'Poet' was the perfect persona for one anxious to construct 'the enigma of a manner'.

Curran wrote that when Joyce formally adopted the mask of poetry, with it came a voice and a performance, which, with his flair for acting, came easily. But Colum noted that while he would recite Jonson and Yeats with a composed, dignified and persuasive lilt far more impressive than Yeats or Russell, he could also switch to a raucous voice when recounting his 'seedy adventures' around Dublin or reciting from his repertoire of deliberately scandalous rhymes.[11] But not everyone was aware of that side of Joyce – both Curran and Byrne would be shocked when they first read allusions to such wayward behaviour in his work

Meanwhile, John was still dodging the rent collector. Between July 1899 and May 1900 he upped sticks three times, moving first from Windsor Avenue (where Joyce had first read Ibsen) to Convent Avenue, also in Fairview, then (for a mere six months) to No. 13 Richmond Avenue (roomy but 'ramshackle and in bad repair', and shared with a family from Ulster) to which a hired float carted what was left of their possessions. As he descended socially, John became more irascible and bibulous, so that his daughters now feared him and Stanislaus detested him ever more intensely.

A few days after receiving his twelve-guinea fee from the *Fortnightly*, James took his father to London for a week, John in high spirits at the prospect of spending the money. While Stannie was always glad to see the back of his father, Jim enjoyed his company on such excursions. On the train journey from Holyhead to London, John happily baited a jingoistic English passenger over the Boer War, while the diplomatic Jim played peacemaker.[12] With Mafeking besieged and opinion sharply divided, British imperialism was on the back foot. As a good Irish nationalist John's sympathies lay with the Boers, and needling the English was a sport he enjoyed. In London they stayed in a cheap lodging-house, sallying out to visit Courtney at the *Fortnightly Review* and to meet T. P. O'Connor, ex-Parnellite MP and editor of the mass-circulation *Sun*. But O'Connor probably decided that Joyce would not make a popular journalist and nothing came of the meeting.

John was showing his son how to enjoy London – visiting music-halls, theatres, pubs and restaurants. Once, in a comic incident beside the statue of Cromwell outside the Houses of Parliament, he outraged one native sightseer by comparing the Protector unfavourably to the Boer leader, Kruger – another palpable hit against the betrayers of Parnell.[13] Years later James told Arthur Power of his reaction to England and the capital of Ireland's oppressors. He had disliked the bustling streets, the muddy pavements, the arc-lights, the sudden fights outside pubs, and could never have lived and worked there, he said. Whereas in Dublin under the British, they enjoyed 'the kind of desperate freedom which comes from a lack of responsibility,' he felt that, 'in that [London] atmosphere of power, politics, and money, writing was not sufficiently important. Also though there is plenty of legal liberty in England ... there is not much individual liberty, for in England every man acts as a censor to his neighbour.'[14] However, Joyce's attitude towards England was highly ambivalent. He resented the English ascendancy over Ireland, but saw the English language, rendered through a Gaelic consciousness, as a means of personal liberation.

Just before the two men left Dublin, on 4 April 1900, Queen Victoria had begun a two-week visit to Dublin. According to Joyce, the Queen 'entered the Irish capital in the midst of a silent people';[15] according to the London *Times* she enjoyed a rapturous welcome from her devoted Irish subjects, drove around the city and its environs practically every day in an open carriage, visited, among other places, Chapelizod, St Stephen's Green, Rathmines, Rathgar, Bray and Blackrock – a royal progress retracing that of the Joyce family – the tour culminating in a dazzling military display in Phoenix Park where a bright sun glinted and sparkled on helmets, bayonets and the shields of Maxim guns.[16] So successful was the visit that she extended it from two to three weeks. She was, therefore, still in Dublin when the two Joyces returned to Fairview, out of money but full of their trip – John singing his own garbled versions of popular songs and James proclaiming the music-hall 'a criticism of life'.[17]

The spring vacation also gave him the freedom to pursue his own writing, and to travel. When John was hired to sort out the voting list in Mullingar that summer, some of his children joined him, including James. They stayed with a photographer called Philip Smith, whose assistant was a girl from Bray. Smith was later incorporated into *Ulysses* as the Mullingar photographer for whom Milly Bloom works. Now he was able to complete his play, *A Brilliant Career*. It was heavily Ibsenite, the story of a doctor who puts career before love and realizes his mistake too late. With all the solemnity of the self-conscious young playwright, he inscribed the manuscript, 'To my own Soul I dedicate the first true work of my life.'[18]

Even as Dublin entertained the Queen a momentous event occurred which propelled Joyce into a wider world than even England offered. On 23 April he heard from William Archer, Ibsen's English translator, that the playwright had written a letter of appreciation of his *Fortnightly Review* article, saying: 'I have read, or rather spelt out, a review by Mr James Joyce in the *Fortnightly Review* which is very benevolent ("velvillig") and for which I should greatly like to thank the author if only I had sufficient knowledge of the language.'[19] To be addressed in this fashion by his literary hero was a profound moment for Joyce, a baptism into European literature, a club to which few of his Irish contemporaries could hope to aspire. He replied via Archer, revealing himself as 'a young Irishman, eighteen years old' and vowing to keep Ibsen's words in his heart for ever.[20]

Shortly afterwards Joyce returned to London alone, lunching with Archer at the National Liberal Club in Whitehall, going to see Eleanora Duse in D'Annunzio's *La Gioconda* at the Lyceum Theatre (afterwards sending the great actress a poem of adulation), and haunting the music-halls, for which he had by now acquired a very special taste.[21] His London theatre visits inspired him to read more D'Annunzio (*La Gloria* and *Sogno d'un Tramonto d'Autunno*, as well as *La Gioconda*) and to acquire a copy of Archer's translation of Hauptmann's *Hannele*.

On 1 May 1900 John gave his Richmond Avenue landlord the slip and decamped to No. 8 Royal Terrace (a grey-faced, cement-clad, two-storey terrace house with basement and sunken garden). Those precious family portraits, 'proof' of his lineage, were this time transported by hand. Behind the houses ran a narrow lane which backed on to St Vincent's Hospital along which, in *A Portrait*, Stephen escapes from his father's wrath, evoking with stylish ease a scene of human desolation: 'The lane behind the terrace was waterlogged and as he went down it slowly, choosing his steps amid heaps of wet rubbish, he heard a mad nun screeching in the nuns' madhouse beyond the wall. "– Jesus! O Jesus! Jesus!"'22

At the college, George Clancy, a keen nationalist, formed a branch of Douglas Hyde's Gaelic League, devoted to promoting the Irish language, Irish music and culture. Joyce, the Ibsenite anti-nationalist, might not have been expected to take an interest in such provincial matters, but he had formed an attachment to a young woman who in *Stephen Hero* he calls Emma Clery. He was clearly smitten, and, as Stanislaus recalled, took her as his muse for several of the poems he then composed. This mystery woman might have been the sister of a Belvedere student named Ennis, though some think she was based on one of the Sheehy girls. She was a keen member of the League and actively encouraged others to attend the Irish classes. Joyce probably went along in pursuit of this alluring young woman. She loved him singing Irish ballads, and thought he could make a career of it. However, in the fragments of their conversation he weaves into his novel, they clearly disagreed about the cultural revival.

Joyce is said to have attended the inaugural meeting of the League and even taken a few classes in Irish ('in a back room on the second floor of a house in O'Connell St.'), but his teacher, Patrick Pearse, bored him by mocking the English language (which was, said Pearse, 'the language of commerce and Irish the speech of the soul') and ridiculing as inadequate such words as 'thunder', which for Joyce was an almost magical word. One of the League's most passionate and strident advocates was the large and booming Michael Cusack, founder of the Gaelic Athletic Association, whom Joyce took as his model for the Citizen in the 'Cyclops' episode of *Ulysses*. In *Stephen Hero*, his relationship with Emma came to a full stop when, in a fit of sexual passion, he waylaid her in the street and proposed they sleep together. Stephen took her outraged rejection as typifying middle-class Irish Catholic girls – passionless virgins, too cowardly to surrender to the pleasures of the flesh and whose seduction would in any case demand the most wearisome and elaborate strategic planning. 'Marsupials' he called them. His preference for the more willing girls of the chambermaid class and *demi-monde* over respectable Catholic virgins rang as true for Joyce as it did for Stephen.23

At the end of August he sent his play to Archer, who found it both interesting and puzzling, writing back to say that he thought Joyce had talent, 'possibly more than talent'. However, for the commercial theatre it was 'wildly impossible'. The canvas was too large for the subject – 'a huge fable of politics and pestilence', in which the central concern of the drama was lost. The symbolism, he thought, might be very good, but he was 'no great hand at reading hieroglyphics'. Nevertheless he praised Joyce's 'gift of easy, natural and yet effective dialogue, and a certain sense of scenic picturesqueness'.[24] That ear for natural dialogue would characterize all his writing, and his liking for hieroglyphics would transform his later works.

As Joyce was spending less time at home, he practised on a piano at the college. For him, what went for singing also went for poetry. 'The voice,' said Curran, who sometimes joined him, 'could be singularly musical, rising and passing away in quotation or at will into characteristic aerial harmonies.'[25] His repertoire now included Yeats's 'Who Goes With Fergus' and 'The Salley Gardens', Mangan's 'Dark Rosaleen', and several Gilbert and Sullivan arias. Then there were ballads, some Elizabethan, some Irish, such as 'Turpin Hero', 'Blarney Castle' and 'The Croppy Boy'.[26] 'Turpin Hero' gave him the title of his first novel, *Stephen Hero*.

> Bold Turpin Hero is my name
> And I from Dublin City came.

He loved poetry that could be set to music, especially sixteenth-century verse. His own poems always invited musical accompaniment, and Joyce would often set them himself. As he turned more and more towards prose, it never strayed far from poetry, and friends like Colum thought that everything he wrote was suffused with music.

In spite of Byrne's claim that he had lost all his friends, Joyce still attended the Sheehys' open nights and in the New Year of 1901 acted in a short comedy, *Cupid's Confidant* by Mary Sheehy, playing Geoffrey Fortescue, a rake and adventurer, a performance described in the *Freeman's Journal* as 'a revelation of amateur acting'.[27] Curran and Skeffington remained his friends, even though he refused to sign 'Knickerbocker's' petition supporting W. T. Stead's 'International Crusade of Peace'.[28] He also found himself popular with the college's medical students who had cheered him so vigorously at his presentation. One of those students, Vincent Cosgrave, told Byrne that Joyce was 'the most remarkable man any of us have met'.[29]

It was while moving among the medics that Joyce first met Oliver St John Gogarty, son of a Dublin surgeon. Gogarty claimed that their initial encounter was on a tram, a suitably rocky means of travel to symbolize what was to become a rocky though important relationship. It gave Joyce one of his most enduring fictional characters (the scabrous Malachi Mulligan) and it gave Gogarty another figure to mock ('Kinch, the knife-blade') and tall tales to add to the already-racy legend of Joyce. Many of the apocryphal stories about the young bard he called 'Dublin's Dante' sprang from the inventive mind of the Mephistophelean 'Mulligan'.[30]

Gogarty had been educated at Stonyhurst, the English Catholic public school, and later at the Protestant Trinity College where he became a pet student of John Pentland Mahaffy, Professor of Ancient History, the celebrated conversationalist and epigrammatist, who had taught and polished the wit of a previous favourite, Oscar Wilde. Gogarty modelled himself on Wilde as a wit and man-about-town. He was stocky, athletic, a racing cyclist and swimmer, who more than once plunged into the not-so-pure waters of the Liffey to save lives. He was waggish, profane and a fount of bawdy limericks. He was more than three years older than Joyce, and found his genius both awesome and amusing, especially as he took himself so seriously and seemed to be asking to be mocked. The two young men shared an attitude of amused cynicism towards the con-temporary Irish cultural scene: against the narrow passions of the extreme nationalists and the philistinism of 'the rabblement' ('Their Intensities' and 'Their Bullockships', they called them). For Gogarty, the answer was to Hellenize Ireland; for Joyce it was to Europeanize it.

Despite his penchant for limericks, Gogarty had serious poetic ambi-tions, and at their meeting on the tram Joyce, he claimed, had shown him a sheaf of his beautifully inscribed poems – 'Tennysonian, exquisite things' inscribed on vellum.[31] This shared commitment to poetry gave them a bond as members of the young Irish literati, and offered Joyce a source of income. Finding it increasingly hard to make ends meet, he fell into his father's habit of borrowing, and Gogarty was rarely without funds. It helped to be seen as a poetic genius to whom it was a privilege to give. His mother also gave him money, usually for an offering when he told her he was going to church. According to *Stephen Hero* he took the money and pocketed it.

The poetic pose, the readiness to recite and his beautifully modulated delivery won Joyce the nickname 'The Bard'. His own collection, *Moods*, had swollen to some forty or fifty poems. William Archer, who saw them, thought them too nebulous, his metrics were eccentric and many of his rhymes inept.[32] If he published his collection as it stood he might one day regret it, Archer told him. Stanislaus was less delicate. Those of the poems his brother called 'love poems' seemed to him inspired by anonymous meetings in Nighttown. Stanislaus called them 'prostitute poems'. Jim was unmoved. 'Well, why not?' he said. 'Doesn't a great part of all lyrical poetry correspond to that description? You're a tiresome moralist.'[33]

The love affair with Ibsen continued and in early March 1901, on the occasion of his seventy-third birthday, Joyce sent him a letter of greetings, admiration and apology in Norwegian. 'I am a young, a very young man . . . an undergraduate,' he wrote, and Ibsen could imagine how inspiring it had been for him to have received a word of encouragement from such an esteemed hand. 'I have sounded your name defiantly through the college where it was either unknown or known faintly and darkly.' He had proclaimed the playwright's true eminence in the history of drama, his 'highest excellence' and 'lofty impersonal power'. He then rather spoilt the effect of his eulogy by drawing attention to Ibsen's age. 'Your work on earth draws to a close and you are near the silence. It is growing dark for you.' He, on the other hand, though obscure, was young – 'joyfully, with hope and with love'.[34] Ibsen did not reply.

In contrast to Ibsenite 'realism', there was also the lure of the mystical. In the spring of 1901 Joyce had been briefly attracted by Theosophy, but, having been, as he later wrote, 'steeled in the school of old Aquinas',[35] was able to resist what he called 'that motley crew' of mystics. In *A Portrait* he mocks George Russell's fascination with spiritualism as he does in *Ulysses*, demonstrating how his talent for satire fed upon his passion for wordplay:

> The lords of the moon, Theosophos told me, an orangefiery shipload from planet Alpha of the lunar chain would not assume the etheric doubles and these were therefore incarnated by the rubycoloured egos from the second constellation.[36]

Stanislaus saw this flirtation with the Hermeticists prompting his brother to explore two opposing extremes in his literary imagination – 'the attraction of mysticism and the call of reality' (each of which he found attractive). And although he rejected mysticism as unedifying, he could view it with detachment and allude to it for his own literary purposes, as is evident in *Ulysses* and *Finnegans Wake*.

One seriously important discovery arising from Joyce's study of Italian was Giordano Bruno, the sixteenth-century philosopher burnt at the stake for heresy whom, according to *A Portrait*, he discussed with his tutor, Ghezzi. 'He said Bruno was a terrible heretic. I said he was terribly burned.'[37] Bruno would inspire in him the belief that the artist is champion of truth against the weight of mindless convention, which would express itself most clearly in his attack on 'the rabblement'. Encouraged by Ghezzi he had begun to further elaborate his Aquinean aesthetic, stressing truth and beauty as the main purpose of art rather than instruction which was conventional Catholic teaching.

Stanislaus was now freed from Belvedere. So unreservedly atheistic had he become, the Jesuits were doubtless happy to see the back of him. He took an unsalaried job in an accountant's office as a way of getting a foothold in some profession. However, like his brother, family poverty and his own slender means did not prevent him finding money for theatres, books and concerts. Once, visiting the Dublin Rotunda to hear Clara Butt sing, he got into conversation with a middle-aged married woman who contrived to run into him again later. The incident, as relayed to James, juxtaposed with the suicide of a married woman at Sydney Parade station, would form the basis for his story 'A Painful Case'. It so intrigued him that the funeral of the dead woman he calls Mrs Sinico is mentioned three times in *Ulysses*.

The two brothers had resumed their old habit of exploring the city streets together, mostly in the evenings. Their parents became unhappy about these twilight expeditions. John thought James was spending too much time away from his studies and made vague threats about taking him away from the university. May was concerned that her faithless eldest boy would also lead Stanislaus into apostasy, apparently unaware that he had already found his own way there. What is more, he had also found a new role for himself, noting down their conversations as well as his own reflections on his unusual brother. Eventually Stanislaus would leave a lasting record of their relationship through good times and bad. And, although some of his claims have been questioned, his Dublin diary offers the most intimate account we have of the young Joyce.

In his passion for accumulating epiphanies, composing and reading poetry, Joyce was indeed neglecting his work and did poorly in his second-year examinations. He even thought of abandoning his degree and going on the stage under the name of 'Gordon Brown', his English translation of Giordano Bruno. Perhaps in pursuit of this dream, he had memorized two stories of Yeats, 'The Adoration of the Magi' and 'The Tables of the Law', both of which captured his passing fascination with the occult. (Stanislaus recalled how he spoke the lines, 'almost chanting ... like incantations woven out of magic words'.)[38] That summer on another trip with his father to Mullingar, he turned his hand to translating, and soon completed English versions of Hauptmann's *Vor Sonnenaufgang* and *Michael Kramer*. In 'A Painful Case', we glimpse a manuscript of the latter in the desk drawer of James Duffy, 'a little sheaf of papers held together by a brass pin ... the stage directions ... written in purple ink'.[39]

The poet and playwright Padraic Colum first encountered Joyce and Gogarty at a party given for followers of the Irish Literary Theatre to which they had been invited. Colum recalled how the two newcomers sat apart from the rest of the company, Yeats included, seeming to regard the rest of their artistic contemporaries with a degree of superior scepticism. To Joyce, those not in sympathy with his Ibsenite position were little more than 'trolls', and Gogarty looked loftily down upon all of those around him – including, it transpired, on Joyce too. But, even though he made 'Kinch' the butt of his humour, his victim was always taking note and biding his time – something Gogarty suspected but only knew for certain when first *A Portrait* and then *Ulysses* finally appeared.

Colum eventually got into conversation with Joyce at the National Library. He was soon drawn into one of Joyce's peregrinations around town, and found himself deeply impressed. 'Looking back on that promenade, I know that I could have had no better introduction to the personality and the mind of that unique young man. He talked as a formed person talking to one whom he suspected of being unformed; he delivered, as he often did in those days, some set speeches. What maturity he had then!' Colum found him heretical and schismatic, distrustful of all enthusiasms.[40] Conversations for Joyce were mostly monologues in which he aired his ideas while his companions were expected to listen and offer only the occasional comment. Passages in *Stephen Hero* and *A Portrait*, said Colum, faithfully capture the tireless monologist in action.

Although Joyce admired Yeats as a poet, he was by no means enamoured of the Irish Literary Theatre or the cultural revival. After it had produced plays by Yeats and Edward Martyn, he had pressed for the company to perform something by Ibsen but they had opted for exclusively Irish plays and so, he thought, 'surrendered to the trolls'. According to Curran, it was after watching performances of *Diarmuid and Grania* by Yeats and George Moore, and Douglas Hyde's *Casadh an tSúgáin* (during which he sat 'inwardly seething') that, on 14 October, Joyce wrote a diatribe mocking the efforts of the revivalists, provocatively entitled 'The Day of the Rabblement'. The editor of *St Stephen's*, his old enemy Hugh Kennedy, had requested a submission, but when he saw it he passed it to Father Henry Browne, the journal's official 'adviser'. Browne recommended rejection on the grounds that D'Annunzio's *Il fuoco*, cited by Joyce, was on the Roman Index and so forbidden reading for Catholics. Skeffington, now college registrar, had, also by invitation, sent Kennedy an article on university co-education, which was similarly vetoed. The rejected authors decided to publish their essays (including a preface declaring themselves the victims of censorship) and on 21 October had eighty-five copies printed by the Dublin printers, Gerrard Brothers. Stanislaus helped with the distribution, delivering one into the hand of George Moore's maidservant on his doorstep in Ely Place.

Joyce's essay began with a clear statement and a deliberate mystification – 'No man, said the Nolan, can be a lover of the truth or the good unless he abhors the multitude; and the artist, though he may employ the crowd, is very careful to isolate himself.' On the one hand he stated directly his opposition to the parochialism and popularization of the cultural nationalists, but his teasing allusion to 'The Nolan' was intended to baffle. Was he citing an obscure Irish writer or what? In fact it was a reference to his current hero, Giordano Bruno of Nola, heretical martyr to freedom of speech. 'The Irish Literary Theatre gave out that it was the champion of progress, and proclaimed war against commercialism and vulgarity,' he complained, '[But] after the first encounter it surrendered to ... the rabblement of the most belated race in Europe.'[41] For him the Irish literary movement had placed politics and popularization above art and squandered the prospect of contributing in any serious way to world drama. This broadside stood as a clear statement of a position Joyce never abandoned, that art is a high calling and not for sale to any movement or passing fashion. Although he despised the rabblement, the lives of the 'lower orders' greatly intrigued him, and when in October he heard John F. Taylor, a Dublin barrister, defend the power of 'the rude vernacular', his speech found its way into *Ulysses* where Stephen hails it as 'The finest display of oratory I ever heard'.[42]

Joyce's final university year saw great changes in his home life which grew increasingly tense, especially when John returned drunk to confront a fearful May and a resentful Stanislaus. The family's only means of income now was John's meagre pension, and more and more the children were having to go without. James was rarely at home, using the house mostly as a dormitory and often staying at the National Library till closing time at 10 p.m. The Sheehys' place also became a home from home for him. David Sheehy was an urbane liberal man and the mood at Belvedere Place was relaxed and jovial, far removed from the strained atmosphere which pervaded 8 Royal Terrace and from where yet another quick exit was impending.

In *Stephen Hero* Joyce reveals John's *modus operandi* as he contemplated a fresh move. Following a tip-off from a friend at the Sheriff's office giving him a few days' notice, 'every morning he brushed his silk hat very diligently and polished his eyeglass and went forth humming derisively to offer himself as a bait to landlords'.[43] This well-practised confidence trickery failed to improve the family fortunes which slipped ever downwards. Undoubtedly John's grimmest move to date had been to Glengariff Parade, a solitary float again bearing the last remnants of a once-large furniture collection. In Royal Terrace they had backed on to a madhouse; now they backed on to Mountjoy Prison. It was a poor-looking place, poorly situated – one storey in front and two out of sight at the rear. The squalid conditions meant bedbugs and lice, but James, who as part of his Rimbaud act was sedulously avoiding soap and water, claimed that dirt was the best vermin-repellent.

On 1 February 1902, the day before his twentieth birthday, Joyce once again addressed the Literary and Historical Society. This time he abandoned iconoclasm for panegyric in a further attempt to define and justify his own poetic role. His chosen subject was 'James Clarence Mangan', the Irish Romantic (drunkard and opium-eater), not widely known, although well-considered by Yeats and a few others. Joyce's appreciation of Mangan was highly personal. He had descended into poverty, living the life of the *poète maudit* much like Mallarmé and Rimbaud. Joyce had been reading Verlaine on the subject and saw Mangan's failure as his own likely fate, should he remain in Dublin. It matched his mood of melancholy and reinforced his sense of being different. Such poets, he thought, were too often judged for their morals rather than their verse.

Although he praised the poet's imaginative power, it was clearly Mangan's outsider status to which he was drawn. Irishmen who knew of Mangan's work, he said, were surprised that it came from 'a man whose vices were exotic and who was little of a patriot ... A stranger in his own country, he became a rare and unsympathetic figure in the streets, where he is seen going forward alone like one who does penance for some ancient sin.' His childhood was one of both poverty and coarseness in a world inhabited by cruel demons, including his 'human boa-constrictor' of a father – an expression Joyce gave to Shem in *Finnegans Wake*. 'Mynfadher was a boer constructor,' he says.[44] Mangan's consolation was his inward life 'where for many ages the sad and the wise have elected to be'. It was not his ill-written verse that interested Joyce, said Arthur Power, but his almost morbid single-mindedness.[45]

His address, with its wide literary reference sprinkled with the odd quotation in Norwegian lent the paper an air of erudition, and delivered in Joyce's flat impersonal metallic voice, made a considerable impression. Padraic Colum thought it was composed under the influence of Walter Pater; Felix Hackett remembered it as 'soaring to a conclusion of musical and oracular utterance'.[46] Stanislaus wrote, 'The essay was no mere literary exercise, nor yet simply an appreciation of Mangan; my brother was clearly feeling his way in it towards the literary tenets that were to dominate his work.'[47] Professor Magennis, again in the chair, is credited with giving one of the best summing-ups in the Society's history. But the star turn of the evening was obvious. The next day's *Freeman's Journal* reported, 'James Joyce was deservedly applauded at the conclusion of what was generally agreed to have been the best paper ever read before the Society.'[48]

On 13 March, as Joyce approached his finals, his young brother George fell ill. He had followed his older siblings to Belvedere where, like James, he had displayed effortless brilliance. Since James's falling away from his parents and sisters, George – good-looking with light curly hair and an infectious but knowing laugh – had replaced him as the family favourite. Certain gossips thought that May, having lost James to atheism and determined to see one of her sons take up the priesthood, pushed him too ruthlessly. Occasionally Jim and Stannie would take the boy swimming to the Bull Wall, where some remarked on his frailty, putting it down to incipient consumption.[49] But George had been struck down with typhoid fever, and instead of sending him to the nearby Mater Misericordiae Hospital, his over-protective mother decided to nurse him at home. At first he seemed to respond to treatment and the doctor (Frank Winder – inclined to drunkenness, it was rumoured) advised May Joyce that she could try feeding him. But on 26 March, after she had done so he quickly deteriorated. The disturbing scene is recorded in *A Portrait* (where it becomes Stephen's sister Isabel who lies dying). James was at George's bedside a great deal and would go into the parlour below, leaving open the doors, to play and sing his favourite songs – 'Who Goes With Fergus?' and 'Impetuous Heart, Be Still, Be Still'. Everyone knew the boy was unlikely to survive, including George himself, and these haunting airs must have sounded like songs of sad farewell. Two months short of his fifteenth birthday, on 3 May he died of enteric fever complicated by perforation of the intestine.

May Joyce was distraught, blaming herself for trusting the doctor whose advice had brought about the boy's death. James, too, was deeply shaken. The moment is captured in a neatly turned epiphany ending, 'Poor little fellow! ... I am very sorry he died. I cannot pray for him as the others do.'[50] He seemed to blame his country for the state to which his family had been reduced, saying shortly afterwards to Stanislaus, 'Ireland is an old sow that devours her farrow.'[51]

He had a great quarrel with his mother over his refusal to observe his Easter duties that year, and, when challenged about this by Byrne, replied in Satan's words, 'I will not serve.'[52] Having lingered long on the brink of total apostasy, George's death had tipped him over the edge. Medicine might have failed poor George, but prayer had been of no avail either. In *Stephen Hero*, as Dedalus and 'Cranly' walk around St Stephen's Green, he suddenly announces, 'I have left the Church.'[53] His mother told all to her confessor who advised her to distance herself and her children from the heretic, but she was unable to excommunicate her favourite child from her deepest affections. That child too was passing through intense inner turmoil. He felt deeply about his mother's plight, married to an abusive drunk and worn down by endless pregnancies and invasive poverty. But now he found himself in open disagreement with her and she was horrified and distressed by his outspoken blasphemy. If this and George's death left her feeling numb, James's way of handling things was to retreat behind his mask of feigned indifference.

George was buried in the family plot in Glasnevin Cemetery. Afterwards, James, his father and Uncle William Murray repaired to a pub on Finglas Road where, to his father's dismay, he called for a pint of stout. 'Who taught you to drink stout?' asked John. The comparatively abstemious James had turned to alcohol and it would become a presence in his life from that time onwards.[54] William D'Arcy (whose father Bartell appears undisguised in *Ulysses* as a lover of Molly Bloom) recalled that the day after George's funeral he went looking for a new house with John, who kept muttering, 'We must get out of Glengariff Parade.'[55]

The death of George propelled Joyce finally away from his religion and also into an unqualified commitment to literature. The problem was how to make a living. He had no wish to sell his pen and considered himself incapable of writing best-sellers. At home finding money often meant resorting to the pawnbroker, while John, unable to deny himself the pleasures of the pub, spent most of what he had on Guinness and porter. In *Stephen Hero*, Stephen curses 'the publicans and the pawnbrokers who live on the miseries of the people and spend part of the money they make in sending their sons and daughters into religion to pray for them'.[56]

Gogarty suggested a medical career, which could make him rich enough and leisured enough to write as he wished. Joyce was persuaded, but said later that he started medicine as 'an escape from the spirit of the college ... to go from mysticism to science'.[57] Whatever his motivation, in April he went with Gogarty and Cosgrave to meet the head of the University College Medical School.

In an unsettled state of mind following George's death, Joyce's final examination results were again poor. Joyce seems to have come to consider examinations a great joke and took every opportunity to subvert them. Never reluctant to add to his own mythology, he told Eugene Sheehy how he had shown his contempt for his examiners and their questions by dismissing the poet Cowper as only fit to compose rhymes for Christmas crackers, and, writing about one of his poems, simply quoting Hamlet's farewell to the dead Polonius: 'Peace tedious old fool!'[58] Another despised writer, Addison, he wrote off as 'the world's greatest hypocrite'. Asked in his final oral examination, 'How is poetic justice exemplified in the play of *King Lear*?' he answered 'I don't know.' The examiner, knowing Joyce could do better than that, tried again. 'Oh, come, Mr Joyce, you are not fair to yourself. I feel sure you have read the play.' 'Oh yes,' he replied, 'but I don't understand your question. The phrase "poetic justice" is unmeaning jargon so far as I am concerned.' Having failed to play by the rules, failed to stick to the prescribed books or answer in the prescribed fashion, he failed Honours and had to settle for a Pass degree. In view of what he claimed to have done in his finals, Eugene Sheehy thought it was to the university's credit that they passed him at all. But a poor degree would not keep Joyce down, and before he left Language and Literature behind he had the satisfaction of his essay on Mangan appearing in the May issue of *St Stephen's*.

The impressions Joyce left on his university contemporaries varied. Curran wrote a sympathetic memoir of him, and his friend, Tom Kettle, recalled him as 'wilful, fastidious, a lover of elfin paradoxes ... the very embodiment of the literary spirit'.[59] Byrne, while finding him attractive, noted his cold frigidity and unsympathetic attitude towards the elderly while Mary Sheehy and Padraic Colum, although liking him, noticed his ability to change from charming gentleman to someone unrecognizably coarse and uninhibited. The jaundiced Hugh Kennedy later denounced him for having brought discredit upon the Jesuits, while Gogarty's mentor, Mahaffy, told the Limerick-born journalist and critic, Gerald Griffin, 'James Joyce is a living argument in defence of my contention that it was a mistake to establish a separate university for the aborigines of this island – for the corner-boys who spit into the Liffey.'[60] To the loftily disdainful Mahaffy, Joyce was himself little more than one of the rabblement.

7

An Uncertain Future

(1902)

'Keep thy foot out of brothels, thy hand out of plackets, thy pen from lenders' books, and defy the foul fiend.' Shakespeare, *King Lear*

Moving from Belvedere to University College had allowed Joyce to escape the invisible nets of the Jesuits; moving from University College into an uncertain future would liberate him from academic constraints and the demands of an insecure home life. Now he had to decide what to do with his new-found freedom.

Gogarty and Joyce had become almost inseparable. Joyce found Gogarty's wit and commitment to poetry impressive; Gogarty found in Joyce ('The Bard') the perfect straight man for his Wildean one-liners. And there were obviously moments of utter hilarity. As Joyce told his mother later, 'An old woman shook her umbrella in my face one day in Dublin – I was laughing so loudly.'[1]

Just before taking leave of University College's Jesuits, Joyce enquired about the possibility of teaching at the college but his poor degree weakened his academic prospects. Father Darlington suggested journalism or a clerkship with Guinness, both of which he rejected with contempt. The idea of any routine job was anathema to him, something to avoid at all costs.

That summer, Joyce was determined to pursue his writing career and bring himself to the attention of the Dublin literati. Yeats was living in London and his protégé John Millington Synge was in Paris. However, Moore, back in Ireland after many years abroad, Lady Gregory and George Russell were around, always on the look-out for new talent. In early August, Joyce visited Russell at the office of his paper, the *Irish Homestead*, in Lincoln Place. He showed him some of his epiphanies and shortly afterwards Russell wrote to Yeats:

I want you very much to meet a young fellow named Joyce whom I wrote to Lady Gregory about half jestingly. He is an extremely clever boy who belongs to your clan more than to mine and more still to himself. But he

has all the intellectual equipment, culture and education which all our
other clever friends here lack. And I think writes amazingly well in prose
though I believe he also writes verse and is engaged in writing a comedy
which he expects will occupy him five years or thereabouts as he writes
slowly. Moore who saw an article of this boy's says it is preposterously
clever. Anyhow I think you would find this youth of 21 with his assurance
and self-confidence rather interesting.[2]

His reputation was already growing – a reputation for being awkward as
well as brilliant, as Russell informed his friend Sarah Purser. 'I expect to
see my young genius on Monday and will find out more about him.
I wouldn't be his Messiah for a thousand million pounds. He would be
always criticising the bad taste of his deity.'[3] The following Monday (18
August) Joyce walked out to Russell's home in Rathgar, taking along those
carefully copied sheaves of his poetry. AE is said to have been bemused
by the haughty young man who quizzed him unendingly about aspects
of mystical understanding – 'proud as Lucifer', he told a friend.[4] Joyce's
own allusion to their encounter is buried in *Ulysses*:

> —What do you think really of that hermetic crowd, the opal hush poets:
> AE the mastermystic? That Blavatsky woman started it. She was a nice
> old bag of tricks. AE has been telling some yankee interviewer that you
> came to him in the small hours of the morning to ask him about planes
> of consciousness. Magennis thinks you must have been pulling AE's leg.[5]

Russell was impressed not only with his interest in matters mystical but
also with his verse, telling a friend later that 'Joyce writes with perfect art
poems as delicate and dainty as Watteau pictures.'[6] But he is also reported
as telling Joyce, 'You have not enough chaos to make a world' – probably
one of Russell's least profound insights.[7]

Aware of his eagerness to meet Yeats, Russell told him that he would
be in town that October attending rehearsals of his play, *Kathleen ni
Houlihan* (written with Lady Gregory), starring Maud Gonne. Having
spoken to Yeats, he wrote to Joyce saying that the poet would like to meet
him, either at the *Irish Homestead* office or the Nassau Hotel where he
would be staying.[8] But Joyce chose his own way of meeting the poet, as
if by accident in the street outside the National Library.[9] Russell had
already issued Yeats with an Ibsenesque warning, telling him that 'The
first spectre of the new generation has appeared. His name is Joyce. I have
suffered from him and I would like you to suffer.'[10]

It would be a famous encounter. Joyce, the young man, knocking at
the door of the man he saw as presently wearing the crown of Irish poetry;

the older man not quite knowing what to make of the brash young pretender. They repaired to the smoking room of a Sackville Street restaurant where Joyce soon displayed his critical panache. If he was rude and arrogant to Yeats, it was perfectly consistent with his behaviour towards Father Darlington and towards Stanislaus who suffered his slights continually. All were regarded as whetstones on which to sharpen his wits.

The two men were from different backgrounds with different interests – Yeats a child of the Protestant Ascendancy, fascinated by aristocracy and peasant superstition, Joyce from the Catholic lower middle class, intrigued by Dublin's *demi-monde*; Yeats embracing the beauty of nature, Joyce drawn by the ugliness of the city; Yeats seeing in Homer the true expression of high art, Joyce preferring Dante and the journey to Hell and back. They were also two different kinds of creative intelligence – Yeats's originality moulded by considerations of poetic form; Joyce's wanting always to spill into shapes beyond the formal. Yeats was also committed to a cultural nationalism which Joyce thought a betrayal of poetic genius.

Asked by Yeats to read some of his poetry, Joyce replied, 'I do so since you ask me, but I attach no more importance to your opinion than to anybody one meets in the street.' In fact he seems to have read from his epiphanies which Yeats later described as 'beautiful though immature and eccentric ... meditations'.[11] When Yeats complimented him, he was told dismissively, though 'with a gentle and engaging smile', that 'It is likely both you and I will soon be forgotten.' Joyce then quizzed him about his earlier poetry and when Yeats said that he was moving in a more experimental direction, Joyce replied, 'Ah, that shows how rapidly you are deteriorating.' At Yeats's mention of Balzac and Swinburne, Joyce roared with laughter and told him that he spoke in generalizations like a man of letters and not at all like a poet. Overlooking his apparent rudeness, Yeats asked Joyce to write a play for the Irish Literary Theatre, and he said he would produce one within five years. His parting shot was, 'We have met too late. You are too old for me to have any effect on you.' This story got blown up through repetition and gossip into him saying, 'It is too late for me to help you,' which casts the encounter in a somewhat different light.[12]

Joyce left his epiphanies and poems for Yeats to read and later received a kindly appreciation of them, praising his technique and the 'delicacy' of his talent, but quoting Dr Johnson: 'Let us wait until we find out whether he is a fountain or a cistern.'[13] Although the young critic's remarks left Yeats with what Ellmann called 'a permanent impression of a brilliant but cruel mind',[14] he was no doubt flattered by how much of his work Joyce knew by heart. Some eighteen months later (in 1904), on republishing his stories 'The Tables of the Law' and 'The Adoration of the Magi', Yeats appended a note saying, 'I do not think I should have reprinted them had I not met a young man in Ireland the other day, who liked them very much and nothing else that I have written.'[15] Joyce in his turn, although decidedly unconverted to Yeats's vision, would continue to admire his imaginative powers and afterwards confine his criticism to parody and mild mockery in the pages of *Ulysses*. Buck Mulligan, for example, lampoons 'Who Goes with Fergus?', transforming the lines 'Being forbid to marry on earth,/They blossomed to immortal mirth' into 'Being afraid to marry on earth/They masturbated for all they were worth.'[16]

Still intrigued by 'The Tables of the Law', Joyce spent time reading 'the fading prophecies of Joachim Abbas' in what he called 'the stagnant bay' of the two-hundred-year-old Marsh's Library adjacent to St Patrick's Cathedral. There, there were books containing marginal notes in the hand of the one-time dean of the cathedral, Jonathan Swift, his 'furious Rabelaisian dean' and 'Irish Rabelais'. Joachim and the library crop up in *Stephen Hero*, *Ulysses* and *Giacomo Joyce* – a lasting trace of a youthful attachment to the hermetic tradition; Swift lurks behind some of his stories, flits briefly into *Ulysses* and stands centre-stage in *Finnegans Wake*, woven deeply into the text and permeating the nocturnal consciousness of Humphrey Chimpden Earwicker.

That October, Joyce joined Byrne and Cosgrave at University College Medical School in Cecilia Street. These were friends off whom he could bounce his ideas and an audience for his capers. Thenceforth his most convivial moments in Dublin would be spent in the company of such young medics. He was adopted as what Gogarty called 'a medic's pal' – one who by association enjoyed the licence afforded to medical students thanks to the aura of mystery surrounding their craft.

Cosgrave, a perpetual student, indolent and hedonistic, had a good bass voice and shared Joyce's love of Palestrina, attending concerts at the Pro-Cathedral (St Mary's) with him whenever Gregorian chants were to be sung. They also plunged together into Dublin's netherworld of whoring and carousing,[17] often joined by the devil-may-care Gogarty. Mary Colum described Joyce's reputation at this time as 'distinctly Byronic'. 'He had given up religion, it was said, and went in for evil frequentations of all kinds.'[18] In the public imagination the rake was progressing. Gogarty seemed to take special delight in debauching the one-time priestly Jesuit, a knockabout performance beautifully captured in the opening scenes of *Ulysses*.

With his godfather's legacy now spent, Joyce was in need of funds. However, just when he might have welcomed a handout from his father, the family fortunes again took a downturn. In October, finally abandoning the moonlight flit, John took the risky step of commuting part of his meagre pension in return for a lump sum and bought a house at No. 7 St Peter's Terrace in Cabra, a move which halved his income to £5 10s 1½d per month, and was widely regarded as an act of folly for a man with a large family to support. According to William D'Arcy, rumours had it that John had been pushed into cashing in part of his pension by May who wanted a more settled home life, but she then proceeded to hand out unspecified sums to Catholic charities she supported.[19] This piece of tittle-tattle was meant to explain John's increasing hostility towards her over his perilous finances. There was, however, one mouth less to feed at home: Charlie had left Belvedere that summer and entered a seminary. With two sons lost to atheism and one to medical incompetence, only Charlie remained to fulfil May's dream of having a priest in the family.

Alf Bergan told how, on the day he took his lump sum, John got drunk and was spotted by him and a friend close to Nelson's Pillar in Sackville Street, heading uncertainly homeward. Thinking he lived at Dollymount, these kindly Samaritans handed him over to a tram conductor with strict instructions to see that he reached his destination safely. When John sobered up enough to realize what had happened, he attempted to disembark but was restrained by the dutiful official until they reached the terminus. As it was the last tram, all he could do was sit on the seawall and cry before having to walk the seven miles back to St Peter's Terrace where he fainted into May's arms. He later told Bergan, 'I was in bed all next day and could not walk as I had a blister on my heel as big as a pigeon's egg.'[20] This is the incident which Joyce commandeered for his story, 'Grace' in which a helpless drunk is rescued by friends and persuaded to attend 'a retreat for businessmen'. Stanislaus thought it highly amusing that the old reprobate should be doing something so contrary to his nature, but noted that on each day of the retreat he returned home drunk.[21]

In his newly penurious state, John immediately took out a mortgage for £50 on the new house, then in December another for £50 and two more for £50 and £65 in April and November the following year. But life at St Peter's Terrace was no more congenial to young James than it had been at previous addresses. Gogarty gave a vivid picture of the circumstances Joyce was attempting to escape and the emotional turmoil through which he must have been passing:

Once I was in Joyce's home in St Peter's Road, Cabra, and it was miserable. The banisters were broken, the grass in the back-yard was all blackened out. There was laundry there and a few chickens, and it was a very very miserable home. He spent most of his time in the National Library. I think he went home rather reluctantly. He couldn't desert his mother and he found her caught in the middle of this misery and that burned and made him very miserable.[22]

The Kildare Street library offered him not just a way of escape, but also some of the best intellectual company in Dublin – George Russell, John Eglinton, Thomas Lyster, Richard Best. All would find themselves cast in the play of Joyce's fiction.

On 31 October, at a ceremony disturbed by noisy students (himself included) during the playing of the National Anthem, Joyce received a B.A. degree of the Royal University, no doubt in the presence of his proud family. Afterwards he happily donned his white-fur-collared gown and natty bow tie, and, looking suitably scholarly, posed for the obligatory graduation photograph, his emphatic jaw highlighted against the shadows and with what Stanislaus described as 'a far-away look' in his eyes. Yet despite this conferring of academic laurels, he told his brother that he wondered whether university studies were at all worth the trouble.[23]

That 'far-away look' (which a sardonic Colum put down to defective eyesight)[24] probably betrayed his true state of mind at the time. Although he attended a few classes at the Medical School, he found Dublin claustrophobic and was considering emigrating. Apartness had long been essential to Joyce's posture, and exile would fulfil his sense of separation. Many of the Irish authors he took as literary forebears – Swift, Goldsmith, Congreve, Sheridan, Shaw and Wilde – had left their native shores in search of a more creative climate, and their examples afforded a more attractive prospect than anything on offer at home. Even Yeats and Moore had migrated. More crucially for him, Ibsen, escaping from Norway in search of cultural freedom, and writing in a language familiar to little more than four million people, had revolutionized European drama. Here were lofty achievements to be emulated.

The mass of Irish emigrants since the Potato Famine had headed west; Joyce was looking to the east. He set his sights on Paris, city of Villon, Rimbaud and Verlaine, where Laurence Sterne had been lionized, Moore, Synge and Turgenev had preceded him, and Wilde, on his release from prison, had sought sanctuary from the prurient rabblement. Abandoning his medical studies in Dublin (as his father had done in Cork) and taking them up in Paris sounds contradictory until it is remembered that Baudelaire, Verlaine and Flaubert were students there and Rabelais and Zola in particular studied medicine. Furthermore, Zola, who had died only a few weeks earlier that year, had, like Joyce, chosen science over mysticism. He would not be the first or last to hope that the spirit of a place would nourish his creativity. His plan was to continue his studies at the Sorbonne, but before being able to do so he was faced with the usual problem – want of money,

Lady Gregory – folklorist, dramatist, widow of an Irish MP and doyenne of the Irish cultural revival – was the next literary personage Joyce set out to entrance. He wrote to her in early November, telling her that he had abandoned his studies for lack of money. He thought the university, by not offering him teaching work, was discriminating against him on grounds of his disbelief. Furthermore, the Churches hated 'human beings', and he wanted to escape the atmosphere of religious intolerance which, as a writer, he found inhibiting. A medical degree would provide him with the security he needed in order to work, and he would continue his studies in Paris, teaching English to support himself. 'I am going alone and friendless ... into another country, and I am writing to you to know can you help me in any way. I do not know what will happen to me in Paris but my case can hardly be worse than it is here.' The prospect of failure did not dishearten him, he said, because failure proved very little. He ended in the ringing tones with which he would later conclude *A Portrait of the Artist*:

> I shall try myself against the powers of the world. All things are inconstant except the faith of the soul, which changes all things and fills their inconstancy with light. And though I seem to have been driven out of my country here as a misbeliever I have found no man yet with a faith like mine.[25]

This spirited and eloquent letter had its effect, and at the beginning of November Yeats summoned him to dine with his father and Lady Gregory at the Nassau Hotel.[26] The evening yielded no promise of money, but he had aroused the lady's interest and felt sufficiently encouraged to apply, on 18 November, to study at the Faculty of Medicine at the University of Paris.

Meanwhile, Russell busied himself searching out Parisian contacts for him. Moore was moodily uncooperative, but Lady Gregory suggested Maud Gonne, now living in Paris and about to marry Major John Mac-Bride.[27] She then tried to persuade Joyce to remain in Ireland, adding that she was unsure how to help a young atheist as the only 'real friend' she had in Paris was 'a very devout Catholic Churchman'. However, Yeats had a flat close to London's Euston Station and would surely give him breakfast on his way through to Paris, she said.[28]

She arranged for him to meet Synge, the thirty-one-year-old emerging playwright, just back from a summer in the Aran Isles. Synge gave him the address of the Hotel Corneille, the Paris hotel recommended to poor medical students by Thackeray, and once home to Irish nationalists John Mitchell and John O'Leary. The Corneille stood just opposite the Théâtre de l'Odéon in the rue de Corneille, close to the Luxembourg Gardens, convenient for the cafés of St-Germain and a short walk from the Sorbonne. It was also the place where in 1896 Synge had first met Yeats and become his protégé. Lady Gregory arranged an introduction to Dr Joseph Rivière, founder of the Institut Physicothérapique in Paris, and wrote to Yeats herself about his plans. She also mentioned him to E. V. Longworth, editor of the Unionist Dublin *Daily Express* who, she told him, had 'French connections'. Through his father he got the address of Joseph Casey, an old comrade of John Kelly, and William Archer gave him another contact – an old friend, Blanche Taylor – but warned him that Paris was swamped with English teachers.

Undaunted, his mother having packed his 'new second-hand clothes', on 1 December Joyce embarked for the City of Light. With him he carried a letter from Timothy Harrington, the Mayor of Dublin, an old friend of his father, introducing Joyce as 'a young man of excellent character ... whose career as a student has been distinguished by industry and talent'.[29] He also took along several books to review for the *Express*. The fact that he was prepared to write for such a 'West British' newspaper shows how determined he was to distance himself from the cultural nationalists, albeit that his reviews would be written under a cloak of anonymity.

This was his first expedition away from the English-speaking world towards what he now considered his creative homeland, Europe. Later it would take on an even greater significance as he saw himself on a great cultural mission – to save his own country not by remaining in Ireland to take on the British, but by leaving to take on their language and assert by intelligence and cunning the inventive power of the Irish genius.

'I was a fierce-looking infant. Was I not?' Joyce wrote after sending this photograph to his sweetheart, Nora Barnacle.

The Joyce family in 1888: John Joyce looking suitably patriarchal; May Joyce looking suitably maternal; her father, John Murray, who disapproved of his son-in-law, looking suitably tight-lipped; and young James, about to enter Clongowes Wood College at age 'half-past six', looking suitably eager to learn.

James Joyce, B.A., in graduation robes, with what his brother Stanislaus called 'a faraway look' in his eyes. He was known at the university as 'the Mad Hatter' and only scraped a pass degree, but in distant Trieste he was happy to style himself 'Dr James Joyce'.

Among the Jesuits: Joyce (standing, second from left) with fellow students and staff at University College Dublin, including Father Joseph Darlington (in academic robes), and beside him the mustachioed Professor Edouard Cadic, Joyce's French teacher. Constantine Curran (at the end of the front row, right) sits next to Michael Lennon, who later betrayed Joyce's friendship by writing a scurrilous article about him and his family.

Second Part — Opening which tells of the
journeyings of the soul.

All day I hear the noise of waters
    Making moan,
Sad as the sea-bird is when going
    Forth alone
I hear the winds cry to the waters'
    Monotone:

The grey winds, the cold winds are blowing
    Where I go;
I hear the noise of many waters
    Far below,
All day, all night I hear them flowing
    To and fro.

Hotel Corneille
5 Rue Corneille, Paris

The Bohemian: Joyce sent this carefully posed photo-card from Paris not only to his
mother but also to J. F. Byrne ('Cranly' in *A Portrait of the Artist*) and other friends.
He sent one carrying an obscene message about prostitutes to Vincent Cosgrave.
Cosgrave showed it to the pious Byrne, who refused to talk to Joyce for a time.

Oliver St John Gogarty ('Buck Mulligan' in *Ulysses*), medical student, poet and wit who modelled himself on Oscar Wilde: he mocked Joyce and dubbed him 'the Bard' while secretly envying him.

The Martello Tower at Sandycove, where Joyce lived briefly with Gogarty and the trigger-happy Englishman Trench ('Buck Mulligan' and 'Haines' in *Ulysses*). It became the setting for the opening ('Telemachus') episode of the novel.

The 'Bard' comes to call: Joyce in Constantine Curran's garden. Asked later what he was thinking when the picture was taken, he said, 'I was wondering whether Curran could lend me five shillings.'

William Butler Yeats, the great Irish poet, would encourage and help the young Joyce, even though he was rude at their first meeting, telling him, 'I attach no more importance to your opinion than to anybody one meets in the street.'

No. 7 Eccles Street, the home of Joyce's friend Byrne, which in *Ulysses* became the home of Leopold Bloom and his unfaithful wife Molly.

Joyce's Irish muse, Nora Barnacle, the girl he met in Nassau Street, who became the model for Molly Bloom. The day of their first date, 16 June 1904, became 'Bloomsday', the much-celebrated date on which *Ulysses* is set.

Alessandro Francini Bruni, a close friend, fellow teacher and drinking crony of Joyce's in Pola and Trieste, who later gave what Stanislaus Joyce called a 'vulgar', 'riff-raffish' lecture on him in the city.

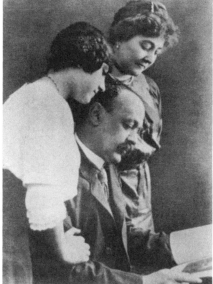

Ettore Schmitz was a pupil of Joyce's in Trieste, who, as 'Italo Svevo', had published two unsuccessful novels. Joyce thought highly of his work and promoted him in France and England, bringing him belated recognition and acclaim as a brilliant and subtle modernist. Joyce borrowed Livia Schmitz's name for 'Anna Livia Plurabelle', the spirit of the River Liffey, and her long red hair as an image for the river in *Finnegans Wake*.

Obscure object of Joyce's desire, Amalia Popper, a student of his and likely object of the sexual fantasies of his alter-ego 'Giacomo Joyce'.

The Joyces had the habit of leaving their children, Giorgio and Lucia, behind in their flat while they went to the theatre. On one occasion the children were heard to complain, 'And now we shall be shut up again like pigs in a sty!'

8

'Sinister genius'

(1902–1903)

'I will not jump with common spirits
And rank me with the barbarous multitudes.'

Shakespeare *The Merchant of Venice*

Joyce arrived in London at 6 a.m. on 2 December 1902 on the Irish Mail from Holyhead. Yeats met him at Euston Station and took him to his flat at Woburn Buildings off the Euston Road. That district would assume an iconic significance for Joyce, and in *Finnegans Wake* he makes mock obeisance to 'the flushpots of Euston and the hanging garments of Marylebone'.[1] Yeats gave him breakfast, and afterwards took him to meet the editors of two magazines he hoped might publish him. Finding them unavailable, they called on Arthur Symons, the symbolist poet whose translation of D'Annunzio's *Francesca da Rimini* he thought Joyce might review. Symons, a Wagnerian, regaled them with Good Friday music from *Parsifal*, and, seems to have taken to Joyce more readily than Yeats (calling him 'a curious mixture of sinister genius and uncertain talent').[2] He would do a great deal to help this 'sinister genius' get his poems known and published.

In London, Joyce was obviously on his best behaviour. Two days after his departure, Yeats reported to Lady Gregory: 'I have had Joyce with me for a day. He was unexpectedly amiable and did not knock at the gate with his old Ibsenite fury. I am trying to get him work on the *Academy* and *Speaker* and I have brought him to Arthur Symons. I have been twice to the *Speaker* about his affairs and have otherwise wasted a great deal of time.'[3]

On the night of 2 December, Joyce took the boat train from Victoria Station, then the Newhaven–Dieppe ferry, arriving at the Gare du Nord the following morning still suffering the effects of seasickness. He went straight to the Hôtel Corneille and settled into a third-floor room overlooking the Théâtre de l'Odéon whose cloistered arcades housed mostly bookshops. The hotel (with its darkened staircases, bare wooden floors, linen-covered walls and antiquated furniture) was just a short walk from the St-Germain hotel where Wilde, the betrayed artist, had died exactly two years earlier.

He contacted Dr Rivière who, he told his mother, treated him to a seven-course lunch, after which he took himself off to the university, hoping to register. That, however, proved more complicated than he had imagined – either he would have to take a baccalaureate, the French equivalent of his Dublin degree, or hope the Minister of Public Instruction would judge him already suitably qualified. There were only two weeks left of the autumn term at the École de Médecine, but he obtained a temporary pass to classes in physics, chemistry and biology. His parents were now sending him regular small sums through Lloyds Bank, and although there were no course fees, he was often broke.

His father's contact, Joseph Casey, was an old Fenian with a whiff of dynamite about him, who, after a spell in London's Clerkenwell Prison, had followed the flight of the 'wild geese' (Irish Jacobite exiles) for France. He had a flat in the rue de la Goutte d'Or close to the Gare du Nord, and worked as a typesetter for the Paris edition of the *New York Herald*. Joyce joked about his rolling 'gunpowder cigarettes' with inky fingers in a Montmartre café. Casey, who drank absinthe (the lethal 'green fairy') rather than coffee, and spent his time reliving old Fenian days, would feature as the rebel Kevin Egan in the 'Proteus' episode of *Ulysses*, and as an illusory interloper in the 'Circe' episode.

However, Joyce's contacts in Paris were sparse and a life of bare subsistence loomed – the romantic life of the *poète maudit* suffering for his art. He spelled out his situation with not a little relish to his mother: 'I can get breakfast for 3d, dejeuner (soup, meat, dessert, coffee) for 8d or 9d and dinner (soup, fish, meat and vegetables, dessert, coffee) for 1s 8d. But I am obliged to take coffee constantly through the day ... This I find to my taste as the weather here is very severe, sometimes going down to 7 or 9 degrees below zero.'[4] He ate cheap meals at a café-restaurant on the Place des Deux-Écus on the Right Bank, or, closer to home, at a *crémerie* in the rue Saint-André des Arts or rue Monsieur-le-Prince, where for an extra few francs he could get the rice cooked with cinnamon. One consequence of these letters home was a healing of the breach with his mother, with whom he shared not just his tales of privation but also his hopes of success as a writer. She in her turn was anxious to give him good homely advice. Probably thinking of the typhoid that had carried away George, she warned him not to drink Paris water unless filtered or boiled.

Joyce's tales of bohemian life around the Latin Quarter cafés tell of strange companions, some as eccentric as himself. A café in the Carrefour de l'Odéon was their favourite meeting place. Later he recalled some of the young intellectuals who gathered there: an Italian, a German poet, an Englishman[5] and a Spaniard. To overcome language barriers they would sometimes converse in Latin. All, except the willowy Joyce, were large men and their argumentation was vigorous – he once clashed violently with the German poet, Theodor Däubler, barely avoiding a duel.[6] Asked by Stanislaus what he would have done had the challenge been issued, he replied promptly, 'Started for Dublin by the first train leaving Paris.'[7]

Not all of his times in French cafés were disputatious. There were many occasions for levity. As he told his mother, 'I have more than once upset a whole French café by laughing.' But his tales of poverty and suffering suited the image he was attempting to project, and while he told her that he could not really afford theatres, he told Gorman of his attending an early performance of Debussy's *Pelléas et Mélisande* at the Opéra-Comique and Heijermans's *La Bonne espérance* at the Théâtre-Antoine. He was present at the final performance of the Polish tenor Jean de Reszke in *Pagliacci* and thought his voice very like his father's.[8] He also saw the celebrated Gabrielle Réjane in *Lysistrata* and in Henri Meilhac's *Ma Cousine*. Even the Corneille was not really that uncomfortable, rating a mention in Baedeker. He was, however, fascinated by the underbelly of society, so cheap cafés and mingling with the Parisian *demi-monde* suited both his artistic purposes and prevailing mood.

He soon sent off his first contributions to the Dublin *Daily Express*, a withering review of William Rooney's *Poems and Ballads*, but a kindlier one of Walter Jerrold's monograph on George Meredith. Both appeared in the 11 December issue, and he told his mother to look out for them. Now launched into a wider world, he was still pursuing his long-term literary ambitions, still committed to watching and listening. To his collection of epiphanies he added impressions of Paris, capturing images of 'unloved' 'perfumed' women promenading the Boulevard St-Michel or sitting in cafés silently eating pastries or dismounting from carriages 'with a busy stir of garments, soft as the voice of the adulterer'.[9] In the event of his death, he told Stanislaus, his epiphanies were to be sent to all the great libraries of the world, including the Vatican, hoping no doubt to shock His Holiness and his fellow celibates, as he liked to shock others.[10]

Yeats finally persuaded *The Academy* to give Joyce some reviewing and, perhaps encouraged by this, he composed a poem which he sent to his friend Byrne on a picture postcard of himself dressed as a *poèt de Bohème* – wide-brimmed hat, ankle-length coat, that 'far-away look' in his eyes, mimicking (as Gogarty observed) the very expression to be found in a famous portrait of Rimbaud. The poem has a haunting resonance, especially its opening lines:

All day I hear the noise of waters
Making moan,
Sad as the sea-bird is when going
Forth alone.

It hints at the sense of loneliness echoed later in *Stephen Hero* – a feeling which had first led him to retreat into himself and now to retreat to another country. It was the loneliness of the gifted imagination in an alien world. It left him with a feeling of persistent restlessness. 'I am afraid I shall not easily settle down,' he told his mother. 'I should not like to live in Paris but I should like to divide my existence.'[11]

He sent her one of his picture postcards complaining about his poverty and one to Cosgrave on which he wrote a scurrilous verse in dog Latin about Paris prostitutes. Cosgrave showed this to the devout Byrne who was horrified. He was, it seemed, continuing to disgrace the Jesuits. But Joyce was trying to capture the seductive image of Paris, and later has Ignatius Gallaher telling the impressionable Little Chandler in 'A Little Cloud', 'I've been to the Moulin Rouge ... and I've been to all the Bohemian cafés. Hot stuff!'[12] And *Ulysses* carries many allusions to Paris's climate of intellectual excitement, its free-ranging political debates and above all its air of intoxicating sexuality.

At first Archer's warning about a lack of English-language students in Paris appeared exaggerated. On 15 December he informed his mother that he had been offered a job with the Berlitz School starting at 150 francs (six pounds) a month, and had he not been attending medical classes so diligently he would have taken it. He did, however, find one private student – a bluff, bearded champagne salesman and socialist, Joseph Douce. From Douce he earned just 25 francs (one pound) a month, to which he was able to add what little came from home, his reviewing fees, and occasional small loans from Casey and his son.

He borrowed Douce's name for his sexy Irish barmaid in the 'Sirens' episode of *Ulysses*, where some passages about her and Mina Kennedy seem cunningly encoded. Both are women to lust after. 'Rose Douce' sounds like code for 'Sweet Briar' (the play that had excited young Joyce), and 'sweetbriar' was sixteenth-century slang for female pubic hair. 'Miss Douce composed her rose to wait.' ('Rose' was eighteenth-century slang for a virgin vagina; Mina in Gaelic means 'small and smooth'.) Joyce's work is shot through with such obscure imagery.

The tales of wretched living and bare subsistence alarmed his mother. She worried about his lack of money but was hardly in a position to help him much, especially when he asked for funds for a ticket home for Christmas. She was clearly anxious to see him again. 'We will be united very soon thank God for home you must come if only for a week,' she wrote, suggesting they send his return ticket from Dublin. Still concerned for his well-being (living as he was in a freezing room lit by candles), she suggested he buy a lamp and a spirit stove on which to boil water, but then worried that he might have an accident with it. He must have tried, stricken with remorse for having hurt her by his apostasy and arrogance, to write about it to her but was unable to do so in straightforward terms. She was clearly troubled that he was trying to tell her something she was unable to understand. 'As you so often said I am stupid and cannot grasp the great thoughts which are yours much as I desire to do so. Do not wear your soul out with tears but be as usually brave and look hopefully to the future.'[13]

The Dublin literati were anxious to keep tabs on Joyce, and Yeats wrote to say that he had managed to interest the editors of *The Speaker* and *The Academy* in him and the poems he had sent from Paris. 'Perhaps I will make you angry,' he added, 'when I say that it is the poetry of a young man, of a young man who is practicing his instrument, taking pleasure in the mere handling of the stops. It went very nicely in its place with the others, getting a certain richness from the general impression of all taken together and from your own beautiful reading.'[14] Lady Gregory enquired after him and he reported on his work for Longworth at the Dublin *Daily Express* and his disillusionment with medicine. He found Paris 'amusing', he told her, but had not been won over by life in France which was impossible for the creation of poetry. But he wished the French long life, if only because of their cooks and dancing masters.[15]

Just before Christmas his parents sent him his ticket home, booked, as he had asked, for the shorter Calais–Dover crossing in the hope of avoiding seasickness. By Christmas Eve he was back in Dublin, where he remained for a month, picking up again with friends, especially Gogarty and Cosgrave, his companions in nocturnal mischief.[16] The group had acquired another member in John Elwood, a Republican who, Jacobin-style, called everyone 'Citizen', the title Joyce chose for his bigoted Irish nationalist in *Ulysses*. He spent Christmas at St Peter's Terrace, and thought his father had never looked better – 'brown, healthy and neat' – although the truth was that he was approaching the end of his financial tether and becoming ever more prone to drunken outbursts. As his long-suffering mother (whose health was beginning to deteriorate) wrote later, 'Yr Pappie has been in a curious state of mind for some time past.'[17] Her eyes and teeth were troubling her and he vowed to save up to get her decent treatment. But his own teeth needed attention, and with his sight also beginning to weaken before long he would have to resume wearing glasses.

Joyce's fasting had become part of his persona and Gogarty thought his low alcohol threshold was due to his consuming too much Guinness on an almost permanently empty stomach.[18] 'The Bard', he noticed, would often withdraw to the toilet where, he suspected, their conversations were recorded, and he noted Elwood's comment that with Joyce having chosen writing over medicine, they were 'all on stage' now.[19] ('He fears the lancet of my art,' thinks Stephen, as Buck Mulligan taunts him on the gun platform of the Martello Tower.) However, probably none of them realized just how they would feature in his future fiction. Gogarty and Cosgrave would be pained, but Elwood's portrayal in *A Portrait* as 'a raw Gipsy-looking youth with a shambling gait and a shambling manner of speaking' was less unflattering.[20]

He had sent Lewis C. Hind, editor of *The Academy*, a sample review and, passing through London on his return to Paris, he called at the magazine's office in Chancery Lane, expecting a positive editorial verdict and further commissions. But Hind had not been impressed by his critical tone. In his memoirs, *May It Please the Court*, Eugene Sheehy tells Joyce's story of his comic encounter with the editor. Told that his review 'would not do', Joyce merely said 'Sorry' and went to leave the room. 'Oh! Come, Mr Joyce,' said Hind, 'I am only anxious to help you. Why won't you meet my wishes?' 'I thought,' replied Joyce, 'that I was to convey to your readers what I considered to be the aesthetic value of the book you gave me.' 'Precisely,' said the editor, 'that is what I want.' 'Well!' replied Joyce, 'I don't think it has any value whatsoever, aesthetic or otherwise, and I have tried to convey that to your readers, and I presume that you have readers.' Annoyed by this, Hind told him if that was his attitude he couldn't help him. 'I have only to lift the window and put my head out, and I can get a hundred critics to review it,' he said. 'Review what?' replied Joyce, 'your head?' and walked out.[21] On a more pleasant note, Archer again took him for a meal at the National Liberal Club, a meal he must have hoped would not end up in the English Channel.

By 23 January Joyce was back at the Hôtel Corneille, no longer pretending to pursue his medical studies. Now he devoted himself to a course of reading more to his taste. He obtained a ticket for the Bibliothèque Nationale and resumed the philosophical and literary studies broken off the previous summer at university, copying out passages from Dante's *Inferno* in a meticulous hand as if dwelling on and digesting them as he wrote. At night he preferred the Bibliothèque St-Gervais, 'sheltered from the sin of Paris' according to *Ulysses*,[22] and there befriended a Siamese student called Chown – a useful source of occasional loans, he found.

At the Bibliothèque Nationale he read the complete works of Ben Jonson, whose poetry he particularly admired, and at the Bibliothèque St-Gervais he tackled a long list of books on Irish history and read religiously through Aristotle's *Metaphysics*, making page after page of detailed notes – 'a garner of slender sentences', he called them.[23] He also kept up his reviewing. He was asked by *The Speaker* to review the French translation of Ibsen's early play *Catilina* containing the lines 'I dreamed that, winged like Icarus of old,/I flew aloft beneath the vault of heaven,' which seemed to speak directly to the embryonic Stephen Dedalus. And although he saw 'little merit' in it and later came to doubt Ibsen's achievement, his personal identification with his Norwegian hero remained important to him.

Occasionally Joyce had just a bit more cash than usual. Shortly after his return to Paris, he received a pound from Gogarty, borrowed ten francs from Chown, and in early February acquired a new pupil through Douce – a M. Auvergniot – a gift from the gods for his twenty-first birthday. In addition to the usual family greetings, he received a letter from his father regretting that things were not what he had hoped they would be on the occasion of his majority. However, said John, he remained the son who would eventually amount to something that would have made his grandfather Joyce proud of him. 'I now only hope that you may carry out his ideas through your life and if you do, you may be sure you will not do anything unbecoming a gentleman.'[24] Be that as it may, James was certainly his father's son when it came to getting by on little money. He had discovered a new dodge. If he asked a French acquaintance what he was doing for lunch he would invariably be stood a free meal, but, he said, the same trick didn't work with the English or Americans. As a birthday treat he borrowed another 10 francs from Chown, took a train to St-Cloud, returned along the Seine on a river ferry and capped the evening with a visit to the theatre.

On 7 February he went to the Théâtre Sarah Bernhardt in the Place du Châtelet (the amphitheatre cost just one franc) to see Bernhardt as Hermione in Racine's *Andromaque*, with incidental music by Saint-Saëns ('Miss Bernhardt is inexhaustible in the power she possesses of adding role to role and triumph to triumph,' reported *The Times*.)[25] Perhaps the sight of the handsome actress encouraged him one evening to call on Maud Gonne at 7 Avenue d'Eylau, but he was told that she was in bed and could not be disturbed. She wrote afterwards to apologize, saying that she had been nursing a child sick with diphtheria and did not wish him to become infected, but promising to meet him in the Trocadero Gardens – 'a pleasure deferred' she called it.[26] She did later call at the Corneille but found him out. Joyce felt slighted by his earlier rebuff and told his mother he had no further intention of contacting Gonne, who on 21 February married Major John MacBride at the Church of St-Honoré d'Eylau. Joyce, it seems, was not present.[27]

Gogarty, eager for gossip, wrote to Joyce asking for 'a full account of the MacBride nuptials',[28] but Joyce, uninterested, did not respond. His mother wrote urging him not to ignore her, saying, 'You will make a big mistake by not keeping as yr Pappie says "in touch with her".' Gonne features in *Ulysses* somewhat disreputably (as a 'beautiful woman, *La Patrie*' linked to names of her past lovers), and in *Finnegans Wake* jokingly, as if at an auction ('Gowan, Gawin and Gonne'). Little escaped the voracious mind of the observant epiphanist, whose collection of sketches and poems continued to grow.

Stanislaus's drab office routine was at least enlivened by an occasional letter from brother Jim in good vituperative mood and 'feeling very intellectual' up to his eyes in Aristotle's psychology. He was fed up with AE who probably would not approve of his Parisian epiphanies, but, 'so help me devil I will write only the things that approve themselves to me and I will write them the best way I can'. He then cursed all the self-righteous Dublin cultural revivalists and cranks he could think of: 'Damn Russell, damn Yeats, damn Skeffington, damn Darlington, damn editors, damn free-thinkers, damn vegetable verse and double damn vegetable philosophy!'[29] Then, quite casually, into his letter he dropped two poems, including one of his best – 'I Hear an Army Charging upon the Land'. This was the poem of his Yeats liked most, perhaps attracted by the sense of violence captured by the force of his imagery.

Joyce decided that the best way to economize was to 'fast' occasionally and to do his own cooking, which meant smuggling items of food into the Corneille against hotel rules. But he did have his moments of festivity. On 25 February, with money from his father, he dined well, treating himself to a cigar and some confetti to scatter around at the Paris Carnival that evening. *The Times* reported the event as an outbreak of hooliganism: *les Apaches* on the rampage, 963 arrests by midnight, 150 weapons – knives, knuckle-dusters and revolvers – confiscated, a girl of eighteen stabbed in the Faubourg St-Martin. Joyce's own report for the *Express* never appeared, but in the 'Proteus' episode of *Ulysses* he has Stephen suspected of murder in Paris at carnival time in 1904.

What money he had was soon spent. 'I bought a stove, a saucepan, a plate, a cup, a saucer, a knife, a fork, a small spoon, a big spoon, a bowl, salt, sugar, figs, macaroni, cocoa &c and got my linen from the laundry,' he told his father. His home-cooking was the usual basic fare drummed up by students in garrets: hard-boiled eggs, cold ham, bread and butter, macaroni, figs and cocoa. But, he added – just in case it might be thought he was living too well and no longer suffering – 'I am sorry to say that after my dinner on Tuesday I became very ill and at night I had a fit of vomiting. I felt very bad the whole of the following day but I am better today except for attacks of neuralgia – induced, I imagine, by my constant periods of fasting.'[30]

A letter from his mother in early March was full of family news – May and Mabel were 'showing cleverness' and Poppie wanting to go into business or to college. But Charlie bewildered her. He had forsaken the seminary and returned home to give everyone a bad time – drinking, refusing to find work, cursing his father and even turning on her.[31] The one son who had not abandoned her religion was now behaving like a morose young delinquent. May's distress can hardly have improved her health which continued to fail.

She urged Jim to write to his father as he grew jealous when letters from him arrived addressed only to her. But, according to Stanislaus, absence had intensified his feelings for a mother whose image, confused with that of the Virgin, had come to him in a dream. Although upset by his apostasy, she continued to express her love for him, and he was now eager to please her. However, he continued to plead poverty and feed her sad tales of near-starvation which, even though he passed them off as his 'Lenten regulations', can hardly have calmed her anxiety over his well-being. When he did write to his father, a brief postcard (signed without greeting) on 6 March, it was about money matters, with instructions for Stanislaus to carry a message to Longworth at the *Express*, and complaints about not hearing from editors at *The Speaker* or the *Irish Times* who had promised him some reviewing.

Synge returned to Paris briefly in early March to clear his flat before heading back to Ireland. He was a tall, dark, brooding man of thirty-one, reserved with most people but not, it seems, with Joyce. He left his card at the Corneille and suggested they meet in the Odéon Cloisters. It was an appropriate enough meeting place, under the colonnade of a great theatre lined with bookstalls. Synge lent Joyce the manuscript of his recently completed play, *Riders to the Sea*, which Joyce recalled Yeats telling him was 'quite Greek'. However, he was unimpressed. 'I am glad to say that ever since I read it I have been riddling it mentally till it has [not] a sound spot,' he told Stanislaus. 'It is tragic about all the men that are drowned in the islands: but thanks be to God Synge isn't an Aristotelian. I told him part of my aesthetic; he says I have a mind like Spinosa [*sic*].'[32] He thought the dialogue of Synge's Aran islanders was probably fabricated, but not having been there himself he could not judge exactly.

Over the next week they met regularly for lunch, invariably arguing about literature – Synge, aggressively opinionated, garrulous and edgy; Joyce, scholarly and erudite. The playwright was surprised to discover his young acquaintance's disdain for French literature, and they disagreed on what was relevant to art. Joyce took him back to his hotel room and showed off his notebook crammed with what he called 'Memorabilia' – a collection of solecisms committed by famous authors, including Yeats. After glancing at it Synge swore, threw the book down and said, 'What of it? It is not important at all.'[33] Joyce studied too much for a poet, he said. The Spinoza-like mind of Joyce and the literary mind of Synge were not on this occasion happy to meet. When Joyce suggested a trip to the Parc de St Cloud together, Synge reacted angrily, saying, 'You want to behave just like a bourgeois going out and sitting in a park on holiday.'[34] He had seen through the bohemian pose to the essentially middle-class rebel beneath. Despite what Joyce said about *Riders to the* Sea, he memorized speeches from it and recognized that Synge would be a major player in Yeats's cultural revival.

His fasting and economizing paid off, and he was able to afford the odd trip away from Paris – to Clamart and Charenton, where the insane Marquis de Sade had once been incarcerated, and to the Bois de Vincennes where he observed the confluence of the Marne and the Seine. Rivers intrigued him, and Leopold Bloom, 'waterlover, drawer of water, water-carrier', also admired 'continental lakecontained streams and confluent oceanflowing rivers with their tributaries and transoceanic currents, gulf-stream, north and south equatorial courses'.[35] On trips to Nogent and Tours, Chown went along and no doubt picked up the bill.

At a railway station kiosk on one such trip Joyce bought a copy of Edouard Dujardin's *Les Lauriers sont coupés*. It was a revelation to him. Written as a *monologue intérieur*, it offered a stylistic device enabling the far more elaborate expression of consciousness than was possible in the short poems and epiphanies he continued to accumulate. On 9 March he wrote to tell Stanislaus, 'I have written fifteen epiphanies – of which twelve are insertions, and three additions.' Then, after trying, as if by habit, to squeeze money out of his penniless brother, he urged him to encourage their mother to get out more in the warmer weather. Evidently he was growing concerned about her health.[36]

Longworth sent him Lady Gregory's *Poets and Dreamers* to review which prompted Joyce to resume his attack on the rabblement. Having been befriended by the author did not inhibit the fearless critic. The folktales in this collection, recounted by old people in the west, he wrote, were often the product of feeble, meandering and sleepy minds, and were not as ironically and delicately treated by her ladyship as they had been by Yeats in *The Celtic Twilight*. Although unkind to Gregory's book, he was not dismissive of Irish folklore and legend, as his final many-layered novel, itself a modern meandering Irish legend, would demonstrate. To distance himself from Joyce's views, Longworth broke the rule and printed the review over his initials. Fortunately there were no repercussions, and he continued receiving books to review for the *Express*.

By mid-March his mother's letters sounded a little brighter. On the 19th, she wrote to say that John was working in Mountjoy Square organizing a by-election campaign, and Charlie was behaving much better. However, she was concerned about James's clothes, his diet and work prospects, and feeling sad that he had missed the St Patrick's Day Ball in Paris where he might have made good contacts. One of his sisters was having eye trouble and she, too, was hardly able to read the letter she was writing. Otherwise, she assured him that she was in good health, and sent him a postal order for nine shillings (around 11 francs).[37] He replied that he was just about managing to pay his hotel bills and economizing a little, but his shirt was indescribable, one boot was worn through and his flies were held together with safety pins. Nevertheless, his mother's money and a cheque from Longworth had raised his spirits. 'Today,' he told her, 'I came laughing and singing to myself down the Boulevard Saint-Michel without a care in the world because I felt I was going to have a dinner – my first dinner (properly speaking) for three days. This shows what simpletons we all are.'[38]

Although his sister Poppie could not afford even a pair of gloves, his mother, worried about the state of *his* clothes, offered to pay for his suit to be cleaned and then to buy him a new one. Now in his mood of reconciliation, he told her he attended vespers regularly, either at Notre-Dame or at St-Germain l'Auxerrois. Anyone in the know would have been unsurprised. 'An Irish atheist,' said John Pentland Mahaffy, 'is one who wishes to God he could believe in God.'[39] And, after all, he had what Buck Mulligan in *Ulysses* calls 'the cursed jesuit strain' in him, even though 'injected the wrong way'.[40]

The mood also brought forth confidences, and he told May of his hopes and plans as a writer: 'My book of songs will be published in the spring of 1907. My first comedy about five years later. My "Esthetic" about five years later again. (This must interest you!).' Clearly he valued her good opinion. 'Tell me what you think of me,' he wrote.[41] His deep interest in aesthetics had taken him to Aristotle again and in his ruled student notebook he teased away at such questions as 'What is beauty?' and 'What is Art?' And far removed from such aesthetic uncertainty were the favourite Ben Jonson verses he copied down to add later to his repertoire:

> As bright as is the Sun her Sire,
> Or Earth her Mother, in her best Attire,
> Or Mint, the Mid-wife, with her
> Comes forth her Grace! . . . [42]

He composed and then destroyed some Jonsonian dialogue, which, he told Stanislaus, although nonsensical had captured the style.

In late March, Synge sent Lady Gregory the latest news about the vagabond poet.

> He seems to be pretty badly off, and is wandering around Paris rather unbrushed and rather indolent, spending his studious moments in the National Library reading Ben Jonson. French literature I understand is beneath him! Still he interested me a good deal and as he is being gradually won over by the charm of French life, his time in Paris is not wasted. He talks of coming back to Dublin in the summer to live there on journalism while he does his serious work at his leisure. I cannot think that he will ever be a poet of importance, but his intellect is extraordinarily keen and if he keeps fairly sane he ought to do excellent essay-writing.[43]

Things suddenly seemed to be looking up. Joyce managed to pay Casey 5 francs he owed him, his review of Ibsen's *Catalina* appeared in *The Speaker*, and he sent two more reviews to Longworth. He was also pleased and amused to hear from Stannie that Eglinton had said, 'There is something sublime in Joyce's standing alone.'[44] Furthermore, he had finally broken into the *Irish Times* with an interview with Henri Fournier, the French racing driver, who planned to go to Dublin to take part in the second James Gordon Bennett Cup race that July. The interview, published on 7 April 1903, seemed bored and blasé; sports reporting was not Joyce's strong point. But, characteristically, he still drew on it for his story 'After the Race'.

The omens were looking good and he wrote home asking May to send him a Holy Week book in time for Tenebrae on 8 April (the 'Spy Wednesday' celebrations which Stephen and Cranly attend at the Pro-Cathedral in *Stephen Hero*). This office of the Church in which candles are extinguished after each prayer was a favourite and had inspired an early poem, one in which William Archer had seen 'real promise'. Joyce attended Tenebrae at Notre-Dame on all three nights before Good Friday, walking back to the Corneille afterwards through the gaslit streets.

But the omens had been misleading. On the evening of Good Friday, 10 April, he returned to his hotel to find a telegram awaiting him: 'Mother dying come home father.'[45] Although it was midnight, he rushed off through the deserted streets to his student Douce's apartment to borrow 75 francs for his fare home. He left for Dublin next day ('Hurrying to her squalid deathlair from gay Paris'),[46] taking the cheaper Dieppe–Newhaven route, on which inevitably he was seasick.

His homeward journey is captured in an epiphany which reveals his woeful state of mind. Lying exhausted on the deck of the Channel ferry, consumed by fear and remorse, he observed the mists moving against the cliffs along the French coast and imagined hearing the chanting choirboys of Notre-Dame, still fresh in his memory. 'Beyond the misty walls, in the dark cathedral church of Our Lady, I hear the bright, even voices of boys singing before the altar there.' The most recent letters from his mother, expressing her love for him, evoked that dream image of the Madonna from whom, it seems, he had not been able fully to separate himself. 'She comes from her ancient seat to visit the least of her children, mother most venerable, as though he had never been alien to her.'[47]

9

A Death in the Family

(1903–1904)

'I perchance hereafter shall think meet
To put an antic disposition on.'

Shakespeare, *Hamlet*

May Joyce had been diagnosed with cirrhosis of the liver. Not known to be a drinker, most likely she had contracted hepatitis (the other known cause of the disease) because of the poor living conditions at St Peter's Terrace.[1] On James's arrival, her health seemed to improve, but now she only rarely left her bed. If she haunted his thoughts and dreams, she would also haunt his fiction and his conscience – the woman whose faith and love he had betrayed. ('Venus has twisted her lips in prayer. Agenbite of inwit: remorse of conscience.')[2] His sister May later recalled that the rest of the family were sent from the room while Jim read his latest writing to his mother.[3] Absence and guilt had inspired in him a new sense of maternal devotion, but not to the point of abandoning his unbelief. It is said that faced with the prospect of death, May pleaded with James to make confession and take communion, but he was unyielding. He was prepared to indulge his religious feelings to the extent of visiting churches and bathing in their ambience, but he would not bow a deceitful knee to any priest of the Church he had left. Ellmann suggests that he stopped short, out of fear and respect, at pledging false allegiance to so ancient and venerated an icon.[4]

In the street in late April he ran into Yeats who reported to Lady Gregory, 'I saw Joyce in Dublin. He said his mother was still alive and it was uncertain whether she would die or not. He [then] added "but these things really do not matter." I spoke to him about his behaviour at *Academy* office and other things of the kind rather sternly. He took it unexpectedly well.'[5] From Paris he brought his bohemian persona and costume – his 'Hamlet hat' and 'cloak of inky-black', long hair and small beard which Gogarty claimed he shaved off after being told he had Dante's profile.[6] This bizarre outfit was completed with an ashplant, lending him a final touch of the magus. W. J. Lawrence, a theatrical historian associated with the Abbey, left a verbal caricature of Joyce: 'an odd creature with his strange eyes and long hair, walking along the street with huge strides, seven-league-boot style, with his arms waving constantly'.[7] He had begun to call himself a socialist, though some considered his manner more that of an anarchist with a bomb in his back pocket.[8]

Stanislaus thought Paris had wrought a fundamental transformation in his brother. He had acquired a taste for Continental living; he had discovered that hunger and privation were preferable to the constraints of religion and the demands of nationalism, and acquired an attitude to money which would be a source of irritation between them for years to come.[9] But his stories of impoverishment also revealed the depth of his commitment to his new religion of art. In moments of painful hunger, he said, he had learned to stave off the pangs by reciting poetry. He was, as Stanislaus put it, truly 'a believer in the vivifying grace of the imagination by which the soul lives'.[10]

Now back in touch with his Dublin friends, Joyce was especially anxious to repair his relationship with Byrne, fractured by Cosgrave's showing him his obscene dog-Latin verse. At first Byrne told him there was no chance of reconciliation. But Joyce valued 'Cranly's' friendship and pursued him until he relented. Others, like Moore, who snubbed him when he gate-crashed a party given by Lady Gregory, he did not mind offending.

Yet the bad reputation he was acquiring through gossip did not prevent him attending open Sunday evenings at the Sheehys', where, although often withdrawn, he would happily sing – his own songs as often as old favourites. That June, Hanna married Francis Skeffington, and Joyce for a time succumbed to a secret passion for Mary, the prettiest and wittiest of the sisters, who wore her soft black hair in a long plait. Mary was, said Stanislaus, 'the only girl who had ever aroused any emotional interest in him', and became for a while his muse.[11] After a conversation with her, during a walk in the hills with Skeffington, James composed the poem, 'What counsel has the hooded moon/Put in thy heart, my shyly sweet.'[12] But his real taste in women remained with the more uninhibited ladies of the *demi-monde*.

On 4 July, John Joyce's birthday, at a Dublin municipal meeting, his friend Tim Harrington, the Mayor, supported a demand (by the 'Extreme Disloyalty Party', which included Maud Gonne MacBride) that no address of welcome be delivered to King Edward when he arrived for a ten-day visit on the 21st. The King, as Joyce said in his 1907 lecture, 'Ireland, Island of Saints and Sages', had to be content with a reception given by the Sheriff. But the spurned monarch does rate a mention in 'Ivy Day in the Committee Room', and is a cavorting presence around Nighttown in the 'Circe' episode of *Ulysses*. If the King was unwelcome in Dublin he was certainly welcome in the house of Joyce's fiction.

The doctor treating May, Dr Bob Kenny, an old friend of John's and Visiting Surgeon at North Dublin Union Hospital, was a short lean dandyish figure whom she nicknamed 'Sir Peter Teazle' (after the character in Sheridan's *School for Scandal*). She was an excellent mimic and clearly kept her sense of humour to the end. Over the coming months her condition slowly deteriorated and she began to suffer violent fits of bilious vomiting. The image of his dying mother spewing green bile haunts Stephen in the 'Telemachus' episode of *Ulysses*: 'The ring of bay and skyline held a dull green mass of liquid. A bowl of white china had stood beside her deathbed holding the green sluggish bile which she had torn up from her rotting liver by fits of loud groaning vomiting.'[13] Her sister-in-law, the children's Aunt Josephine, moved into the house to nurse her. Fourteen-year-old May was the most attentive of her daughters, while James again played and sang – some of her favourite songs – through the open doors from the piano downstairs. John, at first the caring husband suffused with a 'new warmth', took out yet another mortgage of £50 to cover her medical expenses. But he grew increasingly restless as the months dragged on, and by degrees transformed himself into the villain of the piece.

One evening, returning home drunk with a bunch of his equally inebriated pals in tow, he came into May's bedroom where James, Stanislaus and Aunt Josephine were sitting with her, and began pacing up and down, evidently in an evil mood. Suddenly he shouted, 'I'm finished. I can't do any more. If you can't get well, die. Die and be damned to you!' Stanislaus, in a great fury, yelled, 'You swine!' and went for him. But, when May attempted to get out of bed to separate them, he turned to look after her instead, while James led his raving father out of the room. May pleaded with Stannie never to do that again. 'You know that when he is that way he doesn't know what he is saying,' she told him. However, Stannie never forgave him, recalling how often he had said to May, 'I'll break your heart! I'll break your bloody heart!'[14] And that's exactly what he thought finally his father *had* done.

May gradually fell into a coma and died on 13 August; she was just forty-four. At her bedside, apart from John and the family, were Aunt Josephine and some of her family, including a canon of the Church. John Murray, John's *bête noire*, knelt down and began to pray loudly, motioning to the others to join him. James and Stanislaus remained standing, much to their uncle's disgust. Stannie couldn't have cared less, but James was consumed by a deep sense of guilt. The deathbed scene, said Stannie, 'burnt itself into my brother's soul' and in an epiphany he captured a nightmare in which the hideous vision of his decomposing mother appeared to him in her grave-clothes, a nightmare visited in turn upon Stephen Dedalus in *Ulysses*.

When news of the incident reached Gogarty's ears, he made great play of it, embroidering it into a version which had Joyce's mother pleading with him to pray for her and him callously refusing. For those who came to hate Joyce because of his apostasy and later writing, Gogarty's cruel fiction was readily accepted as evidence of the evil which comes of sinful disbelief. Inevitably it surfaced in *Ulysses* in the taunting of Stephen by Buck Mulligan, showing Joyce's skill in capturing a scene through mock-dramatic speech.

> You wouldn't kneel down to pray for your mother on her deathbed when she asked you. Why? Because you have the cursed jesuit strain in you, only it's injected the wrong way. To me it's all a mockery and beastly. Her cerebral lobes are not functioning. She calls the doctor sir Peter Teazle and picks buttercups off the quilt. Humour her till it's over. You crossed her last wish in death.[15]

Mulligan also offends Stephen by saying jovially on meeting him, 'O, it's only Dedalus whose mother is beastly dead.' The offender cannot understand his offence, explaining that Stephen had only seen his mother die, while he, as a medical student, dissects corpses every day and so is immune from such feelings. Even though the story comes to us as a fiction it rings true of the wittily sardonic Gogarty who could never resist the opportunity to be cleverly outrageous.

Joyce believed his mother had died of cancer, although her death certificate states 'cirrhosis', and that she had endured four months five days of persistent bilious vomiting.[16] May was interred at Glasnevin Cemetery where her son George lay buried. From this point on, Poppie, the eldest daughter, now twenty, ran the household as best she could. Aunt Josephine took on the role of surrogate mother to the numerous young Joyces who became progressively alienated from their irascible father. Not only was it increasingly difficult to extract money from him in order to eat; Stannie wrote of how John would threaten to break their 'bloody hearts', as he had done to their mother, then adding, 'I'll break your stomach first though, ye buggers. You'll get the effects of it later on. Wait till you're thirty and you'll see where you'll be.'[17] Visits to the Murrays' would at least guarantee a meal and a tranquil refuge from hunger and drunken violence. Faced with these trying circumstances the older girls (Eva thirteen, May fourteen and Eileen fifteen) all bore up, while Charlie, now eighteen, despite having abandoned the priesthood, had, according to Stannie, become 'intolerably' Catholic.

In what might be seen as a symbolic gesture of renunciation, Stannie burned all John's love letters to May after Jim had read them through, without even looking at them himself. His hatred of his religion and country had only been intensified by his mother's wretched life and death, for which he blamed her unquestioning loyalty to an unenlightened Church at war with freedom of thought and the joy of living,[18] and 'the hateful country and hateful times in which she lived'.[19] For James, who was closer to her than his casual remark to Yeats seemed to indicate, her death was not just shattering but another turning point. Thereafter he would always seek mother-substitutes (Aunt Josephine being the first) from whom he would demand the enduring loyalty and devotion due from a mother to a son. Any deviation, or suspected deviation, from that expectation would be considered betrayal.

His youngest sister Mabel ('Baby') was distraught beyond consolation at her mother's death. James took the time and trouble to talk things through with her, assuring her that their mother was in heaven and happier than she'd ever been, and the girl was finally calmed.[20] Stanislaus claimed that he found his father sitting alone at home 'whining' and attacked him bitterly 'forgetting very little', but John simply said, 'You don't understand, boy.'[21] Jim was more forgiving and as always managed to retain a fond attachment to him.[22]

With his mother no longer a moral presence in his life, Joyce was intent upon following William Blake's youthful slogan that the road of excess led to the palace of wisdom.[23] Gogarty and company were only too willing to accompany him down that road. (Gogarty, claimed Stanislaus, was becoming increasingly annoyed by Jim's stubborn air of superiority derived from reading D'Annunzio and had told Elwood that he planned to get him drunk 'in order to break his spirit'.)[24] Persuaded that excess was the way of the Elizabethans (in whose poetic ambience his mind often dwelt), Joyce was soon drawn back into nights of heavy drinking, wenching and singing bawdy songs around Monto, on which Gogarty, the diabolical Lord of Misrule, held sway. In his diary Stannie recorded his brother's descent into degeneracy:

> He has or seems to have taken a liking for conviviality, even with those whose jealousy and ill-will towards himself he well knows, staying with them a whole night long dancing and singing and making speeches and laughing and reciting, and revelling in the same manner all the way home ... [but] ... one must judge him by his moments of exaltation, not by his hours of abasement.[25]

Not for nothing had Gogarty once sent Joyce a poem in Paris decorated with a winged phallus.

In the same spirit of the ridiculous, the story of the origins of the title of his poetry collection, *Chamber Music* (which Stanislaus claimed to be his suggestion), now took its due place in Joycean mythology. The story goes that while Joyce and Gogarty were entertaining a lady of easy virtue, an acrobat called Jenny ('my lady of love ... a good soul', according to Gogarty), Joyce began to recite his poems. When Jenny retired behind a screen to make use of a chamber pot, Gogarty suddenly exclaimed, 'There's a critic!' and the title, now a delicious irony, duly suggested itself. Joyce passed on the story to his biographer Gorman and a letter from Gogarty to Joyce seems to confirm this version of events – 'Chamber music immediately springs into my mind from the appearance of the above abbreviation [PO for Post Office]' – followed by a suggestion that Joyce visit Jenny ('the holy woman') and send him a report on 'her condition'.[26] The title might well have been Stanislaus's, but the double-entendre in response to Jenny's 'criticism' certainly has the authentic Gogartian ring to it.[27]

But the months following his mother's death were not all bacchanalia. After turning in fourteen reviews on the trot for the *Express* Joyce quarrelled with Longworth, who threatened to throw him out if he ever showed his face there again. And his further attempts to contribute to the *Irish Times* came to nothing. As a result he now needed to find some means of earning a living. He was offered some temporary French teaching at University College, but he saw it as an attempt to buy him back for the Jesuits and declined. He considered applying for a position at the National Library, but found no one to support him, and he made a feeble effort to interest himself in the Law before returning to his medical studies. With Skeffington he planned to launch a newspaper to be called *The Goblin*, but they failed to get backing. There was a hare-brained scheme for getting parcels of books out of pawn and passing them off as rare volumes, but booksellers quickly saw through the deception and Joyce ended up the loser. Now he was reduced to cadging from any likely donor, even accepting Gogarty's old clothes and was now almost always to be seen wearing creased flannels, tennis shoes and a yachting cap. On one occasion he borrowed Gogarty's .22 rifle and pawned it, repaying him by contributing the final line to a Gogarty poem which won him a first prize at Trinity.[28]

His break with Longworth would not have surprised his friends. He seemed to set out deliberately to provoke, as if motivated by a demon of the perverse. And some of his attitudes would not have commended themselves to the editor of a popular daily paper – what Stanislaus called his 'tiger-like, insatiable hatred' for what he called the 'rabblement', his deliberately speaking truths which others found indigestible, and shocking with his obscene limericks. He was, thought Stannie, a mixture of cruelty, gentleness and simple openness, and few people would love him.[29]

With Gogarty around again, the rake's decline progressed, but all the time the artist was awake, observing and noting. The city, Joyce told Stanislaus, was suffering from 'hemiplegia of the will' and he was determined to live, even if it meant he never wrote another line.[30] Stannie, now clerking for a pittance at the Apothecaries' Hall, was disgusted with him, believing that in his misguided friendship with the medics he was squandering his genius. But although Joyce did not believe in genius, considering it 'a fake of vanity',[31] he was the alchemist who turned the dross of everyday gossip into literary gold. And while he dismissed Stannie's attempts at writing, he readily appropriated his ideas for his own fiction, and later, when they were apart, found that he missed his ever-reliable whetstone.

In the wake of his mother's death, Joyce was reviewing and re-assessing his own life. Early in the New Year of 1904 he wrote a short auto-biographical essay (a studied self-portrait) called, at Stanislaus's suggestion, 'A Portrait of the Artist'. He offered it to Eglinton for his new magazine, *Dana*. But Eglinton rejected it, saying that he was not prepared to publish anything he could not understand himself. This essay, however, would form the kernel of a novel Joyce now began, *Stephen Hero* (also *his* suggested title, claimed Stanislaus), which would chart the journey of his alter ego, Stephen Daedalus, away from innocence – the necessary prelude to a life dedicated to art.

This can be seen as a critical moment in Joyce's adult writing career. From the start he set his sights extremely high. It would be no simple account of his life to date, but a meditation on an emerging literary and philosophical consciousness. Some of his epiphanies would be developed and expanded and woven into his narrative. Some were dreams, often nightmares, such as the shock of coming across that monkey's skull at his aunt's house at Usher's Island; others captured his drinking cronies, like flies in amber. As Stanislaus wrote, 'I don't think they will like themselves in it.'[32]

In mid-January there was some respite from revelry when Gogarty departed for Worcester College, Oxford, to try for the Newdigate Prize for English verse, as Wilde had done. There he gained a reputation for wit and erudition, and forged some enduring friendships, including George Bell, future Bishop of Chichester, and Samuel Chenevix Trench, the Anglo-Irish son of a British general and a passionate Irish nationalist. Trench, who called himself Dermot, became the model for the somewhat demented Englishman, Haynes, in *Ulysses*. Before he left, Joyce told Gogarty about his novel, and its progress would be a matter of curiosity thereafter among the nervous medics, conscious that they would more than likely be skewered by the Bard's sharpened pen. By 10 February he had completed the first chapter.

Gogarty did not win the Newdigate, but took second prize, and achieved some fame with his Oxford limericks, most notably: 'There was a young man from St John's/Who wanted to Roger the swans./"Oh no," said the porter,/"Oblige with my daughter,/The birds are reserved for the dons."' And when Joyce was in Paris, Gogarty wrote him letters in a deliberately archaic language as if in shared contempt of modern life and letters – 'Inform me how thou liltest: – Yokoko! Yokoko! Yokoko! ... I am subsidised to article the post ere a moon be waned. At present I wind the pastoral pipe ... O preposterous Poet! write to thine impossible friend. Oliver Gogarty.'[33]

On Joyce's twenty-second birthday, John returned home drunk and went straight to bed, leaving the others to celebrate the occasion with – for once at least – a hearty dinner followed by a birthday cigar. Stanislaus caught brother Jim's mood: '[He] says he is not an artist. I think he lives on the excitement of events.'[34] In pursuit of that excitement, he indulged his passion for brief encounters on long nights out around Nighttown followed, much to his father's disgust, by long sleep-ins.

But on his occasional forays into the respectable world of the Sheehys his dubious reputation made him strangely attractive to the middle-class girls he despised. Stanislaus records how Dublin's 'wise virgins' were delighted by the company of the impecunious genius suspected of 'wild ways', pressing their attention on him with 'secret, shy admiration'.[35] He in turn regarded them all in a crudely sexual fashion. 'Jim says he has an instinct for women. He scarcely ever talks decently of them, even of those he likes. He talks of them as of warm, soft-skinned animals. "That one'd give you a great push." "She's very warm between the thighs, I fancy." "She has great action, I'm sure."'[36] But his libertine life suddenly caught up with him; in March he wrote to Gogarty reporting a sexual infection and asking his advice.

Gogarty was amused at Joyce's visitation and replied in suitably Elizabethan fashion: 'Congratulations that our holy mother has judged you worthy of the stigmata ... it would be absurd and pernicious for me to prescribe for a penis in a poke so to speak. I enclose a letter for you to hand to my old friend Dr Walsh one of the best ... If I would venture an opinion – you have got a slight gleet from a recurrence of original sin. But you'll be all right.' He warned him not to neglect the condition, otherwise it could become incurable.[37] Writing to Walsh, he explained

Joyce's problem, hinting that he might have gonorrhoea. Two weeks later, he was back in Dublin, anxious to help his friend with his 'importunate particle'.[38] Stanislaus did later wonder how on earth his reckless brother had managed to avoid the more perilous scourge of syphilis.

But Joyce, at sober moments, was getting down to his novel. He found living at home increasingly intolerable, and, after his father sold the family piano, he moved out. Recommended by George Dempsey, he took a part-time teaching job at a small private school in Dalkey and rented a room at 60 Shelbourne Road from a Mrs Elizabeth McKernan, who, fortunately, was not punctilious about collecting his rent.

The Dalkey school gave him the setting for the 'Nestor' episode of *Ulysses*. Francis Irwin, the owner and head, a Loyalist Ulsterman, provided the model for Mr Deasy, whose jokey anti-Semitism introduces an important running theme into the novel, and whose parsimony prompts Stephen to review his own finances, all borrowings. Mulligan nine pounds, Curran ten guineas, Mrs McKernan five weeks' board, and so on. His meagre pay from Deasy – £3 12s monthly– was, he concludes 'useless' and, in any case, would not remain in his pocket for long.

In March Joyce met a promising young singer, John McCormack, just returned from Italy after winning the annual Feis Ceoil (Irish Music Festival) tenor competition the previous year. Both McCormack and Best encouraged him to enter the Feis that coming May. Curran helped him hire a grand piano and he tapped Gogarty for money to pay for singing lessons. (According to Gogarty, Joyce never paid for the piano but simply waited for it to be repossessed.) He chose as his singing teacher Benedetto Palmieri, said to be the best in Dublin, but managed only a few lessons before running out of funds and having to borrow again. He had friends hunting for sheet music on the bookstalls along the Dublin Quays, and kept himself in practice by singing at any local concert where there was room on the programme. However, he was not always paid and had to pawn books in order to scrape up the competition entrance fee.

Occasionally he did actually earn some money. Eglinton accepted a poem he called 'Song' for *Dana* magazine, a poem asking to be sung, as all Joyce's poems did. He set it to music and it became one of his favourite party-pieces: 'My love is in a light attire/Among the appletrees/Where the gay winds do most desire/To run in companies.'[39] Eglinton paid him a sovereign for the poem, later recalling how Joyce 'chortled' as he pocketed it.[40] The same poem was accepted for the May issue of the *Saturday Review*. It had been passed on by Symons who had seen several of Joyce's poems and told him they were remarkably good and should be published. 'The Bard' now had a valuable advocate, and publishers and editors would soon be hearing about him as a coming man. The romantic sentiment of his verse, however, contrasted starkly with the coarse attitude towards women which Stanislaus had noted. As he wrote later of a poem of yearning from the pen of Henry VIII, 'It is strange from what muddy pools the angels call forth a spirit of beauty.'[41]

By the end of the month, Joyce had completed enough of his novel to elicit a judgement from Stanislaus: 'The chapters are exceptionally well-written in a style which seems to me altogether original. It is a lying autobiography and a raking satire. He is putting nearly all his acquaintances in it, and the Catholic Church comes in for a bad quarter of an hour.' But nor was Stannie exempt from his brother's unrelenting contempt, as he religiously recorded. He reminded him, said James, of Gogarty's description of Eglinton – 'that he had to fart every time before he could think' and added, for good measure, that he was commonplace, 'a thick-headed bloody fool' with a voice that was 'unpleasant and expressionless', and that he'd hate to be a woman waking up and seeing his face on the pillow in the morning.[42] But Stannie still regarded his brother as 'heroic' and 'noble' and appeared to suffer this abuse uncomplainingly, which only encouraged the mockery. There were very few Joyce did not regard as belonging to the contemptible rabblement, even in his own family.

10
Nora
(1904)

'From women's eyes this doctrine I derive:/They are the ground, the books, the academes,/From whence doth spring the true Promethean fire.' Shakespeare, *Love's Labour's Lost*

Early in 1904, a young woman escaped from an oppressive family situation in Galway and found refuge in Dublin. Nora Barnacle, barely twenty, buxom with long auburn hair, fine brows and enticing slightly hooded blue eyes, found work as a chambermaid at Finn's Hotel in Leinster Street, and was soon catching the eye of young men around town. She had a wild, adventurous streak, was too nonconforming to be considered a good Catholic, and on occasions, as a girl in Galway, would make forays into town with her friends disguised as boys. She had had two serious relationships. Her first beau, Michael Feeney, died of typhoid aged seventeen; a second, Michael Bodkin, died of tuberculosis aged twenty. Both were buried in Galway's Rahoon Cemetery. For this she had earned the nickname 'man-killer' at the Presentation Convent where she worked as a laundress. When she began meeting a Protestant boy, Willy Mulvagh, her uncle and guardian Thomas Healy forbade her to see him, and, finding them together again, had beaten her, so precipitating her flight to Dublin. Apart from that, she had been drawn into a risky flirtation with a young curate, and was clearly primed for further liaisons and unafraid of what amorous adventures might come along.

What inhibitions James Joyce had against using obscenities had now been abandoned along with his sobriety and once-neat dress, though Padraic Colum thought it was all part of an elaborate performance.

The gestures he made with the ashplant he now carried, his way of making his voice raucous, were surely part of an act. And wasn't there, too, in his behaviour the assertion of a young man conscious of his hand-me-down clothes ... who was familiar with the houses in Nighttown? The raucous voice, the obscene limericks delivered with such punctilio ... Was he playing Rimbaud? Villon?[1]

Gerald Griffin recalled encountering him at the National Library holding forth to Skeffington, Colum and Kettle:

> A tall gaunt youth in a shabby grey suit, quondam white canvas shoes down at heel and a tennis-shirt open at the neck, Joyce stared fixedly with his steely grey-blue eyes into space, while he scornfully anathematized the Irish National Theatre movement, using crisp Anglo-Saxon monosyllables to express his contempt for George Moore, Yeats, Synge, Standish O'Grady, Lady Gregory, O'Neill Russell and other exponents of the movement. As he warmed to his subject, the variants ... became more vivid and vitriolic.[2]

Act or no act, Joyce's once-fastidious Jekyll was being overtaken by his slovenly, coarse, inebriate Hyde.

But he could turn sober and smart when necessary. On 16 May he entered for the Feis Ceoil tenor competition. As Curran recalled, things did not go quite according to plan:

> He appeared on the platform in spotless linen and with a butterfly tie, he was young, but he looked even younger than his age, and he fascinated an old lady who was sitting behind me. 'Oh, what a nice boy,' she said to me. Joyce sang the recitative, I remember, splendidly – 'Whom the Lord Chasteneth', and an aria by Sullivan, 'Come Ye Children'. Then the sight-reading test was presented to him, and he gave one look at it, jumped off the platform, and took refuge in a hostelry adjacent to forget.[3]

Herbert Gorman, with whose biography Joyce assisted, wrote that 'This [test] seemed to the budding tenor a monstrously inartistic thing to do (much like asking a blindfolded sculptor to carve a statue) ... He did not regard it as a test of the beauty of the voice or the musicianship of proper delivery to sing at sight.' For days afterwards he spoke scathingly of the festival regulations.[4] Being unable to complete the test he was awarded only an honourable mention but when one of the medal-winners was disqualified he was sent the bronze for third place. He told Gogarty that he had tossed it into the Liffey in disgust, but in fact he threw it into his Aunt Josephine's lap saying he had no use for it. After her death and Joyce's, it ended up in the possession of Stanislaus.[5]

The next day Curran wrote him a letter of commiseration:

> My dear Joyce ... I don't know whether to offer you my congratulations or sympathy. It is simply scandalous that you let the first prize be

thrown away, for your singing particularly of the oratorio business was throat, chest and head above the rest of the rabblement. I hope the inclusion in the list will mean that you sing at the concert on Saturday night, to take your place of honour as Dublin's Prime Platform Favourite.[6]

The judge was Professor Luigi Denza of the London Academy of Music, composer of the famous 'Funiculi-Funicula' and other popular pieces. In adjudicating, Denza spoke admiringly of Joyce's performance and recommended that he take up singing seriously. Shortly afterwards, on hearing the results, Palmieri wrote offering him singing lessons in return for a percentage of his professional earnings. But Joyce declined, having already decided to leave Ireland, hinting that his failure in the competition was the final straw.

A week after the competition he received an invitation from Gogarty to spend a week in Oxford at his expense, an offer he did not take up. However, he was definitely in the mood to get abroad, planning a visit to England that summer, telling Gogarty that he intended to acquire a lute from the celebrated instrument maker, Arnold Dolmetsch, a friend of Yeats, and tour the south coast of England from Falmouth to Margate singing old English songs by Dowland and Byrd. However, when Dolmetsch told him that the instrument would cost sixty-five guineas and pointed out the difficulties of caring for such an instrument the idea was quietly dropped. Nevertheless, he continued singing around Dublin, and in early June asked Gogarty for the loan of a decent suit and clean shirt in order to sing at a garden fête.

He would sometimes surface from the round of concerts and retreat to Monto to see old friends. He turned up one day at Curran's home at 6 Cumberland Place where his friend took a photograph of him dressed in baggy trousers, tennis shoes and yachting cap. It became an iconic image of the youthful Joyce – the insouciant-looking, unsmiling poet with that same far-away look in his eyes. Asked later what he was thinking when the picture was taken, he said he was wondering whether Curran could lend him five shillings. He also attended open evenings – sometimes at the Sheehys' and occasionally at the home of another Irish poet, James Cousins, a vegetarian-Theosophist Ulsterman and friend of George Russell. His wife Gretta would lend her name to the wife of Gabriel Conroy in Joyce's story 'The Dead', though the character would come from someone closer to him, Nora. If he held himself back from respectable chit-chat, he was always ready to sing. On 8 June, the diarist Joseph Holloway attended one such occasion and recorded his impressions of the young troubadour in action.

Mr J. Joyce, a (mysterious kind of) strangely aloof, silent youth, with weird, penetrating, large eyes, which he frequently shaded with his hand and with a half-bashful, far-away expression on his face, sang some dainty old world ballads most artistically and pleasingly, some to his own accompaniment. As he sings he sways his head from side to side to add to the soulfulness of his rendering. Later he sat in a corner and gazed at us all in turn in an uncomfortable way from under his brows and said little or nothing all the evening. He is a strange boy; I cannot fathom him.[7]

The unfathomably 'strange boy' image was of course carefully cultivated for such occasions.

At another evening with the Cousinses, on 15 June, Joyce's singing was heard by Professor Michele Esposito, Professor of the pianoforte at the Irish Academy of Music, who was there with his wife and two handsome daughters, Vera and Bianca (invariably referred to as 'the refined Misses Esposito'). He sang Henry VIII's 'Pastime with Good Company', the ballad of 'Turpin Hero', and a couple of his usual sentimental Irish ballads. The girls, who also sang, had a somewhat jaundiced view of the young tenor, however, recalling him as one of those involved in disrupting the University College degree ceremony two years previously. But their father was sufficiently impressed, comparing his voice flatteringly to that of de Reszke, to invite him to a musical evening at their home in Sandymount.

On the afternoon of 10 June 1904, Joyce was booked to sing at a garden fête. Walking along Nassau Street, his eye was caught by a shapely, 'proud' and 'sauntering' young woman with rich auburn tresses and an inviting air. It was Nora Barnacle. Her biographer suggests that probably the myopic Joyce saw only her silhouette and curvaceous movement.[8] But in *Finnegans Wake* there is a hint of something more dramatic – instant sexual magnetism: 'He's fane, she's flirty, with her auburnt streams, and her coy cajoleries, and her dabblin drolleries, for to rouse his rudderup, or to drench his dreams.'[9] For him this encounter was an instant epiphany, seeing in her what he could never hope to find in the Belvedere Place virgins. Years afterwards she said that, because of the yachting cap, she thought he must be a sailor, possibly Scandinavian.[10] If she thought him Scandinavian, to him she was one who bore the name of an Ibsen heroine, and, as he soon discovered, had escaped from her own doll's house in Galway. They struck up a conversation and Joyce secured a date to meet her the following Tuesday evening at 8.30 p.m. outside Oscar Wilde's childhood home at No. 1 Merrion Square. When the lady failed to show up (possibly kept late working at the hotel) he returned home dejected.

Next day he wrote to her, 'I may be blind. I looked for a long time at a head of reddish-brown hair and decided it was not yours.'[11] He hoped she had not forgotten him and asked her to fix another day for a meeting. She suggested the following day, 16 June. Unknowingly, Nora Barnacle from Galway had made a date with history. She was not alone. That night Millicent Bandmann-Palmer tackled the role of Hamlet at the Gaiety Theatre. If her performance was not celebrated in theatrical history it was memorialized in *Ulysses*, as were many other Dublin events of that day, as reported in the press.[12]

Nora was born on the night of 21 March 1884, in Galway city workhouse. Not that the family was impoverished – her father Thomas was a baker and her mother Annie a seamstress – but the workhouse then served as the city's general hospital. She had five sisters and one brother, and was popular with other girls. She had spent much of her childhood living with her grandmother, and was educated by the Sisters of Mercy until the age of thirteen when, because of her father's drunken violence, her parents separated and she was sent to the Presentation Convent. She could read well enough, but had not yet mastered the art of writing grammatically. However, she was handsome, bright, witty and intelligent, and was at ease with her evident sexual allure. Her lively personality and good looks had attracted admirers and the early deaths of Michael Feeney and Michael Bodkin had affected her profoundly. Feeney, hearing that she was about to leave for the convent, waited at her garden gate all night in pouring rain, hoping to see her. When, a few months later, she learned of his death (complicated by pneumonia) she was convinced he had died for love of her. The story haunted her thereafter and came to haunt also the man she eventually married.[13]

Even after her escape to Dublin, Nora was not entirely free to be herself. The duplicitous proprietor of Finn's Hotel made her attend mass while using her to smuggle alcohol into his unlicensed premises from Fanning's pub nearby. What flirtations or dangerous liaisons she had enjoyed since arriving in the city, and before her June encounter with Joyce, remain a mystery and probably remained a mystery to him. But her readiness to defy both family authority and the unwritten law of Catholic exclusivity indicates an independence of mind which would make future acts of defiance and renunciation easier for her.

The celebrated rendezvous of Dublin's Dante and Galway's Nora on 16 June would be enshrined as the day of Mr Leopold Bloom's Ulyssean perambulations around the city (with Stephen Dedalus as his youthful shadow). On the actual day, the young couple's evening stroll led them to Ringsend, well away from the heart of respectable Dublin, and there in the heat of mutual passion, Nora took the rampant young Bard in hand (saying, he recalled, 'What is it, dear?')[14] and deftly satisfied his immediate urge. (For him, he told her, that night and that deed were 'a sacrament'.) Joyce had found himself a girl who combined a knowing sexuality with an unformed mind eager to learn – a *tabula rasa* who would have delighted Aristotle. One bird in flight had met one poised to take off. The trick with the ungloved hand was, it seems, the way she kept her more ardent admirers in check. Within a very short time he was her 'Precious Darling' and she was his 'Little Pouting Nora'.[15] He purloined the glove that fitted the hand that did the pleasurable deed and kept it lying open on the bed beside him. It gave him the excuse to buy her a new pair – his first present to her. 'Exchange is no robbery,' he told her.

If he was besotted with Nora, it did not prevent him from getting drunk in the usual way in the usual company. On the evening of the 20th, after a Rabelaisian binge around town, they turned up at the Camden Street rehearsal rooms, the temporary home of the Irish Literary Theatre, but got no further than the darkened passage in the front entrance. There Joyce collapsed in a heap and threw up, with Gogarty and Cosgrave supine beside him. At that moment 'the refined' Miss Vera Esposito, accompanied by her equally refined mother, emerged into the pitch blackness at the other end of the passage and tripped over the recumbent poet, who found himself lying under the petticoats of a beautiful young actress. When her startled cry produced what she called 'some disgusting maudlin grunts', she and her mother retreated to the theatre and alerted the Fay brothers (the company's producers) and some of the actors, including George Roberts, who hurried to the scene of the outrage and turned up the gaslight. Gogarty, however, had already managed to remove the offending drunkard from the building and the door was slammed and bolted after them. Joyce then began battering at the door with his ashplant, shouting, 'Open the door at once, Fay, you can't keep us out of your bawdy house, we know you.' At this, the knights-to-the-rescue threw open the door and told Joyce not only what they thought of him but who it was that had stumbled into him as he lay in a pool of his own regurgitation. Gogarty, probably more sober than Joyce, dragged him away before the police arrived. The moment was captured in Mulligan's jocular flashback in *Ulysses*: '– O, the night in the Camden hall when the daughters of Erin had to lift their skirts to step over you as you lay in your mulberrycoloured, multicoloured, multitudinous vomit!/– The most innocent son of Erin, Stephen said, for whom they ever lifted them.'[16] Miss Esposito never forgave the drunken Bard. 'He was,' she said later, 'overwhelmed by a mean inferiority complex,' not having 'a decent home' and having to put up with 'slum dwelling'.[17] It was such social and cultural snobbery among some in Dublin which inspired Joyce to wreak his literary vengeance upon them.

Still drunk, later that night, he and Cosgrave were navigating through Nighttown when they encountered a young woman, apparently alone. When Joyce accosted her, her soldier escort emerged from the shadows and attacked him, leaving him, he told Curran a few days later, with a 'black eye, sprained wrist, sprained ankle, cut chin, cut hand'.[18] He admitted later that while he was 'morally intrepid' he was 'abjectly cowardly in a physical sense' and that his politeness was 'a form of physical cowardice'.[19] During this assault Cosgrave stood by and watched, hands in pockets. Thereafter he became a figure of contempt for Joyce who noted his 'reptilian' eyes – 'a shrivelled soul, poignant and embittered'.[20] Abandoned by Cosgrave, Joyce was rescued by Alfred (Hugh) Hunter. Hunter, a tall, dark friend of his father's (and reputedly a Jew and a cuckold), on hearing of his distress took him (possibly via the Mater Misericordiae Hospital in Eccles Street) to his home off Clontarf Road, where he had lived with his wife Marion.[21] The street, the wife and Hunter, the good Samaritan, supplied the germ of the idea which later evolved into *Ulysses*, with Hunter as the prototype of Leopold Bloom and his wife lending her reputation and name at least to Molly Bloom, née Marion Tweedy.

Three days later, he was sufficiently sober and recovered to send a batch of his novel to Curran, asking him to read it and then meet to discuss it with him 'on some altitude where we can utter our souls unmolested'.[22] They met at various times, mostly at Bewleys in Westmorland Street, their favourite café, to discuss the evolving opus. Curran, now editing *St Stephen's*, had asked Joyce for a contribution, but he found his *Hero* very strong meat. For the first time he saw the sordid circumstances underlying his friend's life. 'Our earlier talks . . . had been the not exceptional converse of students who cared about literature . . . I had little idea of the true extent and harshness of the situation which was hidden under his wry humour. The reading of his manuscript was therefore an experience as painful as it was engrossing.'[23] It was, he decided, mainly an elaborate work of self-justification. Now that the 'harshness of his situation' was revealed, Joyce invited himself to Curran's office (he worked for the Accountant General) hinting that he was 'in a bloody hole', and ready as ever to take a loan, if offered.[24]

It was fortunate that Russell, then editing the *Irish Homestead*, the house magazine of the Irish Agricultural Organization Society, had invited Joyce to submit a story suitably simple and rural with perhaps a touch of pathos. Knowing his potential contributor, Russell added that it should not be shocking to his readers, but for a fee of £1 it was 'easily earned money if you can write fluently and don't mind playing to the common understanding and liking for once in a way'. If he wished, he could write under a pseudonym. The timing was just right. Joyce had accumulated a considerable collection of characters and incidents, gleaned from his father's storytelling, gossips with Stanislaus and direct experience. He told Curran that he planned to write ten '*epicleti*' (prayers of consubstantiation) which he would call *Dubliners*. By the beginning of July he had already finished one story called 'The Sisters', submitting it to Russell as from 'Stephen Daedalus', together with a chapter of *Stephen Hero*.

Things were looking up for the young writer. The novel was going well, his story was accepted by Russell who sent him his sovereign, Eglinton had published one of his poems in *Dana*, John Baillie, editor of the London literary annual *The Venture*, asked for a contribution, and Arthur Symons wrote saying that, although the publisher Duckworth had turned it down as 'too slight', he would submit his poetry collection next to Grant Richards.

On the day *Chamber Music* was sent to Richards, Joyce attended a funeral. John's friend Matt Kane (Chief Clerk to the Crown Solicitor) had drowned in the sea off Kingstown, and James and Charlie kept their father company in the cortège as it wound through the streets of Dublin up to Glasnevin Cemetery. Alfred Hunter (not in fact Jewish but a Unitarian Ulsterman who later converted to Church of Ireland) was there too, and the scene at the cemetery would transform itself via Joyce's imagination into the funeral of Paddy Dignam in *Ulysses*, with Kane in the role of Martin Cunningham. Paddy had died in a drunken stupor, the same fate that would overcome the immortal Finnegan, at whose wake (and awakening) we are informed that 'Hubert was a Hunter'. Among the mourners, reported the *Freeman's Journal*, was the respectable-sounding 'James A. Joyce, B.A.', and what John's biographers call 'the old crowd'[25] – a procession of names reading like the cast list of the 'Hades' episode of *Ulysses*.

Stanislaus, now mooning over his fourteen-year-old cousin 'Katsy' Murray, was reading Tolstoy and, having decided that his brother was a 'genius', pondering on the meaning of the word. Returning home from visiting his cousin, he faced a tirade from his drunken father for having patronized the despised in-laws, 'Oh, ye bloody-looking Yahoo of hell! Down with the Murrays were ye?' He threatened to sell the house and throw them all out. 'I'll pelt the Murrays with you. Pelt them, by God.' In his diary Stannie recorded his misery, blaming the blighted prospects of his siblings, and the deaths of his mother and brother George on his profligate father, and trying to record the rambling thoughts of someone up to the point of falling asleep. He based this essay into fading consciousness on a passage from Tolstoy's *Sebastopol Sketches*, the thoughts of a dying Russian officer. When James saw it he was contemptuous, calling it 'youthful Maupassant', and tossed it aside. Later, when he adopted the *monologue intérieur* and attributed it to Edouard Dujardin, Stannie, annoyed, reminded him of the Tolstoy story and his casual dismissal of it.[26] Clearly he thought it was he rather than Dujardin who had first put the idea into his brother's mind.

John, three days drunk, according to Stannie, was now shouting about 'breaking Jim's arse with a kick'. He had, he knew, long ago lost his favourite son to literature, and to the company of others. His daughters he despised – May had been sent to a convent and Eileen would soon join her there. Jim, meanwhile, having stepped well outside his father's circle of hell, told Stanislaus that his ambition in life was 'to burn with a hard and gem-like ecstasy'.[27] To this end, perhaps, he was serenading his lady-love by post – quoting Henry VIII's love songs, and Yeats's 'Down by the Salley Gardens' – and urging her to leave her stays behind or by powers invested in him by the Pope, to come without a skirt, in order 'to receive the Papal Benediction' when next they met. From the outset she can have had few illusions about his impiety and ardent sensuality. Cosgrave (a darkly jealous rival) told him that he was in love, but merely for the first time.[28]

However, Joyce had discovered not just a passing fancy, but a muse. One of the first poems he wrote after meeting Nora began 'O Sweetheart', in which he bemoaned the treachery of friends, but asserted that one would come to him 'And softly woo him/In ways of love,' and, with his hand beneath her breast, his sorrow would pass.[29] Thanks to Symons and Edward Garnett at Duckworth's, in July *The Speaker* took two of his poems, including 'O Sweetheart'. Joyce saw Nora as one who could both satisfy his carnal desires and remain true while others betrayed him. He had found his faithful long-term mother-substitute. On 13 August, he sent her a copy of the *Irish Homestead* carrying his story 'The Sisters' hoping it would interest and impress her.

The want of funds continued and when Gogarty returned from Oxford that summer Joyce told him grandly, 'I never borrow anything but guineas now'. Gogarty mentioned that, on being told of his poverty, his Oxford friend George Bell had wept, to which the impoverished Bard replied, 'We'll make him shed golden tears.' This remark the 'faithful' Gogarty duly reported to Bell. But when Joyce wrote to the future bishop requesting three guineas, sportingly the good man paid up. Missing the scholarly congeniality of Oxford, Gogarty conceived the idea of establishing a writer's colony based in the Martello tower at Sandycove. This deserted stone fortification set above rocks (known as 'the Forty Foot'), from which gentlemen-only bathing took place, was available for rent and he soon had possession of the keys to the weighty door. Joyce knew that if ever he needed a sanctuary he could always find room in Gogarty's citadel.

Curran was still pressing him for a contribution to *St Stephen's*. But when he received 'The Holy Office', a satirical broadside in 100 lines blasting the self-satisfaction of the literary nationalists, although Curran found it amusing he rejected it as 'unholy'. However, it was Joyce's manifesto of contempt for, and rejection of, the literary figures who then bestrode the Dublin scene, especially Yeats and Russell, who had abandoned poetry for nationalist propaganda. His target, as ever, was their suffocating limitations, their dishonesty in pandering to the rabblement when their eyes should have been turned outwards, like Ibsen's and his own.

> Myself . . . who dishevelled ways forsook
> To hold the poets' grammar-book,
> Bringing to tavern and to brothel
> The mind of witty Aristotle . . . [30]

The Literary Theatre people were 'that mumming company' and its women followers 'giddy dames'. Colum, Eglinton and George Roberts, acolytes of the leading torchbearers, were lampooned mercilessly, as self-deceiving hypocrites. His own position was for honesty, sensuality, the freewheeling imagination and cosmopolitan vision. Like Parnell he was a stag at bay, defiant – 'I flash my antlers on the air' – an enduring Joycean self-image. Byrne, seeing it, was bewildered as to why his once-close companion should satirize his own friends so mercilessly, wondering if it was because they had refused him money or offended him in some other way. But, undeterred at being turned down for *St Stephen's*, Joyce decided, as he had with 'The Day of the Rabblement', to have it printed for private distribution. However, unable to afford a printer immediately, he saved his ammunition for later.

Some indication of Nora's feelings for her new beau is revealed in the letter she wrote him on 16 August on flowered paper, which, from its stilted phraseology, Joyce guessed had been lifted from a book on letter-writing. Her words were borrowed but the desire to please him was her own. He in turn wooed her in both word and song, telling her that he was cutting people in the street, wanting only to hear her voice. On 22 August he invited her to an afternoon concert at which, he told her, he was singing – just for her – 'My Love She Was Born In The North Countree', and 'The Coulin', which contains the prophetic lines:

> To the gloom of some desert or cold rocky shore,
> Where the eye of the stranger can haunt us no more,
> I will fly with my Coulin, and think the rough wind
> Less rude than the foes we leave frowning behind.

At that time Joyce was, according to Stanislaus, obsessed with 'the syphilitic contagion in Europe', reading about it and even contemplating 'a series of studies in it in Dublin'. The result was invariably madness, he declared, and he even seemed to 'delight in the manias and to humour each to the top of its bent'.[31] Following his earlier 'gleet' he had, it seems, finally become alert to the dangers of his excursions into Monto, and the desirability of acquiring a steady partner.

Nora was always enthralled by his voice, and she was impressed yet again when one evening that month, at the Antient Concert Hall, he appeared on the same programme as McCormack and the baritone J. C. Doyle – both 'topnobbers', as Bloom would have it.[32] But expectations were not matched by the quality of all the performers. The concert started late, the audience became noisy and impatient and the accompanist failed to show up. The stand-in pianist was incompetent, unable even to 'strum out' Joyce's two chosen songs – 'In Her Simplicity' and 'The Croppy Boy' – and he had to accompany himself. Even so, he acquitted himself well enough. 'Mr Joyce possesses a light tenor voice, which he is inclined to force on the high notes but sings with artistic emotionalism,' wrote Joseph Holloway. 'One of his selections, "Down by the Salley Gardens," suited his method best; and, as an encore, he tenderly gave "My Love Was Born in the North Countree," a short and sweet piece.'[33] The experience was not wasted on Joyce; it became the basis for his story, 'A Mother', reliving the events from the point of view of the wretched pianist and her ambitious mother.

With Nora 'tugging at his elbow' his plan to tour seaside resorts as a troubadour began to lose its attractions. After trying to explain himself to her he felt she had failed to understand him or his intentions. ('I know what's talking now,' she had told him the night before, implying that she thought his motives for seeing her could only be carnal.) At the end of August he wrote her what amounted to a confessional letter, explaining his feelings about his family, Ireland and the Church. It was a shared confidence which would draw them even closer together – a manifesto and justification for a life of exile and intimacy into which he was now attempting to draw her. But he was sick with worry that he had alienated her from the start by telling her that marriage and a conventional family life were not for him. His own miserable experience of it – his mother worn down and destroyed by childbearing and ill-treatment, other lives ruined by a wastrel father, siblings he did not care for – underlay this hostile attitude. 'My mind rejects the whole present social order and Christianity – home, the recognised virtues, classes of life, and religious doctrines.'[34] He was at war, too, with the Catholic Church and the whole system that had made his mother 'a victim'. He tried to interpret her reactions to all this in the look in her eyes and the tone of her voice, and to assure her he was not the ignoble and unfathomable character she might think he was, and that no one had ever been so 'close to his soul' as she was. 'Can you not see the simplicity which is at the back of all my disguises?' he asked her. 'We all wear masks.'[35]

Although Stanislaus admired his clever brother and envied 'the strength of his emotions, the beauty of his mind at times, his sense of honour, his pride, his spontaneity', he did not like him, he said.[36] He was too full of contradictions, for one thing, and had acquired the lying habits of a drunkard, talking coarsely and enjoying the sound of his own voice. And while openly despising the sentimentality of clerks, he behaved just like one, walking out at night and canoodling with 'Miss Barnacle' while she called him 'My Love'.[37] In fact, apart from her, Joyce had become acutely aware of his loneliness and was writing to her every day and meeting her whenever she was free.

At the end of August the McKernans asked Joyce to move out while they went on their summer holidays. He stayed briefly with the Cousinses, then with the Murrays and then with a medical pal before returning to St Peter's Terrace to pen a note to Nora. Finally, on 9 September, he took refuge with Gogarty at the Martello tower, having agreed to do the housekeeping in return for bed and board, and the freedom to work at his novel. (Stanislaus claimed he was 'there on sufferance'.) The tower already had another lodger, Dermot Chenevix Trench, Gogarty's Oxford friend. Trench assisted George Russell at the *Irish Homestead*, which published Joyce's story 'Eveline' the day after he moved in. Although he respected the Englishman, Joyce found his unquestioning dedication to Irish nationalism and the cultural revival irritating, as he did Gogarty's constant teasing. However, for the time being he still considered Gogarty a friend, even allowing him, on their first morning at the tower together, to shave him.[38] All were now present – characters, setting and unfolding events to be written later into literary history.

Initially he felt settled enough at the tower to invite Nora to visit, but she never made the journey. However, 'various friends' came to call, having heard of the strange trio holed up in their bastion on the rocks. One visitor was William Bulfin, an Irish-Argentinian then touring Ireland. Bulfin heard that the three young bohemians were 'creating a sensation in the neighbourhood' and went to investigate. In the tower, he reported finding 'some men of Ireland'. Trench, he recalled, was 'a most strenuous Nationalist . . . with a patriotism . . . which moved him to pour forth fluent Irish upon every Gael he encountered'; Gogarty, 'the poet', was 'a wayward kind of genius, who talked in a captivating manner, with a keen, grim humour, which cut and pierced through a topic in bright, strong flashes

worthy of the rapier of Swift'; Joyce, 'a singer of songs which spring from
the deepest currents of life ... listened in silence, and when we went
on the roof he disposed himself restfully to drink in the glory of the
morning.'[39]

For Joyce, living in the tower would be a defining experience, even
though it lasted less than a week. His tendency to be apart, refusing to
bathe from the Forty Foot, and his air of detached superiority continued
to irritate Gogarty. Matters between the three came to a head in a way
forever enshrined in *Ulysses*. On the night of 14 September, Joyce's fifth
day in the tower, Trench woke screaming that he was about to be attacked
by a black panther and, grabbing his revolver, loosed off a couple of shots.
Gogarty managed to calm him down and confiscate the gun, but Trench,
having settled back to sleep, again woke up screaming and this time it
was Gogarty who fired a shot, bringing down a shelf of pots and pans on
the head of the slumbering Bard. This was too much for Joyce who quickly
decamped, leaving his belongings behind. He told Stanislaus that he had
been thrown out, and it was not beyond Gogarty to have planned this
nightmare scenario with Trench to frighten him away. Ignoring his tor-
mentors, he wrote from St Peter's Terrace asking James Starkey ('Seamus
O'Sullivan'), a frequenter of the tower, to pack his trunk for collection
next day, then took refuge with the Murrays. Joyce and Gogarty never
recovered their old camaraderie. He never again saw Trench who five
years later, frustrated in love and still trigger-happy, blew out his brains.

Living in Ireland had lost all meaning for Joyce. The lure of 'exile' and
the notion of returning to the Continent began to possess him. But if he
was to elope with Nora he would need to secure an income. The job once
offered by the Berlitz School in Paris suddenly seemed very appealing. He
discussed this with Lady Gregory who offered to help him financially if
he obtained such a posting. But he worried that Nora might not want to
go with him. She had asked him if he loved her, to which he had replied
that he was deeply fond of her and wished to possess her completely – if
that was 'love' then he did indeed love her. He had expressed his fears of
being deserted at the dockside by a hesitant lover in 'Eveline', but he need
not have worried; she was now as captivated by him as he was by her.
'When I wake in the morning I will think of nothing but you,' she told
him.[40] Without each other they felt isolated and alone, but they both
knew that leaving together without marrying in so Catholic a country
would be social death, so that secrecy was essential. He consulted Byrne,
who urged him to act. 'Don't wait and don't hesitate,' he said. 'If she
agrees to go away with you, take her.'[41] Fortunately for him, she agreed.

Seeing an advertisement for teaching posts in Europe, Joyce applied,
and on 18 September received an encouraging reply from an Evelyn

Gilford, the proprietor of an agency based at Market Rasen, saying that a post had been reserved for him at a Berlitz School on the Continent. In return for a payment of two guineas he would be told exactly where. As a precaution he contacted the London Berlitz, enquiring after Gilford's credentials, and was told they had no such agencies in England, although Continental schools might have their own arrangements. He then consulted the Market Rasen police who confirmed Gilford's respectability. Meanwhile the Berlitz sent news of vacancies in Amsterdam and London, but he told them it was Paris he wanted. While awaiting a reply he shared his sense of excitement with Nora, referring to their impending elopement as 'this adventure of ours' and saying that once they were safely abroad the Dublin gossips could say what they liked. He told her that if her family got wind of their plans she should leave her job at Finn's immediately.

Joyce now decided to return home and remain there till they left. John had been kept in the dark about Nora and of his sisters only Poppie knew about her. On 4 October a telegram arrived from Gilford, to whom he had sent the two guineas, asking if he could go to Zurich immediately. The cheapest fare, he discovered, was £7 10s, and he immediately used Gilford's cable to persuade Lady Gregory to help. Generously, she sent him five pounds. Having delivered a short story, 'After the Race', to the *Irish Homestead*, he also wrote asking Russell to send his fee as a matter of urgency. George Roberts was invited to donate but declined, as did Eglinton. But he did manage to extract two guineas from Skeffington and ten shillings from a grandson of Morris Harris, the old Jewish art dealer on Nassau Street, whose shop he visited occasionally.[47] He tried Alf Bergan without success but John Joyce claimed later to have chipped in a pound. Joyce then received conflicting messages from the Berlitz in London and from Gilford. London told him to wait; Gilford told him to go. On the 7th Berlitz informed him that there was no vacancy in Paris and that made up his mind. On the brink of departure, he asked Starkey (O'Sullivan), whose father owned a chemist's shop, to supply him with a toothbrush and toothpowder, a nail brush and '1 pair of black boots and any coat and vest you have to spare'.[43] It was a shabby near-destitute poet who now stood poised to take himself and his young companion away into exile. Nevertheless, with just enough money to get them to Paris, he decided to leave.

There was a last encounter with Gogarty, a chance meeting in Nassau Street. Gogarty seemed anxious to see him again, but Joyce gave no hint of his plans. In any case, the breach was now too wide to be easily bridged. The man who had started the myth of Dublin's Dante would become the unreliable source of many a Joyce story, even claiming that while studying psychiatry he had diagnosed him as schizophrenic. The joke in Dublin was that as a poet Gogarty made a good doctor and as a doctor he made a good poet.

Aunt Josephine and sister Poppie tried to dissuade him from his 'adventure', though Poppie did help Nora prepare for the journey. On 8 October 1904, John Joyce, still in the dark about James's plans, accompanied the rest of the family to the North Wall, the traditional point of departure for many Irish emigrants, believing he was there to see his eldest son set sail alone on the morning tide. In order not to alert him, Nora, with no one to wave her goodbye, boarded separately, and the two lovers joined up only after a tearful farewell from John and the girls and after the ferry had sailed. Unfortunately for them, John's friend Tom Devin, who happened to be on board, saw them together, guessed what was happening, and on his return informed John of his son's deception. On hearing about it and learning the name of his son's companion, he is said to have remarked, 'Barnacle? Well, she'll always stick to him.'[44]

In London Joyce took the opportunity to visit Arthur Symons, hoping for a hand-out, leaving Nora in a park for so long that she feared he would never return. But Nora was his one link to Ireland and to Dublin, a link and a relationship he was never able to break. Not finding Symons at home he rejoined her and they headed for the station and the boat train to Paris.

When Joyce left Ireland that October day, he had evaded the enticements of the priesthood, the grim vision of a wasted life portrayed in his story 'The Sisters', the suffocation of office routine which has Farrington, the lawyer's scrivener, in its grip in 'Counterparts', and the treadmill of domesticity to which his Little Chandler is enslaved. Ahead lay the flight-path of the wild geese and a vague dream of artistic fulfilment. Undoubtedly Joyce saw his departure from Ireland as an integral part of the personal myth he was then in the process of composing. This was not simply the conventional exit of a failed youth in search of a future abroad; it was a man embarking, like Dante, on a journey of self-discovery, a man intent on offering a new awareness to those he left behind, enshrouded as they were in the darkness of religious superstition, parochial narrow-mindedness, and solipsistic nationalism. All this he hoped to achieve through 'silence, exile and cunning'.[45] The exhilaration he felt would be celebrated with one of the most stirring flourishes in literature: 'Welcome, O life, I go to encounter for the millionth time the reality of experience and to forge in the smithy of my soul the uncreated conscience of my race.'[46] Behind him he left a mixed reputation. Yeats and Synge thought highly of him; Elwood considered him 'a great artist'; Kettle, Curran, Skeffington and his old teacher, Mr Dempsey, never doubted his genius. Gogarty, his Mephistopheles, not only respected him but also feared him, knowing that Joyce had it in him to wreak a painful revenge for both real and supposed wrongs. Moore called him a mere carbon copy of Symons, while others spoke bitterly of his apostasy. And when he was known to have failing eyesight there were rumours of syphilis. The story of his running off with a barmaid was soon swirling around the Dublin gossip mill, as was the story that they had married secretly before leaving Ireland. Joyce was never anxious to deny this (even giving 8 October 1904 as the date of his marriage), and this tale was still being repeated right up until his death.

The cynically superior Mahaffy, whose distaste also extended to Moore, told Gerald Griffin after they had both departed: 'Thank God they have both cleared out of Dublin, but not before they had squirted stink like a pair of skunks on all the decent people with whom they came in contact. It's an ill bird that fouls its own nest.'[47] But the departing 'skunk', Joyce, the harbinger of a new kind of Irish writer and literature, would return to haunt Dublin with a vengeance.

11
Birds of Passage
(1904–1905)

'It is suicide to be abroad. But what is it to be at home ... what is it
to be at home? A lingering dissolution.' Samuel Beckett, *All That Fall*

After two trips to Paris, Joyce must have felt himself to be a seasoned
traveller, and, with his command of French and Italian, well able to
handle himself, come what may. But for Nora, leaving Ireland was an
expedition into the unknown in the company of a man she barely
knew and to whom she was bound by nothing stronger than youthful
passion.

Boarding the ferry for France and then the train for Paris, with
Switzerland in prospect, Joyce was taking with him not just a beautiful
twenty-year-old companion, but the manuscripts of an unfinished
novel, a treatise on aesthetics, his epiphanies, his Dublin stories, copies
of his poems, his various notebooks, magazines containing his published
work, and what books he could cram into his trunk. These, together
with his cumulative memories, a well-stocked mental library and a
subtle, finely tuned brain, were the tools with which he would fabricate
a world and create a unique consciousness focused upon the city he
had left.

In Paris they drove in an open-topped fiacre between the Gare St-
Lazare and the Gare de l'Est, where they left their luggage. Then, after
again leaving Nora in a park, Joyce set off to find enough money to
see them through to Zurich. He ran into Con Curran who happened
to be in Paris, but was unable to help, and Douce was away in Spain.
However, Dr Rivière, who was at home, gave him sixty francs, more
than enough for their immediate needs. Just before leaving Paris, Nora
sent her mother a postcard couched in suitably vague terms, probably
intended to ensure that she did not advertise for her 'missing' daughter
in the Dublin press. They arrived in Zurich early in the morning of
11 October 1904.

They checked into the nearest hotel, the Gasthaus Hoffnung, close
to the Bahnhofplatz, where Joyce was amused to find that the pro-

prietor's name was Dubliner. They were soon in bed engaging in what Joyce called 'the ecstasy of combat'. The glove which had kept Joyce satisfied this far was finally discarded. Nora's sexual enthusiasm was evident, and, as her biographer puts it, 'she needed no tutoring'.[1] She often initiated their love-making and encouraged James with whispered obscenities, which would not have been out of place in Bella Cohen's Monto.[2] She also had a small repertoire of risqué songs such as 'Old Tom Gregory Has a Big Menagerie' which delighted him. Next morning he reported proudly in a letter to Stanislaus that Nora was no longer a virgin.[3]

After breakfast, full of hope and self-confidence, he set out for the Berlitz School, equipped with his letter from Gilford, only to find that there was no vacancy and no one had heard of any agency in Market Rasen. The director wrote a letter to Gilford for Joyce to forward. While awaiting a reply he found time to do some work on Chapter 12 of *Stephen Hero* and draft another short story, 'Xmas Eve'. Stanislaus was instructed to ask 'the mystical' Russell if he would like another 'Stephen Daedalus' story for the *Irish Homestead*.

Gilford sent him a copy of a seemingly official letter offering him the non-existent teaching post in Zurich, which explained nothing. Fortunately, the Berlitz director found Joyce impressive. He mentioned a possible vacancy in Trieste and offered to pay his and Nora's travelling expenses. Still uncertain of what awaited them, Joyce left his trunk with a friendly Berlitz teacher and they travelled south into Austria. On the 20th they arrived at Trieste station. Emerging into the palatial arrivals hall, they must have presented a sorry spectacle – Nora in her shabby dress, Joyce in his long black Parisian overcoat and bohemian wide-brimmed hat. Once again, Nora was deposited, this time in the garden square in front of the station, on a bench beside the statue of Elisabetta, the assassinated wife of Emperor Franz Josef. Joyce was probably unaware how a woman sitting alone in a public place would be regarded and she was subjected to coarse comments and ogling from passing sailors and dockworkers.

Meanwhile, in search of a hotel, Joyce made his way along the sweeping esplanade to the Piazza Grande, the splendid square located on the Trieste waterfront overlooking the Adriatic. There, at a café, he encountered some drunken English sailors who the police were about to arrest. Naively thinking he could help by translating for them, he offered to accompany them to the police station where he was promptly locked up with the others – not surprisingly perhaps, since a policeman had been injured during the arrest. Joyce protested that he was not a sailor but a respectable Irishman hired to teach at the Berlitz School. He demanded to see the

British Consul who at first seemed unwilling to help but did finally materialize. Harry Lionel Churchill was a rather grand figure, once Queen Victoria's Special Envoy to the Shah of Persia. To him, the shabby, smooth-tongued Joyce must have seemed a suspiciously disreputable character to be keeping company with three drunken sailors. Although he finally secured his release, this cold encounter left Joyce with a deep suspicion of English officialdom, which later events would only intensify. And now his arrival in Trieste had been officially recorded. Not only had the police got his name but the local newspaper, *Il Piccolo della Sera*, reported the incident the following day.[4]

He rejoined the patient Nora at the station, full of apologies and explanations and promising to make things up to her. They found a room at the Hotel 'Central' (Haberleitner) at 15 via San Nicolo, close to the Berlitz at No. 32.[5] At the school they were dismayed to be told by the director, Giuseppe Bertelli, that he too had no vacancy.

The couple remained in the city for some ten days, moving addresses as funds allowed. For a while they took a flat overlooking the beautiful Piazza Ponterosso flanking the Canale Grande whose bustling street market gave a flavour of Trieste's rich ethnic mixture. Stanislaus, who had been appealed to for help, cabled to say he had no money, and so, close to broke, Joyce sought work as an English correspondent at the various banks around the port, and scrounged for funds howsoever he could. After scouting for students wanting to learn English and quickly signing one up, he told Stanislaus he thought he could build a decent private teaching practice in the town. But time was against him, and when he learned that the owner of the local Berlitz franchise, Almidano Artifoni, was to visit the city, he arranged to meet him.

Artifoni, a socialist like himself, was eager to help. He advised Joyce to apply formally to the school as a married man, and so (he claimed later) he arranged to go through a form of marriage, with Nora calling herself 'Gretta Greene' – a suitably joky Joycean alias for a love-smitten runaway. The ceremony was supposedly overseen by one il Cavalieri Fabbri, with Joyce claiming jokingly that 'I did not want a clerk with a pen behind his ear or a priest in his nightshirt to interfere in my matrimonium.'[6] Now that he was 'respectable', Artifoni hired him to work at the school he had recently opened in Pola (Pula in today's Croatia), the principal base of the Austrian Imperial Navy, and gave Joyce enough of an advance to get them there and settled in. Finally they had a more established existence in prospect.

On the morning of 29 October, the 'newly-weds' boarded the Austrian Lloyd steamer for the 109-nautical-mile trip along the Adriatic coast to Pola on the southern tip of the Istrian Peninsula, arriving, according to

Alessandro Francini Bruni (the Berlitz teacher sent to meet them), looking decidedly down at heel:

> Ragged and tattered as a beggar, he [Joyce] dragged along nonchalantly a hyena of a suitcase that had lost its fur ... From every rent in it things hung dangling in the breeze but he did not trouble himself to tuck them in. Mrs Joyce, a little to one side, almost lost in a wide-brimmed straw hat and a man's overcoat that hung below her knees, looked like a pile of rags. Erect and motionless, she shifted her glance from one man to the other, without a trace of expression on her face.[7]

The town was 'en fête', celebrating the unveiling of yet another statue to Franz Josef's Elisabetta; Joyce was also 'en fête', having achieved a 'position' with which he could confound all those in Dublin who had predicted he would fail.

They found a tiny second-floor flat at 2 via Giulia – 'a furnished room and kitchen, surrounded by pots, pans and kettles' – directly opposite the school. To Joyce's delight, immediately following their arrival, Artifoni inserted a notice in the *Giornaletto di Pola*, saying, 'The Berlitz School begs to inform those [naval] officers and imperial and royal employees who could not enrol as pupils in English because the times desired were already taken, that yesterday evening the second English teacher arrived,/James A. Joyce B.A./Bachelor of Arts Mod. Lit./One may therefore enrol for English lessons on any day for any hour between 9 and 12./The Management.'/ Not long afterwards a larger advertisement appeared promoting him to '*dottore in filosofia*' – Doctor of Philosophy – which, Joyce persuaded his father, was the Italian equivalent of his BA. The trunk containing their best clothes had still not caught up with them. The much-lauded '*dottore in filosofia*' and his 'wife', therefore, would spend just a little longer looking 'ragged and tattered' and 'a pile of rags'.

Two days after arriving James wrote to Stanislaus asking for 'all the news' from Dublin. Isolated from the place which continued to fire his imagination, he was more than ever dependent on his brother to contact people for him, send Irish newspapers and feed him the latest gossip. News came back that the 'mystical' Russell had told him in less than 'mystical' terms that his brother was 'a cad' for having run off with Nora – he would soon abandon her – and that 'a touch of starvation' would do him good. Now, armed with news of Jim's Berlitz appointment, Stannie had great pleasure in trekking out to Russell's house at Rathgar in the middle of the night, rousing him from sleep and telling him, 'My brother has wired me that he has obtained a position in a school.' 'I am very glad to hear it,' replied Russell, eyeing his visitor suspiciously. 'That's why I came to see you,' said Stannie, 'I knew you'd be delighted; but I'm afraid that "touch of starvation" will have to wait a little longer.' When Russell replied that Joyce would benefit from regular work, Stannie interrupted him, saying it was a pity he hadn't said all this to his brother's face while he was in Dublin. Russell protested, 'I would have done so, if I had thought of it,' to which Stannie retorted, 'I didn't say you wouldn't. I said you didn't,' and abruptly wished him goodnight.[8]

For teaching Austro-Hungarian naval officers at the Berlitz, Joyce received £2 for a sixteen-hour week, beyond anything he could have hoped for in Dublin where that was equivalent to a head teacher's pay. He and Nora began to improve their appearance and, at Artifoni's suggestion, Joyce bought himself a brown suit. While Stanislaus was writing about the family 'living on practically starvation rations' they were both thriving and putting on weight. Their daily life was leisurely enough, as Joyce reported:

> We get out of bed at nine and Nora makes chocolate. At midday we have lunch which we (or rather she) buys, cooks (soup, meat, potatoes and something else) in a locanda opposite. At four o'clock we have chocolate and at eight o'clock dinner which Nora cooks. The[n] [we go] to the Caffè Miramar w[here we read] the 'Figaro' of Paris and we [come] back about midnight.[9]

Soon he was urging Stanislaus to consider a Berlitz job, too.

However, despite its superficial glamour – royalty, naval displays, Austro-Hungarian pomp and ceremony – life in Pola turned out to be grimly tedious. Although situated on the spectacularly beautiful Istrian coast, it was for Joyce 'a naval Siberia ... swarming with faded uniforms ... boring'. The town was small and 'peopled by ignorant Slavs who wear little red caps and colossal breeches';[10] they were pestered by mosquitoes, and his students were uninspiring – mostly officers from either the shore establishment or the flotilla anchored in the harbour. (One was warship commander Miklos Horthy, later 'His Serene Highness the Regent of the Kingdom of Hungary'.)[11] The main languages spoken were German (the official language), Italian and varieties of Slavic, but he found the Italian 'very corrupt'. The language of Dante was not spoken in the streets of Pola.

His sixteen hours of teaching a week only added to his boredom. The Berlitz method was wooden – the sometimes comical question-and-answer technique he later satirized in the 'Ithaca' episode of *Ulysses*,[12] but, notwithstanding the tedium, he enjoyed colleagues such as Francini, a colourful Florentine, who, like himself, had eloped with a young wife, Clothilde, an opera singer. After a year in Trieste, they had arrived in Pola shortly before Joyce and Nora, and the couples soon became firm friends. Francini had a comic wit and gift for mimicry which appealed to Joyce, and became one of the few people outside his family with whom he was on first-name terms. His other colleague, a young Englishman called Eyers, 'a lovely pianist', said Joyce, was 'falling under the Daedalian spell' and 'we sometimes have music'. But once he had to turn Eyers out of their flat for making Nora cry by casting aspersions on her social origins – the kind of hated class snobbery he had hoped to have left behind in Ireland. Although they were said to get on badly, the two Britons shared a common interest in Oscar Wilde and an article on the impending publication of his *De Profundis* drew them into animated discussion about the man who turned agenbite of inwit into such moving prose. (Later Joyce would lecture on Wilde, allude to him several times in *Ulysses* and thread his name throughout *Finnegans Wake*.)

If Pola was boring for Joyce, it was totally isolating for Nora, cut off from her family and culture by secrecy and distance, and from those around her by mutual incomprehension. Like Joyce she was eager for news from home and curious to know how those at Finn's had reacted to her sudden departure.

With winter approaching, because their room had no heating they ate mostly at the Caffè Miramar on the seafront, where Joyce did most of his writing. As he became more engrossed in his work, Nora, in need of company, began urging him to persuade Stanislaus to think about leaving Ireland too. Joyce was already doing so, and had told his father that there was a probably a job for his brother with the Berlitz if he wanted it.[13] Now he was back into his literary stride, he was missing his whetstone. And, if Stannie came, he would bring Dublin with him.

In celebration of his 'unvirgining' of Nora, he wrote what he called 'my obscene song' 'Bid Adieu to Girlish Ways', ending:

> Begin thou softly to unzone
> Thy girlish bosom unto him
> And softly to undo the snood
> That is the sign of maidenhood.

He sent it to Eglinton who refused to publish it. In certain Dublin circles Joyce, 'the cad', was now *persona non grata*. But in London he was just another poet. In November John Baillie published two of his poems entitled 'Songs', in his literary annual *The Venture*,[14] and more were published in *The Speaker*. Then Symons informed him that Grant Richards, who was considering *Chamber Music*, had gone bankrupt, and advised him to retrieve his manuscript. He also urged him to try his short stories on magazines in both England and America.

As Joyce settled down to work he was both dreaming up ideas for short stories, and reading those of others, including Henry James. But he was beset by distractions, first mosquitoes and then by the tantalizing presence of Nora, as he hinted to Stanislaus – 'I really can't write. Nora is trying on a pair of drawers at the wardrobe.'[15] In this atmosphere *Stephen Hero* stalled, and with his creativity blocked, he turned to translation, co-opting his friend Francini to help with an Italian version of George Moore's *The Celibates* for a Florentine publisher. The plan foundered, but Moore's stories would leave their impression on both *Dubliners* and *Ulysses*. His other major recreation was music. Amalija Globočnik, Artifoni's deputy at the Berlitz, had a piano and invited them for 'musical evenings'. She was, he told his brother, 'a melancholy little Androgyne and very sentimental with me. I daresay there is something in me which interests women.'[16]

By December he knew that Nora was pregnant. As their intimacy grew, she began to share with him details of her life – her broken family, life with her grandmother, her indulging in 'the gentle art of self-satisfaction', her sad love affairs with the boys who died, her encounter with the curate who put his hand up her skirt and told her to confess that it was someone else, her walking out with Mulvagh and her beating by her Uncle Tom. But, she told him, her family were 'toney' and her rich uncle Michael Healy supported them. Anxious to understand what Nora was now going through, James asked Stannie to do research for him on midwifery and embryology, and send him the results. He also suggested that Aunt Josephine should write to 'Signora Joyce' with words of advice and encouragement. 'She is away from all women except a little Fräulein and is of course adorably stupid on these points. You might write some kind of a generalising "Don't-be-alarmed-my-dear" letter as my own steely cheerfulness in what does not afflict me personally is in need of some feminine supplement.'[17]

The prospect of fatherhood encouraged Joyce to come to terms with life in 'boring' Pola, and in December he returned to the novel, telling Stanislaus that he had completed Chapter 12 and was well into Chapter 13. But after reading extracts to Nora he declared that 'she cares nothing for my art', something he might already have gathered from the fact that she had already lost her copy of *The Speaker* containing 'O Sweetheart', his poem written 'just for her'. But her indifference did not worry him too much and her naivety delighted him. One evening he took her to a bioscope. 'There were a series of pictures about betrayed Gretchen. In the third last [act] Lothario throws her into the river and rushes off, followed by rabble. Nora said "O, policeman, catch him".' So it amused him that she called *him* 'very childish' and 'simple-minded'. She also told him he had 'a beautiful character' and 'a saint's face', when in fact he thought it more that of 'a debauchee'.[18]

Stannie regarded his brother as a man of 'strange impulses', including a prurient curiosity about other men's attraction to Nora. One evening, for example, having arranged to meet a colleague at the Caffè Miramar, he sent Nora along first. Turning up later, he sat at a separate table as she conversed with another customer, and passed her a note asking, 'Is this fellow annoying you?' The resulting arguments Nora tended to dismiss as 'misunderstandings' or 'lovers' quarrels', but finally Joyce seems to have felt the strain. One night in December he had severe stomach cramps and Nora prayed out loud for God to 'take Jim's pains away'. But he knew that all she cared about was that he should finish his novel quickly and get rich so that they could go and live in Paris. Replying to Stanislaus, who had written to say she was unworthy of him, he explained just why she appealed to him. Her mind might be untrained, he said, but 'Her disposition, as I see it, is much nobler than my own, her love also is greater than mine for her. I admire her and I love her and I trust her.'[19] And he was proud to announce that while he was learning German, she was learning French.

His story 'After the Race' had appeared in the December issue of the *Irish Homestead*, but his subsequent offerings had been rejected. Nevertheless, with completion of his novel still a long way off, Symons's advice to try more short stories prompted him to return again to his 'epicleti'. 'Xmas Eve' was rewritten as 'Hallow Eve', then as 'The Clay' and finally entitled simply 'Clay', in which he took his cousin Willie Murray's sister-in-law, Maria O'Donohoe, as his model for the diminutive laundress beset by ill-omens. No longer caring to please the puritanical Russell, he felt free to write as his imagination dictated. 'Stephen Daedalus' would be replaced by 'James Joyce' who would never again masquerade under a pseudonym.

Approaching fatherhood concentrated his mind on the immediate future. His child, he had decided, would not be encumbered by religion. 'Why should I superimpose on my child the very troublesome burden of belief which my father and mother superimposed on me?' he asked.[20] His antipathy to Catholicism was undimmed, and after concluding a letter to Aunt Josephine with a jibe at his and Nora's Dublin detractors who had predicted that he would leave Nora in the street, he could not resist a gesture of contempt towards the new Pope: 'In conclusion – I spit upon the image of the Tenth Pius.'[21]

By the beginning of the New Year 1905 he was working on Chapter 15 of *Stephen Hero*, reliving his time at Belvedere. He included a self-portrait which hints at how Nora was now making her silent contribution to his fiction:

> His [stiff] coarse brownish hair was combed high off his forehead but there was little order in its arrangement ... A girl might or might not have called him handsome: the face was regular in feature and its pose was almost softened into ... beauty by a small feminine mouth. In ... a general survey of the face the eyes were not prominent: they were small light blue eyes which checked advances. They were quite fresh and fearless but in spite of this the face was to a certain extent the face of a debauchee.[22]

Nora not only fed him with amusing and telling phrases, but also with stories, folklore and songs from Galway which he absorbed along with anything else Irish that came his way. This helped him accept the distance between himself and the country which continued to captivate him. Nevertheless, he said, he had already come to terms with having become what he called 'a voluntary exile'.[23]

He welcomed Stannie's criticism of the book, and, having previously scorned his diary-writing, now asked him for any documents or diary entries dealing with University College – the subject of his next chapter. As ever, he wanted news of home and the latest literary gossip. (The Irish Literary Theatre now had its own venue, the Abbey, and a publishing house, Maunsel & Co., had been established in Dublin by Joseph Hone, Stephen Gwynn and George Roberts, with the aim of promoting the work of the Abbey playwrights and poets.) By mid-January the Joyces had moved into a new room, with 'very cosy stove and writing-desk', at 7 via Medolino, a house rented by the Francini Brunis.[24] But their lives still had their drawbacks. Writing was taking its toll on James's eyes so that a doctor recommended pince-nez, and Nora's life was still confined to the flat and café. They did manage one break from routine – a steamer trip to a cheese-fest on the island of Brioni on Joyce's twenty-third birthday, 2 February: a rare venture for a timid sailor always apprehensive about sea travel.

In March, Joyce and Francini were transferred to the Berlitz School in Trieste – reputedly because a spying scare led the Austrians to clear all foreigners out of Pola, but probably in this case because they were offered better jobs. It would be an extremely important move for Joyce because

Trieste would provide the very atmosphere he needed for his writing to flourish and for his imagination to evoke Dublin at long range through the spyglass of tranquil recollection.

12

At a Crossroads

(1905–1906)

'He had put in the people he knew with almost "libellous" freedom [making it] ... impossible for him to live in Dublin. The desire for originality defeated its own ends.' Stanislaus Joyce.

Trieste at the beginning of the twentieth century was a particularly good place for Joyce to embark on his great literary odyssey. Experimentation and adventure were key elements of his quest for authorship; they would come dramatically together in the strangely evocative twilight of a dying empire. Austro-Hungary, of which this was the principal port, was home to Kafka, Stefan Zweig, Karl Kraus, Hugo von Hofmannsthal, Arthur Schnitzler, and Rainer Maria Rilke. There, too, Freud was busily 'discovering' the unconscious.

Trieste itself is a city haunted by literary ghosts. Dante is said to have written part of *The Divine Comedy* at the nearby Duino Castle; Thomas Mann stayed at the Hotel de Ville while writing *Buddenbrooks*; Richard Burton, the pornographer and sexual anthropologist, died there; Stendhal and the Irish novelist Charles Lever were consuls there, and Joseph Conrad had visited and written about the port in his sailing days. Apart from the Duino, the other noteworthy Triestine prominence was Duke Maximilian's Miramar, a white marble mock-Norman folly. For Ibsen, journeying through the Alps in 1868, his first glimpse of it ('a strange luminosity, shining like white marble'), was a momentous epiphany.[1] And Joyce wrote longingly to Nora from Dublin four years later of 'the lights twinkling along the *riva* as the train passes Miramar'.[2]

As well as numerous theatres where plays by Strindberg, Sudermann and Ibsen were performed, Trieste boasted an opera house dedicated to Verdi, which, during the spring of 1905, offered operas by Donizetti, Bellini, Offenbach, Mascagni, and Massenet as well as by Verdi himself. Joyce and Nora could afford only the cheapest seats, sitting among the less than fragrant members of the audience, but after the cultural famine of Pola, this was a veritable feast of European culture at which Joyce was happy to gorge himself.

They had also landed up in a great trading centre, the meeting place of many races, religions and cultures. The opening of the Suez Canal had increased the importance of Trieste as one of the major gateways for Oriental goods imported into Central Europe, so beside the majority German and Italian speakers, the streets teemed with Hungarians, Czechs, Albanians, Jews, Serbs, Slovenes, Croats and transients from all parts of the world – sailors and traders in colourful native costume speaking a strange confusion of tongues. Images and echoes of 'the exotic East' would leave their impressions on Joyce's work, and the freewheeling business atmosphere would inspire the entrepreneur in him.

To begin with, the couple took a fourth-floor room at 3 Piazza Ponterosso, again overlooking the teeming marketplace beside the Canale Grande, which they had loved on their previous stay in the city. Nora was now wearing a veil like the fashionable women of Trieste, and was, thought Joyce, looking 'very pretty'.[3] She continued to amuse him with her unconscious humour, looking at an article on Ibsen in *T.P.'s Weekly* one day and asking 'Is this the Ibsen you know?' – the kind of remark that invariably triggered that famous guffaw. However, she was four months pregnant, and there was the growing danger of eviction.

Everything in Trieste was of considerable curiosity to Joyce, especially the various religions practised there. After visiting the Greek Orthodox church of San Nicolo on the Riva Corelli (now Riva 3 Novembre), he wrote to Stanislaus dilating on the strange liturgy. 'Damn droll! The Greek priest has been taking a great eyeful out of me: two haruspices.' Strangely enough, he said, it made him realize that his story 'The Sisters' was 'rather remarkable'.[4]

As eating and drinking in style became an everyday affair, shortage of money continued to haunt Joyce. Well aware that they would soon have to cater for another hungry mouth, he was trying to economize, haggling with shopkeepers and questioning restaurant bills. To make a little extra, he undertook to write a six-page pamphlet for the Berlitz School in Japan and even followed his father's example by entering newspaper competitions for cash prizes. Another idea was to secure the franchise to sell Foxford Irish tweed in Trieste, and he did manage to clinch a dozen or so deals over the following years, giving him something for the Citizen to boast about in the 'Cyclops' episode of *Ulysses*.

Nora always felt he should have pursued a singing career, and that summer he approached Giuseppe Sinico, a Triestine maestro, who told him that in two years he could make him fit for the opera stage. 'My voice is extremely high,' he told Stanislaus, '[and] he says it has a very beautiful timbre.'[5] He continued his lessons with Sinico until the end of the year when he could no longer afford the fees. However, he borrowed his singing-master's name for the woman who dies in 'A Painful Case' and is buried in *Ulysses*.

His novel had reached Chapter 22 where Stephen, beset by demands on his future from his father and the Jesuits, spars with the college president over his paper on Ibsen. With his confidence rising, he began to feel that teaching English to foreigners was a waste of his talents. 'I cannot tell you how strange I feel sometimes in my attempt to live a more civilised life than my contemporaries,' he wrote. 'I cannot believe that any State requires my energy for the work I am at present engaged in.'[6] To assert his difference, he took to drinking in cheap workers' cafés around the Città Vecchia (old Trieste) declaring himself 'a socialist artist'. But talk of revolution among the drinking classes also made him conscious of the narrow irredentist passions of most Italian-speaking Triestines. The movement for union with Italy would gain momentum in the years running up to 1914. Its chief mouthpiece was *Il Piccolo della Sera*, the daily paper founded by Teodoro Mayer and edited by Roberto Prezioso, a sprucely dressed Venetian who became a student of Joyce.[7] Prezioso was a model for Robert Hand in *Exiles*, while Mayer contributed something to Leopold Bloom.

Like the streets of Dublin, the streets and alleys of Trieste were there to be explored, its churches, a fine cathedral and a synagogue to be visited, cafés and bars and a brothel quarter to be sampled, as he is reputed to have done during Nora's last months of pregnancy. When his landlady gave them notice to leave he had a further reason to wander the streets, this time in search of a home. But his luck was out, and once Nora's pregnancy was noticed there would be 'no room at the inn'.

Things were particularly bad for Nora. Because she spoke no Italian, people treated her rudely, and the stylish Triestine women sniggered at her short four-crown dress, her unfashionable hairdo and unshapely figure so that she became nervous about venturing out alone. However, because she disliked cooking in other people's kitchens, they mostly ate out, even though Italian food made her sick and she found the summer heat intolerable.

Each day Joyce managed to get through three English newspapers, including the London *Standard*, in which he found confirmation of Grant Richards's bankruptcy. He promptly wrote asking for his *Chamber Music* manuscript back, and was so dispirited that he decided to abandon poetry. From then onwards – except for an occasional moment of inspiration – the Bard would use his poetic gifts mainly to infuse his fiction with symbolic resonance.

Finally, on 1 May, they found a home at 30 via San Nicolo, next door to the Berlitz, where the landlady, Signora Moise Canarutto, seemed impressed with the grandeur of the school and Joyce's position there. However, when Bertelli, the director, saw Nora he told Joyce he must be mad, presumably believing that teachers he paid so modestly should not begin families. Ironically, just as Joyce found a secure address in Trieste, John Joyce was about to be dispossessed of his home in Dublin. The City Corporation, no longer prepared to tolerate his unpaid rates, ordered that the Cabra house be legally sold and the debt recovered. Those Joyces still living at home moved on 7 June to Whitworth Place, Drumcondra, with what sticks of furniture remained. John had finally frittered away his whole inheritance. 'John Joyce,' said some unkind person, 'pissed his money away into the Liffey.'

That month James had fifty copies of his satirical broadside 'The Holy Office' printed in Trieste and sent to Dublin for Stanislaus to distribute to people he wanted to impress or shock. Copies were to go to Byrne, George Roberts, Eglinton, Russell, Gogarty, Best, Cousins, Starkey, Moore, Elwood, Cosgrave and a few others. It was the first that most of his 'victims' would learn of his hostility towards them. Hostility towards *him* was often tempered by nervousness, and the Dublin cauldron was bubbling with jealous rivalries. Cosgrave was jealous of Joyce, Joyce was as jealous and fearful of Gogarty as Gogarty was of him, and the stay-at-homes were all jealous of the wild geese, a theme explored by Joyce in 'A Little Cloud'. Now they all awaited nervously the appearance of his novel.

In June Stannie was sent the just completed Chapter 24 of *Stephen Hero*. All who saw it agreed that this would be 'one of the novels of the century'. Gogarty's suspicion that Joyce would put them all into a novel one day had been fulfilled. Cosgrave, while admiring the subtlety of the satire, objected strenuously to being called 'Lynch' (after the Mayor of Galway who hanged his own son), but said he would not like to be Gogarty when Joyce got to the tower episode.[8]

In July the exile marked his ninth month abroad by writing a series of self-revealing confessional letters to Stanislaus, a style of letter he reserved only for the few close to him.

You will remember the circumstances in which I left Ireland nine months ago. Like everything else that I have done in my life it was an experiment. I can hardly say with truth that it was an experiment which has failed seeing that in those nine months I have begotten a child, written 500 pages of my novel, written 3 of my stories, learned German and Danish fairly well, besides discharging the intolerable (to me) duties of my position and swindling two tailors. I believe, besides, that I write much better now than when I was in Dublin and the incident in Chap. XXIII where Stephen makes 'love' to Emma Clery I consider a remarkable piece of writing.

He was, he reported, well fed, having his teeth fixed and had acquired some spectacles and a watch. His salary was not going far, but Bertelli had taken possession of his passport and degree certificate to ensure that he would not look for work elsewhere. Nora was not in good health – frequently in tears, often silent in company, feeling miserably alone and saying she could not continue as they were. She had succeeded in destroying his 'natural cheerfulness and irresponsibility', he said, and he had become concerned for his future offspring. 'I do not know what strange morose creature she will bring forth after all her tears and I am even beginning to reconsider the appositeness of the names I had chosen ("George" and "Lucy").'[9]

But, whatever her shortcomings, Nora was, he thought, utterly incapable of deceit – a quality he valued above almost all others. She had also shown an unexpected side of herself, during one melancholy scene between them quoting his poem 'O, Sweetheart, Hear You Your Lover's Tale',[10] and making him think that he was a poet after all. However, since he was so ignorant of women, he asked Stannie to show his letter to Aunt Josephine in the hope that she could help. He wanted a hopeful and passionate life, not merely one of 'mutual tolerance'.[11]

Despite this morbid frame of mind, in short bursts of creativity Joyce was driving on with *Dubliners*, anxious to earn money. He revised 'A Painful Case', and on 12 July finished 'The Boarding House' and 'Counterparts'. His pen was, he thought, being driven by a 'mischievous' spirit under the influence of Maupassant, and he was hoping, he implied, to stir up the Dublin critics by his moral 'obliqueness'.[12]   A shape was emerging which would eventually determine the order in which the stories would be placed, and he decided there was a sequel to be written, called *Provincials*.

In a café at three o'clock on the afternoon of 27 July he found Nora in pain. Neither was aware that she was in labour; Joyce had estimated it would be another month before the baby arrived. He took her back to via San Nicolo, and Signora Canarutto called a midwife while he summoned one of his students who happened to be a doctor. Nora was very stoical and barely cried out during her labour, but the nervous father chose not to be present. At 9 p.m. Signora Canarutto's old Jewish aunt came to him to announce, '*Xe un bel maschio, Signore.*' The name he needed from his list of two would be George (or 'Giorgio') after his dead brother. He immediately cabled Stanislaus, breaking the glad tidings. The mischievous Cosgrave reported to Gogarty that the message had read, 'Mother and bastard doing well.'

John sent a congratulatory telegram and Stanislaus wrote saying how pleased he was to think that a child had been born on whom no church could lay claims and who would not be required to take religious super-stitions seriously. Accordingly, a year later Joyce would register his son's birth but categorically refused to have him baptized. For his family, unaware of this, congratulations were in order and Aunt Josephine sent the simple message 'Bravo Nora!'[13] At the sight of his vulnerable young son, it dawned on him that at last his life of self-indulgence would need curtailing. Later, Stanislaus found a note addressed to Giorgio written on the manuscript of *Dubliners*: 'Before you were born I had no fear of fortune.'[14]

Family life was beginning to change him in subtle ways. He knew his nature was artistic and whatever seemed to stifle it made him unhappy. Both he and Nora had been finding the hot summer intolerable. Joyce cursed 'the damn silly sun that makes men into butter', and sought solace and refreshment by walking in the woods outside Trieste, with the Bora wind roaring around him, enjoying the fragrant smell of the soil. But he embraced fatherhood and took delight in his son's development. Now two months old, the boy seemed healthy (despite 'the paternal inheritance', he said). He was 'very fat and very quiet', with Nora's eyes, and reminded him of the photograph of his 'fierce-looking' two-year-old self. But he worried that he might have to 'hawk' him 'from one beggarly lodgings to another, from land to land'.[15] Unhappily, that worrisome prospect would become a self-fulfilling prophecy.

By September, *Dubliners* was taking on a broadly biographical shape, following the path from childhood to death. Now there were nine stories altogether and, fearful of losing them, he sent them to Stanislaus for copying. Compared with the stories he had submitted to Russell, the allusions were darker, more subversive and complex. For example, 'The Sisters' had been revised, so that the old priest's death now symbolized the paralysis at the very heart of the society he had escaped. Father Flynn's palsy and dementia, it was implied, sprang from a source of unmentionable sin, one with which he thought the whole city was infected. So the story at the beginning spells out the theme of the whole collection – death in life and life in death and all confined within the purlieus of a single city.

He was delighted when Stannie, having read his latest stories, compared him to Rousseau, Lermontov, Turgenev and Maupassant, although he considered the subject of 'A Painful Case' too big for its form and titles such as 'A Mother' and 'The Clay' more appropriate for paintings than stories. Yet, while flattered by the European comparisons, Joyce thought he was doing something new for Ireland. He hoped that by getting the collection published he would earn enough money and reputation to bring his brother to Trieste and help turn Dublin into another Christiania.

On 23 September he offered *Dubliners* to London publishers Heinemann, stressing that it was 'not a collection of tourist impressions but an attempt to represent certain aspects of the life of one of the European capitals'.[16] However, he was still asking Stanislaus to check certain facts about Dublin needed for his stories. Could a priest be buried in his habit? Could a municipal election take place in October? Even when shot through with symbols, his fiction, he thought, should also be utterly realistic. On the same day Grant Richards wrote saying that although he thought highly of *Chamber Music*, which had been resubmitted to him, he could not afford to publish it without Joyce's financial assistance. Joyce declined the proposal but asked Richards to keep the manuscript until he could see his way to publishing it.

At the end of September he informed Stanislaus that there was a job for him at the Trieste Berlitz from 20 October – on a six-month contract or for longer. He would earn a salary of 40 crowns (£1 13s) a week for a maximum of forty hours of teaching a week with the chance of extra classes at a crown a lesson. His third-class travel expenses would be refunded and there was a spare room (with board) next to theirs at 30 via San Nicolo. If his brother could not raise the fare he would send him the necessary 100 crowns. He should learn a little Italian, just to get by, and make sure he dressed smartly. After some thought, Stanislaus decided to leave Whitworth Place, cut his ties and take the job. Asked for money for the fare, John told him to 'Go to Hell!' So Jim cabled 180 crowns to cover all his expenses. Soon he would have someone with whom he could discuss his work and talk about Dublin to his heart's content. There was also the prospect of doubling the household income to 85 crowns (£3 11s 0d) per week, over twice the pension John Joyce received to support his near-destitute family.

Stanislaus arrived in Trieste on 27 October. Meanwhile, Cosgrave was keeping him abreast of news from Dublin, and sent two poems of Gogarty's, including 'The Song of the Cheerful (but slightly sarcastic) Jaysus', beginning:

> I'm the queerest young fellow that ever was heard
> My mother's a Jew; my father's a Bird
> With Joseph the Joiner I cannot agree
> So 'Here's to Disciples and Calvary ...'

which Joyce would later appropriate for *Ulysses*. Gogarty had finally passed his M.B., and the following May wrote to Joyce asking him to agree to forget the past, but Joyce replied that to do so was 'a feat beyond my power'.

When, 'after careful consideration', Symons's publishers Constable rejected both of his books he sent *Dubliners* (now a total of twelve stories) to Grant Richards. If his writing was not bringing in any funds, at least his position at the Berlitz seemed secure after one of his students, Count Francesco Sordina, a wealthy Greek trader and the best swordsman in Trieste, spoke highly of his teaching and brought along several other well-heeled customers – 'real live ladies and gentlemen' (including the wife of Baron Ambrogio Ralli) – to sign up for classes. Even Bertelli was impressed.

Stannie's arrival did not, as it happened, quite work the magic Joyce had anticipated. Rather than as a soulmate, he came to see his dour respectable brother primarily as a source of income, treating his salary as a contribution to the housekeeping, often drawing it himself at the school. Domestic life was beginning to pall, and in November he complained to Aunt Josephine about Nora's indifference to his artistry and the fact that she regarded him as much the same as the other men she had known. He hated the situation into which he had allowed himself to be trapped, and the wearisome necessity of having to make allowances for people. Back in September he had hinted to Stanislaus that he might flee the scene, as he believed Ibsen had done. 'If I once convince myself that this kind of life is suicidal to my soul, I will make everything and everybody stand out of my way as I did before now.' He feared himself, he said, to be in danger of committing 'the atrocities of the average husband'.[17] However, when Nora wrote to Aunt Josephine a little later she gave no hint of any tension, asking advice on nursing Giorgio, the baby's teething pains, and the pudding they had conjured up for Christmas. The couple survived by turning their hostility on Stanislaus, who was irritated but for different reasons – mostly to do with his brother's drinking.

Joyce's home life was about to change. Francini had suggested that he, Nora, Giorgio and Stanislaus share a large apartment with him, Clothilde and their son. Joyce readily agreed; it would save money. On 24 February 1906, they moved into a ground- and first-floor flat in a poor working-class district. Via Giovanni Boccaccio was a dark, narrow street of tall apartment buildings running north on the east side of the railway line. Although the couples sometimes dined out together, Joyce took to dodging off to workmen's cafés, carousing, dancing and finally returning home drunk. Sometimes Stanislaus would hunt him down and haul him back home barely able to stand. By now Nora, James and Stanislaus were gradually adopting the Triestine dialect as their *lingua franca*. Francini, who had a taste for horseplay and scatological humour, used a strong Triestine vernacular to tell his off-colour stories.[18] Joyce enjoyed the crude humour, joining in the laughter, but Nora considered it childish, telling him that since he had met the Italian, he was hardly recognizable. Nor did this frivolity commend itself to Stanislaus. He was upset not only to see his brother falling into his father's dissolute ways but also to see his genius dissipated in a haze of alcohol.[19]

At the end of January 1906, Joyce had written to Richards about *Dubliners*, mentioning a thirteenth story, 'Two Gallants', and hoping that, with Irish Home Rule again in the British headlines following that month's general election, he might think it timely to publish a book of Irish stories. But Richards disagreed, saying that unfortunately books about Ireland did not sell. Nevertheless, in this case, because he and his colleagues so admired Joyce's stories, he was prepared to take a chance, and offered him a 10 per cent royalty on every copy sold after the first five hundred, while demanding first refusal of all his future works for five years. A delighted Joyce (still barely twenty-four) replied that on the question of terms he was happy to place himself in Richards's hands, and, anticipating spring publication, suddenly saw the prospect of his novel quickly following the stories into print. By 13 February he had Richards's contract offering publication in the UK and overseas territories.

The great sense of euphoria Joyce felt at this breakthrough with Grant Richards did not last. By the end of April there were early signs that *Dubliners* might be running into difficulties. On the 23rd Richards informed him that 'Two Gallants', 'Counterparts' and 'Grace' had been refused by the printers, who in those days stood in danger of prosecution if complaints about obscenity were raised with the Home Secretary. Richards asked him to make small alterations in the latter two stories and either suppress or alter parts of 'Two Gallants' in which a pair of cynical ne'er-do-wells set out callously to dupe a susceptible housemaid. There were also objections to the word 'bloody' in 'Grace' and a reference to a man 'running two establishments' in 'Counterparts'. Seemingly ignorant of the power of the British printer to suppress books, Joyce replied saying that he was unable to do what Richards asked. He had taken great pains to write the book, despite all kinds of obstacles in accordance with the classical canons of his art, and the views of a printer were no concern of his. He could make no concessions over 'Counterparts' nor remove the word 'bloody' from 'Grace'. He would be sending Richards a fourteenth story, 'A Little Cloud', he said, and suggested he try another printer. If he could not publish the book 'as written' they would have to agree to end their relationship; it would be a disaster for him, but he was simply unable to alter what he had written.[20] Joyce then explained his somewhat grandiose conception for the stories:

> My intention was to write a chapter of the moral history of my country and I chose Dublin for the scene because that city seemed to me the centre of paralysis. I have tried to present it to the indifferent public under four of its aspects: childhood, adolescence, maturity and public life. The stories are arranged in this order.[21]

They were, he said, written 'in a style of scrupulous meanness' with a complete commitment to representing exactly what he had seen. He could not write, he had decided, without offending people and if he had taken the view of the printer the stories would never have been written. English literature was the laughing stock of Europe, he said, but would one day return to its Chaucerian roots and rejoin the Continent. Clearly he saw himself blazing a trail – a literary adventurer and pioneer.

When Richards warned him that he would not find an English publisher for the collection as it stood[22] Joyce asked why this had not been made plain before his contract had been issued. He offered to cut two of the three 'bloodys' out of the book, but then asked why Richards had not also taken exception to 'the allusions to the Royal Family, to the Holy Ghost, to the Dublin Police, to the Lord Mayor of Dublin, to the cities of the plain, to the Irish Parliamentary Party &c?'[23] He seemed unaware that by drawing attention to these other aspects of the book he was inviting further problems and further delay. But he was not prepared to prostitute his art for money, and to submit to the blue pencils of timid publishers and cowardly printers. However, he did make some concessions to render 'Grace', 'Ivy Day in the Committee Room' and 'The Boarding House' acceptable to Richards. Even so, the publisher (or his printer) still had problems with parts of 'Counterparts' and 'Two Gallants' and now wanted 'An Encounter' excluded completely. Here Joyce drew a line in the sand, affirming once again his high purpose in writing the stories. 'I fight to retain them because I believe that in composing my chapter of moral history in exactly the way I have composed it I have taken the first step towards the spiritual liberation of my country.'[24]

Unable to accept that his book might not be published, he later made more concessions over his stories but would not apologize for what he called 'the odour of ashpits and old weeds and offal' which pervaded them. The Irish, he declared, needed to look at themselves.[25] He was still a man with a mission to embrace high art even while attending to the conscience of his race. This exchange with Richards was just the first of

many such fights with publishers, printers and official censors which
would dog his literary life.

Stanislaus was depressed at how Jim and Nora's relationship had deteriorated. Nora was now openly dissatisfied with her life. Bringing up a small
child, having to do housework, cooking, washing and cleaning for two
men (both inclined to be morose and uncommunicative) was getting her
down. She would lash out with all the harsh words she could summon
from her chambermaid's vocabulary to tell Jim what she thought of him
and their impoverished life together, threatening to return home and take
Giorgio with her. Stanislaus, wretched at being made use of and largely
ignored by his brother, wrote a long letter to Aunt Josephine piling on
the misery and wishing he were back home. The tenseness and claustrophobia of their home life and Jim's sense of creative frustration are
well-captured in his story 'A Little Cloud'.[26]

To make matters worse, Bertelli had embezzled the Berlitz School funds
and absconded to America. Artifoni took over as principal and told the
Joyces that the school's parlous financial state meant that he might be
unable to afford two English teachers. Joyce took that as a cue for moving
on – perhaps hoping that a change of scene would reinvigorate his work
and marriage. He saw an advertisement in the Italian newspaper *La
Tribuna* for a correspondence clerk fluent in English, French and Italian
at the Nast-Kolb & Schumacher Bank in Rome. He had often thought of
relocating to Italy and long wanted to see Rome, and such a move would
also secure Stanislaus his post in Trieste. He had good references, one
from his pupil Prezioso, the editor, and the one he had received from Tim
Harrington in Dublin. After some long-distance haggling he was offered
a two-month trial in Rome starting on 1 August at 12 guineas a month.
His friend Francini was also ready to move on and in June he joined
Prezioso's paper, *Il Piccolo della Sera*.

Joyce felt sufficiently excited by the thought of moving, and confident
enough about his future, to tell Richards that in Rome he expected to
finish his novel, suggesting that he 'buy' a couple of critics, 'strong men'
able to boost *Dubliners* and thereby insure it against adverse criticism.
These expansive feelings led him to soften his attitude towards Gogarty,
and he wrote inviting his old Mephistopheles to visit them if he were ever
in Italy. He was so anxious to remain in touch with Ireland and Dublin
gossip that even Gogarty's company was worth contemplating.

13

The Conception of *Ulysses*
(1906–1907)

'The more books we read, the sooner we perceive that the only function of a writer is to produce a masterpiece. No other task is of any consequence.' Cyril Connolly, *The Unquiet Grave* (1944)

On 30 July 1906, Joyce, Nora and Giorgio set off for Rome. Stanislaus was left with the unpaid bills and an empty flat. They took the train to Fiume, then a boat to Ancona. Their first impressions of Italy were not good. Ancona, he wrote, was a 'filthy hole: like rotten cabbage'. They spent the night on the deck and, not having got the hang of the currency, Joyce was swindled three times – by a money-changer, a cabman and a railway official. At Ancona they took the train to Rome where they arrived exhausted on the 31st, the day before he was due to start work at the bank.[1] They found a room at 52 via Frattina, close to the Spanish Steps, where the rent was high enough to make a serious hole in his salary.

The ghosts of Keats and Shelley hovered nearby. Keats had died at a house on the Steps, and on the via Corso was the house where Shelley had written *The Cenci* and *Prometheus Unbound*. Joyce showed little interest in Keats; apart from Shakespeare, Wordsworth and Byron, Shelley was the English poet to whom he gave 'the highest palms', so his spirits were lifted by the thought of treading in the footsteps of one so inspired. But, for him, Rome was less a place of literary pilgrimage than of religious fascination. Here lay one of the main sources of Irish paralysis, the city at the centre of the faith which had held his mother in thrall, had so ensnared him as a youth and had left its lasting scars. He attended services at St Peter's, fascinated not by its architecture but by its priestly rituals. He also visited the Biblioteca Nazionale Vittorio Emanuele to examine the records of the 1870 Vatican Council which declared the infallibility of the Pope – a casual and empty decision, it seemed to him, embodying what he most hated: tyranny.

He found getting to the bank through the confusing maze of Roman streets difficult, and the bank itself, an imposing edifice on the corner of Piazza Colonna and the via San Claudio, somewhat intimidating. Nevertheless, he survived his first interview – a close quizzing by one of the bank's partners, the surly unsmiling Schumacher – and was paid his travel expenses plus a 100 lire advance. He was startled to discover that his hours would be 8.30 a.m. till 7.30 p.m. with a two-hour lunch-break, and the prospect of doing much writing in Rome suddenly looked bleak. Even so, a band playing selections from Wagner's *Siegfried* in the Piazza Colonna that evening cheered him up and he was pleased to report that Romans were 'excruciatingly well-mannered'.[2]

Nora, left alone for so much of the day with Giorgio, resorted to taking him to the various neighbourhood cinemas. Once weaned, he soon began to eat with as much gusto as his parents and started to grow appreciably. He was also acquiring better Italian so that it became normal for the family to converse in that language and thereafter his parents were always 'Babbo' and 'Mamma'. But this proximity to his mother in the early years meant that Giorgio would grow up much closer to her than to his father. She, in turn, became deeply attached to Giorgio, sharing with him her Roman isolation.

The bank job was undemanding and mechanical, little better than the Berlitz, Joyce thought. In the first week he took in the main sights of the city – St Peter's, the Pincio, the Forum, and the Coliseum. As a former altar-boy, what fascinated him about St Peter's was the layout, the liturgy, the music, and the number of altars, at which different masses took place. At the Coliseum he was more interested in the visitors and recorded an epiphany – a group of Cockney tourists quoting Byron: '"Whowail stands the Coliseum Rawhm shall stand/When falls the Coliseum Rawhm sh'll fall/And when Rawhm falls the world sh'll fall – but adding cheerfully: – /Kemlong, 'ere's the way aht –"'[3] He noted the importunate touts and souvenir sellers, and the parties of carefully chaperoned American girls (whose accents he disliked) complaining about not understanding the language. 'Rome,' he said, 'reminds me of a man who lives by exhibiting to travellers his grandmother's corpse.' He wished himself far away – beside the sea at Bray or at some English seaside resort eating English bacon and eggs and enjoying English sunshine, beefsteak, boiled potatoes and onions, a pier at sunset, a beach and some smokes.[4]

He found the Roman cafés disappointing, and preferred to eat at a Greek restaurant (Caffè Greco) on the via Condotti which had been patronised by Henri Amiel, Thackeray, Byron, and Ibsen, and where the latest *Daily Mail* and *New York Herald* were available. This was one place he and Nora could meet during his long workday. And wherever they went Giorgio was very popular. People laughed with pleasure when they saw him and gave him biscuits and fruit, and the proprietor of the café made a fuss of him. He was a well-behaved child and even their landlady, Signora Dufour, seemed fond of him. Joyce sent instructions to Stanislaus about how to handle his debts – pay the baker, give a false address to his tailor and the correct one to his doctor. Once his situation in Rome was secure, he said, he would arrange for him to join them.

From the Irish papers Stanislaus was forwarding (*Sinn Fein* and the *Irish Independent*) Nora learned that Gogarty had married, and she hurried to meet Jim from work with the hot news. He was amazed and amused, unable to imagine the cynical old blasphemer in wedding suit and high silk hat. However, in charitable mood, he wrote to Stannie, 'I suppose we had better wish Mr and Mrs Ignatius Gallaher health and long life'[5] – a reference to the unpleasantly boastful character who so impresses the frustrated Little Chandler in 'A Little Cloud'.

After only two weeks in Rome, Joyce, almost out of money, was asking Stanislaus for a loan (he had already borrowed 50 lire), suggesting he request a week's salary in advance and wire it to him immediately. The problem, he explained, was that they were eating 'enormously'. Nora was at last enjoying Italian food. Most evenings they ate roast beef, Italian meatballs, stuffed tomatoes and salad at the wine shop across from the apartment. Once they ate a whole roast chicken with ham, bread and wine.[6] Ironically, a few months later he was complaining of indigestion and chronic constipation, which he put down to his inactive life – the first signs perhaps that his inner organs were not as robust as his appetite.

Living as they were, partly at Stanislaus's expense, Joyce was surprised to discover that his brother was subsisting on bread and ham and could not understand why he didn't wheedle an advance from Artifoni. He was worried about Richards's proposed cuts to his stories and asked Stannie's opinion, adding mysteriously, 'Yesterday we went to the cemetery.'[7] The mystery had a literary explanation. It was the place where Shelley's ashes had been buried. Joyce had also been reading Wilde's *The Picture of Dorian Gray* and decided there were too many concealing lies in it. Perhaps prompted by thoughts of the dead Shelley and the ageing Dorian dying inside a youthful body, suddenly he was suffering from hideous and terrifying 'dreams of death, corpses and assassination' and asked Stanislaus if he knew of a cure for this malady. These thoughts of mortality conjured up a vision of Nora's lost love, Michael Bodkin, dead and buried in the graveyard at Rahoon.[8] Within weeks the title for a new *Dubliners* story had surfaced in his mind – 'The Dead'.

Although he was finding his job at the bank wearisome, handling between 200 and 250 letters a day and sometimes not getting away until eight-thirty, he was trying to rewrite 'A Painful Case'. The result of these prolonged sedentary labours was that the seat of his trousers wore through. He also found the stuffy formality and attitudes of the other bank employees tiresome. Provoked by the reactionary views of a German colleague, he launched into what he called 'a socialist outburst' at the bank – attacking capitalism in one of its own bastions. Speaking his mind and not giving a damn about the consequences was not just reserved for publishers and the wine-shop.

His frustration over Richards's procrastinations was growing, especially when he learned of works being published by Dublin contemporaries he despised. In letters to Stanislaus he wrote as if, like one of his Dubliners, he was still trapped by invisible nets cast for him by malevolent gods.

> Here am I (whom their writings and lives nauseate to the point of vomiting) writing away letters for ten hours a day like the blue devil on the off chance of pleasing three bad-tempered bankers and inducing them to let me retain my position while (as a luxury) I am allowed to haggle for two years with the same publisher, trying to induce him to publish a book for which he has an intense admiration. Orco Dio!⁹

His next communication from Richards was a rejection letter with a hint of blackmail, telling him that, although his objections did not reflect the firm's views, he thought *Dubliners* would damage his reputation as well as Joyce's own future prospects. However, if Joyce sent him his novel, Richards said, he would give him a decision within a fortnight. Publication of *Stephen Hero* would make the eventual publication of *Dubliners* more likely.¹⁰ But Joyce was not to be so easily fobbed off. He complained to Arthur Symons who advised him to insist that Richards publish the twelve stories he had undertaken to publish and said that he himself would write urging him to do so. On 2 October, Joyce consulted a lawyer who advised him to try to settle the matter out of court, as legal actions were expensive and could jeopardize his chances with other publishers.

Two weeks later Joyce made his final concessions to Richards, offering to omit 'Two Gallants' and 'A Little Cloud', to delete passages in 'Counterparts', and cut the word 'bloody' out of 'Grace'. But Richards was in no mood to change his mind. On the 26th he replied, 'I am afraid you think we have treated you badly, but ... although what we have done has been in our own interest it is also, although you may not see it now, in yours too.'¹¹ His manuscript would be returned. On receiving this letter Joyce collected all the money in the flat and went off to drink himself into forgetfulness. Returning home drunk at midnight, he managed to stumble and smash the landing windows. Next morning his landlady demanded immediate payment for the repairs.

But his life had some compensations, and he especially enjoyed observing his son's reactions to the world around him. Giorgio had learned from Nora to blow soap bubbles, loved beating time to the band in the Piazza

Colonna and had added the word 'Brava' to his vocabulary. He was so popular with the wine-shop proprietor that they were invited one night for a free dinner.

Joyce had hoped that by publishing *Dubliners* he would be able at a single stroke to pay off his debts and consider writing full time, like George Gissing about whom he had been reading. But that hope had been dashed and for the moment his situation was dire. In September he was only saved from complete destitution by finding a language student willing to pay 20 lire in advance, but that extra student, while helping to keep his head above water, meant not finishing work till nine o'clock. At one point he was reduced to borrowing 5 lire from another student, and to economize he decided in future they would eat their meals at home.

Politics had a way of intruding itself into his life and thoughts. Word came that his college friend Tom Kettle had been elected to Parliament, but Joyce was antiparliamentarianist. His own politics, a brand of socialism, sprang from a hatred of the burgher class. He much preferred the working class because they were honest, even though brutalized and cunning. However, although he read the socialist *La Tribuna* and the anticlerical *L'Asino* and became fascinated by the activities of the various socialist factions in Rome, his own socialism would ebb and flow as circumstances changed. As for Irish politics, he favoured Sinn Fein's programme over that of the other Irish parties, mainly because they were uninvolved with the Church. He supported the independence of Ireland but not its cultural isolation. Even so, he saw himself outside of, and above, all parties. 'If the Irish programme did not insist on the Irish language I suppose I could call myself a nationalist,' he wrote. 'As it is, I am content to recognise myself an exile: and, prophetically, a repudiated one.'[12]

By mid-September he had been moved to the bank's reception room – a rise in status if not in salary. Eating at home and his evening teaching helped them get by and he continued to advise Stanislaus in Trieste to pay no bills and keep pressing Artifoni for advances. He could find no more teaching and at times was reduced to asking for further advances from his private student, once even borrowing a single lire from him. In this gloomy, downcast mood, a terrific thunderstorm had him shaking and agitated at his desk, so much so that the banker's son closed the office shutters. When someone was struck dead by lightning outside a nearby church, Joyce was convinced that next time it would be him.

He became acutely nostalgic for Irish company and good Irish talk about what he called 'the isle ... full of voices',[13] even though he had to admit that he preferred Italy for its climate and intellectual ferment. However, a series of anarchist bombings in the city that November (including one at St Peter's which he barely avoided, one at the Caffè

Aragno close to his office, and another close to where he was living) somewhat blunted his enthusiasm for Italy, and for good Irish conversation he substituted voluminous letters to Stanislaus.[14]

The disheartening news from 'the isle of voices' was that the family had moved yet again. In October, evicted from Whitworth Terrace for non-payment of rent, they moved to Millmount Terrace where John had difficulty raising the £32 annual rent. Brother Charlie was also in a bad way – without decent clothes, diagnosed tuberculous and in and out of hospital. James's image of Ireland was one of poor hygiene and rampant disease, not a picture alluring enough to tempt him back home, despite the seductive voices. However in its favour, he discovered, more books were now being published in Dublin, mostly by George Roberts and Joseph Hone at Maunsel.

To add to his worries, his one language student had left Rome for the summer; at the end of September Giorgio suffered an attack of bronchitis, and the landlady (probably as an inducement to them to leave) raised their rent to 40 lire. They were living above their income and, having just repaid Stannie 43 lire and splurged what they had left, Joyce had to ask him to lend it back again until the end of the month. But this financial crisis came at the very moment when his creativity had taken off again. In a letter to his brother postmarked 30 September he said that he had a new story in his head about Mr Hunter (the man who had rescued him after his beating in Dublin and taken him home to recover). This was the moment of conception of *Ulysses*.

Symons said he would urge Elkin Mathews in London to publish *Chamber Music*. If he did so he would review it himself and arrange for a couple of other critics to give it 'proper' notices. He was as good as his word and on 8 October sent the collection to Mathews, calling it 'A Book of Thirty Songs for Lovers'. 'I am offering you a book which cannot fail to attract notice from everyone capable of knowing poetry when he sees it,' he wrote. 'I should make a point of reviewing it myself in the *Athenaeum* or *Saturday [Review]*, and would tell others about it.'[15]

Within a week, Joyce began to bounce back. Giorgio, he reported, had recovered, become very active and acquired eight teeth. His son was, he thought, the most successful part of his life. He was reading Gissing and Hardy (who made him realize how boring English novels were).[16] It emboldened him to carry on revising *Dubliners*. On 13 November, he updated Stanislaus, saying, 'I thought of beginning my story "Ulysses" but I have too many cares at present.' Although he had got no further than a title, the idea had already begun, magnet-like, to draw fragments towards itself. When he took up *Stephen Hero* again, he said, he would treat Gogarty for the betrayer he was – Malachi Mulligan, it seems, was conceived as a villain from the very outset. Perhaps with his projected hero, Mr Hunter/Bloom, in mind, he was anxious to obtain a Dublin newspaper carrying a report of a recent Jewish divorce case, and on reading Guglielmo Ferrero's history of Rome, *Grandezza e decadenza di Roma*, he told Stanislaus that it included 'a fine chapter on Antisemitism'. He commented on the 'apocalyptic' vision of Marx and reflected that Ibsen's friend Georg Brandes was Jewish.[17] From the very beginning, his thoughts about 'Ulysses' were drawing him towards a wider vision.

It also led him back to Ireland in a very specific fashion. His imagination, he thought, was not sufficiently powerful to be able to conjure up accurately the details of Dublin life he needed and he wished he could be transported there for a short time. He was, after all, writing something like a chapter in the history of Ireland. However, he was sickened, he told Stanislaus, by the attacks in *Sinn Fein* on the 'venereal excesses' of the English and the implied 'purity' of the saintly Irish (as portrayed by Skeffington and Arthur Griffith). If he lowered a bucket into the sexual department of the well of his soul he would draw up more than just his own water, but theirs, too, plus that of Shelley, Ibsen and St Aloysius, he said. 'I am going to do that in my novel (inter alia) and plank the bucket down before the shades and substances above mentioned to see how they like it: and if they don't like it I can't help them. I am nauseated by their lying drivel about pure men and pure women and spiritual love and love for ever: blatant lying in the face of the truth.'[18] It sounded like a declaration of war, and he would not be taking on just his old Irish antagonists.

Still dwelling on the city he had left behind, he was amused to recall what his Dublin friends had predicted for him when he left Ireland. 'Eglinton was sure I would come back begging to Dublin and J.J.B. [Ellmann thought that Joyce meant J.F. Byrne] that I would become a drunkard and Cosgrave that I would become a nymphomaniac. Alas, gentlemen, I have become a bank clerk, and ... bad as it is, it's more than either of my three prophets could do.' But his greatest antipathy was reserved for Gogarty whose regular column for *Sinn Fein* he called 'stupid drivel'.[19]

By taking on extra evening teaching at a language school and working four hours on Saturday's Joyce found he could save up to 100 lire a month and urged Stanislaus to do the same. However, unable to find a new room for less than 70 or 80 lire a month, with the use of a kitchen, and with landlords hostile towards children, he now considered Rome 'the stupidest old whore of a town ever I was in'. And Romans, he decided, were far from the subtle characters portrayed by Henry James; their main concern being 'the condition ... of their *coglioni* and their chief pastime and joke the breaking of wind rereward ... it is an expletive which I am reserving for the day when I leave the eternal city as my farewell and adieu to it.'[20] It is the epitaph Bloom writes for himself and his farewell gesture to Daly's Bar at the end of the 'Sirens' episode of *Ulysses* – 'Pprrpffrrppff'.

He managed to arouse the interest of the publisher John Long who asked to see the manuscript of *Dubliners* and wanted to know who had so far rejected it. But his work stalled when he, Nora and Giorgio were suddenly evicted from their room on 3 December. They removed themselves first to a restaurant where they enjoyed a large dinner before leaving at eleven-thirty to look for a room. Finally, after four nights in a hotel, they found a single room at 51 via Monte Brianzo and had to sleep head to tail to get a comfortable night's sleep in the narrow bed. These cramped quarters would be their home for the next three months.

To Joyce, that Christmas offered a bleak prospect – 'a low-water mark in Xmases', he said. He was worth just 11 lire (less than 10s) and was again begging Stannie for money. Ironically, his father, no doubt thinking his son the banker was now flush with lires, asked him for a pound, a request he passed on to Stanislaus, telling him to send the money via himself rather than directly to Dublin. Despite his antipathy towards the old man, Stannie sent both money for Jim to forward and money directly from himself. In the New Year he began a new diary, his 'Book of Days', picking up the story he had broken off in Dublin.

Although Joyce had ideas, he thought, for 'three or four little immortal stories' in his head, the Roman weather was too cold for him to write them. His situation seemed miserable all round, but that only inspired his ability to transform his wretchedness into prose, including a scene-setting description of their room:

> [Scene: draughty little stone-flagged room, chest of drawers to left, on which are the remains of lunch, in the centre, a small table on which are *writing materials* ... and a saltcellar: in the background, small-sized bed. A young man with snivelling nose sits at the little table: on the bed sit a madonna and plaintive infant. It is a January day.] Title of above: *The Anarchist*.[21]

Unsurprisingly perhaps, given their small bed, by early January Nora was again pregnant.

To Joyce's delight, Elkin Mathews accepted *Chamber Music* and on 11 January sent him a contract. It proposed no royalties on the first 300 copies sold and 15 per cent of the sales price afterwards. This time he signed the contract only after consulting his lawyer. Its publication would at least give him a book to his name, but financial success was still eluding him. He was again reduced to begging 10 crowns from Stanislaus who thereby had to forgo the new boots he was saving up to buy.[22]

Joyce's imagination was now fully possessed by his novel. Over the next six months he would lose confidence in it and consider rewriting it, but he was already thinking beyond even that. As he later said, 'In Rome, when I had finished about half of [*Stephen Hero*], I realised that the *Odyssey* had to be the sequel, and I began to write *Ulysses*.'[23] He later told H. L. Mencken (co-editor of the American magazine the *Smart Set* and later the *American Mercury*) that *Ulysses* was a continuation of both *Dubliners* and his first novel. The greater project was already conceived and had come to embrace and reach beyond his current work; but there would be a fifteen-year gestation before it finally reached the point of delivery. From thenceforth, his *Künstlerroman* would be viewed as a prequel to be adapted with the grander conception in mind.

As re-conceived, the chapter that was supposed to follow Stephen's departure for France was sketched but then abandoned. It was meant to cover his mother's death, his return to Ireland and sojourn in the Martello tower with Gogarty (called Doherty in this version) which would later become the mock-epic opening chapter of *Ulysses*. The death of his mother was therefore left a blank between one novel and the other. This enabled him to make more of a point of Mulligan's jibe about him ignoring her dying request to kneel and pray for her. But it also suggests that he sidestepped a scene he preferred not to relive[24] – although her ghostly form surfaces momentarily and horrifyingly in Stephen's solitary reflections on the roof of the Martello Tower.

At the beginning of February 1907 news filtered through from Dublin about protests on the opening night of J. M. Synge's *The Playboy of the Western World* at the Abbey Theatre. The police were called while Yeats and Lady Gregory attempted to calm things. Joyce felt upset at being so far from the scene of the action. The whole *Playboy* rumpus had put him off starting on his story 'The Dead', which shows how the tentacles of his home town could reach out to excite or stifle him. The idea for both 'The Dead' and 'Ivy Day' he attributed to Anatole France, although the latter story also owes something to Stannie's account of his father at work during a Dublin by-election three years earlier. But exactly how his ideas came to him remained a mystery, even to Joyce. All he could say was that beyond his novel and beyond 'The Dead' he had had 'some kind of thing' stirring in his head.[25]

Not unusually, Joyce was beset by numerous further tribulations. He had unwisely abandoned his evening classes, his lawyer's bill had come to 30 francs, and, having bought new clothes for himself and Giorgio, he was in financial trouble yet again. Nor did it cheer him to hear that

Gogarty's mother was 'beastly dead', leaving his old adversary both independent and rich. Worse still, the publisher John Long had still not
returned the manuscript of *Dubliners*, his glasses were troubling him, his
teeth were decaying, he was struck down again with an attack of stomach
cramps, and the newly pregnant Nora was complaining about the state
in which they were living. It was a bleak outlook for his twenty-fifth
birthday, and he asked Stanislaus for an immediate loan of 10 Austrian
crowns and of 30 lire later in the month. However, he 'squandered' a lire
on a gallery ticket for Wagner's *Götterdämmerung*, sitting next to a man
who smelt of garlic, and coming away feeling unmoved.[26]

Under pressure to leave their room once again, Nora finally found one
on the Corso (at 35 lire) and left a deposit on it. But they were both
depressed and had lost their appetites. Seemingly at the end of his tether –
no money, unable to write, cold and dispirited, tempted to lapse into
drunkenness – Joyce cabled Stanislaus telling him that he had given in
his notice at the bank and asking him to talk to Artifoni about his
returning to the Trieste Berlitz, as he had been promised he could. He had
only resigned on the strength of that understanding. But while Artifoni
was happy to lend him 40 crowns he said he had no immediate vacancy.
Joyce felt that his 'spiritual barque' was 'on the rocks', he was 'a fish
out of water', and without people with whom he felt temperamentally
compatible. Remembering how congenial he had found Trieste, he
decided to 'save his soul' by leaving Rome ('this last mad performance of
mine', he called it), asking permission to remain in his flat a bit longer
while he sorted out his next move.[27]

But leaving would not be that simple: the disappointed landlady of the
reserved quarters on the Corso confronted him in a café demanding a
month's rent, which he was obliged to cough up. He wrote to ask Stanislaus
whether he thought he could get enough private teaching in Trieste to
survive, but Stannie, reluctant to resume the role of 'brother's keeper',
replied that the prospects were bleak and urged him to withdraw his
resignation. Joyce said that was impossible and began to consider finding
a job in France, preferably in Marseilles where a French-Italian friend of
his had connections.

A letter from John Long on 21 February turning down *Dubliners* seemed
finally to present him with a stark choice – either to become a writer or
to settle for a full-time job; he could do nothing else. He had stopped
writing, and even reading made him tired. He had lost interest in politics,
and, after the bombings in Rome, he was no longer feeling the urge to be
a socialist or anarchist or even a reactionary. A conversation he overheard
at their local wine-shop captured well his change of heart and mind –
'Uncle, is Mr James a socialist?' Proprietor: 'He's a little of everything.'[28]

The prospect of receiving page-proofs of *Chamber Music* from Mathews cheered him and he told Stanislaus he would get him to correct them. Some of the poems he thought pretty enough to put to music of the Old English sort he liked. This accumulation of events and feelings seemed to concentrate his mind. The way ahead for him was a singular one, he decided. 'I have certain ideas I would like to give form to: not as a doctrine but as the continuation of the expression of myself which I now see I began in *Chamber Music*.'[29] But when Stannie saw the poems he was unimpressed. The poems, he thought were 'of the prettiness of passion', but that in the writing of them, Jim had not brought the full powers of his mind to bear upon them and his moral courage had failed him.[30]

There was neither prettiness nor graceful dignity in Joyce's final workday in Rome. That evening he drew a month's salary (250 lire) at the bank and went on a farewell spree – a drunken adieu to the Eternal City, which he had come to consider 'vulgar' and 'whorish'. When suitably drunk, two congenial bar-flies took him to a backstreet and relieved him of his bulging wallet. He returned home penniless and completely soaked from an evening downpour.

Now all but stony-broke, he decided to head directly for his one sure source of funds. Stanislaus, thinking his brother was bound for Marseilles, was surprised and not exactly pleased to receive a telegram on 7 March informing him that the family would be arriving back in Trieste at eight o'clock that evening.

14

Going Freelance in Trieste

(1907–1909)

'Freshly blows the wind homewards: my Irish child,
where are you dwelling?' Wagner, *Tristan and Isolde*

Stanislaus was at Trieste station to meet them. They were, he wrote, 'almost as thin and poverty-stricken as Italian immigrants'. James, thinner than ever, was looking hung-over and unshaven 'in a manky shapeless capecoat', Nora, 'more bedraggled than ever' cradling in her arms the plump, fresh-faced Giorgio.[1] Joyce said that he left Rome with a mouth full of decayed teeth and a soul full of decayed ambitions. His ideas, he felt, had atrophied under the influence of dull bank colleagues. Now he looked forward to re-engaging with the self-reflective line of thought he had begun with his epiphanies and poems.

Stannie was again faced with the constant distraction and drain on his meagre purse of an improvident penniless brother and his hungry family, now homeless. He found himself other accommodation and let them have the room he had been subletting at 32 via San Nicolo, next door to the Berlitz. Artifoni offered Joyce six hours teaching for 15 crowns a week, little more than 12 shillings. On 26 March Nora felt her baby move, and with the prospect of another mouth to feed, Joyce began to search for private students. Meanwhile, alerted to his return and want of funds, Prezioso, editor of *Il Piccolo della Sera*, commissioned him to write a series of articles on Ireland, seeing a parallel between an island under British rule and Trieste under the Austrians. Joyce was delighted and quickly got to work on the first, on Fenianism, which appeared on 22 March. 'The Home Rule Comet' would follow in May and 'Ireland at the Bar' in September. For these he was able to draw both on his own family history and his copious reading of Irish history in Paris, arguing how the struggle for Irish independence was confounded all too often by treachery from within.

More free time meant more time to drink. Stanislaus had by now become cynical about his brother's waywardness. He had, he wrote, never been able to live in the same town as Jim and know where to find him at any hour of the day.[2] On 6 April he recorded a drunken conversation between Francini and his brother – Jim lamenting having written stories which no one would publish and considering unlearning English and writing in French, a language in which literature was appreciated. He even contemplated returning to Ireland, but the idea of submitting his stories to George Roberts at Maunsel, or any narrow cultural nationalist, he considered unthinkable.

Old heroes were losing their charm for him. D'Annunzio, he said, had become a charlatan,[3] and Ibsen he now saw as an imbecilic old man. Discussing *A Doll's House*, he said, 'For us woman is an aperture. We make no difference between a whore and a wife except that a whore we have for five minutes, a wife for our life.' Ibsen might write like a gentleman but *he* wouldn't.[4] Inside the mercurial, articulate intellectual there still lurked the man from Monto. Continuing this conversation later, he said he had never met an Ibsenite woman – to the playwright, women were just symbols. They 'were never happy unless they were pattering after children'. He dwelt on how Maupassant and Flaubert dealt with adultery, arguing that men did not feel jealousy but merely an offended sense of proprietorship.[5] With Nora now heavily pregnant, his feelings of attraction to other women and his ponderings on betrayal, emotions and ideas which would feature prominently in his future work, were becoming more intense.

On 22 April, at the Stella Polare café beside the Canal Grande, as if making a new start, he read his brother the eleventh chapter of *Stephen Hero*. Stannie was struck by its 'Russian power'. It was, he said, unlike anything he'd ever heard before, and he urged his brother to carry on with it. But Joyce didn't think he could recapture that earlier style, and the Russian parallel did not impress him. He wanted to write the moral history of the life he knew and not stories about epileptics, he said. And yet the stories he had written, about his Dublin 'paralytics', seemed to please him.

A self-pitying letter from John suggested that life at home had descended into chaos, and he blamed his situation partly on his delinquent son and his irregular 'marriage'. 'I need not tell *you* how your miserable mistake affected my already well crushed feelings,' he wrote, 'but then maturer thoughts took more the form of pity than anger, when I saw a life of promise crossed and a future that might have been brilliant blasted in one breath.'[6] Joyce in turn blamed the situation on his wretched country, and spoke angrily to Stanislaus about the state of Ireland. The Irish thought themselves intelligent, he said, because they lived next to the second stupidest people in Europe. Even so, he continued to back Sinn Fein's programme for independence, until the party's flirtation with violence became apparent and his support ebbed away.

Ironically, considering that he was broke, Artifoni offered to sell Joyce the lease of the Trieste Berlitz for 1,000 lire. But, even had he had such a sum he probably wouldn't have wanted the responsibility. Then fortunately, he was invited to give a series of lectures on Ireland at the Università del Popolo at 25 crowns a time. He offered three – one on Irish politics, one on the poet J. C. Mangan, and one on the Irish cultural revival. In the event he ended up giving just one. 'Ireland, Island of Saints and Sages', was delivered on 27 April 1907. He turned up in Artifoni's borrowed black coat and read his written-down lecture stiffly in Italian. Because of her shabby dress, Nora stayed away.

Joyce knew he was speaking to a sympathetic audience, many of them his former pupils, committed to returning Trieste to Italian rule. He was able to draw parallels between the city and Ireland, a Catholic country with its own language suffering under the domination of a foreign power. The main difference, he said, as if by way of warning, was that what had forever frustrated hopes of Irish Independence was the history of betrayal. Prezioso thought his Italian impressive; Silvio Benco, the novelist, who had checked his *Piccolo* articles, thought it 'a bit hard and cautious'. However, his message and the flat, unemotional delivery seemed to please his listeners and he was warmly applauded.

On 7 May, Elkin Mathews published *Chamber Music*. Now at last he had a book in print. Although at one stage he had told Stannie that he wished he could cancel the book as it was insincere – all fakery – he proudly sent copies to his friends, even offering Curran the manuscript copy, and was delighted when it was favourably reviewed. Later he portrayed it as an important part of his creative development, telling Herbert Gorman that 'I wrote *Chamber Music* as a protest against myself.' He asked Mathews to send copies to various composers in the hope that they might be tempted into putting some of the poems to music. Arthur Symons quickly produced a review for *The Nation*, advising everyone who cared about poetry to buy a copy. It contained 'a rare kind of poetry ... full of ghostly old tunes ... all so singularly good, so firm and delicate, and yet so full of music and suggestion, that I can hardly choose among them.'[7] His old friend Tom Kettle, writing in the *Freeman's Journal*, referred to the 'rare and exquisite accent' of the poems which held one strangely by their 'integrity of form', the best having 'the bright beauty of a crystal'.[8] There were appreciative reviews also in the *Daily News, Evening Standard, Manchester Guardian, Irish Independent, Scotsman* and *Country Life. Chamber Music* was a *succès d'estime* and he would happily insert slips quoting from these notices in his later books.

Early in May, Stanislaus returned to 32 via San Nicolo while the Joyce ménage moved to 45 via Nuova. There finally he began work on 'The Dead'. Soon after the move, on 16 May, his eyes began to trouble him. The following day they were worse, and Nora had to read for him. On the 23rd he was struck down with rheumatic fever and unable to leave his bed. For the following month he was laid up with painfully inflamed joints, his right arm disabled, incapable of work, and Artifoni had to lend him the money to cover his medical costs. It was 13 June before he was recovered enough to leave the flat, though barely able to crawl and with his right arm still useless.

Nora would soon be needing the hospital maternity ward, admission to which required a marriage certificate. Joyce consulted the doctor, explaining the true nature of his 'marriage', and was advised to buy Nora a ring which might do the trick. She gave the place and date of her wedding to 'Giacomo Joyce' as Dublin on 5 February 1904, more than four months before they actually met.

With Nora's delivery imminent, on 25 July 1907, Joyce, taking Giorgio with him, was able to convey her to the hospital.[9] There, suitably equipped with her fake wedding-ring, she entered the Ospedale Maggiore Stabilimento di Maternità (General Hospital Maternity Ward) as Signora Giacomo Joyce. At 5.30 a.m. on the 26th, Nora gave birth to a daughter – 'female, mature, live, Lucia Anna, 3,500 gr. 49cm', said the hospital record. The names had been carefully chosen – 'Lucia', after the saint who, for the Scandinavians, 'brought light in time of darkness', a message that cannot have escaped her Ibsenite father whose sight was now threatened; 'Anna' after Nora's mother and the mother of the Virgin. The birthday, 26 July, also happened to be the feast day of St Anne.

In his diary Stanislaus recorded, 'Both wanted a boy', but Joyce would come to love this strange yet mercurial child, would see 'genius' in her and draw her into his increasingly labyrinthine world of fiction. She was a delicately formed, blue-eyed child with her mother's dark looks and a slight cast in her left eye which only seemed to enhance her good looks. Giorgio enjoyed having a tiny sister and would climb into her bed, kissing her and telling her not to cry.[10] When word of her arrival reached Dublin, Aunt Josephine was the first to congratulate them. 'A thousand welcomes to the little lady,' she wrote.[11] The attitude of the little lady's mother was more ambivalent, however, and while Giorgio had been kept at the breast for eighteen months, Lucia would be weaned after only four.[12]

In July, through his contacts with *Piccolo*, Joyce was given free tickets to the opera. There would be no more gallery seats among the rabblement for the Joyces. That year they saw *La Bohème, Tosca, Siegfried* and *Carmen*, after which he was proud to boast that Giorgio could sing the 'Toreador song' as well as snatches from other operas. Reading press reports of John McCormack's Covent Garden debut that autumn, he commented that he had done the tenor a favour by not pursuing his own singing career. Music was still an important part of his life, and he was delighted that July when the Anglo-Irish composer Geoffrey Molyneux Palmer asked permission to set some of his poems to music. Molyneux Palmer would eventually set thirty-two of the thirty-six *Chamber Music* verses.

Needing more space, in mid-August the family moved to two rooms in 'the very large old and dirty-looking remains of what was once a very fine house' in the via Santa Caterina.[13] Stanislaus also moved in. Although this halved the rent, the arrangement was inconvenient because getting to Jim and Nora's room meant passing through Stannie's. This led to upheavals, especially when Jim returned home late and drunk. On more than one such occasion Stannie attacked him yelling, 'Do you want to go blind?'[14]

When he had recovered, urged by Stannie, Joyce returned to 'The Dead'. It took much labour and application and was not completed until the end of September. When he finally read it, Stannie thought it 'a magnificent story ... worthy of any of the Russians I have read, Tolstoy or Tourguéneff. The comedy of the supper table is excellent and so is the end ... [But] ... he seemed to think my opinion of it too favourable.'[15]

Dubliners took Joyce beyond poetry and epiphanies, although every story was touched by poetry and embodied one or more moments of revelation. Consequently each story, rather than presenting a neatly tailored narrative, captured a mood. The influences were wide and varied, but two stand out – Maupassant and Zola. Few stories in Irish or English had been written in this vein and publishers were aware that here was something original, even though controversial. If what Edna O'Brien, in her monograph on Joyce, called 'an air of nervous fragility' hung over them, it is doubtless because they all stem from the fast-receding memory of the exile. Joyce was less delicate writing *about* the stories, telling the publisher Constable that a good selling point was 'the special odour of corruption' which, he hoped, floated over them.[16]

The stories reflect Joyce's personal obsessions – fear of betrayal, the unfulfilled marriage, sexual frustration, thwarted ambition, the smothering effects of religion, cruel and casual bigotry, the wretchedness of wasted lives. Despite the 'scrupulous meanness' of the pared-down prose, the spirit of compassion and imaginative empathy for his often-flawed characters is far from mean. Joyce achieves this effect by occupying the inner world of his characters while also trying to capture what he called 'the drab, yet glistening atmosphere of Dublin, its hallucinatory vapours, its tattered confusion, the atmosphere of its bars, its social immobility'.[17] This sad and seamy underside of respectability, which he subtly reveals, is the world behind the net curtains, inside the seedy boarding house, the Gradgrind's office, the deserted house haunted by the dead. And yet the sordid ambience is captured in prose which is both elusive and exquisite, honed to perfection.

Undoubtedly the best story in the *Dubliners* collection is 'The Dead', which tells of Gabriel Conroy's painful discovery that his wife, Gretta, has had a secret, unforgettable lover – a consumptive boy, Michael Furey, who died shortly after lingering at her gate one freezing night to confess his love. It was for her, she believes, that he died. This haunting memory, evoked by a song, leaves the wife overcome with guilt and sorrow, and her husband stricken by a sense of loss. Joyce shows superb mastery of atmosphere and the moment in creating a Christmas occasion of good cheer, lively gossip, music and dancing, culminating in evocations of past delights and long dead pleasures. Following this brilliantly achieved climax, the poignancy of Gretta's bleak memory and Gabriel's bitter realization brings both 'The Dead' and the whole collection to a sublime if melancholy conclusion. The exquisite finale (much influenced by Bret Harte's short story 'Gabriel Conroy') captures a sense of general despair – the snow-covered landscape mirroring also a man's desolation, his empty marriage and a nation rendered sterile by imperialism and suffocating religion.

> [S]now was general all over Ireland. It was falling on every part of the dark central plain, on the treeless hills, falling softly upon the Bog of Allen and, farther westward, softly falling into the dark mutinous Shannon waves. It was falling, too, upon every part of the lonely church-yard on the hill where Michael Furey lay buried. It lay thickly drifted on the crooked crosses and headstones, on the spears of the little gate, on the barren thorns. His soul swooned slowly as he heard the snow falling faintly through the universe and faintly falling, like the descent of their last end, upon all the living and the dead.[18]

This collection was a prelude to Joyce's 'moral history' of Ireland, with Dublin as its 'centre of paralysis' which he hoped might stir an indifferent public.

Two things now absorbed Joyce. One was *Stephen Hero* which he planned to rewrite and recast; the other was the Jewish religion to which many of his students belonged but of which they appeared to know little.

Reading Israel Zangwill's *Ghetto Tragedies* prompted him to draw parallels between the Irish and the Jews, a people with whom he found it easy to identify. One of his students, a Jewish convert to Catholicism, Ettore Schmitz, manager of a naval paint factory in Trieste, interested him greatly because of a shared interest in literature. He would find Schmitz an invaluable source of instruction about Jewish culture in creating the character and background of Leopold Bloom. When Jim was ill, Stannie took over his teaching duties, and Schmitz began to ply him with questions about *Irish* ways, saying that his brother asked him so many questions about Jewish life, he wanted to get even. James got to know the Schmitz family well, and the long hair of Ettore's wife Livia gave him the image for Anna Livia Plurabelle, the spirit of the River Liffey which flows through *Finnegans Wake*. When he read them his story 'The Dead' at their villa at Servola a few miles outside Trieste, Livia Schmitz presented him with a bunch of flowers. 'It was,' wrote Stanislaus, 'the first genuine and spontaneous sign of pleasure in the literary work of that outcast artist that I can recollect.'[19]

Artifoni eventually leased the Berlitz to two of the teachers, and paid for new suits for the Joyce brothers, which James thought might help if they had to take on private pupils.[20] In fact he did acquire a few fee-paying pupils – Prezioso, Sordina, and Romeo Bartoli, a teacher at the Trieste Conservatory and chorus-master at the Teatro Verdi, as well as the children of wealthy Triestine merchants. However, in certain quarters a reputation for drunkenness led to some young women being barred from his classes by anxious parents.

Out of the blue a letter arrived from Gogarty, regretting the loss of his old drinking partner and offering him 35 kroner and his return ticket to teach him German in Vienna where he was staying. Joyce, however, was able to resist the tempter's offer. It so happened that he had been thinking of Gogarty and other Dublin characters in developing the new story which now gripped him. 'Jim told me,' wrote Stanislaus, 'that he is going to expand his story "Ulysses" (a story set on a single day) into a short book and make a Dublin "Peer Gynt" of it.' *Hamlet* would also feature, and Faust contending for his soul with Mephistopheles. He would, he told Stanislaus, put everything he knew into it. The simple short-story idea conceived in Rome had acquired encyclopaedic proportions in Trieste. Stannie found the conception very impressive. 'It should be good,' he wrote. 'Jim says that he writes well because when he writes his mind is as nearly normal as possible, that what he says is worth listening to because he has an uncommon amount of good sense at times.'[21] By the end of December he was back at work on his novel which now began with young Dedalus going to school. But feeling unhappy after reading D'Annunzio's

The Triumph of Death, he dismissed *Stephen Hero* as 'the same old bag of tricks' following 'the same old grooves'.[22] It is significant that just as *Ulysses* was stirring in his imagination he was expressing dissatisfaction with conventional forms.

By the New Year, Lucia was already weaned, but Nora was still kept busy having to cope alone with one small baby and a very active and quarrelsome Giorgio. When James was not teaching or closeted with his novel he was out enjoying the rich café life of multicultural Trieste, arguing and debating with colleagues and drinking companions drawn by his magnetic personality. Often faced, on his return, with a drunken husband, Nora began to vent her frustration – about the misery of their impoverished existence and his selfish dissipation. She refused to cook for him, threatening to leave and to tell her family about his inability to provide for them, and, worst of all, to get Giorgio and Lucia baptized – something she knew would really nettle him. He responded by accusing her of turning his children against him.[23] In desperation, she took money from his pocket while he slept to pay urgent bills; he retaliated by giving her no money for lunch. Her final volley was to call him a 'Woman-killer'.

Feeling ever more despondent, Joyce was again suffering stomach pains, and at home the bickering became increasingly ill-tempered and petty. During one bitter exchange she snapped, 'Sure Cosgrave told me you were mad,' a remark which would come back to haunt him. His twenty-sixth birthday (2 February 1908) can hardly have been a day of gladsome celebration. However, following these domestic ructions and feeling that his health was under threat, he did try to reform, and in mid-February Stanislaus reported him keeping more regular hours, forswearing alcohol and working conscientiously at his novel. The book, in its rewritten form, would be more focused on the inner life of the hero under the new title *A Portrait of the Artist as a Young Man*. By the beginning of March he had finished Chapters One and Two (covering Stephen's early life, schooldays and fall from grace with the prostitute) and by April, Chapter Three (Stephen's remorse and the hellfire sermon) was completed.

The opening passage of the novel, representing the dawning consciousness of Stephen Dedalus, shows Joyce reaching towards the *monologue intérieur* – an early indication of the direction of his creative impulse. This major revision and re-conception had prompted him to start a new notebook devoted to characters and events from the life he wanted to recreate. In this process, much to the annoyance of Stanislaus, Stephen's brother Maurice was banished to the shadows. But if James was a reformed character, his attitude to the opposite sex seemed decidedly unreformed.

In April Stanislaus recorded that 'Jim's dislike for women has grown almost savage,' and decided that his misogyny was at the root of his very nature. It was, however, not a lasting or defining hatred and probably had more to do with the constraints of marriage and feelings of frustration over his work. It may also have been that he was simply indulging his mischievous impulse to shock. Publicly he was always respectful and courteous to the women he met.

That month, Elkin Mathews wrote to say that Joseph Hone, the business manager at the Dublin publishers Maunsel, had asked to see the manuscript of *Dubliners*. Joyce, who had a poor opinion of George Roberts (the editorial side of the company), was reluctant to agree, and asked for his stories back. He then tried Hutchinson, who rejected them unseen. Over the following year he also received rejections from Alston Rivers, Methuen, Greening & Co., Edward Arnold, Constable, and the London literary agent A. P. Watt. For him, Maunsel would be a last resort.

Jim and Nora were still quarrelling bitterly, and when, during Holy Week, he attended mass at the Church of St Antonio she wondered why he never went to confession, from which he might benefit. Stannie, the atheist, noted his brother's continuing fascination with religion, and suggested that by avoiding the confessional he retained the integrity of his unbelieving soul. It was, of course, the great intricate cathedral of the imagination represented by the Church that most entranced him – the ritual, the music, the ambience, and the drama rather than the superstition.

In July Nora discovered that she was again pregnant, which in her present state of discontent she found decidedly unwelcome. Joyce had other matters to divert him. With the help of one of his students, a lawyer, Nico Vidacovich, he was translating Synge's *Riders to the Sea* into Italian. He was also taking singing lessons again, this time with Romeo Bartoli, and allowed himself to be lured the following year into singing with a quintet '*Selig wie die Sonne*' from *Die Meistersinger* ('pretentious stuff,' he thought). Having somehow squeezed a piano into their rooms, he invited their friends for musical evenings at which he sang duets from Verdi with Clothilde Francini Bruni, and, if she could be persuaded, Nora would sing 'Dark Rosaleen'.

But the bright and tuneful atmosphere would soon darken and turn discordant. *Dubliners* was again rejected that July, and on 4 August Nora suffered a miscarriage. Stanislaus, increasingly fed up with living in such cramped quarters and infuriated about Jim's unpaid bills, decided to move out. Faced with the prospect of their rent doubling, Nora gave Stannie the cold shoulder. The tense atmosphere was hardly conducive to writing, and Joyce grumbled about what he called his 'truncated existence'. Trieste suddenly seemed to be bad luck for him and he considered moving to Florence or Milan to pursue a singing career. For a while in October he drowned his sorrows by attending eight consecutive performances of Puccini's *La Bohème*, and adding '*Che gelida manina*' ('Your tiny hand is frozen') to his repertoire.

Stanislaus, who had finally moved to 27 via Nuova, was openly scornful of his brother's musical ambitions. 'I take little interest,' he wrote, 'in the budding *tenorino* that has failed as a poet in Paris, as a journalist in Dublin, as a lover and novelist in Trieste, as a bank-clerk in Rome, and again in Trieste as a Sinn-Feiner, teacher, and University Professor.'[24] But Jim ignored his brother's disdain and, ironically, Stannie later took lessons himself with Bartoli, even though the maestro considered his singing 'disappointing'. Like his father, he considered Jim's elopement with Nora a sad error. His attitude to her was ambivalent. His diary suggests that he was greatly attracted to Nora, was pained by her indifference and reacted accordingly. After she had visited him alone one day, he wrote lamenting how some men could be made fools of by 'some totties', and ruin themselves for a thing they could get anywhere for tuppence and which was worth no more than tuppence anyway.[25] His attitude towards Nora would change over time as he came to see the important part she played in his brother's emotional and creative life.

With Charlie no longer at home, the remaining Joyces had become the targets of John's drunken spleen. Poppie wrote asking Stannie to return to look after them. Jim proposed that his brother should take Giorgio with him to Dublin for a six-week visit in the summer, hoping it would calm his father down and spread a little peace and light around Millmount Terrace. He reassured Poppie about his health. 'I feel a little better of the rheumatism and am now more like a capital S than a capital Z,' he wrote.[26]

The year 1909 would be an important and traumatic one for Joyce, challenging him once again as a writer, and enticing him back to the novel over which he had laboured so long and which he had come to neglect. But it took a moment of mutual discovery to galvanize him. In February, Ettore Schmitz, his student, mentioned to him shyly that he too was a writer and had published two novels under the pseudonym 'Italo Svevo'. These were *Una Vita* and *Senilità*, published ten years earlier. Joyce took them to read and was deeply impressed, telling him, 'Do you know that you are a neglected writer? There are passages in *Senilità* that even Anatole France could not have improved.' His words moved Schmitz almost to tears. From then on he talked to Joyce openly about his frustrated ambitions.[27] Joyce's enthusiasm had reignited his will to write, and he would soon embark on the novel that would bring him literary recognition.[28] His brother, said Stanislaus, was more than a teacher to Schmitz, he was 'an influence'.

That 'influence', however, had been undergoing his own crisis of confidence. With his disappointment over *Dubliners* and the feeling that readers would be put off by the hellfire passages in *A Portrait*, Joyce's inspiration had run out. He showed the first three chapters to Schmitz who disagreed with him about the sermons, saying that he knew many Triestines who would be greatly struck by them. 'Every word of these sermons acquires its artistic significance by the fact of their effect on poor Stephen's mind.' He did, however, object to the first chapter. 'I think it deals with events devoid of importance and your rigid method of observation and description does not allow you to enrich a fact which is not rich by itself. You should write only about strong things. In your skilled hands they may become still stronger. I do not believe you can give the appearance of strength to things which are in themselves trivial, not important.'[29] Schmitz's serious interest in his novel was sufficiently encouraging for Joyce to take it up again.

With his mind refocused on Dublin, it also became focused on Oscar Wilde when the Strauss opera of his controversial *Salomé* was performed in Trieste that March. *Piccolo* commissioned an article from him on the playwright and he produced an essay which said almost as much about himself as about Wilde. He began by reflecting on the name, Oscar Fingal O'Flahertie Wills Wilde, which implied descent from Fingal, King of the ferocious O'Flahertie clan. 'Like that savage tribe, he was to break the lance of his fluent paradoxes against the body of practical conventions, and to hear, as a dishonoured exile, the choir of the just recite his name together with that of the unclean.' The sentence rings strangely prophetic of Joyce himself – the exile already regarded as suspicious and morally tainted by many conventional Dubliners. Wilde, he wrote, again sounding strangely self-referential, 'grew up in an atmosphere of insecurity and prodigality'. He then got in a shot at the rabblement who threw stones at Wilde, quoting his comment in *The Picture of Dorian Gray* that the sins we perceive in Dorian are our own.[30] Finally he lamented a life which ended not only in public disgrace but with Wilde's conversion. He could identify with a genius betrayed; it was the prospect of grovelling recantation that he himself was determined to avoid. So engaged did he become with Wilde that he wrote to his literary executor, Robert Ross, asking permission to translate his *The Soul of Man under Socialism* into Italian. Unfortunately, no Italian publisher seemed interested in publishing it.

The revolutionary spirit was present in Trieste not just in the form of socialism but also in the new doctrine of futurism. In March 1909, Filippo

Tommaso Marinetti came to the city to unveil his Futurist Manifesto which declared that:

> Literature having up to now glorified thoughtful immobility, ecstasy and slumber, we wish to exalt the aggressive movement, the feverish insomnia, running, the perilous leap, the cuff and the blow ... We intend to glorify the love of danger, the custom of energy, the strength of daring. The essential elements of our poetry will be courage, audacity and revolt.[31]

Such iconoclasm was not without its appeal to Joyce. There were certain established conventions on which his ambitions depended – the conventions of publishing, the theatre, criticism and scholarship, for example – but where conventions of language and the novel form were concerned he would show himself to be a Marinetti in his own right.

By the end of March the Joyces had moved to 8 via Vincenzo Scussa, the 600 crowns deposit coming from several of his students, including Schmitz and a Greek fruit merchant, Nicolas Santos, whose well-endowed wife was yet another source for Molly Bloom. In anticipation of Giorgio's Dublin visit, Joyce sent a photograph of Nora and Lucia to his father. John was clearly impressed, and his attitude towards his son's 'miserable error' began to soften. Now living at 44 Fontenoy Street, he was in his usual financial plight and full of self-pity. Clearly thinking that Jim was on the rise, he sent him a desperate plea for help, saying, 'I feel certain I have seen my last Xmas.'[32] Jim and Stannie clubbed together to send what they could.

On 24 March, J. M. Synge, one of the few of his Irish contemporaries Joyce admired, died aged thirty-seven, a creative life cut short with so much left unwritten. Having published very little so far, Joyce was no doubt haunted by the prospect of meeting a similar fate. In April, he finally bowed to the inevitable and wrote to Joseph Hone asking whether Maunsel would be interested in *Dubliners*. The response was 'Yes', and later that month he sent him the manuscript which thereby fell into the hands of George Roberts, something he had previously declared 'unthinkable'. If Joyce had known the train of circumstances he had now set in motion he would never have posted it.

When, on 1 June, Dermot Chenevix Trench, the unstable, trigger-happy Anglo-Irish nationalist who had helped scare Joyce away from the Martello tower, shot himself, there was the sense that a chapter of Joyce's life had ended. The actors had dispersed. Gogarty had removed himself to a circle of upper-class respectability, and now another of his 'betrayers' was gone. That summer, having received a year's fees in advance from one of his students, he changed his plans and decided that *he* and not Stannie would take Giorgio to Ireland. It would prove to be a fateful decision. On 25 July, the exile, now ready to confront his past, set out with his son for Dublin.

15

The Exile's Return

(1909–1910)

'The ear of jealousy heareth all things.' Wisdom of Solomon

Disembarking at Kingstown Pier four days later, the first thing he saw was 'Gogarty's fat back' which he succeeded in avoiding. The newly qualified surgeon happened to be meeting someone else, but it must have seemed to Joyce an ominous sign of his past returning to haunt him.

The family welcoming party at Westland Row Station were expecting Stannie and were surprised to see Jim. Giorgio was an instant favourite with his grandfather and with the Joyce sisters, especially Poppie, now a nun called Sister Mary. Aunt Josephine declared that Jim had lost all his boyishness, Eileen thought him very foreign-looking. His father urged him to move somewhere nearer home and took him off to a country pub with a piano. There he sat down and sang the aria which Alfredo's father sings to his son in *Traviata* – a song of remorse for opposing his love for Violetta. 'Don't torture me more ... My soul is too eaten by remorse ... Ah, foolish old man! Only now I see the harm I did.' Peace between them was thus restored. Back at the family home, now in Fontenoy Street, John, the patriarch, surveyed his children and first grandchild and, indicating the portraits of his grandparents and father, declared proudly, 'We have five generations in this room' – a good excuse for a toast.

Venturing into town, Joyce began to encounter old friends and betrayers. Russell told him that he looked 'like a man of business', Eglinton that he looked 'very ecclesiastical', Cosgrave that he looked 'in splendid health', while Gogarty, struck by his gaunt appearance, declared, 'Jaysus, man, you're in phthisis.' Meeting the Sheehy-Skeffingtons, Hanna pronounced him 'not a bit changed' while 'Knickerbockers' (Francis) thought him 'somewhat blasé'. All said he looked 'melancholy'. Only Curran, he told Stanislaus, seemed 'ugly' and ill-disposed towards him. He tried to contact Joseph Hone at Maunsel, but he was away and George Roberts said he was rarely in touch with him. Nevertheless he was still hopeful of getting a contract from them for *Dubliners*.

Gogarty recalled that he invited Joyce to lunch at the Dolphin in Essex Street, then had to cry off in order to see a patient. When, later, Joyce visited his home in Ely Place, he sat looking out of the window in silence for some time before saying, 'Is this your revenge?' and leaving.[1] The version Joyce gave Stanislaus was that he and Gogarty had passed each other in Merrion Square, and Gogarty, realizing who he was, ran back, buttonholed him, and, rambling on at him in a confused way, insisted that he go to his house. The atmosphere between them, however, was far from relaxed. To everything Gogarty said, he replied, 'You have your life. Leave me to mine.' Gogarty then invited Joyce to motor with him and his wife to Enniskerry for lunch, but he declined. He offered Joyce drinks which he also declined. Finally, he said, 'Well do you really want me to go to hell and be damned?' to which Joyce replied, 'I bear you no illwill. I believe you have some points of good nature. You and I of 6 years ago are both dead. But I must write as I have felt.' According to Joyce, Gogarty then said '"I don't care a damn what you say of me so long as it is literature." I said "Do you mean that?" He said "I do. Honest to Jaysus. Now will you shake hands with me at least?" I said "I will: on that understanding."'[2] They never met again.

His worst encounter was a second meeting with Cosgrave who informed him mischievously that he too had gone for long walks down by the river after dark with Nora (on nights she had told Joyce she was working), implying some sort of clandestine intimacy. Joyce was devastated and rushed home to write an impassioned letter to Nora in Trieste, putting the allegation to her. Had she gone with 'a friend of mine' on the same route along the canal and down by the Dodder and shared her favours with him in between their own evenings together? He seemed convinced that she had broken faith with him. Was it all over between them? She must write and put him out of his misery. This he followed up with another dawning horror. Was Giorgio his son? There had been little blood when they first made love. Had she lain down with his 'friend' on the river bank? His fond memories of her were shattered. 'How old and miserable I feel,' he wrote. He would not take Giorgio to Galway but would return to Trieste as soon as Stannie could send the fare.

The following day, still in despair, he visited Byrne, now living at 7 Eccles Street where he broke down. 'I had never before seen anything to approach the frightening condition that convulsed him,' recalled Byrne. 'He wept and groaned and gesticulated in futile impotence.' Byrne calmed him down by saying that Cosgrave was out to cause trouble and that what he had said about Nora was 'a blasted lie', probably cooked up by Gogarty and company. He insisted that Joyce stay for lunch and dinner, and also overnight. Next day, after breakfast, Joyce set off cheerfully, returning that afternoon with a gold chain with five pieces of ivory attached – a present, he said, for Nora. 'Beautiful,' said Byrne, 'one ivory for every year you've been with her.' Joyce was delighted, saying he hadn't thought of that but now he would add one to it every year.[3]

There was no reply from Nora to his frantic letters of accusation, and he did not immediately write to tell her that he had been wrong about Cosgrave. If he had hoped she would reply to his charges and questions he was to be disappointed. The haunting prospect of being deceived by Nora, however, had again excited his imagination and would be explored in depth later in his play *Exiles*. He returned to Eccles Street for supper and asked Byrne to retrace with him their walks around Dublin. They spent the night walking the city streets. Their perambulation ended outside a chemist's shop where there was a weighing machine and Joyce suggested they weigh themselves. Back in Eccles Street Byrne found he had left his key inside. To avoid waking others in the house, he climbed the railings and dropped into the basement area, effecting an entrance that way. The incident stayed with Joyce and was duly inserted, weighing machine and all, into *Ulysses*, where 7 Eccles Street becomes the home of Leopold and Molly Bloom – scene of her repeated adultery with Blazes Boylan.

Now enjoying the Triestine title of 'Professor' he decided to apply to his old college (part of the new National University of Ireland) for their Chair of Italian, after obtaining promises of testimonials from Prezioso, Trieste's Università del Popolo, the bank in Rome and his old friend Tom Kettle. Unfortunately, enquiry revealed there would be no professorship of Italian at the newly constituted University College, just a lectureship for evening classes. What he did succeed in doing, however, was to give the impression in Dublin that he was more qualified than he really was. Writing of Joyce in his diary, Joseph Holloway, the Dublin diarist, noted, 'He got high honours in Italian in the University before he left Ireland.'

He finally made contact with George Roberts, the man at Maunsel, he had heard, who made the final decisions. Roberts told him that *Dubliners* was unlikely to make much money and Joyce then offered to cover part of the costs if a royalty were paid to him from the outset. Roberts promised to review the situation, and on 16 August he received Maunsel's draft contract offering royalties five per cent higher than those proposed by Grant Richards. If all went to plan the book would be published the following spring. On the 19th, the agreement was signed and returned to Roberts.

In a mood of euphoria, and perhaps hoping to make Nora feel less lonely, he announced that his seventeen-year-old sister Eva would be returning with him to Trieste. She had always rather worshipped her older brother and would not have taken much persuading to join him. A camp bed would have to be found and she could have Stannie's old room to share with Giorgio.[4] Then, after two weeks with still no reply to his accusations from Nora (and doubtless having made her miserable by delaying matters), he finally wrote her a letter of grovelling contrition. 'My sweet noble Nora, I ask you to forgive me for my contemptible conduct but they maddened me, darling between them. We will defeat their cowardly plot, love ... Just say a word to me, dearest, a word of denial and O I shall be so transported with happiness!'[5] Two days later she wrote telling him that Stannie was being very kind to her during this time, and she was looking forward to Eva joining them. She was also, she said, reading *Chamber Music*. He immediately began wooing her, telling her that she had been his 'dream muse' while writing the poems. But now he worried that he might learn something about her in Galway that would make him even more jealous of her past loves. Betrayal, the ever-recurrent theme, both terrified and excited him. In both *Exiles* and *Ulysses* he would plumb the depths of his insecurity about Nora as he had already done in his story 'The Dead'. The insecurity of Gabriel Conroy was his own.

By late August he was becoming sick of Dublin. Away from Nora his desire for her had grown intense, almost violent. 'I will not write on this page what fills my mind, the very madness of desire. I see you in a hundred poses, grotesque, shameful, virginal, languorous. Give yourself to me, dearest, all, all when we meet. All that is holy, hidden from others, you must give to me freely.' He hinted that he would like her to write to him privately a letter to match his desire for mutual debauchery with himself in command. 'I wish,' he wrote, 'to be lord of your body and soul.' He reminded her of the three words he had used to describe her body in 'The Dead', 'musical and strange and perfumed', and he urged her to prepare herself for his return.[6]

His offer to interview the Italian tenor Caruso, then in Dublin, and to review the Abbey première of Shaw's *The Shewing-Up of Blanco Posnet*, banned in England, was rejected by several English papers. But finally *Piccolo* commissioned him to cover the play, so now he could present himself to the Abbey crowd as a drama critic for a reputable Italian newspaper. As a reviewer, the theatre manager, William Henderson, reserved a seat for him and he had a press card printed saying '*Piccolo della Sera*, Trieste'. He also claimed to be in touch with Synge's brother over his Italian translation of *Riders to the Sea*, but publication rights were refused. Then, card in hand, he presented himself to the manager of the

Midland Railway as an important foreign correspondent writing travel articles on Ireland and extracted free tickets to Galway for himself and Giorgio.

Although anxious to leave Dublin, he had to see the Shaw play first and could not resist taking in *The Playboy of the Western World*, also playing at the Abbey. There, during the interval, he met the diarist Joseph Holloway who thought this once 'sneering youth' 'much improved'.[7] The following night, 25 August, hoping for some Abbey 'fireworks', Joyce donned his critic's cap for the Shaw première which left everyone puzzled as to why the play was banned in England. Joyce dashed off his notice for *Il Piccolo* and mailed it to Stanislaus, asking him to check it before passing it on to the paper. Although he thought it 'a crude melodrama' and the art 'too poor to make convincing drama', he questioned whether there might be 'a crisis in the mind of this writer', and 'some divine finger has touched his brain'.[8]

Next morning he and Giorgio travelled to Galway to stay overnight with Nora's mother at Bowling Green. She had long reconciled herself to her daughter's elopement, and she and Nora exchanged letters regularly. Annie Barnacle and her 'son-in-law' got on well and she sang him 'The Lass of Aughrim', the sad song of seduction and betrayal which in 'The Dead' prompts Gretta Conroy to relive her tragic parting with the doomed Michael Furey. The song moved him to tears. They talked about Nora and he met her sisters Dilly (whose name he gave to Stephen's sister in *Ulysses*), and Kathleen (with whom, walking on the beach, he talked about 'taking lessons' from the sounds of the sea). Meanwhile, Giorgio was the centre of much attention from all the women. At the house where Nora had lived with her grandmother, he posed as a prospective buyer in order to get a glimpse of the room she had slept in. He also visited her uncle, Michael Healy, who had always taken a close interest in him and occasionally sent him money.

Back in Dublin he wrote urging Stannie to send money immediately, telling him to tap his best student for it. To Nora he wrote another passionate letter, declaring his undying love and expressing his hopes for the future: 'I would wish you to be surrounded by everything that is fine and beautiful and noble in art. You are not, as you say, a poor uneducated girl. You are my bride, darling, and all I can give you of pleasure and joy in this life I wish to give you.' Nothing, not even their children, he said, would ever come between them. If coarse words offended her they also offended him, but he then told her how he would like to kiss her in an unmentionable place.[9]

Despite having written about being offended by coarse language he immediately penned her a letter so indecent that next day he felt ashamed.

He quickly wrote excusing himself, saying that he felt in an impossible situation away from her and implying that he had not found himself universally welcomed in the town which had so inspired his imagination in far-away Trieste. 'Dublin is a detestable city and the people are most repulsive to me.' He felt drained and incapable of writing, he told her, before switching from self-disgust to unconcealed lust, launching into a masochistic fantasy of being flogged by her, and recalling a night of shared abandon in Pola. 'Are you too, then,' he asked her, 'like me, one moment high as the stars, the next lower than the lowest wretches?' She, he saw, as 'a powerful simple soul' acknowledging the power she had over him.[10] For him she was both worshipful Madonna and licentious Circe.

He had a brown leather case made for the necklet of ivory cubes with a card written in gold ink saying simply: 'Nora 1904–1909'. It contained a small tablet of yellow ivory, engraved on one side in fourteenth-century-style type, with 'Love is unhappy' and on the other with 'When love is away', taken from the last line of the ninth poem in *Chamber Music*. The five dice, he explained meant 'the five years of trial and misunderstanding'; the tablet signified 'the strange sadness we felt and our suffering when we were divided'.[11]

Stannie had sent £3 5s 0d, but was told that £12 was needed to cover Eva's travelling expenses. He sent a further £4 which, Joyce said, would cover him and Giorgio, but he required an additional £2 for Eva, who would cost very little anyway and would spare him having to hire a servant. His motive in inviting her to Trieste, it seems, was somewhat less than brotherly.

Tom Kettle was to marry Mary Sheehy, and on 5 September he and Joyce spent four hours talking together. Joyce hoped they would spend some days of their honeymoon with him and Nora in Trieste. Once again, with things looking up, he was 'high as the stars', he said. More good cheer was to follow. 'Tonight,' he told Nora, 'I was in the Gresham Hotel and was introduced to about twenty people and to all of them the same story was told: that I was going to be the great writer of the future in my country. All the noise and flattery around me hardly moved me.'[12] It was, after all, a reputation based on hardly anything published.

Then, worried at Nora's silence, he feared she might have found his lustful letters offensive. 'Some of it is ugly, obscene and bestial, some of it is pure and holy and spiritual: all of it is myself,' he told her, but they showed the intensity of his love and desire for her. He went on to imagine his return and to dwell upon the 'naughty' sensuous body that awaited him. Love, he told her, was a curse, especially when coupled with lust.[13] They were letters Leopold Bloom might have written to the flirtatious

Martha Clifford, and letters Bloom would have enjoyed reading himself. He told both Nora and Stannie that his nerves were shattered and not to worry him about debts he had run up. He wanted his homecoming to be a happy one.

When the issue of *Piccolo della Sera* carrying his review arrived from Trieste he showed it proudly to Holloway and Henderson, to whom he also gave the manuscript of his Italian version of *Riders to the Sea*. His plan, he told them, was to spread the word about the Irish. He was delighted when the *Freeman's Journal* and the *Evening Telegraph* reported his *Piccolo* review, and told Stanislaus to make sure that Ettore Schmitz saw copies.

Finally, on 9 September, having wrung a £3 advance from Maunsel & Co., Joyce, Eva and Giorgio embarked for Trieste. Stanislaus received a telegram announcing their impending arrival. It also informed him that he, Stannie, would be sharing the cost of singing lessons for Eileen on top of subsidizing the rent, fares and presents for Nora. Using his press pass, he wangled first-class tickets from Holyhead to London.[14] It took a five-day trek across Europe for the weary travellers to reach Trieste, and not unusually Joyce arrived back completely broke. However, he brought back one important thing – material for his play, *Exiles*, a story of paranoia, supposed treachery and betrayal, with, he claimed later, similarities to Swift's relationship with Stella and Vanessa.[15]

Their reunion burned itself into his memory and later he recalled the pleasure of his first glimpse of Nora on his return to the via Vincenzo Scussa: 'I see you in the corridor, looking young and girlish in your grey dress and blue blouse and hear your strange cry of welcome.'[16] That night, she came to bed as he lay asleep, her hair down and wearing a chemise with blue ribbons. Afterwards they had what he called 'nice talks together' in which they spoke more openly than before about their feelings for each other. It was an ecstatic reminder of the honeymoon he still dreamt of having.

Jim and Nora's 'lovers' reunion' sickened the unromantic Stanislaus who had received few thanks for taking on his brother's teaching load, supporting him financially in Dublin and caring for his family during his absence. For Eva, her first trip away from Ireland was a great culture shock. She was a pious and naive young woman and already somewhat disturbed by her brother's apostasy. The life and values of Trieste were far removed from life at home, and what suited her brothers was alien to her nature. There were political arguments at breakfast-time, dinners at trattorias and, above all, visits to cinemas. She was homesick from the start.

A chance remark from her about the absence of cinemas in Dublin gave Joyce an idea. He would open one himself. The idea failed to excite

Stanislaus who knew he would be left to look after Nora, settle bills recklessly incurred by his absent brother and expected to take over his teaching. Nor did Nora relish the idea of again becoming a grass widow while her husband lived well off others in the city she had not seen for five years.

Without funds he would need backers. He had no difficulty finding partners for his project among a group of Triestine businessmen, acquaintances of his friend Vidacovich who had already financed cinemas in Trieste and Bucharest: an upholsterer Antonio Machnich, a leather merchant Giovanni Rebez, a draper Giuseppe Caris and a bicycle-shop owner Francesco Novak. Joyce persuaded these men that opening a cinema in Dublin offered a great business opportunity, and they should send him there as their agent to make preliminary arrangements in acquiring the necessary premises. They agreed to send Joyce on this mission, covering all travelling costs (500 crowns from Rebez), and to pay him 10 crowns a day expenses. In return he would earn 10 per cent of the profits. The cinema would be called the Volta after Alessandro Volta, the Italian inventor of the electric cell, whose name would figure in the 'Cyclops' episode of *Ulysses* in the company of Dick Turpin and Buddha.

A contract with Joyce was signed, and on 18 October he prepared to leave again for Ireland. A few days before he left, while he and Nora were out shopping in the via Stadion, they passed a priest and Joyce said, 'Do you not find a kind of repulsion or disgust at the sight of one of those men?' to which Nora replied, 'No, I don't,' a rebuff which he found particularly hurtful. When he took her to see *Madame Butterfly*, hoping to share the delicacy and beauty of the music with her, she was rude to him. Another night, when he was wanting to share with her his hopes and dreams about his writing, she did not want to know.[17] On his departure, her parting shot was 'Imbecile!' His last memory of her, as the train pulled out of Trieste, was of her turning her head 'in grief with ... a strange posture of helplessness'.[18] He would be away for two and a half months. The honeymoon was postponed indefinitely.

He arrived in Dublin on 21 October, this time well shod and well dressed and with a good wad of money in his pocket, and got to work immediately. On his first day he viewed three likely premises for the cinema and made an appointment to see the city's theatre inspector about a licence to show films. Trudging the streets and having to deal with 'ordinary people' rekindled his old disdain for the rabblement. 'I feel the day all wasted here among the common Dublin people whom I hate and despise,' he told Nora.[19]

Her stinging farewell still rankled and for a time he refrained from writing. Then he received a letter from her asking if he had tired of her, to be deserting her so soon after their reunion. He quickly replied assuring her that he would never tire of her (his 'strange little love', his 'little bad-tempered bad-mannered splendid little girl') if she 'would only be a little more polite' and not use insulting language to him again. She had him captive, but if she was fretful and moody she would spoil his chances of doing *anything*. He conjured up images of handsome profits from his cinema project, and said he was planning to buy her a sable fur cap, stole, and muff. 'I *know* and *feel* that if I am to write anything fine or noble in the future I shall do so only by listening at the doors of your heart.' He needed her to be brave and support him in his work, and hoped that she would write him 'a nice letter'.[20]

His yearning for his young wife had again begun to engulf him. Any pleasure he had in returning to Dublin, he told her, had quickly palled, and even a trip to the theatre with his father and Eileen left him feeling disgruntled – 'a wretched play' and a 'disgusting audience'. And, as always, he felt a stranger in his own country. The Sheehys were snubbing him, his relations with Tom Kettle were, for some reason, strained, and when people stared at him in the streets, he felt sure they sensed his hatred of them – 'I see nothing on every side of me but the image of the adulterous priest and his servants and of sly deceitful women.' He was, he admitted, 'a jealous, lonely, dissatisfied, proud man'.[21] That loneliness may have led him to pick up another infection – what he referred to as 'that damned dirty affair of mine' – perhaps after encountering one of those 'sly deceitful women' who, he told Nora, lurked around Nighttown. Not surprisingly, perhaps, after confessing this he heard nothing from her for a while.

Although suddenly stricken with sciatica, it did not take him long to find a likely location for his cinema, at 45 Mary Street – a shop with a large warehouse at the rear, not far from busy Sackville Street. Anxious not to lose it, he wrote suggesting that one of his partners, Machnich, should come to inspect it. While awaiting his arrival, he cast around for other business opportunities, thinking again about selling Irish tweeds and of importing fireworks into Ireland.

Joyce was determined to impress those who had spurned him as a lost cause before he left Dublin. Encountering another of his old acquaintances, Richard Best, at Bewley's café, he asked if he would be working at the National Library that evening. Best said he would finish at 10 p.m., so Joyce met him there at closing time, then walked home with him. But rather than reliving past walks together, Best found him uncommunicative, saying little more than 'Huh huh' whenever he expressed an opinion. Arriving at his door, he invited Joyce inside, but he declined. Instead, as Best recalled, 'With a very decisive gesture ... Joyce took out his wallet and waved it in front of me with about a hundred pounds in it.' He said nothing and then walked off. Best took this to refer to his once having refused to lend him ten shillings, and as an indication that he was no longer needed.[22]

Writing to Nora, his 'dear little Butterfly', he reassured her that, unlike Cio Cio San, she had not been deserted. He sent her a pair of reindeer-skin gloves and twelve yards of Donegal tweed with directions about what sort of dress to make with it – a long skirt 'collared, belted and cuffed with dark blue leather and lined with bronze or dark blue satin'. His passion for her and the prospect of making money had aroused a desire to dress her up, and now he had a set of squirrel furs in mind for her. But he still wanted her to value him for his writing. He had had sheets of parchment cut specially and was copying all the *Chamber Music* poems on to them in indelible Indian ink. These he planned to have bound for her 'in a curious way', so that she would have the only copy of its kind.[23] That 'curious way' meant having the Joyce family crest bound into it. He wrote asking Stanislaus to send his copy of it to the binder. Finally, the gloves did the trick and the silence from Nora was broken. In a burst of comic irony (recalling his first present to her) she replied, as if from Finn's Hotel, hoping to see him soon but unable because of work to get away immediately.

Meeting George Roberts, he extracted a promise that he would soon be seeing the proofs of *Dubliners*, and, having heard that Herbert Hughes, a Belfast composer, wanted to put some of his *Chamber Music* poems to music, he suggested that Maunsel might also consider publishing Moly-neux Palmer's settings. Pursuing his cinema project, he managed to per-suade the landlord of 45 Mary Street to agree to a three-year lease on the property, sending news of this to his partners in Trieste and leaving them to close the deal. By 18 November plans for the cinema were to go before the Council and a licence to operate would, he felt sure, follow automatically. Machnich, finally convinced that Joyce was getting some-where, agreed to travel to Dublin with their fellow partner, Rebez, to help get the show on the road.

But other problems were about to beset him. The Joyce family was still disintegrating and still suffering the consequences of John's profligacy. He was in hospital with an eye infection (conjunctivitis and iritis); Charlie, having made a girl pregnant and been forced into a shotgun marriage, was now destitute and out of work in America, and Poppie, the nun, was about to leave for New Zealand. In an attempt to help out, Jim now suggested that Eileen return with him to join Eva in Trieste. As Stanislaus had fallen silent, he wrote urging him to take his singing lessons with Bartoli seriously, and asking for the money he needed to buy squirrel furs for Nora. All he received in reply was a telegram announcing that their landlord at via Vincenzo Scussa had issued a writ for non-payment of two months' rent. Shaken at the prospect of Nora and the children being put out on the street, he sent 20 crowns, telling Stannie to ask Vidacovich for 32 crowns for business expenses and to pay the landlord one month's back rent, with a promise of double rent in December. Eviction must be prevented at all costs. Meanwhile, a notice to quit 44 Fontenoy Street had been served on John, and there was the prospect of the family being roofless for Christmas.

To add to his sense of helplessness, Joyce received a 'sad and scornful' letter from Nora, no doubt prompted by the desperate financial situation in which he had left her and the children. To her, a man who could not support his family was beneath contempt. Crushed by the scathing tone of her letter, his reply was one of cringing self-mortification. He had not slept for two days and nights, he told her, advising her to get herself and the children away from his evil influence, and make a new life for themselves. 'It is wrong for you to live with a vile beast like me or to allow your children to be touched by my hands.' There was no affectionate greeting or signature to his letter, he wrote, because his endearments would not be welcome and the sight of his name would disgust her.[24] After receiving two more kindly and emollient letters from her a day later, Joyce went to Finn's Hotel, visited Nora's old bedroom and wept. After dining there, he sat at the table and wrote to her, sobbing as he did so. Still unable to bring himself to open with any greeting, he referred to her throughout in the third person — this 'foolish-hearted' Galway girl who had such power over him and whose eyes were 'like strange beautiful blue wild-flowers growing in some tangled, rain-drenched hedge', a phrase Robert Hand would use about Bertha in *Exiles*. When she wrote again he felt somewhat reassured and even began to hope they could exchange more intimate letters of the sort he craved. For now he just ventured a few comments about her underwear. 'I wish you had a great store of all kinds of underclothes, in all delicate shades, stored away in a great perfumed press.'[25]

Once Machnich and Rebez had arrived in Dublin and were installed at Finn's, Machnich sent off sufficient funds to Trieste to ensure that Joyce's rent was paid. The Mary Street premises passed muster and he undertook to help them look for suitable sites in other cities around Ireland. Novak was to be brought in to manage the new cinema, together with a skilled Triestine film projectionist and some Italian carpenters to help with the conversion. Padraic Colum, who met Joyce at the time, was impressed by the air of authority he exuded in ordering the workmen around in fluent Italian, but, as Mary Street was something of a slum, he doubted that the cinema would succeed. Some were sceptical about the Italians. John Joyce found Machnich, a bearded character in a fur coat, amusing and dubbed him 'the hairy Mechanic in the lion-tamer's overcoat'. At the end of November Joyce and his partners headed for Belfast looking for more cinema sites.

Three days later he was back at Fontenoy Street writing the first of a series of explicit and revealing pornographic letters to Nora. On his earlier forays to Monto, excited by a sense of unforgivable sinfulness evoked by hellfire sermonizing, he had acquired a taste for extreme forms of sexual debauchery, including excremental fetishes and sado-masochistic practices, acted out with a running commentary of obscene cries and whispers. The letters shed considerable light on what bound James to Nora – her toleration of his four-letter excesses and overt lechery, and eagerness to share in his more deviant sexual fantasies. Unable to allay his jealousy, he began questioning her about her sexual contacts with Michael Bodkin, with a man at Finn's who had fancied her, and about Cosgrave. Where did they touch her? Where did she touch them? How far did they go? How far did she go? When, honestly and truly, *was* the first time for her? Rather than torturing himself, he had now become excited by thoughts that she *had* done secret things with others, and was inviting her to share in his fantasy of betrayal. If she had done these things and confessed all to him, it might well bind them closer together, he assured her in gloating anticipation of some salacious response to his questions.

The language of abandonment and obscene fantasy clearly anticipates the absurd theatre of Bella Cohen's whorehouse in the 'Circe' episode of *Ulysses*, not to mention the 'Penelope' episode starring Molly Bloom. Now she was his 'Dear little fuckbird', his 'darling little convent girl', his 'sweet little whorish Nora'. When she wrote telling him that she could not afford any new underwear and was walking around without any, it only served to set him off again.

These bizarre and crudely licentious letters always ended in the flowery language of his most delicate love poems. How, he asked Nora, could she possibly love this wretched man who was intent on degrading and depraving her? She delighted him by replying in like terms (worse than his, he told her) and he rose to the occasion, stimulating himself to orgasm and urging her on to ever greater excesses. Always feeling half-guilty about what he had written, he pleaded with her to keep the letters secret and worried that they might excite her so much that she would find some other, more convenient lover.

Following that outpouring and with all lustful passion spent, James's subsequent letters returned to a more romantic, even mawkish, register, recalling in minute detail his reactions on finding himself in her room at Finn's – the sight of her bed, 'the four little walls', 'the little curtains' she had drawn at night, the thought of her undressing there. He would never leave her again, he vowed. Then he again reverted to sexual fantasy, this time a masochistic one. She could punish him as much as she liked and he would thrill to the tingle of her hand. Flog him, he pleaded, capturing the style and flavour suggestive of high Victorian pornography. Continuing in the same vein, his expressions of lust turned ever more excremental, and, fearing that he had lit an unquenchable fire in his young 'wife', he assured her that she could have him as much as she liked and in all sorts of positions when he returned. But at one point he worried that he might have reactivated his 'little problem' ('that cursed thing') by exciting and then satisfying himself so much.[26]

In early December projection equipment was being imported from London. By the 17th the Volta was ready to open its doors. By now Joyce's ostentatious display of wealth had attracted spongers, including, unsurprisingly, his father, anxious for handouts and loans. He didn't disappoint them, he told Stanislaus, because he was thinking of his book.[27] He escaped his family for a day in Cork looking for sites for other Voltas, but without success.

On Saturday 20 December, the cinema finally opened, and with a music licence applied for, Joyce planned to be home in Trieste for New Year's Day. These events did not interrupt the flow of erotic letters and he celebrated the opening day by penning one of his fantasies about accessing Nora's underwear and stimulating her to orgasm with onanistic and coprophilic imagery. For Christmas he sent her his newly bound, crested copy of *Chamber Music* with their initials, 'J' and 'N', intertwined on the cover, which, he told her, had cost him a great deal. Journeying home to her was now very much on his mind. Every station and especially the sight of the Miramar and the long quays of Trieste, would bring him closer to his 'soul's peace'. 'I am a poor impulsive sinful generous selfish jealous dissatisfied kind-natured poet but I am not a bad deceitful person. Try to shelter me, dearest, from the storms of the world.'[28] He borrowed 24 crowns from Rebez to send to her.

On Christmas Eve he reported a bustling crowd queuing outside the cinema needing a policeman to control them. To his amazement the constable had known Nora in Galway, 'a handsome girl with curls and a proud walk', he said, and inevitably Joyce felt a stab of jealousy at the thought.[29] Five days later, on 28 December, a letter was sent to Stanislaus from their sister Mabel bearing the ominous message, 'Jim is ill with his eyes.'[30] He had been struck down, like his father, with conjunctivitis. Finally, after more than six weeks away, on 2 January

1910 Joyce set off with Eileen for Trieste. He arrived, so he claimed, with 'black bandages over both my eyes', but with notes and sketches to be woven into *A Portrait* which would consume much of his attention from then onwards.

16

Portrait of the Artist in Retrospect
(1910–1912)

'It is dangerous to abandon one's own country but it is more dangerous still to return to it, for then your fellow countrymen, if they can, will drive a knife into your heart.' Joyce to Italo Svevo

When the weather improved in Dublin in late February 1910, the queues at the Volta grew and the business began to flourish. 'House Full' notices were often posted outside. But then, according to William D'Arcy, prompted by the Church, a boycott targeting the cinema was launched – queues were picketed and a whispering campaign began, aimed at ridding Dublin of this evil influence on the minds of the faithful. Women would approach those queuing, ask if they were Catholics, and, if so, tell them that going to the cinema was 'a sin'. D'Arcy claimed that he saw one queue of around a hundred melt down to fifty after the women had worked along the line. But once inside there were wonders to behold. D'Arcy was full of admiration for the conversion work, recalling a large white sign above the entrance with bold red letters announcing 'Volta Picture Theatre', a stained wooden floor with carpet down the centre aisle, two hundred Windsor chairs for top-price customers, deep-cream-painted walls, lights with fancy shades and palms in tubs around the 'orchestra' enclosure – 'the most elegant hall in Dublin', it was claimed. The films shown were mostly French and Italian imports, and included *The First Paris Orphanage*, *La Pouponnière*, *Nero – a Sensational Dramatic Story of Ancient Rome*, and *Manœuvres of the Italian Navy in the Mediterranean*.

After Joyce's departure, the Volta staggered on until June. Then, having sustained losses of £1,600, the partners, never comfortable with the language of the people or the climate of the city, sold it at a loss of £600 to Provincial Cinema Theatres, a London company which ran it as a cinema until it closed in 1948. Despite its failure, Joyce's association with it has ensured the Volta a place in the history books of both Ireland and Irish literature.

The 'conjunctivitis' turned out to be iritis (inflamed iris), accompanied on this occasion by arthritis of the right arm, and Joyce was ordered to rest for a month. Confined indoors, he could spend more time with his children – Giorgio now four and a half and Lucia two years younger – singing his daughter to sleep with a lullaby he had composed for her: '*C'era una volta, una bella bambina/Che si chiamava Lucia.*' She was, says her biographer, her father's 'first siren'.[1] Eva and Eileen also made much of the children, entertaining them and taking them to cinemas.

The devout sisters only now discovered to their dismay that Jim and Nora were unmarried, and their children unbaptized. If and when Jim did attend, as he usually did in Holy Week, it was merely for the liturgy and music and he made a point of sitting well apart from his sisters. As true daughters of their Church, they were scandalized by their brother's irregular, unobservant life, especially Eva who was finding adjusting to the exotic atmosphere of freewheeling Trieste very difficult. Eileen, however, was soon at ease with the city. Later she recalled: 'Those were the happiest years in my life ... I did most of the housekeeping ... they were an awfully happy couple ... Jim was so devoted to her ... they had their rows of course ... she was always at him to teach more and spend less time at "the silly writing" and earn some money.'[2]

Suddenly beset by creditors, on 12 February Joyce wrote to Stanislaus in desperation saying that until he started teaching again the following week he had no money. But Stannie was slow to respond, preferring to stay away from the expanded ménage following rows with Eva and Nora, and fed up with being made use of by his brother. A month later the situation was still perilous and Joyce's piano, on hire-purchase as usual, was threatened with seizure. Pleading once again for help, he reminded Stannie that he had agreed to share the expense of having their sisters in Trieste, and begged him to avoid the constant rows between them over money which only added to his many other worries. Sometimes when playing the imperilled piano, unable to keep creditors from his door, he would invite them inside and charm them with talk about music or politics before sending them away empty-handed and returning to the piano.[3]

But his literary prospects were again looking better. George Roberts of Maunsel had sent word that proofs of *Dubliners* were expected shortly. Work on his novel could now recommence. In his notebook he had continued recollecting, rehearsing and reflecting upon his own life, penning character sketches, rehearsing encounters and recreating dialogue. Eileen recalled how he worked.

He wrote at night mostly, and he lay always across the bed on his stomach when he wrote. He had a huge blue pencil, like a carpenter's pencil, and a white coat on to reflect on the paper because his sight was so bad. He always wrote with a white coat on – it gave a kind of white light.[4]

However, things were not as bright on the Maunsel front as Roberts suggested. He did not send a full set of proofs but simply those of 'Ivy Day in the Committee Room', asking for changes to passages referring to Edward VII as 'this chap come to the throne after his bloody old bitch of a mother keeping him out of it till the man was grey', and 'an ordinary knockabout like you and me ... fond of his glass of grog and ... a bit of a rake'.[5] Joyce agreed to revise the passages but returned the proofs having merely substituted 'old mother' for 'old bitch of a mother'. When, in June, a dissatisfied Roberts asked him to rewrite the whole passage Joyce declined on the grounds that there had been no objection to this story from Grant Richards or his printer, even when the recently deceased King Edward had been alive. After that, for some time Roberts fell silent.

In the midst of all this he heard that, with the Volta sold, he would not receive his expected 10 per cent of the proceeds. Ettore Schmitz, who met Joyce at the time, saw for himself how cheated and betrayed he felt. 'I remembered your face so startled by such wickedness,' he wrote.[6] The fact that Joyce seemed surprised by his partners' chicanery, he observed, was a mark of true literary character. A mere businessman would have accepted such a thing as normal.

But this 'true literary character' still needed to earn a living in Trieste, which meant teaching. As recalled by colleagues and students, Joyce cut a bizarre and almost pathetic figure at this time. Francini remembered him as 'skinny as an underdeveloped capon, cowardly, and in poor physical shape';[7] Benco at *Il Piccolo*, described him as 'an overgrown schoolboy who had developed too rapidly'.[8] As a teacher he was not always punctual or well prepared, preferring impromptu conversations rather than slavishly following Berlitz-style formulae as once required to do. Occasionally he would read from his own work and his students were all familiar with *Chamber Music*, of which many had bought copies. As Maurice Furlan recalled, 'His lessons were – at least where I was concerned, a little bit particular: he could ask me to describe a petrol lamp – of course I was unable to do so with my knowledge of English, and then he started describing it himself for about half an hour. I was again and again astonished at the particular way his brain worked.' He would spend time discussing Schopenhauer and Nietzsche or stories in *Dubliners* before asking Furlan to run out and bring back some fivepenny rock-drops from the corner-shop.[9] As to his view of his students, he told Francini that although he was impressed that most of them were 'noblemen and signori and editors and rich people', he found them pretty awful to teach.[10]

The love-hate relationship between the Joyce brothers persisted. Particularly galling to Stannie were Jim's constant demands for money to fund a prodigal lifestyle while his own clothes grew threadbare and he often went hungry. In late August he was again prevailed upon to contribute to the cost of moving the family to roomier quarters (furnished with made-to-order mock-Danish furniture) on the third floor of 32 via della Barriera Vecchia (over Picciola's pharmacy), while he remained in his poky room in the via San Nicola. The new apartment suited Joyce very well. That autumn he managed to secure some evening teaching at the Scuola Superiore di Commercio Revoltella, a commercial high school in Trieste, and to help with his expanded ménage he hired a live-in maid, Maria Kirn. His more demanding private students such as Schmitz now came to the apartment for their lessons.

At Christmas, Roberts wrote complaining that the corrected proofs of 'Ivy Day' Joyce had promised had not arrived. On 22 January 1911 he wrote again saying that publication of *Dubliners* had been postponed until the requested changes had been made.[11] Throughout the spring Joyce argued that Maunsel was in breach of contract and made veiled threats about taking court action. In June, Roberts told him that it was he and his unjust complaints, and not they, who were the problem. Joyce had agreed to make 'certain alterations' but the changes he had made were negligible. While Roberts had no wish to have a quarrel with his author he thought Joyce should at least give Maunsel the opportunity to recoup their money by making 'the necessary corrections' without further delay.[12] But Joyce's powerful sense of paranoia was triggered. Here was yet another betrayal by a treacherous son of a treacherous city.

In pursuing what had now become a vendetta with Roberts, Joyce wrote to King George V, son of Edward VII and grandson of Queen Victoria, sending the disputed passage of 'Ivy Day in the Committee Room', and asking whether *he* found it offensive enough to be omitted. On 11 August he received a reply from the King's private secretary at Buckingham Palace, saying that it was 'inconsistent with rule' for His Majesty to express an opinion in such cases.[13] Joyce took this royal 'No Comment' as a signal that the monarch was not offended by the reference to his grandmother as a 'bloody old bitch'.

Encouraged by this, he informed Roberts and his partner Joseph Hone that, as they obviously had no intention of publishing his book, he would circulate an account of his problems with Maunsel to the Irish press. The circular was a blow-by-blow account of his dealings with them, alleging breach of contract for which, as a non-UK resident (he now admitted) he was unable to sue; all he could do was publicize his grievances, and other writers should take note.[14] The circular was published in full by *Sinn Fein* and in edited form by the Belfast *Northern Whig*. Having also taken a swipe at Grant Richards he took the precaution of sending a copy to him too. Richards replied saying that he didn't think Joyce understood the difficulties facing publishers, but restating his interest in his future work.

One day, when his self-confidence was already dented following Roberts's last letter, Nora told him he was wasting his time with his scribbling. Joyce, who was working in the kitchen on *A Portrait*, suddenly lost control. 'All right,' he said, 'I'll give up writing,' and in a fit of despair thrust the manuscript into the burning stove while, according to Eileen, Nora stood by laughing, saying 'He's mad! He's mad!' Eileen, so she claimed, quickly snatched the burning pages from the fire and, with the maid Maria's help, spread them around the kitchen. Thus a minor masterpiece that linked Joyce's life to all his later work, was rescued from an act of desperation. Eileen recalled that next day Jim told her, 'Some parts of it I could never have written again,' and presented her with three bars of multi-coloured soap, some mittens, a collar and a bow.[15] Re-energized, he sat down to rewrite the novel, which, from here on, would not only consume him but point him towards *Ulysses*.

Earlier, in June, word had come that Mabel ('Baby') Joyce was ill in Cork Street Fever Hospital. Eva, wanting to be with her sister and, happy to escape the strange confusion and petty quarrelling surrounding her brother, returned to the familiar confusion and petty quarrelling surrounding her father. On reaching Dublin she was met by a shabby-looking John, who first borrowed a shilling from her and then told her that they were all evicted from Fontenoy Street and she would have to find a place to stay. Eventually sister May scraped up the cost of a week's rent for her in a Drumcondra boarding house.[16]

At first, reports about Mabel were good, but on the 12th, the seventeen-year-old finally died of typhoid fever, the infection that had taken George nine years earlier. Joyce sent a wreath and (with Stanislaus) money for the funeral, again (as he had for his brother's death) blaming his blighted homeland and the wretched conditions to which his family had been reduced by a feckless father. John wrote, self-pityingly as usual, thanking him for his help and claiming that 'Baby' was his last real link to her mother. His health was failing, his life was over, he said, and his remaining daughters had turned against him, not even wanting to walk with him at their sister's funeral. He promised Jim that his colourful hunting waistcoat – foxes' head, brown satin lining, mulberry buttons and all – and the family portraits would now pass into his safe-keeping. Not surprisingly perhaps, Jim's reply was, wrote his sister May, a 'strange and bitter' one.[17]

That summer, Joyce had allowed Eileen and Maria, their maid, to take the six-year-old Giorgio on holiday to Maria's family home at Corso in the hills outside Trieste. Giorgio found the relaxed country atmosphere and absence of tension within the household so enjoyable that he was reluctant to return. Joyce, distressed by this 'rejection', wrote a strong letter asking Maria to bring Giorgio home at once.[18] He enjoyed playing with his son and openly showered him with affection. He hated the idea of sending him to school where he might be taught religion, yet feared that if he brought up the boy himself he would make a mess of it. That autumn, therefore, Giorgio entered the Civica Scuola Popolare where religion was not on the curriculum.

Joyce's thirtieth birthday celebration on 2 February 1912 was followed by a threat from his landlord (Giuseppe Picciola, the pharmacist) to evict him for rent arrears. In search of more income, he applied to teach at the Istituto Tecnico at Como in Italy but was turned down because his qualifications were not recognized there. He would need to pass examinations in English and Italian to qualify for employment at an Italian public school. To save the situation, in March Joyce gave another series of lectures at the Università del Popolo, this time on 'Realism and Idealism in English Literature', focusing particularly on Blake and Defoe.[19]

He admired Blake's powerful verse and mystic vision, and his readiness first to support the French Revolution and then abandon it with the coming of the Terror. This matched Joyce's own support for Irish freedom and his revulsion at the use of violence to achieve it. Blake's attitude to women clearly echoed something of Joyce's own relationship with Nora.

> Like many other men of great genius, Blake was not attracted to cultured and refined women ... Mrs Blake was ... in fact ... illiterate, and the poet took pains to teach her to read and write ... In the early years of their life together there were discords, misunderstandings easy to understand if we keep in mind the great difference in culture and temperament that separated the young couple.[20]

He saw the shades of Milton and Homer, the two great blind poets, as Blake's chief inspirations but thought his Albion less representative of 'the Anglo-Saxon spirit' than Defoe's Crusoe – the masculine self-reliance, unthinking ruthlessness, determination, ponderous but workmanlike intellect, callous sexual indifference, religious equanimity and purposeful taciturnity.[21] Exploring these inspired and inspiring characters gave him the opportunity to explore his own nature in its dual aspect of realist and poet.

Having applied to enter for the teaching diploma in English, Joyce was allowed to sit the examination at the University of Padua on 24 April, giving him just three days to prepare for it. There would be three days of formal written examinations followed by an oral test. On his first day in Padua he wrote essays in Italian on 'The Universal Literary Influence of the Renaissance' and on Charles Dickens. Obviously his lectures on Blake and Defoe meant that he was well prepared for the written papers.

He portrayed the Renaissance as a philosophic movement of consciousness from idealism to materialism, from 'scholastic absolutism' to humanistic liberation, much like his own intellectual journey from Jesuitry to Ibsenism and beyond. Despite Stanislaus's claim that his brother never cared for Dickens,[22] it is evident from his early writing that he had read 'the great Cockney' extensively. While not ranking Dickens highly among European writers, Joyce wrote, he admired his brilliance in conveying the sense of a particular city. No writer before or since had so felt the life and breath of London in his nostrils, except perhaps Defoe. He then dilated on 'the well-crowded Dickensian gallery' of Hogarthian caricatures, and in his umbilical attachment to the odour and noises of a city, it is evident that he saw in Dickens a reflection of himself.

There followed a day of translating. Then, after a short break back in Trieste, he returned to complete the examinations on the 30th. Joyce's results, when they came through, were impressive – 421 marks out of a possible 450. Nevertheless, the diploma was denied him on the grounds that his Irish degree was unrecognized in Italy. But no experience was left unused by Joyce, and in *Giacomo Joyce*, the fragmentary fiction he produced later, there is a memory of Padua which suggests that while there he was drawn as ever to the nether regions of yet another city.

Padua ... The silent middle age, night, darkness of history sleep in the Piazza delle Erbe under the moon. The city sleeps. Under the arches in the dark streets near the river the whores' eyes spy out for fornicators. Cinque servizi per cinque franchi. A dark wave of sense, again and again and again.[23]

Eva wrote from Dublin to say how much she missed the children, especially Lucia, and that Charlie and his family had returned from America impoverished.[24] Eileen, meanwhile, had taken a job as governess to a family in Udine some 60 kilometres north of Trieste, and Jim was trying to fix her up as a language and piano teacher to Letitia, the daughter of Ettore and Livia Schmitz at their villa in Servola.

By the end of May he had heard nothing more from George Roberts at Maunsel, even though he wrote to him regularly. However, he had bought himself an American desk at which he now worked, and that month published an article about Charles Stewart Parnell – an enduring passion and defining part of his identity. The recurrent theme of treachery loomed very large in his mind following the Roberts 'betrayal'. The essay, 'The Shade of Parnell', reveals his grasp of Irish history, packing it with details of Parnell's speeches, the conspiracy against him, the O'Shea case and 'the Chief's' betrayal by the Irish clergy. 'The citizens of Castlecomer threw quicklime in his eyes. He went from county to county, from city to city, "like a hunted deer", a spectral figure with the signs of death on his forehead.'[25] The exile at bay standing up against the howling rabblement was exactly how he saw himself and was to become a recurrent leitmotif in his fiction. He sent copies to his family but received no acknowledgement. Next time, he told Eileen, he would send a pair of old trousers, which was 'more in their line'.[26]

Within his immediate circle in Trieste – Schmitz, Prezioso, Francini, and painters such as Argio Orell – he was the focus of much attention and admiration. To Francini he sometimes recited Dante, often reducing him to tears. The friends all shared a love of music and often enjoyed musical evenings together – Mrs Francini singing to Joyce's piano accompaniment. Prezioso had introduced him to many of these friends and also to the wealthy students he taught – Sordina, Ralli, Ettore and Livia Schmitz. One of his students, Frantisek Schaurek, a Czech bank cashier, asked to be taught by Eileen to whom he had taken a strong fancy, declaring himself by saying 'Love is the best teacher.' They would marry two years later.

Giorgio's first school report listed his achievements for the year: 'Behaviour: Commendable; Diligence: Satisfactory; Italian Reading: Adequate; Italian Language: Adequate; Arithmetic and Singing: Very Good.'[27] However, he had inherited a family weakness – poor sight. Joyce sent him to have his eyes tested and soon he would be wearing spectacles, while his father preferred the 'poetic' pince-nez favoured by Yeats. Lucia too had her slight strabismus, which some found attractive.

Nora now decided to take her daughter to Galway to meet her family. They would visit the Joyces, and stay for a few nights in Dublin at Finn's Hotel. There was also the fond hope that in Galway she could wheedle some cash out of her generously disposed Uncle Michael Healy to pay for Jim and Giorgio to join them. On 8 July, the Dublin Joyces turned out in force to meet the visitors at Westland Row Station. At the sight of Lucia, John Joyce broke down and began lamenting his breach with his favourite son. They were escorted to Finn's and next day taken to visit the Murrays, to whom Nora took an instant dislike, before managing to escape to Galway.

After a while Joyce began to grow anxious about Nora, who had not written since her departure. Finally she sent him no more than a scribbled postcard, and his old fears about losing her to someone else resurfaced. He wrote back a letter oozing with self-pity, upbraiding her for having passed through Dublin, staying at Finn's, and yet failing to mention where and how they had met. He was unable to sleep, he said; he had pains in his side and feared he might die in his sleep, even waking Giorgio several times during the night, frightened of being alone. Troubled by jealous thoughts, he was now determined to follow her, whatever the cost, and relive their first meeting in Nassau Street. 'I shall go *alone* to meet and walk with the image of her whom I remember,' he told her.[28] He obtained some advance fees from Schmitz and Ralli and on 12 July left hurriedly for Dublin with Giorgio, arriving five days later.

He stayed first at 17 Richmond Place with Charlie and his family. The Murrays visited, and when Katsy and Mabel heard that Giorgio was still unchurched at the age of seven they secretly 'baptized' him themselves in the bathroom. It is difficult to know whether Joyce, had he known, would have been furious or simply amused by this piece of amateur theatricals.

Joyce was anxious to refresh his memory of the city which he had made the centre-point of his creative imagination. There were places to revisit and fragments of gossip to be gleaned from every encounter, every visit to a bar, every edition of a Dublin newspaper. One story he found particularly amusing concerned his hapless classmate Reuben J. Dodd Jnr, son of the man who had brought his father to ruin. The previous August, Dodd Junior wanted to marry and, when his father opposed the match, had jumped into the Liffey as his parent looked on. A passing docker, one Moses Goldin, seeing what had happened, dived into the river and rescued the sodden youth, ending up in hospital and losing a day's work. When his poor wife approached Dodd Senior, she was told that her husband should have minded his own business before grudgingly being handed a florin. To Joyce this was hilarious and he stored it away to use later, in the 'Hades' episode of *Ulysses*. When Martin Cunningham tells the story, mentioning Dodd's reward of two shillings, Simon Dedalus comments, 'One and eightpence too much.'[29] No doubt he got this story and all the latest gossip from John, who was delighted to see Jim and Giorgio again.

When he visited the Maunsel offices it was to be told that George Roberts now wanted changes to more than one story. Offending passages in *Dubliners*, the publisher proposed, should be replaced by asterisks with a prefatory note from Joyce, or else he could take the printed sheets and get the book published himself.[30] But by this time Joyce was finding the whole matter, and Dublin, too depressing,[31] and, after spending just a day in the city, he left with Giorgio to join Nora and Lucia to spend a few days at her mother's home at Bowling Green in Galway. Michael Healy gave them lavish meals and Joyce went cycling around the Galway coast, and visited the grave of Michael Bodkin, whose ghost so haunted 'The Dead'. Then he obeyed the call of Miss Ivors in that story and visited the Aran Islands, making notes for two articles promised to *Il Piccolo*. One about Galway, 'The City of the Tribes', appeared on 11 August and one on the islands, 'The Mirage of the Fisherman of Aran', on 5 September. He also tried to get an interview with Guglielmo Marconi at his wireless telegraphy station at Clifden, but failed. However, everything was material to his authorial mind and in *Finnegans Wake* this becomes

> the loftly marconimasts from Clifden sough open tireless secrets (mauveport! mauveport!) to Nova Scotia's listing sisterwands. Tubetube![32]

To Schmitz he sent a picture postcard of an ancient fisherman inscribed as a portrait of the artist 'as an *old* man.'[33]

Wanting to settle matters with Maunsel, he consulted George Lidwell, a solicitor friend of John's, who appears in *Ulysses* as a flirtatious customer of Miss Kennedy and Miss Douce in the 'Sirens' episode. When he returned to Dublin on the 16th to keep an appointment with Roberts, Lidwell accompanied him. The publisher now voiced his suspicion that some of the stories carried indecent allusions. He asked Joyce whether sodomy occurred in 'The Sisters', what 'simony' meant, for what reason the old priest might have been suspended other than breaking a chalice, and whether there was more to 'The Dead' than met the eye. After a two-hour interview, Lidwell agreed to vet the script. His opinion was that vulgar expressions and references to Victoria and Edward in 'Ivy Day in the Committee Room' would cause no problems, but 'An Encounter' could lead to trouble because such 'vices' were considered so repugnant they were rarely given publicity. He therefore advised Joyce not to take the risk of leaving the story unaltered.[34] Before leaving Dublin, Joyce agreed in writing to the omission of 'An Encounter' on condition that the book included a note explaining the excision.[35] But Roberts again postponed a final decision until he had received the opinion of his London lawyer.[36]

Strangely enough, next day he was happy to discuss with Joyce the binding of his book, and, hearing about his novel, encouraged him to finish it. This time Joyce left Roberts in a more hopeful frame of mind, seeing the possibility of his literary career taking off after all. In a mood to celebrate, he took a double room at 21 Richmond Place, a few doors away from Charlie, and wrote asking Nora to join him. She could wear her prettiest clothes and tightest blouse, he said, and should remember to clean her teeth or he might send her straight back to Galway. He hoped she would come with him to the Abbey to see plays by Yeats and Synge and after they returned to Trieste would read books with him as her guide.[37]

But the moment of elation soon passed. Next day Roberts sent him a flat rejection of *Dubliners*, Maunsel's London solicitor having deemed it full of prima facie libels. Changing a few names would not eliminate the risk of prosecution. Joyce was fuming. He told Stannie that if he had had a revolver he would have 'put some daylight' into Roberts.[38] But despite his murderous feelings, he had two more fruitless meetings with the publisher, after which he was offered the printed sheets for £30 if he would return next day to collect them. Arthur Griffith, editor of *Sinn Fein*, told him that these sorts of games were typical of Roberts, and the suggestion that he might be sued for publishing *Dubliners* was a bluff.

By now Joyce had decided to publish the book himself under the imprint of the Liffey Press, but the printer, John Falconer, refused to hand over the proofs. When asked what would happen to them, Falconer said they would be burned. Dublin morality had passed its final judgement upon its disreputable Dante. But Joyce was not so easily frustrated, and 'by a ruse' (he said) he managed to smuggle a set of proofs out of the printer's offices. Like it or not, Falconer *would* contribute to the book's ultimate appearance. Nevertheless, Joyce felt that he had been treated abominably by all at Maunsel. It had taken Roberts and his benighted printer three years to decide that his book was unpublishable and he felt that the decision had marked him – much as Parnell had been marked once the truth about him and Mrs O'Shea had been made public. Now, like 'the Chief', he was truly a stag at bay; there were those in Ireland who would gladly see him obliterated, and he developed a talent for dramatizing himself in that way. 'The excuses put forward day after day are easily seen through,' he wrote later, 'and I find it difficult to come to any other conclusion but this – that the intention was to weary me out and if possible strangle me once and for all. But in this they did not succeed.'[39]

Frustrated, angry and homicidal as he felt, having his book burned was somehow a fitting martyrdom to suffer for the high art of literature. *Dubliners* had not just been rejected; it was condemned to the stake. Few writers could boast such an honour; he would not let the world forget it. In fact, according to Roberts, the book was not burnt but guillotined and the sheets used for packing; however, for Joyce, a burning was far more dramatic. If his book was terribly heretical, let it be terribly burned. He would have his revenge, first in verse, then in the 'Circe' episode of *Ulysses* where Bloom is symbolically burned at the stake and the paralysed city which had rejected Bloom's author is also put to the torch – 'Dublin's burning! Dublin's burning! On fire, on fire!'[40]

A telegram from Stannie urging his brother to return to Trieste immediately or risk eviction did nothing to lessen his feelings of despair. Joyce told him to threaten Picciola, their landlord, with legal action should he carry out his threat during their absence. Stannie, however, decided to act alone and found the family another apartment in a new building on via Donato Bramante. 'While Jim and his family were in Dublin,' he said, 'I moved "carefully and horizontally" into a smaller, newer, cleaner flat, instead of bothering about legal actions and so on.' It was his brother, he said, who had illusions about the law. The Dublin adventure having ended in anticlimax it was time to leave. Braving the sea, on 11 September Joyce took his family back to Trieste via the longer Channel crossing from Harwich to Flushing. There he wrote a card to Padraic Colum and began composing 'Gas from a Burner', a satirical broadside aimed at Roberts and those in Ireland who had censored and betrayed him.

> This lovely land that always sent
> Her writers and artists to banishment
> And in a spirit of Irish fun
> Betrayed her own leaders, one by one.

And he did not forget what that lovely land had done to its uncrowned King —

> 'Twas Irish humour, wet and dry,
> Flung quicklime into Parnell's eye.

The indictment ends with Roberts penitently baring his buttocks awaiting punishment – the mark of shame from the ash-smeared hand of his printer's foreman: '[A] sign crisscross with reverent thumb/*Memento homos* upon [his] bum.'[41]

Composing this impassioned tirade – showing Joyce at his satirical best – occupied the whole train journey between the Hook of Holland and Salzburg. Arriving back in Trieste on the 15th, Joyce arranged for it to be printed the next day, sending copies for Charlie to distribute around Dublin. This he did, despite John's calling his son 'an out and out ruffian without the spark of a gentleman', and *Dubliners* 'a blackguard production'.[42]

Joyce saw himself as the victim of a conspiracy by shadowy and nameless figures, later telling an Italian friend, 'Some say it was the doing of priests, some of enemies, others of the then Viceroy or his consort, Countess Aberdeen. Altogether it is a mystery.'[43] He would return at various times to England but the Island of Saints and Sages would never see him again.

17

A Portrait Completed; A Masterpiece Begun
(1912–1915)

'The writer's only responsibility is to his art. He will be completely ruthless if he is a good one.' William Faulkner

Back in Trieste it must have been hard for Joyce to accept that the past three years had been lost waiting for Maunsel to publish *Dubliners* and that his original instinct to steer clear of Roberts had been correct. If he had to make a new start, free of Irish entrapments and memories of past betrayals, he had a good place from which to launch himself.

The new apartment (on the second floor of 4 via Donato Bramante) stood on a gentle rise above the Piazza Vico and below the cathedral-citadel of San Giusto. It was roomier than the previous flat, with more space for books and a large drawing room in which to work and hold classes. Apart from the reception room, which had a window overlooking the street, there were two bedrooms – one a 'guest room' in which Joyce kept his piano – and a separate kitchen. There was space enough for his American desk and a wall on which to display the five family portraits, now gifted to him by his father. He had arranged to have them cleaned in Dublin before being shipped to Trieste. His other heirloom, the hunting waistcoat, when he wore it, added a raffish touch to his normally correct and dapper appearance. At this new address he would spend three comparatively happy years during which he would finally publish *Dubliners*, begin writing *Giacomo Joyce*, complete *A Portrait of the Artist* and *Exiles*, and write the first chapters of *Ulysses*.

Denied the rewards of authorship, Joyce remained entirely dependent on teaching for a living. To his list of Triestine celebrity students he had now added the families of wealthy Jewish merchants, who were to play their part in advancing his creative imagination. Although his income from private tuition was modest, he secured more lecturing at the Università del Popolo – this time a series of twelve talks on Shakespeare's *Hamlet*, beginning with a history of Elizabethan society and theatre, with passing reference to 'The Dark Lady of the Sonnets'.[1] This frustrated academic (who, as a teacher, always styled himself 'James Joyce B.A.' or even '*dottore in filosofia*') would find ultimate artistic and intellectual fulfilment in the comic encyclopaedism of *Ulysses* and *Finnegans Wake*. *Ulysses* is shot through with allusions to Shakespeare, and in the telegraphese he developed for the *Wake*, he seems to offer various Shakespearean identities of his own. 'Be irish. Be inish. Be offalia. Be hamlet. Be the property plot. Be Yorick . . .'[2]

With Charlie still unable to find work, it seemed that all he ever heard from Dublin was news of poverty, failure and dying. In December Uncle William Murray, Aunt Josephine's husband, his mother's brother (and Richie Goulding in *Ulysses*), collapsed and died. Jim liked Willie – the only one of his mother's family, he said, who had taken any pride in his existence and with whom he had had 'many wild nights . . . many arguments . . . a good-hearted lively companion of my youth'. He sent his condolences to Aunt Josephine and for a while used black-bordered writing-paper as a mark of respect.[3]

As the year turned, he sent out *Dubliners* once more – to the publishers Elkin Mathews and Martin Secker, again offering to pay the printing costs – only to have it refused a second time. Mathews (who had sold less than half the 300-odd copies of *Chamber Music* printed) passed the manuscript to John Long who also turned it down again. After that he seems to have abandoned hope for the time being. But by 1913 things were looking up for Joyce. During the first part of that year, thanks to the efforts of his former students Schmitz and Vidacovich, he was offered a full-time job at the Scuola Superiore di Commercio Revoltella; he had three poems included in Kathleen Tynan's *The Wild Harp, A Selection of Irish Poetry*; and his ornately framed family portraits arrived from Dublin. From then on he would rarely be without them, displaying them proudly and adding to the collection from time to time.

Notwithstanding his extra income from high-school teaching, Joyce's lifestyle continued to exceed his earnings, and he was often threatened with legal action for non-payment of bills. His previous landlord was still chasing him for back rent, and now a music-shop proprietor pursued him through the Scuola Revoltella for money owing for sheet music. But, with his lofty imperturbability towards money, he brazened his way happily through such situations. He and Nora continued to eat and drink at good restaurants, the children were well clothed and Nora herself now dressed in the latest fashion.

At around this time he made two new friends: the irredentist poet Leone Dario de Tuoni and the 'impressionist' painter Tullio Silvestri would become members of Joyce's circle, often meeting at his flat or in cafés in the Città Vecchia where on at least one occasion Silvestri saw Joyce helplessly drunk. The two men would perambulate around Trieste reciting their verse and passages from Verlaine to each other. As one of Joyce's students, Tuoni later recalled lessons from the reluctant pedagogue at his apartment. Formal teaching, for which he had an aversion, would quickly give way to talk about art and literature and uttering ironies, in which he took great pleasure.[4]

Prezioso had been a friend of the Joyces for some time. On postcards he sent every Christmas, he always addressed them as 'little Ireland', and he was one of the few people allowed to address Joyce as 'Jim'. He had long been fascinated by Joyce as a man; now he transferred some of this interest to Nora and took to dropping in at their flat, often in the afternoons when she was alone. When she mentioned this to Jim, he did not object, finding the situation rather intriguing. The idea of her having an admirer cast him into an agony of jealousy but at the same time came to possess him to the point of fixation, as thoughts of Michael Bodkin and Cosgrave still did. Now the flirtation was closer to home, something he could observe, and even encourage. Notes made later for *Exiles* underline his fascination with adultery as an experiment to be observed, a theme he would use that play to explore. Given the green light, Nora responded to Prezioso's interest by further improving her appearance, and so attracting the attention and admiration of other friends of Joyce's.

However, matters threatened to get out of hand when the Italian, waxing adoringly familiar, told Nora: '*Il sole s'e levato per Lei*', 'The sun shines for you.' It provided Joyce with an expression he gave to Molly Bloom ('the sun rises for you he said the day we were lying among the rhododendrons on Howth head'),[5] and to Brigid the maid in *Exiles* who tells Bertha, 'Sure he [Richard] thinks the sun shines out of your face, ma'am.'[6] Joyce suddenly decided to end the experiment. He confronted Prezioso in the Piazza Goldoni where Silvestri caught sight of them and, he claimed, saw Prezioso weeping. The artist guessed that Joyce had upbraided him over his advances to Nora and determined to end the affair by humiliating Prezioso. Whatever Silvestri thought had happened, Joyce did not end his friendship with the *Il Piccolo* editor. They continued exchanging Christmas cards, and, when it finally appeared, Prezioso would receive a signed copy of *Dubliners* from its proud author. That autumn, when Joyce began work on *Exiles*, he centred it around a triangle much like that between himself, Nora and Prezioso, represented there by Richard Rowan, his 'wife' Bertha and the journalist Robert Hand – with a fourth character, Beatrice Justice, a music teacher, no doubt representing his 'Dark Lady'. Prezioso's attraction to his 'little Ireland' has been construed as an attraction to James as much as to Nora, a construction sometimes also placed on *Exiles*. This, if true, might explain Joyce's wish to end the affair and also Prezioso's tears of disappointment and humiliation.

That summer, perhaps encouraged by further interest in his poems from Geoffrey Molyneux Palmer, after a pause of ten years Joyce returned to writing poetry, this time inspired by a needleboat race in which Stanislaus participated at San Sabba. He presented 'Watching the Needle-boats at San Sabba' to his brother and his rowing-club friends with 'the rheumatic chamber poet's (or pot's) compliments'.[7] As they rowed they sang an aria from the last act of Puccini's *The Girl of the Golden West*, a song which Joyce echoed in his poem.

> I heard their young hearts crying
> Loveward above the glancing oar
> And heard the prairie grasses sighing:
> No more, return no more![8]

He sent it to the *Saturday Review* in which it was published on 20 September. It was his first appearance in an English literary magazine for three years.

With his lyrical humour upon him he also wrote a poem that autumn for Lucia, his 'wonder wild', called 'A Flower Given to my Daughter',

> In gentle eyes thou veilest,
> My blueveined child.[9]

The line and no doubt the sentiment recur in *Giacomo Joyce* which hints at who gave Lucia the flower. 'A flower given by her to my daughter. Frail gift, frail giver, frail blue-veined child.' And Nora's past love, Michael Bodkin – 'the dark boy whom she ... embraces in death and dis-integration' – still haunted him,[10] a poignant train of thought that produced the poem 'She Weeps over Rahoon':

> Rain on Rahoon falls softly, softly falling,
> Where my dark lover lies.
> Sad is his voice that calls me, sadly calling ... [11]

The lyricist could still emerge when summoned.

In November Joyce wrote to Grant Richards again offering him *Dubliners* plus a contribution towards the cost of production and, as a proposed preface, a version of his letter about the book's past life, entitled 'A Curious History'. It took Richards two months to reply and then it was to ask what alterations Joyce had made to satisfy publishers' fears about possible obscenity charges. Although this looked promising, there was still no saying what might upset their cautious negotiations.

But Joyce's luck was about to change quite dramatically. Amidst this uncertainty, in mid-December he received a letter from Ezra Pound, the manic young American poet, part-genius, part-charlatan,[12] with a mission to revolutionize English Literature. After being fired from a teaching post at Wabash College, Indiana, for alleged immorality, Pound had headed for England and insinuated himself into London literary circles through Elkin Mathews and Yeats, who thought him 'queer' but attractive and gifted. According to Douglas Goldring, who helped Ford Madox Hueffer (later Madox Ford) edit the *English Review*, Pound 'with his mane of fair hair, his blonde beard, his rimless pince-nez, his Philadelphian accent and his startling costume, part of which was a single turquoise ear-ring, contrived to look "every inch a poet"'. Yeats was more than just impressed by the newcomer, he was reinvigorated as a poet. 'One of [Pound's] greatest triumphs in London,' said Goldring, 'was the way in which he stormed 18 Woburn Buildings, the Celtic stronghold of W. B. Yeats, took charge of his famous "Mondays" ... and succeeded in reducing him from master to disciple.'[13] Pound had rooms in Holland Place Chambers in Kensington, but since July 1913 had been acting as secretary to Yeats at his Sussex cottage, where Joyce was spoken of as a young literary tiger who probably shared many of Pound's own pet hates.

In his letter, Pound told Joyce that he was connected with two literary magazines, *The Egoist* and *The Cerebralist*, which paid little or nothing ('we do it for larks') but had space for 'markedly modern stuff'. He also mentioned two well-paying American magazines, *The Smart Set* and *Poetry* (edited in Chicago by Harriet Monroe) for which he collected material. Pound sensed that he was writing to someone out of the ordinary, telling Joyce, 'This is the first time I have written to anyone outside my own circle of acquaintance (save in the case of French authors). These matters can be better dealt with in conversation, but as that is impossible, I write.'[14]

He wrote again ten days later, after Yeats had shown him Joyce's poem 'I Hear an Army'.[15] Pound wanted it for a proposed anthology, *Des Imagistes*, and offered Joyce a guinea and a proportion of the profits. He was as good as his word and sent him his guinea by return, saying he now wanted Joyce for *The Egoist*. For Joyce, knowing Pound would open doors for him which had so far been closed, meant that dreams of greatness suddenly would seem achievable. It was as if he had been visited by Literature's own fairy godfather and been dragged from a dark and painful obscurity into the bright light of literary stardom.

With Rebecca West as assistant editor, *The Egoist* had been launched in 1911 by Dora Marsden, as *The Freewoman*, a suffragist fortnightly which became notorious for outspoken discussions about sex and procreation.

In June 1912 it became the *New Freewoman*, but by December 1913, with Richard Aldington as assistant editor and Pound in charge of the literary pages, Marsden was persuaded to change the title to *The Egoist* to reflect a less ideological, more individualistic line and to publish younger, more radical writers, such as Wells, Eliot and Aldington, geared to the modern age. In January 1914, in the first issue of *The Egoist*, Joyce's 'A Curious History' appeared, heralding the arrival of a new force in English letters. Pound chose to print it in full in place of his usual fortnightly book column.

Encouraged by Pound liking his poem, Joyce sent him copies of his stories, which the American then submitted to H. L. Mencken for *The Smart Set*, recommending 'The Boarding House' and 'A Little Cloud'. He then wrote to Joyce assuring him that stories which had shocked the modesty of Maunsel would certainly not shock them at *The Egoist*. 'We want it to be a place where a man can speak out,' he wrote, and, even though they could not pay him, magazine publication of stories often led to whole collections appearing in book form. Joyce was now desperate to get the complete *Dubliners* into print in order to feel free to finish *A Portrait*, which was still only three chapters long. Meanwhile he continued to push Grant Richards, informing him that *The Egoist* had published 'A Curious History', hoping it would encourage him at last to bring out his seemingly cursed story collection.

Taking Pound at his word, Joyce sent him the first chapter of his novel, and by mid-January Pound had written back pronouncing it 'damn fine stuff ... clear and direct like Mérimée'. He had sent it straight to *The Egoist*, he said. After all the delays and discouragement over *Dubliners* it must have been exhilarating for Joyce when just two weeks later, on 2 February – his thirty-second birthday – the first of twenty-five instalments of *A Portrait of the Artist as a Young Man* appeared in Dora Marsden's magazine. She had recognized its worth immediately and so, thanks to her and Pound's good judgement, it quickly saw the light of print. The coincidence of publication and birthday was to Joyce highly propitious, and contriving other such concurrences on future occasions became important to him. As Pound had warned, he received no payment, so to help stave off debt collectors and bailiffs, Joyce took a part-time job as English correspondent at the paint factory of Gioachino Veneziani, Ettore Schmitz's father-in-law, at 100 crowns a month. Living by writing alone was still but a distant prospect.

The publication of *A Portrait* was not the only good news. On 29 January 1914, finally satisfied with Joyce's reassurances, Richards wrote agreeing to their original contract for *Dubliners* on the understanding that Joyce himself would purchase the first 120 copies at trade price. He also wanted to replace the dashes Joyce used to denote dialogue with the usual quotation marks. Reluctantly Joyce agreed to this, but thought quotation marks 'unsightly', giving the impression of unreality. And so, within a very few days, Joyce's fortune had turned through 180 degrees; his sense of achievement was inspiring.

The feeling of exultation continued, and on 1 March 1914 he turned to the projected novel that had long possessed him. It would mean a switch from the humourless self-obsessed student narrator of *A Portrait* to the hilarious, omniscient satirist of *Ulysses*. But eager though he was to plough on with the new book, initially other works, notably *Giacomo Joyce* and *Exiles*, kept interrupting him.

On the brink of making his mark as a writer, and with Dublin on his mind as ever, Joyce wrote inviting his father to visit them in Trieste to have his portrait painted for the family gallery. John replied from a convalescent home in Drumcondra where he was recovering after two months hospital treatment for gastric problems. He would have his portrait done, he said, as soon as he could 'get up some flesh' and would happily come if he could pay his own way. He was anxious to know something about Frantisek Schaurek whom Eileen – 'the *only one* of my daughters (*now alive*) who never gave me insolence, or showed contempt for me' – had told him she wished to marry.[16]

Pound had now received the second chapter of *A Portrait* and told Joyce that it was already attracting the admiration of his contemporaries, such as Wyndham Lewis and Ford Madox Hueffer. He also mentioned that Lewis was about to launch what he called 'a new Futurist, Cubist, Imagiste Quarterly'. He might take some essays but not Joyce's stories which he was not very keen on. *Blast: A Review of the Great English Vortex* appeared in June with contributions from Pound, Lewis, Hueffer and Rebecca West, and a list of those writers Lewis thought deserving to be blessed or blasted. Joyce's name appeared among the ranks of the blessed.[17] With Lewis's benediction, he was already being recognized as an innovative presence on the wider literary scene.

Joyce had accumulated a dozen complimentary reviews of *Chamber Music*, which he had printed on slips, and, when proofs of *Dubliners* arrived in May, he sent sixty-five of them to Richards asking him to include one inside each copy sent out for review. And with an eye to publicity, he suggested the story of the burning of the book as a preface.[18] *Dubliners* was published on 15 June 1914, the eve of the tenth anniversary of the day on which *Ulysses* was set. It was another auspicious coincidence. Arthur Symons gave the book his blessing: 'I find a great deal to like in *Dubliners*,' he wrote, ' – unequal as the short stories are, but original, Irish, a kind of French realism, of minute detail, sordid ... a sense of Dublin as I saw it – a lurid glare over it ... But the best is the last: the end imaginative.'[19]

First reviews were not encouraging. On the day of its publication, *The Times* ran one headed 'Studies in the Dismal', complaining that Joyce was concerned not with ordinary Dubliners 'but almost exclusively with those of them who would be submerged if the tide of material difficulties were to rise a little higher' while admitting somewhat grudgingly that '*Dubliners* may be recommended to the large class of reader to whom the drab makes an appeal, for it is admirably written.'[20] The *Athenaeum* reviewer admired Joyce's skill but thought that three of the stories (unspecified) 'would be better buried in oblivion'.[21] One of the few Irish reviews came in the *Irish Book Lover* which declared that 'Mr Joyce here gives us pen portraits of great power,' but wished 'that the author had directed his undoubted talents in other and pleasanter directions.'[22]

But in a review by Gerald Gould in the *New Statesman*, for the first time in print Joyce was hailed as 'a genius'. While he had an original outlook and special powers and method as a writer, said Gould, it was impossible to say how he would develop. 'Certainly the maturity, the individual poise and force of these stories are astonishing ... Mr Joyce seems to regard this objective and dirty and crawling world with the cold detachment of an unamiable god.'[23] The anonymous reviewer in *Everyman* was also highly appreciative and used the word 'genius' twice.[24] But it took a longer review from Ezra Pound in *The Egoist* to locate *Dubliners* in its wider literary context. Pound recognized that in Joyce he had found a writer of enduring importance with a rigour which marked him not only as one of the modern generation, but also worthy of comparison with Flaubert, Strindberg, Herman Bang, and Galdós.[25]

Having received Chapter Three of *A Portrait*, Pound congratulated Joyce on his handling of the hellfire sermon and added, somewhat ominously, that he had 'done a little punctuating'. Pound's tendency to act as self-appointed copy editor to Joyce would lead to future difficulties between them. It must have given him a moment of grim satisfaction recalling their earlier battles when Grant Richards, delighted with the critical coverage of *Dubliners*, wrote asking him what he was doing next. Joyce promised him first refusal on the novel.

The euphoria of his success was soon overtaken by world events. On 28 June, the Archduke Franz Ferdinand and his wife Sophie were assassinated in Sarajevo and their bodies returned to Vienna through Trieste. By 1 August, Germany had declared war on Russia and two days later on France. The following day, after German troops entered Belgium, Britain declared war on Germany and on the 12th Germany's ally, Austro-Hungary, invaded Serbia. The whole deck of European cards was collapsing and Joyce and his family found themselves trapped behind enemy lines and in danger of internment as unwelcome aliens. For Joyce, with two more chapters of *A Portrait* to send to *The Egoist*, the most worrying thing was that mail between Trieste and London was disrupted.

Meanwhile, Lucia, just coming up to her seventh birthday, had completed her first year at the Civica Scuola Popolare. According to her first school report, she clearly outshone her brother in Italian and arithmetic, and matched his 'very good' score for singing. In her proud father's eyes she was not just good or very good; she was, he came to think, exceptional.

During July and August, Joyce was working on *Giacomo Joyce*, exploring the obsession of a teacher for a student – his Dark Lady, thought to be based on one or more of his female students: Amalia Popper, Annie Schleimer or Emma Cuzzi. Popper, on whose character and dark 'oriental' looks he drew for Molly Bloom was the daughter of Leopoldo Popper, a Jewish businessman whose name Joyce gave to his Ulyssean anti-hero. Cuzzi, a strapping, somewhat masculine outdoor girl, probably attracted the masochistic side of him expressed in his letters to Nora and in the 'Circe' episode of *Ulysses*. All would come to his flat for classes or he would visit them at their homes. He was still only thirty-two, a handsome, lively, unconventional, charismatic teacher, and these young women were to excite his sexual interest and imagination (and probably he theirs), resulting in the fragmentary and highly impressionistic *Giacomo*. It remained incomplete, and perhaps was meant to be no more than an extended prose poem, but it was important in a number of ways. It indicated his highly erotic cast of mind, showed the direction in which his prose was moving as *Ulysses* continued to incubate, and pointed towards his magnificently achieved portrayal of the voluptuous Molly Bloom.

This sketchy sexual meditation shows Joyce more decidedly embracing the *monologue intérieur*, used tentatively in *A Portrait* and more fully later in *Ulysses*. But for the moment he set aside both his novel and *Giacomo Joyce* to work on *Exiles*, taking him away from his flirtatious meditations in Trieste and back to his enduring love affair with Dublin. But his security in exile was now under threat. On 17 September he was informed that he was suspended from his post at the Scuola Revoltella until his contract had been officially approved by the Ministry of Public Instruction in Vienna.

Joyce now became entirely dependent on his job at the paint factory and his private pupils, but at least he had more free time to complete *A Portrait*. In October he heard from Harriet Shaw Weaver, the new editor of *The Egoist*, now a monthly, asking after the latest two chapters of *A Portrait*. Unlike Pound, who had swept into Joyce's life like a hurricane, Weaver's entrance was comparatively silent but would be nonetheless just as significant and more long-lasting. The chapters she had requested (Four and Five) came fluently: Chapter Four tracing Stephen's transformation from God-fixated Jesuit to young writer dedicated to art, and his revelatory meeting with his 'Bird-girl'; Chapter Five following him to university and his debates with Cranly and Lynch about religion and art and with Davin about nationalism. Finally having resisted these tempters, he stands alone. The coda, in often humorous diary form, culminates in Stephen preparing to leave Ireland on his quest to forge 'the uncreated conscience' of his 'race'. The postscript of his return – his mother's death, his sojourn with Gogarty and Trench at the Martello tower with its dramatic climax – would be saved for *Ulysses*. The completed *Portrait* charts the intellectual and moral progress of an artist striving towards a state of unfettered creativity. Its ruthless honesty and elegantly original style were to mark him out now as more than just a coming man. In the process he created the Myth of James Joyce, a myth he would now have to live up to. (The question remains: Was Joyce writing directly from his own consciousness or writing as he imagined Stephen Dedalus would have written with the changes of style throughout reflecting the artistic evolution through which he was passing?)

As mail between Austria and Great Britain was no longer flowing freely, he would need another means of getting his manuscripts to *The Egoist* in London. Finally he persuaded Gioachino Veneziani to allow him to use his Venetian address for the purpose, and serialization of *A Portrait* resumed in the November issue.

In December, not having heard about his teaching status, Joyce wrote to the Lieutenancy of Trieste asking for a decision. In January 1915, his position became suddenly more vulnerable. Stanislaus, who had not hidden his strong irredentist opinions was arrested and interned for the duration of the war, first at Schloss Kirchberg an der Wild, about seventy miles north of Vienna, and later at Katzenau near Linz. Although unaware of it, both he and his brother had been under surveillance by the Austrian secret police since hostilities began and both had been listed as foreign residents. What may have saved Joyce from the fate of his brother was that, unlike Stanislaus, he no longer voiced strong political views; he was too immersed in his work. By the end of the month Pound had sent all the chapters of *A Portrait* to Grant Richards and suggested that Joyce acquire an agent. Coincidentally, on 10 February, prompted by H. G. Wells who spoke of his 'unstinted admiration' for his work, J. B. Pinker (agent to Joseph Conrad and Ford Madox Hueffer, Wells and many other distinguished authors), wrote offering Joyce his services at the usual 10 per cent commission. Joyce agreed, except for those rights already assigned to Richards.

He was still unmolested, he told Pound, but the situation in Trieste was 'very unpleasant'.[26] On 23 March he heard from Mencken that 'The Boarding House' and 'A Little Cloud' would appear in *The Smart Set*. Mencken hinted that a US edition of *Dubliners* was about to be published by Benjamin W. Huebsch, 'one of the few intelligent publishers in New York'.[27] But on enquiry, Huebsch said that as they sold badly he was not interested in story collections. However, he was attracted by *A Portrait* which he had been reading in *The Egoist*. There was obviously a growing American interest in the new man.

With Stannie locked up and his own status less than secure, Joyce decided to try to get himself and his family out of Austria to a neutral country such as Switzerland. As diplomatic relations with Great Britain had been severed, he approached Ralph Busser, the American Consul, who began putting out feelers in the hope of persuading the Austrians to allow him to leave the country. Other influential friends in Trieste – Count Sordina and Count Ralli in particular – would also pull strings for him.

He was not the only one who would retreat from Trieste in the face of war. In April, Eileen married Frantisek Schaurek, with Joyce as best man dressed in an ill-fitting borrowed suit. Then, in May, when Italy came into the war on the Allies' side and the sound of gunfire could be heard in the city streets, the happy couple quickly left for the comparative safety of Prague. Suddenly Trieste was swarming with soldiers and policemen. Most civilians were evacuated, and Joyce came under increasing scrutiny from Austrian intelligence.

The sense that it was time to turn the page and move on was confirmed for him in May when Grant Richards declined to publish *A Portrait* on the grounds of a diminished intelligent readership in time of war. The serialization of his novel would be completed in September, but its publication as a book would be postponed. In England the interest was still only lukewarm. In May, Richards had also informed Joyce that at the end of 1914 sales of *Dubliners* had reached no more than 499, including the 120 he had bought himself and around two hundred bought by his various friends, relatives and acquaintances in Ireland. There would, he added, be no author royalties until more than five hundred had been sold. (Richards later sold the remainders to America.) Pound tried to comfort him. Short-story collections were normally unsaleable and his new wife Dorothy had read them twice over and declared them 'excellently good'.[28]

His play was now finished. With both *Portrait* and *Exiles* out of the way and *Giacomo Joyce* seemingly abandoned, Joyce produced a handful of poems which, thanks to Pound, appeared in *Poetry*, Harriet Monroe's magazine. More importantly, he had finally got back to working on *Ulysses*.

The new novel, the story of a single day in Dublin, 16 June 1904 (the day on which James had first walked out with Nora Barnacle), was designed, roughly, to follow the trajectory of Homer's *Odyssey*. From the start he saw it falling into three main sections. On the tenth anniversary of that day, he told Stanislaus: 'The first part, the Telemachiad, consists of four episodes: the second of fifteen, that is, Ulysses' wanderings: and the third, Ulysses' return home, of three more episodes.'[29] Quite quickly, however, he reconceived it with a first part of three episodes, a middle section of twelve, and a final part of three. This movement through three phases can also be seen as following the three-phase historicist cycle described by the Italian philosopher Giambattista Vico – the divine, the heroic, and the human – (and mirrored in the triptych of Dante's Inferno, Purgatorio and Paradiso). He had probably discovered Vico's theory from reading Benedetto Croce, and would sometimes discuss both thinkers with his students, who were now the best sounding-boards he could find.[30] He identified with Vico in part because he too was terrified of thunderstorms. In Vico it was a titanic crack of thunder which moved history from chaos into the divine; in *Finnegans Wake*, that crack rips along a hundred-letter 'thunder word', precipitating the fall of Humphrey Chimpden Earwicker, and sets the cyclical narrative in motion.

The influence of Freud on *Ulysses* is less clear, but, like Freud, Joyce was an interpreter of dreams and fascinated by apparently incoherent utterances – in the wandering mind of Leopold Bloom, for example. His student Paolo Cuzzi recalled them discussing Freud's theory of slips of the tongue and Joyce claiming that Vico had anticipated Freud. Ettore Schmitz's nephew, Dr Edoardo Weiss, had studied with Freud in Vienna and brought psychoanalysis to Trieste in 1910. In Trieste, Joyce, it was found, possessed copies of Freud's *Leonardo da Vinci: A Memory of his Childhood*, and Ernest Jones's study of Hamlet and the Oedipus complex.[31] But his focus on the interior lives of characters was directed more by Edouard Dujardin and his *monologue intérieur* than by any Viennese doctor.

With Trieste now beleaguered, Joyce formally requested permission to leave with his family for Switzerland. Ralph Busser finally obtained travel visas allowing them to enter Switzerland, and, through the good offices of Counts Sordina and Ralli, exit visas were granted on condition that Joyce swear to remain a non-combatant for the duration of the war. This he did happily. And so, at the end of June 1915, the family headed for the Swiss border. With him, Joyce carried the most immediate of his notes, but more significantly the first-written chapter of *Ulysses* – the 'Calypso' episode in which Leopold Bloom, lover of 'the inner organs of beasts and fouls', with mutton kidneys fried in butter on his mind, is introduced, and his sybaritic wife Molly Bloom (née Tweedy), lover of more human organs, luxuriates in the marital bed.

Somewhat riskily, he had agreed to act as a courier between an Italian student of his, Mario Tripcovich, son of the shipping tycoon Count Diodata Tripcovich, then living in Graz, and his fiancée, Sylvia Mordo, whose father had fled to Italy and was regarded by Austria as a traitor. So when Joyce and his family left Trieste he was carrying letters which, if they had been discovered, could have led directly to his arrest. The critical moment came at Feldkirch where the train was stopped and border guards checked passports and luggage. To Joyce's relief his 'hot' letters went undetected and he was at last free to cross into neutral territory. Revisiting the town years later he told a friend (Eugene Jolas): 'Over those tracks ... the fate of *Ulysses* was decided.'[32] In return for this service, and for forwarding letters for him, too, the Count had agreed to pay rent on the Joyce apartment during their absence.

They would remain in Switzerland for the rest of the war. But Joyce would never lose his deep affection for the liberal culture of Trieste and would look back with nostalgia on the happy times spent overindulging around its convivial cafés. As he sang in celebration of it in *Finnegans Wake*, '*trieste, ah trieste ate my liver!*'[33] And as he told Stuart Gilbert, a later friend and collaborator, 'I cannot begin to give you the flavour of the old Austrian Empire. It was a ramshackle affair but it was charming, gay, and I experienced more kindnesses in Trieste than ever before or since in my life ... Times past cannot return but I wish they were back.'[34]

18

The Exile in Exile

(1915–1917)

'Falsity of purpose was the literary sin against the Holy Ghost, and he [my brother] was vigilant to detect it. In his fashion not unlike Carlyle's ideal of the poet as priest, he watched, though he did not pray.' Stanislaus Joyce, *My Brother's Keeper*

The Joyces arrived in Zurich on 30 June 1915 and checked into the Gasthaus Hoffnung where eleven years earlier James had brought Nora on their Swiss 'honeymoon'. It would be the first of seven addresses in Zurich over the next four years. Behind in Trieste were left most of his possessions, including books, notes and manuscripts, except for that first fragment of *Ulysses* with its sketchy glimpse of Leopold Bloom, the freelance advertising salesman, child of an East European Jewish *converso*, who had also converted in order to marry the one-time Molly Tweedy. With him he carried the idea of an Odyssean day (or eighteen hours and forty-five minutes to be exact) in the life of 'dear dirty Dublin' observed through the eyes of Stephen, Bloom, Molly and Joyce's poetic other.

Into wartime Zurich had flooded a mixture of refugees and revolutionaries, artistic and political, of many nationalities and ethnic origins. The city's main street, Bahnhofstrasse, thronging with exiles, spies and deserters, had become known as 'Balkanstrasse', and so intense was the political debate and agitation that, according to the Austrian writer Stefan Zweig, 'Landscape, mountains, lakes and their enfolding calm went unnoticed in this bewitched world; life meant newspapers, bulletins and rumours, opinions, explications ... one lived the war in one's mind more intensely than at home in a country at war ... '[1] But this climate of cultural ferment suited Joyce, as it had in Trieste, and his mood while living there was recalled as being 'very gay'.[2]

Like Dublin, Zurich was bisected by a river, the Limmat, joined within the city limits by a tributary, the Sihl, and like both Dublin and Trieste it had a thriving theatrical and operatic scene and was a hotbed of gossip, especially in time of war when the established intellectual and artistic world was being challenged. Jung was there developing his own version of psychoanalysis; Lenin was awaiting his moment to instigate a Russian revolution and transform the new century, and the subversive Dadaists, inspired by the Romanians Tristan Tzara and Marcel Janco, were creating works and ideas which would lead to Surrealism and beyond.

Amid this chaos of war, pacifists like Stefan Zweig and Romain Rolland took their own stand for culture and civilization in their anti-war *International Review*, for which Joyce worked briefly. The shades of Mozart, Goethe, Wagner and Casanova stalked the city streets, and at its two main theatres, the Stadttheater and the Pfauen, the teenage Lotte Lenya, future wife of composer Kurt Weill, was acting and singing in plays including Shaw's *Caesar and Cleopatra*, and operas by Lehár and Strauss. Even during wartime, orchestras and opera companies were drawn to Zurich by its long musical tradition. Far from the sound of guns, here was a milieu which could strike sparks from the imagination and stimulate the revolutionary instinct. Here the ambience and topography of the town would provide Joyce with the tranquillity and stimulus needed to create the masterpiece now evolving in an imagination at its most fertile.

After a week in the city, the Joyces moved to a small apartment at 7 Reinhardstrasse. In a tight spot financially they were fortunate enough to receive an unexpected gift of £15 (some 375 Swiss francs) from Nora's uncle Michael Healy which eased their immediate situation. That situation was also very much in the mind of Ezra Pound in London, who was bending his efforts to secure a grant for Joyce from the Royal Literary Fund, and had begun canvassing potential supporters. H. G. Wells said he had no clout with Edmund Gosse, who administered the fund with Sir Henry Newbolt, and, with unconscious irony, Ford Madox Hueffer offered to find Joyce work with the War Office Censorship Department. Yeats was more than ready to help, and found Gosse sympathetic but wanting to see examples of Joyce's work. Wisely, while mentioning *Dubliners* as 'a book of satiric stories of great subtlety, a little like Russian work', he first focused Gosse's attention on the inoffensive *Chamber Music*, extolling in particular 'I Hear an Army' as 'a technical and emotional masterpiece'. Later he wrote declaring Joyce 'a man of genius ... [with] the promise of a great novelist and a novelist of a new kind'.[3] Joyce also wrote stressing the misfortune that had led him to Zurich, the expense of moving, the threat from Italian airships to his home in Trieste, and his difficulty in having to support his young family. He asked Elkin Mathews to send Gosse a copy of *Chamber Music* but left Yeats to send him *Dubliners*. The Fund's committee still needed some persuading and it would be a while before Joyce heard their decision.

Having declared his inability to help with Gosse, Wells now wrote expressing admiration and interest in Joyce's work. Thrilled to hear from so celebrated a writer, Joyce wrote back, 'I shall be very pleased indeed to make your acquaintance and shall be glad of an opportunity of thanking you personally for your friendly interest in my writings.' Forgetting, it seems, that Europe was off the itinerary of most English travellers except soldiery, he said he hoped that if ever Wells was in his neighbourhood he would call on him.[4]

Joyce's agent Pinker wrote saying that he had recommended *A Portrait* to the British publisher Martin Secker, and Pound promised he would pass *Exiles* to a leading American agent. Duly encouraged, Joyce found a woman willing to type his play in return for two English lessons. In London, Pound stressed to Yeats the need for warm clothing in a country like Switzerland, and reported Joyce's iritis attacks which could incapacitate him for two to three weeks at a time. Whatever the state of his eyes, his memory remained as sharp as ever. When Harriet Weaver sent copies of *The Egoist* containing episodes of *A Portrait*, even though the manuscript was still in Trieste he was able to make corrections from memory. But, ominously enough, soon afterwards Weaver reported that *The Egoist*'s printer had refused to typeset certain passages of the novel in the August instalment, and as the episode was already in print he would have to wait for *A Portrait* to be published in book form before the expurgated passages could be restored.

At the end of July the Royal Literary Fund sent Joyce a form asking for a detailed description of his situation and the names of two referees. Pound supported him enthusiastically. 'I consider Joyce a good poet, and *without exception* the best of the younger prose writers,' he wrote, adding that *A Portrait* was 'a work of indubitable value, and permanence' and that his work had been 'absolutely uncorrupted'. For a decade he had lived remotely and in poverty in order to perfect his style and was therefore uncontaminated by commercial influences.

> His style has the hard clarity of a Stendhal or a Flaubert ... He has also the richness of erudition which differentiates him from certain able and vigorous but rather overloaded impressionist writers. He is able, in the course of a novel, to introduce a serious conversation, or even a stray conversation on style or philosophy without being ridiculous.

But the splenetic Pound then risked jeopardizing Joyce's case by attacking the government for 'investing in wrecks' by paying pensions to the likes of Walter de la Mare rather than men like Joyce who were producing 'lasting work'.[5]

Yeats, his second referee, wrote to Gosse, saying that he considered Joyce one of the most promising of Irish writers. In a second letter, responding to an enquiry from Gosse about his politics and wartime loyalties, he wrote:

He had never anything to do with Irish politics, extreme or otherwise, and I think disliked politics. He always seemed to me to have only literary and philosophic sympathies. To such men the Irish atmosphere brings isolation, not anti-English feeling. He is probably trying at this moment to become absorbed in some piece of work till the evil hour is passed. I again thank you for what you have done for this man of genius.[6]

Finally, at the end of August, Joyce received the first £25 of a £75 grant through the Credit Suisse. He wrote a suitably gracious note of thanks to the members of the committee, something for which he demonstrated a nicely judged talent over the years.

The embryonic *Ulysses* was now at the centre of his creative focus. Behind his novel stood the Homeric myth, for, he believed, 'The most beautiful, most human traits are contained in the Odyssey.'[7] His imaginative world was peopled by the ghosts of great writers and their characters. Molly Bloom, for example, is a reincarnation of a female type celebrated in literature – the Greek goddess 'Calypso', Chaucer's 'Wife of Bath', Defoe's 'Moll Flanders' – who delights in her sensual being, and in fantasy at least, freely and shamelessly indulges her carnal appetites. (In the 'Ithaca' episode Bloom lists twenty-five suspected lovers and his reaction to her supposed infidelities.) Joyce's sexually uninhibited letters from Dublin in 1912 suggest an equally sexually uninhibited Nora, a willing partner in a sado-masochism fantasy – the masochistic Joyce pleading with his dominatrix Nora for humiliation, much as Bloom pleads with Bella Cohen. In his library Joyce had *Venus in Furs* by Sacher-Masoch (first name Leopold), a book which gave him some of the more deviant excesses in the 'Circe' episode, and Richard and Robert in *Exiles* embody something of Masoch and de Sade.[8]

In September 1915, Pound, having read the final chapter of *A Portrait* in *The Egoist*, was immensely impressed – 'I think the book is permanent like Flaubert and Stendhal,' he wrote. 'Not so squarish as Stendhal, certainly not so varnished as Flaubert. In English I think you join on to Hardy and Henry James – I don't mean a resemblance, I mean that there's has [sic] been nothing of permanent value in prose in between. But I think you must soon, or at least sooner or later, get your recognition.'[9] The brilliance of the novel he put down to the fact that Joyce had spent so much of the early part of his creative life in Trieste rather than huddled in the British provinces.

Joyce was growing desperate to get *A Portrait* out in book form so that he could concentrate on *Ulysses*. But London publishers were not enthusiastic. Grant Richards, Secker and Herbert Jenkins turned it down; Duckworth simply dithered. John Lane then expressed an interest, but

Harriet Weaver, equally concerned to see it out in book form, suddenly suggested that *The Egoist* might publish it.[10]

By the end of October the Joyces had moved to 19/III Kreuzstrasse, a large apartment house on a busy street sloping gently down towards Lake Zurich. As they settled into their newly adopted city, so they adjusted to its social life. Nora was ever anxious to keep abreast of the latest fashion and ensure that her children and husband were well turned out. Lucia, now eight, adapted more successfully to her new school and having to speak German than Giorgio, becoming her class 'entertainer', telling tall stories about Trieste and Galway, while her brother, aged ten, found himself demoted to a lower form almost immediately. Family life underwent changes, too. In Zurich, unlike Trieste, it was conventional for wives to accompany husbands to theatres and restaurants and so the children were often left alone. On one occasion when their parents set off for the theatre they were heard to complain bitterly, 'And now we shall be shut up again like pigs in a sty!'[11] But more often it was Nora who grumbled when Jim got drunk and had to be carried home.

Since Stannie's detention in Trieste, Jim had kept in touch with him, sending money and food parcels, and exchanging birthday and seasonal greetings. Over time Stannie gained the impression that his brother, well out of harm's way, was on easy street, especially when told about his 'pension' from the Royal Literary Fund. He had now been transferred to a castle, Schloss Grossau bei Raabs, in Lower Austria, grown a beard and kept fit by playing tennis – a fairly civilized internment by all accounts. Both Jim and Nora wrote to him, and the children sent postcards, but he replied more often to Nora (pretending to the other internees that she was his wife – perhaps, indulging the secret fantasy that she had 'married' him rather than Jim).

Eileen wrote from Prague saying that she and her husband Frantisek, who had been excused national service, were safe. Charlie Joyce, working for the telephone company in Dublin, having been widowed, had married a devout Catholic and was now the father of five children. Nora received news from her distraught mother that her brother Tom had enlisted in the British Army and might soon be sent to France. Meanwhile, Michael Healy had sent them another £9. In thanking Healy, a pious man, Joyce said he had just been celebrating the festival of St Justin Martyr, patron saint of Trieste, and if he could discover who was the patron saint of men of letters he would pray just to remind himself that he existed. Pound told him that *Exiles* would never find a theatre in England, so he trudged around Zurich trying in vain to interest producers there, even getting to know the director of the Stadttheater for the purpose.[12]

He began acquiring friends in Zurich. At his favourite café, the Pfauen in Heimplatz, adjacent to the Pfauen Theatre, he met Ottocaro Weiss, a student of political economy and friend of Oscar Schwartz, one of his Triestine students. (The idea of Black introducing him to White amused Joyce.) While Weiss's brother, Edoardo, had been a student of Freud, Ottocaro was an acquaintance of Jung. Talk at the Pfauen ranged over theatre, art and the new 'science of the mind', as well as literature. Although Joyce took a poor view of psychoanalysis he was certainly interested in Freud's theory of the interpretation of dreams. He recorded his own dreams in a notebook during 1916 and encouraged Nora to describe hers which he also noted down.[13] Weiss interested Joyce partly because he was Jewish and through him he could, as he had with Schmitz, continue to explore the Jewish consciousness. This fascination led him to works by Otto Weininger, such as *Sex and Character* which suggested, more than a little irrationally, that Jewish men are naturally womanly, a quality he ascribed to Bloom and which reflected something in himself.

Although Joyce advertised in the Zurich newspapers he had little success in recruiting students. The few he did attract were often people he already knew. He disliked being solely dependent on teaching so was pleased to hear from Pound in the New Year that Harriet Weaver had been persuaded to pay him £50 from *The Egoist*. Pound also informed him that so far *A Portrait* had been rejected by Werner Laurie, John Lane and Jonathan Cape, then an editor at Duckworth, whose reader Edward Garnett complained of its formlessness and use of 'ugly words'. Pound called the likes of Garnett 'vermin' and 'lice' who needed exterminating if there were to be any hope for the future of English literature.[14]

Like Pound, Harriet Weaver thought highly of *A Portrait* and told Joyce that, having found a willing printer, she was now ready to publish his 'wonderful book', and would soon send the promised £50 in two instalments. Joyce was so relieved that he instructed Pinker to accept whatever terms Weaver offered.

He was further encouraged in February when the Secretary of the Stage Society which generally produced Shaw's plays, asked to see *Exiles*. When the Society turned it down, Joyce blamed Shaw, but Shaw later denied having vetoed it, saying that he had merely recommended cuts to avoid action by the Lord Chamberlain, the official English theatre censor in those days.[15] In fact, records of the Stage Society reveal that Joyce's play was voted down by four to two.[16] Shaw, who did not vote, submitted the comment: 'Just the thing for the S.S.'[17] Interviewed later, he said that while he liked the play he had recommended cuts because Joyce always thought he had to include some obscenity in his work, which he found boring. When *Exiles* was not performed he simply took it that Joyce was not prepared to wield the blue pencil.[18] Joyce's own version of events was, 'It was put in the programme of the Stage Society together with Congreve's *Way of the World*, and d'Annunzio's *Dead City* ... but then removed again, owing to a protest by Bernard Shaw, who found it "obscene".'[19]

Not long after arriving in Zurich, Joyce had reported to the Consulate and on 1 March he was sent a circular informing him that under the new UK Military Service Act 'any British subject ... who would be willing to serve in His Majesty's forces if called on, and who is considered physically and otherwise suitable' was invited to register himself and report for physical examination.[20] Joyce ignored this summons to the flag, but three months later received a reminder inviting him to respond. He did so by informing the Consul that he was under a signed obligation to the Austrians to remain a non-combatant in return for permission to leave the country. For the time being he was left alone, but his unwillingness to register had been noted and would be held against him later.

Harriet Weaver's optimism about being able to publish *A Portrait* proved premature. When her printer backed out she found no others willing to print certain passages unaltered – probably scared off by the prosecution of D. H. Lawrence's *The Rainbow* the previous November. Pound suggested that if a printer could be found to print what was 'safe', he would fill in any blanks with typewritten insertions. By April nine printers had refused the book in England, and at Pound's suggestion, Miss Weaver decided to find an American printer who would send the pages for her to have bound in London.

By this time the Joyces had moved to a slightly larger ground-floor apartment at 54 Seefeldstrasse, in a small enclave off the main street leading south from the city along the Zurichsee. There they would remain for nine months, during which time, on 24 April 1916, the Uprising in Dublin, followed by the execution of the ringleaders (including his one-time Gaelic teacher, Patrick Pearse), disturbed not just the peace of Ireland but the peace of the British Empire itself. Joyce was shocked by the violence and what remaining sympathy he had for Sinn Fein evaporated. The incident touched him personally when his old friend 'Knicker-bockers', Francis Sheehy-Skeffingon, leading a pacifist demonstration, was shot dead by a demented British officer recently back from France and ready to shoot 'conchies' on sight.

In mid-May, Joyce heard from a New York publisher, John Marshall, wanting to publish *A Portrait* in full. This was particularly welcome news as, with his Royal Literary Fund grant about to expire, his financial situation had again become acute. Marshall sent him a £10 advance and the Irish-American lawyer, John Quinn, a friend of Yeats with a passion for Irish literature, sent him £10 as a pledge of support and admiration for his work. His circumstances were further improved in June when Pound, after much effort, persuaded the Society of Authors to award him grants of £2 (50 Swiss francs) a week for thirteen weeks from its War Emergency Fund. In July Pound helped again by forwarding him £20 'from an anonymous donor'. The following year, still in dire straits, Joyce asked Harriet Weaver to approach the scholar-poet and civil servant Edward Marsh on his behalf for help, which she did.[21] Marsh would occasionally help indigent writers from a parliamentary grant awarded to his family after the assassination of his great-grandfather, Prime Minister Spencer Perceval in 1816. Joyce was duly granted a handout from what Marsh jokingly called the Perceval 'murder money'.

John Marshall's business, which was poorly funded, collapsed in July and his plan to publish *A Portrait* evaporated, but Pound felt sure that Joyce would soon find a US publisher. His judgement was confirmed when, on 16 June (an emblematic date for Joyce) Benjamin Huebsch wrote to Miss Weaver with his proposal: publication of the complete novel, with sheets printed in the US going to the English publisher under joint imprints, the costs being shared. He also wanted to take sheets of *Dubliners* from Grant Richards and an option on Joyce's next book.[22] He was anxious, he said, to see Joyce properly launched in America, and Pound recommended that Huebsch's offer be accepted. In England the situation was still unresolved. Heinemann, briefly interested, was the latest London publisher to refuse the book. Now it would be up to Harriet Weaver and her Egoist Press.

That summer Pound, knowing that Yeats enjoyed a Civil List pension, asked what chances Joyce had of obtaining one. Yeats said that, although it required a parliamentary grant, the Prime Minster had the discretion to make such awards himself. So, through Lady Emerald Cunard, whom he had met on his rounds of literary London, Pound sent copies of Joyce's books to Edward Marsh, who was also Prime Minister Herbert Asquith's Private Secretary in charge of Civil List pensions. Marsh liked what he read and wrote to George Moore and Yeats asking their opinions of their fellow Irishman. Moore, despite his dislike of the young Joyce, and despite thinking the *Dubliners* stories uneven, wrote admiringly of 'The Dead', assuring Marsh that Joyce had not been around when 'the Sinn Fein seed' was being sown, and had last left Dublin with a good reputation. 'I am sure,' he concluded, 'that from a literary point of view Joyce is deserving of help.'[23]

Marsh wrote eloquently in his support to Asquith, saying that Joyce's work was occasionally 'outspoken' but not excessively so, and although he had once drunk quite heavily he had since recovered and was now above reproach. On 19 August, Asquith, who was also considering the case of the novelist Leonard Merrick, noted on the papers submitted, 'Yes, with some doubts as to Joyce.'[24] Nevertheless, next day Marsh issued a directive to the Treasury authorizing the Paymaster General to pay Joyce 'one hundred pounds Sterling (£100–0–0) as of His Majesty's Royal Bounty'.[25] (Lawrence later received £50.) When the news came in a letter bearing the 10 Downing Street address and crest, Joyce immediately informed his father who (despite his rebel inheritance) was overwhelmed by the 'Royal Bounty' reference, and expressed pride at his son receiving 'such an honour from His Majesty'.[26] Congratulations also arrived from Eileen in Prague, from Poppie (Sister Mary Gertrude) at her convent in New Zealand, and from Stanislaus in his Austrian prison camp.

Joyce's supporters, such as Yeats and Moore, knew of his youthful debauches around Dublin, of course, but nothing of his drinking in Trieste or Zurich. The fact that he could now write as he evidently was writing, must have led them to believe he was now a sober, hard-working author. During the day he certainly was; he had learned to confine his alcoholic indulgences to the evenings, often ending up legless and in no condition to deserve the honour of a government subvention. Joyce was only too aware that being 'a mystery' had its advantages. It also helped to be called 'a genius' in influential literary reviews.

In the hope that the pension might be renewed for a second year, at Pound's suggestion Joyce composed the most polite and punctilious letter of thanks imaginable to a British Prime Minister from a descendant of one of the Whiteboys of Munster, ending 'Your faithful and obedient servant'.[27] Other letters went to Marsh, Lady Cunard, Yeats and Moore. In thanking Yeats for his support over the pension, he wrote, 'I hope that now at last matters may begin to go a little more smoothly for me for, to tell the truth, it is very tiresome to wait and hope for so many years.' He also took the opportunity of acknowledging the wider help he had received, especially from Yeats and his dynamic American protégé. 'I can never thank you enough for having brought me into relations with your friend Ezra Pound who is indeed a wonder worker.'[28]

That wonder worker had in fact worked wonders on Joyce's reputation. He was, remarked Pound, becoming famous for being spoken and written about more than for being read. As proof of that, he was welcomed even further into the British Establishment with an entry in the 1916 edition of *Who's Who*, the pages of which were mostly reserved for the Empire's great and good. (It cannot have lessened the suspicion in certain Irish quarters that he had become a British agent.) When publishers asked for biographical information for publicity purposes it saved time for him to be able to refer them to his entry in *Who's Who*. But for the benefit of Harriet Weaver and Huebsch (who was also interested in publishing

Chamber Music) he supplied a 500-word mini-biography, placing his work in the context of his life so far.[29]

For a brief moment in late September the ferocious war engulfing the Western Front touched Joyce, when news came that Captain Tom Kettle of the Dublin Fusiliers had been killed leading his company 'over the top' at the Battle of the Somme. Writing to his old friend's widow, Mary Sheehy, and thinking also of her deceased brother-in-law Francis Skeffington, he wrote: 'I am grieved to learn that so many misfortunes have fallen on your family in these evil days,'[30] one of his few recorded comments on the Great War.

Although Joyce's financial circumstances had been alleviated, his sense of anxiety had not: in an uncertain world his and his family's security and his own long-term literary prospects were equally uncertain. At the end of October he suffered several collapses (each lasting around twenty minutes) which he feared might be due to a heart condition, but his doctor diagnosed a nervous breakdown. (Nora also suffered bouts of depression with similar symptoms.) It took him a while to recover properly and get back to *Ulysses*.

Huebsch published *A Portrait* in New York on 20 December. The same day, Pound, having seen a photograph Joyce had sent, wrote saying that he was horrified by the condition of his eyes, and decided to offer him the benefit of his diagnostic skills. 'It is a bit terrifying. I suspect your oculist of believing that your astigmatism is harmonic and not inharmonic. Hence the lines of eyestrain in the forehead. I'd like to see your glasses prescription.' He was anxious to put Joyce in touch with an American oculist who had treated him.[31] But the health of Joyce's reputation also concerned Pound. In January his essay on *Exiles* would appear in the American magazine *Drama* and he would pass the play to Yeats who had told him, 'If it is at all possible the Abbey should face a riot for it.'[32]

Once Huebsch had published *A Portrait*, things moved quickly. On 22 January 1917, having received the printed sheets from America, Miss Weaver telegraphed Joyce to announce that the Egoist Press five-shilling edition would be out in England on 15 February, just missing his thirty-fifth birthday. Now he could relax and await reviews of the book which had taken him fourteen years to complete and see published. However, he would have difficulty reading them because on 4 February he suffered yet another painful attack of rheumatic iritis. He was unable to write for a month and for a while he feared he might lose his sight completely.

Pound, in his *Egoist* review of *A Portrait*, called it 'real writing' and again compared him favourably to Flaubert.[33] Yeats, who rarely read novels, had obtained the US edition and on 11 February told Pound *A*

Portrait of the Artist was 'a very great book – I am absorbed in it.'[34] Pound forwarded Yeats's letter to Joyce, but said that he could expect 'a few violent attacks from several sheltered, and therefore courageous, anonymities'.[35]

In the *Freeman's Journal*, one such 'courageous anonymity' declared that 'Mr Joyce plunges and drags his readers after him into the slime of foul sewers,'[36] and the *Irish Book Lover*'s 'Anon' concluded that, 'No clean-minded person could possibly allow it to remain within reach of his wife, his sons or daughters.'[37] But the *TLS*'s Arthur Clutton-Brock described it as 'wild youth, as wild as Hamlet's, and full of wild music,'[38] while in the *New Statesman*, 'Solomon Eagle' (J. C. Squire) called Joyce 'a genuine realist' whose 'prose instrument is a remarkable one'. It was not a book for the easily disgusted, he said, and what Joyce would do with his powers was unclear but it was doubtful that he would make a novelist.[39] Wells, writing in *The Nation*, said that while he objected to Joyce's 'cloacal obsession', it was 'a book to buy and read and lock up, but ... not a book to miss'.[40] In *The Smart Set*, Mencken foresaw 'a Joyce cult'[41] and *The Dial*'s John Macy said that 'If they ever put up a statue of Joyce in Dublin it will not be during his lifetime. For he is no respecter of anything except art and human nature and language.'[42] It was both a shrewd observation and an accurate prediction.

Joyce was delighted with the reception of *A Portrait*, even enjoying the expressions of disgust, saving some for quotations on the book blurb, and writing to thank all his reviewers. Then, as if to celebrate the news of his book's British publication, the Joyces moved to a large third-floor apartment at 73 Seefeldstrasse, where Giorgio had to sleep on a camp bed and Lucia shared the bedroom with her parents. (Nora's biographer Brenda Maddox suggests that these sleeping arrangements in Zurich plunged nine-year-old Lucia into the highly charged sexual atmosphere which then existed between her parents. Joyce did say later that among his writings the best source for understanding his daughter was *Exiles*.) The apartment belonged to the uncle of his student Paul Ruggiero and the rent was high, but they found it comfortable and liked their neighbour, Philipp Jarnach, assistant to the composer Ferruccio Busoni. But Jarnach did not much care for Joyce's singing, considering his voice 'disagreeable and rather loud ... penetrating and not always correctly pitched'. When he complained, Joyce agreed to sing only at certain hours, and the two men became friends despite their differences in musical taste: Jarnach, a modernist who admired Schoenberg; Joyce, essentially an opera buff who preferred what Jarnach called 'the old Italian hackneyed things'.[43]

In March, just as the Swiss winter was passing, the sun broke through for Joyce. He received a letter from a firm of London solicitors advising him of a gift from an anonymous 'admirer'.

> We are instructed to write to you on behalf of an admirer of your writing, who desires to be anonymous, to say that we are to forward you a cheque for £50 on the 1st May, August, November and February next, making a total of £200, which we hope you will accept without any enquiry as to the source of the gift. We trust that this letter will reach you, the address having been taken by our client from 'Who's Who' for 1917, Yours faithfully, Slack, Monro Saw & Co.

That last sentence was a clever ploy to put him off the scent. His anonymous 'admirer' was someone known to him who knew exactly where he lived. Joyce was overwhelmed but was too ill to reply until 6 March when his eyes had improved, but even then the letter had to be written for him. 'Allow me to express my sincerest gratitude both for the munificence of your gift and for the delicacy of its giving. I hope that the future may justify in some measure an act so noble and considerate.'[44]

After the wide review coverage, the book began to sell respectably. Miss Weaver informed Joyce that two hundred had been sold in one week, including orders from two Dublin booksellers. He had copies sent to various friends and acquaintances in England and Ireland, including his family. Their reactions were mixed. Forty-five years later his sister May recalled that while taking pride in Jim's success, 'When the *Portrait* was published, it really embarrassed us a lot to see the family details given to the public.'[45] Yeats's friend John Quinn reported good sales in America and offered £20 for the corrected proof sheets.[46]

The first reaction to the book from an old friend came from Con Curran who wrote saying how much pleasure parts of it had given him. However, he lamented the absence of some episodes from *Stephen Hero* and felt that Stephen's classmates were too easily recognizable. He also thought Joyce had been unkind to the 'harmless' and 'rather pitiable' Father Darlington, and found the passages on aesthetics 'dead'. No doubt, he said, 'another volume of unamiable observation [was] threatening' – about the Abbey crowd, for example – but he hoped Joyce would turn from autobiography towards something deeper and more imaginative.[47]

By its very achievement, *A Portrait of the Artist* demonstrated the fulfilment of the ambition it expressed – to create a distinctive Irish consciousness. The young man had indeed become an artist in something like the manner charted in his book. And although it was, as Stanislaus had declared of its forerunner, 'a lying autobiography', it was still a portrait, and the representation of a real intellectual journey, an escape from despotic religion through art to free expression, a journey made magically alive through the most stylistic mastery of the language. The musical ear had led him to a musical prose.

Pound was now cultivating the editors of the *Little Review*, a Chicago-based literary magazine, which John Quinn was funding, trying to find an outlet for his own work and that of his other protégés Wyndham Lewis and T. S. Eliot. It had given Joyce a 'puff' in the February issue, and its editors, Jane Heap and Margaret Anderson, had become enthusiastic about *A Portrait*. Heap saw it as 'a living thing, new and soaring, and beautiful, impalpable, imperishable',[48] while Anderson wrote, 'There is no doubt that we will have novels before long written without even as much of the conventional structure of language as Mr Joyce has adhered to – a new kind of "dimension in language" which is being felt in many places.'[49] Before long Anderson and Heap would be presented with just such a novel by Joyce himself.

With *A Portrait* now a *succès d'estime*, there was the real prospect of *Exiles* (which the English Stage Society was again asking to see) also being published. Yeats still had the manuscript and Joyce asked Pinker to resubmit it to Grant Richards as he wanted it in print before the end of the year. As ever, he needed to clear the decks before he could engage fully with his next project. What he was now aiming to produce was not simply another novel, but his *magnum opus* – the book that would place him alongside the great writers he admired and enable him to explore the farthest extents of his intellectual and imaginative capabilities.

19

The Coming Forth by Day of Leopold Bloom
(1917–1918)

'Great literature is simply language charged with meaning to the
utmost possible degree.' Ezra Pound, *How to Read* (1931)

Work on *Ulysses* progressed slowly, as did recovery from his eye complaint.
Joyce could not face the daylight without dark glasses, and, when working,
could only proceed cautiously, often using Nora or certain friends as
amanuenses. His powers of recollection were sharp, however dim his
vision grew from time to time, and he recreated his 'times remembered'
in an ever more dream-like form. Behind that dreamlike vision he was
trying to recapture a world he knew was passing away. He told his future
friend and the biographer of *Ulysses*, Frank Budgen, 'I want to give a picture
of Dublin so complete that if the city one day suddenly disappeared from
the earth it could be reconstructed out of my book.'[1]

In late March, Pound invited him to contribute to a magazine he hoped
to edit, but Joyce was reluctant to be diverted from his new project and
replied, 'Unfortunately, I have very little imagination. I am also a very
bad critic' – an ironic comment since he was then working on the 'Scylla
and Charybdis' episode of the novel in which he portrays himself imaginatively as an informed and extremely adept Shakespearean critic, albeit of
the biographical school, and a self-analyst, perceiving parallels between
himself and the darkly brooding Hamlet. But he was curious to know how
others would react to its experimental mode and structure. In April 1917
he asked Pound, 'I wonder if you will like the book I am writing? I am
doing it, as Aristotle would say, by different means in different parts.'[2]

On 6 April America declared war on Germany, becoming directly
involved for the first time in a European war. Three days later Lenin left
Zurich en route to revolutionize Russia. Meanwhile, still comparatively
detached from world affairs, Joyce engrossed himself in *Ulysses*. The stress
of what he was trying to do – to transform the story of his rescue by Alfred
Hunter into a great Dublinesque satire – led to another nervous collapse.

Once he had recovered, he read through Huebsch's edition of *A Portrait*,
and listed 365 misprints. Printers would be increasingly confused by his

language and textual innovations. He was disappointed with sales of the novel in England. In May, Miss Weaver informed him that during the first three months, just 435 copies had been sold – a slow start but there were only 240 copies left and she had sent his corrections to Huebsch. To Pound, he blamed what he called the book's 'collapse' on its lack of inverted commas.[3] However, sales in America were better, and John Quinn sent word that his payment of £20 for the novel's manuscript was on its way.

Harriet Weaver was playing a strange double game with him. While receiving friendly letters about the sales and reviews of *A Portrait* from her, Joyce was also receiving messages like this from her via Monro Saw, Weaver's London solicitors:

> Dear Sir ... Our client ... requests us to reply expressing thanks for the books and the courteous words written in them ... Our client is sorry to hear that you have been suffering for several weeks a painful and dangerous illness of the eyes and hopes that you are now better, and that the danger is over./Our client would like the arrangement as to quarterly cheques to continue whilst the war lasts, and until you are able to settle down again. Perhaps you will kindly notify to us any change in your address ...[4]

It was perfectly in character for Weaver to have concealed her generosity. She was forty, daughter of a Cheshire doctor ('hopelessly English', she said) and heiress to a small fortune – money derived from the cotton trade and built by investment which she viewed with distaste, seeing it as the ill-gotten product of usury. She was unmarried and driven by a strong urge to improve the world. Having helped fund *The Egoist* she was now funding its most brilliant contributor. In her eagerness to divest herself of this guilty burden of wealth, she was fortunate to come across Joyce who was more than eager to relieve her of it. Her odd relationship with Joyce at this time saw him sending her a money order for £2 6s 4d for extra copies of his book while she was sending him 1,300 francs (some £50) a quarter, anonymously, to cover his expenses.

In March, Joyce got involved briefly in a fruitless film project. However, having suffered an attack of glaucoma at the end of April, he found preparing a scenario difficult, so an English actor, Claud W. Sykes, was asked to type what he wrote. After the enterprise collapsed, Sykes agreed to undertake the typing of *Ulysses*. It was a friendship which would blossom and persist. At the same time Joyce's circle of friends continued to expand, all of them attracted to what Symons called his 'sinister genius'.[5] But he could be comical as well as sinister. When drunk he would unbend and launch into a string of obscene limericks or an operatic aria, or leap up and perform what friends called his 'spider dance', a wild caper enhanced in its comedic effect by wild contortions – a waving of his ashplant, a flinging of his spindly legs, arms shooting out from under the wide cloak he wore. He could break into this dance while walking with friends along Bahnhofstrasse, or start quoting poetry – his favourite Verlaine or sometimes Felix Beran's war poem.

> Des Weibes Klage
> Und nun ist kommen der Krieg der Krieg ...
> ('The woman complains
> And now is come the war the war ...')

Despite the bouts of drunken ribaldry, some friends denied that he ever used coarse language, except in his books, though one of his students, Paul Suter, recalled that he loved obscene words, 'savouring them like candy'.[6]

To add to his impaired eyesight, in early July Joyce was laid up for a week with fever and tonsillitis followed by attacks of nervous anxiety brought on by worry about the fate of *Exiles*, still in the hands of the Stage Society. Getting it into print, he told Grant Richards, would make it easier to interest theatres and would set his mind at rest. He was now convinced that it was the Zurich climate that was damaging his health and clouding his clarity of thought. But it was not just his health that prevented him throwing himself into the new book; his family life was also problematic. Nora seemed to share his ill-health – coming close to a breakdown herself, starting to lose her hair and having disturbing dreams. Lucia was also beginning to worry her fraught parents. In August, Joyce told Miss Weaver, 'I wrote you a letter a few hours ago but my daughter who is an "absentminded beggar" lost it somewhere in the street. So I repeat it here.'[7] For Maddox, Nora's biographer, that comment juxtaposed with the blank look Lucia presented in photographs taken at this time suggested something 'disturbing' about the girl.[8]

Joyce was delighted to see *A Portrait* reviewed in Germany (the *Berliner Tageblatt*), Holland (the *Nieuwe Amsterdammer*), Greece (the *Επερία*) and France (where *La Revue* compared him to Zola and Flaubert, saying, '*L'auteur se place du premier coup parmi les personnalités marquantes de la littérature anglaise réaliste*'). In Switzerland he elicited promises of reviews from the *Journal de Genève*, *La Semaine Littéraire* and *Neue Zürcher Zeitung*. In making his name as a man of European letters Joyce was never too proud to seek publicity. He asked Richards to be sure to insert a sheet of his *Portrait* reviews into *Exiles*, which he had at last agreed to publish.

A New York ophthalmologist, consulted by Quinn, had recommended a famous Zurich eye specialist, Ernst Sidler-Hugenan. When Joyce saw Sidler in early August, he was told that he had synechiae (adhesion of the iris to the cornea), and that the only cure was an iridectomy to his right eye. Delay would only make matters worse.

Yet however ill he was, Joyce was never fully able to dismiss *Ulysses* from his mind. He had a long discussion with his language student Georges Borach that summer, eulogizing the *Odyssey*, and Odysseus as above all other comparable literary heroes, arguing that 'The most beautiful, all-embracing theme ... the most beautiful, most human traits are contained in the *Odyssey*.' He had been entranced as a twelve-year-old schoolboy, he said, by the mysticism of Ulysses. For him, Ulysses was the only great man to survive the siege of Troy, and his own motives were now intertwined with those of his hero. 'The motif of wandering ... The motif of the artist, who will lay down his life rather than renounce his interest.' It sounded like a personal manifesto. Borach recalled him speaking (incorrectly) of fifty-year-old Odysseus encountering the seventeen-year-old Ariadne – the theme of the older man and the young girl clearly fascinated him and he told Borach that that, too, was 'a great motif!'[9]

In need of a break, Nora left for a holiday in Locarno, taking along the children and the family cat. The Italian-speaking city reminded her of Trieste, especially when she heard the shouts of the street-market traders. The people, she reported, were 'lively and dirty and disorderly', and the climate – apart from one terrifying thunderstorm – she felt was healthier. Her hair began to grow again and she began to unwind.[10] She hoped that without her and the children around Jim would be able to get on better with 'OOlysses'. But Joyce felt that his illnesses had dulled his brain and he was still worrying whether *Exiles* would ever be performed. Trying and failing to persuade theatre companies had become an irritating drag on his writing. 'My whole life,' he complained, 'seems to be taken up with useless correspondence.'[11]

In Locarno, at the Pension Daheim, Nora was enjoying herself, socializing, mountain-walking and taking trips on Lake Maggiore. She relaxed by reading a book sent by Jim (probably *Venus in Furs*) by their favourite pornographer. 'I am very glad to get it, especially as it is by Masoch,'[12] she wrote, and teased him with hints of flirtations by beginning one letter, 'Dear Cuckold'.[13] But the children were less serene. By mid-August they were anxious to get back to Zurich to prepare for the new school year, and, as they grew up, their mother was finding them something of a handful. 'I havent any trouble with them,' she reported, 'except in the morning before they get up it's a regular game with them they have a boxing match in the bed and of course I have to pull the two of them out on the floor Georgie is very shy he is afraid of his life I might see his prick so that he rolls himself up in the quilt.'[14] Why she allowed her ten-year-old daughter to sleep with her sexually aroused brother remains a mystery, as Lucia's biographer points out, but in Locarno Nora seems to have been less preoccupied with the children than with herself and her absent husband. She told him how much she was missing him, and hoped he was writing 'Ulisses [*sic*]' and not staying up too late at night.[15] Now back at work, Joyce was doing both.

There had been yet another hiccough over the Egoist Press edition of *A Portrait*. The printer who had agreed to print further sheets had gone off to war and his successor was refusing to set it up without deletions, so once more Miss Weaver was having to search for another. Ironically, however, Grant Richards, seeing the way the wind was blowing with Joyce, especially in America, decided to buy back some of the copies of *Dubliners* he had remaindered.

On 17 August, Nora and the children returned to Zurich to find him still beset by anxieties about *Exiles* and the failure of Quinn's money to arrive from New York. At that point, without warning, his health again collapsed. Out walking, he had suffered 'a violent *Hexenschuss*' (lumbago attack) and was unable to move for twenty minutes. Finally he managed to crawl on to a tram and get home. Although he felt better that evening, next morning he again had symptoms of glaucoma, and again blamed the Zurich climate, fearing that he would be unable to afford to heat the apartment during the approaching harsh winter.[16]

Meanwhile, there was no putting off the inevitable. On 23 August at the Augenklinik, Sidler performed his iridectomy – a complicated and difficult operation, Joyce was told. He emerged with bandage and eye-patch, looking more aloof and mysterious than ever. Afterwards he suffered another nervous collapse and it was three days before he was well enough to see Nora. Money worries and the strangely intense engagement he had with his novel probably lay at the root of his breakdowns, and Sidler advised him to seek a more relaxed climate. However, his eye was still bleeding and painful and it was not until mid-September that he was thought well enough to return home. Then, within two days he had a relapse and was back in the Augenklinik for another operation. Fortunately the Perceval 'murder money' arrived in time to pay Sidler's bill.

Pound had somehow got the impression that his novel would be finished by the New Year and Miss Weaver said she was keen to serialize it in *The Egoist*. Aware of his present need, she offered Joyce a £50 advance, sending him £25 on account and adding, 'I think that the publication of the book as a serial would give *The Egoist* the right of publication later in book form.'[17] Pound wrote two days later saying that the *Little Review* (now based in New York) would publish *Ulysses* in instalments in America, even though it would mean adding extra pages to the magazine and incurring a higher printing bill. He would, he hoped, get Joyce a £100 fee for it.

If *Ulysses* was now guaranteed publication, *Exiles* was still being denied a theatre. At least Yeats had finally written explaining why he had not recommended it to the Abbey – the company never did such plays well and a dispute had robbed them of certain players while their best women actors had been lured away to the commercial theatre. Although Yeats had thought the play sincere, it was nothing like as good as *A Portrait* which he had found exciting and recommended widely. But not all Abbey theatregoers agreed with him. On 22 September, the diarist Joseph Holloway wrote, 'I finished reading James Joyce's crudely compiled book, *A Portrait of the Artist as a Young Man* in which he succeeds in introducing more downright coarseness of language and filthy expressions than any book I ever came across.' Yeats, however, was not so readily offended. Having heard about *Ulysses* he awaited it, he told Pound, 'with impatience'.[18]

Giorgio also had weak eyesight and perhaps for that reason was no great reader. Once, when Claud Sykes came to visit, Joyce asked him, 'What was Giorgio doing when you came in?' 'Reading,' said Sykes. Joyce feigned surprise, exclaiming, 'My son with a book!' Giorgio in his turn could be equally rude about his father, saying that he couldn't write anything as good as Wild West stories. Sykes was struck by the permissive chaos of the Joyce household. 'The children brought up themselves,' he recalled, 'and the house was a pigsty . . . The Joyces wouldn't have people in to tea because they were ashamed of their china and furniture.'[19]

The problem that most occupied him that autumn was that of transforming his novel into more than a sequel to *A Portrait*. He wanted to abandon the Daedalian myth and relate it more to that of the Odysseus legend. He took Walter Leaf's *Troy: A Study in Homeric Geography* and Victor Bérard's *Les Phéniciens et l'Odyssée* as his chief guides, in particular Bérard's idea that the *Odyssey* had Semitic origins which lent itself to Joyce's image of Bloom as Wandering Jew.[20] To bring his Edwardian Dublin alive he studied books on period slang, filling pages of his notebooks with words and phrases appropriate to the characters he was now conceiving.[21] When his notebook was not to hand, he made jottings on small scraps of coloured paper, menus and cigarette packets, often forgotten and later discovered in pockets, under ornaments or behind pictures. These notes were entered on to notesheets and, when used, scored in coloured crayon, each colour corresponding to an episode.

By late October the Joyces were in Locarno, lodged first at the Villa Rossa, and then at the Pension Daheim, where Nora had previously stayed. Away from the damp Zurich climate, the demands of students and landlords, Joyce hoped to make better progress with his novel. Working to reconstitute it, he listed and arranged his notes, ideas and turns of phrase culled from books and newspapers, sketches of scenes and characters under key headings. The schema he produced later, relating chapters of *Ulysses* to organs of the body, probably derived from the theosophical notion, recorded in the same notebook, that stages of occult development corresponded to various parts of the anatomy. These notes would feed into *Ulysses*, especially into his 'Circe' chapter and much later into the great confusion of words and ideas that would make up *Finnegans Wake*.[22]

He soon finished the first part of *Ulysses*, the 'Telemachia', and sent it to Sykes for typing. On 10 November he wrote a revealing letter to Edouard Dujardin, wanting to know if his novel *Les Lauriers sont coupés* was still obtainable. This, he claimed, was the source from which he adopted the *monologue intérieur*, now to be his main means of accessing the consciousness of his chief characters – Stephen Dedalus, Leopold Bloom and the voluptuous Molly – and his own copy was still in Trieste. This journey into the interior as a literary quest captured perfectly the spirit of the times, when the European mind was turning, under the guidance of Freud and Jung, in the same direction in its quest for an understanding of the human psyche. Joyce did not exactly declare his purposes to Dujardin but simply told him, 'I am a sincere admirer of your work, so personal, so independent, and also am a humble labourer in the vineyard of the Lord.'[23] His letter does not seem to have elicited a reply, but they would meet later when Joyce was no longer an obscure writer toiling among the celestial vines.

The continuity of Joyce's writing would become evident as *Ulysses* unrolled. Into it would be incorporated insights, epiphanies and images from his earlier work. The *monologue intérieur* also linked it back to *A Portrait*, where he had first flirted with the technique. In England it was adopted (by Virginia Woolf among others) as the 'stream-of-consciousness', a term coined by the American psychologist William James, and there are passages in Dickens, Tolstoy, Dostoevsky and Melville, as well as the dramatic soliloquy, which foreshadow its more sustained use to portray the flow of human consciousness. Dujardin had taken the idea from the operatic aria, and adopted it in a more sustained fashion than previously. Joyce only gradually came to grasp its full possibilities, but because he employed it to such brilliant effect with such subtle brilliance he is often credited, wrongly, with having invented it. Its effect can be to bemuse – Stephen's philosophical meanderings, Bloom's daydreaming, and Molly's nocturnal reveries required a new kind of reading and a new kind of readership.

But Joyce would deploy more than one technique. To achieve the effect he wanted he could switch from one register, one form of utterance or narrative mode to another – third-person narration, mock liturgy, stylistic pastiche, catechism, newspaper headlines and surreal drama, as well as verbal representations of conscious states and cinematic devices such as the fade and the flashback. The verbal mischief, the nimble turns and twists of mind, the time-shifts, the switches of consciousness, the protean imagery, the mirrored hall of memory, all of which characterize the text, offer a confusion of voices orchestrated around a series of powerful myths and recurrent motifs. Joyce was in the process of demonstrating a new and quite astonishing virtuosity.

Receiving another 1,000 francs from Monro Saw, he had the page-proofs of *Exiles* sent via the solicitor to his anonymous English admirer with his thanks. For the time being things were looking up. Richards had acted quickly to get his play into print, and Miss Weaver sent news that a second edition of *A Portrait* was pending. He promised her signed copies of *Dubliners* and *Chamber Music* and one of *Exiles* in due course. Meanwhile, the poet Thomas Sturge Moore, a board member of the Stage Society, told him that he had every hope that the Society would include the play in its spring programme. But Moore's confidence was misplaced; *Exiles* was kept for some five months without a clear decision. As Joyce told the story, the Society hung on to his play for three years – yet another 'betrayal' to add into his catalogue of treachery.

Nora complained that at the Pension Daheim Jim never spoke to her. Her biographer read this as a sign that Joyce's interest in sex had moved away from her.[24] If so, the reason was his new immersion in *Ulysses*. In the process of his novel being re-conceived, his narrative turned inwards, as did his own sexual impulse, towards recreating the libidinous worlds of Stephen Dedalus and the Blooms. Insofar as he indulged in sexual play it was in rehearsing the lubricious acts and fantasies of his principal characters. Nora's reaction was to withdraw. Joyce told Sykes that he had to apologize for her 'taciturnity' towards his wife Daisy and to the wife of a German friend, but she had been persistently ill and had suffered a number of nervous breakdowns. That, at least, was his explanation.

One of his playful indulgences was a strangely inept flirtation in Locarno with a tall, willowy, delicately attractive young German doctor, Dr Gertrude Kaempffer, who was recuperating from tuberculosis. He inveigled her into a correspondence, sending her letters declaring his love and recounting his first sexual experience – masturbating at the sound of that nursemaid urinating – and telling her that he enjoyed the thrill of clandestine sex and the risk of discovery.[25] The doctor's reaction was not as he had hoped; she was unmoved and thought him sad and sick rather than sexy and attractive. He was both recreating the sexual triangle he had explored in *Exiles* and exploring the sexuality of one of his characters (Bloom, who also indulged in similar fantasies with Martha Clifford and Gerty MacDowell, named, apparently, after the offended doctor). The urinary sexual fantasy which had surfaced in his obscene letters to Nora in 1909 would recur in *Finnegans Wake* where Humphrey Chimpden Earwicker stands accused of a similar indulgence. Probably not unaware of her strange husband's strange role-playing, it can be no wonder that Nora felt ignored. She did not react well. Joyce told Sykes that it was partly her nervous breakdowns that prompted him to consider returning to Zurich.

The first chapter of his novel, Stephen's Telemachian adventure with Buck Mulligan and Haines, the wild Englishman in the Martello Tower (with its mock dogma, mock liturgy and mock incantations) was followed by the 'Nestor' episode in which our hero confronts first a class of pupils, then the ethnocentric headmaster, Deasy, and finally the 'nightmare' of history. In the following episode, 'Proteus', he plunges into a sea of imagery and words, ebbing, flowing and whirling through the mind of Stephen as he walks the beach, self-absorbed to the point of abstraction, cloaked in thoughts both philosophical and sensual:

> Ineluctable modality of the visible: at least that if no more, thought through my eyes. Signatures of all things I am here to read, seaspawn and seawrack, the nearing tide, that rusty boot. Snotgreen, bluesilver, rust: colour signs. Limits of the diaphane. But he adds: in bodies. Then he was aware of them bodies before of them coloured ... Diaphane, adiaphane. If you can put your five fingers through it it is a gate, if not a door. Shut your eyes and see.[26]

The resonances from Dujardin's *Les Lauriers sont coupés* and the *monologue intérieur* method were now evident. The old balance between realism and symbolism would slowly tilt as *Ulysses* unwound towards the dream-like ebb and flow of *Finnegans Wake*.

Sykes, his typist, was having to unpick and decipher Joyce's entangled text. Although, as he said, he tried to write clearly with a large margin on the left-hand side of the page, there were important interlineations. As time went on, these wordy insertions and convolutions would extend themselves – such was the movement of Joyce's mind during the act of creation, much like that cavorting dance of his, the manuscript recording all the twists and turns of an intricate mental odyssey.

The first chapter of the novel reached Pound in early December and on the 17th he wrote back, 'Wall, Mr Joice, I recon your a damn fine writer, that's what I recon'. An' I recon' this here work O' yourn is some concarn'd litterchure. You can take it from me, an' I'm a jedge.'[27] Five years later he called it 'an epoch-making report on the state of the human mind in the twentieth century'.[28] Twenty years later, in his *Guide to Kulchur* (1938) he was even more fulsome:

> The katharsis of 'Ulysse', the joyous satisfaction as the first chapters rolled into Holland Place, was to feel that here was the JOB DONE and finished, the diagnosis and cure was here ... the whole boil of the European mind, had been lanced.[29]

Such was Pound's enthusiasm that Margaret Anderson felt able to announce in her *Little Review* that Pound had assured her the book was not just better than *A Portrait*, but 'rather better than Flaubert'. They were, she announced, about to start publishing a prose masterpiece.[30] Like *A Portrait*, *Ulysses* would first show itself in print in serial form in an obscure if radical literary magazine.

With a way forward for his novel now clear to him, worried about Nora's health and now bored with Locarno, Joyce decided to return to Zurich. It meant the children again changing schools and languages (from French back to German), but like Nora, they were merely guests at the moveable feast that was James Joyce, and were obliged to follow.

Early in 1918 Joyce was back in Zurich with the novel decidedly in progress. By late January the family was settled in a first-floor flat at 38 Universitätstrasse, just a short walk from the Pfauen where Joyce soon rejoined his old companions. His circle of friends was constantly expanding. He especially enjoyed the company of Greeks, such as Nicolas Santos, whose language fascinated him and who would recite bits of the *Odyssey* to him.

His reputation was spreading around Zurich, and probably through Ottocaro Weiss his name had reached the ears of Mrs Edith Rockefeller McCormick, a wealthy American patron of the arts and of psychoanalysis, who resided grandly at the Hotel Bauer au Lac. Mrs McCormick, an imposing and sympathetic figure, who dispensed largesse to struggling artists and intellectuals, among them Jung, now invited Joyce to visit her. She took to him and when she enquired what he was doing he lent her a manuscript copy of *Exiles*.

Joyce was so absorbed in his work that the great battles which were tearing Europe apart never seemed to intrude much into his private world – except that he was secretly under surveillance. He had been spied on in Trieste and was still being spied on in Zurich because of his pledge to avoid combat and because the Austrians had discovered his role as go-between on behalf of young Mario Tripcovich and his father. Probably aware that one of his students was an Austrian spy, Joyce was careful to cultivate an image he thought would please the Austrians. The spy duly reported to his masters that Joyce was more Fenian than pro-British.[31]

For Margaret Anderson at the *Little Review*, the arrival of the first chapters of *Ulysses* in New York was a key moment both in her own life and in the history of modern literature.

> I shall never forget the day in February, 1918, when Ezra Pound, as foreign editor of the Little Review, sent us a package from London. It contained the manuscript of Ulysses./I read straight through to Episode III. When I came upon 'Ineluctable modality of the visible: at least that if no more, thought through my eyes. Signatures of all things I am here to read, seaspawn and seawrack, the morning tide,' I remember calling out to Jane Heap, 'This is the most beautiful thing we'll ever have to publish. We're going to present a masterpiece to America.' [32]

Anderson began publishing *Ulysses* in the March 1918 issue of the *Little Review*. It was a fateful move for all involved, especially for the editors and for Joyce.

A friend in Trieste, the newspaper editor Roberto Prezioso, declared a passion for Nora, telling her, 'The sun rises for you.' Joyce may have feigned outrage, but he encouraged her to have affairs ('So he'd have something to write about,' she said). The character Robert Hand in *Exiles* seems to be modelled on him.

His brother's keeper: as a young man, Stanislaus Joyce was in awe of his brother's brilliance, but over time he became frustrated by his dissolute lifestyle and disenchanted with the way his genius developed.

A fateful union: Joyce's sister Eileen married Frantisek Schaurek, a Czech bank cashier, in 1914 before leaving Trieste for Prague. In 1926, Schaurek committed suicide after 'borrowing' 75,000 francs from the bank.

Nora surprised and delighted her husband by her performance as the Galway girl Cathleen in John Millington Synge's *Riders to the Sea*. 'I think Synge's words were spoken with the genuine brogue,' he told a friend.

The young family: Nora with Giorgio and Lucia in Zürich in 1918. As the family fortunes improved, Nora enjoyed dressing herself and her children in the latest fashions. Some think that the strange sexual tensions in the marriage were disturbing for the children, especially Lucia.

While in Trieste, Joyce brought out his first book, *Chamber Music*, a volume of lyrical poems, which gave him a pretext for cultivating a poetic image.

Frank Budgen, Joyce's 'Boswell' in Zürich, who, in his book *James Joyce and the Making of 'Ulysses'*, recorded the process by which the author created his masterpiece.

BELOW Although he was deeply engrossed in writing *Ulysses* while living in Zürich, Joyce cut a strange figure there, often having to be carried home dead drunk after a late-night binge. Among the chorus girls at the city's Stadttheatre, he was known as 'Herr Satan'.

Marthe Fleischmann and Rudolph Hiltpold, her 'guardian': she was briefly the target of Joyce's sexual passion, which led him to plan an elaborate seduction in Paul Suter's studio. Afterwards he told Budgen that his hands had just explored every part of a woman's body, both hot and cold.

Dazzled by fame: when Man Ray put him under the lights in his studio not long after an eye operation, Joyce showed distress and finally put his head in his hands, a moment captured here by the photographer.

Publisher and author: at her Paris bookshop, Shakespeare & Company, Sylvia Beach offered to publish *Ulysses*, which most other publishers would not touch for fear of prosecution.

Joyce owed much of his success to the enthusiastic support of a number of influential literary figures. Here he is seen in Paris in 1923 with Ezra Pound (second from right), who had helped *A Portrait of the Artist* to be published in 1914; John Quinn (far right), who helped him financially; and Ford Madox Ford (far left), who gave *Ulysses* a glowing review and later was the first to publish an episode of Joyce's latest work, entitled 'From Work in Progress', in his *transatlantic review*.

The bourgeois family man: behind the Bohemian imagination stood the man who craved respectability, disliked obscene language and enjoyed luxury.

Lucia's lost love: her passion for the young Samuel Beckett was unreciprocated, and after his rejection she began her slow descent into madness.

A lunch in honour of the author of *Ulysses* on Bloomsday 1929 at the Hôtel Leopold at Les Vaux de Cernay, near Versailles, was organized by his Paris publishers, Sylvia Beach and Adrienne Monnier, and attended by both expatriate and French admirers.

The Brancusi sketch of Joyce on the right was rejected by the publishers who had commissioned it for his book *Tales Told of Shem and Shaun*, but they accepted the one on the left, the artist's 'Symbol of Joyce'. On seeing this, John Joyce remarked, 'Jim has changed more than I thought.'

Unlikely revolutionaries: Jane Heap and Margaret Anderson (pictured here with Ezra Pound) began publishing *Ulysses* episode by episode, until they inadvertently sent a copy to a lawyer's daughter and ended up in court charged with publishing an obscene book.

20

Earthly Trials

(1918)

So Daedalus designed his winding maze;
And as one entered it, only a wary mind
Could find an exit to the world again—
Such was the cleverness of that strange arbour.

Ovid, *Metamorphoses*

The launching of *Ulysses* was not the only good thing to happen to Joyce that March. On the 1st he learned that he had been gifted 1,000 francs a month for a year from an anonymous source (Mrs McCormick, he later discovered) to be paid through the Eidgenossische Bank of Zurich. With his money from England he now enjoyed the comfortable monthly income of around 1,100 francs. Characteristically, he did not conserve this new-found wealth, but dispensed it merrily, entertaining friends at the Pfauen and investing generously in a project he was devising with Claud Sykes.

In Zurich there was a propaganda war in progress. The Germans were subsidizing German operas, plays and art exhibitions and the French were matching them. In 1917 Max Reinhardt's company had performed Shakespeare and Strindberg, while the Comédie Française had offered Molière. Richard Strauss had conducted *Elektra* and *Don Giovanni*. Claud Sykes, like Joyce under pressure from the British Consulate to make himself available for military service, conceived a way of demonstrating support for his country's cause without having to don military uniform or fire a gun in anger. He even thought he had tacit approval from the Consul for this. With Joyce's support, he and his wife, the actress Daisy Race, planned to form a semi-professional theatre company to be called the English Players, to perform plays by British playwrights. Sykes would do the producing while Joyce would be business manager. He hoped to gain kudos with the Consulate without violating his parole, and perhaps acquire financial backing from the government for this contribution to British propaganda. It would also provide him with a stage on which *Exiles* could be performed. Having decided to open with Wilde's *The Importance of Being Earnest*, they began casting around for players. Joyce was particularly keen to see Irish plays staged and the company would tackle works by Shaw,

Synge and Edward Martyn (for whose play, *The Heather Field*, he produced the programme notes).

Miss Weaver's reaction to *Ulysses* soon followed that of Margaret Anderson: '[It] is bitter reading, to me at least – difficult too, the third section, but of vital interest.' Her printers, she informed him, were refusing the 'Telemachus' chapter and she was looking for one prepared to take a risk.[1] Pound pre-empted any censorship of the 'Proteus' episode for the *Little Review* by excising the passage about the dog pissing against a rock on the beach, so making a mockery of the magazine's claim to be 'A Magazine of the Arts, Making no Compromise with the Public Taste'.

By the end of March, the 'Calypso' episode, featuring Bloom's morning ingestions and evacuations, was also with Pound. On Good Friday he sent Joyce his opinion. He found some passages difficult to stomach and worried about the danger it posed to the *Little Review* which at least offered him a modest source of income.

[It] has excellent things in it; but you overdo the matter … The excrements will prevent people from noticing the quality of things contrasted./ At any rate the thing is risk enough without the full details of the morning deposition. If we are suppressed too often we'll be suppressed finally and for all, to the damn'd stoppage of all our stipends. AND I cant have our august editress jailed, NOT at any rate for a passage which I do not think written with utter *maestria*.[2]

Pound told Quinn, the *Little Review*'s chief backer, who also found it repugnant, that he had taken his blue pencil to the offending episode. 'I rec'd the fourth chapter some days ago, and deleted about twenty lines before sending it off to NY.' Yet, despite his distaste for Bloom's sanitary habits, Pound continued to regard Joyce as the shape of things to come. 'It still seems to me,' he wrote, 'that America will never look *anything* – animal, mineral, vegetable, political, social, international, religious, philosophical or ANYTHING else – in the face until she gets used to perfectly bald statements,' and he deplored 'the English and American habit of keeping their ostrich heads carefully down their little silk-lined sandholes …'[3] Nevertheless, when this episode appeared in the *Little Review*, the critical moments of Bloom's visit to the outhouse had been excised as Pound had indicated, another compromise with public taste which Joyce did not appreciate.

Episodes V and VI ('Lotus-Eaters' and 'Hades') soon followed. The 'Lotus-Eaters' chapter tracks Bloom around Dublin and to the post office which serves as the post restante address of 'Henry Flower', his amatory alter ego, in pursuing his secretive erotic correspondence with Martha

Clifford. Joyce was working at full steam. In the 'Hades' chapter he took himself back to Glasnevin Cemetery where he had been part of the cortège at the funeral of Matt Kane, which in the novel becomes the burial of Paddy Dignam. En route to the cemetery, Bloom's carriage passes the perambulating Stephen (a boy not only in search of himself but in search of a father), and the rampant Blazes Boylan bound for an assignation with Bloom's wife Molly, so at that moment the main characters of the novel are fleetingly conjoined. The crossing and re-crossing of paths was emerging as a feature of the novel. At Glasnevin, Bloom's mind dwells on hideous images of death and decay, and his outsider status is emphasized through the malicious whisperings and contemptuous remarks of the other mourners: 'In God's name, John Henry Menton said, what did she marry a coon like that for?'[4] Bloom was destined to be scorned in Dublin, much as his creator thought *he* was (for marrying 'a barmaid').

In Weaver's quest for a publisher for *Ulysses*, Eliot suggested Leonard and Virginia Woolf, who had recently established the Hogarth Press at Richmond and were printing books on a hand-press. Encouragingly enough, in an article for the *Times Literary Supplement* on 10 April Virginia had named Joyce as 'the most promising' of the young writers then challenging 'the conventions of their predecessors'.[5] Weaver found herself invited to tea shortly afterwards, and, dressed with scant regard to fashion, as was her wont, she took along Joyce's manuscript, appropriately enough under a plain cover. Reports of the meeting read like drawing room comedy. In his autobiography Leonard Woolf recalled the occasion. 'On Sunday, April 14, 1918, Miss Weaver came to tea, bringing with her a large brown paper parcel containing the MS ... We put this remarkable piece of dynamite into the top drawer of a cabinet in the sitting-room ...'[6] But Weaver seemed ill-at-ease in the over-refined atmosphere chez Woolfs. While Leonard saw her simply as 'a very mild blue eyed advanced spinster', Virginia viewed her through the disdainful eye of a Bloomsbury snob as the unappealing and dowdy proprietress of a questionable periodical.

> I did my best, [she wrote in her diary] to make her reveal herself in spite of her appearance, all that the editress of the Egoist ought to be, but she remained unalterably modest, judicious and decorous. Her neat mauve suit fitted both soul and body; her grey gloves laid straight by her plate symbolized domestic rectitude; her table manners were those of a well bred hen. We could get no talk to go. Possibly the poor woman was impeded by her sense that what she had in the brown paper parcel was quite out of keeping with her own contents. But then how did she ever come in contact with Joyce and the rest? Why does their filth seek exit

from her mouth? Heaven knows. She is incompetent from the business point of view and was uncertain what arrangements to make ... And so she went.[7]

A month later, Woolf wrote to Weaver saying that the length of the manuscript precluded them from undertaking the work on their small hand-press in less than two years, which she thought would be unacceptable to Joyce.[8] She might not have read it through at the time because she reserved her most caustic comments for the book until it finally appeared. Her servant was instructed to return the brown paper parcel.

The Importance of Being Earnest opened on 29 April at the Theater zu den Kaufleuten on Pelikanstrasse. Complimentary tickets were sent to Mrs McCormick and the British Consul, Percy Bennett, from whom both Joyce and Sykes thought they had received official blessing. The cast included a professional opera singer, Tristan Rawson, as Jack Worthing, Mrs Matthias, an American actress, as Lady Bracknell, and Evelyn (Poppy) Cotton, an English actress, as Gwendolyn. Sykes's wife, Daisy Race, played Cecily and Sykes himself took the role of the Reverend Chasuble. (Ruggiero acted as usher and Borach undertook to lead the applause.) There had been difficulty finding an actor to play Algie Moncrieff, and finally the part went to Henry Carr, a tall handsome twenty-six-year-old repatriated prisoner of war employed at the Consulate. By all accounts the evening was a success. The theatre was sold out, the applause at the curtain enthusiastic (Borach shouting, 'Hurrah for Ireland!'), and even the self-important Percy Bennett was moved to congratulate Joyce, telling him it was far better than he had expected.

A vexatious problem arose immediately afterwards. From the outset it was clear that Carr disliked Joyce, seeing him as a column-dodger. As business manager, Joyce had arranged with the actors that professionals would be paid 30 francs and amateurs 10 francs. But the amateur Carr had thrown himself into his role fully, even going to the trouble of buying a new pair of trousers, a hat and gloves for the part, and expected the company to cover the expense. When Joyce handed him a 10-franc fee, Carr dismissed it as 'a tip' and left in high dudgeon, boycotting the cast's celebratory dinner and complaining next day to Sykes. Hearing about the complaint, Joyce became angry. Sykes, anxious to retain the Consul's support for a company tour of French Switzerland, asked him to let sleeping dogs lie. But Joyce decided to confront Carr at the Consulate, demanding payment for tickets he had been given to sell. The money for only three out of eight tickets was handed over, and a row erupted (witnessed by two Consulate employees, Toad Smith and Joe Gann). Carr, in a rage, demanded 150 francs for the clothes purchased, and that being refused called Joyce 'a cad and a swindler' and threatened to throw him downstairs, shouting, 'Next time I catch you outside I'll wring your neck.' Joyce, for once, could think of nothing to say except, 'I don't think this is fit language to be used in a Government office, Mr Carr.'

Afterwards, he wrote to Percy Bennett, begging to inform 'His Excellency' of the encounter, reporting Carr for abusive and threatening language and demanding an apology from him. He sent a copy of his letter to Sir Horace Rumbold, British Minister in Berne, requesting police protection. It all seemed alarmingly reminiscent of the occasion on which he had been beaten up by a soldier in Dublin, and this time there might be no Alfred H. Hunter to come to his rescue. On 3 May, he hired a lawyer to issue two writs against Carr (in the name of Dr James Joyce), one for libel and one for 25 francs (plus six months interest at 5 per cent) owed on the tickets. Carr, in return, claimed eighteen times that amount as what he saw as his share of the English Players' profits.

Joyce was up against a formidable Establishment pair. Rumbold (a 9th Baronet) had been UK chargé d'affaires in Berlin at the outbreak of war. Bennett, a career diplomat, had served in New York, Athens, Vienna, Rome and Bucharest. Both men took Carr's side. Bennett, known to his own family as 'Pompous Percy',[9] had a poor opinion of Joyce anyway – a man who had spurned his country's call to the flag with the unlikely excuse of having given an undertaking to the Austrian enemy not to fight. There was also the possibility that he was an Irish rebel and therefore anti-British. Having taken up this position, the Consul refused to budge and set about discrediting Joyce to the Foreign Office in London. Although he had once enjoyed excellent relations with British diplomats in both Austria and Switzerland, he was now perceived as a scrimshanking trouble-maker, becoming, in Herbert Gorman's words, 'the best-hated British subject (by British bureaucrats) in the country'.[10]

Although Joyce wanted the respect and support of the Consulate, he vented his anarchic contempt for jingoists like Bennett in a typically apt piece of satirical verse no doubt to be sung to a suitably comic tune by an Irish tenor after a few glasses of absinthe or Swiss white wine.

> Who is the man when all the gallant nations run to war
> Goes home to have his dinner by the very first cablecar
> And as he eats his cantelope contorts himself in mirth
> To read the blatant bulletins of the rulers of the earth?
> It's Mr Dooley,
> Mr Dooley,

The coolest chap our country ever knew
'They are out to collar
The dime and dollar'
Says Mr Dooley-ooley-ooley-oo.

Five verses followed in celebration of 'the funny fellow who declines to go to church', 'the meek philosopher who doesn't care a damn', 'the tranquil gentleman who won't salute the State', and 'the man who says he'll go the whole and perfect hog/Before he pays the income tax or license for a dog'. All are heroes of 'Mr Dooley-ooley-ooley-oo'.[11] Joyce's flair for the telling mock-heroic jingle, so evident here, was at its best when his temper ignited.

Bennett may have detected this spirit of insolence in Joyce's manner and doubtless resented him having informed his superior, Rumbold, of the incident. His favourable opinion of the English Players changed utterly; he withdrew the Consulate's backing, and the company's plans to tour French Switzerland were suddenly in jeopardy. Bennett made it clear to Sykes that his future goodwill depended on the company dispensing with Joyce. To him, Rumbold and Carr, Joyce's indifference to the war was blatantly unpatriotic, so now he was under suspicion from the British as well as the Austrians.

Despite these stressful distractions Joyce's literary career continued to inch forward. In May, *Exiles* was published by Grant Richards in London and by Huebsch in New York together with *Chamber Music*. Now it was in print, critics could judge for themselves. In June, under the heading 'Ibsen in Ireland', the *Freeman's Journal* found *Exiles* more Norwegian than Irish. It was like 'Ibsen without the energy and dramatic reality', or 'Shaw without the humour'.[12] But the *New Statesman*'s Desmond MacCarthy acclaimed it 'a remarkable play', adding 'I am more sure of this than of having understood it. I could never undertake to produce it unless the author were at my elbow; and when a critic feels like that about a play which has excited him it means he has not quite understood it.'[13] Arthur Clutton-Brock in the *TLS* found that '*Exiles* ... reveals resources of spiritual passion and constructive power which should greatly cheer the friends of [Joyce's] talent', and called on the Stage Society or the Pioneer Players to 'let us and the author see this play'.[14] On reading this, Joyce immediately asked Pinker to send copies of the play and the review to both companies.

He now tried to persuade Richards to bring out a second edition of *Dubliners* to cash in on any interest the play had aroused. However, with *Exiles* things seemed destined to move slowly, and it would not be until the autumn that copies reached Zurich. Conscious of his isolation and anxious to keep abreast of new developments in English literature, Joyce ordered Lawrence's *The Rainbow* and asked Harriet Weaver to send him Virginia Woolf's novel *The Voyage Out*.

Sykes agreed to Joyce's suggestion that the English Players produce a short run of three one-act plays – J. M. Barrie's *The Twelve-Pound Look*, Synge's *Riders to the Sea*, and Shaw's *The Dark Lady of the Sonnets* – for which he supplied the programme notes. The net for actors was cast wide and Nora was roped in to play Cathleen in *Riders to the Sea*. Her Galway lilt suited the part well and she acted with confidence, in effect playing herself. She was a great success and Joyce was very proud of her performance. 'I think Synge's words were spoken with the genuine brogue,' he wrote later.[15] *Exiles* was considered, but no one could be found to play the part of Richard. Joyce refused to play his own alter ego and Sykes said he could not act as well as direct.

By mid-May Joyce had sent six episodes of *Ulysses* to Pound who passed them to *The Egoist* and *Little Review*. However, at that point he was still unsure of how the book would turn out, telling Miss Weaver that he did not even know how much of it was actually written. Several further episodes had been drafted and re-drafted, one of which had taken him two hundred hours before he had produced a satisfactory copy. 'I fear I have little imagination,' he told her. 'However, if all goes well the book should be finished by the summer of 1919.'[16] He was worried that she might find his explanations tedious but she told him that, on the contrary, she *was* interested. After that he rarely hesitated to confide in her over what he was writing.

That summer Joyce made a significant new friend. Frank Budgen was of Cornish-Welsh extraction, an ex-sailor, one-time Marxist, autodidact, painter and sculptor attached to the Consulate, helping to promote British culture. A colleague of Budgen's, the stage designer Horace Taylor, had met Joyce at the Stadttheater. When he mentioned him to Budgen his reaction was, 'Who is James Joyce?' Taylor explained, saying they would get on well and should meet. A dinner was arranged in the restaurant of Taylor's pension at Zürichberg out beyond Fluntern. Joyce arrived late and Budgen recorded his first impression:

I saw a tall slender man come into the garden through the restaurant. Swinging a thin cane he walked deliberately down the steps to the gravelled garden path. He was a dark mass against the orange light of the restaurant glass door, but he carried his head with the chin uptilted so that his face collected cool light from the sky. His walk as he came slowly across to us suggested that of a wading heron. The studied deliberateness of a latecomer, I thought at first. But then as he came nearer I saw his

heavily glassed eyes and realised that the transition from light interior to
darkening garden had made him unsure of a space beset with iron chairs
and tables and other obstacles.[17]

And the sculptor in Budgen sized him up.

The form of his head is the long oval of heads of the Norman race. His
hair is dark enough to look black in this light. His beard is much lighter,
orangey-brown and cut to a point – Elizabethan. Behind the powerful
lenses of his spectacles his eyes are a clear, strong blue, but uncertain in
shape and masked in expression ... The colour of his face is a bricky red,
evenly distributed. The high forehead has a forward thrust as it issues
from under the front rank of hair. His jaw is firm and square, his lips thin
and tight, set in a straight line. Something in Joyce's head suggests to me
an alchemist. It is easy to imagine him moving around in a room full of
furnaces, retorts and books full of diagrams. And something in his poise
suggests a tall marshfowl, watchful, preoccupied. But I feel reassured.
What I had imagined under a well-known writer is not there. He might
easily be a painter.[18]

To begin with, Joyce was 'watchful and defensive', thinking Budgen
had been sent by Bennett to spy on him over the Carr affair. Later, as
they walked together back down towards his apartment on Universitätstrasse, Joyce unbuttoned and questioned him about his life and
work, saying he hoped they would meet again. When Budgen asked
him what had persuaded him that he was *not* a spy, Joyce replied that
he bore a striking resemblance to Arthur Shrewsbury, the old English
cricketer.

Shortly afterwards, they met by chance in the street and, strolling
together along the lakeside, Joyce told Budgen about the novel he was
writing based on the *Odyssey*. 'You seem to have read a lot, Mr Budgen,'
he said. 'Do you know of any complete all-round character presented by
any writer?' Budgen suggested, 'Faust, Hamlet ...' Joyce then made his
point, saying, 'Far from being a complete man, [Faust] isn't a man at all.
Is he an old man or a young man? Where are his home and family?
We don't know. And he can't be complete because he's never alone.
Mephistopheles is always hanging round him at his side or heels. We see
a lot of him, that's all.' As for Hamlet, 'Hamlet is a human being, but he
is a son only.' On the other hand, Ulysses was 'son to Laertes, but ...
father to Telemachus, husband to Penelope, lover of Calypso, companion
in arms of the Greek warriors around Troy and King of Ithaca. He was
subjected to many trials, but with wisdom and courage came through

them all.' Furthermore, when the history of Troy ended, that of Ulysses had just begun.[19]

Following his visit, Joyce sent Budgen a copy of *A Portrait*, enclosing press notices of *Dubliners* and *Chamber Music*. When Budgen returned the book with a letter of appreciation, Joyce became even more forthcoming about his work. Hoping to talk to him about *Ulysses*, Budgen began visiting the Joyces' apartment in Universitätstrasse. It was, he found, a polyglot household. Joyce and Nora conversed in English, spoke Italian to their children who spoke to one another in Züri-Deutsch – a veritable Tower of Babel. Where Sykes had found Lucia 'strange' and Giorgio 'a lout', Budgen with his sculptor's eye, saw Lucia as 'slender and elegant' and her brother 'powerfully-built and energetic', tall for his age and a good competitive swimmer. Nora he found 'a stately presence', warm, quick to judge and forthright, with a scale of values all her own. As he and Joyce talked alone about *Ulysses*, she came in and said, 'And is he talking to you again about that old book of his, Mr Budgen? I don't know how you stand it. Jim, you ought not to do it. You'll bore Mr Budgen stiff. What do you think, Mr Budgen, of a book with a big, fat, horrible married woman as the heroine? Mollie Bloom [sic]!' She often told people *'Das Buch ist ein Schwein!'* According to Budgen, Joyce greeted these sorts of remarks with 'suppressed laughter'. Nora's lack of appreciation of his work mystified him. He knew his writing had an effect on people, he said, but, 'My wife's personality is absolutely proof against any influence of mine.' Their mutual attraction and love was rooted firmly in mutual toleration.

Despite his elaborate politeness, around Zurich Joyce cut a distinctive if sometimes sinister figure – slim, dapper, with a pointed beard and powerful stride. Budgen's Bavarian landlady found him scary, and the chorus girls in the Stadttheater nicknamed him 'Herr Satan'.[20] But with copies of *A Portrait* in the bookshops, he had also become a minor celebrity around town, and the book was another good excuse for a celebration.

After the Pfauen, Joyce's favourite cafés were the Terrasse and the Odéon, Lenin's preferred haunt, close to the Bellevue Platz and the Quai-brücke. At the Odéon, Stefan Zweig found him sitting alone in a corner-seat one day, an enigma behind 'strikingly thick lenses' – ever ready to assert his independence from the English in whose language he wrote but did not wish to think. 'I cannot express myself in English without enclosing myself in a tradition,' he told Zweig. 'I'd like a language which is above all languages, a language to which all will do service.'[21] In writing *Ulysses* he was more and more moving towards producing a language of his own – a language subversive of the rules and constraints he despised. At the Restaurant zum Weissen Kreuz close to Universitätstrasse and at meetings of the Club des Étrangers, he communed with fellow exiles; at the Kronenhalle at the foot of Ramistrasse, where he came to love and know the family who owned it, he entertained his special friends. It was there that Philipp Jarnach introduced him to Ferruccio Busoni, but their musical tastes were at odds and the composer was unimpressed when Joyce praised Shakespeare as a poet but dismissed him as a dramatist.[22] More to his taste were Budgen's artistic friends, August and Paul Suter, Rudolph Maglin and Daniel Hummel. On one occasion they all sneaked into the Commercial Department at the British Consulate for a night of drunken antics, virtually wrecking the place and doubtless affording Joyce some satisfaction at having desecrated this *sanctum sanctorum* of the Establishment enemy.

To celebrate the arrival of his monthly slice of Mrs McCormick's munificence, he would take Budgen and Paul Suter to the Zimmerleuten, a restaurant on the Limmatquai, and there treat them, the proprietress and the rest of the staff, to champagne all round. On such occasions, he might entertain with his spider dance, or take off on impulse to visit a statue in the Uraniastrasse representing 'Labour', for which Budgen had modelled. This bohemian carousing often ended with Joyce being carried home, much to Nora's disgust, draped drunkenly across Budgen's powerful shoulders. To her, it was too reminiscent of the bad old days in Trieste. But she knew just how to handle him, and once scared him into sobriety by telling him that she had destroyed the manuscript of *Ulysses*.

These spats aside, Suter thought Joyce and Nora had a wonderful marriage. When she disparaged *Ulysses*, Joyce would smile and produce a copy of a cheap romance magazine, *Perl-Romain*, saying, 'This is the sort of thing my wife reads.' Few experiences were wasted on him and he mimicked the style of such magazines in the 'Nausicaa' episode of the novel on which he was now engaged. Suter noted that almost all his conversation revolved around *Ulysses* which was never far from his thoughts. He was continually making notes on scraps of paper, and was hardly able to join in any discussion that was not related to his novel. Whatever they began talking about, probably quite unconsciously, Joyce automatically changed the subject to *Ulysses* or some related topic.[23] Others interested him only insofar as they aided and abetted the writing of his book. Some, like Budgen, found this fascinating; others did not. August Suter once refused Budgen's invitation to dine with Joyce, saying, 'Why should I? [He] always wants to talk about himself.'[24]

The Joyce family also left its impression on Suter. He remembered Lucia for her rather attractive squint, but she was, he thought, spoiled by her father who considered her unusually gifted. Giorgio, on the other hand, was regarded with puzzlement by both his parents. He was always flush with money, though how he acquired it remained a mystery.[25] Nevertheless, Joyce was deeply fond of both children and neither was ever smacked; physical punishment was anathema to the pacifistic Joyce.

Two days before the preliminary hearing of the case of Joyce vs. Carr, scheduled for 8 June, Joyce received a registered letter from Consul Bennett requesting him to register for military service. He replied that there must be an error – he had already explained his presence in Switzerland to the Consulate. By its timing, Bennett's letter was clearly calculated to unnerve him and affect his performance in court. It had its effect, and he was too debilitated to write.[26] But the Consul did not leave it at that. On the 11th he wrote another letter, demanding to know why he had not responded to the earlier one. Two weeks later Sykes received a similar demand; the Consul had his knife out not just for Joyce but for the English Players too. A letter from Rumbold to the Foreign Office about the affair confirms the point:

> Mr Bennett was of the opinion that Mr Joyce and his company are most undesirable people, that their performances are very mediocre and are neither socially nor professionally in the interests of British propaganda. Mr Joyce is an Irishman of military age and returned to the Consulate General a circular which had been sent to him on the subject of military service with the remark that it had been evidently sent to him by mistake./In view of this I replied to Mr Joyce that I could give him no assistance in his theatrical undertakings.[27]

Bennett's deputy, George Beak, suggested to London that Joyce be relieved of his British passport.

At the Foreign Office, memos went back and forth on the subject, the concluding note reading, 'Mr Joyce is a novelist of some note. His novel ("Portrait of the Artist as a Young Man") was received very favourably here some few months ago. His later work is bad and what he is doing in Switzerland is not very much to our artistic credit. But these are hardly reasons for revoking his passport.'[28] The wise heads of two Foreign Office officials, Alec Randall and Stephen Gaselee, then decided that Bennett and Beak should 'hold their hand' for the time being. Joyce was fortunate. Gaselee was a distinguished classicist and bibliographer who later contributed to Eliot's literary magazine *Criterion*. He wrote to Rumbold saying that nothing could or should be done to hinder the English Players; any books they required should be provided through the diplomatic bag, and assistance be given them on any foreign tours they undertook.[29] But Sykes received no confirmation of such assistance and, with the Carr case now set to run, the Players found themselves *persona non grata*, and the subject of a boycott instituted by Bennett, which some (himself, Beak, Carr, Smith and Gann) observed but others (like Budgen and Taylor) ignored.

The first case of Joyce vs. Carr dragged on for over five months. Although Carr had the benefit of being represented by the Consulate's lawyer, Dr George Wettstein, on 15 October the court decided in favour of Joyce over the money owed for tickets; Carr was ordered to pay Joyce 60 francs plus costs of some 39 francs. Honour having been settled on one score there was still the matter of Carr's slander in calling Joyce 'a swindler'. That matter was deferred.

Perhaps in the hope of repairing relations with British diplomats in Switzerland, on 30 November Joyce wrote to Rumbold in Berne, outlining the whole Carr case from his point of view. He itemized not just Carr's misbehaviour but Consul Bennett's boycott of the English Players and his persecution of himself and Sykes over the matter of military service, adding:

> I believe that Your Excellency will hold, as I hold, that it is no part of the duties of consular officials, as set forth in the acting instructions issued by the foreign office, to commit or to aid and abet blackmail and assault or to organise a calumnious boycott of English literature or to invite British subjects to compound a felony and threaten to penalise them if they decline to do so.[30]

For good measure he enclosed a letter to Sykes from the Prime Minister, Lloyd George, wishing the English Players well. Unsurprisingly, there was no reply from Rumbold, but Bennett's card seems to have been marked and he was soon removed from the Zurich Consulate. Joyce's other persecutor, Carr, was repatriated to England. According to his widow, although he hated Joyce, he regretted causing the storm in a teacup which put an end to his career with the Foreign Service.[31] Only Joyce gained from the affair, not financially but by providing him with yet more grist to his mill – his letter to Rumbold conveying the sense of persecution which underlies key parts of *Ulysses*.

A formal end to legal proceedings came in the New Year, but in the absence of Carr, and with those able to corroborate Joyce's claim (Bennett, Smith and Gann) refusing to do so. With his case thus weakened, his lawyer advised him to withdraw the charge before the case came to court, which he did. The final adjudication was delivered on 11 February when Joyce was ordered to pay 10 francs in court costs and 120 francs to Carr, as well as his attorney's fees of 142 francs. Together with his own lawyer's fees, the action had been financially (if not imaginatively) costly for Joyce and it rankled with him that he had finally, as it seemed, been trumped by the British Establishment. Afterwards he complained of having been deserted by his lawyer and having to defend himself, but the court record reveals that there was simply no trial.[32] He got his revenge by writing his persecutors into the 'Circe' episode of his novel – a chapter he began later in Trieste but which would be wrestled through nine drafts before its completion.

Receiving no reply to his letters, Joyce again wrote to Rumbold accusing Bennett of misusing his office in threatening to have him expelled from Switzerland (either by conscripting him to the UK for military service or by depriving him of his British passport). This time the Minister replied saying that he had spoken to Bennett who denied instigating a boycott of the English Players or threatening to have Joyce expelled (a denial on which internal memos of the Foreign Office cast serious doubt). He then told Joyce that the Consulate had no knowledge whatever of his having been released from Austrian captivity on parole and that his contention that Bennett had blackmailed him was pure fabrication. Joyce, incensed by this brush-off, wrote a long letter accusing both Bennett and Rumbold of high-handedness, of false accusation and failing to support British artists working in the Allied cause. He ended with a wonderfully indignant flourish. If it was Rumbold's intention to extend the mantle of his royal master's protection over hooliganism and breach of public faith, he took the occasion to inform His Excellency that it was his intention to bring all the details of the case to the notice of friends in the UK and the US who would ensure that a distinguished member of their craft could not be blackmailed, blacklisted and menaced with impunity.[33] Nothing more was heard on the matter from the British authorities, but shortly afterwards, for whatever reason (probably for having demonstrated poor diplomatic skill in this case) Bennett was shipped off to the backwater of Panama and spent the rest of his career in the diplomatic wastes of Latin America.

The Players' tour of French Switzerland was aborted when one of their actors died, a victim of the great post-war flu pandemic. The company returned to Zurich and on 30 September, at the Pfauentheater, they staged Shaw's *Mrs Warren's Profession*, a play about prostitution banned in England. It was, according to Stanislaus, a play his brother disliked for its falsity,[34] but in mounting it he and Sykes could show their contempt for the British Establishment. Joyce held all Establishments in contempt. As he told his friend Borach shortly afterwards, 'As an artist I am against every state.'[35]

21

Settling Scores and Moving On

(1918–1920)

'If I am a sun, as you say, it is a sun which is often under an eclipse.'
Joyce to Fanny Guillermet, February 1919

The effect of the Carr case on *Ulysses* had been to stem the flow. During three months in Locarno Joyce had completed three episodes, and between March and May 1918 three more. But the seventh took until July – the 'Aeolus' episode, in which the paths of Bloom and Stephen almost cross again in the offices of the *Freeman's Journal* and Dublin *Evening Telegraph*. In this episode, conversation threading between news headlines and advertising copy touches on the enslaved Israelites, the colonized Irish, and Moses and Parnell who would lead them out of bondage. In line with the myth of Odysseus (Ulysses), the Aeolian winds of rhetoric play ironically throughout the scene. But Joyce was finding the work hard-going and the next episode would take three more months to complete.

By the end of October, the Joyces had moved across the street to 29 Universitätstrasse. According to Bugden the apartment was 'not a bad apartment as apartments go', in 'a modernish house of no particular character', with 'a superfluity of mice and a shortage of culinary utensils'.[1] Over Joyce's desk hung photographs of two important Ulyssean muses, one of a man full figure standing two feet high, elegant and bourgeois in black striped trousers, possibly his Triestine friend Schmitz (Svevo) who, he told visitors, was a model for Leopold Bloom – both of them Jews who had converted for love. The other showed a Greek statue of 'Penelope' with forefinger raised 'trying to recollect what *Ulysses* looks like', he said.[2] One day shortly after meeting Budgen, Joyce left a copy of *Dubliners* and copies of the *Little Review* carrying the first six episodes of *Ulysses* at his apartment. Having read the first chapters of the novel about which Joyce had talked so compulsively, a dialogue could begin. Budgen found himself becoming ever more engaged with its emergence as he was drawn ever deeper into the consciousness behind its creation. Joyce had found his new whetstone.

He was now working on the 'Lestrygonians' episode which included Bloom's lunchtime visit to the Burton Restaurant where the gluttony of the diners repels him, and to Davy Byrne's pub where he ruminates on images of ravenous greed. Joyce took the oesophagus as the prevailing human organ and Bloom's interior monologue is shot through with alimentary and gastric imagery, so that a line of constables 'Goosestep. Foodheated faces ... Bound for their troughs.'[3] When Budgen asked him how *Ulysses* was progressing, he said, 'I have been working hard on it all day.' 'Does that mean that you have written a great deal?' asked Budgen. 'Two sentences,' said Joyce. 'You have been seeking the *mot juste*?' 'No,' said Joyce. 'I have the words already. What I am seeking is the perfect order of words in the sentence.' Seduction, he explained, was a motive in his book, and was expressed as a shop-window display of women's silk petticoats. The words over which he was struggling were to convey the effect of this display on his hero and read, 'Perfume of embraces all him assailed. With hungered flesh obscurely, he mutely craved to adore.' 'You can see for yourself [he said] in how many different ways they might be arranged.'[4]

Budgen learned that Victorian female undergarments were a powerful fixation of Joyce, who carried a miniature pair of women's drawers (from a doll) in his pocket. One evening at the Bahnhofbuffet Joyce joined a group of artists and, to disconcert one of their number, the homosexual poet Siegfried Lang, he slipped them onto two fingers and 'walked' them across the table.[5] When Joyce mentioned women's clothes, said Budgen, he understood him to mean 'those garments visible only on the clothes-line or on privileged private occasions'. This enduring fascination with 'the underclothing of ladies of the Victorian era' is a recurrent motif in his novels.[6] In *A Portrait* Stephen waxes lyrical at a glimpse of the frilly drawers of the wading 'Bird-girl' and in *Ulysses* the voyeuristic Bloom describes in lip-smacking detail, 'a pair of outsize ladies' drawers of India mull, cut on generous lines, redolent of opoponax, jessamine and Muratti's Turkish cigarettes and containing a long bright steel safety pin, folded curvilinear'.[7] (Bloom undergoes numerous changes of costume, including, most melodramatically, a switch to female clothing during the sado-masochistic shenanigans in the 'Circe' episode.)

When it was completed Joyce sent the 'Lestrygonians' episode to Pound. A few weeks later, Pound wrote congratulating him on 'the glorious & wily *Ulysses* of blessed memory ... Bloom is a great man, and you have almightily answered the critics who asked me whether having made Stephen, more or less autobiography, you could ever go on and create a second character.'[8] Harriet Weaver was so impressed she was considering making a further settlement in Joyce's favour. He had now moved on to the 'Scylla and Charybdis' episode which follows Stephen into the hallowed reading-room of Dublin's National Library to debate with Eglinton, Byrne, Gogarty and company theories about Shakespeare, his life and identity. This would take him four months to complete.

With their new-found affluence, Nora began taking her daughter shopping for fashionable clothes. Lucia was now eleven and Giorgio thirteen. Joyce was proud of his well-dressed family, and urged friends to visit, saying, 'Come early so that you can see the children and hear Giorgio sing.'[9] However, his family, friends and acquaintances had to get used to him using them as research fodder for his fiction. Nora was well aware of what he got up to where she was concerned – dramatizing her love of Michael Bodkin, encouraging and then agonizing over her admirers. As she told Budgen tearfully one evening, 'Jim wants me to go with other men so he'll have something to write about.'[10] This was the 'Dear Cuckold' she regarded with such bemused indulgence. Lucia was also aware of this strange conspiracy in which her parents appeared to engage,[11] in a household in which sex and her father's strange libidinous obsessions were an ever-present source of tension.

At 11 a.m., on the 11th day of the 11th month of 1918, the signing of the Versailles Treaty brought the Great War to an end. Peace on the battlefield was quickly replaced by revolution on European streets. When things erupted in Zurich the English Players were preparing to mount Stanley Houghton's Ibsenite drama of Lancashire life, *Hindle Wakes*. Despite strikes, marches and police charges against rampaging crowds, Joyce and Sykes continued rehearsing. The audiences, however, were sparse because of the influenza epidemic, and the play lost money. Hoping to broaden their audience appeal, Joyce proposed a multilingual programme of three plays – one Italian, one French using French and Italian-speaking actors, and thirdly Browning's *In a Balcony* – performed by the English Players. At the performance on 11 December, as the curtain rose for the Browning play, from backstage Joyce sang Giovanni Stefani's canzona, 'Amante Tradito' (Betrayed Lover – a suitably Joycean lament), accompanied on the guitar by his friend Ruggiero. It would be his last formal theatrical performance.

In England and America the first responses to *Ulysses* had begun to emerge. That summer Eliot had written recommending 'the superb new novel of Joyce' to Scofield Thayer, editor of *The Dial*.[12] Yeats wrote to John Quinn saying, '[Joyce's] new story in the *Little Review*, looks like becoming the best work he has done. It is an entirely new thing – neither what the eye sees nor the ear hears, but what the rambling mind thinks and imagines from moment to moment. He has certainly passed in intensity any novelist of our time.'[13]

With the war over, myths were beginning to circulate in Ireland about Joyce's wealth and wartime activities in Trieste,[14] which further fuelled the idea that he had become a lackey of the British – not a healthy reputation in a country moving towards violent rebellion. He was well aware of the dangers and when Budgen asked him why he would not be returning to Ireland, he said, 'Because I'm a coward and afraid of being shot.'[15] Perhaps he recalled Shaw's line in *The Shewing-Up of Blanco Posnet*, 'Assassination is the most extreme form of censorship.' And wasn't Ireland a country of censorious extremes?

In early December Joyce had an opportunity to indulge a sexual fantasy which fed directly into his novel. One day, at 29 Universitätstrasse, he saw through the window of an apartment at the rear a young woman pulling the chain, having just used the toilet. As ever, thoughts of female urination excited an immediate reaction. Shortly afterwards, walking in the street, he saw the same woman dressed in black and wearing a big hat decked with feathers. To his astonishment she resembled the 'Bird-girl' he had once seen wading in the shallows on Dublin's Dollymount Strand, the girl who had thrown Stephen Dedalus into 'a holy silence of ecstasy'. Her soft regular features and gentle eyes led him to think she was Jewish, and even her slight limp enchanted him. By now obsessed, he followed her home, put a note through her letterbox and eventually wrote her strange letters professing love and confessing his sexual passion. When she replied, she became 'Martha Clifford' to his 'Leopold Bloom', and, strangely enough, shared the same first name.

She was Marthe Fleischmann, a well-born Bernese, a kept woman, living in a flat adjacent to her lover, Rudolf Hiltpold, at 6 Culmannstrasse which stood immediately behind the Joyce apartment. Her niece, Frau Walter Bollmann, described her as, 'a haughty, proud, sweet and soft, languishing beauty' with 'a natural aristocratic bearing', but 'hollow and superficial', obsessed with her own good looks, sexually frigid, prone to neuroses and suicidal.[16] But to Joyce she was no fragile ice-maiden. 'There was,' he told her later, 'something frank and almost shameless in your allure ... a pretty animal.' He continued spying on her, and having sent her a letter and observed her through a window reading it, wrote to her, 'How graceful you were yesterday evening, as you sat at the table, in a dream, then suddenly lifted my letter up to the light. What is your name? Do you think of me sometimes? Write to me at the address I give you.' He was disappointed when she drew her shutters. 'I want to see you,' he protested. The intensity of his overtures (couched in the style of schoolgirl romances later employed in 'Nausicaa') must have been overwhelming for a vain, neurotic young woman who so often had her head stuck in romantic novels.

I imagine a misty evening to myself. I am waiting – and I see you coming towards me, dressed in black, young, strange, and gentle. I look into your eyes, and my eyes tell you that I am a poor seeker in this world, that I understand nothing of my destiny, nor of the destinies of others, that I have lived and sinned and created, and that one day I shall leave, having understood nothing in the darkness which gave birth to both of us.[17]

She agreed to meet him and he presented her with a signed copy of *Chamber Music*, which seems to have had the intended effect. Joyce's pose as the successful poet, thought her niece, appealed to Marthe's snobbish pretensions; her readiness to indulge his bizarre sexual overtures appealed to his fancy for a compliant female. As his fixation grew, he lurked in the street hoping to catch sight of her, a little fearful that her reputedly hot-tempered 'minder', Hiltpold, might read his letters and waylay him.

Joyce was no longer satisfied merely to have an erotic pen-pal; unlike Bloom, he contrived to meet *his* Marthe, visiting her apartment for tea occasionally, and once, according to Budgen, questioning her closely about the women's underwear that so fascinated him. Before long he began to win her affection, drawing her into an even closer encounter of his own devising. For this purpose Budgen was recruited. The sculptor had the use of Paul Suter's studio on Bellevueplatz, and on Candlemas Day 1919, his thirty-seventh birthday, Joyce arranged to bring her there, having primed his friend beforehand. Budgen was to draw a female nude and display it prominently, and, from another friend, Joyce would borrow a menorah – the seven-armed candelabrum used in Jewish ceremonial – for some undisclosed purpose, but presumably to create a suitable atmosphere of bewitchment. Then, having brought Marthe to the studio and having invited Budgen to call him 'Jim' (a rare privilege), after a while he took her off. Later that day he told his friend that his hands had just explored every part of a woman's body, both hot and cold.[18] How far the explorations had taken him is unclear, but afterwards he wrote to her, 'Through the night of the bitterness of my soul the kisses of your lips fell upon my heart.'[19] That evening there was the usual birthday celebration which ended with Joyce and Ruggiero singing the Greek national anthem 'Hail Hail oh! Liberty!'[20]

There is no suggestion, however, that his various flirtations ever threatened his growing dependency on Nora, the woman who probably understood him best. She, it seems, was unaware of what her rakish husband was doing with Marthe Fleischmann, since her own sex life had all but ceased. Deceiving Nora was, on his own admission, part of the pleasure he derived from the affair, and ironically, later that year when he asked Budgen to paint Nora's portrait, it was to the same studio that she came to sit for him. He found her 'an exceptionally good sitter', and Joyce liked his preliminary sketch, telling him, 'It seems to my barbarian eye a delicate and provocative object.'[21] However, Nora hated the result, which made her look moody and sensual and petulant (she thought), and tore it from its frame in disgust. Budgen also did a full-length portrait of Joyce but found him a restless sitter who could not stand a bright light. He preferred to pose lying down and they compromised with him sprawled in an easy chair.[22]

Early in the year Joyce had put the final full stop to the 'Scylla and Charybdis' episode. Copies were sent to Pound for *The Egoist* and the *Little Review*. Margaret Anderson, increasingly nervous that the magazine might be seized, made excisions – something he discovered only later. Miss Weaver, however, wrote to say that it was so absorbing, it had kept her awake all night reading it.

Joyce's own nights were often nights of carousing. To please Nora he had given up absinthe and turned to wine. Celebrating at the Pfauen with the recently demobilized Ottocaro Weiss, Joyce was offered a Swiss white wine new to him, Fendant de Sion. He was delighted with it. 'To impress me,' said Weiss, 'he held up his glass against the light much as a doctor would hold up a specimen. "What does that look like to you?" he asked me. I replied, to mock his enthusiasm, "Urine" ("Orina"). "Yes," said Joyce, "but it's an archduchess's" ("Si, ma di una arciduchessa").'[23] Thereafter Joyce would refer to his favourite wine as 'the Archduchess' or 'the Archduchess's most excellent piss'.[24]

The momentum of Joyce's writing had picked up. He soon plunged into his next episode, 'Wandering Rocks', which follows 'the superior, the very reverend Father Conmee S.J.' through the streets of Dublin and features almost every other character in the novel, passing and re-passing, conversing with and ignoring one another, taking in headlines, advertisements, bookstalls and book titles, the Liffey quays and the Guinness distillery. It is Joyce's personal tour of 'dear, dirty Dublin'. That too was sent off to Pound who at the end of January forwarded him a second advance of $50 from the *Little Review* for US serialization rights.

But the first signs of the trouble awaiting *Ulysses* in America appeared when the US Post Office, acting on information received from the New York Society for the Suppression of Vice, confiscated the January 1919 issue of the *Little Review* containing the first part of his 'Lestrygonians' episode and burned it. A Post Office official who complained of the episode to the Chief Postmaster wrote, 'The creature who writes this Ulysses stuff should be put under a glass jar for examination. He'd make a lovely exhibit.'[25] Joyce would have been much amused. Thereafter,

Ulysses would run into as many impediments as its heroic Greek prototype on his legendary travels.

For the moment there was no trouble with the book in England. Miss Weaver had decided that the best she could do was publish only what passed her printer's critical inspection. And so the troublesome 'Telemachus' was by-passed, and the January–February issue of *The Egoist* carried the next episode, 'Nestor'. Between then and December, the magazine carried five extracts from the 'Proteus', 'Hades' and 'Wandering Rocks' episodes.

But in America the *Little Review* was now under close scrutiny, and the May issue containing the conclusion of the 'Scylla and Charybdis' episode, despite a stout defence sent by Quinn to the Post Office solicitor, was again consigned to the flames. With revolution sweeping Europe and even affecting America, a book so subversive of literary, moral, imperial and religious conventions and beliefs was bound to attract conservative hostility.[26] Joyce, however, relished the attention. 'This is the second time I have had the pleasure of being burned while on earth,' he told Harriet Weaver proudly, 'so that I hope I shall pass through the fires of purgatory as quickly as my patron S. Aloysius.'[27]

Despite a recurrence of his eye problem (this time in his 'good' right eye), he began work on the 'Sirens' episode in which Bloom sees Blazes Boylan hurrying along to Molly's bed and sublimates his own libidinous urges in sly letters to Martha Clifford as from 'Henry Flower'. In 'Circe', Henry Flower, of no fixed abode, would be charged, with allusive tact, with 'Unlawfully watching and besetting'.[28] Guilt and risk of discovery were a great sexual thrill for Joyce. As he wrote cryptically to his passing 'muse', the spied-on Marthe Fleischmann, 'I would like to send you flowers, but I am afraid.'[29]

On 8 May, Joyce left with Budgen for a short break in Locarno to escape the *foehn* (the warm dry wind from the south that could leave inhabitants exhausted, with throbbing headaches) and hoping a change of climate would forestall another eye attack. But he was also hoping to escape bailiffs pursuing him for non-payment of damages in the Carr case, and to make up for lost time by completing the 'Sirens' episode in the city where the first three chapters of his book were written so effortlessly.

In Locarno he heard of the sixty-three-year-old oft-married Russian baroness Antonietta de St Léger who lived on the Isle of Brissago on Lake Maggiore making dolls. She had a reputation for wild living and was known locally as 'The Siren' or 'Circe', after the mythical enchantress who lured men to her island and to their doom. Joyce wrote explaining his interest and found himself invited to St Léger's lair. There she introduced him to her library of erotica, entertained him with tales of her debauchery, and finally insisted he take away with him a trunkful of books and letters describing many varieties of sexual perversion. Later he told Budgen, 'I got some of the absurdest things in "Circe" out of it.'[30] What he never revealed was exactly which perversions in the 'Circe' episode owe their inclusion to the seductive Lady of the Lake.

The tide of Joyce's life was about to turn dramatically. On 14 May, a telegram arrived from Nora informing him that 'Monro client wishes to settle 5,000 pounds 5 per cent war loan upon you' and adding her congratulations. The sum involved, the equivalent of over £200,000 in today's money, coming out of nowhere, was staggering by any standards. Harriet Weaver, his anonymous English sponsor, had made him a man of means, independent of teaching. Through her lawyer she explained the qualities in him she admired – 'your searching piercing spirit, your scorching truth, the power and startling penetration of your intense instants of imagination' and 'power of expression', qualities lacking in most other contemporary writers, she thought.[31] Now, with Mrs McCormick's 1,000 francs a month and the prospect of a steady income from his war loans (around 500 francs or £21 monthly), Joyce's financial future seemed fully secure. To add to this, Pound forwarded money from the *Little Review* and Quinn was expressing interest in purchasing the manuscript of *Exiles* which had been published by Huebsch the previous October and which, he said, had left the New York critics 'baffled'.[32]

Joyce quickly returned to Zurich and on 17 May wrote to Monro Saw thanking his still-anonymous donor for her generosity. The news had arrived at a time of depression brought on by worry and illness and had brought to his life a brighter prospect.[33] His new financial security made him again determined to leave the city whose climate he blamed for his eye attacks. Many were already leaving, now that peace was declared – the spies, deserters, war profiteers, artistic exiles and revolutionaries. The ambience of ferment and flux which had prevailed over the previous four years was slowly evaporating and Zurich was losing its magic. Only the Swiss were happy to see their city return to peacetime normality.

Joyce hoped that summer to return to Trieste, where Stanislaus, home from prison, was living in a large apartment with the repatriated Schaureks. The tenancy of his old flat for which Count Tripcovich had paid the rent during his absence, was about to end. It had been damaged by bombs, then ransacked after the Italian takeover, and Stannie had stepped in to help salvage his property. However, he felt resentful that his brother had escaped internment, and although he agreed to pack up and clear his flat, it had cost him nearly 300 lire to do so. He was no longer prepared to be treated as a soft touch. 'I have just emerged from four years of hunger and squalor,' he said, 'and am trying to get on my feet again. Do you think you can give me a rest?'[34]

But Joyce had more pressing matters on his mind. In June he received a letter from Marthe Fleischmann's 'guardian', Hiltpold, demanding a meeting. The whole Candlemas incident with Joyce had disturbed the delicately balanced Fräulein Fleischmann who had suffered a nervous breakdown and had spent time in a clinic recovering. Finally, she had confessed all to Hiltpold, who now wrote demanding to know what Joyce had been doing playing with the young girl's affections. Joyce had gone to see the 'guardian' in 'the lion's den', he told Budgen, and described with good Joycean mock heroics how he had 'displayed all that suave human diplomacy, that goodness of heart, that understanding of others, that timidity which yet is courage, those shining qualities of heart and head which have so often ... Result, *stasis: Waffenstillstand* [Armistice].'[35] But, if the affair with Marthe was over, he would appropriate it for the 'Nausicaa' episode of *Ulysses*, begun a few months later, in which Bloom ogles the sexually precocious Gerty MacDowell at play on the Sandymount Strand and arouses himself to a climax to the accompaniment of exploding rockets. (Fleischmann is said to have received a handwritten postcard from Joyce later, addressed to 'Nausikaa' from 'Odysseus'.)[36]

Refreshed from his time in Locarno, Joyce was again working on the 'Sirens' episode. Discussions he had had with Otto Luening, an American music student in Zurich, reveal a particular interest in the polytonal music which Luening and Jarnach were then composing. Joyce showed him how he could transfer a flute solo by Gluck into language equivalents.

> He began going through the piece, note by note and phrase by phrase, literally transposing it first into word inflections and then into verbal images. At the end of this evening with Joyce I had learned more about the relationship of language to music than ever before or since.[37]

The opening three pages of the episode certainly seem to capture the sound and rhythms of verbal mimicry in the manner described by Luening. They also telegraph sequences and moments in the chapter ahead.

> Bronze by gold heard the hoofirons, steelyringing Imperthnthn thnthnthn.
> Chips, picking chips off rocky thumbnail, chips. Horrid! And gold flushed more.
> A husky fifenote blew
> Blew. Blue bloom is on the.
> Goldpinnacled hair.[38]

The 'Sirens' episode had taken Joyce five months to write and when it was finished in June he felt exhausted. As he told Harriet Weaver, offering an insight into the mental world of his creativity, 'Always when I have finished an episode my mind lapses into a state of blank apathy out of which it seems that neither I nor the wretched book will ever more emerge.'[39]

On reading the 'Sirens' episode neither Miss Weaver nor Pound much liked it. Pound said he thought the focus should have been on Stephen rather than the 'cloacal' Bloom and even pencilled in some suggested changes before sending it to New York; Weaver wrote saying that the episode fell short of his 'usual pitch of intensity'.[40] His writing, she thought, had obviously been affected by depression over the Carr affair. But Joyce was not ready to admit that he had got anything wrong. For him, if there were any fault with *Ulysses* it lay in the incomprehension of his readers. Later, in explaining to Weaver the stylistic problem of capturing the shifts of mood and tempo in the novel, he wrote of 'the seductions of music beyond which Ulysses travels'.[41] He was going his own way and the reader would have to follow.

Now, with the hope of returning to the old normality of Trieste, work could be resumed. On 19 June he told Budgen, still in Locarno, about the latest episode which they had discussed at length. 'The chapter of the "Cyclops" is being lovingly moulded in the way you know.'[42] The episode, set in Barney Kiernan's tavern, sees Bloom confronting and rebuffing the ultra-nationalistic and anti-Semitic Citizen. It also allows the reader to eavesdrop on the chorus of scandal-mongery surrounding Molly and Blazes Boylan. Someone to whom Joyce showed the episode in Zurich said it was futuristic, while Budgen declared it cubistic.

His contract gave Grant Richards first refusal of *Ulysses* until the end of June 1919. But Joyce had already told Harriet Weaver that he didn't think Richards would be interested in publishing it at any time, and offered her the book rights on any terms she cared to propose. When Richards was told that Joyce would not finish the novel until long after his claims on it had passed, he wrote implying that, having published *Exiles* without prospect of recovering his costs, it was unfair to deny him the option of publishing *Ulysses* 'on technical grounds'. Joyce, however, could now afford to ignore such emotional blackmail from a man who had so often failed him. In any case, he foresaw troubles ahead and did not believe that anyone in the UK would publish it or even find printers willing to print it.[43] With six extracts safely out in *The Egoist*, however, Miss Weaver was more optimistic, and even prepared to discuss the cost of binding. But, since it took him between four or five months to complete a chapter, he was unlikely to finish *Ulysses* before the end of 1920.[44]

Still unaware of the identity of his English patron, Joyce wrote to Monro Saw asking if by any chance it was Lady Cunard (who had earlier recommended him to the Royal Literary Fund) as he would like to write and thank her directly. But Miss Weaver had already decided to reveal her hand and at the end of a letter dealing mostly with *Ulysses*, she added, 'Perhaps I had better add that it was I who sent the message through Messrs Monro, Saw and Co and that I am sorry I sent it in the way and in the form I did . . . It is rather paralysing to communicate through solicitors. I fear you have to withdraw all words about delicacy and self-defacement: I can only beg you to forgive my lack of them.'[45] She had committed herself to funding him and would continue to do so as long as he needed her help. When word of his good fortune reached Dublin, Joyce received the inevitable begging letters, one from Charlie, still struggling to maintain his large and impoverished brood. Jim sent him two pounds; Stanislaus, struggling to pick up his teaching career, sent five.

Replying to Miss Weaver, Joyce expressed surprise and regret at not having known that she was behind the gift. But he was also perplexed, he said, since at the moment she made her money over to him she was expressing reservations about his novel and he feared he had alienated her. She reassured him that he was not to worry on that score, but from that moment onwards he felt he had to explain to her the thinking behind his book and so involve her more in the creative process. This shift in their relationship would eventually lead to her greater involvement in his well-being and that of his family too.

In America his old friend Padraic Colum, who had published a sympathetic article about him in *Pearson's Magazine* a year earlier, set up a sympathy fund for Joyce to enable him to pay his legal costs, and $1,000 would eventually be sent (including $700 from *The Dial* editor Scofield Thayer) – far more than required. The bailiffs were duly paid off. When the money arrived in June, Joyce, feeling affluent, gave $200 to Claud Sykes for the English Players, whose funds had been embezzled by his successor as business manager.

In one of his occasional moods of despair and self-doubt and with memories of being struck down with excruciating glaucoma in the great Zurich thoroughfare, Joyce had composed the poem 'Bahnhofstrasse', still clinging to Elizabethan lyricism and lamenting the passage of time:

> Ah star of evil! star of pain!
> Highhearted youth comes not again.[46]

It would also sound as a note of sad farewell to the city that had offered him sanctuary for the past five years.

In August, the arrival of £100 on account from Miss Weaver gave him cause to cheer as did the news that *Exiles*, in German under the title *Verbannte*, was to be performed in Munich on the 7th. However, his spirits were dashed when the Munich newspapers declared the play 'a flop'. The reports, he told Weaver, indicated that it had been 'a stormy evening', and the play was immediately withdrawn. Clearly German bourgeois susceptibilities had been outraged. Ironically enough, at that very moment *Il Piccolo della Sera* in Trieste was quoting a Joyce admirer acclaiming him not just as a novelist but as 'a playwright celebrated by all the critics in Europe'.

Now determined to return to Trieste in October, he sent his notes to Stanislaus and his books, pictures and typewriter a month later. 'The Sirens', he complained, was still not published, and some cuts had ruined it anyway.[47] But his 'ruined' text was still too strong for some. Eliot had been claiming that the only two people in England who truly appreciated Joyce were himself and his wife Vivien, but after she had seen the first part of 'Sirens' in the September issue of *Little Review*, she wrote to her friend Mary Hutchinson, 'What do you think of Joyce now? I am in trouble. I am *almost* giving him up! He is abominable. Is he laughing? . . .'[48] Fortunately it did not disturb the sensibilities of the Post Office inspectors sufficiently to have them reaching for their matches.

Joyce's friendship with Ottocaro Weiss came to an abrupt end at about this time, seemingly due to a tiff over payment for a bottle of Fendant at the Pfauen.[49] But it was also recalled by Lucia that Weiss, like Prezioso, had been unduly attentive to Nora – another possible source of tension between the two men. Shortly afterwards, Joyce discovered, on turning up at the bank for his monthly cheque from Mrs McCormick, that her support had been suddenly withdrawn. He never found out the reason for this but suspected Weiss, who was close to her, of having turned her against him. However, she was already unhappy with him for refusing to submit to psychoanalysis by Jung, her other main beneficiary. Hoping to repair their relationship, he asked to see her, but she refused, saying she was too busy. Then, as a peace offering, he sent her part of the manuscript of *Ulysses* which she acknowledged briefly but said only that she would happily keep it for him until he needed it. She was unable to support him further, she added, but wished him *bon voyage*.[50] It was, Joyce concluded, one more betrayal, even though McCormick had continued her payments six months beyond the year intended.[51]

The 'Cyclops' episode had gone off to Pound. The fearful Margaret Anderson excised mention of a hanged man's excited member and this time the episode would scrape past the Post Office's watchdogs safely enough to appear in the November *Little Review*.

Joyce was now working to complete one of the most ambitious chapters of *Ulysses* – the 'Oxen of the Sun' episode. Stephen has joined carousing medical students at Dr Horne's Hollis Street Maternity Hospital where Mina Purefoy is undergoing a prolonged labour. The drink is suitably plentiful, the talk suitably bawdy and the air suitably expectant – all of which Joyce captures in a suitably impressionistic and convivial opening: 'Send us bright one, light one, Horhorn, quickening and wombfruit. Send us bright one, light one, Horhorn, quickening and wombfruit. Send us bright one, light one, Horhorn, quickening and wombfruit./Hoopsa boyaboy hoopsa! Hoopsa boyaboy hoopsa! Hoopsa boyaboy hoopsa!'[52] The drunken prose dissolves into a series of brilliant parodies of English styles from Anglo-Saxon times to the twentieth century. Joyce was drawing not only on his encyclopaedic reading of English literature but also on his considerable powers of mimicry.

Later, urging Budgen to come to Trieste, Joyce offered the prospect of his helping with the episode. The idea behind it, he said, was 'the crime committed against fecundity by sterilizing the act of coition'. He concluded with a flourish of symbols, ending, 'Bloom is the spermatozoon, the hospital the womb, the nurse the ovum, Stephen the embryo./How's that for High?'[53] The target in using the various styles he had used, he said, was the English anthology tradition and the national identity and conventions affirmed by such collections which he believed inhibited literary fecundity. When Pound read it, he told Quinn, it was 'perhaps the best thing he has done ... better even than Rab[elais]. Our James is a grrreat man.'[54] But the 'grrreat man' did not always feel so good about what he'd written. According to Arthur Power, 'Joyce's sensitivity was such that during the composition of the episode, he was put off his food because his imagination was filled with half-born foetuses, swabs, and the smell of disinfectants.'[55] Harriet Weaver was both impressed and horrified. 'I think this episode might also have been called "Hades",' she wrote, 'for the reading of it is like being taken the rounds of hell.'[56]

Encouraged and now confident that he would have the book ready by the autumn of 1920, Joyce asked Pinker to draw up a contract, specifying an advance on signature and the right to revise at first proof stage. Furthermore, with the actions of the *Little Review* editors in mind, he wished it to stress that his manuscript was 'not to be tampered with'.[57]

In Europe things were progressing more smoothly. His poem 'A Memory of the Players in a Mirror at Midnight' appeared in the April *Poesia*, *Il Convegno* ran Carlo Linati's translation of *Exiles* through April to June, and in May, Benco wrote about the play in *Piccolo*. With his poem 'Bahnhofstrasse' appearing in the *Anglo-French Review* two months later, Joyce's dream of becoming a European author was slowly being realized.

The greatest worry haunting him was that Miss Weaver, like Mrs McCormick, would suddenly drop him, especially as she had compared his 'Oxen of the Sun' episode to 'Hades'.[58] Then, realizing that she had caused him some disquiet, she asked him 'not to pay the slightest attention to any foolish remark I may make', which she would try to avoid in future. She was, she wrote later, unfamiliar with 'the curious doctrines and legends of the Holy Roman Catholic and Apostolic Church which (or so it seemed to me) formed much of the groundwork of Oxen'.[59] Probably to reassure him of her continuing faith in him, she told him she was making over to him stocks and war bonds yielding some £100 a year inherited from an aunt.[60] In thanking her, he said he hoped to finish *Ulysses* in order to repay her for her generosity. He did not know, he confessed, exactly what he had done in his book, but working on it had left him close to exhaustion.[61]

Joyce now wanted to shake the accumulated dust of Zurich from his feet. However, he found that Trieste had changed. The cultural climate which had so suited the young exile had evaporated. The busy centre of commerce and intellectual excitement under tolerant Austrians had been replaced by just another port under Italian rule.

The Joyces moved into 2 via Sanita with the somewhat reluctant Schaureks and the decidedly reluctant Stanislaus. Including Eileen's two daughters (Nora and Bozena), a cook and baby's-maid, it was a ménage of eleven. It was a temporary arrangement which was to last nine months with the children having to sleep on sofas. His Danish furniture had been 'adopted' by the Schaureks for their own use. To his relief, however, his papers had been kept safe, and he promised the manuscript of *A Portrait* to Harriet Weaver. Despite his reputation for imposing on Weaver's generosity, Joyce often made her gifts of his most valuable manuscripts.

In Trieste, empty flats were in short supply. Rents were sky-high and he was as ever short of funds, so the prospect of establishing a separate household seemed remote. As transferring his money from Zurich was proving difficult, Joyce sent urgently to Pinker for royalties due from the American publisher Huebsch, and now regretted having given so freely to the English Players.[62] Feeling desperate, he wrote hoping to persuade Mrs McCormick to resume his monthly stipend, but again received no reply. Finally and reluctantly he accepted a post to teach English for an hour a day back at the Scuola Superiore di Commercio Revoltella, now upgraded to a university.

He was missing Budgen, the one friend who understood his work, and, still hoping to lure him to Trieste, told him, 'I avoid all contact with people [here]. Need I tell you what a great privation it is to me to have not within earshot your over-patient and friendly self?' He asked Budgen to keep his whereabouts secret, lamented the absence of 'the Archduchess' in Trieste, and reported that *Ulysses*, like himself, was 'on the rocks'.[63] To make matters worse, after an altercation with Stanislaus, the Joyces drew apart from the others and began to take their meals alone.

Unlike Edith McCormick, John Quinn was only too eager to acquire his *Ulysses* manuscript, offering £25 (or $125) on account and stressing that he wanted the whole thing, not just fragments. He already had a large collection of literary manuscripts, and was keen to add to it anything Joyce cared to relinquish. Despite his need of funds, however, Joyce preferred instead to offer it again to Mrs McCormick. When he still received no reply, Quinn offered double, with no suggestion that he would not go further.

With the old *joie de vivre* knocked out of Trieste, Joyce found the place dispiriting. Meeting his former student Maurice Furlan in the street one day he told him, 'This city has become a dungheap,'[64] and asked by Pound how it was under the Italians, he replied that one should not speak ill of the dead. But he could at least attempt to recapture some of the good old times through a few remaining good old friends. One day he walked into Silvio Benco's office at *Il Piccolo della Sera*, taking the editor by surprise. To Benco he cut an odd figure in a shapeless overcoat, and showing signs of age.

> After a few minutes he asked me to lower the lampshade, since the direct light hurt his eyes. And then we talked of his weakened sight, of Trieste, where he hoped to settle for good, of the chaotic times which had not, however, shaken his imperturbability.[65]

Benco was too busy to accept Joyce's invitation to lunch, but Francini was happy and eager to wine and dine the whole family in his fourth-floor apartment – Tuscan dishes and white Chianti – after which Joyce would entertain with song, and sometimes with dances too. Occasionally Joyce and Francini would disappear for an evening of feasting, drinking and endless talk at the Restaurant Bonavia, leading to the inevitable late, unsteady journey home.

His long-suffering family were facing an uncertain future. Nora, at thirty-five, was looking tired and having medical problems. Giorgio was now a very tall fourteen-year-old with a good embryonic tenor voice. Lucia was twelve going on thirteen, and getting dangerously close to the female early-teen-years that so fascinated Leopold Bloom. Like Nora, she was not unaware of how her father regarded young girls like herself and how he wrote them. But the question of how much she acted as his muse in drawing as he did the adolescent objects of desire in his fiction, and how far she came to identify herself with them, is a question at the heart of the mystery of Lucia's subsequent life.[66]

Apart from forays to the Francini Brunis, the Joyces' social life was distinctly impoverished by their move. There was good opera in Trieste but tickets were expensive, Joyce's dress-suit had been purloined, he had no decent boots and he was often reduced to squeezing into Giorgio's cast-offs. Nor was Nora able to keep abreast of rapidly changing post-war fashions, although she and the children were well enough dressed in their Swiss outfits.

For six weeks following their arrival Joyce felt unable to work. His despondency had not been alleviated when he saw that 'the erection allusion' had been cut from the 'Cyclops' extract printed in the *Little Review*. Then came news that, with no English printer willing to set further episodes, *The Egoist's* December issue carrying the first part of the 'Wandering Rocks' would be its last. Only his deep engagement with *Ulysses* enabled him to overcome such disappointments. During this final short stay in Trieste he would complete 'Nausicaa', rewrite 'The Oxen of the Sun', and start on 'Circe' and 'Eumeus'. However, he felt his isolation acutely, telling Budgen, 'Not a soul to talk to about Bloom. Lent two chapters to one or two people but they know as much about it as the parliamentary side of my arse.'[67]

His daily round was less than exciting. Apart from short walks down the street to buy the *Daily Mail* at midday and the evening paper later, he spent most of his time sprawled across two beds surrounded by notes, grappling with the most difficult episode he had so far tackled. His mood was close to desperation. If Budgen would only visit for a week, he said, he could stay in the apartment for nothing and Joyce would share his travel costs. 'Writing *Ulysses* is a tough job enough without all this trouble,' he lamented, but 'to abandon the book now would be madness'. 'Nausicaa', he wrote, was being written 'in a namby-pamby jammy marmalady drawersy (alto là!) style with effects of incense, mariolatry, masturbation, stewed cockles, painter's palette, chit chat, circumlocution, etc., etc.' and was shorter than the other chapters.[68]

Unaware of his son's newly reduced circumstances John wrote in his usual wheedling, self-pitying fashion, hinting at his lack of money and holding out a vague hope of future gain.

Do, like a good fellow, write me and let me know if I may expect to see you again before I die. My time is very nearly up. So that there is no time to lose ... I have made a fresh will, leaving you all I have, some £150.[69]

But Joyce, who had learned the art of wheedling at his father's knee, was not to be so easily beguiled.

The New Year got off to an unpromising start for him. On 9 January 1920 Jane Heap wrote to say that the Post Office had informed her that she had been banned from sending that month's *Little Review* (carrying part three of the 'Cyclops' episode) through the mail, but it had also threatened that, if she continued running *Ulysses*, it would be banned altogether. The future for Joyce's novel looked bleak, the exchange rate had weakened and he was again feeling under-financed.[70] However, throughout January 'Nausicaa' continued to take shape in its 'namby-pamby jammy marmalady drawersy (alto là!) style'.

In trying to capture the consciousness of Gerty MacDowell, Joyce had been reading novelettes aimed at young girls and asked Aunt Josephine to send him more, plus a penny hymnbook, and details about Sandymount – of trees and steps beside houses visible from the shore.[71] He also wanted 'tittletattle, facts etc, about Holles Street maternity hospital'.[72] By early February 'Nausicaa' was finished and sent to Budgen for comment. When Miss Weaver read it she told him, 'You are very good [for] the soul ... the Reverend James Joyce S.J., M.D. and if you are "Herr Satan" you are also the creator; for when you say, in Stephen's words, "Let there be life" there certainly is life – and morning and evening are one day!'[73]

He told Jane Heap that after the 'Oxen of the Sun' episode there remained only 'Circe' to complete for section two of the novel. The three-part 'Nostos' (homecoming) was already part-written. And he told Quinn, who had finally cabled a 3,000-lire advance ($150 or £30) for his *Ulysses* manuscript, that he hoped the book would be finished by the autumn, after which he planned a two-year-long rest from writing. Meantime things were not going smoothly for him – books being burnt, or censored, unfinished translations, and publications which never happened – which made his literary life very wearisome.[74]

He had hopes, he said, of joining Budgen in Cornwall, and, perhaps wanting to reacquaint himself with Mr Bloom's Dublin, even considered risking a brief visit to Ireland.[75] But at the end of March Aunt Josephine wrote saying 'There is nothing but raids and murders here.'[76] 'Ireland,' he told Budgen, 'is impossible.'[77] There would be no homecoming for this particular Ulysses. In May, Pound wrote inviting Joyce to meet him in Venice. Five days later he wrote to say that he and his wife were moving to Sirmione on Lake Garda. He urged Joyce to visit him there, hoping they would be joined by Eliot who was keen to meet the author of whom he had heard so much and of whom that summer he would write, 'Mr Joyce's mind is subtle, erudite, even massive.'[78]

After the long labour to deliver the maternity hospital episode he was able to relax and sum up progress on *Ulysses*. After 'Circe', his next chapter, he thought the rest would be plain sailing. All he needed was a quiet place in which to finish the book, but was desperately short of money and unable even to afford new clothes. Pound, always eager to help, recommended France as the cheapest place he knew of, offering to find him accommodation there plus 1,000 lire towards the fare.[79] When Joyce at last agreed to visit him in Sirmione, Pound was delighted. It would take nine hours by train from Trieste to Desenzano, he said, then half an hour by boat.

By 8 June, Joyce was on his way to Sirmione where he would finally meet the man who had done so much to get *A Portrait* and *Ulysses* into print. Two of the greatest modernist innovators of the century were about to come face to face, although Joyce probably did not recognize Pound's stature and seems to have read little of his work. Nervous because thunderstorms were reported in the area, he took the lofty Giorgio along 'to act as a lightning conductor', he said.[80] It was a strange encounter, with Pound collecting the two Joyces from the station in his car to save them the experience of a lake-crossing. To Joyce's surprise, instead of wanting to discuss *Ulysses* Pound seemed more interested in the identity of his anonymous patron. Joyce thought it hilarious when Pound guessed it was John Quinn,[81] whom he saw as more grasping than giving. He probably never did divulge the name of his benefactor to Pound whose impression of Joyce he later shared with Quinn:

> Joyce – pleasing; after the first shell of cantankerous Irishman, I got the impression that the real man is the author of *Chamber Music*, the sensitive. The rest is the genius; the registration of realities on the temperament, the delicate temperament of the early poems. A concentration and absorption passing Yeats' – Yeats has never taken on anything requiring the condensation of *Ulysses*.[82]

Joyce's impression of Pound is not recorded but he later implied that he thought him slightly mad. Nevertheless, this remote lakeside encounter would launch Joyce into a completely new phase of his life, in which Pound would help him establish himself as the 'grrreat man' he thought him to be. After two days, Joyce returned with Giorgio to Trieste (complete with ill-fitting suit and boots supplied by Pound) to pack and get his family on the road to France.

At first his intention was to remain in Paris only briefly before proceeding to London. He was still at work on the 'Circe' episode and looked upon the trip as a working holiday. But he kept changing his plans – now telling Quinn that he intended to spend just a few months in some tranquil corner of France or England to finish the novel. Having already dispatched five chapters to New York, he asked Quinn for the final payment for his manuscript to see him through his time in France. The novel would, he thought, be published in book form in January by the Egoist Press in London and by Huebsch in New York.[83] Despite the threat of Post Office seizure, the *Little Review* was still publishing episodes of *Ulysses*, and Joyce informed Margaret Anderson that the end was written and would, he hoped, be with her by the autumn.

The Joyces left Trieste on 3 July 1920. The Schaureks were at the station to wave them off, but Stanislaus, no doubt thankful to see the back of his bothersome brother, stayed away. After two days in Venice and a stopover in Milan to meet Carlo Linati, the Italian translator of *Exiles*, the family journeyed on to Paris where Pound had reserved rooms in a hotel. Joyce planned to remain for three months to complete 'Circe' and if possible finish off the whole book.

But, unknown to Joyce, a time-bomb had been set ticking. Miss Anderson had distributed unsolicited copies of the July–August issue of the *Little Review* containing the last part of 'Nausicaa'. By ill fortune, one copy was delivered to the daughter of a New York lawyer, who, shocked by what she read, immediately asked her father to start a prosecution. The matter was referred via the County District Attorney to John Sumner, Secretary of the New York Society for the Suppression of Vice, and a prosecution was instigated. The battle between Sumner and the editors of the *Little Review* would see a confrontation between the defenders of Victorian propriety and the reforming forces of unabashed realism. Bloom's encounter with the youthful Gerty MacDowell, and his sexual fantasies prompted by glimpses of her underwear, challenged the deep-seated taboo against the corruption of innocence, as did Gerty's knowing reaction to his evident lubricity.[84] The fate of the *Little Review* and *Ulysses* in God-fearing America would, it seemed, be left hanging in the balance.

22
Ulysses: Inside the Dismal Labyrinth
(1920–1921)

'So we only groped through the dismal labyrinth ...'
Mark Twain, *Innocents Abroad*

Joyce's debt to Ezra Pound was about to mount. Not only had he arranged accommodation for the family in a hotel at 9 rue de l'Université, but had spread word of the coming of one of modern literature's geniuses, and distributed copies of *A Portrait* to people he thought influential in the city. The rich cultural atmosphere which was about to engulf Joyce would transform him from a language teacher who wrote occasional verse and somewhat obscure fiction of questionable taste into a major figure at the cultural heart of Europe. In those immediate post-war years Paris was a bustling centre of creative ferment, its cafés thronged with artists and poets and would-be artists and poets.[1] It was also, of course, a city Joyce knew well, especially the Left Bank. Now he would get to know it all over again.

The family arrived at the Gare de Lyon on 8 July 1920. Many in Paris and London were eager to meet the new man. On 3 July, Eliot had written to Pound, 'Is there any chance of Joyce staying in Paris or coming to London, so that he could be seen?'[2] and a week later he wrote asking for his address. Within days of his arrival, Pound arranged a late-afternoon supper party in Joyce's honour at the Neuilly home of the poet and Zionist André Spire. There he met a select number of Parisian *littérateurs*, among them Jenny Serruys Bradley, a literary agent, who would translate *Exiles*, Aurélien-Marie Lugné-Poë, the actor-manager who would consider producing it at his Théâtre de l'Oeuvre, and Natalie Clifford Barney, the American 'Amazon', whose famous Paris literary salon in the rue Jacob catered mostly for what one observer called 'ladies with high collars and monocles'.[3] At Pound's urging, his friend, Ludmila Bloch-Savitsky had undertaken to translate *A Portrait* and lend the Joyces a flat – the servants' quarters of her house in Passy. The flat was small and bare, there was no electricity and just one double bed. However, it came rent-free until they found something more permanent. Pound was determined that everything be done to help his genius settle in Paris and flourish there.

At Spire's soirée Joyce first encountered the American bookseller Sylvia Beach, daughter of a Princeton clergyman, whose English-language bookshop, Shakespeare and Company, had opened the previous November at 8 rue Dupuytren. Beach had heard of Joyce well before his arrival in Paris. She had sold and displayed *A Portrait*, *Chamber Music* and *The Egoist* in her shop window, and was now eager to meet the author who Pound was telling everybody was 'a grrreat man'. Her descriptions of the couple offer the first glimpse we have of them after their arrival in Paris.

> Mrs Joyce was rather tall, and neither stout nor thin. She was charming, with her reddish curly hair and eyelashes, her eyes with a twinkle in them, her voice with its Irish inflections, and a certain dignity that is so Irish also. She seemed glad to find that we could speak English together. She couldn't understand a word of what was being said.[4]

When food was served she noticed that Joyce refused to drink, turning his glass upside down at the table. After supper he disappeared and Beach eventually found him sitting alone in Spire's small library. His problem was that he was not very interested in modern French literature and wanted only to speak about himself. 'Mr Pound introduced me to a number of people here on whom I created anything but a good impression,' he told Harriet Weaver.[5] But the impression he made on Miss Beach in their library encounter could hardly fail to be good. Already a worshipper, and nervous in his presence, she asked, 'Is this the great James Joyce?' to which he replied simply, 'James Joyce' and held out a 'limp boneless hand' for her to shake.

> He was of medium height, thin, slightly stooped, graceful [she recalled]. One noticed his hands. They were very narrow. On the middle and third fingers of the left hand, he wore rings, the stones in heavy settings. His eyes, a deep blue, with the light of genius in them, were extremely beautiful. I noticed, however, that the right eye had a slightly abnormal look and that the right lens of his glasses was thicker than the left. His hair was thick, sandy-coloured, wavy, and brushed back from a high, lined forehead over his tall head. He gave an impression of sensitiveness exceeding any I had ever known. His skin was fair, with a few freckles, and rather flushed. On his chin was a sort of goatee. His nose was well-shaped, his lips narrow and fine-cut. I thought he must have been very handsome as a young man.

His voice, she noted, was sweet and 'pitched like a tenor's' and 'charming' (that of an English actor), but she was astonished at his terrified reaction when a neighbourhood dog began to bark. 'Is it coming in? Is it fierce?' he asked, and pointing to his goatee beard, told her it was there to cover the scar from that dog-bite as a five-year-old. She told him about her bookshop and he took down the address and promised to visit her.[6]

The major English bookshops in Paris were Brentano's, Galignani's and W. H. Smith's – all on the Right Bank. Beach catered mostly for denizens of the bohemian Left Bank, where, after the war, Americans came flocking, drawn by the favourable exchange rate and in flight from Prohibition. Apart from selling books, Beach's shop housed a lending library and became a centre of gossip and point of contact for Paris's English-speaking artistic exiles. Pound had been one of her first customers, soon followed by Sherwood Anderson, Gertrude Stein, Alice B. Toklas, and George Antheil, the composer, who later rented a room over her shop. Her first library subscriber was André Gide. Now she had acquired her most illustrious customer.

Beach's friend and lover, Adrienne Monnier, ran a French-language bookshop, La Maison des Amis des Livres, in the nearby rue de l'Odéon. The two women, who shared a flat, were a curious contrast – Beach, a slim, girlish, enthusiastic woman, modern and broad-minded, with bobbed hair and stylish if masculine dress, and the solidly built, seriously dedicated Monnier, an austere feminist, with long hair coiled, and draped from head to foot in sober peasant costume. Monnier was the dominant partner whose advice Beach usually took unquestioningly.

The day after their meeting, Joyce walked into Shakespeare and Company carrying an ashplant, wearing a dark blue serge suit and a grubby-looking pair of white plimsolls, a black felt hat perched on the back of his head. He joined her library and the first book he borrowed was Synge's *Riders to the Sea*, becoming one of those regular customers for whom Beach would cash cheques, order books, provide a convenient poste restante, and offer coffee too, if required. She was astonished when he told her that he understood eleven languages, including Yiddish and Hebrew. She was also taken aback to discover how bad his eyes (his 'gropesarching eyes')[7] were, leaving him liable to bump into things and unable sometimes to distinguish objects clearly. Beach's shop had a very particular ambience, its walls crowded with posters, drawings by Blake, and photographs of her favourite writers – Whitman, Poe and Wilde – framed letters and manuscript fragments. Joyce's photograph would eventually join her other literary heroes – Pound, Hemingway, Scott Fitzgerald and Lawrence. He must have thought he had walked into a literary Elysium.

By 15 July, the Joyces had moved into Madame Bloch-Savitsky's tiny flat at Passy. Though the quarters were cramped, living expenses were manageable – no rent to pay, a favourable exchange rate and prices half what they were in Trieste. Now more settled, Joyce had decided to remain in Paris to finish *Ulysses*, revising 'Cyclops', completing 'Circe', 'Eumeus' and 'Ithaca', and adding an eighteenth chapter – 'Penelope', the novel's finale. All he had achieved in Paris so far, he told Harriet Weaver, was due to Pound. But he might have to return to Trieste for his notes if he wanted to finish his book by December. After that, he said, he planned to sleep for six months.

With the £25 balance of Quinn's down-payment for the *Ulysses* manuscript still awaited, and no money from Huebsch (who was hesitating over a novel which had been so frequently seized and burned), Joyce was upset at not being able properly to celebrate the birthdays of Lucia on 26 July and Giorgio on the 27th. Fortunately, Pound's friend, the London poet, John Rodker, and his wife (a daughter of Madame Bloch-Savitsky) turned up and insisted on taking the whole family out to dinner.[8] Before leaving for London, Pound introduced Joyce to Fritz Vanderpyl, the Belgian art critic, who became a friend and with whom he took strolls in the Luxembourg Gardens. But he was still anxious to see Budgen. 'I want to hear you on the *Oxen* episode,' he wrote, 'and I want to bore the life out of you with 'Circe' which is half written.'[9]

The charming and refined Eliot came to Paris that August, accompanied by the pugnacious and sardonic Wyndham Lewis. They stayed at the Hôtel de l'Elysée, and Eliot, having brought over a large parcel from Pound for Joyce, invited him to the hotel. Joyce arrived at 6.30 p.m. accompanied by Giorgio. Lewis, who left an ironic account of the meeting, found him 'an oddity in patent-leather shoes, large powerful spectacles, and a small gingerbread beard, speaking half in voluble Italian to a scowling schoolboy: playing the Irishman a little overmuch perhaps, but in amusingly mannered technique'. However, as the meeting progressed, he warmed to this strange character. 'I took a great fancy to him for his wit, for the agreeable humanity of which he possessed such stores, for his unaffected love of alcohol, and all good things to eat and drink.' But Lewis knew little about his work, except for the extracts from *A Portrait* in *The Egoist*. Joyce, by contrast, appeared to have read everything of his and seemed impressed to meet him. What followed was, in Lewis's words, 'a Punch and Judy show'.

Eliot placed the mysterious parcel on the table in the hotel bedroom and they all stood contemplating it before Joyce collapsed into a chair and Giorgio, uncertain how to react, stood around scowling. When Eliot announced the parcel was from Pound, Joyce approached it and struggled to undo the knots until Eliot produced a pair of nail scissors. The brown-paper wrapping was removed and the contents revealed – Pound had sent him a used pair of brown shoes and some old clothes, which were now sitting at the centre of 'a large Second Empire marble table, standing upon gilt eagles' claws'.[10] While Eliot and Lewis chuckled, Joyce simply said 'Oh' and sat down again. When Eliot invited him for dinner, Joyce had a heated argument with Giorgio in Italian ('a good imitation of an altercation between a couple of neapolitan touts', wrote Lewis), then handed him the indecorous package to carry home with a message to Nora saying that he would be dining out that evening. Giorgio rushed off with the parcel under his arm, 'his face crimson and his eyes blazing with a truly southern ferocity – first having mastered himself for a moment sufficiently to bow to me from the hips, and to shake hands with heroic punctilio'.[11]

With Giorgio gone, Joyce relaxed and turned Eliot's invitation to dinner into his own. They would be *his* guests. He led the way to a nearby restaurant, hurrying ahead of them, and having selected a table was already consulting the menu before they sat down. Without much ado, Joyce then ordered what Lewis called 'a large and cleverly arranged dinner as far as possible for all palates, and with a great display of inside knowledge of the insides of civilized men and the resources of the cuisine of France, discovering what wines we were by way of liking if any'. At the end of the meal he produced a bundle of notes from his pocket and settled up with a generous tip on top. That very day John Quinn had cabled him $125 (1,750 francs) to add to the $400 (6,000 francs) he had already advanced for the *Ulysses* manuscript. It was this money which enabled Joyce to play the open-handed plutocrat and so retrieve his Irish pride after the humiliating handout of old clothes from Pound. From then on, said Lewis, he and Eliot met Joyce over 'several days' (Eliot said they met twice) and were not allowed to pay for anything –, beers, coffees, taxicabs were all paid for with massive tips. Lewis claimed their stay in Paris was 'one long fête' at Joyce's expense, but that Eliot had found his pretentiousness 'objectionable' and 'arrogant'. However, writing to his mother from Tours on 24 August, Eliot mentioned having dined with Joyce and enjoying himself 'very much'.[12] To John Quinn, he later wrote, 'I met Joyce in Paris . . . I found him quite charming, and liked him.'[13]

Joyce now thought Huebsch's attitude towards *Ulysses* was 'dubious'. But if American attitudes were questionable, and English attitudes unpredictable, in Ireland (now descending into boycott, riot and Black and Tan violence), there was a hopeful glimmer. Nora's uncle Michael Healy had sent him a copy of the *Dublin Review* carrying an article about some recent books including *A Portrait*, which it described as 'Flaubertian' and 'a work of genius', and – a somewhat backhanded compliment – 'a remarkable record of the personal journey by one "sick of soul"'.[14]

Gradually it dawned on Joyce that he had landed on his feet. 'Paris,' he told Lewis, 'is the last of the human cities,'[15] and there was no reason for him to proceed to England where there seemed no future for his book or to Ireland where there might be no future for himself. Remaining in France meant Nora and the children having to make major adjustments – in particular to learn a new language. Initially Lucia would receive private tuition while Giorgio, having finished school, was found a job in the office of Jenny Serruys' brother.

At the end of August, Joyce had lots of news for Stanislaus. Budgen had visited Paris en route to England and Claud Sykes and his wife were due to arrive any day. Eliot, Rodker and Lewis were becoming frequent visitors, so that dinners and lunches were 'the order of the day'; an American admirer had presented him with an army greatcoat; Giorgio was in line for a job with an American Trust Agency at 200 francs a month, while Lucia had become obsessed with Napoleon. As to himself, the case of books and manuscripts he had dispatched from Trieste before leaving had still not arrived, Huebsch had lost interest in *Ulysses* and no English printer would take it on. Now it was proposed that Rodker produce it in Paris for the Egoist Press, naming himself as printer.

Joyce was still grappling with 'Circe'. In August, he told Miss Weaver, 'Circe herself had less trouble weaving her web than I have with her episode.'[16] To Linati shortly afterwards he wrote more dramatically that 'The episode of "Circe" has changed me too into an animal.'[17] And to Stanislaus, 'Have written "Circe" about five times. It allows me about four or five hours sleep every night.'[18] On 3 September he sent Quinn a complete breakdown of the eighteen chapters which would finally make up *Ulysses*.

Although the narrative had already included some shift to dramatic dialogue, in the 'Circe' episode, he plunged directly into one of the most brilliant and original pieces of surrealistic drama (anticipating Antonin Artaud's Theatre of Cruelty), in which the whorehouse is presented as theatre. It was the perfect platform from which to wreak revenge on all who had betrayed him, notably Bennett, Rumbold, Georg Wettstein, Carr, Smith and Gann – the British Establishment in Zurich who had persecuted and tormented him. Rumbold appears as demon barber and hangman, who executes 'the Croppy Boy' (an Irish rebel with whom Joyce identified), Bennett as 'Sergeant Major Bennett, the Portobello bruiser', Wettstein as his cowardly second, and Smith and Gann as hanged criminals. Carr is a drunken redcoat who threatens Stephen, and then delivers Joyce's own verdict on his chief persecutor: 'God fuck old Bennett. He's a whitearsed bugger. I don't give a shit for him.'[19] To Francini in Trieste he wrote, 'I think ["Circe"] is the strongest thing I have written in spite of my expulsion in circumstances known to the goddess who protects me.'[20]

For the benefit of Carlo Linati who had been asked to write about *Ulysses* for an Italian magazine, Joyce promised an aid to the understanding of his 'three-time blasted novel' – a sort of skeleton key or summarizing scheme for his personal use only. 'It is an epic of two races (Israelite-Irish),' he wrote, 'and at the same time the cycle of the human body as well as a little story of a day (life) ... It is also a sort of encyclopaedia. My intention is to transpose the myth *sub specie temporis nostri* [in the light of our own times]. Each adventure (that is, every hour, every organ, every art being interconnected and interrelated in the structural scheme of the whole) should not only condition but even create its own technique.' But now, he added, there was a movement against the book headed by 'Puritans, English Imperialists, Irish Republicans, Catholics – what an alliance!' For achieving that, he said, he deserved the Nobel Peace Prize.[21]

In late September, Huebsch came to Paris and Joyce, who met him for the first time at his hotel, was not impressed by what he took to be the American publisher's threatening manner, and when he asked for cuts to *Ulysses* Joyce refused even to discuss the matter. He said later, 'I perceived a few minutes after my meeting him that he considered me an embarrassing person and my books bad sellers but could not make up his mind to take a definite step.'[22] When Huebsch asked Joyce if he thought anyone would publish his novel as it stood, he said that if necessary he would have it published in Paris. Huebsch replied that if he did so there would be nothing to stop him bringing out a pirated edition in New York – something Joyce probably hadn't considered. He tried to make Joyce feel beholden to him by telling him that he had made a sacrifice for art by publishing *A Portrait*, but Joyce knew that Huebsch would do well enough if he brought out a private edition of *Ulysses*.[23]

Despite the urgings of Quinn and Pound, Joyce refused to withdraw the novel from the *Little Review*, even though they told him that future prosecutions would only discourage Huebsch further from publishing it. He thought it would look as though he were passing sentence on his own book and putting the *Review* editors in the dock himself. In any case, he felt sure that other things would discourage Huebsch – such as the 'Circe' episode – still being revised. To weaken now would only damage the reputation he had acquired among his admirers for courage in having written the novel.[24] Harriet Weaver, who met Huebsch in London, reassured Joyce that he was merely indicating that the book's publication in Paris would not guarantee copyright protection in America. Rodker, therefore, had promised not to publish a Paris edition and handed his manuscript copy to Huebsch.[25]

At the end of September Joyce told Frank Budgen that Huebsch was talking about only a small private edition of *Ulysses* costing 150 francs, that 'Circe' was becoming 'wilder and worse and more involved', and that Madame Savitsky had given them notice to quit their flat. He was therefore dashing around looking for a new home.[26] Fortunately, to ease his immediate financial situation, Miss Weaver had sent him, in addition to the gift of bonds, a cheque for £200. With that money in hand he could at least consider taking a decent apartment, if one were to be found. Their present one was damp, a mere matchbox with furniture (in Lucia's words) 'stuck together with spit'. But in seeking help, he gathered that, despite Pound's efforts, he had not made much of an impression on the city; he told Budgen that he detected 'a furtive attempt' to promote the merits of 'a certain Marcel Proust' against him by people who would be glad to see him fail. 'I have read some pages of his, but cannot see any special talent but I am a bad critic,' and too preoccupied with 'problems raised in "Circe" (of good taste, tact, technique, etc.)', to afford any distractions.[27]

In New York on 29 September, as a result of John Sumner's complaint a Greenwich Village bookseller who sold the *Review* was summoned to appear before Jefferson Market Police Court to answer charges of publishing material which was 'obscene, lewd, lascivious, filthy, indecent and disgusting'. Attempts by Quinn to persuade Sumner to drop his complaint against the *Little Review* failed, but he managed to get the charge switched from the bookseller to Margaret Anderson and Jane Heap. They hardly helped matters by declaring that they 'gloried' in what they had done in publishing *Ulysses*. They would, they said, 'do it again', and, like true martyrs, welcomed the prosecution which they thought would be the 'making of the *Little Review*'.[28]

At the preliminary hearing on 21 October, Quinn, who despised both women (considering them communist lesbians, which they were), told them to stay out of the proceedings and took it upon himself to defend *Ulysses*, arguing that literature could not be obscene as it tended to disgust and discourage whereas filth made vice alluring. 'Joyce's treatment of sex would not drive men to whorehouses or into the arms of lewd women,' he declared, 'but would drive them away from them.' As for corruption, the average innocent person would not comprehend the sexual allusions in the novel, which must mean that the judge himself had a corrupt and depraved mind to have understood them. The magistrate is reported to have found this suggestion amusing but still committed the two editors for trial. It cannot have helped that the most recent issue of the *Review* carried a photograph of Joyce giving a very credible performance as 'Herr Satan', a latter-day collector of souls. Now the fate of the *Little Review* and *Ulysses* in God-fearing America was now decidedly in peril. The first part of the 'Oxen of the Sun' would appear in the September–December issue of the *Review*, but, with the trial now set, publication of *Ulysses* in the magazine came to a dead stop.

Still unable to find a flat, at the end of October the Joyces moved back to one small room in rue de l'Université – from one matchbox into another. It was the twentieth and coldest address, he said, at which he had written *Ulysses*.[29] But his sense of displacement was allayed somewhat when Lugné-Poë said he would put on the now-translated *Exiles* at his theatre in December, and by the arrival of his long-lost case of books and manuscripts from Trieste.

To Quinn he bemoaned the fact that he was without a decent place to live and was missing his possessions in Trieste. His children were also a source of worry; their multilingual education had equipped them to speak Italian and German but not French, which made them unable to make friends in Paris. Giorgio seemed to be going nowhere and he did not know what on earth to do with Lucia. As for the much-vaunted Paris restaurants, 'We are obliged to eat in a popular restaurant, both lunch and dinner. The food is bad, the cooking worse, and the wine is worst of all. The restaurants are chock full but only for two hours, because at nine o'clock (which was my dinner hour), they close the restaurants and go to sleep under the tables ... If I were alone, rather than enter one, I would buy food and eat it in the street.'[30] He wrote of his suspicions about Huebsch and listed his complaints against him – no contract or decent advance offered for *Ulysses*, no replies to letters and demands for cuts and alterations. Quinn replied that Huebsch was withholding commitment to the book until after the *Little Review* trial. If he decided against publication, Quinn suggested approaching the publishers Boni and Liveright.

On 22 November the violence in Ireland reached a new level of intensity when some fourteen British officers were shot dead in their quarters in Dublin by gunmen commanded by Michael Collins, and later that day Black and Tans machine-gunned a Gaelic football crowd at Croke Park. The fate of the British in Ireland had been sealed and the country was to become ever more polarized between moderate and extreme Republicans. Within a month the War of Independence would be raging out of control: there would be riots, terror and carnage in Cork, leaving the city in flames. For a pacifist anti-nationalist apostate who had taken money from British kings and had dealings with British prime ministers, there would be no comfortable place in such a country.

During November, Joyce was creating at full throttle, poring for hours over his bundle of notes and relics of his life, wearing a white coat as if needing that reflected light, and writing late into the night. He was working on two chapters of *Ulysses* simultaneously – finishing off 'Circe' and drafting 'Eumeus', the sojourn of Bloom and Stephen in the cabman's shelter following their night of surrealistic debauchery in Monto. His plan was to finish these episodes, send them off in January, then apply himself to the final two – 'Ithaca' and 'Penelope', both of which he had sketched out in 1916. However, November saw him struck down again with eye trouble, and at times it was almost impossible for him to read or write, a set-back he put down to the shivering damp of his living conditions. He pictured himself to Pound, sitting in the cold 'writing about tiresome Bloom with Mrs Pound's shawl round my head and Miss Serruys' two blankets round the rest of my body'.[31]

Finally, on 1 December Joyce took a six-month lease on a luxury apartment at 5 Boulevard Raspail at Notre-Dame-des-Champs in Montparnasse, costing £300 a year. Now that he had the means he did not see why he should not live well. The state of his health demanded this sort of place, he told Rodker – one he could heat whatever the cost. And this flat had both a telephone and a piano, so now he could talk to his friends and entertain them with song. On reflection he was amazed at his transformation since coming to Paris, from 'homeless and barefoot' to 'living in luxury'. In his new quarters his eyes had recovered sufficiently for him to resume work, though now he was plagued with painful neuralgia, and what he called the nerves of his head which were 'in a bad way'. 'Circe', he decided, was having her revenge for what he had done to her legend in *Ulysses*.

A few days after moving in, Joyce re-established contact with John McCormack, then giving a concert in Paris. The tenor's career had blossomed since they had last met in Dublin. He had recently completed a world tour and had achieved a wide reputation with his recordings – a star of the new age of the gramophone. In Paris he was grandly lodged at Claridge's on the Champs-Elysées, bound next for an opera season in Monte Carlo. Following the concert, Joyce wrote congratulating him on 'a feat of breathing and phrasing – to say nothing of the beauty of tone' which no Italian lyrical tenor could match – and especially applauding his aria from *Don Giovanni*.[32] He tried to interest him in Molyneux Palmer's settings of his *Chamber Music* poems, sent him a copy of *A Portrait* and told him that if his daughter ever found her afternoons 'too boresome', Lucia, who found every afternoon 'boresome', would be pleased to keep her company.

Missing Budgen still, Joyce wrote to him nostalgically about their 'Pfauennights' in Zurich, and asked urgently for his help from London. 'The whirligig movement in "Circe"' was on the refrain 'My Girl's a Yorkshire Girl' and he needed the words and music. This music-hall song of working-class love, 'played on Mrs Cohen's pianola with lights', he said, he would balance, 'to unify the action', with Stephen's lone star Elizabethan lament for lost love. He also looked ahead to his final chapter, saying, 'I am going to leave the last word with Molly Bloom, the final episode being written through her thoughts and tired Poldy being then asleep.'[33]

Five days before Christmas, Joyce wrote to Pound, Budgen and Harriet Weaver, '"*Circe*" finished this morning at last.'[34] Later he told John Quinn that the episode had been rewritten nine times over seven years of hard labour through eight illnesses and nineteen changes of address, across Austria, Switzerland, Italy and France.[35] Now able to relax somewhat, he was happy for Sylvia Beach to extend his circle of acquaintances. One of her earliest customers, a friend of Adrienne Monnier's, was Valery Larbaud, the distinguished French novelist, critic and translator. She arranged a meeting between Larbaud and Joyce at Shakespeare and Company on Christmas Eve, and the two struck up an immediate rapport, even though the Frenchman knew nothing of Joyce other than what Beach and Monnier had told him.

It had been a difficult year for Joyce and he told Michael Healy he hoped the Devil would take it as quickly as he liked. His first problem in 1921 was to find a typist for 'Circe', and he worried that, if it were a woman, she might find it disturbing. Altogether nine typists had refused it, some finding his writing too difficult to fathom, others simply too horrified by what they read. One, said Beach, came to Joyce's flat and, as he opened the door, simply threw the manuscript down and fled.[36] Beach then decided that she and Joyce would do the typing together at her shop, but that proved difficult because of customers continually coming and going. So another of Beach's friends took it up – a lawyer who had once studied and defended prostitutes, so nothing in 'Circe' was shocking to her. She passed her legible copy ready for final typing to another friend, the wife of Norman Harrison, a minor official working at the British Embassy. Added to these difficulties, Joyce had lost patience with Huebsch, was unhappy with his agent Pinker,[37] and Lugné-Poë had given him no date for the production of *Exiles*.

However, Larbaud, who had now read copies of the *Little Review*, had decided that *Ulysses* was a work of genius. He wrote to Joyce saying that he was 'raving mad' about it, had been unable to sleep at nights after reading it, deemed it 'as great and comprehensive and human as Rabelais', and was writing an essay on it for the *Nouvelle Revue Française* (*NRF*).

At the end of January, Weaver reported an increased interest in *A Portrait* suggesting that a further edition might be necessary, and that she had already received 150 orders for *Ulysses*. It was something to celebrate on his thirty-ninth birthday. A fortnight later Joyce sent word that he had completed the 'Eumeus' episode and was back working on 'Ithaca' and 'Penelope' throughout the night, until three or beyond. However, the prospects of bringing the book out that summer were fast receding.

Quinn was still urging Joyce to withdraw *Ulysses* from the *Little Review*, but the decision was made for him on 21 February 1921 when the case against the *Review* finally came to court in New York. Quinn put up what was thought to be a brilliant defence, but the three presiding judges found against him, and Anderson and Heap were each fined $50, given a criminal record and ordered to cease publishing *Ulysses*.[38] (They were, thought Quinn, lucky to have avoided jail). Although the novel was a great talking-point, its serialization in the US was terminated forthwith. Some, however, saw the ban as an opportunity. Earlier that month in a note sent to him from London's Savoy Hotel, an aspiring New York magazine proprietor, Samuel Roth, asked why *Ulysses* had not yet appeared in book form.

No longer constrained by the demands of a deadline, Joyce felt free to indulge his fantasy even more and the chapters of *Ulysses* became longer and stranger.[39] At the end of February, with two episodes to go, he informed Budgen that 'Ithaca' was being written in the form of a mathematical catechism. 'All events are resolved into their cosmic, physical, psychical etc. equivalents, e.g. Bloom jumping down the area, drawing water from the tap, the micturating in the garden, the cone of incense, lighted candle and statue so that the reader will know everything and know it in the baldest and coldest way, but Bloom and Stephen thereby become heavenly bodies, wanderers like the stars at which they gaze.' The last 'all-too-human' word was left to 'Penelope', who was, he said, 'the indispensable countersign to Bloom's passport to eternity'.[40]

Joyce first learned the outcome of the *Little Review* trial on 1 March when he was shown a press cutting from the *New York Times* of 22 February, announcing 'IMPROPER NOVEL COSTS WOMEN $100'. It quoted Quinn for the defence saying that, although cast in 'a curious style', *Ulysses* was not unlike other books which had *not* been prosecuted, and 'There may be found more impropriety on display in some of 5th Ave show windows or in a theatrical show than is contained in this novel.' Joyce sent the cutting to Harriet Weaver with the comment that the offence was less grotesque than the defence.[41] He had copies made of similar reports in other newspapers.

As Quinn had predicted, on 24 March, a month after the trial, Huebsch finally informed him that before publishing *Ulysses* he would require alterations to the 'Nausicaa' chapter condemned by the New York court. Quinn, knowing Joyce's attitude to censorship, told Huebsch that it must be published unaltered or not at all. Despite his hopes for 1921, Joyce decided it was not a good year for him, adding up, as it did, to thirteen.

There was still no fair copy of 'Circe'. What had been completed, he told Miss Weaver, looked a complete mess, 'typed by several different people using different machines and all colours and kinds of paper is a horrible thing to look at – much less to read'.[42] More encouragingly, however, on Larbaud's recommendation, Gaston Gallimard had asked for a full translation of the novel for the *NRF*. Joyce was also increasingly in demand by visiting Americans. A friend of Quinn's, the psychiatrist, Dr Joseph Collins, invited him to lunch and suggested he rewrite passages of *A Portrait* 'in the language of the consulting room' to make it more saleable in the US. But the author of *Ulysses* did not share the American taste for Freud and the subject was quickly changed. For his pains Collins got himself written into the 'Penelope' episode as a doctor for women's diseases. (After reading extracts from the novel, Collins commented, 'I have in my files writing by the insane just as good as this.')[43]

A friend of Pound's, Robert McAlmon, who had met Joyce at Beach's bookshop, had asked Miss Weaver for his address. McAlmon, recently married to the English poet Winifred Ellerman, known as 'Bryher', was a literary playboy intent on spending as much of his wealthy father-in-law's money as possible. Now determined to get to know Pound's 'genius', he presented himself at the Boulevard Raspail apartment. There he was struck by Nora's prettiness, 'simple dignity' and 'reassuring manner', and Joyce's obsession with words, often to the point of weeping over them. After that, the two met often – for aperitifs most evenings and for sessions during which Joyce would read to him long passages from *Ulysses*. Not everybody cared for McAlmon. Hemingway once threatened to 'knock his block off', and Scott Fitzgerald said he was 'a pretty good person to avoid'.[44]

Joyce's American friends in Paris, mostly met through Shakespeare and Company, included poets William Carlos Williams and e.e. cummings, musician George Antheil, artist Myron Nutting, and illustrator Richard Wallace. One who spurned him was the envious Gertrude Stein who declared Joyce a passing fancy and that her work had long anticipated *Ulysses*.[45]

On 5 April, Huebsch finally wrote declining to publish *Ulysses* unexpurgated and proposing to send the manuscript back to Quinn. Knowing there was no prospect of Miss Weaver finding a printer in England, Joyce immediately requested that it be returned directly to him. He had good reason. On receiving Quinn's message, he went to the rue Dupuytren to share his feeling of despair with Miss Beach. She recalled him 'sighing deeply in a tone of complete discouragement' and saying, 'My book will never come out now.' On an impulse she said, 'Would you let Shakespeare and Company have the honour of bringing out your *Ulysses*?' Joyce was overjoyed, accepting the offer immediately.[46] Feeling that they both might have acted rashly, Beach consulted Miss Monnier and Larbaud, who thoroughly approved, and next day, when Joyce returned, the matter was agreed. One of the greatest novels of the century would be published by a woman who had never published a book before, from a small backstreet bookshop which had been in business for barely six months.

23

An Eventful Labour

(1921–1922)

'Whilst others have been at the balloo, I have been at my book, and am now past the craggy paths of study, and come to the flowery plains of honour and reputation.' Ben Jonson, *Volpone, or The Fox*

Once it had been decided that she would publish *Ulysses*, Sylvia Beach lost no time. She quickly produced a prospectus for subscribers in English and French, carrying press notices of Joyce's previous books and of *Ulysses*. An announcement was also placed in the *Bibliographie de la France* to bring the book to international attention. Within days she was able to announce the first subscriptions.

The plan agreed with Joyce was to publish in October, an edition of 100 signed copies on Holland hand-made paper at 350 francs, 150 copies on vergé d'arches at 250 francs, 750 copies on linen at 150 francs – 1,000 copies in all. Joyce would be paid a royalty of 66 per cent of net profits, far beyond anything he would have received from any other publisher. American subscribers could be sent the Paris edition by mail or buy it over the counter in Paris. By 10 April, the first chapters had gone to Miss Beach's printer, Maurice Darantière of Dijon. The Shakespeare and Company bookshop soon became Joyce's second home and the easily bored Lucia was also a frequent visitor.

Harriet Weaver, still anxious to publish the book in England, suggested that Beach supply the sheets of her edition for the proposed English (second) edition and she would provide her with the names and addresses of all the Egoist Press subscribers and booksellers with whom she dealt. When the Paris edition had been fully subscribed, she would publish her edition at 9 or 10 shillings a copy, of which Joyce would receive a royalty of 25 per cent on sales, until costs had been recouped, and then 90 per cent of profits for this and any future editions. And, since he had written saying how desperate he was for money, she would also send him £200 on account. Furthermore, by dealing with him directly they would cut out Pinker and his 10 per cent. Joyce was happy to agree and gave Weaver a free hand to publish the book as she thought fit. He quickly got Beach's agreement to the arrangement and estimated that he could bring around

110 names to the list from his own friends and contacts. The two women would co-operate over publicity, the prospectus and subscription lists, and become good friends in the process.

On 8 April 1921, Joyce's prediction of an 'unlucky' year appeared to be confirmed. Mrs Harrison, his typist, called on him, 'in a state of great agitation', to say that her husband had discovered the manuscript of 'Circe' lying around at their home, had read a little and then, in disgust, had torn it up and burned it. There followed, Joyce gathered, hysterical scenes which spilled out into the street. Fortunately, she had kept most of it hidden. Greatly distressed, he begged her to return the manuscript at once, but she failed to do so until the following day, after what he called 'twenty-four hours of suspense'. It transpired that only the last half-dozen pages of the copy left beside her typewriter had been destroyed, and he was comforted by the thought that Quinn had his original manuscript which would enable him easily to recoup the missing pages.

Shortly after the deal was struck with Miss Beach, there was a celebration party at the famous Bal Bullier in Montparnasse. There Joyce first met the young Irish writer and art critic Arthur Power. He was impressed that Power, like him, was from Dublin, had left the Church, chosen exile and had read all his books. Power in turn was impressed by Joyce's sensitivity and courteous manner. The evening culminated with Miss Beach proposing a toast to the success of *Ulysses* and Joyce inviting Power to join them for a final drink at the nearby Closerie des Lilas.

Pound, who had left England for good, was in Paris on 16 April, and Joyce gave him what he had of 'Circe' and 'Eumeus' to read. The poet was, said Joyce afterwards, 'very excited', and talked of producing a manifesto about it. One American in Paris by no means excited was Gertrude Stein, who, on hearing of Beach's plan, came to her shop and announced that she and her companion Miss Toklas were cancelling their library subscriptions.[1]

In mid-April Quinn finally wrote explaining in typically long-winded detail what had transpired at the *Little Review* trial and with Huebsch. The letter only confirmed to Joyce that he had been wise to withdraw his book from America, and he replied, with barely concealed disdain, that the publication of *Ulysses* (complete) had been arranged in Paris in a couple of days.[2] He explained what had happened to the 'Circe' manuscript and asked Quinn if he would return the last six or seven pages of the original manuscript for copying. However, having got his hands on it, the possessiveness of the collector overcame him, and Quinn refused Joyce's request. According to Sylvia Beach, he also rejected a request from her, and refused point-blank when her mother in New York telephoned suggesting that she come to his office to make a fair copy of the ruined passages, exploding with rage and using 'language unfit for a lady'.[3] Finally, and grudgingly, he allowed the pages to be photographed and from these Joyce had copies typed for the printer. Quinn later excused himself, pleading tiredness and anger over his time taken up defending *Ulysses*, 'the cursed *Little Review*' and its 'shameless' editors.[4]

Richard Aldington gave *Ulysses* some useful publicity that month with his promised article in the *English Review*. While declaring it 'a remarkable achievement' he thought its influence on younger writers might be 'deplorable'.[5] Eliot disagreed, believing its effect would be salutary, and telling Robert McAlmon, 'Joyce I admire as a person who seems to be independent of outside stimulus, and who therefore is likely to go on producing first-rate work until he dies ... Joyce has form – immensely careful. And as for literary – one of the last things he sent me contains a marvellous parody of nearly every style in English prose from 1600 to the *Daily Mail* ... One needs a pretty considerable knowledge of English Literature to understand it.'[6] A week later Eliot wrote to Quinn saying how charming he had found Joyce but adding, 'I can see that he is certainly a handful, with the true fanatic's conviction that everyone ought to forward the interests of his work. It is however the conviction of the fanatic, and not the artfulness or pertinacity of ordinary push; and the latter part of *Ulysses*, which I have been reading in manuscript, is truly magnificent. I hear that he has captured some of the French literary elite who profess to know enough English.'[7]

With the second edition of *A Portrait* almost sold out, Miss Weaver was planning a third, and asked Joyce if he wanted to make revisions. When, shortly afterwards, Pound sent her the 'Circe' episode, she was struck by his extraordinary new style of writing, telling him that it showed no symptoms of fatigue, as she had feared. Joyce, in thanking her for her 'generous' advance, said that her aid illuminated what he called 'the dismal labyrinth I seem to walk in'.[8] But her generosity did not end there. She had two thousand prospectuses for *Ulysses* printed, sending a large batch to Miss Beach and was soon able to announce that a Dublin bookseller had asked for 100 'for judicious distribution', and an American export agent had ordered ten books. The birth of *Ulysses* was now widely and eagerly anticipated.

Towards the end of May, still working to complete his final two chapters, Joyce again suffered a sudden eye-attack. Miss Weaver thought him in need of a holiday, but Joyce had his own way of unwinding; at the fashionable Michaud's restaurant in the rue Jacob, he resumed his old Zurich style of living. 'Had several uproarious allnight sittings (and dancings) with Lewis as he will perhaps tell you,' he told Budgen.[9] On similar occasions at the Gypsy Bar or the Noctambule, Wyndham Lewis would declaim Verlaine and Joyce recite Dante in Italian in a priestly incantatory fashion, entrancing the 'girls' who frequented the place. McAlmon often drank along with them till beyond midnight, and Joyce would sleep late next morning.[10] Having McAlmon around had one advantage – he was a useful source of loans, to the tune of around £30 ($150) a month, loans he was quite happy should remain unrepaid. Unsurprisingly perhaps, Joyce told Budgen that he found McAlmon 'very simple and decent'.

But sometimes it was Joyce who appeared the simpleton. Once, dining out at the Brasserie Lutétia, drinking *vin mousseux*, McAlmon sensed a nervous foreboding on Joyce's part. Some disaster, he thought, could so easily prevent his book appearing, and he saw omens of doom every-where – cutlery wrongly set at table, an inexplicable toothache, the rumble of thunder, the thought of fire at the printers consuming his work. When McAlmon reported seeing a rat in the restaurant Joyce passed out and then had to be ferried home in a cab. Nora, who had seen him carried home drunk many times was on the point of scolding him, but when McAlmon explained that he had fainted, she became suddenly tender and caring.[11] There was nothing straightforward in this complex inter-dependency.

The lease of Joyce's expensive Raspail flat was about to expire, and Valery Larbaud, who was going to England that summer, offered him his flat rent-free during his absence. On 3 June the Joyces moved to the French writer's newly decorated, tastefully furnished flat at 74 rue Cardinal Lemoine, close to the Seine just opposite Notre-Dame – their fifth address in Paris in eleven months. Joyce liked his new surroundings, 'a charming little quarter situated in a kind of park', he wrote,[12] 'with ... absolute silence, great trees, birds ... like being a hundred kilometers from Paris'.[13] It was not far for Lucia to visit Shakespeare and Company where she had befriended Myrsine Moschos, Miss Beach's new Greek assistant, or for Giorgio to be sent for a sub when cash ran out. He began to rely heavily on the Beach account for day-to-day expenses.[14] Two days after moving in, Joyce wrote to Larbaud saying how comfortable they were and how well he was proceeding with 'Ithaca'. 'I have left "Circe" and the pigs, sows, chitterlings, grunts etc. on Boulevard Raspail,' he wrote. Nora and Lucia were also delighted with the place.[15] When proofs from Darantière started arriving shortly afterwards, he became completely engrossed, returning each batch with not just corrections but copious additions. Printing costs escalated and he had to ask Miss Weaver for further advances.

Although he was now working with a new sense of freedom, he still found it hard-going, especially the mathematical aspects of the 'Ithaca' episode and the barely drafted 'Penelope', his 'last and stormiest cape' to round. Needing more background on Molly, Budgen was recruited to supply books and relevant information about Gibraltar where she had grown up and received her first amorous kiss. Joyce had already chosen the colours for the binding (white letters on a blue field, like the Greek flag, symbolic of the Odyssean myth – white islands scattered across a blue sea) and among the subscribers for the book he could now boast a nephew of Hungarian communist leader Bela Kun, an Anglican bishop, a leader of the Irish revolution, and Winston Churchill. He had, he told Francini, become 'a monument'.[16] On 16 June, the 'monument' and Nora were able to mark the seventeenth anniversary of their soon-to-be-widely celebrated first night out together.

The mood of satisfaction did not last. Having been informed of his excesses by Lewis and McAlmon, his patron wrote to enquire whether Joyce thought he was drinking too heavily and was being led astray by his new Parisian friends. Fearful of losing her goodwill, he immediately forwarded the letter to Budgen seeking his advice, and on receiving it back with his suggestions, wrote Miss Weaver a clever letter of self-justification, listing some of the legends circulating about him. His family thought that he had lined his pockets in Zurich by spying, in Dublin it was said that he was done-for and dying in New York, in Aberdeen that he was an eccentric who carried four watches and spoke nothing but the time of day, in Trieste that he was a cocaine addict, in Liverpool that he owned a chain of Swiss cinemas, in America that he was either blind, emaciated and consumptive or an austere guru, in Paris that he was a petit bourgeois whose ultra-politeness was intentionally offensive. 'People in Zurich,' he went on, 'persuaded themselves that I was gradually going mad and actually endeavoured to induce me to enter a sanatorium where a certain Doctor Jung (the Swiss Tweedledum who is not to be confused with the Viennese Tweedledee, Dr Freud) amuses himself at the expense (in every sense of the word) of ladies and gentlemen who are troubled with bees in their bonnets.' In fact, Joyce said, he was perfectly ordinary and unworthy of such inventions, but had acquired the reputation of a hopeless drunk too lazy to complete anything. As for his Paris friends, most had been introduced to him by Pound.[17]

Misfortune, he complained, continued to dog him. Since arriving in Paris he had been ignored by the French literary press and had no success with *Exiles*. However, at least translations of *Dubliners* and *A Portrait* were under way and work on *Ulysses* was mostly completed. He avoided literary occasions, he said, and had no time for idle gossip, nor had he read a work of literature for years – all of which might have affected him. 'My head is full of pebbles and rubbish and broken matches and bits of glass picked up most everywhere. The task I set myself technically in writing a book from eighteen different points of view and in as many styles, all apparently unknown or undiscovered by my fellow tradesmen, that and the nature of the legend chosen would be enough to upset anyone's mental balance.' Long as it was, he said, his letter had not even touched on what he called 'the darker aspects of my detestable character'.[18] Two days after writing this, he suffered another violent eye-attack, and McAlmon found him in a bed, the room darkened and Nora bathing his eyes with ice-water.

John Quinn, in Paris that summer, spoke contemptuously of Beach's tiny, obscurely situated bookstore, but on 27 July she moved Shakespeare and Company to more spacious premises at 12 rue de l'Odéon – 'Stratford on Odéon', Joyce called it. Quinn, finding Joyce too unwell to dine out, met him at rue Cardinal Lemoine, and there gave him a further 2,000 francs on account for the *Ulysses* manuscript. He was horrified by Joyce's ill appearance, especially the poor state of his teeth, and was irritated that he was not prepared to take his medical advice.

By August, 5,000 prospectuses had been sent out and 260 subscriptions collected. Despite his iritis, and sometimes being able to use only one eye, Joyce was writing around twelve hours a day and his brain was reeling – as he imagined would be those of his readers, he said. A draft of 'Ithaca' was now completed as well as the first sentence of 'Penelope' which he outlined to Miss Weaver. It would consist of eight or nine sentences, the first of which would be 2,500 words long, each sentence loaded with long words ('sesquipedalian', he wrote) but ending in a monosyllable. 'Bloom and all the Blooms,' he said wearily, 'will soon be dead, thank God. Everyone says he ought to have died long ago.'[19]

In a letter to Larbaud he revealed the final monosyllable of 'Penelope' and of *Ulysses* – 'Yes'.[20] 'Penelope', he told Budgen, was the *clou* to the book, and revolved slowly but surely around four 'cardinal points' of the female anatomy – 'breasts, arse, womb and cunt'. Although he thought it probably the most obscene chapter in the book so far, he considered it 'perfectly sane full amoral fertilisable untrustworthy engaging shrewd limited prudent indifferent.[21] *Weib. Ich bin das Fleisch der stets bejaht.*' (Molly was the flesh that always affirms.)[22] But to understand this chapter you had to understand 'Ithaca', he said. The book's web of meaning was deeply woven and required careful unpicking.[23]

With the complex core of his work now completed, Joyce had reduced his workday from sixteen hours to six and tried to get out of the flat more. One day in late August, he said, he went out looking for unpleasant news, and walking back from the Gare du Nord, a 'filthy rat' ran past him, a sure sign of bad luck. Not long afterwards he went with Giorgio to the

Alhambra music-hall. During the show he suffered a repetition of the nervous attack he had suffered on Zurich's Bahnhofstrasse, collapsing, being hardly able to breathe, and having to be taken in a taxi to a nearby night pharmacy for a dose of ether.[24] Determined to exercise more, he took walks every day across the river and along the Champs-Elysées to the Etoile and back – taking in the new bookshop in the rue de l'Odéon, where the third (London) edition of *A Portrait* was now on sale. He also strolled along by the Seine looking, he said, for a suitable place to throw Bloom in with a fifty pound weight attached to him.[25]

Following the Harrison incident, he had become nervous about typists and got McAlmon to type the final episode. Having recovered his great phantasmagoric 'Circe' chapter from disaster, he added what he called 'a Messianic scene', a parody of Christ's cross-examination by the High Priest of the Sanhedrin. Harrison, in seeking to destroy this dark diabolical chapter had, it seems, unleashed something even darker and even more devilish in its author.

In October the Joyces returned to 9 rue de l'Université where this time separate rooms were taken to accommodate the children. 'Penelope' was with the printers and he had only 'Ithaca' to finish. But, even with the novel still unfinished, Larbaud had undertaken to appear at a séance to discuss it, and a young intellectual, Jacques Benoît-Méchin, was recruited to translate passages to illustrate Larbaud's talk. Asked persistently about the schematic diagram he had made for Carlo Linati, Joyce finally relented, giving Benoît-Méchin a copy and copies also to Beach, Quinn and Monnier. All were asked to keep this to themselves but it soon began to circulate, much to Joyce's later annoyance.

Miss Beach had obtained subscriptions from some prominent writers including George Moore, Harold Monroe and Ronald Firbank. She wrote hoping to get one from Shaw, but in reply received a delicious piece of Shavian satire. He had, he said, read fragments of the novel in serial form.

It is a revolting record of a disgusting phase of civilisation; but it is a truthful one ... I have walked those streets and known those shops and have heard and taken part in those conversations. I escaped from them to England at the age of twenty; and forty years later have learnt from the books of Mr Joyce that Dublin is still what it was, and young men are still drivelling in slackjawed blackguardism just as they were in 1870.

He found some consolation, Shaw said, in finding someone prepared to confront it and, by means of his literary genius compel others to confront it too. He wished the book well, but, as to purchasing it, 'I must add ... that I am an elderly Irish gentleman, and that if you imagine that any

Irishman, much less an elderly one, would pay 150 francs for a book, you little know my countrymen.'[26] When Pound challenged Shaw over what he had said about the book, Shaw replied that he would see Joyce and his lady bookseller 'damned' before he would pay 'fifty times what M. Joyce could buy my entire works for'.[27] The publicity-conscious Joyce thought the letter worth printing and he bet McAlmon that Shaw would subscribe anonymously and get his copy through a bookseller.[28]

Even with the book all but complete, he was still asking Aunt Josephine about Dublin families featured in *Ulysses*, and how easy she thought it would be for someone to climb over the railings and drop into the basement area of 7 Eccles Street. He also wanted to know whether, during the cold February of 1893, the canal was sufficiently frozen for skating on, and enquired after Alfred H. Hunter, who had set the Ulyssean hare running by a simple act of charity back in 1904. Hunter, he would have found, was now an advertising salesman, a job he gave to Bloom, in addition to the name of Hunter's wife (Marion) to Bloom's wife. Feeling ever more alienated from what he called 'the slaughterhouse' of Ireland, he insisted that, apart from Aunt Josephine, he wanted no help from his fellow Irishmen, either moral or material. John Joyce had written an amusing letter to Lucia but his son, not even aware of his current address, had to enquire after that too.[29]

The rights of *Chamber Music*, *A Portrait* and *Exiles* had now been transferred from Elkin Mathews and Grant Richards to the Egoist Press, but this did not affect Joyce's income from them. Still living beyond his means and desperate again for funds, he prevailed on Miss Beach to solicit support from Quinn and McCormack, amongst others, in order that he might complete his masterpiece free of money worries. At last, with the aid of a loan from McAlmon, on the evening of 29 October, he put the final full stop to the 'Ithaca' episode. Revisions apart, the composition of *Ulysses* was over. He immediately sent the glad tidings to Pound, Larbaud, Weaver, Budgen and McAlmon.

By the beginning of November Joyce firmly expected *Ulysses* to appear within a few weeks and money to start flowing in. When that was obviously not going to happen, the date of publication became talismanic for him. *A Portrait* had first appeared serially in *The Egoist* on 2 February, *his* birthday; *Ulysses* was begun on 1 March, the birthday of Budgen, and had been finished on Pound's birthday. On whose birthday, he wondered, would *Ulysses* be published?[30] His obsession with dates, especially saints' days, could still determine his choices.

His impaired sight did not prevent him, on 5 November, from taking his family to see Charlie Chaplin's first full-length film, *The Kid*, and perhaps recognizing something of his own wild dancing in Chaplin's antics. Certainly it struck a chord with Lucia who, showing off her talent as a dancer, dressed herself up as the little tramp and performed her own Chaplin act at a party that Christmas, complete with baggy pants, twirling cane and toothbrush moustache. It gave a light-hearted counterweight to her more stolid hero Napoleon, and she would later, with the help of Larbaud, publish an article about the comic.

By now the passages to be read at Larbaud's séance had been chosen – the exchange about execution from the 'Cyclops' episode, the romantic passage in 'Sirens', some extracts from his favourite chapter, 'Ithaca', and six pages of 'Penelope'. His schematic outline of the book sent to Larbaud would, he told Weaver, help add a further element of confusion to the proceedings. He now regretted sending him the schema and would ask for it back, he said, but did offer to send it to the ever-trusted Miss Weaver. With tickets for the séance now selling, he sent Nora to Shakespeare and Company to borrow 100 francs from the takings. Fortunately for Joyce, his hints and tales of suffering to his benefactress resulted in a draft for £100 plus an unspecified 'gift'. From this he paid Miss Beach 300 francs of what he had borrowed from her, but he would eventually end up owing her some thousands – all meticulously recorded in her accounts. By July of the following year she calculated it had grown to 40,565 francs (around eight hundred pounds).[31]

Preparations for the séance were suddenly complicated when Joyce saw Benoît-Méchin's translation of the 'Sirens'. He thought it deficient, and it was decided that the passage should be read in English by a young American actor, Jimmy Light, whom Joyce carefully rehearsed for the occasion. Other translated extracts were revised with help from Larbaud's friend, the poet Léon-Paul Fargue. Finally, at Miss Monnier's Maison des Amis des Livres at 7 rue de l'Odéon on 7 December, a fortunate few got a first taste of the intricate poetry and sometimes discordant music of one of the century's greatest works. To prepare listeners in advance for what was to come, the notice for the séance warned that some words and expressions not in common use might prove shocking.

The event was oversubscribed and the room packed. Larbaud had an attack of stage-fright and needed a glass of brandy in order to get started. Then there was a moment of drama when the lights failed during the reading of the 'Cyclops' episode but the audience sat it out patiently, and, according to Sylvia Beach, the whole event was a triumph, each reading being greeted with loud applause. Finally, when Joyce, who had been hiding in a back room, was dragged out, overcome with embarrassment, to be kissed on both cheeks by Larbaud, there were even louder cheers.[32] Joyce, of course, feared that some of those present, such as Fargue, might

have found the evening boring.[33] But the success of the readings convinced him that, despite his earlier doubts, *Ulysses* could be translated
into other languages. The séance, he said later, was the opening of his
Paris career.

Just before Christmas, Nora had a lucky escape when a bus mounted
the pavement close to the bus-stop where she was waiting and pinned
her against a lamp-post. Joyce dismissed it as 'hardly an accident'. It must
have been in this same cold frame of mind that he met Eliot again, this
time accompanied by his wife. Vivien Eliot felt the chill. 'I have seen
Joyce several times,' she wrote to Mary Hutchinson, 'and find him a
most unsympathetic personality. Vain! Egoist! Unseeing ...'[34] There was
a Christmas party with friends of Budgen, where Lucia did her Charlie
Chaplin act and Joyce and Giorgio sang. Nora, still recovering from her
close encounter with the Paris omnibus, stayed at home.

In January 1922 Joyce got a taste of Irish opinion about *Ulysses* (albeit
a favourable one) when Joseph Hone, the silent partner at Maunsel when
Dubliners was turned down in 1912, published 'A Letter from Ireland' in
the *London Mercury*. Perhaps trying to make amends for the tribulations
to which he and George Roberts had subjected Joyce, he wrote that:

> For us in Ireland Mr Joyce's significance lies in this, that he is the
> first man of literary genius, expressing himself in perfect freedom, that
> Catholic Ireland has produced in modern times. Mr Joyce is as Irish as
> M. Anatole France ... is French. It was perhaps not really strange that
> when this writer did appear, his implied criticism of Irish life should be
> so much bolder than anything that could be found in the books of his
> Protestant contemporaries.[35]

Confirmation that he was now considered something of a celebrity in
America came when Joyce was interviewed for the magazine *Vanity Fair*
by the twenty-nine-year-old Djuna Barnes. They met at the Café les
Deux Magots in the Place St-Germain-des-Prés, he in a blue overcoat and
sporting his colourful hunting-waistcoat. Barnes had read *Dubliners* and
A Portrait and had been struck by the singing quality of Joyce's prose.
Although they had met before, now in broad daylight she was able more
fully to size up the man Pound had told her had been 'more crucified in
his sensibilities than any other writer of our age'. Immediately after the
limp, 'peculiarly pulpy' handshake, he began talking. 'The pity is, the
public will demand and find a moral in my book – or worse, they may
take it in some more serious way, and on the honour of a gentleman,
there is not one single serious line in it.' All great talkers, he told her,
sipping chilled wine and puffing on a cigar, had spoken 'the language

of Sterne, Swift, or the Restoration'. 'Even Oscar Wilde ... studied the Restoration through a microscope in the morning and repeated it through a telescope in the evening.' In *Ulysses* the great talkers were all there. 'I have recorded, simultaneously, what a man says, sees, thinks, and what such seeing, thinking, saying does to what you Freudians call the subconscious – but as for psychoanalysis, it's neither more nor less than blackmail.' He looked sad and tired, she wrote, his eyes pale, ill and unfocused, while occasionally the curve of his upper lip suggested that he was jeering. But he had, she decided, fulfilled the intention of Stephen in *A Portrait* of freeing himself to write against what he no longer believed in, armed only with 'silence, exile and cunning'.[36] The interview was published with a sketch of Joyce by Barnes's friend Mina Loy.

Loy was not the only one who caught his likeness that winter. Sylvia Beach persuaded a reluctant Joyce to be photographed by Man Ray at his Montparnasse studio. Ray recalled the occasion and the unhappy subject. Joyce came to his studio 'like a man who had to perform a distasteful chore'. His eyes being bad, his poses were 'very stiff' and finally, unable to bear the lights, he dropped his head in his hands and refused to go on. At that point Ray took the photograph which he sent to Beach. She was not, he thought, particularly enthusiastic, but, as he put it, 'it served its purpose, at the time'.[37]

The complete *Ulysses* was in page-proof form by 5 January 1922, and although he was still revising through early January, he told Miss Weaver that he had vowed to make no more changes after 1 February. In fact he finished sooner and began to hope that its publication would again coincide with his birthday, 2 February. Myron Nutting had been asked to reproduce the exact colour of the Greek flag for the cover, but no precise date had been set for the launch. Joyce was on tenterhooks awaiting its appearance. After the backwash from the launching of his 'Dreadnought' had subsided, he said, he planned to go to London.

With the publication of *Ulysses* imminent, even though the end of 'Penelope' was still being written, the Joyces took Misses Beach and Monnier for a celebration meal at Ferrari's, a popular Italian restaurant on the Avenue Rapp. The following day, in Dublin, the Dáil Éireann voted 64 to 57 in favour of the treaty with Britain which established the Irish Free State. It looked as though *Ulysses* and the new state might share more or less the same birthday. Both would have a mixed reception, but the book would outlive the state.

Still unsure when *Ulysses* would appear, on 22 January Joyce told McAlmon that he was 'in a state of energetic prostration', expecting it to be out by the end of that week. Finally, on the 30th, he announced to Miss Weaver that after much sending of letters and cables, *Ulysses* would be published on 2 February, his fortieth birthday, which, in his mind, could only bode well for its future.

But no road for Joyce ever ran entirely smoothly. Djuna Barnes told the American journalist and editor Burton Rascoe of a last-minute fright the superstitious Joyce received. As publication day approached she was walking with the Joyces in the Bois de Boulogne, when a man brushed past Joyce and mumbled something inaudible to her. Joyce turned pale and began trembling. 'That man,' he said, 'whom I have never seen before, said to me as he passed, in Latin, *"You are an abominable writer!"* That is a dreadful omen the day before the publication of my novel.'[38]

24

Ulysses: Birth and Afterbirth
(1922–1924)

'There is no past, no future; everything flows in an eternal present
... [*Ulysses*] is a tower of Babel ... The history of people is the history
of language.' Joyce to Jacques Mercanton.

Having been urged by Miss Beach to have the book ready for sale on
Joyce's birthday, Darantière wrote on 1 February saying that three copies
would be dispatched from Dijon by express mail and should arrive the
following day. But Joyce, fearing they would arrive late and his lucky day
would be missed, urged Beach to phone the printer, emphasizing how
important the day was to the author. Darantière then offered to send two
copies in care of the guard of the Dijon–Paris express, arriving next
morning at 7 a.m. Miss Beach was at the Gare de Lyon as the train pulled
in, to collect the first copies of *Ulysses*. From there she took a taxi to the
rue de l'Université and delivered one into the hands of the expectant
Joyce. The other went into the window of Shakespeare and Company.

Joyce could now bask in the open admiration of his friends. There were
phone calls, telegrams, and flowers from Myron Nutting's wife Helen.
Miss Weaver, John Quinn, and Pound all received cables announcing the
coming forth of the great work. Darantière was sent a telegram of thanks
and Miss Beach a *pneumatique* and signed copy of his *Ulysses* schema. That
evening there was a private celebration at Ferrari's at which the book was
the guest of honour. The Joyces were joined by the Wallaces (Richard and
Lillian), the Nuttings and Helen Kieffer, their young niece, daughter of
Quinn's partner and a friend of Lucia. In her diary, Helen Nutting
described the scene: 'Joyce at the head of the table, sitting sideways,
melancholy, eating nothing sighing now and then over ordering the
dinner.' Nora, Giorgio and Lucia sat saying nothing. The book, which
everyone was anxious to see, was parked under Joyce's chair, as if he was
reticent about unveiling it. Finally, after dessert, the parcel was unwrapped
and a copy of the blue-and-white-covered book was laid reverentially on
the table. Joyce was deeply moved and the whole party then toasted
Ulysses, the product of sixteen years of agonizing, reflecting and composing, and its author, the self-proclaimed forger of the conscience of his

race. The waiters, duly impressed, took the book to show to the *padrone*.

After dinner they went to the Café Weber in the rue Royale, and Joyce showed Helen Nutting and Mrs Wallace where their and Mrs Pound's names appeared in the book. Afterwards he was anxious to go on elsewhere with Myron Nutting, but found himself bundled into a cab by Nora. As she did so he told Wallace, 'I must be saved from these scenes.'[1] Nora knew, however, that if she did not get him home at once the evening would never end.

Lucia was now quite close to the Nuttings. She was, wrote Helen in her diary later, 'the most normal of the family, tactful, with humour and good sense. A wonderful girl.' She visited the Nuttings' studio in Montparnasse, and joined Helen Kieffer, their niece, who was studying dance at the Jaques-Dalcroze Institute on the rue de l'Annonciation. This was her first true Parisian friendship and would set a course for her own creative talent in which Joyce had come intensely to believe. Soon Lucia was also at the Institute, studying dance not just with Helen but also with the daughters of Larbaud and William Bird, an American journalist, who ran a small Paris publishing press (the Three Mountains Press) and who also became friendly with the Joyces. The Emile Jaques-Dalcroze method – eurhythmics – was fundamentally a method of teaching music through the natural rhythms of human movement, bringing with it an awareness of the body as a subtle means of communication. By contrast, Giorgio, the singer, never lost the stiff formality witnessed by Eliot and Wyndham Lewis.

Joyce sent a signed copy of his novel to Stannie in Trieste. Copy no. 1 of the *édition de luxe* went to Miss Weaver to whom he wrote, 'In conception and technique I tried to depict the earth which is prehuman and presumably posthuman,' and he was amused to tell her that by chance she bore the name of his heroine – Penelope the weaver.[2] At Shakespeare and Company, in Miss Beach's copy (no. 2), he inscribed his thanks and inserted an envelope containing the words of the song 'Who Is Sylvia?' Copy no. 3 went to Margaret Anderson. Thus the three women who had done most to help bring his great creation to birth were appropriately rewarded.

He presented copy no. 1,000 to Nora who immediately offered to sell it to Arthur Power who was present, a joke which Joyce pretended to find amusing. Although it was widely believed that Nora had never read *Ulysses*, according to Power it was evident that she had. She admitted to McAlmon that she had read the last pages of the book, adding, 'I guess the man's a genius, but what a dirty mind he has, surely!' When McAlmon told her that it was her down-to-earth presence that had transformed her husband from 'the word-prettifying bard' and 'martyred sensibility',

Stephen Dedalus, she told him, 'Go along with you! What they'll be saying next is that if it hadn't been for that ignoramus of a woman, what a man he would have been! But never you mind, I could tell them a thing or two about him after twenty years of putting up with him, and the devil take him when he's off on one of his rampages!'[3]

Further copies of *Ulysses* were only dribbling in to Shakespeare and Company and being snapped up immediately. The shop, Joyce told Harriet, was in a state of siege – a nerve-racking conclusion to the book's publication, he said. Then, as there were no royalties from the book yet, he asked for a £50 loan from the war stock held in trust for him.

He had become anxious about American copyright, even though Quinn had advised him that the episodes published in the *Little Review* were already copyrighted there and should be safe from piracy. Another concern was that the Post Office and Sumner's New York Society for the Suppression of Vice would be on the look-out for copies entering the country. This raised the question of how Americans who had paid in advance would obtain their copies safely.

On 26 February, Stanislaus sent his reactions to the book, and in particular the 'Circe' episode which he had read earlier in typescript.

> I suppose 'Circe' will stand as the most horrible thing in literature, unless you have something on your chest still worse than this 'Agony in the Kips'. Isn't your art in danger of becoming a sanitary science? I wish you would write verse again ... I should think you would need something to restore your self respect after this last inspection of the stinkpots. Everything dirty seems to have the same irresistible attraction for you that cow-dung has for flies.

Francini, he reported, had given a caricature talk about him at the Philharmonic Hall in Trieste – not a caricature in good taste 'worthy of its subject', but a 'vulgar and silly' one worthy of the '*Coda del Diavolo*' ('the devil's arse'). '*Dagli amici mi guardi Iddio*' ('God protect me from my friends'). He took the opportunity to ask his now-famous brother for the £10 he had lent him two years earlier in Trieste, saying he could hardly have any need of it now.[4] Joyce did pay up, but couldn't resist mentioning a further gift from Miss Weaver, making a sum of £8,500 in total (close to a quarter of a million in today's money), together with 'the reversion of a country house somewhere'. Had the audience at the Philharmonic known about this they 'might have laughed themselves to death', he said.[5]

The reviews of *Ulysses* were beginning to trickle in. One of the first, in the *Observer* of 5 March, was by Sisley Huddleston, who knew Joyce through Sylvia Beach. The widespread belief in literary circles that Joyce was a genius, he wrote, was unprecedented, but it was a belief he shared. There were obscene passages but if the thoughts of men and women were obscene, how else should they be depicted? It was not pornography. The quality of his prose testified to his genius. Although Molly's *monologue intérieur* was 'the vilest ... in all literature ... yet its very obscenity is somehow beautiful and wrings the soul to pity ... '[6] This review, Joyce claimed, brought in 136 orders for the book and 145 requests for prospectuses. A week later the 150-franc edition was completely sold out. George Slocombe was also complimentary in the *Daily Herald*, declaring that, 'No other writer in the world ... has ever attempted anything so stupendous. And few writers have flung at the world Mr Joyce's amazing precocity, untrammelled licence, prodigious patience, and shameless unreserve.' He recommended reading the end first and 'skipping the interminable and elaborate syntheses of the middle part'.[7]

Ulysses had made Joyce a celebrity in Paris, too, and on 10 March he and Nora were guests at the wedding of the wealthy socialite Peggy Guggenheim and the artist Laurence Vail, the so-called 'King of Montparnasse'. The reception was held at the Hôtel Plaza Athénée in the Avenue Montaigne, with all the expatriate glitterati in attendance. The new literary 'star', however, was still living out of suitcases in a crowded 'matchbox' in the rue de l'Université. And stardom, he found, could also bring unwelcome attention. When one young man approached him in a restaurant and asked, 'Could I kiss the hand that wrote *Ulysses*?' he replied, 'Oh no, don't do that; it did other things too.'[8]

Friends and acquaintances reacted mostly with awe to his achievement. Harriet Weaver wrote that she found 'the peculiar ingenuity' of its 'confused unschooled literary style' in the 'Eumeus' episode 'very refreshing'. And Dora Marsden declared it both 'fearful and wonderful'. On 8 March Yeats wrote to his one-time lover and muse, Olivia Shakespeare, that he was reading 'the new Joyce', and was 'impressed'. 'It has,' he said, 'our Irish cruelty and also our kind of strength and the Martello Tower pages are full of beauty. A cruel playful mind like a great soft tiger cat – I hear, as I read, the report of the rebel sergeant in '98: "O he was a fine fellow, a fine fellow. It was a pleasure to shoot him."'[9]

Signs of the puritan backlash against *Ulysses* in Britain soon appeared. The London *Daily Express* of 25 March had set the tone by announcing that 'Reading Mr Joyce is like making an excursion into Bolshevist Russia: all standards go by the board.'[10] A week later in the *Sporting Times* (known as the *Pink 'Un*), their columnist 'Aramis' wrote, 'In *Ulysses* [Joyce] has ruled out all the elementary decencies of life and dwells appreciatively on things that sniggering louts of schoolboys guffaw about ... The main contents of the book are enough to make a Hottentot sick.'[11]

The first French reaction came in the April issue of the *NRF* with Larbaud's 'The *Ulysses* of James Joyce', based on his lecture at Miss Monnier's séance. He began by pronouncing Joyce the greatest living English writer, comparing him to Swift, Stern and Fielding, Flaubert and Baudelaire. What some would consider lewd and salacious in the book was Joyce's attempt to show man complete with all his virtues and vices, his high and low mindedness. 'With this [book],' he declared, 'Ireland is making a sensational re-entrance into high European literature.'[12] Such an opinion from so revered a figure in so august a journal was bound to establish Joyce as a major European novelist, something he had dreamt of achieving as a young ambitious student. That same month, in the *Mercure de France*, Pound presented him as a Flaubertian who had moved beyond Flaubert's final unfinished novel, *Bouvard et Pécuchet*. 'It is ... one of those books that any serious writer needs to read.'[13] Joyce believed it was the French reviews of *Ulysses* which finally aroused the interest of the serious English critics.

Intimations from Dublin suggested that *Ulysses* would meet fierce resistance there, as it had in London. At Trinity College Library an indignant assistant librarian told a friend of Joyce, 'Had we known it was such a vile production we would not have thought of allowing it into the library.'[14] The response from the National Library was no more encouraging.[15] Gogarty was reported as being furious about his depiction as Buck Mulligan, saying, 'That bloody Joyce whom I kept in my youth has written a book you can read on all the lavatory walls of Dublin.'[16] Shaw, it was rumoured in Ireland, had tossed his copy of *Ulysses* onto the fire in disgust. Despite all the Irish hostility *Ulysses* was never prohibited in Ireland, although works by Shaw, Huxley and even Wells were.[17]

More considered Irish reactions came from various points of view. In the *New York Tribune*, Ernest Boyd dismissed Larbaud's 'myth of a "European" literature', declaring that 'no Irish writer is more Irish than Joyce'.[18] Mary Colum, in the *Freeman's Journal*, saw *Ulysses*, like *A Portrait*, as a piece of confessional literature – with the interior monologue allowing us inside the confessional, to penetrate the mind of a sinful supplicant in a way no priest ever could. Joyce, she declared, had created a new literary form.[19] Unsurprisingly, perhaps, one of his most hostile Irish reviews came from a Catholic convert. In the *Dublin Review*, the Anglo-Irishman Shane Leslie denounced *Ulysses* as 'devilish drench', which should be banned from Catholic houses. In the *Quarterly Review*, he described it as 'an Odyssey of the sewer ... literary Bolshevism ... anti-Christian ... totally unmoral ... unreadable ... unquotable and ...

unreviewable'. Even the book's innocent appearance struck him as sinister – resembling in size and colour nothing more threatening than the London telephone directory.[20] In *The Dial*, John Eglinton, while applauding 'the unfailing vitality and purity of [Joyce's] phrase, of his superb powers of mimicry and literary impersonation', thought that rather than a good augury for Irish literature, it was 'a violent interruption of what is known as the Irish literary renaissance'.[21] Joyce had reason to be quietly satisfied with Irish reaction generally. His long-range bombardment, it seemed, had reached its target, and Eglinton's review showed a 'softening of heart towards the longquesting hero of my telephone directory'.[22] Even Shane Leslie, he thought, secretly liked the book.

The weightier English reviews were the ones Joyce most wanted to see take notice of *Ulysses*. At first they seemed to ignore it – even the *TLS*, which annoyed him. However, early in April, John Middleton Murry reviewed it in the *Nation and Athenæum*. Murry also contested Larbaud's claim that Joyce belonged to high European literature, seeing him instead as 'the egocentric rebel in excelsis, the arch-esoteric ... He is the man with the bomb who would blow what remains of Europe into the sky. But he is so individual that very few people will know when the bomb has exploded.' The driving impulse of *Ulysses*, he said, was 'an immense, a prodigious self-laceration, the tearing-away from himself, by a half-demented man of genius, of inhibitions and limitations which have grown to be flesh of his flesh.' He should be given his head, but even if restrained he would still be a tremendous genius, but a European one, never.[23]

After meeting Joyce, Murry realized how little of *Ulysses* he had understood, so invited him to tea at the Victoria Palace Hotel to discuss the novel. When they met on 27 April, Katherine Mansfield, Murry's wife, joined them. Later she told Violet Schiff,

> Joyce was rather ... *difficile*. I had no idea until then ... how closely [*Ulysses*] was modelled on the Greek story, how absolutely necessary it was to know the one through and through to be able to discuss the other. I've read the *Odyssey* and am more or less familiar with it but Murry and Joyce simply sailed away out of my depth. I felt almost stupefied. It's absolutely impossible that other people should understand *Ulysses* as Joyce understands it. It's almost revolting to hear him discuss its difficulties. It contains code words that must be picked up in each paragraph and so on. The Question and Answer part can be read astronomically or from the geologic standpoint or – oh, I don't know! And in the midst of this he told us that his latest admirer was *Jack Dempsey*.

But shortly afterwards Joyce told Violet and her husband, Sydney Schiff (the novelist 'Stephen Hudson'), that 'Mrs Murry understood the book better than her husband.'[24]

Arnold Bennett, reviewing *Ulysses* in *Outlook*, referred to its difficult dullness and immorality, but acclaimed Joyce 'a very astonishing phenomenon of letters', and declared some sections of his book 'immortal'. He cited in particular the orgiastic scenes in the 'Circe' episode and Molly's monologue in 'Penelope', saying, 'I have never read anything to surpass it, and I doubt if I have ever read anything to equal it. My blame may have seemed extravagant, and my praise may seem extravagant; but that is how I feel about James Joyce.'[25] Joyce was pleased with both Bennett's and Murry's reviews, telling Harriet Weaver that Murry's had broken the British dam.[26]

Eliot's long-awaited essay on *Ulysses* did not appear until the November 1923 edition of *The Dial*. He sided with Larbaud in seeing the importance of the novel's Odyssean parallels and the styles and symbols accompanying each episode, and dismissed Richard Aldington's claim that it was a mere scaffolding around which the novel had been constructed. Nor, he argued, would it have the deleterious effect on the novel form that Aldington anticipated, though he saw it as a significant shift away from traditional narrative towards myth.[27]

Even in private, members of Joyce's own profession were as divided over the book as the published critics. The American poet Hart Crane, for example, overcome with enthusiasm, wrote to a friend that *Ulysses* was 'easily the epic of the age'.[28] The aggressively puritanical D. H. Lawrence (whose *Lady Chatterley's Lover* lay six years ahead) told his wife that 'This *Ulysses* is much more disgusting than Casanova',[29] while that summer Virginia Woolf confided to her diary that she found it 'an illiterate, underbred book ... the book of a self-taught working man ... egotistic, insistent, raw, striking; and ultimately nauseating. When one can have the cooked flesh, why have the raw?'[30] Ernest Hemingway, who had met Joyce just before Christmas, wrote to Sherwood Anderson that he had produced 'a most goddamn wonderful book'.[31]

The book was slowly percolating into the USA, where, for the moment, the Post Office seemed unaware of its existence. The *New York Times Book Review* gave the novel to the psychiatrist Joseph Collins whose review read more like a case-history. Having privately compared Joyce's writing to that of the insane, Collins now declared him 'one of the sanest geniuses that I have ever known', who 'transfers the product of his unconscious mind to paper [and] holds with Freud that the unconscious mind represents the real man.'[32] Gilbert Seldes, in *The Nation*, argued that *Ulysses* was essentially a burlesque of the *Odyssey*, like 'a satyr-play', a masterpiece written as caricature. But the American review Joyce found most pleasing came from Edmund Wilson in the *New Republic*. Wilson called the book 'perhaps the most faithful X-ray ever taken of the ordinary human consciousness' and 'probably the most completely "written" pages to be seen in any novel since Flaubert'. His conclusion was encomiastic. If he never picked up his pen again Joyce 'must know that the hand which laid it down upon the great affirmative of Mrs Bloom though it never write another word, is already the hand of a master'.[33]

The old world celebrated in *Ulysses* was slipping away. News came that Yeats's father (who had championed Joyce in America) had died and in the same week J. B. Pinker passed away, to be succeeded by his son Ralph. Old Ireland, too, was passing, and the Free State's Minister of Propaganda, Desmond Fitzgerald, called on Joyce, asking when he intended returning home. Once the Anglo-Irish Treaty had been ratified, he said, he would propose him for the Nobel Prize. Joyce was amused, telling Robert McAlmon that his chances of winning the Nobel were nil and he was willing to bet that if Fitzgerald stuck with his promise once he had read the book, he'd be fired.[34] Joyce also noted that with a new Irish Postmaster General and a vigilance committee dominated by clergy empowered to censor, the future for his book in Ireland was at best uncertain.[35] The future of the country was also uncertain and it would soon be plunged into civil war. Subsequent Irish governments, under greater Catholic influence, would not be sympathetic to the likes of Joyce, though by the end of the year he would have one staunch supporter in the new Irish Senate, W. B. Yeats, and one somewhat less staunch, the Mephistophelean mythmaker, Oliver St John Gogarty.

On April Fool's Day, Nora had finally decided to leave for Ireland, taking her children with her. She was determined to get away from the rue de l'Université, from the book that had dominated her life for so many years, and from her self-obsessed husband and the circle of sycophants his celebrity had attracted. Returning to Galway, among her own people, she would have some chance to be herself again. Having failed to persuade her to remain, Joyce sent Giorgio to Miss Beach to draw 2,000 francs from his royalty account for the journey. When she arrived in London, however, she wanted to stay and do some shopping and cabled for more money – some for a fur and £2 a week to keep her going – and asked him to join her. Joyce took it that she had decided to settle in London and replied that he would go anywhere in the world to be alone 'without family and without friends'.[36] It was as if he wanted to recapture the early months of their relationship. Desperately lonely, he once fainted in Beach's bookshop from worry. He implored Nora to read 'that terrible book' which had so broken his heart, and take him and do with him what she would.

Nora and the children were met in Dublin by her uncle Michael Healy who took them to dinner with John Joyce and his old friend Tom Devin. Nora seemed oblivious to the fact that Ireland was on the brink of a civil war and proceeded merrily on to Galway where the city was divided between pro-Treaty Regulars and anti-Treaty Irregulars. Robberies and murders brought the conflict onto the streets but despite this, Nora and the children remained in Galway for two weeks. They were not staying with her mother this time because the children refused even to enter the house, with its primitive living conditions and pervasive odour of cooking. They stayed instead at a boarding house at Nun's Island and ate out at cafés. Meeting her family again and showing the children the Presentation Convent where she had worked as a girl, Nora even thought of staying on.

In Paris, McAlmon, who had been away, returned to find Joyce feeling desolate and abandoned without his family around. Stories of political clashes in Dublin left him distracted and fretful – 'a lost spirit wailing in the wilderness' – bombarding Nora with telegrams and letters and agonizing about their well-being. She had no idea, he told her, how worried he was and how his fears for them were affecting his eyes. Despite his sighs and other expressions of distress, McAlmon decided Joyce rather enjoyed 'the martyrdom of his trials and tribulations'.[37]

But he had reason to worry. Giorgio had been accosted in a Galway street by a drunken officer demanding, 'How does it feel to be a gintleman's son?'[38] and Free State soldiers entered their bedroom to set up a machine-gun post there. Nora decided to return to Paris and they made a run for the station. However, between Galway and Dublin, their train was raked by gunfire and they all had to hit the deck of their carriage and remain lying flat for the rest of their journey. Such anarchic chaos only seemed to justify Joyce's fears for his own safety in Ireland. When she arrived back home with the children Nora was still very shaken. She had left a blithe spirit, Joyce said, and returned a nervous wreck. After that she could never bring herself to cross water without panicking, not even trusting herself to one of the *bateaux-mouches* that plied the Seine. And persuading her to cross the Channel to England, he said, became 'a frightful job'.[39] Less affected, apparently, Lucia left for a summer camp at Deauville on the Normandy coast where she celebrated her fifteenth birthday, and Giorgio departed for a short holiday to the Austrian Tyrol. Nora's experience left Joyce with a hardened attitude towards the new Ireland. He referred to the Free State as the 'free fight' and Galway as a 'dunghill'.[40]

Although exhausted and needing a break, on 18 May Joyce was drawn by some of his 'admirers' into a strange encounter with Marcel Proust. It was an evening devised by the wealthy Sydney Schiff, a grand celebration at the Hotel Majestic marking the première of Stravinsky's burlesque ballet *Le Renard*. Schiff's secret purpose, however, was to bring together five great icons of modernism – Proust, Picasso, Joyce, Stravinsky and Diaghilev. To this event came the cast of Paris's High Bohemia and their hangers-on – a great carnival of courtesans, pimps, voyeurs, pederasts, and even a communist-lesbian duchess – the satellites of high art orbiting their chosen geniuses.[41] The set-piece of the occasion was an encounter between Proust and Joyce, for whom chairs were set at a table with their supporters in attendance. The evening was a disaster. Joyce, whose day was ending, was drunk and uncommunicative; Proust, whose day was just beginning, found Joyce uncouth and equally unforthcoming. They talked about anything but literature – truffles, said some, mutual ailments, said others. According to Joyce, 'He wanted to talk about dukes; I wanted to talk about chambermaids.' In fact the two had more in common than they probably realized, including an interest in sado-masochism, an obsession with historical detail, and a fascination with epiphanies. Afterwards, a tipsy Joyce joined Schiff in Proust's cab and wanted to follow them back to the Frenchman's flat, but Schiff managed to shake him off and send him home. Later Joyce told Padraic Colum that Proust in his fur coat reminded him of the decadent hero of *The Sorrows of Satan*. Proust's impression of Joyce remained unrecorded.

Four days after the party, Joyce again suffered a severe attack of iritis. He was attended by Dr Victor Morax, a leading Paris ophthalmologist, who treated his left eye which was now threatened (as his right eye once had been) with glaucoma. At the end of May he had an especially acute attack and, as he was unable to get to the surgery, Morax sent along his student, Dr Pierre Mérigot de Treigny. De Treigny was surprised at the disordered squalor in which so famous an author was living – clothes strewn everywhere, Joyce in dark glasses squatting on the floor wrapped in a blanket, an unfinished meal and half-empty wine bottle on the table. There was no chair and the doctor had to crouch beside the patient to examine him and administer something for the pain. Called back after a second attack, Morax explained that an operation might be necessary. Joyce was so upset that he sent the children to fetch Miss Beach.[42] At the rue de l'Université she found him in intense pain, quite exhausted, with Nora bathing his eyes from a bucket of ice-water. 'When the pain is unbearable he gets up and walks the floor,' she said.[43] Joyce had no intention of submitting to an operation at the height of an attack, the very mistake he had made in Zurich. He asked Beach to arrange for him to see her oculist, Dr Louis Borsch, a fellow American, at his clinic at

39 rue du Cherche-Midi. After an agonizing wait, he saw Borsch who agreed that an operation would be too dangerous until the iritis had passed. He was able to relieve the more acute symptoms, but Joyce was left unable to write and Giorgio was enlisted as amanuensis.

By 8 June the first edition of *Ulysses* was fully distributed to buyers and booksellers. On 22 July, Weaver informed Beach that Samuel Roth was now seeking permission to publish *Ulysses* in serial form in his magazine *Two Worlds*, and refused to take 'No' for an answer. It was, it transpired, the same Samuel Roth who had written to Joyce eighteen months earlier. Asked to investigate, Quinn reported that Roth was a former Columbia University student, 'a nut poet ... full of crazy ideas'. 'He must,' declared Quinn, 'be either a fool or a wild man, otherwise he would not waste paper suggesting the printing of *Ulysses* in one issue of a magazine.' He would be arrested immediately and was not worth worrying about.[44]

Joyce decided to go to England for a holiday and to get a second opinion on his eyes. Still barely able to read, on the morning of his departure, 17 August, another attack threatened. Nevertheless, by that evening he, Nora and Lucia were safely ensconced at London's ornate Euston Hotel, which became his favourite London hotel because, he told Gerald Griffin, the nearby Euston Station was 'the Gateway to Ireland', where the Irish Mail left for Holyhead and the Dublin ferry. Furthermore, he liked the manager, the night porter, and the English breakfast, and managed to obtain a special rate for long stays. The hotel and its manager, E. H. Knight (a very 'knice' man) would earn a mention in *Finnegans Wake* – 'Here's dapplebellied mugs and troublebedded rooms and sawdust strown in expectoration and for ratification by specification of your information, Mr Knight, tuntapster, buttles; his alefru's up to his hip.'[45]

His first meeting with Harriet Weaver was, to her at least, a revelation. Joyce was impressed by her honesty and generosity but refused to conceal his own extravagance, ordering taxis and tipping lavishly when she would have taken the bus or tube train. Now she knew that Wyndham Lewis's reports of profligacy were not exaggerated, but she tolerated this self-indulgence and was unfazed by his unpredictable responses. He urged her to read the *Odyssey* before reading *Ulysses*, and when she asked him, like an importunate journalist, what he would write next he replied, 'I think I will write a history of the world.'[46] What sounded like an impish reply would not be that inaccurate a description of the work upon which he was soon to embark.

After just two days in London Joyce suffered an attack of conjunctivitis. He consulted various London eye specialists, all of whom declared his condition 'critical'. Some recommended an operation; others advised against it. He was caught in a dilemma – whether to continue his holiday in England or return to Paris and consult Borsch, to whom he now wrote for advice. However, more than once he went to the Westminster Hospital to have leeches attached to his eyes, and he told Miss Beach that coming to England with its damp climate rather than heading to the French Riviera was probably a mistake.[47]

The assassination of Michael Collins on 22 August seemed to symbolize an Ireland tearing itself apart. But if Joyce no longer wished to go to Ireland, Ireland could always come to him. While at the Euston, he met his cousins Kathleen ('Katsy') and Alice Murray, Aunt Josephine's daughters, taking them to an Italian restaurant in Soho. Kathleen remembered him wearing 'a big coat with a cape, a wide hat and double glasses', and showing off by ordering in Italian. Having received no acknowledgement of the copy of *Ulysses* he had sent to their mother, he asked what she had thought of it. According to Alice she had said that *Ulysses* wasn't fit to read, to which Joyce replied, 'If *Ulysses* isn't fit to read, life isn't fit to live.'[48]

Borsch wrote finally, advising him against an operation, and by 18 September, after a few days recuperating beside the sea in Folkestone,[49] the travellers were back at the rue de l'Université where workmen's hammering robbed them of all tranquillity. Borsch was away, Joyce was reduced to the use of only one eye, and the family was unable to eat locally because people insisted on greeting the famous writer. Finally, from 1 November they secured an apartment, at 26 Avenue Charles Floquet, close to the Champ de Mars in the 7th arrondissement. There was also the cheering news that Edmond Jaloux, the eminent French author and critic, had declared *Ulysses* '*au-dessus de tout éloge*' ('above all praise'). Ominously, however, Rodker had heard rumours of a pirated edition being launched in New York and had decided to publish the book quickly in Paris, leaving no time to insert Joyce's corrections.

It was decided that, to avoid police seizure, this second English edition should also be private but cheap. Two thousand copies would be published in Paris by Rodker at two guineas each and shipped quietly to Britain. A large number had been ordered in advance by an American agent and it was hoped to smuggle them into the US somehow. However, Quinn reported that the Customs had already seized several copies of the first edition which was now fetching up to $100 in New York. Quinn blamed the seizures on Beach's amateurism and suggested smuggling the books in bulk across the Canadian border where Sumner's agents would not be active.[50] Later Hemingway arranged for a friend to shuttle back and forth from Canada posing as an artist and smuggling in a few copies at a time. Another scheme involved an English bookseller taking 800 copies, cutting them into sections and sending them hidden inside newspapers for rebinding in America.[51] By the end of September Miss Beach's first edition had been distributed and many bookshops were left waiting for Rodker's second, into which Joyce had finally agreed an errata slip could be inserted.

In October, Eliot published Larbaud's review in *Criterion*, the magazine he had just launched in London, intended as a successor to *The Egoist*, but carrying the kind of work he favoured. The issue also included the first printing of *The Waste Land* and the first of two essays by Sturge Moore on *Tristram and Isolde*.[52] The former echoed *Ulysses* in 'mythical method', shifting registers and intellectual depth, and together they heralded a new, fractured, unstable vision for a new age. The latter may have helped prompt a fresh line of thinking which drew Joyce ultimately towards *Finnegans Wake*.

Harriet Weaver had circulated 5,000 leaflets carrying reviews of *Ulysses*. Several days before its launch, the second edition was fully subscribed, half from America, raising again the problem of getting copies past US Customs. But Joyce's main concern was to get himself down to the Riviera. Two nights before they left, the Nuttings called to take him and Nora to dinner at Les Deux Magots where they talked about Proust and it emerged that Joyce had at least read and admired *Du côté de chez Swann*. He spoke enviously of Proust's working conditions: 'He has a comfortable place at the Etoile, floored with cork and with cork on the walls to keep it quiet. And I, writing with people coming in and out, I wonder how I ever finished *Ulysses*.'[53] But Arthur Power reported Joyce saying, 'I don't like being shut up. When I am working I like to hear noise going on around me – the noise of life', and he thought his ability to write depended on his ability to work wherever he happened to be.[54]

When Borsch returned to Paris, he saw Joyce on 3 October and decided that the trouble in his left eye stemmed from the root abscesses in his teeth, which needed to be drained or extracted. However, he said, there was no immediate risk of another attack and approved his taking a holiday in Nice. On 10 October, Joyce, Nora and Lucia, in blooming health after her summer camp, finally left Paris, while Giorgio remained in the city. By the 17th, they were installed at the Hôtel Suisse in Nice, enjoying the sunshine of the Côte d'Azure, and in the bright light, his eyesight improved.

But the weather in Nice soon deteriorated and the place was swept by rain and high winds. At the end of October Joyce's eye pain returned and he again suffered the leech treatment from a local oculist, Dr Louis Colin. To decrease the nebula formed by accumulated blood, Colin also administered large doses of salicylate of soda, and said he thought that rheumatism rather than bad teeth was the source of his eye trouble. Strangely enough, despite some inflammation, Joyce told Miss Weaver his eyesight had improved slightly. But his letters were short because

Lucia was writing them and she was, he said, 'not such a distinguished english writer as her troublesome father, thank God'. He signed himself 'James Job Joyce'.[55] He now realized that the feared eye operation was inevitable. Colin agreed and Joyce thought it wiser to return to Paris to have it done by Borsch.

Despite his impaired vision, Joyce had managed to list corrections for the first third of the book, and in November sent them to Rodker for inclusion in the second edition. One note inserted into his notebook listing corrections for the 'Cyclops' episode – 'Polyphemous is Ul[ysses]'s shadow' – is thought to show Joyce's mind turning towards another book. Then, in the first number of *Criterion* he came across Larbaud's review of *Ulysses*. One sentence he liked in particular read, 'The English language has a very great store of obscene words and expressions, and the author of *Ulysses* has enriched his book generously and boldly from this vocabulary.'[56] This may have prompted him in the same notebook to continue listing and juggling with words that took his fancy – word combinations which would lead ultimately to the brilliant word-play and contrived confusion of tongues which became *Finnegans Wake*.

Hearing that the Egoist Press had been visited by a policeman, he urged Miss Weaver not to keep copies of *Ulysses* in her office, advice which wisely she took. Another person not wanting to keep his book around was Aunt Josephine, who wrote saying that she had passed her copy to Charlie. She herself, finding it difficult, had not got far with it. Joyce warned her that she risked being overtaken by his wife. 'I think Nora will beat you all in the competition. She has got as far as page 27 counting the cover.'[57] He advised her to first read Charles Lamb's *The Adventures of Ulysses*, and asked Sylvia Beach to send her a copy of Larbaud's *Criterion* article to help her comprehend the book. However, he could not resist asking her for 'any news you like, programmes, pawntickets, press cuttings, handbills' – he enjoyed reading them, he said.[58]

At the end of October the London *Sunday Chronicle* reported a talk at the Royal Society of Literature by the poet Alfred Noyes, Professor of Literature at Princeton University and soon-to-be Catholic convert. He applauded Shane Leslie's attack on the book, attempting to refute the claim that Joyce was a great, if slightly mad, genius, saying: '[Ulysses] is simply the foulest book that has ever found its way into print … there is no foulness conceivable to the mind of madman or ape that has not been poured into its imbecile pages.' 'The only sound analysis of the book', said Noyes, was the *Sporting Times* review which had declared it 'the work of a madman'. It was no more than 'literary Bolshevism'. The current battle being waged against the 'great Victorian writers' was, he claimed, an indication of 'a destructive spirit which may lead us far along the road to barbarism'.[59] Thereafter Noyes, who, perhaps unsurprisingly, had failed at Oxford, would never let *Ulysses* entirely out of his sights.

Joyce seemed to relish such hostility, and suggested to Harriet Weaver that extracts from Noyes's talk and Leslie's review should be quoted in her leaflet among the eulogies already included. The effect of these attacks could only enhance the book's reputation, he wrote, asking her to send copies to Larbaud, Jaloux and Pound. He drafted a letter for Miss Beach to send to Leslie, informing him that copies of *Ulysses* sent to Trinity College and the Irish National Library had been acknowledged, while the British Museum had actually ordered and paid for one, and no press copies had been sent to Irish papers. It finished cheerfully, saying that a second edition was already subscribed. What Joyce could not know was that Leslie's review would have serious consequences for the book in England.

In London, Huddleston's and Leslie's reviews had come to the attention of the Director of Public Prosecutions. Guy Stephenson, Assistant to the Director, received a memo from a colleague noting tersely, 'Shane Leslie finding [*Ulysses*] "unreadable, non-quotable and unreviewable" has promptly proceeded to read it, to review it and to quote from it.' Stephenson, who had already noted Huddleston's *Observer* review, wrote back that, 'It would appear to be of a nature calling for . . . a possible prosecution.' The Director, Sir Archibald Bodkin, having obtained a copy and dipped into it, found 'glaring obscenity and filth'. He had read through the entire 'Penelope' episode before deciding that Molly's rambling thoughts were 'written as they are as if composed by a more or less vulgar woman'. Although it was published in a limited private edition, the fact that copies were getting into the country justified the Customs in confiscating them. All Chief Constables were alerted. All borders – land, sea and air – would be carefully scrutinized to ensure that this subversive book was prevented from corrupting England's innocence.[60] America was well ahead of them. In December, news came that between 400 and 500 copies of the second edition of *Ulysses* had been stopped by US Customs and destroyed.

By mid-November the family were back in the Avenue Charles Floquet where Joyce was faced with the realities of what he had left behind. Miss Beach was increasingly annoyed over the decision to rush out a second edition while her more expensive first edition was still in certain shops. She told Joyce that she had been besieged by booksellers angry because they felt their unsold first editions were rendered less valuable by the cheap upstart – 'a dishonourable fraud', they called it. They would, they said, boycott it. But Rodker, who was seen as the chief villain, was preoccupied trying to find ways of outwitting censorious Customs officials.

Still trying, when he could, to read more Proust, on the 18th Joyce heard that the French writer had died in his cork-lined room on the Boulevard Haussmann. On the 21st he attended Proust's sumptuous funeral at the Père Lachaise Cemetery in Ménilmontant. It was a bizarre reprise of the grand night at the Majestic, with High Bohemia now in mourning black. In retrospect, that occasion of drinking and celebration now seemed like a premature wake.

The new apartment was, recalled Arthur Power, fine and airy, 'the most attractive of [Joyce's] many habitations'. 'It looked out onto the Eiffel Tower, and since it was near the École Militaire, through the trees one occasionally caught glimpses of uniformed officers riding past in the Parc du Champ de Mars.'[61] Power was very struck by the Joyces' bourgeois lifestyle – Nora and Giorgio acting as guardians of the family's respectability. He once arrived at the flat with his pockets full of bottles, hoping to enjoy a drink with a fellow Irishman, but, receiving a cool reception from the family and finding the atmosphere unwelcoming, made his escape. When he did return he became used to 'the Rule of Nora' and Joyce's amused reaction to it.

> [In] the late afternoon ... he used to come into the room from his study wearing that short white working-coat of his, not unlike a dentist's, and collapse into the armchair with his usual long, heart-felt sigh. As often as not Mrs Joyce would say to him, 'For God's sake, Jim, take that coat off you!' But the only answer she got was his Gioconda smile, and he would gaze back humorously at me through his thick glasses.[62]

But, Power claimed, 'He hated anything to do with bohemians, and always showed contempt for their way of life. Once, when I asked where he liked to go for his holidays, he answered abruptly: "To some place where honest people earn an honest living."' When they discussed *Ulysses*, Power asked him what had happened between Bloom and Gerty McDowell. 'Nothing happened between them,' Joyce replied. 'It all took place in Bloom's imagination.'[63] The life may have been bourgeois but the mind was a land of bohemian fantasy.

Frank Budgen finally turned up in Paris. What he did not know was that Joyce was anxious to retrieve the letter he had sent to him about Miss Weaver and his drinking, fearful that it might fall into the hands of his enemies. He asked Budgen to bring it along one night on the pretext of wanting to see what he had written and then proceeded to get his friend drunk. When he was so incapable that he had to be helped back to his hotel, Joyce took the opportunity to remove the wallet into which Budgen had tucked the letter. Next morning, the wallet was returned with a note from Joyce saying that he had taken charge of it to prevent him from being robbed. But Budgen saw that his letter was missing and knew that Joyce had tricked it out of him. He was so offended that he did not communicate with Joyce again for several years.

Joyce's daemon was prodding him towards another book which, inevitably, would evolve from what had gone before. His interest in his past did not end with *Ulysses*, and Aunt Josephine was still being bombarded with detailed questions about known and curious characters from that vanished world – their failings, looks, voices, pastimes, manner of dying.[64] Fragments were what he was now looking to find, pieces for a mosaic he was contemplating. As a clue to how Joyce's mind was moving, for Christmas he sent Miss Weaver a Studio Edition of the *Book of Kells*. It was, he told Power, a book he always kept with him and to which he went for inspiration. Now it had helped inspire him to ruminate along lines which would lead him away from his day-long odyssey into human consciousness towards a long night's excursion into *un*consciousness.

Pain, fear and terror were Joyce's dominant emotions of the first part of 1923. Faced with a serious eye operation and radical dental surgery, his capacity to concentrate was much diminished. 'If only I could wake up and find myself – operated,' he wrote to Miss Weaver. 'It is not the pain so much as the idea in itself, the circumstances and the hideous boredom of it.'[65] Added to that, his work was under threat on two fronts – in the UK by the British Public Prosecutor and in the US by the Postal Department and New York Society for the Suppression of Vice. Rodker ordered an additional 500 copies to replace those seized by US Customs. These would be sent to England for smuggling into America. But officialdom was now on the alert for this 'disgusting' book, and it would also have to get past the vigilant eyes of the UK Customs.

News from Dublin continued to spell danger. John Joyce's old Fleet Street office (one-time home of the Collector General) had been blown up, and on the night of 12 January, Senator Oliver Gogarty was kidnapped by Irregulars while taking a bath, escorted to a deserted house on the banks of the Liffey and seemed about to be shot. But the wily Buck Mulligan feigned a bowel seizure and, when his simple captors took him outside to relieve himself, he threw his greatcoat over their heads, leapt into the Liffey, and swam through the sewery waters to safety on the opposite bank. Asked about this later he said, 'I wasn't swimming, I was just going through the motions.'

The Joyce family was now more settled. Lucia was enrolled at a Paris *lycée*, Giorgio had found paid employment at the Banque Nationale de Crédit, and their father's money situation had eased somewhat. At the end of January he received £150 (10,950 francs) in advance royalties for the second edition of *Ulysses* from Rodker. A further royalty cheque came from Miss Weaver in February, and the *Little Review* reported first editions fetching up to $500 in New York. But suddenly word came that Rodker's extra 500 copies of *Ulysses* had been seized at Folkestone, earmarked for destruction.[66]

After Dr Louis Berman, an endocrinologist recommended by Pound, advised total tooth-extraction and a pupillary sphincterectomy (partial reconstruction of the pupil), Joyce consulted Borsch who decided on less radical treatment. But the uncertainty left him feeling anxious. On 14 February he started dionine treatment to his left eye and within a week found his sight dramatically improved as the film which had so obscured his sight began to dissipate. Although the improvement had so far done little for his reading, he now reported that he could see the lights in the Place de la Concorde which had previously been no more than a blur. Borsch confirmed his belief that the operation on his right eye in Zurich at the height of an attack had been a mistake as 'the exudation flowed over into the incision and reduced the vision of the eye considerably and permanently'. He had been wise to resist an operation in London when he was in pain there. The question of his eyes, Joyce told Miss Weaver, was 'almost as complicated as *Ulysses*'.

As a measure of the improvement, he announced, 'Yesterday I wrote two pages – the first I have written since the final *Yes* of *Ulysses*.'[67] A corner had been turned. With some difficulty, he said, he had copied them on a double sheet of foolscap in handwriting large enough for him to read. Two of these climactic sentences, a sketch of King Roderick O'Connor and one of Tristan and Isolde, survived into *Finnegans Wake*.

> King Roderick O'Conor, the paramount chief polemarch and last pre-electric King of Ireland, who was anything you say yourself between fiftyodd and fiftyeven years of age at the time after the socalled last supper he greatly gave in his umbrageous house of the hundred bottles with the radio beamer tower and its hangars, chimbneys and equilines ... [68]

His creative daemon was leading him into the strange world of Irish myth and legend, and the innovative verbal style of the novel-to-come was already evident. As he composed more sketches, he sent them to Miss Weaver who typed them and became more involved in this curious new composition than she had ever been, even with *Ulysses*. When he next met Larbaud he read from his sketches, and won him over by the sheer power and dash of his delivery. His own curiously encoded prose carried its own peculiar sense and air of exuberance when read by Joyce himself.

Pleased by the partial return of his sight, he wrote a long letter to his father who had the impression that his eldest son was now, as he said, 'going strong' in Paris. In anticipation of the inevitable begging letter, Joyce quickly played down his good fortune. Investments donated to him by 'a lady' were bringing him in £450 a year, with which he had to support a family of four in an extremely expensive city; he also had to find 600 francs a month to cover medical expenses. Set beside that, he told his father, *his* pension of £150 (actually a half of that) to support just himself did not look too bad. Despite this plea of relative poverty, he proposed that John should have his portrait painted at his expense by Power's friend, Patrick Tuohy, a Dublin art school teacher[69] (affordable because he had received £600 in royalties from Weaver).

By 13 March Joyce's conjunctivitis had flared up again, and, unable to write, he was back dictating to Giorgio. Borsch told him, 'Your eye is as puzzling as the money-market,' to which he commented, 'And as ruinous.' He spent several sleepless nights trying to allay his fears by composing mentally what he then dictated the following morning. The last passage he had sent Harriet (which came towards the end of the book) had been taken down without notes, and it was hers, he told her, as was the manuscript if it were ever completed.[70] It seems that he already had an idea of the end towards which his daemon was directing him.

Ulysses continued to excite critical opinion in England. In March 1923 the *Sporting Times* mischievously announced that it could be purchased from Shakespeare and Company for as little as 10s, while the *Evening News* included *Ulysses* in a shortlist of books, the first editions of which would one day become highly valuable.[71] The *Manchester Guardian* carried a thoughtful appreciation of the book from Stephen Gwynn, proclaiming Joyce and James Stephens the outstanding writers of Georgian Ireland, and Joyce himself 'the first notable force to appear in it from the Catholic population'.[72]

Yet despite these good opinions, the future of *Ulysses* looked more precarious than ever. In May, following the seizure at Dover, a confidential letter was sent by the Home Office in London to all British Chief Constables requiring them to report any sales of Joyce's *Ulysses* and Frank Harris's pornographic autobiography, *My Life and Loves*, both published in Paris, both of which contained 'numerous passages of a grossly obscene nature'. Their importation into Britain was banned.[73] Joyce was in good Irish company. Frank Harris was a Galway man.

Once his conjunctivitis had subsided, Borsch proposed that they proceed with his eye operation. Yet, amid all his discomfort and nagging fear, Joyce managed to compose a further passage for the new book, using a charcoal pencil and a large sheet of paper, his handwriting, he said, resembling Napoleon's when irritated. He entered the *maison de santé* on

3 April. Over the next two weeks he underwent two dental operations which left him toothless, and unable to talk or eat properly until he could get a decent plate fitted. As soon as he recovered he entered Borsch's clinic, presenting the doctor with a shamrock plant for good luck to them both, and finally, on the 26th, a sphincterectomy was performed. It was a dangerous operation and his recovery would be slow.

On returning home he was faced with hefty bills from Borsch and the dentist, so he was relieved when Miss Weaver sent him a royalty cheque for £300 and informed him that she would be gifting him more money which she had inherited unexpectedly from a recently deceased aunt. Despite his painfully slow recovery, Joyce was optimistic, saying that every night he 'dreamed of his eye performing feats of vision'. In May he managed his first theatre trip in a year, wearing what he called 'that sempiternal black patch'. On the 22nd he went to another concert by McCormack and was struck to see that he sang with his eyes shut. If only *he* could read and write in that way, he said, all would be well.[74] In September McCormack would receive the freedom of the city of Dublin, but for Joyce the freedom of the mind was what mattered, and the twilight which now surrounded him drew him ever deeper into that private world, its danks and darks, and fleeting shadows.

In June, when the lease on the flat in the Avenue Charles Floquet expired, having again set his mind on some English seaside resort, Joyce put his furniture and possessions into storage. The place decided upon was Bognor in Sussex. On 18 June, leaving Giorgio behind with his friends, the rest of the family left Paris. Storms in the Channel made Joyce nervous and they waited three days in Calais before the sea calmed enough for him to face the crossing. On the 21st they were booked into London's Belgrave Hotel, close to the British Museum, where they were joined by Nora's sister Kathleen on her first trip away from Galway. Joyce found her naive excitement about being in London amusing, while for Nora she brought a welcome breath of home. To Kathleen the 'Joyces' made an incongruous pair – 'Nora all go, Jim all stand-still,' she said. And 'all-go' Nora did not hesitate to sneer at 'stand-still' Jim. 'He's a weakling, Kathleen,' she told her, 'I always have to be after his tail. I wish I was married to a man like my father. Being married to a writer is a very hard life.'[75]

Joyce was soon in touch with English friends and acquaintances. Wyndham Lewis sketched him at his Kensington studio, and, as the weather in London was sweltering, Miss Weaver took the family to the Royal Botanical Gardens in Regent's Park where they could lunch and talk in the shade. It was a somewhat awkward meeting between a preoccupied Joyce and an uncomfortable Weaver. However, they did manage to discuss after some fashion the next edition of *Ulysses* and a third edition of *Chamber Music*, which, it was hoped, Joyce's new-found celebrity would help to sell. Meeting Lucia for the first time, Harriet noted her good, slightly accented English. If the girl seemed somewhat unpredictable to her she put it down to her unsettled childhood.[76] Joyce also joined Eliot for lunch at the fashionable Frascati's in Oxford Street, where Lady Ottoline Morrell, the literary hostess, wished to meet him. Eliot said that when he came down on holiday to Fishbourne near Bognor, he would take him to see 'some of the waste lands round Chichester'.[77]

Although Bognor was not granted the title 'Regis' until 1929, it had enjoyed royal patronage since George III's daughter Princess Charlotte had favoured it in the early nineteenth century. However, the grandly named Alexandra House, where they were to stay, while advertised as 'a private hotel – open all the year; near sea', was just another seaside boarding-house and Mrs Ball, the manageress, just another boarding-house landlady, a recognizable English type beloved of music-hall comedians. She moved the Joyces' luggage without warning, cut off the electric light at 11 p.m. and whisked away their plates before they had finished eating. Joyce found these antics amusing, and, given a chance to move, chose to stay. He liked Bognor. The weather was fine and the town and the countryside thereabouts he found 'very restful'.[78] He became sunburnt, and with Nora now avoiding church and Kathleen keen to attend mass, Joyce took her every morning to the nearby Church of Our Lady of Seven Dolours, strangely suggestive of the church which Gerty MacDowell finds 'a haven of refuge for the afflicted because of the seven dolours which transpierced her own heart'.[79]

For someone like Joyce there was much to enjoy in a town like Bognor apart from the seaside ambience: music-hall and dancing at the newly opened Pavilion, the usual minstrel troupes and Punch and Judy shows, and – something from which he took particular pleasure – simply lying around on the beach listening to the sea. The women went shopping and even Joyce made a few odd purchases: an extraordinary onion-shaped cap and a green suitcase, which doubled as a portable writing-desk.

The money Harriet Weaver was about to bestow on him (that inheritance from her aunt) was some £12,000 (936,000 francs), bringing the total amount he had received from her to £21,000 (some £600,000 in today's money). (This compared more than favourably to the Nobel Prize of £7,500 which Yeats would win that year.) In a letter of 4 July 1923, she told him, 'The amount finally available will come to about £600 a year invested in a security tax-free to persons not resident in this country,' which should take care of his medical bills, the cost of a new apartment and singing lessons for Giorgio. 'Let us hope that in future years he will earn an income rivalling Mr John McCormack's,' she said.[80]

Joyce felt shamed by his patron's generosity, having been in a bad mood when they last met. Her extraordinary beneficence must, he told her, be unique in the history of literature. He only hoped he could justify himself in her eyes, and that fortune continued to favour him.[81] But if her watchword was 'thrift', Joyce's was 'dissipation'. The news was quickly communicated to friends and family. Now he had a good deal to throw around, and to prove it he bought Kathleen an expensive watch.

However inert Joyce might have appeared to the Barnacle sisters, his inner daemon was now in possession, and the new novel was taking shape in his mind – an amoeba which would divide and proliferate in many directions. To begin with, however, he could only follow blindly where his inspiration led. As he told August Suter later, 'I am boring into a mountain from two sides. The question is, how to meet in the middle.'[82] And to Arthur Power he said, 'A book, in my opinion, should not be planned out beforehand, but as one writes it will form itself, subject, as I say, to the constant emotional promptings of one's personality.'[83] Even though he was, by his own admission, working in the dark, the undefined project now gripped his mind and imagination, and at his Bognor boarding house he began to rewrite the sketches he had written in Paris. Nora regarded him with mild exasperation. 'He's on another book again,' she told Kathleen.[84] That book would take him far away from her into the intricate labyrinth of myth he was now in the process of constructing. The notes and sketches he had made began a paper-chase of fragments which scholars have been following ever since in an attempt to uncover the intricate process of composing one of the most enigmatic texts ever pieced together.

In late July, Eliot, true to his word, came to take the family off on a tour of 'the waste lands' around Chichester. One visit was to Arundel Castle, and another to Sidlesham Church in the medieval Hundred of Manhood, where Joyce was struck by the names on the tombstones – Glews, Gravys, Northeasts, Ankers, and most notably Earwickers. Thus was christened the central character of his new epic – Humphrey Chimpden Earwicker whose initials would recur throughout the book in various forms and guises, and who bears the nickname 'Here Comes Everybody'.

With his right eye still not improved, reading continued to be a great strain, and his false teeth were inclined to slip, so by the end of July Joyce was ready to get back to Paris. Nora, Kathleen and Lucia had already left for London. He had a further sketch (a piece about St Patrick in Ireland) to send to Harriet for typing, hoping to meet her in London on his way through.) In early August he said goodbye to sunny Bognor and joined Nora, Lucia and Kathleen at the Belgrave Hotel, staying and working there for the next two weeks.

While in Bognor, Joyce had catalogued some forty pages of notes left over from *Ulysses*.[85] From this modest beginning, a work of such perplexity and magnitude would emerge that it would occupy the next sixteen years of his life. By 13 August he had a first draft of the first part of the book (which he marked 'A') ready to show Harriet when they met the following day. She worried about the effect such intensive work might be having on his eyes, offering to type what he had drafted. On the 16th, the family headed back to Paris via Boulogne, no longer just another Channel port to him, but, crucial to his new project, the birthplace of St Patrick.

In Paris, without a flat and with Lucia again off to summer camp in Deauville, the family checked into the Victoria Palace Hotel, where Joyce had last met the Middleton Murrys. From there he and Nora began flat-hunting, and took to dining at the Restaurant Les Trianons opposite the nearby Gare Montparnasse. This became Joyce's favourite Parisian watering hole and its maître d'hôtel, Jean Cassabel, a personal friend. There he would lavish hospitality on his friends, hold court for his admirers and delight the waiters with his extravagant tips.

When Lucia returned from summer camp she announced her decision to become a dancer, while Giorgio prepared to start singing classes at the Paris Schola Cantorum. Then, when Joyce finally again saw Borsch, he was disturbed to be told that a further eye operation might be necessary. Luckily he could escape into his new novel. He found himself preoccupied by the Tristan and Isolde legend, sketching out 'a description of Isolde's first parent', and getting it typed before dispatching a copy to Harriet. She added it to a folder in which she kept his drafts; he was, he said, already working on another piece. He apologized for his awkwardness in London, saying that it was difficult for him to explain what he was trying to do. It was not yet even clear to him, and, since she herself had been feeling depressed, the two pieces he was sending her – one on earwigs (his 'Earwicker absurdity') and one on Tristan – might bring her some comic relief. They ought to, he told her, because devils bedevil only leprechauns who fail to understand anyone else's jokes – and sometimes not even their own.[86]

By October Joyce's new inspiration seemed to have restored his old self-confidence and he plunged into an unusual flurry of social activity. When Robert McAlmon and William Carlos Williams threw a party at Les Trianons, Joyce drank and sang and danced into the night till Nora decided he was going too far and took him home.[87] On the 4th, in Paris, he attended a riotous performance of the Ballet Suédois at which George Antheil – who had undertaken to compose an opera based on the 'Cyclops' episode of *Ulysses* – performed his compositions *The Airplane Sonata*, the

Sonata Sauvage, and *Death of the Machine* during which a riot broke out. Shortly afterwards he joined Pound, Quinn and Ford Madox Ford (newly appointed editor of the *transatlantic review*) at Pound's studios in rue Notre-Dame-des-Champs. Ford appointed them all editorial advisers, and they allowed themselves to be photographed for the *New York Times*. Quinn was keen to acquire any remaining drafts of *Ulysses*, but Joyce suspected he planned to auction them off in New York.

Ford's backers wanted Joyce excluded from the *review*, but at a party that evening he asked Joyce if he could publish the new work Pound had mentioned to him. The piece in question was the draft Joyce had read to Larbaud and sent to Harriet, called 'Mamalujo' (after the four apostles, Matthew, Mark, Luke and John, and, he later claimed, after 'Mama [Nora], Lucia and Giorgio'). In it the Four Old Men (the four Apostles) – another manifestation of the Four Waves of Erin – were joined by the Four Masters of the Annals of Ireland (four Franciscan Friars), who had already appeared briefly in the 'Cyclops' episode of *Ulysses*. Now they were to be brought centre-stage. The mixing and weaving of narratives, like a mixing and weaving of musical motifs and themes, would distinguish the new work. Pound told him that Ford intended to use the front page of his new magazine to announce him with all trumpets blaring; Joyce said he was not yet ready for any of it to be printed and refused Pound's suggestion to show it to Eliot, fearing that his purpose would be misunderstood. 'The construction is quite different from *Ulysses* where at least the ports of call were known beforehand,' he wrote.[88]

He told Harriet he would send her 'those four fellows' ('Mamalujo') in a cleanly typed copy, adding that he was pleased to rid himself of the troublesome lot of them. When she wrote saying she was finding it difficult to understand a passage in which St Patrick argues about perception and truth with the Irish philosopher Berkeley, he referred her to 'the answer given by Paddy Dignam's apparition: metempsychosis' and the historical theories of Hegel and Vico – about the movement of ideas through time. By now he had begun to see the way forward and his work was taking on a dynamism based on an overall conception. They were, he said, no longer fragments but 'active elements' which would fuse together as they aged together. He sent Harriet a poem about Tristan and Isolde with a stanza from each of his Four Masters and a scheme depicting and delineating them. (The major players in his expedition to the dark side of his imagination – Earwicker, his wife Anna Livia, their sons Shaun and Shem, and daughter Issy, in their various shapes, forms and identities – would not see the light of print just yet.) After this effort he felt tired and unwell, blaming the dark noisy hotel which he suspected was full of germs. People also irritated him, giving him meaningless advice and false information until he silenced them with a look of what he called 'imbecile sarcasm'.[89]

In November he had lunch with Valery Larbaud who, assisted by Léon-Paul Fargue, was working on a French translation of *Ulysses*. Joyce told Larbaud he hoped his new work would continue to interest him, and promised to send him more as it was completed. But his flow was interrupted by another bout of conjunctivitis, leaving him with a heavily bandaged left eye and reducing him again to having to dictate. The disruption to his work was profoundly irritating because, now that it was becoming clearer where his conception was leading him, he wanted to block out certain parts of the book before taking another holiday. When Larbaud asked him why he carried on working in his condition, Joyce quoted, no doubt ironically, the Jesuit motto, '*Ad majorem Dei gloriam*' ('For the greater glory of God'). Religion was never far from his mind and the story of the Fall and the prospect of redemption, an idea explored so brilliantly in 'Circe', would, like the Tower of Babel myth, continue to haunt him through *Finnegans Wake*. His fascination with religion puzzled some of his friends. When Power challenged him, 'Do you believe in a next life?' he looked embarrassed and shrugged, saying, 'I don't think much of this life,' and terminated the conversation.[90]

He was now using a young typist, Lily Bollach, and was impressed by the way she navigated through the sometimes chaotic manuscript, with its many corrections and insertions, sometimes in large crayon scrawls. He arranged to meet her, not at the hotel but at what he called 'the usual place'. It may have suited him to treat a perfectly businesslike relationship as a clandestine flirtation. He probably kept Miss Bollach secret, because Giorgio claimed that his father hated professional typists and never employed one. Secrets were embedded throughout his work – enigmas, allusions, hidden meanings. To McAlmon he revealed a concealed subtext in his writing. Occasionally where he wrote in a veiled way, he said, he was replying directly to the critics of his previous work.

With *Ulysses* now banned by the British Home Office, Misses Weaver and Marsden agreed that Miss Beach could publish a further Paris edition. Harriet proposed calling it the fourth edition, counting the 500 replacements for the copies seized in the US as the third. Of these, just one copy got through and so became a publishing rarity. New Yorkers were afforded a glimpse of another rarity that December when the *Herald Tribune* reprinted 'The Day of the Rabblement' from a copy supplied by Mary Colum. Across the Atlantic Joyce was now newsworthy.

The year 1923 would end little better than it had begun. On 17 December he told Harriet that in the last weeks he had been sinking into a morass of despair, stopping and starting work regardless of day or night.

'I work like a person who is stunned. I cannot imagine any position more grotesque.' 'Stunned grotesquery' could well describe aspects of his new work. His eyesight, he reported, was reasonably functional, and Borsch had recommended deferring any decision about an operation. His dentist had agreed to make him a new plate free of charge; with his present one, he said, he could neither sing, laugh, shave nor, despite the boredom of his writing, yawn. He anticipated 'a wretched Christmas'.[91] But he did manage a faint smile at the sight of the fourth edition of *Ulysses* published by Miss Beach just as the New Year dawned. It was half the size of the first edition, bound in white with blue lettering, and this time with the Greek flag upside down.

Paris was flooded that January, and Joyce's imagination was also in flood. He had already decided on a title for his new novel but had revealed it to no-one, except Nora who was sworn to secrecy. The title had its own angles of reflection. There was the jolly Irish ballad, *Finnegan's Wake*, one of John Joyce's favourites, which tells the story of Tim Finnegan, a hod-carrier whose fondness for liquor proves fatal. Killed in a fall from his ladder when drunk one day, he is laid out 'with a gallon of whiskey at his feet,/And a barrel of porter at his head.' With the assembled mourners soon drunk and riotous, the missiles begin to fly. In the melee, whiskey is splashed over Tim, who resuscitates – the cue for a roisterous song and dance in which the whole the company, including Tim, join.

> Whack folthe dah, dance to your partner,
> Welt the Rure, yer trotters shake,
> Wasn't it the truth I told you,
> Lots of fun at Finnegan's Wake.

For Joyce the song was a celebration of life against death, of resurrection for sinners as well as saints, and a merry resurrection at that. It was also a satirical sideswipe at the Irish Church which disapproved of alcoholic wakes.

On 16 January 1924, passages about Shem the Penman, Shaun the Post and their mother Anna Livia were sent to Harriet. Shem owes something to James Townsend Saward, a famous English cheque forger of the 1850s. 'Forge away Sunny Sim!' says Dolph (Shem) recovering from an attack by Kev (Shaun) in the Geometry Lesson scene in Book II, Chapter 2 of the novel.[92] This choice of alter ego is manifestly a self-mocking version of the young idealist, Stephen Dedalus, who set out to forge the conscience of his race but ended forging fictions and letters of woe in return for cash.[93]

Ettore Schmitz (Italo Svevo) had produced a new novel, *La Coscienza di Zeno* (*Confessions of Zeno*) and sent a copy to Joyce, saying he was dispirited by the Italian critics ignoring it. Joyce read it immediately and thought it Schmitz's best novel so far; he urged him to send copies to the *NRF*, *Revue de France*, *Criterion* and to Ford's *transatlantic review*, and promised to write to them himself about it. As well as talking to Larbaud and others about the book he recommended his friend to the editor of *Il Convegno*. Svevo was not the only writer he was boosting to Larbaud. Lucia had written a short article on Charlie Chaplin, and with Larbaud's help it was published that year in the Belgian magazine *Le Disque vert*.

Lucia was now making her own friends – Myrsine Moschos, Adèle, Yva, Yolande and Emile Fernandez – and sometimes eating away from home. She was learning dance from Raymond Duncan, brother of Isadora, and through the Nuttings and the Fernandezes, meeting many of Paris's avant-garde. Among those frequenting the Fernandezes' Champ de Mars apartment were Jean Cocteau, Erik Satie, Francis Poulenc and Jean Renoir.[94] According to her biographer, in this company she was encouraged to redefine herself as a creative artist in her own right. 'She took from these loose affiliations with surrealist youth a confirmation of her own legitimacy as an artist; one didn't have to be a genius to be a dancer; one had only to give oneself up to the project of expression. She took from them the idea of social license; bourgeois life was boring; to grow artistically, one needed to confront and outrage the commonplace.'[95]

Yet another American writer who met the family at that time, Kay Boyle, saw how the children were desperate to move out of the shadow of their celebrated father. Lucia, she noted, was obsessed in her rage against 'being the child of a famous man'. 'Both she and Giorgio used to argue with me about this, and when I suggested that Joyce was, after all, not that famous (which he actually wasn't at that time), Lucia would become very angry and insist her father was as famous as Rabelais.' Although Boyle thought this resentment 'senseless and unjustified', it seemed to dominate their lives.[96]

Ford was still pressing for Joyce's manuscript, reminding him of his past support and promising to challenge the British ban on *Ulysses* at the highest level in London. Finally Joyce relented, on the understanding that he would get two goes at revising the proofs. When Ford saw the contribution, he became suddenly fearful that he might be about to publish something obscene or blasphemous which would sink his *review* and asked Sisley Huddleston for a second opinion. Huddleston managed to reassure him on the point, but Joyce was still uncertain about publishing it. When he refused to give it a title, Ford suggested *Work in Progress*, which is what it now came to be called until the real title was revealed fourteen years later.

His new work had now come to possess him as completely as *Ulysses* had. He was working non-stop from 8 a.m. to 12.30 and from 2 to 8 p.m. – working like a 'galley-slave', which at least, he said, kept his 'admirers' at bay.[97] He now realized the enormity of what he had undertaken, given his circumstances, 'writing in the dark' inside a dreary room inside a dreary hotel. However difficult the task might be, he thought it could still be done, and wondered with a metempsychotic flourish, 'O dear me! What sins did I commit in my last incarnation to be in this hole?'[98] Those 'sins' were leading him on a quest to forge a language with which to describe the stream of unconsciousness that was the dream.

Concerned that Harriet might find the material he was sending her too confusing, and anxious to win her approval for his new project, he offered her some clues about his characters and their identities – that Shem was Irish for James, that Anna Livia meant Mother of all the Living, and that Dublin was built on the River Anna Livia whose winding shallows were the colour of dark brown hair.[99] The name of Earwicker's wife, he told Schmitz, he had borrowed from *his* wife, Livia, and asked that she should not 'take up arms' about this as his Anna was 'the Pyrrha of Ireland (or rather of Dublin) whose hair is the river beside which ... the seventh city of Christianity springs up'.[100] Writing later, he explained that, 'Anna Liffey, which would be the longest river in the world if it were not for the canal that comes from afar to join the celebrated *divo*, Anthony the Worker of Miracles, and then, having changed its mind, returns whence it came.'[101] This concept of the circular river would give his book its revolutionary form.

His borrowing came closer to home as aspects of Lucia, which had already crept into the 'pubescent delinquent' Milly Bloom and knowingly seductive Gerty MacDowell, began to recur in Issy or Isabel, the object of her father/Earwicker's illicit fantasies.[102] Joyce considered the theme of the young girl and the older man 'a great motif', and as he had entertained adulterous thoughts about Nora for *Exiles* and *Ulysses*, so he entertained incestuous ideas about fathers and daughters for *Ulysses* and *Finnegans Wake*. Lucia's biographer thinks she was not unaware of this and by responding to it, created a dangerously incestuous symbiosis between them. Giorgio's involvement with her in this creative play also seems to underlie some of the other suggestive imagery in the *Wake*.

On 7 March he had finished his 'Anna Livia' episode and sent it to Harriet with the following explanation: 'It is a chattering dialogue across the river by two washerwomen who as night falls become a tree and a stone.' The river was called Anna Liffey. The piece began, he said, with hybrid Danish-English words. The Vikings founded Dublin, whose Irish name was Ballyclee or Town of Ford of Hurdles. Within it teemed all the ills of body and soul. The river was brown, salmon-rich, sinuous and shallow. 'The splitting up towards the end (seven dams) is the city abuilding. Izzy will later be Isolde (cf. Chapelizod).'[103] As soon as he had mailed the episode to her, he began revising it, sending on rewritten pages as they were completed.

The Joyce industry in America was gathering pace. On 1 March, Huebsch published Herbert Gorman's book, *James Joyce: His First Forty Years*; another book, Paul Jordan Smith's *On Strange Altars*, devoted a chapter to *Ulysses* and, without consulting Joyce, Quinn sold the book's manuscript for $1,975, offering the author a percentage which he declined. He then sent Joyce a letter of introduction to the purchaser, Abraham Rosenbach, a Philadelphia book dealer, suggesting that, if he wished to have it, he could offer to buy it back at cost price. Joyce was piqued and not only ignored the suggestion but when Rosenbach approached him in a Paris restaurant he snubbed him,[104] and decided to break with Quinn. Joyce was so angered by someone profiting from the manuscript that thereafter people approaching him to sign copies of *Ulysses* would be courteously rebuffed.

Perhaps hoping for good luck, he asked Miss Bollach to type in his latest insertions and return his manuscript on St Patrick's Day – 'a mere whim' of his, he explained later. That day, too, Joyce was greatly encouraged by Larbaud's expressions of enthusiasm – he was 'in a trance about it', he said, and would say as much to his friend Arnold Bennett. In mid-March Joyce announced that he was about to start 'Shaun the Post', the next section of the book, and sent Harriet a list of the signs which, for brevity's sake, he had designated for each of his main characters – a Greek M for HCE (Earwicker), Λ for Shaun, Δ for Anna Livia (nicknamed Mrs Delta) and ☐ for the unspoken title of the book, he told her,[105] although, as it turned out, a circle would have been more appropriate. One layer of symbols was being laid upon another and that was the method by which the new work would proceed.

25

A Conspiracy of Concealment

(1924–1926)

'One great part of every human existence is passed in a state which cannot be rendered sensible by the use of wideawake language, cutanddry grammar and goahead plot.' Joyce to Harriet Weaver

April the 1st 1924 was a good day for Joyce. The first fragment of his new novel appeared in the *transatlantic review* and he sent Harriet a copy together with an article by Ford in the *Chicago Tribune*, saying that 'For myself ... the pleasure – the very great pleasure – that I get from going through the sentences of Mr Joyce is that given me simply by the cadence of his prose.' That for him, he said, took precedence over any obscenity, blasphemy or Bolshevism that might be found in Joyce's writing.[1] And, further enhancing his French reputation, Madame Bloch-Savitsky's translation of *A Portrait*, *Dédalus*, was now on sale in the shops.

Joyce had been reading Gorman's book, which he thought 'well and carefully written', but, in evoking for him all the heartache and trouble of his life, it had triggered a nervous collapse. Added to this, his eye trouble recurred. He was forbidden to read and told to cut down on the work he was doing – up to ten hours a day for the past seven weeks in near-darkness, he told Harriet.[2] She had news for him too: she and Dora Marsden were returning all rights to their authors and winding up the Egoist Press. (Eliot would take over its office for the *Criterion*, and Jonathan Cape, now a publisher in his own right, wanted to take over its list.) After some negotiations a contract was agreed and Joyce became a Cape author. Sylvia Beach, however, retained the rights to *Ulysses*.

Hearing that Harriet was unexcited and mystified by his 'Mamalujo' episode Joyce felt dispirited and exhausted and was left thinking that his book would remain unfinished for years ahead.[3] But his mood soon changed and he was able to report that although Shaun was proving exceedingly difficult, what he had written struck him as very amusing. He was hopeful, he said, that if he succeeded with it, he and his book would be quite revivified.[4] In that same spirit of optimism he sent a copy of 'Anna Livia' to Larbaud, whose excitement over the new book was so invigorating. Despite this, and despite the steady income from his investments, he continued to worry about money, and, when the pound fell that April, took 6,000 francs of his royalties from Miss Beach to compensate.

At the end of April, Patrick Tuohy turned up with the portrait of Joyce's father, entitled *A Dublin Gentleman*. It was a striking image. A half-seated figure, with glaring eyes, a rubicund complexion and once-proud now-crestfallen moustache, thrusts itself into the painting, hands clasped – a fallen angel lost in his own lost world. Tuohy, 'a small, nervous, manic, sarcastic and irritating character with a withered arm', according to Arthur Power, offered to paint Joyce, too, then the rest of the family. Soon he was a fixture around the place, trying to get a restless Joyce to sit still while he worked. When the sitter grew impatient, Tuohy told him that he was trying to paint his soul, to which Joyce replied, 'Don't worry about my soul, just get my tie straight.' He agreed to fifteen sittings (which extended to twenty-six), after which Tuohy announced that he would take the portrait for exhibition in Dublin and bring it back to be shown at the 1925 Paris Salon alongside that of his father.

Joyce was reluctant to leave Paris after Borsch proposed another eye operation and he did not want to disturb the intense concentration his present work demanded. The 'Shaun' piece was 'long, long as the night he travels through', he told Harriet, but he was halfway there and hoped he would make it to the end.[5] The image of the blind poet venturing into the dark wood of nocturnal confusion came increasingly to dominate his imagination. Sceptics, like his later friend Samuel Beckett, however, thought he exaggerated his blindness so that it had become part of an act.

When, in May, the weather grew suddenly very hot and people at the hotel threw open their windows, laughing and talking in loud voices, Joyce decided he had had enough. He stopped writing and put all his manuscripts into storage at Beach's bookshop. In a letter to Harriet he explained why he couldn't work, and at the same time revealed to her the nature and form of his latest mystery – 'Shaun . . . is a description of a postman travelling backwards in the night through the events already narrated. It is written in the form of a *via crucis* of 14 stations but in reality it is only a barrel rolling down the River Liffey.' He really needed a study of his own with his books and papers to hand to make the writing of this book possible.[6]

He saw Borsch again on 2 June and they settled on Saturday the 7th for the operation. Beset by doubts, he began to fret about the work he felt unable to continue, telling Harriet that maybe it had been a mistake to undertake so difficult a book immediately following *Ulysses*. However, that same morning he had begun to see quite clearly how the second and third parts of his book would work out, and was tempted to retrieve the typescript of 'Shaun' from Miss Beach and finish him off.[7] But his sense of despair again intensified when Borsch, having failed to remember the Whitsun holidays, postponed the operation.

In England, Joyce's puritanical conservative opponents were never quiet for long. Edmund Gosse, who had once supported him but had now recanted, wrote to Louis Gillet, a friend, and editor of the *Revue des Deux Mondes* in Paris, saying how much he would regret him 'paying Mr J. Joyce the compliment of an article' in his review.

> He is of course not entirely without talent, but he is a literary charlatan of the extremest order. His principal book, *Ulysses*, has no parallel that I know of in French: It is an anarchical production, infamous in taste, in style, in everything ... He is a sort of Marquis de Sade, but does not write so well. He is the perfect type of the Irish fumiste, a hater of England, more than suspected of partiality for Germany ... There are no English critics of weight or judgement who consider Mr Joyce an author of any importance ... He [has] prostituted [his talent] to the most vulgar uses ... Do not think I have any personal prejudice ... I speak in an exclusively literary sense.[8]

Gillet ignored Gosse's advice, and the following year produced a critical article in his *Revue* which would further enhance Joyce's French reputation. When Gosse died three years later, Gillet made the letter public at an exhibition of the *Revue*. It was the first Joyce knew of Gosse's hostility.

After a despairing letter from Ettore Schmitz, Joyce urged Larbaud to mention his book, *Confessions of Zeno*, in the next issue of *Commerce* and to quote some pages of it.[9] Having assured his friend that he had nudged Larbaud towards action on his behalf, Schmitz wrote back to say that he had acquired a copy of *Ulysses* and would read it chapter by chapter with the assistance of Stanislaus. 'I think that next to you I could not have a better guide,' he concluded,[10] apparently unaware of Stanislaus's low opinion of his brother's 'latest inspection of the stinkpots'.

On 8 June Harriet sent him 8,600 francs to cover his medical expenses. Thanking her, Joyce said that, for his post-operative convalescence, he had taken a flat in Nice for seven months from 1 October, costing 9,000 francs, with the right to sublet if a flat were found in Paris in the meantime.[11] Finally, on 10 June, ironically the twentieth anniversary of the day on which he first saw and spoke to Nora Barnacle, Joyce underwent his fifth eye operation and second iridectomy at Borsch's clinic – a long, painful procedure which, Joyce suspected, was due either to his nervousness or to insufficient local anaesthetic. Regular progress reports were sent to Harriet and Miss Beach by Lucia and Nora. Harriet wrote a sympathetic note; Beach, more gushing, said she had thought about him all day and suffered as much as he had, even dreaming that his operation had been a success.[12] Joyce's relationship with Beach was an emotional and complex one – close and yet liable to mutual misunderstandings and petulant outbursts from the highly strung American.

When Myron Nutting visited Joyce at the clinic he found him trying to communicate by writing in a notebook, but his words were encoded and incomprehensible.[13] Power also visited and reported him 'lying in a small low-ceilinged room with one single dim light burning over his bed'. He worried that all the atropine injections Joyce had received might have poisoned his system, and that the place, despite Borsch's eminence, was so dilapidated. Joyce remained there while recovering, though the sounds of traffic along the busy rue du Cherche-Midi made sleep difficult. To pass the time, he managed to memorize five hundred lines of Scott's 'The Lady of the Lake'. Finally discharged after sixteen days, he was back at the cheerless Victoria Palace Hotel, feeling well enough[14] but complaining gloomily to Harriet that his sight showed 'practically no improvement', despite the surgeon's reassurances.

Lying, as he was obliged to do, with eyes closed, he was haunted by endless cinematographic evocations of the years of drudgery and failure in Trieste. But he took satisfaction in Ernest Boyd's claiming him for Ireland and was also amused that some Joyce enthusiasts had decided to call 16 June 'Bloomsday', sending him a bunch of white and dyed-blue hydrangeas to mark the occasion.[15] Such popular appeal would be difficult to sustain with his new work. *Ulysses*, he reflected, was a book about which he could talk intelligibly; *Work in Progress* was a completely different matter:

> If ever I try to explain to people now what I am supposed to be writing I see stupefaction freezing them into silence. For instance Shaun, after a long absurd and rather incestuous Lenten lecture to Izzy, his sister, takes leave of her 'with a half a glance of Irish frisky from under the shag of his parallel brows'. These are the words the reader will see but not those he will hear. He also alludes to Shem as my 'soamheis' brother; he means Siamese.[16]

At the hotel, they moved to a new brighter room with a higher ceiling. Joyce now had sufficient sight to get about but his eyes were still too painful for the close, careful work he required of himself.

On returning from the clinic, he had to decline an invitation from Edouard Dujardin to meet George Moore who was visiting him. However, he did finally venture out, once to Shakespeare and Company where he told Miss Beach that he didn't feel like meeting anyone. While he was lurking at the back of the shop a tall, pink-faced man came in and announced himself as Moore. Remembering Joyce's words Beach did not introduce them. Afterwards Joyce asked who the man was and when she told him he expressed disappointment, saying, 'I would like to have thanked him for his kindness in obtaining the King's Purse for me.' Moore later wrote to Beach asking whether the man with the black patch in her shop happened to have been Joyce as he would like to have met him. The two did not meet for another five years.

Joyce was keen to get away from Paris, after some altercations between him and the editors of *Commerce* over fragments of *Ulysses* (translated by Larbaud, Fargue, Auguste Morel and Miss Beach) which were scheduled for the summer issue. Miss Monnier then commissioned a full French translation of the novel. Larbaud felt unable to undertake the work and Morel was asked to produce a first draft which Larbaud, Fargue, Monnier and Joyce would then consider for revision. This arrangement was cumbersome and the team would be riven by disputes and disagreements, with Larbaud sometimes in and sometimes out of favour. Monnier thought Larbaud's reluctance to take on the task by himself stemmed from his annoyance over Joyce's lack of interest in his work.[17]

Borsch finally gave him permission to leave Paris in July. Just before departure, Joyce was cheered to hear that Harriet had invested a further 47,000 francs (around £500) plus £550 worth of war stock in his name – some compensation for the declining exchange rate that summer.[18] The family headed for St Malo to tour through the land of the Bretons, whose ancient culture and language were not so dissimilar to those of the Irish, taking in such places as Dinan, Mont-Saint-Michel, Dol and Carnac. On one occasion touring the countryside with Lloyd Morris, the American critic, and his mother, they came across a field of druidic stones. When they stopped for lunch Joyce took Morris aside and said that if the womenfolk were to comment on the shape of the stones no mention should be made of their phallic significance. Such talk among ladies, Morris concluded, was taboo for Joyce.[19]

News came via Miss Beach that in New York John Quinn was dying.[20] When he died shortly afterwards, Joyce reflected on his insensitivity in selling off his *Ulysses* manuscript cheaply without consulting him first. Nevertheless he recalled the help the lawyer had given him over the years and duly sent his family a letter of condolences. He noted sadly other recent deaths – his old Belvedere teacher, Mr Dempsey, Ferruccio Busoni and Joseph Conrad, whose manuscripts Quinn had also auctioned off.

A marathon letter from Stanislaus commiserated with him over his operations, expressed admiration for Tuohy's portrait of their father, approval of Gorman's book on him, distaste for a vulgar, 'riff-raffish' lecture on him given by Francini in Trieste, and bewilderment over his *Work in Progress* in the *transatlantic review*. 'You began this fooling in the Holles Street episode in *Ulysses*,' he complained, wondering whether it was a leg-pull or simply showed a softening of the brain. What had been published, he said, was 'unspeakably wearisome' and might be 'the last word in modern literature ... the witless wandering of literature before its final extinction ... I refuse to allow myself to be whirled round in the mad dance by a literary dervish.' With *Ulysses*, at least there was much to like, especially the farcical humour, though even that was flawed.

> You try to shift the burden of your melancholy to the reader's shoulders without being yourself relieved. To me you seem to have escaped from the toils of the priest and the King only to fall under the oppression of a monstrous vision of life itself. Where so much has been recorded, I object to what has been omitted. There is no serenity or happiness anywhere in the whole book.

The 'Circe' episode, he went on, was 'worked out with a fantastic horror of which I know no equal in literature, painting or music'. Moreover, his brother's temperament being 'like Catholic morality ... predominantly sexual', he confused the sexual urge with the imagination. And yet while Bloom's often-confusing wool-gatherings vitiated the book, 'The close ... with its dream figure of Bloom's young son and the suggestion that children are the real lambs who take away just these sins of the world is so unexpected and so unexpectedly tender, that one reader at least could not read it unmoved.' 'You see,' he concluded, 'I write rarely but with a vengeance.'[21]

It emerged that the Italian Fascist authorities wished to conscript Giorgio, and Joyce's reaction was grimly ironic. 'Born in Austria, now Italy, of British subjects, now Irish Free State citizens or not, and resident in France he has a choice of armies.' He had tried to resolve the matter with the Consul of the new Italian state in St Malo, but was not impressed by 'Italian government ways'.[22] He decided to sort it all out at the British Consulate in Paris on his return. Pinning him or his son to a particular nationality would take some doing, especially when it came to taking sides and joining armies.

The break from Paris enabled Joyce to think about his new book in broader terms. 'I have been thinking and thinking how and how and how can I and can it – all about the fusion of two parts of the book – while my one bedazzled eye searched the sea like Cain-Shem-Tristan-Patrick from his lighthouse in Boulogne. I hope the solution will presently appear.'[23] The 'brief stay' extended to eight days and by now he was reading intensely and wondering how long his eyes would hold out – the sight in his operated left eye, he told Miss Beach, had almost gone.

Joyce had three reasons for wanting to return to Paris – to see Borsch, to receive visits from Stanislaus and Charlie, now working as a telephonist in London, and to establish Giorgio's nationality. His trip to Brittany, he decided, had yielded valuable research for *Work in Progress*. Even so, he felt oppressed by his own compulsion to work, wishing he could suppress 'the clockwork' in his head. He might compensate, he said, by visiting a few music-halls when he was in London later that year.[24]

By early September he was back in Paris and there found a battle in progress over the translated fragments of *Ulysses* for *Commerce* magazine, involving its American proprietress, Marguerite Caetani (Princess di Bassiano), Fargue, Beach and Monnier, with Larbaud (who disagreed with the others over aspects of the translation) being declared *persona non grata* by the booksellers and warned away from rue de l'Odéon after switching sides.[25] Joyce stayed well clear of the battlefield, finding diversion in the company of his brothers, Stanislaus and Charlie, and Charlie's new wife Ann, a devotee of St Patrick, who gave him a pocket breastplate in the new Irish colours bearing part of the saint's famous prayer and the words 'all rights reserved'. This must be, he thought, the first case of copyright in history. The motto on the front appealed to him especially – 'The shield of God protects me from the hand of every man who plots against me, near or far, alone or with others.'[26]

Joyce was still in search of a new home, and worried that his sight had worsened, an impression confirmed by Borsch who again promised a full recovery in due course. Finally he and Nora found a flat, back in the Avenue Charles Floquet, which they took for six months. He would now have a home to which to return after his trip to London, where he wanted to consult Monro Saw about Giorgio's nationality as well as doing the rounds of his literary contacts. The one immediate bright prospect was that, with the fourth edition of *Ulysses* sold out, a fifth was scheduled for the end of September.[27]

Although Joyce was taking the whole family to London, he didn't book a hotel in advance, wanting to see how rough the Channel was before embarking. It was several days before he judged the sea smooth enough to carry him to England unimperilled. In London, he busied himself with consular officials, publishers and lawyers. He saw Jonathan Cape who was about to reissue *A Portrait*, Rodker who updated him about the doomed second edition of *Ulysses* and visited Eliot, now a publisher with Faber and Gwyer and anxious to see the 'Mamalujo' piece in the *transatlantic review*. By the time they left for Paris, thanks to Monro Saw, Giorgio's nationality had been clarified (he was not Italian) so there was no risk of him being dragged from his singing studies into the ranks of Il Duce's army. He also left the Euston's manager, Mr Knight, impressed enough to inform Miss Beach that their state apartment would be ever at his disposal.[28]

Settling into a new apartment meant retrieving his furniture and his library from storage and his manuscripts and the rest of his books from Miss Beach. In between all that he hoped to meet Harriet who was in Paris but whom he kept missing – at the bookshop, at a restaurant and at her hotel. She was being chaperoned around Paris by the McAlmons, intent upon melting her reserve and allaying any remaining doubts she might have about Joyce, his lifestyle and friendships. They took her to cafés and cabarets and to meet many of Joyce's American friends of whom she had only heard. While she was careful not to match the hard drinking of the others she found that it took very little alcohol to affect her. On one occasion Pound turned up at a restaurant mildly tipsy, and seeing Weaver said, 'Why, Harriet, this is the first time I've ever seen you drunk.' She was so visibly upset by this that Hilda Doolittle, one of the company, took her back to her hotel. Although next day McAlmon was able to soothe her hurt feelings, the incident had reawakened Harriet's fear of seeing Joyce under the influence of drink. After that she withdrew herself from the McAlmon crowd and went to introduce herself to Misses Monnier and Beach, with whom, according to the latter, she got on 'like a house afire'.[29]

Having been told of his readings from *Work in Progress* by McAlmon, when they finally did meet Harriet asked Joyce to read some of it to her. He was happy to do so and invited Miss Beach to join them for the occasion at the new flat.[30] There Joyce talked about Vico and his cyclical theory of history and the language of myth which would underlie and infuse his new novel. As he read, Harriet gradually came to terms with what he was writing and committed herself to learning more of what he was about. Although, on one visit to Les Trianons, she did, to her horror, see him drunk, she also acclimatized herself to his drinking (it was almost always white wine and only in the evening), and her support for him held steady.[31]

Charlie wrote to say that Aunt Josephine was terminally ill, leaving Joyce guilt-stricken that they had become estranged. He wrote immediately saying how grateful he was for her kindness following his mother's death and how much he wanted to see her again.[32] But she never replied and died shortly afterwards. Despite the deep sense of remorse he now felt, he plunged on with his book, handing his crayon-scrawled pages to the trusty Miss Bollach for typing. Work as ever kept him sane and focused.

With the death of Aunt Josephine, Joyce had lost his most valued pair of eyes in Dublin and an irreplaceable memory of times past. Now he would depend more and more on information gleaned from visitors who knew the city. Friends such as Power, Tuohy and Tuohy's young Dublin friend, Thomas McGreevy (newly graduated from Trinity), could be cross-questioned about specific places and how things were changing. But the reality, if he ever returned to see it, would only destroy the image that inspired him.

When Larbaud described a dinner which the Princess Marguerite Caetani had given for him and Eliot, Joyce wrote into his 'Shaun' episode a reference to 'the proprietoress of the roastery who lives on the hill and gaulusch gravy and pumpernickel to wolp up and a gorger's bulby onion (Margareter, Margaretar Margarasticandeatar)'.[33] And when Eliot, again visiting Paris, invited him to meet the princess, Joyce declined, but Eliot too would find a couple of friendly coded references to his name buried in a line or two of the new novel. 'I kickkick keenly love such, particularly while savouring of their flavours at their most perfect best when served with heliotrope ayelips.'[34] 'Even unto Heliotropolis, the castellated, the enchanting.'[35] The sources for *Work in Progress* lay all around him and all were grist for the Joycean word-mill.

He now caught a glimpse of the end of his great endeavour. On 9 November he told Harriet, 'I think that at last I have solved one – the first – of the problems presented by my book. In other words one of the partitions between two of the tunnelling parties seems to have given way.'[36]

When Joyce next saw Borsch, he was very upset to be told that another iridectomy was necessary to remove a cataract, but he felt too tired and resigned to question the doctor. In any case, there were other matters preying on his mind. For example, he was trying to memorize the speech of John F. Taylor from the 'Aeolus' episode of *Ulysses* for a phonograph recording arranged by Miss Beach. It was, he told Harriet, like awaiting execution while faced with too much to do beforehand. His life as well as his work was full of complications, and, he said, echoing the eccentric turn of phrase that now marked his writing, 'from time to time I lie back and listen to my hair growing white'.[37]

In 1924 Joyce's income from investments amounted to almost £1,000, averaging something over 70,000 francs in a fluctuating money market.[38] But payment was quarterly, and as funds ran out from time to time, the children would be sent to Shakespeare and Company for a loan on account. As a return favour, although in some discomfort, he travelled with Miss Beach to the HMV factory in Billancourt to record the Taylor speech from 'Aeolus'. Thirty copies were produced under her bookshop label, most of which she gave to Joyce for distribution among his friends. He was quite proud of the result, and would sometimes play it as after-dinner entertainment, although he said it was not his natural voice. But he recognized that the quality of the acoustic recording was wanting, telling Harriet that she would need 'a rather strong machine' for the spoken voice to be properly heard. Seemingly now converted to the new work, she actually bought a phonograph simply to listen to the recording, while Beach kept a copy in her shop to play for anyone who was interested.

Editors were now eager to publish fragments from Joyce's *Work in Progress*. In mid-November, Eliot came to Paris and extracted a promise from him to submit a piece to the *Criterion*, and McAlmon wanted a passage for his *Contact Collection of Contemporary Writers* which William Bird's Three Mountains Press was to publish. This would be dedicated to Harriet and include contributions from Hemingway, Ford, Djuna Barnes, Bryher (McAlmon's wife), Norman Douglas, Gertrude Stein, and McAlmon himself.

On 29 November, following another iridectomy where the cataract was removed from Joyce's right eye, he saw magnificent but fleeting visions, he told Harriet. Borsch had again sounded positive, assuring him that his sight would return, but had added, more fatalistically, 'The readiness is all.'[39] Harriet, however, was beginning to suspect that Borsch's optimism might be a front, and expressed concern to Sylvia Beach about the surgeon's true intentions. 'Surely Dr Borsch could not go on performing operation after operation unless he felt persuaded of a good result,' she wrote.[40]

Recovering at the clinic Joyce again had what he called 'cinema nights', in which scenes from his past life replayed inside his head. He was treated with ice packs, leeches, iodine and scopolamine drops, leaving him extremely fatigued. He knew he was facing a long recovery before he could return to his 'cinematic text' and it was not until 20 December that he was able to start reading and writing once more. Now he was again faced with the tunnel to excavate.[41] And since he was collecting the names of rivers to keep Anna Livia company, as a New Year's present Harriet offered him the rivers Weaver and Dane.[42]

Coincidences intrigued Joyce and when he pointed out a few in his new work to Harriet, she in turn mentioned some to him. He had won her round to his conspiracy of concealment, to his phantasmagoria of myth and allusion, and finally he believed she saw the ultimate contours of the new book as he did. The work was now flowing steadily. Anxious to get her reactions, on 27 January 1925 he told her that she was about to receive a copy of 'the first two watches on Mr Shaun' (the first part of *Finnegans Wake*, Book III). He was also eager to supply her with a skeleton key to help her unlock the new box of tricks. He cited *Oscar Wilde from Purgatory*, a 'spiritualist' conversation via the ouija board, by Hester Travers Smith, as an inspirational source for one page: 'I perpetually kept my ouija ouija wicket up';[43] 'Pervinca calling, Soloscar hears. (O Sheem! O Shaam!)'[44] There were allusions to the Irish alphabet, Bruno of Nola, Tristan, Norwegian-Danish vocabulary, a line from Ibsen, nightmare expressions in Greek, German, Irish, Japanese, Italian and Assyrian, the Danish names of Irish coastal towns, and old Dublin sea ceremonies mirroring ceremonies for the Doges of Venice. Her replies show Harriet going along with him and, as his intentions became clearer to her, responding with fascination to his letters and even offering her own contributions to the shifting tapestry of his great nocturnal reverie.

At last *Exiles* was to get an airing in America, opening in New York on 19 February 1925. The fact that the actress playing Bertha was called Joyce seemed, he thought, a hopeful coincidence. The play ran for forty-one performances until 22 March. Although Stark Young in the *New York Times* proclaimed it 'one of the events of the theatrical year', reviews were mixed and it was not even the *succès d'estime* Joyce had hoped for. When Jane Heap sent some of the reviews with her congratulations, he told her that he had sent first-night bouquets to the leading actresses when perhaps he should have sent wreaths. Harriet told Miss Beach that, 'Evidently the play needs a very special cast to make its acting a success.'[45]

In mid-February he spent ten extremely painful days at Borsch's clinic with episcleritis, where leeches and ice-packs were again applied to his troublesome eye. Eventually, however, morphine brought some relief until the crisis had passed. By the 25th he was back at the flat in Avenue Charles Floquet which he had taken for a further six months to see him over this bad period. He was still dictating letters to Lucia, but, unable to read print, he passed the time singing at the piano and doing what he called 'octogenarian's exercises' with an elastic stretcher he had found in Giorgio's room. Bad weather, discomfort from his eyes and from an aching tooth fragment, only added to his depression. Fortunately he had acquired a companion, a biscuit-coloured cat from Marseilles, who, like him, was bored by the gloom of Paris but had a good appetite for buttered bread and the *Daily Mail*.[46]

Then another cloud appeared on Joyce's horizon. Ernest Walsh, a twenty-year-old protégé of Ezra Pound, invited him to write a tribute to the poet for his new literary magazine, *This Quarter*. He also asked for something from *Work in Progress* for the following number. But Joyce was in pain and so blind that he could still only dictate, so felt unable, at short notice, to produce anything substantial about Pound. In any case, he had read little of his work and Pound in turn had shown little interest in *Work in Progress*. However, Joyce sent Walsh a short acknowledgement of the poet's encouragement and generosity over the years, and in particular the help given at a time of great difficulty for him long before they met – all this the more valued because emanating from a mind so brilliant and perceptive.[47] But with no mention of Pound's work, this looked like a snub to his poetry and could only help lower the temperature of their formerly warm relationship.

Harriet sent greetings on St Patrick's Day, a day with not only a national significance for Joyce but now a literary one, too. In thanking her, he reported having finished the work promised to Eliot. It had, however, been written under stress. His right eye was again troubling him, a dental operation had been postponed, he had been placed on a diet and told to walk eight or ten kilometres a day. To be able to do this in foul weather with one eye blind and the other inflamed, he said, should earn him the Legion of Honour.[48] He advised her to get a record of McCormack singing 'Molly Brannigan', promising to explain why when she had heard it.

Because he found reading barely possible Joyce asked his typist Miss Bollach to use a heavy black pencil when writing to him, though even to read that would require a magnifying glass, he said. Her latest typescript came back in great confusion because he had been too blind to show her the way through the labyrinth. It took him and Giorgio and three magnifying glasses to read and chop it up so that Auguste Morel could piece it together on *his* machine. Finally he sent the fragment to Eliot to puzzle over. This was one of those rare occasions when his son became involved with *Work in Progress*; both Giorgio and Lucia had their own interests and circles of friends and probably preferred to leave their strangely work-obsessed and all too often self-obsessed father to his own devices.

On 15 April Borsch performed a capsulotomy on Joyce's right eye, which involved cutting into the lens. A week later, Helen Nutting visited him and found him wide awake. He asked her to read from a book about ancient Dublin, and took notes as she read. Afterwards he quoted Goethe saying that when a man wrote he must write as if the book would be read a million times, not skimmed and thrown away. He was particularly interested in places with Danish names or with Irish endings and derivations, and he explained the Four Old Men, or Masters, to her.

The following day, when she went to have tea with the Joyces, she found the whole family there with Mrs Wallace and a friend of Lucia's, Kathleen Neel, known as Kitten. Joyce seemed cheerful to be back home, but was bemoaning the fact that, pending their move, none of his books and manuscripts were to hand. Although she saw how devoted the family were one to another, she sensed a restlessness – Nora looking handsome in a new Chanel dress, Giorgio heading off for a singing lesson and Lucia leaving with Kitten for her dancing.[49] Joyce's 'restlessness' can be detected in a letter written that day to Harriet (in thick black pencil), full of references to Norsemen and St Patrick, and reporting a slight recovery of sight in his operated eye. His other eye remained uncured so he still could not read without a magnifying glass. He was thoroughly fed up, he said, with iodine, aspirin and scopolamine.[50]

He felt that the Paris climate wasn't helping his recovery. To compensate for his inability to read he had acquired a gramophone and spent much of his time listening to records – affording great pleasure to ear and brain, he said. Songs by McCormack and Jean de Reszke prompted Earwicker's speech declaring that 'I introduced her (Frankfurters, numborines, why drive fear?) to our fourposter tunies chantreying under Castrucci Sinior and De Mellos'.[51] Inside his clouded world in which print was melted and blurred, the ear remained keen, and the singer and wordsmith could come together in a harmony of invented sound. The manner in which his mind played and teased and juggled with words is evident in some of the changes he made to his text – 'bike' becoming 'bisexycle' and 'grunted and growled' becoming 'gromwelled'.[52]

Harriet, planning another visit to Paris, soon learned why Joyce had referred her to McCormack's 'Molly Brannigan'. In May he had sent her a ballad dedicated to Molly Bloom to be sung to the same tune. It began, 'Man dear, did you never hear of buxom Molly Bloom at all,/As plump an Irish beauty, sir, as Annie Levy Blumenthal ...' It captured the mood of jollification underlying all his word-sport, and matched the wayward Molly with the singer in Book II, Chapter 2 of *Finnegans Wake* – 'And bemolly and jiesis! For I sport a whatyoumacormack in the latcher part of my throughers.'[53] The inspiration for this, he told Gorman, was a dream – a dream in which he had seen Molly Bloom on a hillock fling a child's black coffin at a passing figure (Bloom), shouting that she was finished with him. From a road nearby there was a shout of laughter from some American journalists with Pound to the fore.

> I was very indignant [he said] and strode up to her and delivered the one speech of my life. It was very long, eloquent and full of passion, explaining all the last episode of Ulysses to her. She wore a black opera cloak, or *sortie de bal*, had become slightly grey and looked like *la Duse*. She smiled when I ended on an astronomical climax, and then, bending, picked up a tiny snuffbox, in the form of a little black coffin, and tossed it towards me, saying, 'And I have done with you too, Mr Joyce.' I had a snuffbox like the one she tossed to me when I was at Clongowes Wood College ... together with a larger one to fill it from.[54]

So much could be read into this dream story (apart from the Freudian symbolism of coffins and snuffboxes): Joyce's insecurities over Nora, guilt over using her in creating Molly, exasperation at her incomprehension of his work, doubts about his own manhood, fears for his reputation and regrets for lost innocence. The Molly Bloom song reflects how he escaped from these and other anxieties – with mirthful song and dance. His *Finnegans Wake* would represent a vaster, more intricate, more bewildering dream, and writing it can readily be seen as self-therapeutic musical comedy.

That spring, Paris hosted the third PEN International Congress which Louis Gillet, the art historian and literary critic, recalled Joyce attending.

> That evening Pirandello ... Galsworthy, Thomas Mann, Unamuno ...
> Stefan Zweig, Jules Romains ... were there – all Europe. It was ... a council
> of intelligences, a communion of all men of good will ... I can still see
> the spectre of the author of *Ulysses* – gaunt and as if disincarnated, his
> profile like a crescent under his thick lenses, eye vexed and obstructed by
> a black felt patch – slide gropingly, with a step at the same time hesitant
> and lordly, among respectful people ready to make room for him.[55]

Joyce was no longer an obscure Irish writer living in distant exile but an international author of distinction moving among equals.

When Harriet visited Paris in May she saw little of Joyce who was busy in his half-sighted way overseeing the family's move to their new apartment. This spacious flat at 2 Square Robiac, just off the rue de Grenelle, cost 20,000 francs per annum, and would be their home for the next six years. However, it required renovation and for two weeks they moved to the nearby Hotel de Bourgogne et Montana while decorators, electricians and curtain-hangers were busy. Harriet was shocked by the chaos, but finally Joyce had found a home he could properly inhabit. There were three living rooms, one decorated with yellow hangings, and a drawing room with blue hangings. Blue and yellow, he said later, were colours he could distinguish one from the other. He had also rented an upstairs room – for a live-in Breton housemaid Nora had engaged.

When Joyce saw Harriet off at the Gare du Nord, the subject of money was not mentioned. But on 13 June, after moving into Square Robiac, one of the first things he did was write to her listing the expenses he had run up (including dental charges, furnishings, and the cost of Giorgio's holiday) totalling 11,600 francs. As a joke he added a PS saying he'd forgotten the wallpaper, but later the same day sent a carpenter's bill for 1,300 francs, and the following day a bill for 4,400 francs for new doors. There were sailcloth awnings still to come, he warned her.[56] There was no mention yet of the piano, a necessity with two singers and a budding dancer in the family. Joyce had had photographs taken to mark Bloomsday 1925, and enclosed them for Harriet with his catalogue of expenses.

He could now rehang the family portraits and unpack his papers, although often he found his pencilling too faint to read, if written, as he put it, 'before the thunder stroke'. However, he had managed to finish what he called his 'Shem piece' for *This Quarter*, and sent copies to Ernest Walsh and Miss Beach. Next he had completed a five-page extract about Earwicker for McAlmon's *Contact Collection*,[57] having inserted 'a few more puzzles', he said, and was now working on 'Anna Livia Plurabelle' for the *Calendar of Modern Letters*, an English review which had already published a sympathetic article on *Ulysses*.[58] Despite these preoccupations, he still managed to entertain Lloyd Morris and his mother, took Arthur Symons and Larbaud out to dinner and began daily meetings with Morel, who, when Miss Bollach was unavailable, did his typing.

Meanwhile, *Work in Progress* was gradually finding its way into print. The July *Criterion* included 'Fragment of an Unfinished Novel', the episode prepared the previous February, which became 'The Manifesto of ALP', and Book I, Chapter 5 of *Finnegans Wake*. When the proofs arrived from *This Quarter*, at Walsh's suggestion Joyce sent them to Pound for checking, assuring him that he really preferred to correct his own proofs. But Pound was offended and wrote an obscure letter to the *Chicago Tribune* saying, 'I am not a receiving station for manuscript, typescript, drawings, photographs or other paraphernalia, accompanied or unaccompanied by return postage,'[59] which Joyce believed was directed at him.

Harriet was now his closest confidante. His letters to her invariably concerned money, but increasingly he dilated upon aspects of his work. Sending her his manuscripts followed by comments and explanations had become a habit. She should read St John Ervine's life of Parnell, Bédier's *Tristan et Iseult*, the Cain and Abel story, or Swift, to comprehend this or that passage. Miss Beach was also sent copies, with corrections hinting at the comic playfulness underlying his prose – 'Cancel *up their sleeve*,/insert *daggers down their back*,'[60] 'Cancel women insert houris',[61] and 'for God insert Goggle'.[62] The close work (aided by magnifying glass and reflective white coat), going ever 'deeper into Liffey water', was wearying, he said, and he wished the three pieces in preparation ('Shaun', 'Shem' and 'Anna Livia') were finished and he was sitting in a railway carriage heading away from Paris.[63]

Once 'Anna Livia' was finished and sent to Sylvia Beach, to be forwarded to the *Calendar*, Joyce felt free to consider escaping the capital.[64] On 23 July the Joyces left for Fécamp on the Normandy coast, birthplace of Maupassant. There they were greeted by three thunderstorms, an appropriately Joycean start to three months of hotel-hopping which would take them to Rouen, Niort, and Arcachon near Bordeaux. He would return with the names of some forty-five more rivers for 'Anna Livia Plurabelle', and hundreds of changes to give to Beach. He had also become possessed with the idea behind 'The Last Watch of Shaun' as he wandered about Normandy. It ought to be 'about roads', he wrote, 'all about dawn and roads, and I go along repeating that to myself all day as I stumble along the roads hoping it will dawn on me how to show up them roads so as everybody'll know as how roads etc.'[65] He had become the creature of his own creation, trapped inside his own Daedalian labyrinth.

In Rouen he received the announcement that his 'confirmed bachelor-brother' Stanislaus, now a professor at the University of Trieste, was engaged to be married to one of his students. Unable to write himself he got Lucia to send congratulations. Replying, Stanislaus said he had met Ettore Schmitz, but did not share his brother's high opinion of his work.[66] Before he left Rouen for Arcachon, Joyce heard that the Stage Society in London intended to include *Exiles* in their next season's programme. He was also threatened with another eye attack and wrote asking Miss Beach to get him eye-drops from Dr William Collinson, Borsch's assistant.

That summer, Gillet published his 'Du côté de chez Joyce' in the *Revue des Deux Mondes*. *Ulysses* was, he wrote, an 'impossible' work, 'one of those indigestible books which seem generally to rebuke the public'. Joyce was merely pushing the technique of Henry James, Proust and Rimbaud to its extremes. But his dislocating and pulverizing of language and grammar destroyed all forms of representation which assured exactitude of description. The style was Dada – verbal tricks and feats of skill, but ultimately meaningless. What was the point, he asked, of wasting so much talent on disrupting the art of writing and exploding centuries of literary convention?[67] Despite its critical tone, Joyce, as usual, saw it in a positive light. Giorgio, on reading the article, was angry, but Joyce said the tone did not matter – what did matter was that Gillet was the son-in-law of a French Academician.

After bad weather in Arcachon and Bordeaux, where Nora received the bad news that both her sister Annie and Uncle Tom had died that summer, the family returned to what Joyce called 'the semi-arctic climate' of Paris, to an apartment finally ready to settle into. Joyce immediately succumbed to a fresh attack of conjunctivitis and was back seeing Borsch on an almost daily basis. Herbert Gorman, who was visiting France, had written saying that he had plans for a new and enlarged edition of his book about Joyce and, never having met the author, requested an interview. Joyce replied that he never gave interviews but agreed to meet Gorman 'on other terms' before he returned to the US, when he could supply him with any information, documents or reviews he required.[68] Gorman was invited to Square Robiac, but when he suggested they should meet instead at Boulogne where he was about to embark for New York, Joyce, fearing the effects of the Channel winds on his eyes, declined.

The doctors still had him on scopolamine, what he called 'the truth-compelling drug', normally used in Germany and America 'to compel criminals to tell lies', and this had turned his writing 'very spidery'. The drug was captured in the spider's web of *Finnegans Wake* with a reference to 'love and lie detectors in venuvarities, whateither the drugs truth of it',[69] showing how little escaped the sharp inner eye of his imagination.

But not everyone appreciated the subtlety of what he was creating. 'Anna Livia Plurabelle', so laboured over for the *Calendar of Modern Letters*, would not be appearing as its printers refused to set it. Edgell Rickward, the *Calendar*'s editor, wrote of his 'regret at losing such a masterly example of his genius', and apologized at being unable to cope with 'the crude forms of convention' followed by their printers.[70] On a more cheerful note, the December issue of the *NRF* would be running the first instalment of Morel's *Ulysses* translation (the 'Hades' episode), and the *Navire d'Argent*, Adrienne Monnier's new journal, would run 'Anna Livia' in its October issue, followed in November by an article on Joyce by Jean Prévost. But there had been no cheques from Eliot or Walsh and nothing from what he called his 'Three Shylocks', Huebsch, Cape and Pinker.

By late September Joyce's eyes had improved and he began to see where his obsession with roads was taking him. He had begun work on 'The Last Watch of Shaun', and (revealing the almost accidental fashion in which he created his textual mosaic) told Harriet he had 'composed some wondrous devices for [the episode] during the night and wrote them out in the dark very carefully only to discover that I had made a mosaic on top of other notes so I am now going to bring my astronomical telescope into play'.[71] During the day, as in the night, as Joyce composed, an air of silent concentration hung over the Square Robiac apartment, and Nora, Lucia and Giorgio simply had to live with it.

When in mid-October another set of proofs of 'Shem the Penman' arrived from Walsh, Joyce added another layer of mystification, and returned them by express post. To Harriet he listed some of the 'advance press opinions' he had had on his latest work – including 'I don't understand a single word,' from Wallace's wife Lillian, to 'I thought I knew English until I read it,' from the French poet and dramatist Paul Claudel, and 'I'm afraid he's gone off his head,' from his father.[72] But he made no compromises, and 'Shem', heavy with enigmas and word puzzles, appeared in the Autumn–Winter issue of *This Quarter*, which also included a twenty-six-page musical supplement – part of Antheil's unfinished operatic score for 'Cyclops'.[73]

In November came news of the piratical printing of extracts from *Work in Progress* in *Two Worlds*, the monthly published by Quinn's 'nut poet', Samuel Roth. *Two Worlds*, which included titillating stories alongside serious literature, had been running these fragments since September. It raised the question of Joyce's American copyright and how vulnerable he was to losing control of his work in the USA. He was at a loss to know what to do. On hearing about it, Harriet wrote to Sylvia Beach, 'What a rogue that Samuel Roth is! I suspect there won't be a second number.'[74] She would be disappointed; Roth was both ingenious and persistent.

Joyce had listed corrections he thought necessary for any future edition of Gorman's book. Sending these to Gorman, he asked him to use them as if he had collected the new information himself rather than having it offered by his subject. He also mailed him a copy of his *Ulysses* schema, which, he claimed later, was sent in confidence – something Gorman would deny.[75] But this readiness to supply material was an indication of Joyce's determination to control anything biographical published about him, and project a public persona to his own liking. His aversion to giving interviews or writing journalistic pieces was an aversion to allowing editors to use his words to justify their own image of him. And, as elusive in reality as he was in his fiction, he had mastered the art of saying 'No' in several languages by sighs, gestures and evasions.[76] However, he had no compunction about using the lives and personas of others for his own purposes. Livia Schmitz had become concerned that he had depicted her in his new novel, but he wrote assuring Ettore that it was only his wife's hair he had borrowed.

That November another Irishman, George Bernard Shaw, won the 1925 Nobel Prize for Literature, the second Dubliner in two years to do so, and Joyce duly offered his congratulations.[77] Although Shaw had pretended to scorn *Ulysses* and was critical of *Exiles*, Joyce never ceased to admire him and his name would be woven into *Finnegans Wake* – mostly by way of puns.

Borsch had already indicated that Joyce required further treatment, and on 5 December, his eyes dilated from scopolamine, Joyce returned for his seventh eye operation which lasted forty minutes. As usual, Borsch was optimistic that his sight would be fully restored, even though immediately afterwards, according to Lucia, her father collapsed and became delirious – the effects of too much scopolamine, it was decided. It took until seven that evening for him to recover consciousness, after which he passed a particularly good night.[78] When she visited him on the 14th Miss Beach found him in good spirits and next day he was back at Square

Robiac. However, the result of Borsch's work was still unclear, and all that Lucia could report was that her father still had no sight in the operated eye, and was suffering pain and dizzy spells.[79] Over Christmas his agony was relieved only by painkillers, and his depression was deepened when Dr Collinson, who had fallen out with Borsch, told him that in truth there was little hope of recovery in his blind left eye.

Locked in his own world of pain and darkness, Joyce was not the best of company. To Livia Schmitz, who met him soon afterwards, he appeared distant, like a sleepwalker; the Belgian poet and painter, Henri Michaux, said he was *'le plus fermé'*; *'il n'existait pas'*. But his remoteness, as ever, was a form of self-protective detachment. Inside the private world of his imagination, which blindness could not dim, his mind was now perfectly tuned to the coining of words – playing and conjuring with meanings, tantalizing with allusions and ambiguities, burying clues, spinning mysteries, scattering traces, and weaving enigmas. He was turning his weakening eyesight into a creative strength. 'I have the impression always that it is evening,' he told the French surrealist Philippe Soupault, who had noticed that *Work in Progress* contained a great many sounds, smells and atmospheres.[80] He knew that, as a writer and as a man, he was withdrawing into obscurity, and doubted that even twenty people would understand the new work.

The Nuttings visited the Square Robiac apartment around Christmas-time, an occasion noted by Helen:

Misery at the Joyces, he with one eye blind ... thin from fretting and pain, not eating, and taking no exercise. Tired of pain, and hopeless of improvement of his sight./'Twice a day they flash a light before my eyes and say, "You see nothing? Not anything?" I am tired of it all, this has gone on so long.'/While I was waiting for Mrs Joyce, Joyce came in, silent-footed, to ask me, 'Mrs Nutting, have you read The Waste Land?'/'Yes, Mr Joyce.'/'What do you think of it?'/'Why, I was so excited by it I can think of nothing else.'/After a pause he said, 'I was not sure that Eliot was a poet. Now, I know he is.'[81]

Eliot's wasteland of despair was not so very far removed from his own.

The after-effects of Joyce's latest operation had come at a cruel moment. His plan to attend the first night of *Exiles* in February was now in ruins. He was unable to travel to London, he told Harriet, unable to see lights, suffering continual pain from the operation, weeping oceans of tears, highly nervous, and unable to think straight. He was now dependent on kind people to see him across the road and hail taxis for him. All day, he lay on a couch in a state of complete depression, wanting to work but quite unable to do so. He would send bouquets to the actresses, he said, but did not know their names or even that of the theatre.[82] Friends, however, would attend on his behalf.

On Monday 15 February the curtain went up on the London première of *Exiles* at the Regent Theatre, King's Cross, home of the London Repertory Players; Shaw was in the audience and Harriet was accompanied by Wyndham Lewis. Writing to Joyce she declared it a success, although one woman sitting beside her had walked out at the end of Act I, muttering, 'I call this collusion.' She liked the leading actors, Rupert Harvey as Richard, and Gwladys Black-Roberts as Bertha, but Lewis considered Roberts's performance 'too emotional'.[83] Ettore Schmitz, there with Livia, wrote saying that the whole evening had given him 'the delightful feeling of being present at the unfolding of one of your important works', although 'the inner springs of Rowan's actions' had eluded them both. However, Harvey had surprised him by something uncanny. 'I don't know whether it is intentional or not, but he moves, sits down, gets up and looks like you.' Despite the loud applause, there were some dissenting voices, and Schmitz overheard one man say, 'They want to force on us Italian ways. Italians, of course, are known for being jealous even when they are not in love.'[84] Claud Sykes, also there, was scornful of the Regent audience – stupid and typically English in their reactions, he told Joyce. He thought Black-Roberts as Bertha lacked 'vehemence', but scenes between her and Harvey 'always went well', and he was amused to see Shaw (whose *John Bull's Other Island* was showing at the theatre that same evening) talking about it keenly during the interval. Sykes saw a promising future for the play and hoped, he said, to see it performed 'at the Abbey or by a good French company'.[85]

The *Times* critic drew a penetrating portrait of Richard which could equally have fitted his creator – 'a realistic novelist, or a psycho-realistic novelist ... and his "copy" compels him to pry into his own and his friends' minds'. His plot to get Beatrice and his friend Robert together was nothing to do with jealousy but contrived merely as an experiment to satisfy the curiosity of the psycho-realist student of human nature.[86] The *Daily News* said the play was 'dull and pretentious' and 'none of the characters of the slightest interest'.[87] But the *Morning Post* depicted them as 'tormented moderns ... [who] ... must confess to each other, confess again and again; no matter what truth or illusion, dreams or facts ... as long as they can disturb each other's equanimity'.[88] Joyce was not pleased by any of the reviews, and writing to Harriet declared it a 'fiasco'.[89]

In March he reported a very slight improvement in his vision, and was back at work on 'Shaun'. Roth had sent him a cheque for $100 for the fragments he had used in *Two Worlds*, claiming that its circulation ran to only 450 copies which at first Joyce saw no reason to doubt. His work was being published in America and he was paid for it, however little.[90] But Hemingway checked out the magazine in New York and reported its having between 5,000 and 10,000 subscribers. Questioned about Joyce, Roth said that he admired his work and had used his name as a draw, but his readers wanted something more amusing and he had now finished using him. In any case, he added, he did not believe in paying contributors much at all. Hearing this, Joyce said he wished he had an American agent and would send no more work to New York.

Giorgio, advised to rest his voice and learn to pitch it higher, dropped his studies and took a temporary office job. Harriet had sent him a book of Elizabethan songs which Joyce now appropriated, using the rhythm of William Byrd's 'Woods so Wild' to describe Isolde in 'The Book of Shaun' – the passage beginning 'Night by silentsailing night while infantina Isobel (who will be blushing all day to be, when she growed up one Sunday, Saint Holy and Saint Ivory ...)'[91] He had experimented with musical forms before, in *Ulysses*, and the shifting themes and variations of the *Wake* were integral to the creation of his own strange song of the night. He had read the Isolde passage the week before to an audience of Miss Beach, the Wallaces and the Nuttings, he said, only to meet with general 'stupefaction'.[92]

Because of his dimmed vision, Joyce had recruited a band of willing women to read aloud to him – Mary Colum, Sylvia Beach, Adrienne Monnier, Helen Nutting and Helen Fleischman, the wife of Leon Fleischman, the American publisher. Mary Colum recalled the scene:

> In Joyce's study in his apartment in Square Robiac, he would have a bottle of white chianti on the table, a medley of books and notebooks, a gramophone somewhere near: surrounded by such items, he and his helper set to work. The amount of reading done by his helpers was librarious, as he might have written himself, as were the notebooks filled with the results of their reading which generally boiled down to only a line or a paragraph.[93]

Now he had a spacious apartment, Joyce enjoyed displaying and showing off his portrait gallery. Viewing the collection, one visitor, the writer Frank O'Connor, a Corkman, noticed a small landscape with a curious frame. What was it? he asked. 'That's cork,' said Joyce. 'Oh, yes, I know it's Cork,' said O'Connor, 'but what's the frame made of?' 'That's cork,' said Joyce. This Joycean joke, claimed O'Connor, left him feeling dizzy. 'It struck me,' he wrote, 'that the man was suffering slightly from association mania.'[94]

Other visitors from Ireland included Mary Sheehy-Skeffington and Harry Sinclair, nephew of the old Jewish art dealer from Nassau Street, both of whom were quizzed about latest happenings in the city. When the Colums told Joyce they had met a Dubliner who knew *Ulysses* back to front and many of the characters in it, they were asked to bring him round. This man, Thomas Pugh, was blind in one eye and born in 1883, close enough to him for Joyce to think it significant. He got Pugh to read aloud from the 'Cyclops' episode in what the Colums called 'a low-down' Dublin accent and sat there smiling. But when Mary Colum laughed he said, 'I can read it in a more low-down Dublin accent than that.'[95] Michael Lennon, a Dublin district judge and Belvedere contemporary of Joyce, paid a visit, questioning him about his family history, a subject on which he was always happy to dilate. After being shown over the portrait gallery, the judge was sent away with an inscribed copy of *Ulysses*. The Irish mountains, he told Harriet, were all coming to Mahomet. Eileen would be stopping in Paris en route for Ireland and Stannie was coming for two weeks at Easter with his fiancée, Nellie Lichtensteiger.[96]

That spring, Joyce came under attack from an unexpected quarter. Wyndham Lewis in his new book, *The Art of Being Ruled*, described Joyce's work as 'demented', 'stuttering', 'perishable', 'punning' and 'squinting', among other things, associating him with followers of Gertrude Stein, producing, in Bloom's case, 'a photograph of the unorganised word-dreaming' of the unfocused, illogical mind. Joyce was trying to grasp Lewis's use of these terms, he told Harriet, but having seen his drawing of her, and thinking it 'wonderful', made it difficult for him to return fire.[97] He was also amused by Lewis comparing Bloom's wool-gathering to the fitful and disjointed speech of Mr Jingle in *Pickwick Papers*. Unlike the explosive Lewis, Joyce preferred the indirect riposte, and this reference to 'Mr Joyce and Mr Jingle' found its way as 'Mr Jinglejoys' into *Finnegans Wake* (Chapter 2 of Book III) in Shaun's farewell speech to the girls of St Bride's Academy. Joyce, the mocker, was never averse to a little self-mockery.[98] Despite having attacked him, Lewis came to Paris and persuaded Joyce to contribute to a review he was launching. Joyce, who bore him no grudge, said he would be pleased to do so.[99]

Having finished 'Shaun' he sent the manuscript to Harriet. By now, he told her, he had the book more or less mapped out in his mind. Next he would turn to the twilight games of Shaun and Shem. As to Vico, she should not take him seriously in trying to understand what he was writing. What interested him more was a fear they both shared – his fear of thunderstorms, practically unknown among male Italians.[100] To the Swiss writer Jacques Mercanton he said later, 'I don't know whether Vico's theory is true; it doesn't matter. It's useful to me; that's what counts.'[101]

When Nora's uncle, the pious Michael Healy, came to Paris that June and needed a hotel close to a church, she asked Thomas McGreevy to take Joyce around to find a suitably situated hotel. McGreevy, like his other friends, noted how dependent he had become on Nora.[102] According to Power, he was now rarely seen in public without her. His other indispensable female support, Harriet Weaver, was, Joyce hoped, busily reading and enjoying his 'Four Watches of Shaun' (to become Part III of his novel). He was eager to have her reaction to how he was using words and trying to shape the book:

> While reading it could you make a complete list of words misspelt. Some, of course, are intentional, most, but there must be others overlooked by my dim sight. Will you let me know whether the 'plot' begins to emerge from it at all?

After recommending certain helpful sources, he told her, 'I shall leave it to your own interpretative discernment.'[103]

Harriet's reaction suggests she was striving hard to become the reader he hoped for. What she saw, she told him, was 'not a plot exactly', but 'a shadowy pattern, intricate in design is emerging "repeating itself" too, or parts of itself, from time to time. The various characters of the book are rather like Jack-in-the-boxes, popping out their heads at intervals to remind us that they are never very far away, always there ready to appear promptly when called for.' The fragment had 'a Jacobean flavour' and related to a darkness which 'lifts and falls, lifts and falls (like a safety curtain in a theatre)' leaving the reader 'stumbling ... and fumbling'.[104] The 'plotless plot' of the final work was already established.

The intense effort of finishing 'The Four Watches' was followed by another eye-attack, and yet another operation. This time things went more smoothly and Joyce was soon back home. But it took a month before he could tell Harriet that slowly but surely the sight of his left eye seemed to be returning.[105] On 19 June he was well enough to attend a performance of Antheil's *Ballet Mécanique* at the Théâtre des Champs-Elysées.

In England, at Cambridge, the young lecturer F. R. Leavis asked permission to import a copy of *Ulysses* for teaching purposes. Not only was his request denied, but the Home Office had him spied on and attempted to have his lectures suppressed. Joyce, oblivious to all this, was kept occupied with Anna Livia, HCE and their offspring, the continuing interest in *Ulysses*, and friends' demands on his time. There was also an opera of Pound's and six concerts by Antheil to attend. Encouragingly enough, Miss Beach reported that 'A Cambridge student told me that they had no other god before you in Cambridge, and said that no man would dare to say anything against a line you had written. He would be beyond the pale. The professors lecture principally on the works of James Joyce and the students of English have *Ulysses* given to them and are obliged to read it twice.'[106] Clearly, censorious officialdom had been well and truly outwitted.

In July, Lucia, approaching her nineteenth birthday, was back enjoying herself among her friends at Deauville, while Giorgio would celebrate his twenty-first far from a concert platform. To escape the Paris heat-wave, Joyce and Nora left for Ostend. They settled at the Hôtel de l'Océan where, much to Joyce's delight, the porter answered the phone saying 'Ici le portier de l'Océan' – 'Porter of the Ocean.'[107] Never able to resist a good language he soon got down to learning Flemish.[108] Most of all he enjoyed the seafront, and took up running, one day covering six or seven kilometres between Middelkerke and Mariakerke. Ostend, he told Harriet, was 'by far the best place' they had been to for a summer holiday.[109]

However, his enjoyment did not last. First there was a thunderstorm which kept him awake all night; then word came that Samuel Roth had started publishing *Ulysses* serially in *Two Worlds*, claiming he had 'an arrangement' with Joyce to do so. The 'Telemachus' chapter had already appeared, and, even more infuriatingly, the issue had been dedicated to him, 'with admiration'. He was at a loss to know what to do. Suddenly he decided that the summer was 'tiresome' and 'bad-tempered', and that Nora had become unhappy, and they considered moving to Ghent.[110]

But then an epiphany captivated him and he lingered a while longer. Sitting under the lighthouse, a little girl of about four climbed up the rocks beside him and began filling his pockets with tiny shells until he sent her away with a coin. It was only then that he remembered that St Patrick's father was keeper of the Boulogne lighthouse, and that the mad Caligula, its founder, had ordered his soldiers to gather seashells as loot along this coast.[111] This conjunction of ideas surfaces in the first chapter of the *Wake*: 'Haroun Childeric Eggeberth', master mason, 'would caligulate by multiplicables the alltitude and malltitude until he seesaw by neatlight of the liquor wheretwin 'twas born ...'[112]

The spell was broken when Georg Goyert arrived with the 900-page proofs of the German edition of *Ulysses*, translated by him and Ivan Goll for Rhein-Verlag in Basel. The publishers were anxious to launch it in November, so they quickly got down to proofreading. Joyce found it full of idiotic errors and breaks – but that, he decided, was only to be expected with 'financial literature'.[113] Unhappy with the translation, he told Rhein-Verlag that if they published it uncorrected he would remove his name from the book. Before Goyert left, Joyce asked Miss Beach to give him a copy of his *Ulysses* schema.

With the German translation now corrected and the French translation still struggling through storms, the autumn issue of *900: Cahiers d'Italie et d'Europe* carried Auguste Morel's translation of the musical 'Calypso' episode.[114] Obtaining this translation was a triumph for the magazine's Paris editor, twenty-two-year-old Nino Frank. Frank had visited Square Robiac seeking Joyce's permission to list him as one of the magazine's editorial consultants. He recalled Joyce as sitting behind a wall of silence, looking like a latter-day Quixote, 'the Knight of the Mournful Countenance, the toughest literary hero known', while still essentially the Irishman of Dublin, 'Seventh City of Christendom'.[115] To Frank's surprise Joyce agreed for his name to be used, and that was how the fragment of the French *Ulysses* came to appear in the autumn number.

Joined by their children, the Joyces left Ostend for Antwerp where they were chased by mosquitoes, and headed, by way of Ghent, for Brussels. They took a day-trip to Waterloo where, according to Chapter 1 of the first Book of the *Wake*, 'Willingdone' (on his famous 'white harse, the Cokenhape') helped by 'the Prooshious', defeated 'Lipoleum'.[116] By chance, on the same trip was the aspiring young American novelist Thomas Wolfe. He was too shy to speak to Joyce but was fascinated by him and his family. Nora seemed to him a 'typical middle-class French woman', vulgar and 'not very intelligent looking'. Lucia he thought 'rather pretty ... [like] ... a little American flapper', while Joyce, struck him as 'a bit stagey', with his coat draped around his shoulders. However, he liked the look of him. 'His face was highly coloured, slightly concave – his mouth thin, not delicate, but extraordinarily humorous. He had a large powerful straight nose – redder than his face, somewhat pitted with scars and boils'[117] – probably the work of the Antwerp mosquitoes. Wolfe was struck by the strange way the family sat apart in the bus on the way back to Brussels.

Through Sylvia Beach, acting as his US agent, Joyce learned that *The Dial* had accepted 'The Four Watches of Shaun', for which he was still sending her his corrections.[118] However, having accepted the piece on 10 September, Marianne Moore, editor of *The Dial*, declined it on the 17th. When she suggested publishing one part rather than all four, it was Joyce's turn to refuse, asking for his manuscript back. He immediately began revising 'Anna Livia Plurabelle' for Wyndham Lewis's magazine, *The Enemy*, and sent copies to Harriet and Miss Beach announcing that he had finished with 'Mrs Delta', but she had by no means stopped babbling.[119]

Miss Beach, whose royalties had been funding his holiday, announced a 'bumper' sale of *Ulysses* that summer and on receiving additions to one of his 'Shaun' episodes told Joyce that she could hardly hold her pen for laughing. 'I am enjoying it so much! What "fun for all"!'[120] Pound, seeing a copy, was rather less amused, telling Joyce, 'So far as I make out, nothing short of divine vision or a new cure for the clapp can possibly be worth all the circumambient peripherization.' There was not even the inkling of a joke there. 'And in any case I don't see what which has to do with where . . .'[121]

In late September Joyce reported having chalked up some sixty-four Flemish lessons and was planning to insert Flemish words into his novel. Jokingly he suggested that Harriet should 'order' him to write something. Entering into the spirit of this invitation she sent him a pamphlet about 'The Giant's Grave', a set of stone relics in the graveyard of St Andrew's Church at Penrith, where she was spending the summer with Dora Marsden, helping research her ambitious philosophical work, *Definition of the Godhead*. She appended the message:

> To Messrs Jacques le Joyeux, Giacomo Jakob, Skeumas Sheehy and whole Company:/Sirs: Kindly supply the undersigned with a full length grave account of his esteemed Highness Rhaggrick O'Hoggnor's Hogg Tomb as per photos enclosed and oblige/Yours faithfully/Henriette Vévère.[122]

The cluster of stones was said to mark the burial place of Owen Caesarius, a tenth-century King of Cumbria. The image brought to mind his own 'big cleanminded giant H. C. Earwicker', a modern manifestation of Finn MacCool, the sleeping giant whose head, according to legend, formed the Hill of Howth and whose feet were hills just beyond Dublin's Phoenix Park. This image of the giant he placed at the beginning of the *Wake* where his swerving, bending, recirculating riverrunning Anna Liffey ultimately returns the reader back to Howth Castle and Environs, the initials heralding the novel's hero. The fall of Earwicker, the fall of Humpty Dumpty and the pratfall of the knockabout comedian mirroring the Biblical Fall itself, echo the fearful thunderous crack which sets the Viconian cycle in motion. (In Joyce's cycle, after the Fall would come the confusion of tongues.) He put in a great initial burst of energy working to fulfil Harriet's order, he said, but, 'almost stupefied', spent three whole days recovering, reading Anita Loos's *Gentlemen Prefer Blondes*.

With Stanislaus's nuptials impending, and in no mood to travel to Italy, Joyce declined to attend the wedding but sent the happy couple 6,000 lire and his best wishes. A month after their return to Paris a tragedy was about to engulf the Joyce family. Eileen, holidaying alone in Ireland, cabled pleading for money, saying, that without it her husband Frank would be ruined.[123] Joyce, puzzled, forwarded the telegram to Stanislaus, asking what it could mean. The answer was not long coming. On 7

November Eileen cabled Stannie saying that she was leaving Dublin and wanting to know if there was anything wrong with Frank, with whom she had lost contact. Stannie knew but wasn't going to break the bleak news to her at long distance. After embezzling money from his bank, Frantisek Schaurek had shot himself. Joyce, guilt-stricken at not answering his sister's earlier plea, offered his lame excuses to Stanislaus – his holiday and winter clothes for his children had been extremely expensive, and having sent him his 6,000 lire wedding present he had been unable to raise another large sum at short notice.

When Eileen arrived in Paris on 10 November, she was told nothing, and left for Trieste thinking that Frank had gone to Prague to settle with the bank the matter of some 75,000 francs he had 'borrowed'. Joyce told her he could not help, having no bank account in Paris.[124] Stanislaus could not understand the suicide. When Schaurek had 'borrowed' from the bank before, his manager had covered up for him and would have done so again. Joyce hinted, however, at another aspect to the suicide, by wondering why this 'unfortunate wretch' had been left alone in these circumstances. On being told in Trieste what had happened, Eileen refused to believe it and insisted on having her husband exhumed to see for herself what had happened. She then took to her bed for three months before returning with her two daughters to Ireland. Joyce decided to keep the affair from Giorgio and Lucia, thinking them too young to understand.[125] After discussing their sister's plight with Stanislaus, James agreed to send her £10 a quarter. He wrote explaining in detail why he could not afford more. Samuel Roth had killed his sales in America and now he was engaged in a costly lawsuit against him, he said.[126]

Eileen's tragedy did not stem the flow of Joyce's creativity. Always anxious to please his patron, he gave Harriet an insight into the thinking behind his new work, describing the shape of the book as it would emerge – a registered secret, he told her. It would end in the middle of a sentence and begin in the middle of the same sentence. Joyce's fascination with languages became increasingly evident as he explained himself to her. Clearly he was thinking in a multilingual fashion – resonances, associations, translations and the proliferation of meanings all springing from words and combinations of words. To all this he added a diagram of the circular journey from Hill of Howth via Phoenix Park, across the Plains of Dublin and back to Hill of Howth ('riverrun, past Eve and Adam's, from swerve of shore to bend of bay, brings us by a commodius vicus of recirculation back to Howth Castle and Environs'). On reading the passage and notes, Harriet wrote back, 'I am much interested in your way of beginning and ending (as you say) the book: or rather, not beginning and not ending: making a sort of circle of it, I suppose like those serpents of myth with their tails in their mouths, and adding that without the clues in his key the reader was left floundering.' Would it, she asked, be 'utterly against the grain, your convictions and principles' to publish an annotated edition to accompany an ordinary edition of the book when published?[127] It *was* against his nature and principles, but he did send her a further key, explaining more terms and thought-streams.

Quinn's successor, Paul Kieffer, refused to act against Roth so a direct approach to the US Attorney General was proposed in the hope of restraining the pirate. To this end, Joyce engaged the Paris-based American lawyer, Benjamin Conner, whose US colleagues took up the matter for Joyce in New York. Pound, who had tangled with Roth himself and come close to suing him, warned that Roth was an extremely wily and practised con man, a 'skunk' with no fear of the law. But Pound showed little sympathy for Joyce either. 'You are in worse shape than I was,' he told him, 'as you have taken money from him ... and you have known for some time that he was a crook. All I can suggest is that you write to as many papers as possible, denouncing Roth, and stating that the text is garbled and unauthorized.' He should also make clear that the parts of *Ulysses* that had been printed before its suppression were in copyright, and that he was proceeding against Roth. Alternatively, he told him, 'You can organize a gang of gunmen to scare [him] out of his pants. I don't imagine anything but physical terror works in a case of this sort (with a strong pull of avarice, bidding him to be BOLD).'[128] The gunman solution did not appeal to Joyce who decided to produce instead a letter of protest to distribute to the press.

Meanwhile he was about to make new and important friends who would help determine the fate of his new work. Having finished his Earwicker passage 'to order', he wanted to try it on a slightly larger audience, so around 14 December he invited Eugene and Maria Jolas, Elliot Paul, the Nuttings, and Misses Beach and Monnier to hear the opening pages of his new work. The Jolases and Paul, all Americans, were planning a new review of international literature to be called *transition*, which Sylvia Beach would publish, and were especially eager to hear him. As Eugene Jolas recalled, 'He read in a well-modulated, musical voice, and often a smile went over his face when he reached a particularly witty passage.' The effect was stunning. 'We were staggered by the revolutionary aspect of this fragment.' Afterwards he asked what they had thought of it, but to Jolas there was little to be said at all. 'It was obvious that we were faced with a unique literary work, one before which all critical canons would have to be abandoned.' The 'stream of consciousness' he had used in *Ulysses* had been replaced here with the 'stream of unconsciousness' with which few would sympathize. After the reading Joyce went to bed and collapsed – 'like the old gentleman' (HCE) he had been writing about, he said.[129] But for those present both the reading and work were a revelation,[130] and next day he received letters of congratulation and several bouquets.

26

Fending Off the Pirates and Envisioning the Invisible

(1927–1928)

'**Piracy**, *n*. Commerce without its folly-swaddles, just as God made it.' Ambrose Bierce, *The Devil's Dictionary* (1911)

Joyce's letter of protest against the pirating of *Ulysses* (composed with the help of Ludwig Lewisohn and Archibald MacLeish) was awaiting distribution. Roth's piracy, it declared, was 'a matter of the gravest import not only to all writers but to all honest men' against which American law offered no protection; the good name of American publishing and literature was at stake. 'The undersigned colleagues and admirers and friends of Mr Joyce,' it concluded, 'protest to American publishers and to American readers not primarily in the name of an esoteric masterpiece but in the name of common honour and honesty and of that security of the works of the intellect and the imagination without which art cannot live.' By the end of January it had attracted the signatures of Gide, Wells, Bennett, Larbaud, and even critics of Joyce such as D. H. Lawrence, Wyndham Lewis and Virginia Woolf. Nothing could bring writers together so effectively as a threat to their copyright. And who would want their name excluded from so august a company?

Pound was one of the few dissenting voices, blaming instead the 'infamous' American law which tolerated the robbery of authors. By comparison, he said, Roth's action was a 'minor peccadillo'. Coincidentally, Roth dedicated the April issue of *Two Worlds* to Pound, who for good measure wrote telling Joyce that he considered *Work in Progress* a bad 'stunt'. The *transatlantic review* had published it, he said, only to help fill its pages, and any further publication would only harm his reputation. The Pound who had once proclaimed Joyce as 'a grrreat man' was clearly having second thoughts. Shaw, also suspecting a Joycean stunt, withheld his signature, too. 'The protest is all poppycock,' he told Sylvia Beach. 'Nobody that the pirate cares about will blame him for taking advantage of the law.' And by publicizing the matter Joyce was inviting others to rush out their own editions of his book, which would, of course, only further increase his reputation.[1] However, despite losing the support of one Nobel Prize winner, Joyce was delighted and 'honoured' to win the support of another – Albert Einstein.

To celebrate his forty-fifth birthday on 2 February 1927, the fifth anniversary of *Ulysses*, and to mark the despatch of his protest letter, Joyce planned a party at Langer's on the Champs-Elysées to which Beach, Monnier, the Archibald MacLeishes, Sisley Huddleston, Larbaud, Power, the French philosopher and novelist Julien Benda and McGreevy (now lecturing at the Ecole Normale Supérieure) were all invited. The bill, he told Beach, would be between 1,000 and 2,000 francs which he asked her to lend him until Monro sent him the money. Alternatively, he said, he could pass the hat round among his guests.[2]

The letter had now collected 167 signatures, including George Russell, Lady Gregory, Sherwood Anderson, Benedetto Croce, Julian Green, Julien Benda, Norman Douglas, Edouard Dujardin, Ernest Hemingway, Somerset Maugham and two more Nobel Prize winners – Yeats and Knut Hamsun. When this was despatched with due solemnity, many English and American papers refused to publish it for fear of libel, but it received wide coverage in press comment and reports. On 3 March *The Times* ran a story on the letter under the headline '*Ulysses* Conspiracy' and the *Sunday Express* carried an article of support by Arnold Bennett, stating that 'Joyce is a very important figure in the evolution of the novel.'[3] Yeats, equally enthusiastic, mentioned the petition in the Irish Senate, calling *Ulysses* 'the work of an heroic mind'.

But not everyone thought so. Wyndham Lewis now decided to attack every modernist in sight. In the latest issue of *The Enemy*, he called Pound 'a revolutionary simpleton' and Joyce and Gertrude Stein 'time-obsessed' and driven by unconscious romantic inclinations. Yeats said Lewis was 'philosophically naïve'.[4] Joyce responded by lampooning Lewis in *Work in Progress* as the humourless Ondt against his self-indulgent carefree Gracehoper.[5] Short of money again, through Harriet, Joyce asked Monro to cash in some of his stock. He offered his pen and several manuscripts for sale in Paris but there were no takers, which hardly boosted his self-confidence. More encouragingly, when Joyce gave a further reading to friends of Miss Monnier, it seemed to have had a profound effect on all present, not least on himself. Afterwards he went home and slept for an hour and a half.[6]

When Harriet told him to take it easy for a while, he wrote another joky letter saying that all work was now suspended in 'The JJ Safety Pun Factory' and signed himself 'Wouldbe Pennyman'. However, his fragile ego was again threatened when, aware of Pound's views, she wrote, 'Perhaps when your book is finished you will see fit to lend ear to some of your older friends (E.P. to be included ...) but the time to talk of the matter is not yet.'[7] It seemed that she was siding with Pound and he was clearly hurt, telling her, 'Your letter gave me a nice little attack of brainache.'[8] Didn't she like anything he was writing? he asked her gloomily. Pound could make brilliant judgements but also screaming howlers. He could at least inform her that the editors of *transition* so liked what she disliked that they had taken it for their very first issue in April, with the other episodes following in sequence.

Suddenly aware of how easily he could be upset, Harriet wrote of her distress at having caused him pain. 'It seems to be my mission to upset my best friends,' she said. But, then, in trying to explain herself, she only compounded the offence by saying that while she liked some of his new work, 'I am made in such a way that I do not care much for the output of your Wholesale Safety Pun Factory nor for the darknesses and unintelligibilities of your deliberately entangled language system. It seems to me you are wasting your genius. But daresay I am wrong and in any case you will go on with what you are doing, so why thus stupidly say anything to discourage you? I hope I shall not do so again.'[9] He was nonplussed by this expression of disbelief in his work and the ghost of Mrs McCormick must have risen before him. According to Maria Jolas he was so devastated that he took to his bed, unable to work for several days. Eventually he wrote telling Harriet that the accusation that he was wasting his talent was so grave he would prefer to reconsider his dubious and disheartened defence before replying fully.[10] She, now as distressed as him, replied by return, 'Can you not treat my last two letters as unwritten and unreceived?'[11]

When Roth proposed paying him $1,000 to admit that he had offered him *Ulysses* before publication, Joyce ordered his New York attorney not to reply. (Joyce did later decide to accept Roth's cheque in payment for the fragments of *Work in Progress* he had published, but not for the unauthorized use of *Ulysses* episodes.) Ironically enough, in a separate action in New York, Roth was facing a charge of publishing 'stories and poems that would tend to corrupt and destroy public morals'. It looked as though he had committed the same sin that had nearly sent the *Little Review* editors to jail.

In defending himself to Harriet, Joyce told her how he had shown some of his recent poems to Pound and asked whether he should publish them. Pound had said he had best put them in his family Bible or album along with his family portraits. But, thinking the American's judgement suspect, Joyce passed the poems to Archibald MacLeish for an opinion. He was, he told Harriet, sorry his work had given her no pleasure, but he was soldiering on somehow, even if somewhat deflated. Keeping himself at the right pitch was difficult, what with the Roth affair and the Schaurek suicide. Clearly upset, Harriet replied that had she known the terrible time he was having she would never have written as she had. Hoping to make amends, she told him that the comic interchange between Jeff and Mutt, his primeval versions of Shem and Shaun, in his latest fragment, had amused her. 'I found it more self-explanatory than some of the other cross-word puzzle 'ems.'[12]

Joyce probably found more satisfaction in a letter from MacLeish, who, having read his poems, told him that he could safely publish them without damaging his reputation. 'They have the strangest quality of "existence". They are not things that are in the process of becoming as so much modern poetry – even some of Pound's best.'[13] The collection, which included his poems to Giorgio and Lucia ('On the Beach at Fontana' and 'Simples'), would eventually appear as *Pomes Penyeach*, a title which Stanislaus considered ridiculous.

Lucia was now dancing with a group calling itself Les Six de Rythme et Couleur. When, in February, they appeared at the Théâtre du Vieux-Colombier, one reviewer commended them on their 'comprehensive and lofty' programme and the group's 'great originality', which was well received by the audience.[14] Even Nora, not always sympathetic to her daughter's ambitions as a dancer, must have realized that she had some talent after all. Her proud father certainly thought so.

The PEN Club in London had invited Joyce to be guest of honour at a dinner on 5 April, and, since so many English writers had signed his protest letter, he agreed to go. Nora was unable to travel (due to the state of her nerves, said Joyce) and he limited his visit to three days, taking Auguste Morel along for company, and presumably for helping him across roads when necessary. The dinner was presided over by John Drinkwater, the playwright, who had attended the première of *Exiles* and seemed to know Joyce's work well. Afterwards, when Joyce met Harriet, his new work, which had so baffled her, was a keen topic of conversation. She was as anxious to reassure him that she was well disposed towards it as he was in need of that reassurance. When she asked him what he intended calling it, he suggested that she guess. The mystery of the title became an important game for him, part of the Joycean legend he was never reluctant to foster. He had succeeded in intriguing his patron and over the coming months she would hazard various guesses. The quest for the secret title would ensure that she never entirely lost interest in the work.

Back in Paris he wrote telling her that he had revised what he had discussed with her when they met – his parable of the Mookse and the Gripes (Joyce's working of Aesop's 'Fox and the Grapes', another symbolic representation of strife between Shem and Shaun) – and afterwards had been prostrated for twenty-four hours. She must not think it was nonsense. 'I am really one of the greatest engineers, if not the greatest, in the world besides being a musicmaker, philosophist and heaps of things,' and then he offered another metaphor for his novel – a wheel without spokes. 'It's a wheel, I tell the world. *And* it's all *square*.'[15] To this she replied, 'You are so incorrigibly absurd, solemn though you may feel about it all!' which sounded as though finally she was getting the joke. For a moment she seemed quite carried away by this realization. She took two sentences from his manuscript as a clue:

> 'Well now, let us, by memory inspired, turn the wheel again to the whole of the wall. Let us remember there was a city which had a wall: and the city stood foursquare – four walls square – and its four square walls turned round and round and round – a merry-go-round, an ever-go-round – around and around and around.' Is that how it was? A wheeling square? or squaring the wheel? And somewhere very near there the name of the book is in hiding – isn't that what you were driving at? Haven't I nearly engineered the name? I remember when you made me a list of your signs years ago □ stood for the name of the book: but you did not then add that it must revolve ... But surely there is to be a spoke in the wheel – one crooked mixed spoke at any rate?[16]

She might also have noted in *Ulysses* that there are references to Bloom's one-time ambition of squaring the circle,[17] and that Joyce was attempting to convey a wheeling maelstrom of unconsciousness within the square confines of a book. But his metaphor does suggest that he was consciously attempting to write the impossible novel.

More immediately, faced with his continual pleas of poverty and requests for money, Miss Beach finally exploded with exasperation, feeling she was being taken for a ride by a silver-tongued persuader.

> You said you only had 9,000 francs a month to live on and then I reminded you that *Ulysses* had brought you 125,000 since last August. It makes about 12,000 francs a month doesn't [it], which added to 9,000 makes about 21,000 a month. You didn't consider the *Ulysses* royalties important enough to mention. But it would be more sportsmanlike of you to own to spending this considerable sum of money than to tell a lot of cock-and-bull stories to me who is your friend if ever you had one. You are the greatest writer who ever lived but even Pound has more sense.[18]

Anxious to mollify her, he offered her the manuscripts of some *Dubliners* stories and a dummy of the first edition. And coming from Trieste, he told her, were 1,500 pages of the first draft of *A Portrait* (*Stephen Hero*) which Yeats had told him were valuable and should not be sold cheaply. With peace finally declared between author and bookseller, Beach agreed to publish *Pomes Penyeach*, the manuscript of which Joyce told her she could also keep. To thwart the pirates he assigned world rights to her, much as he had done with *Ulysses*.

In her shop window, Beach had been displaying an open copy of the previous autumn's number of *900*, carrying Morel's translation of the 'Calypso' episode of *Ulysses*. Joyce disapproved of titles being given to the various chapters, and said there should be a footnote saying that such overt parallels with Homer's story were not in the original text. However, not everyone approved the translation. In April 1927 Morel's text attracted the attention of a retired judge from the British Imperial Civil Service. Stuart Gilbert, Oxford-educated son of a British Army officer and grandson of an Indian raja, had read the novel four years earlier in Burma, where he was dishing out British justice to the natives – mostly by hanging them, he claimed.

Obtaining a copy of *900*, Gilbert compared the translation with the original text, and noticed discrepancies between what he called 'the otherwise excellent translation' and the original. He mentioned this to Miss Beach who suggested that he prepare a note listing the errors he found and send them to Joyce. He did so, saying, 'There are others, less apparent, which, nevertheless, might interest you, and I am at your disposal, should you care to hear my observations.' As to his motive, he added, 'I hope the translation of *Ulysses* may do for French literature what the original has done for English and that nothing may be lost in transit,' and he was not interested in any acknowledgement for this or any payment.[19] The offer was accepted, the number of French translators expanded to six, and into Joyce's circle came a brilliant if sardonic observer of the often bizarre Joyce family.

When Harriet sent him a letter with her latest cogitations on the wheel-square conundrum, Joyce told her he had incorporated some of her ideas into his book. She in turn continued urging him to include annotations to enlighten the bemused reader. He ignored the suggestion, but, just for her, when the April *transition* published the first episode of *Work in Progress*, he sent her a list of almost fifty items, explaining their allusions and hidden meanings. The *transition* issue so delighted him that he ordered free copies to be mailed to his various friends every month at the cost of 400 francs a year.

The city was again beginning to tire him and he planned to take a break on the Dutch coast. Depressed by the worldwide chorus of vilification of what he called 'my experiment in interpreting "the dark night of the soul"' (the latest to express a dislike for it was Sydney Schiff), he was tempted, he told Harriet, to lay down his pen and let someone else pick it up for the second part he had outlined, if only he could find someone as 'absurd' as himself. He soon lighted on a suitably 'absurd' person – the poet and novelist James Stephens, who his enquiries revealed had been born in Dublin on the same day as himself (though no record will confirm this). There was also the combination of his name with that of his hero in *A Portrait*, and their initials together, J.J. and S., was colloquial Irish for John Jameson & Sons Dublin whiskey, which would look nice on the title page.[20] Later he put the matter to Stephens, telling him that he needed someone to take on the novel if ever he was too blind to continue.

His escape to the Dutch coast was dogged by bad weather. The plan was to stay in Scheveningen, but the weather was so wretched that he, Nora and Lucia holed up at the Grand Hotel Victoria at The Hague, taking the ten-minute tram ride down to the coast from time to time. The Dutch, he reported, were agreeable and not grasping, and the strand was 'wild and endless'. On 25 May, Joyce took a stroll along the beach before lying down to pore over his Baedeker. Suddenly he was pitched into his own worst nightmare, under attack from a savage dog. He managed to beat off the creature until the owner arrived and pulled it away. But then, when the man's back was turned, the dog attacked him again. In his confusion and panic his glasses were smashed and he lost one of his lenses. After the dog had been dragged off and secured, he and the owner had to grope around the sand on hands and knees before the missing lens was finally found. He felt so defenceless with 'those detestable animals', he said. Even if he had had a revolver the hound would have pounced on him before he had made up his mind to fire.[21]

On 7 June, the family left for Amsterdam where Joyce spent Bloomsday in bed, suffering from a cold. The omens for him were not auspicious. Although he was soon recovered, catastrophic thunderstorms and cyclones, sweeping across Holland and causing many deaths and much devastation, finally drove them back to Paris. There Joyce found that his friend Richard Wallace was dying of gangrene, Miss Beach's mother had committed suicide, *Work in Progress* was unwanted by American publishers, publication of his poems was delayed, he had lost the photograph of his father's portrait which he always carried with him, and he was left unable to concentrate. Strain and tragedy were all about him, he told Harriet, added to which he was again short of funds.[22]

Although she was unhappy that he was eating into his capital, Harriet quietly arranged to have a cheque sent. In thanking her, Joyce had yet more bad news. Wallace was dead and Miss Beach, in dispute with her

New York lawyers, had withdrawn from the suit against Roth. The pirate in turn had launched his own defence fund, declaring Joyce a 'renegade jew' backed by an organization with 'vast funds' behind it. One of Harriet's latest stabs at his title, *Phoenix Park*, he said was 'rather close',[23] but a month later she came up with her closest guess to date – *Finn MacCool*.[24]

Paris that summer was stifling as usual and, with most Square Robiac inhabitants out of town, the place was shuttered, leaving an atmosphere of stuffiness and claustrophobia. Even so, Joyce completed his Chapter 6 for *transition*, sending the typescript, drafts and proofs to Harriet for safe keeping. Meanwhile Miss Beach, who published his poems on 5 July, was accumulating Joyceana of her own – the first draft of *A Portrait*, copies of 'The Day of the Rabblement', 'The Holy Office', 'Gas from a Burner', and a programme for Mary Sheehy's play *Cupid's Confidante*, listing Joyce in the cast.

There were riots in the city following the execution of the anarchists Sacco and Vanzetti in America on 23 August, and foreigners were being rounded up and asked for their identity cards. He considered fleeing Paris but could not face the southern resorts swarming with Americans, and England, he thought, would be too expensive. So Giorgio and Lucia were sent to the Channel coast while he stayed put with Nora, working on his book and tidying up the 'Oxen of the Sun' episode for the German edition due out in September.[25] When Rhein-Verlag finally published it, he was surprisingly impressed – 'a most "kolossal" and princely edition', he said.[26]

Quite unexpectedly, his landlord issued a new contract from the following April requiring a down-payment, and a doubling of the rent from October. Softening up Harriet for another sale of his stock, Joyce again declared himself drained of the will to continue by negative criticism, and pleading general wretchedness. 'My sight is not good, many operations have made [me] more diffident than ever,' and there was that lawsuit against Roth to fight. He had, he said, spent a good 10,000 hours on Parts 1 and 3, and could not begin to embark on Part 2 unless he was no longer under strain.[27]

He was ill in bed at the end of September and then immersed in revising 'Anna Livia Plurabelle' for *transition 8*, weaving in more river names to enhance its fluidity. 'I think it moves,' he wrote, and by mid-October it was finished, 1,200 hours slaving for just seventeen pages, he told Larbaud. Since he had first heard it his Anna Liffey had proliferated. 'Her fluvial maids of honour from all ends of the earth I now number about 350 I think.'[28] Completing it, he said, had left him 'considerably wound up'.[29] But even then he could not resist adding more river names as they occurred to him. He invited a few friends round to Square Robiac for a reading of the finished work.

Around twenty-five people came to the apartment on the afternoon of 2 November, including the Colums, Nuttings and Jolases, Elliot Paul, McAlmon, Hemingway, Larbaud and a few other French writers. Those present, recalled McAlmon, were 'seated about the room, grave as owls'.[30] Reporting later to Harriet, Joyce said that he thought his reading had left the listeners deeply impressed (a mere twenty-five people of the world's many millions) but it had left him shattered.[31] Even after it appeared in *transition 8* that month, the revision machine was still churning. 'Since it came out,' he said, 'I have woven into the printed text another 152 rivernames and it is now final.'[32] This was the form he intended for a de luxe edition for which James R. Wells of Crosby Gaige Books had offered him £300. But his feelings of exhaustion continued and he had to rest from *transition* work for a couple of months.

Even so, his social life did not stagnate. Irishmen, he said, had begun to knock at his door that winter. Among them were McGreevy, planning to lecture on him at the Ecole, and his old friend J. F. Byrne ('Cranly'), who brought news that his erstwhile medical crony and tormentor, Cosgrave, had recently concluded his own riverrun, drowned in the unsavoury waters of the Thames. Byrne was a good reader and Joyce was thrilled when he read aloud passages from *Anna Livia* in a pure Dublin accent. That weekend, Joyce showed him around Paris taking him to meet Miss Beach whom he had asked to have 1,000 francs waiting for him.

Wyndham Lewis had never returned Joyce's 'Four Watches of Shaun', but instead, in *Time and Western Man*, published that autumn, he used it to attack him again for being obsessed with technique. He followed this with a campaign in *The Enemy* against the so-called 'Revolution of the Word' proclaimed by Eugene Jolas's *transition*. No doubt Joyce, like others, was puzzled by this hostile duplicity from the editor of *Blast* who had once included him in his pantheon of the blessed.

For Lucia, dancing had become an escape from the atmosphere of silent intensity which mostly hung over 2 Square Robiac. Although, like Giorgio, she chose not to be part of the complex creative world of her father, she was aware that aspects of her were woven into the characters of the young women (including his own daughter) who arouse the voyeuristic Bloom. Now she had become a key model for her father's mythic muse Isolde or Issy – subjects of the sometime incestuous thoughts of H. C. Earwicker – at least, according to her biographer, she believed so.

Harriet's ambivalence towards his new work continued to trouble Joyce. Sometimes she seemed to enjoy the impish spirit of his word-play and share his fascination with the great moving shifting saga he was creating, but at other times to despair of his 'squandered' genius. Sylvia Beach, who observed his misery, decided to try to ease matters by writing to her. 'He seems to be very unhappy,' she wrote, 'because the new work does not please you for whom it has been written. He wouldn't mind about anybody else not liking it. He often says to me bitterly, "Miss Weaver doesn't care for it." And yet he feels that some parts of his new book are the best work that he has done and that he can do.'[33]

Obviously upset by her friend's letter, Harriet replied that it grieved her to be unable to share Joyce's current enthusiasm, but she preferred his plainer writing. 'Perhaps I shall get really to like his new style in time and it would be a great help towards this, I am sure, if I could share the pleasure and advantage of hearing the pieces read by himself as they are written, for they seem to be essentially oral.' But she liked to see every word and phrase, know what lay behind it and know why it was written. 'I have the feeling all the time that his genius and his immense labours are being to some extent vested in producing what appears to me to be – to put it baldly – a curiosity of literature ... [However] it distresses me to hurt him and I wish he would not always so insistently ask me how I like the pieces. I *do* like immensely the ending of *Anna Livia* and have told him so.'[34] She had not expected this letter to be shown to Joyce, but it was. It depressed him so much he was unable to resume work. It was a fitting end to what he considered a grim year.[35]

The first letter Joyce wrote in 1928 was to Harriet, explaining how he had done no work for two whole months, stricken with fatigue and now colitis, and faced with the prospect of an eighth eye operation by Borsch. His doctor had told him that his intestinal pains were caused by his mental state, and it was her (Harriet's) lack of faith in him which had brought this on. He no longer had the mind or heart to continue 'wasting his genius' on what she had called 'a mere curiosity of literature', or to manage the susceptibilities of others as he had hitherto. He needed to clarify with her what she had meant by her words, which she had repeated, even after telling him she regretted having written them. Perhaps he should come to London to talk things over with her. He was no genius, he said. If he were, he would probably not appreciate the generosity and intuition with which she had inspired him in the past.[36]

On receiving his letter, Harriet immediately wired back saying she would come to Paris to clear up their misunderstanding. His pains disappeared almost immediately, he told her, although the belladonna (atropine) prescribed by Borsch might have helped. Harriet was upset that

Beach had shown Joyce her letter and now regretted having involved herself in his literary life – although it was Joyce who had invited her into it in the first place.

Faced with a demand for a further 4,000 francs for his new lease and a New York lawyer's bill of 6,000 francs, Joyce again asked Harriet to help. He had got into the habit of asking Monro Saw to sell shares to cover unexpected bills and fund his extravagant lifestyle. But Monro had informed him that from 1 April, his investments would be bringing him in £75 a month and, faced with yet another request for money, warned that disposing of too much stock would jeopardize his future earnings.[37] Fortunately, there was a revised offer from James Wells at Crosby Gaige for 'Anna Livia Plurabelle' which they planned to publish with a preface by Padraic Colum, so, for the time being, those evenings at Les Trianons could merrily proceed.

With his appetite for work restored, Joyce soon had his next episode ready for the February *transition*, in which Dolph (Shem) and Kev (Shaun), studying the sweep of human knowledge, come to blows, while their sister dreams of love. Absorption in work temporarily curbed his wander-lust. Invited to attend an International Book Fair in Florence in April he declined, pleading ill-health. He had avoided Italy since the Fascist take-over and their attempt to conscript Giorgio. In what he called 'a fine panegyric' he recommended his 'stand-in', James Stephens, who was delighted to accept.

When Harriet arrived in late January, Joyce spent a good deal of time explaining his book to her and slowly gaining her sympathy and under-standing of what he was attempting. It was a great weight off his mind and he had no recurrence of his stomach cramps. She planned to remain for two weeks, to reacquaint herself with her two bookseller friends and be there for Joyce's birthday. It may have been to celebrate that occasion that he had his photograph taken by Man Ray's assistant, Berenice Abbott. This time he seemed more relaxed than previously, posed nonchalantly at an angle in a chair, stick held lightly against his right leg, staring through dark glasses from under a jauntily angled hat. His attitude sug-gests that old 'far-away look', perhaps indicating either creative silence – or simply Bloomesque woolgathering.

Impressions of his forty-sixth birthday party at 2 Square Robiac were recorded by Helen Nutting.

Miss Weaver sitting on the sofa with Bob McAlmon beside her, she as tongue-tied as he was voluble. He looked at her from time to time as if thinking, Must I say it all? She, dignified and unworldly, with curled locks just over her ears, like a Victorian wooden doll, looked down at her lap and would have daunted most people. One feels a presence but dumb and sealed. I know Joyce has been reading to her a great deal and talking over his work.

Adrienne Monnier, she noted, sat filling a chair, 'immense and shapeless ... bright and talkative, trying to keep the conversation going ... Lucia, Mrs Antheil, and Kitten sat on the sofa. Lucia's face is fine and thoughtful this winter, Kitten handsome and plump, and Mrs Antheil small and dark ... elegant and discreet.' Joyce and Nora hovered in the background until Adrienne turned the conversation to her latest indulgence – spiritualism. The only spirit he believed in, Joyce remarked sardonically, was *'l'esprit de l'escalier'* – the witty riposte thought of too late.

George Antheil then entertained with Old English music while Joyce and McAlmon danced silently and inventively in the back parlour, McAlmon moving to 'negro rhythms', Joyce attempting the delicate-stepping Greek style practised by Lucia. Adrienne exclaimed, *'Mais regardez donc ce Joyce; il est tout a fait Gréque. C'est le satyr sur un vase grec!'* ('But look at Joyce; he is completely Greek ... the satyr on a Greek vase!') Then McAlmon sang a bowdlerized version of a blues number about the sinking of the Titanic, and Joyce ran through his repertoire of Irish ballads. According to Helen, one of them, 'Oh, the Brown and the Yellow Ale!' he sang more beautifully than she had ever heard him, 'his voice charged with feeling ... pauses, long-held notes, rolled rrr's, melancholy, a right-ness of pronunciation'. Arthur Power said, 'You will never hear anything so Irish as that. It is pure Irish.' After three songs he stopped, and there was champagne, more dancing and singing, and the atmosphere grew relaxed. Meanwhile, Harriet remained calm and still while McAlmon got merry on champagne and Irish whiskey.[38] Her visit had left Joyce in good spirits – more carefree, more at ease with himself.

He was amused to note that throughout whatever turmoil surrounded him, Lucia danced serenely. With her dance troupe under the direction of Lois Hutton and Margaret Morris, bohemian disciples of Raymond Duncan, that February she danced the part of a wild vine in a 'Ballet Faunesque' at the Comédie des Champs-Elysées. Joyce, who thought she had great talent, watched her with pride and pleasure, and was especially pleased when Harriet complimented her on her performance.[39] Nora's opinion remained unrecorded, but she was reportedly unhappy at having lost her daughter to the dance, believing it offered her no decent future.

In March, Eileen and her children came to stay for four days, with her brother stumping up 3,000 francs for their boat fares home. Next came Ettore Schmitz, who, thanks to Joyce, was now a literary celebrity as Italo

Svevo in both Italy and France and had just had a French translation of his third novel, *La Coscienza di Zeno*, published. In Paris he was honoured with a PEN Club dinner at La Closerie des Lilas attended by Isaak Babel, Ivan Goll, Jean Paulhan and Benjamin Crémieux, and presided over by the French writer and poet Jules Romains. To Nino Frank, who also attended, hearing Joyce speaking with Schmitz in Triestine-Italian revealed a different, simpler, more vivacious man. Trieste, he thought, was a place of lasting importance to Joyce – his second Dublin – and he and Svevo were 'men of genius, joined by an enigmatic kinship'.[40] Thereafter, Frank found himself part of Joyce's circle, invited to dine at Les Trianons and sent copies of *transition* including Joyce's contributions.[41]

Still needing help, Joyce asked Thomas McGreevy to undertake some secretarial work, typing his handwritten drafts. Revising the 'First Watch of Shaun' for the March *transition* had, he said, nearly flattened him, and he and Nora escaped for a week to Dieppe. He asked Miss Beach to send a copy of *The Canterbury Tales* which he said Nora must see, to meet the Wife of Bath who had also helped inspire her Ulyssean doppelgänger. More immediately inspiring, Harriet wrote to say that she had enjoyed his parable of the Ondt and the Gracehoper (based on the La Fontaine fable of the Ant and the Grasshopper), finding it much easier to follow than many of his others. She wrote in language imitating the text and wondered at 'the boundless number of "entomological" references ...'[42] Joyce was so delighted that he sent her a glossary explaining almost seventy of the strange neologisms in his fable.[43] At least he did not have the delicate task of explaining to the virginal Harriet such emblematic phrases as 'a very sexmosaic of nymphosis' from his *Criterion* contribution or 'private privysuckatary' from his fragment in *This Quarter*.

He was again suffering stomach pains and blamed the Dieppe climate. On 27 March the caravan moved south to Rouen. However, the search for material never ceased. His interest in Lewis Carroll[44] had been stirred by someone suggesting that his new language was imitation-Carroll, and he discovered two curious facts – that Carroll stuttered (like Earwicker) and his pen name was a reversal of his first two names, Charles and Ludwidge, translated as Ludwig (Lewis) and Carolus (Carroll). Both Alice and her author appear in *Finnegans Wake*, encoded as 'Ledwidge Salvatorious', she as the girl lost in 'Wonderlawn'. 'Alis, alas, she broke the glass! Liddell lokker through the leafery, ours is mistery of pain.'[45]

With much to do in Paris, Joyce returned at the end of March. First he saw Dr Thérèse Bertrand-Fontaine, a friend of Miss Beach and now his family doctor ('a gaunt, cold, grey woman', recalled Beckett), who told him that his inflamed intestine was much better, but he still needed to rest and recover from his nervous exhaustion and reverse his dramatic weight loss. He was given, he said ironically, a diet of 'oyster, Turkish Delight, Butter Scotch, coal, strychnine, hypo-phosphates, etc. etc.' – anything, edible or inedible.[46] Fontaine told him that Dieppe had been a mistake and advised him to go south. Next he had to sort out and massage the egos of his feuding French translators. But with pressure also coming from the *transition* editors to complete his next chapter, he felt too weak to do anything.

Ford Madox Ford turned up and took him out to dinner, inviting him to be godfather to his young daughter, and offering him his house in Toulon for a month. Joyce had qualms about promising to see that the girl was raised in accordance with the Catholic faith, considering such sponsorship pointless, but accepted the invitation 'as an act of friendliness'.[47] He had a fondness for the rotund, slightly dishevelled Englishman he nicknamed 'Father O'Ford' and honoured with a comic song celebrating his 'way' with young females and his multiple couplings.

The French general elections were due on 22 April and, because of previous unrest in the city, Joyce decided to escape to the south, as the doctor had recommended. On the 19th, after giving instructions to Beach, Giorgio and McGreevy to keep things going for him in Paris, he and Nora left for Avignon, the City of the Popes (where St Patrick is said to have stayed), intending to push on to Toulon later. On the long two-day train journey he composed riddles, a verse called 'Creeping to the Coast' for Miss Beach, and tried to puzzle out a mystery he had found in Lewis Carroll concerning the Jabberwock and the Cheshire cat. Carroll's word-spinning was now being subjected to Joycean dissection, offering a glimpse of the way his mind took and played with words as he continued to mine the language.

The *mistral* in Avignon was so fierce that he feared for his eyes and sent to Dr Collinson for eye-drops. Finally the unremitting wind drove them out of the papal city to Toulon and Ford's house. He loved the town, but, finding that the house, though picturesque, was entirely without amenities, he and Nora opted for the nearby Grand Hotel. There, unable to resist his daemon, he began to work through the sixteen notebooks he had brought along, diverted only by the 'heaps of proofs' sent from *transition* to be corrected for the summer issue, leaving him exhausted. He tried to relax by learning Provençal but had little energy for that either.

After two weeks in Toulon they returned to Avignon from where, to cover costs, Joyce asked Miss Beach for 3,000 francs on account. He sent her a case of Clos St Patrice (Châteauneuf-du-Pape), said to be from vines planted by St Patrick, which he also asked her to charge to his account, saying there was also one for Adrienne, two for Bird and two for Jean Cassabel, maître d'hôtel of Les Trianons. It was one of the very few red wines he enjoyed. After just five days in Avignon, they moved to Lyon before returning to Paris on 19 May just in time to attend a McCormack concert on the 22nd.

More and more of Joyce's friends and acquaintances were trying to find the most appropriate words with which to write intelligibly about his revolutionary form of writing. Frank Budgen had published an article about him in *transition 13* – 'The *Work in Progress* of James Joyce and Old Norse Poetry'[48] – and in the same issue there was one from Stuart Gilbert called 'Prolegomena to Work in Progress'. McGreevy, Rodker and one of Jolas's assistant editors, Robert Sage, were also working on essays for the autumn issue, and Joyce began to think that a dozen or so articles on the work by friends and admirers might form a publishable collection. He even came up with a suitably Joycean title – *Our Exagmination round His Factification for Incamination of Work in Progress*.

His work seemed particularly attractive to the American mind. According to Sylvia Beach, F. Scott Fitzgerald worshipped Joyce but was afraid to approach him, so she and Miss Monnier persuaded him and his wife Zelda to invite the Joyces to dinner with the French novelist André Chamson and his wife. The story went that Fitzgerald was so overcome at meeting his literary hero that he offered to jump out of the window in his honour. Joyce, however, declined to return this compliment and so both survived the evening. When Fitzgerald gave him his copy of *Ulysses* to sign, Joyce returned it with a photograph of himself signed as from his 'much obliged but most pusillanimous guest'.[49] Fitzgerald told his New York agent, Max Perkins, 'I was encouraged the other day when James Joyce came to dinner, when he said, "Yes, I expect to finish my novel in three or four years at the latest," and he works 11 hours a day to my intermittent 8. Mine will be done *sure* in September.'[50] In fact, *Tender is the Night*, which he had begun three years earlier, took a further six because of Zelda's mental breakdown, and not unsurprisingly perhaps incorporates the *monologue intérieur*.[51]

Having finished the fifth and final revision of 'The Second Watch of Shaun', Joyce was considering leaving for Copenhagen. But Lucia suddenly announced that she wanted to attend the Elizabeth Duncan Dance School in Salzburg that summer. The idea of their young daughter travelling alone through Europe disturbed both her parents. Lucia went to talk it over with her friend Kay Boyle, who was two years older. Boyle thought she cut a rather tragic figure, 'like the high, perishable, wishful tendril of a vine moving blindly up a wall'. Her parents' fears had affected her and she had become nervous about travelling to Salzburg alone. She asked if Boyle would accompany her, but the American was unable to get away. Joyce came later to discuss the matter with her, saying, 'As far as my children are concerned I am always asking the impossible. A father feels at a loss.'[52] He and Nora decided to forget Copenhagen and go to Salzburg themselves.

As soon as *transition 13* appeared in July, the Joyces left for Zurich before going 'on tour' to Austria, while Giorgio went holidaying in the Pyrenees. From Innsbruck, Joyce sent a card to Sylvia Beach saying they had been held up in 'the ALPs' by a thunderstorm which stopped their electric train. HCE, he wrote, thunders every moment. He had collected another river – the Inn, as fast as anything he had ever seen, silvery-grey and 'runs like a windhound loose' – one of those phrases he captured and stored. But there was too much 'Thor' about, he complained.[53] To Harriet he also referred to thunder as HCE, and said he hoped he would 'Exhaust Himself Completely' and withdraw into 'His Celestial Ether', so revealing the thunder at the centre of his book. By the end of the month they were booked into the Hotel Mirabelle in Salzburg, 'a lordly city,' Joyce thought, where they were expecting to be joined by Gilbert, now working on a book about the writing of *Ulysses*.

The Elizabeth Duncan Dance School was based at Klessheim Castle near the city, and there on 26 July they marked Lucia's twenty-first birthday. The place was so grand she became highly excited, weeping and singing in celebration. She had learned how to unleash her emotions through dance and what Joycean reserve she had inherited was clearly slipping away. At Klessheim, life was communal; the girls wore identical imitation silk tunics and shared a communal bath.[54] Under the influence of Duncan's companion, Max Merz, the school's ideology had become one of discipline and physical perfection, with, according to his critics, racist overtones.

The Salzburg Festival that summer offered plays by the Max Reinhardt Company and operas by Mozart and Richard Strauss. Among the visitors were John Drinkwater and his wife, the violinist Daisy Kennedy, who invited the Joyces for lunch and took them for walks. Drinkwater was a fan of both *Ulysses* and *Work in Progress* and wanted to discuss them at length. But Joyce had little energy for long discussions, so invited him to continue the conversation in London the following month. Others expected in Salzburg included his old Zurich acquaintance Stefan Zweig, George Antheil, still no further forward with the 'Cyclops' opera, and Stuart Gilbert and his French wife Moune. Gilbert was now busy on a book about *Ulysses*, though his would be less about the author and more a commentary on the text. When they met on 16 August Joyce suggested that he consider writing his biography, but the Englishman, no doubt foreseeing the shark-infested waters it would involve navigating, politely declined.

For Harriet, Joyce compiled another detailed glossary of his latest contribution to *transition*. It included words from the Maronite liturgy, and twenty-nine words for 'Peace'– the word, he told her, which had sighed around the world in 1918. She was getting all the detailed explanation she had requested. But this close writing and reading took its toll and on 12 August, Lucia, acting as his amanuensis, wrote to tell Harriet that her father's eyes were troubling him again and a local oculist, Dr Anton Toldt, had advised him to stop working.[55]

When Stanislaus and Nellie arrived in Salzburg on their honeymoon, Joyce probably saw them only as a blur. Stannie told his brother that he found his 'book of the night' incomprehensible and Jim, his own lights now dimmed, told him that the sequel would be a reawakening. But Stannie, quite out of sympathy with the project – probably detecting something of himself in the plodding, pedestrian Shaun – told him brusquely to get on and finish it. However, although Shaun the Post no longer had any influence over Shem the Penman, that did not stop him attacking his brother with increasing ferocity for (as he saw it) 'squandering his genius'. But, as he had noted during their youth, Jim was largely unmoved by criticism and refused to allow it to disturb his feelings for the one member of his family to whom he felt close.

At the end of August, with Lucia's summer school over, the family prepared to return to Paris in the company of the Gilberts. Under treatment from Toldt and with eye-drops from Collinson, Joyce's sight had improved, and en route for Paris he informed Miss Beach that he no longer had iritis, just conjunctivitis and slight episcleritis. For Gilbert, the leisurely two-week journey from Salzburg (with its numerous stopovers) was another chance to cross-examine the man whose book was the subject of his own. He took down his dictation and they picked through the text of *Ulysses* together. He was advised by Joyce to use different-coloured pencils for difficult words and phrases and was referred to Bérard's book on the origins of the *Odyssey*. They arrived back in Paris in mid-September.

Once re-installed at Square Robiac Joyce dictated a long letter to Harriet, bringing her up to date with his news. Since his return he had suffered another eye attack requiring daily visits to the eye clinic again, and wondered who was bewitching him. His mind had been blank for weeks, and if his eyes made working impossible – an eventuality, he said, that some would celebrate – he would head for Torquay, in his imagination at least. Word came that on a *real* journey, the Mephistophelean Gogarty had fallen out of a plane and walked away unscathed. More tragically, his good friend Ettore Schmitz, driving to Venice on 13 September, had died of a heart attack following a car accident at Motta di Livenza.

Rebecca West had published a new book, *The Strange Necessity*, in which she claimed that, having read *Pomes Penyeach*, she had discovered a great secret – that Joyce was a 'great man who is entirely without taste'.[56] He dismissed it saying that all she had succeeded in exploding was some 'bogus bogey personality'. More bruising was a *Criterion* article on language in modern literature by Sean O'Faolain which cited *Anna Livia Plurabelle*. 'Here,' it concluded, 'lies the condemnation of such language as Joyce's. It is not merely ahistoric – not merely the shadow of an animal that never was, the outline of a tree that never grew, for even then we might trace it to some basic reality distorted and confused – but it comes from nowhere, goes nowhere, is not part of life at all.'[57] Usually Joyce took such blows on the chin and soldiered on, but in Harriet's opinion this article really wounded him.

In order 'to cheer him up a little', Harriet wrote describing her fraught relationship with Dora Marsden (who was subject to periods of depression), saying, 'I would like to tell you that what has been of most help to me all through has been your friendship and belief in me.' No one can have been more astonished than Joyce for whom Harriet was a self-contained, buttoned-up enigma.[58] But he took the letter as a cue to respond with yet another catalogue of his own woes and miseries. His Michaelmas had been as bad as hers, he said. He had fasted for three days from 24 September in the hope of getting rid of his eye trouble but had had an attack of giddiness, taken to his bed and had a terrible night, only to be followed by a thunderstorm during which he had fainted. Fearing a heart attack he had sent Giorgio for a doctor who pronounced him OK but suffering from nervous exhaustion and in need of a good long rest. He was ordered to bed for a month, but after three or four days felt better and got up. One consolation came from finally seeing Crosby Gaige's beautifully crafted de luxe edition of the *Anna Livia Plurabelle* in print.[59]

In his last chapter, Dolph and Kev had been studying geometry. Now their author was studying botany and asked Michael Healy to get him an elementary book on the subject with illustrations, and to find out the colours of the Dublin coat of arms. Those who thought that in his *Work in Progress* he had deserted Dublin for a wider world, or even a wider underworld, had failed to understand the movement of Joyce's mind. That city was and would ever remain his primary muse, the fulcrum around which everything revolved. He had acquired a painting of the Liffey from the artist Jack Yeats, W. B's brother,[60] and a 'Liffey' carpet, woven for him by Miss Monnier's sister. When Eugene Sheehy and his wife visited Joyce one day, Sheehy recalled that 'Everything in Joyce's rooms spelt "Dublin"' – paintings, sketches, that specially designed carpet. He found himself being quizzed about long-forgotten acquaintances, and Joyce was thrilled to hear that a statue in the city had been relocated. When Eugene's sister Mary met him later that year she asked why he pretended to be cosmopolitan when his thoughts were always with Dublin. He replied that just as Mary Tudor had said she would die with 'Calais' written on her heart, he would have 'Dublin' written on his.[61]

One early response to *Anna Livia* came from Virginia Woolf. Writing to her friend Christobel McLaren on 2 December, she declared it 'unintelligible'. 'Perhaps under morphia his meaning would swim to the surface. But it's a bloated drowned dog as likely as not when you get it.'[62] The following day, Drinkwater sent him a far more subtle and appreciative reaction, expressing his deep interest:

> I do feel that you set your readers a devil of a problem ... Nevertheless, in spite of all difficulties I flatter myself that I have been able to get a good deal of your intention from the book ... What is important is that you have really something to say and have been evolving an entirely personal way of saying it. You may puzzle us, but I do not think anyone can be for a moment in doubt that here is something of real importance, expressing a beauty of its own, however elusive that beauty may be to unprepared minds. I get frequent glimpses of it through the mist of my difficulties and I wish your independent spirit every kind of good fortune.[63]

There was some hint of change in the critical climate, Joyce told Harriet. He had heard that the literary editor of the *New Statesman*, who some eighteen months earlier had compared him to 'a rednosed comedian' and *Work in Progress* to 'the wall scribblings of the inmates of Bedlam Asylum', was to allow a certain Mr Cyril Connolly to pen 'a favourable notice' in either his own paper or in the magazine *Life and Letters*.[64] Joyce prided himself on not giving interviews to journalists but when the man from the *New Statesman* turned up, the twenty-five-year-old half-Irish Connolly, he was made an exception. It must also have been obvious to him that this young man was deeply sympathetic both to him and to modernist literature. Connolly, the Eton and Oxford aesthete, found Joyce's apartment 'rather smart ... and nicely furnished', and found Joyce himself immediately engaging.

> He wore a white cricketing blazer and blue trousers and at once began to ask me about my family, very very interested in Clontarf – he said he had mentioned Brian Boru's sword in the last bit of his book, and that it

belonged to the Vernons. 'I am afraid I am more interested in little things
like that,' he said, 'than in the problems of the solar system.' He asked
me my age, the date of my birth, which fell in the year he left Ireland
and spoke of the lanes round Clontarf, the few cricketing families there
were in Ireland, and the beauty of the Dodder river. He asked about my
languages and education and said he had read my article on Wyndham
Lewis (such a pity he gave up drawing, he added, and showed me one or
two). He seemed tired and worried about his ... eyes, for he was no
longer allowed to read – a quiet sensitive, pedantic, tragic, and rather
embarrassable man – a lot of the usher about him. He didn't put me at
my ease, but I was frightened, and longed to know him better.

Reviewing *Anna Livia* Connolly wrote that, as a writer, Joyce was 'resented
in Ireland, neglected in England, admired by a set in America, and idolized
by another in France'. He was by temperament a medievalist in revolt
against his Jesuit education and Celtic romanticism and his work showed
a steady and relentless retreat from both. And, it should be remembered,
as well as being a lover of words Joyce was an Irishman 'under no
obligation to rest content with the English language'. Literature in
England, unaware of the decline in the West, grew ever more conservative.
However, on the Continent there was a sense of the exhilaration of an
uncertain future which Joyce's work captured.[65]

Since late June, when he finished '*The Second Watch of Shaun*', Joyce
had added little to his *Work in Progress*, except a passage, prompted by the
encroaching shadows, dictated to McGreevy. The passage was described
to Harriet as 'a short description of madness and blindness descending
upon Swift'.[66] He had read it aloud to Gilbert who typed it out, giving an
explanation of every word used, explanations many readers would have
welcomed. McGreevy, who had resigned from the Ecole Normale, had
been succeeded by a shy, young red-headed poet, a recent Trinity College
graduate and cousin of Harry Sinclair, the Nassau Street jeweller. This was
Samuel Beckett ('a bean-pole with glasses ... gravely truculent, like a Synge
character', according to Nino Frank), whom McGreevy had introduced to
Joyce that autumn. Joyce was not long in commissioning Beckett to write
an article on *Work in Progress* for *transition*.

Always eager to share his medical condition with others, he told Valery
Larbaud that although the doctor had examined 'the inner organs of the
beast' and found them healthy, he was receiving injections of arsenic and
phosphorus to calm his nerves and stimulate his appetite. He felt weak as
a kitten and his world was in permanent dusk. To Harriet he complained
that despite new lenses, his vision was no better, and he was unable to
make out individual printed words except large newspaper headlines.

Even though practically sightless he was busy learning Spanish by ear (from phonograph records) and clinging to what he called 'the insane idea' that one day he would find it possible to get to grips with print again.[67] He could, however, look forward to the appearance of the French *Ulysses*, the prospectus for which was out. The de luxe edition was already sold out; Tomas Masaryk, the Czechoslovak President, had been seen with a copy under his arm and, he was amused to report, another early subscriber was Bonaventura Cerretti, Papal Nuncio to France.

But the run of good luck did not last. Nora had become unwell – suspected of having cancer and in need of an operation. Despite his nervous apprehension over this, finding that H. G. Wells was in Paris, Joyce arranged to meet him for lunch on the morning before he took Nora to the hospital. Wells told him that he had expected to meet 'a tall fierce aggressive man in a frieze overcoat carrying a heavy stick', and Joyce decided that was the phantom he had evoked when he read him. After their meeting, Wells wrote saying how he much admired his talent and liked him personally but acknowledged that they were set on different courses. His training, said Wells, had been scientific, constructive and English, whereas Joyce's had been Catholic, Irish and revolutionary. His mental outlook was towards the unifying and concentrating of power and economy and the possibility of progress, but:

> Your mental existence is obsessed by a monstrous system of contradictions. You really believe in chastity, purity and the personal God and that is why you are always breaking out into cries of [cunt], shit and hell. As I don't believe in these things except as quite provisional values my mind has never been shocked to outcries by the existence of water closets and menstrual bandages – and undeserved misfortunes. And while you were brought up under the delusion of political suppression I was brought up under the delusion of political responsibility. It seems a fine thing to you to defy and break up. To me not in the least.

Turning to the issues of *transition* in which Joyce's new work had so far appeared, H. G. went on to explain why he could not contribute to propaganda for work so different from his own. While acknowledging Joyce as a considerable man and a mighty genius, and *Work in Progress* as 'an extraordinary experiment', which he would go out of his way to defend, for Wells it was 'a dead end'. 'I can't follow your banner any more than you can follow mine. But the world is wide and there is room for both of us to be wrong.'[68]

On 8 November, following his meeting with Wells, Joyce took Nora to a *maison de santé* at Neuilly, for an exploratory operation followed by seven days of radium treatment. Joyce was so anxious for her that he took a bed in an adjoining room and remained with her throughout – a week spent, he said, 'in great alarm' only heightened by passing storms.[69] When Nora came through the operation he cabled friends with the news, warning Harriet that when medical bills came on top of legal costs in the Roth affair, an unavoidably large payment would be required. They left the hospital on 15 December, and although there would be post-operative therapy, Joyce felt that Nora had been treated well. Soon he was back to writing, but said that all he could read were children's books with very large print.[70]

Borsch was now trying what he called 'a pilocarpine cure' in the hope of saving and improving what sight Joyce had. His clouded vision meant adopting special measures. He told Harriet he was having the hundred pages of 'The Third Watch of Shaun' typed in 'legal size' – three times the normal size and triple-spaced. He would have these pages read to him three times and hope to memorize them so that he could easily make insertions from the twenty notebooks filled since he began the fragment. Sylvia Beach was urging him to consult a famous eye specialist in Munich but he was undecided, telling Harriet, in pure 'Wake' fashion, 'You know my sluggish, slimy, slithy, sliddery, stick-in-the-mud disposition.'[71]

Fleeting images of Christmas at the Joyces' were again captured by Helen Nutting.

> A room full of soft lights, a piano and [several] Irishmen ... Joyce, who with a pink paper cap on his head, thin-faced, subtle, and keen, was entirely at ease with his countrymen. He sang old ballads ... in a voice rich with melancholy ... Then ... Tuohy, with no graces at all, would make his contribution ... Lucia curled up in a chair, at times bursting into spasms of laughter over Tuohy. She danced a Charleston ... Tuohy was anxious to learn it, and she gave him a lesson. He never got the step, but ... with rosy cheeks and coattails at angles, he did his best. Lucia sweetly and most politely saying, 'Now you must do this.' winking over his shoulder when his head was turned. George came in at midnight and we all sang carols. So ended an unforgettable evening. One felt the deep bond between Joyce and Ireland, the intimate charm of the home, the melancholy charm of music. Nora, handsome and hospitable; Lucia, half-child, half-woman, vital and audacious, gifted child of a gifted father.[72]

Before the year's end Sylvia Beach had learned (probably through Dr Fontaine) that Nora's treatment had failed and she would require another and more radical operation. Nora herself had not been informed and the doctors decided not to worry Joyce either until after the New Year. For him, 1928 was ending under a cloud of worry about his own health and with a compulsion to slave on with his 'Third Watch of Shaun'. It was, he said, 'a dreadful time', but there were odd glimmers of light on his horizon. The New York Supreme Court finally issued an injunction forbidding Roth and his agents, on pain of the law, from using Joyce's name or publishing any further parts of *Ulysses*.[73]

27

A French Connection

(1929)

'It is a riddle wrapped in a mystery inside an enigma.' Winston Churchill

Stuart Gilbert began a Paris journal on New Year's Day, and his first entry recorded a 'fête chez Joyce' to celebrate the New Year. Apart from the usual crowd of Joyce's friends those present included the glamorous and wealthy young Caresse and Harry Crosby. The casually attired guests were clearly upstaged by the 'dressy' Nora, Lucia, and the now-divorced Helen Fleischman enjoying a sexually liberated life in Paris. (Fleischman had slipped almost silently into the Joyces' world but would soon become an intimate and significant part of it.) Adrienne Monnier was bored because the occasion was 'not literary enough', Eugene Jolas, 'thrilled about the new literature . . . absorbed vast quantities of drink and talked of his youth [in Alsace]'; and the 'gentle and amiable, rather languid' John Rodker, said he 'hopes to be known as a French writer'.[1] Nino Frank recalled Gilbert telling slightly risqué stories 'with the mocking tone of an Anatole France canon who had had Dickens do his make-up',[2] while Joyce, in colourful waistcoat, merry on white wine, entertained those present by singing 'Mr Dooley', after which he and McAlmon teamed up to dance a hornpipe.

With a truce declared among the translators, the French edition of *Ulysses* was finally published by Monnier's La Maison des Amis des Livres with Morel named as principal translator 'assisted by Stuart Gilbert' and with the entire translation reviewed by Valery Larbaud 'in collaboration with the author'. On 22 January, Joyce presented a copy to Miss Beach to mark what he called 'her Seven Years' War' since 1922.

Still unaware of it, Nora now faced a hysterectomy, and finally on 14 January Dr Fontaine sent for Joyce to break the news. All this was quickly communicated to Harriet who was distraught to think of the ordeal they would be undergoing. With Miss Marsden's great book now finished (though destined to sink into oblivion), she decided to go to Paris and give what help she could.[3] However, with Joyce's permission required for the operation, the doctors first had to contend with his 'sluggish, slimy, slithy, sliddery stick-in-the-mud disposition'.

It took three agonizing weeks before he could bring himself to make a decision. This only brought on his digestive pains again. Friends rallied round. Gilbert came to the flat to help correct the proofs of 'The Third Watch of Shaun' for the March *transition*, with Helen Fleishman assisting.[4] For Joyce it was a tense atmosphere in which to pass his forty-seventh birthday. The operation was scheduled for 5 February, he told Stannie, asking him not to mention it in replying as, ten days before it was due, Nora had still not been informed.[5]

With Harriet now in Paris, Nora was finally told of her condition. She moved back into the *maison de santé* at Neuilly with Joyce in close attendance. This time the operation was a success. When Gilbert visited them, hoping to continue discussions about his book, the worried husband was too distracted, and Gilbert went home disappointed, to record in his journal, 'Joyce is grumpy, seems unwilling to help with *Ulysses*. A spoilt god. Still, without such pride, he could hardly have carried *Ulysses* through.'[6] Joyce was delighted, however, when Beckett called and read him a passage about the River Thames from *Great Expectations*. Nora was out of hospital by mid-March, in time for her forty-fifth birthday, and with Harriet still in Paris she could be left in her capable hands at Square Robiac. Now at last Joyce could venture out, though, because of his poor eyesight, rarely alone.

Giorgio, whom his father came more and more to consult, considered him far too open-handed with money he hoped one day to inherit, and not demanding enough in payment for his work. When Joyce presented 'velin' copies of *Ulysses* to Nora's doctors, he protested.[7] And, when Harry and Caresse Crosby, who ran the Black Sun Press, offered Joyce $1,000 for three *transition* fragments ('The Ondt & Gracehoper', 'Mookse & Gripes' and 'The Triangle') to be published together as *Tales Told of Shem and Shaun*, Giorgio urged him to hold out for more. Gilbert wrote mockingly, 'If Picasso is getting $500 for three or four hours work, why should he get so little for forty or fifty?' 'I hate this *demi-monde* of "letters",' he went on, 'The *marchand de mots* is worse than the *marchand d'épices*, for he expects flattery as well as cash ... Up to the neck in their muddy intrigues.'[8] But stubbornness paid off; the Crosbys' offer was doubled.

By the end of March, Harriet was back in London and Joyce, 'stupefied by iodine', was busily revising his fragments for the Crosbys. They wanted a frontispiece portrait of the author from Picasso, but he was too busy. So Brancusi was hired, and after producing a sketch which they considered pedestrian, conjured up a pattern of lines and spirals which he called 'Symbol of Joyce', expressing the *'sens du pousser'* ('sense of thrusting') which was, he thought, his main characteristic. When John Joyce saw the symbolic portrait he stared at it for sometime before saying, 'Jim has changed more than I thought.'

D. H. Lawrence was in Paris, seeing the Crosbys and meeting Aldous Huxley. When Nino Frank mentioned this and asked Joyce if he should publish something by Lawrence in *900*, he replied, 'Oh no. That man writes really too poorly. Ask his friend Aldous Huxley for something instead; at least he dresses decently.'[9] Later he told Gilbert that Lawrence's prose was 'lush' and his English 'sloppy', and that the sex was 'imitation pornography' that was better found in the backstreets of Paris. Lawrence, never short of a vituperative phrase, called Joyce's work '*real* pornography' and 'too terribly would-be and done-on-purpose, utterly without spontaneity or real life'.[10]

That spring, Lucia entered a contest in solo dancing at the Bal Bullier in which she danced to Schubert's *March militaire* dressed in a fish costume. She was a great success with the audience and there was disbelief when the judges placed her second. There were repeated cries of '*Nous réclamons l'irlandaise! Un peu de justice, messieurs!*' Afterwards, a group including Beckett, McGreevy and Power took her for a celebratory dinner at La Closerie des Lilas. One judge wrote of her performance, 'This very remarkable artist ... totally subtle and barbaric, gives proof of an unmistakable personality. Barbaric, she forcefully performed to the *Marche militaire*; during the choice morsel of *feu follet* ... she was subtle.'[11] Another judge (a disciple of Rudolph Laban) was so impressed she offered to prepare Lucia for the following year's competition. She gladly accepted and began throwing herself into ballet lessons.

Samuel Beckett was so taken with her performance that he kept a photograph of her in costume which he still possessed at his death in 1989. At that time he was involved in a passionate love affair with Peggy Sinclair, his 'blithe and buxom' German cousin, but was clearly drawn to the slight, expressive, sometimes unpredictable girl two years his junior. In his *Dream of Fair to Middling Women*, written in 1932 (which, he admitted, 'stinks of Joyce'), Sinclair has been identified as 'the powerfully constructed Smeraldina-Rima', against 'the lightly built Syra-Cusa', who 'flowed along ... her body more perfect than a dream creek'.[12] The Lucia-like figure was no less than a personification of Anna Livia Plurabelle, flowing through Joyce's dream. Lucia herself gradually became fixated on the young poet Beckett and whenever he came to Square Robiac to work with her father, she would rush to the door to greet him. They began to meet occasionally, taking tea at the Ecole Normale, eating out and visiting cinemas and theatres together. For her, attraction soon became obsession; for Beckett it remained attraction. He was particularly disturbed that during meals she would eat little and suddenly disappear to the ladies' room to vomit.

Joyce now regularly held court for his admirers. Philipp Jarnach came to Square Robiac one day and found him looking 'fat and bloated', surrounded by young acolytes quoting to him from *Ulysses*. The composer was quickly recruited to set four or five of his *Chamber Music* poems. Joyce clearly enjoyed the readiness of his devotees to serve his every need. As Stuart Gilbert observed,

> He got people ... to follow him wherever he wanted them to accompany him; boring plays and operas, dull expensive restaurants; to [cancel] their arrangements if he wanted their assistance in some trivial, easily-postponed task; to run errands for him, pull strings for him, undertake delicate and distasteful missions which exposed them to snubs, rebuffs and ridicules at his bidding.[13]

He was, Philippe Soupault told Maria Jolas, '*formidable*'. 'You go to see him – he asks which way you are going – to the Etoile – before you know it he's got you to do an errand for him at the Bastille.'[14] And Jacques Benoît-Méchin remembered being deeply impressed by Joyce's magic – 'a Prospero figure', he called him.

Adrienne Monnier had proposed a charabanc trip on 27 June to cele-brate the twenty-fifth Bloomsday and to launch the French *Ulysses*. Joyce agreed to go even though he feared sunstroke and thunderstorms. Nino Frank recalled 'an immense bus', hired for the occasion. The company included Frank, Benoît-Méchin, Paul Valéry, Dujardin, Fargue, Gilbert, McGreevy, Monnier, Beach, Soupault and his then lover Helen Fleisch-man, Giorgio, and young Beckett. Their destination was, appropriately enough, the Hôtel Léopold at Les Vaux de Cerney, near Versailles.

In the bus, Fargue sat with Joyce, speaking fondly of Larbaud and hoping to mend their relationship. He and Valéry wanted to make speeches but Joyce dissuaded them. He enjoyed his celebrity but found public eulogy embarrassing. The feast at the Léopold, which came to be known as the 'Déjeuner *Ulysse*', was obviously a merry one, and the merriest in the party were Beckett and McGreevy. Intoxicated by alcohol and female company, they began demanding that the coach stop at every tavern on the way back to Paris. Finally, according to Joyce, Beckett was 'ingloriously abandoned' by the indignant Valéry and Adrienne Monnier.[15] Nino Frank remembered things slightly differently – that he, Soupault and Joyce were also in and out of the taverns, performing 'antics', and that Beckett finally disembarked of his own accord and simply stalked off.[16]

Helen Fleischman's presence on the Square Robiac scene, which Gilbert now regarded with cynical disapproval, was greeted by Padraic Colum as 'a breath of fresh air in [Joyce's] life'.[17] In particular, she read his work in a way few close to him did or could. Nino Frank thought that the darkly pretty but vampish Fleischman had cast an amorous eye on Joyce and was attempting to work her charms on him. Meanwhile, Beckett, like McGreevy, was also reading to him, taking his dictation, and later helping with a French translation of *Anna Livia Plurabelle*. Joyce once asked the young Irishman which people in Dublin were reading *Ulysses*. When Beckett named them, Joyce said, 'But they're all Jews.' Were there no Irish readers? Beckett explained that most Irish intellectuals were then interested in Kafka, a writer Joyce had barely heard of, and the news left him perplexed and worried.[18]

That long-planned trip to Torquay could no longer be postponed. Giorgio, who had recently ended an affair, his first, with Richard Wallace's wife Lillian, and was now dallying with Helen Fleischman, found an excuse to remain behind. And so it was the Joyces minus Giorgio, but accompanied by the Gilberts, who left for England on 1 July. The following day, after a four-hour train journey from London, they were in Torquay, the south Devon coastal resort celebrated for its Mediterranean climate, and a favourite retreat for English writers.

They were soon ensconced at the sumptuous Imperial Hotel (Drinkwater's recommendation), perched on a cliff overlooking the broad sweep of Torbay. The Imperial boasted of having entertained such notables as the Emperor Napoleon III, the Queen of Holland and King Edward VII, and offered 'breath-taking views of the English Riviera, a tennis court, an orchestra and an electric lift'. Its dramatic location, palatial style and dimensions obviously appealed to Joyce's taste for luxury. What was good enough for a Napoleon and a King of England was good enough for James Joyce. As Miss Beach commented, 'He always put up at palaces. He liked the grand style.'[19]

A week later he was in London for four days, meeting Eliot at Faber and Gwyer, trying to sell him Gilbert's book, *James Joyce's 'Ulysses'*, which Cape had turned down, and which must have seemed to Eliot more Joyce than Gilbert. He had a friendly reunion with John Drinkwater, met James Stephens and Harriet, whom he asked down to Torquay. Stephens told him he was 'much impressed and moved' by Joyce's invitation to take over *Work in Progress* should he become too blind to continue, and declared *Anna Livia Plurabelle* 'the greatest prose ever written by man'. Drinkwater was no less encomiastic, declaring the last part of it 'one of the greatest things in Eng. literature'.[20] These responses banished all doubts about what he was doing and he resolved to press on regardless of critical incomprehension.

He took the liberty of booking Harriet into the Imperial from 7 to 14 August, saying, 'Everyone seems delighted with this place – especially my wife.' But as prices were high he had persuaded the hotel manager to make a reduction for a month's stay. Only Lucia was unhappy, resentful at her dancing lessons being interrupted but also worried that she would find the Duncan programme too physically demanding. Gilbert was still grilling Joyce for his *Ulysses* book, but, lamenting the fact that England had just elected its first Labour government, predicted the death of courtesy and respect,[21] something by no means extinct at the Imperial.

His eyes were rather worse, Joyce reported, and he had only been in Torquay for two or three weeks when he failed to see a wall and fell over it, injuring his right knee, arm and wrist, making it difficult for him to sleep. Fortunately, Helen Fleischman had turned up with Giorgio and now joined Gilbert in taking Joyce's dictation. But Gilbert was not just noting Joyce's words, he was recording his own disdainful impressions of the *ménage en vacance*. 'The wall-vaulting episode. Drop miscalculated. Bruised nose, knees; sprained arms. Leap in the dark. Height of drop increased in reports from 7 or 8 feet till 20 feet.' And, 'His wife enchanted with everything at the Imperial. Nice people, nice food, nice town! Why? Expensive dowdiness, the inferiority feeling absent amongst morons who cannot sparkle. Her own folk. The Great Man interested as usual in himself only.'[22] This self-obsession was only intensified by the darkness which so cut Joyce off from the rest of the world, and his occasional sense of helplessness. Borsch had died recently and he had no idea where to go for further treatment.

He arranged for Gilbert's chapter on the 'Hades' episode to appear in the *Fortnightly Review*, and got Eliot interested enough to ask to see Gilbert's complete manuscript. He also persuaded Jolas to print the chapter on the 'Aeolus' episode in *transition* and was hoping to get further episodes published in France, Italy and America. With so much of the book having come from him, he was pushing himself as much as Gilbert, who admitted that Joyce had actually dictated the passages about music in his 'Sirens' chapter. As for *Our Exagmination*, Joyce told Larbaud, 'I did stand behind those twelve Marshals more or less directing them what lines of research to follow.'[23]

He was also still on the look-out for a suitable biographer. It would not be Gilbert whose low opinion of Joyce's tastes revealed a profound lack of understanding of the subject. 'Went with him to a concert of inferior troupe on pier; he was really amused by the funny old man's jests.' But low comedy was much to Joyce's liking and grist to his mill, as is evident in the 'Circe' episode of *Ulysses*. They also saw a play called *The Yellow Streak* at Torquay's Pavilion Theatre 'about a woman committing adultery but continuing to love her husband', about which Gilbert commented merely that it was a problem play, 'likely to please women'. But he failed to note the parallels with the theme of *Exiles* – adultery as a game of calculation.

Joyce knew that one problem facing him was that his new work was inaccessible even to speakers of his own language – and still more problematic for translators. When the Poet Laureate, Robert Bridges, sent him a copy of his *Testament of Beauty* inscribed 'To Mr James Joyce from the author in hermeneutic sympathy', Joyce sent it to Larbaud as an example of 'most accessible' English. In what he called 'this curious meeting of extremes' (the Shem of Paris versus the Shaun of England) he recognized that he had placed himself among the 'goats' subject only to impulsive thought and writing, and thereby banished to 'the everlasting sleep' visited upon ailing academicians.[24]

In August, *Our Exagmination* was published. It was a carefully prepared boost for *Work in Progress* and its author. Contributors, including Beckett, Budgen, Gilbert, McAlmon, McGreevy, Rodker, Elliot Paul and William Carlos Williams, dwelt on the work's various aspects and influences – Vico, Rabelais, the *Book of Kells*, the Jesuits and Lewis Carroll – and how it extended language games already at play in *Ulysses*. Reactions, as might be expected, varied widely. Arnold Bennett, previously a Joyce admirer, said it had given him second thoughts; Edmund Wilson was much influenced by it in writing *Axel's Castle* and seems to have grasped that it came largely from Joyce himself. The *Daily Dispatch* reviewer, however, while thinking Joyce's 'English' 'weird and wonderful', considered the book a hoax.[25]

Coincidentally, *Tales Told of Shem and Shaun* appeared at the same time. Hamish Miles, reviewing it in the *Criterion*, said that, with only fragments available, judgement of the whole must remain suspended.[26] The *New York Times* called Joyce 'a fashioner or creator and transformer of language' who was extending 'the method of Lewis Carroll' and 'the metathesis system ... attributed to Dr Spooner'.[27] Taking a different slant, in the *New English Weekly* D. G. Bridson recommended reading it aloud 'with an empty mind ... impersonally', so that 'the full beauty of the rhythm and the peculiar turn of the words becomes apparent'.[28] When someone remarked that one of the reviews was 'sarcastic', Joyce became downcast until Gilbert commented that he found it 'ironic but friendly', at which he brightened up.

When Harriet arrived in Torquay, Nora was still recovering from her operation, Lucia was still fretting about her dancing career, and Helen

Fleischman had returned to Paris with Giorgio. So Harriet now kept the Joyce women company, leaving James free to satisfy the demands of his creative daemon. Gilbert was amused to find him studying girls' magazines, including *Peg's Paper*, *Schoolgirl's Own* and *Poppy's Paper*. But what to Gilbert seemed trivial, to Joyce was material he could use. ('Poppypap's a passport out. And honey is the holiest thing ever was . . .')[29] He even suggested the 'wild idea' of getting *Anna Livia* published in a girl's paper.[30]

An expedition with Harriet to Kent's Cavern, a honeycomb of caves embedded with fossils and hung with stalactites, described in the guidebook as 'a fairy grotto', can only have further excited Joyce's imagination. For what was *Work in Progress* but a labyrinth of varied and delicate verbal shades and tones and a fairy grotto of the creative mind? Strangely, he never travelled to nearby Cornwall where the burial stone of Tristram stands at the heart of the legend that now echoed through his book.

Leaving the Imperial on 15 August, the Joyces headed for another grand hotel, the Royal in Bristol, the city where in 1171 Henry II granted 'his city of Dublin to his men of Bristol',[31] a story which finds an echo in *Finnegans Wake* where men of Bristol become men of 'Tolbris'. After two days, they moved on, first to visit Claud and Daisy Sykes in Letchworth Garden City, then to Cambridge to meet C. K. Ogden, inventor of Basic English ('the International Language of 850 words in which everything may be said') at his Orthological Institute, where Joyce had agreed to record a passage from *Anna Livia Plurabelle*.

Ogden, who boasted the two largest recording machines in the world, had had the passages to be read by Joyce photographed and magnified so that he could read them easily. After a false start, when the lights suddenly failed, the recording was accomplished. Joyce's reading echoed the incantatory style of Yeats and Pound – a riveting and strangely haunting performance. The disc was marketed by HMV, the Argus Book Shop in Chicago and the Gotham Book Mart in New York. The author and diplomat Harold Nicolson, who later played it on the BBC, said of it, 'His beautiful voice trilled on slowly like Anna Livia Plurabelle. He has the most lovely voice I know – liquid and soft with undercurrents of gurgle.'[32] When Ogden sent Joyce his copy in November, Lucia broke it – whether 'absentmindedly' or on purpose was never said.

Back in London, Joyce finally met and dined with George Moore, presenting him with a copy of *Our Exagmination*. It was, apparently, a lively encounter, a polite duel of wits with Joyce playing 'the great writer' and Moore matching his performance. According to Moore, 'He was distinguished, courteous, respectful, and I was the same.' They compared careers – Moore born into wealth, Joyce having to struggle against poverty, but both having enjoyed the friendship of Edouard Dujardin. Although Moore claimed he had not yet read *Ulysses*, he knew enough about it to ask Joyce how he related the mundane doings of Bloom to the actions of Ulysses. To this Joyce replied, 'I see I am on my defence.' Moore then apologized and the exchange of courtesies continued with Joyce enquiring if Moore would honour him by accepting a copy of the French translation of his book, to which Moore replied, 'I shall be delighted to accept any book you choose to send me, but I hope you don't mind my reminding you that I can read English.' At that, as Moore recalled, 'He smiled a hesitating smile that reminded me of the Gioconda.'[33]

By mid-September the Joyces were back in Paris. After the crossing Joyce felt exhausted – 'broke and needing a holiday', he said, even though much had been achieved during his absence. A parting shot from London came in an attack on *Anna Livia* from Arnold Bennett in the *Evening Standard*. 'Human language,' he declared, 'cannot be successfully handled with such violence as he has here used to English. And *Anna Livia Plurabelle* will never be anything but the wild caprice of a wonderful creative artist who has lost his way.'[34] Joyce, bemused by Bennett's attitude, asked Larbaud why, if *Work in Progress* was that misconceived, did he keep returning to it?[35] Nora had left England somewhat reluctantly, and Joyce said they had to ring a bell every quarter of an hour to stop her talking about London.

After what Joyce called 'a month's tears', Lucia made the momentous decision to turn down the Elizabeth Duncan School at Darmstadt, having come to the conclusion that her physique was unable to cope with a strenuous dancing career. As Joyce told Harriet, she thought she was forfeiting years of hard work and throwing away her talent.[36] The school's pursuit of physical perfection had also made her self-conscious about her strabismus, and she was intent on having surgery to correct what Beckett, among others, found rather attractive. She was, she told Stella Steyn, an Irish artist, that her father had advised her to take up art instead, and that as he was infallible he must be right.[37] But, as dancing was what had come to define her adult self and bring her admiration, abandoning it had left her feeling painfully insecure. However, Joyce by contrast felt his self-confidence boosted by his English trip and even reported some improvement to his sight.

A close friendship had sprung up between Joyce and the singer John O'Sullivan, now chief tenor at the Paris Opera. Stanislaus, who had met him in Trieste, had told Jim he had read *A Portrait* and Joyce invited him to the apartment for dinner on 15 October. Hearing Giorgio sing at a private party in November, O'Sullivan said he liked his voice enough to promote him wherever and whenever he could. By the end of the year

Giorgio had given up any attempt to alter his vocal range, and had been engaged as a bass at 500 francs (some £4) a month at the American Pro-Cathedral of the Holy Trinity on the Avenue Georges V. And Lucia, unable yet to abandon her calling completely, planned to take a job with the gentler dance school of Margaret Morris, if and when she moved it to Paris.

There was much literary activity to report in October. James Wells at Crosby Gaige wanted to publish more from *Work in Progress* and Joyce decided to send him the fragment he called 'Haveth Childers Everywhere', which would become Book III, Chapter 3 of *Finnegans Wake*. *Transition* received what would be his last piece for a while: Chapter 4, set in the bedroom of Earwicker and Anna Livia as sleep dissolves and consciousness returns. The manuscript for the German edition of *Ulysses* on which he, Goyert and Goll had laboured, was sent off to Rhein-Verlag. And finally Eliot at Faber accepted Gilbert's book, *James Joyce's* Ulysses, chapters of which would appear in the *Criterion*, the *Revue de France* and the *Neue Rundschau* as well as in an Italian review.[38]

On 24 October 1929, the Wall Street Stock Exchange began to falter and five days later it crashed. The cheap living in France for American expatriates came to a sudden end. The London Stock Exchange followed suit almost immediately. Joyce remained fairly well insulated against the worst aftershocks of the Crash by having his capital in government holdings. The only threat to his financial security remained his own irresistible impulse to overspend.

Five days later, he received an unusual visitor at Square Robiac – the Russian *cinéaste*, Sergei Mikhailovich Eisenstein. Now inspired by the idea of 'the intellectual cinema', Eisenstein, had read and re-read *Ulysses* and was intensely interested in the interior monologue and its cinematic possibilities. He recalled visiting Joyce as 'a ghost experience' – the room being dark and they being both in shadow.[39] His blindness, he decided, contributed to 'that particular sharpness of inner vision', enabling him to explore the inner lives of his characters. Joyce also expressed interest in the cinema, wanting to see Eisenstein's films. He explained that in *Work in Progress* he was reflecting linguistically 'the birth of different languages from general chaos ... written in a fusion of undifferentiated linguistic poetry', and then read Eisenstein a fragment from it. The Russian's first clear sight of Joyce was as he was conducted towards the door. 'He is a tall, slightly stooping man: a man almost without a front – so sharply outlined is his profile.'[40] Only as he left, clutching a signed copy of *Ulysses*, did he become conscious of his host's blindness – the dedication was indecipherable.

Cinematic techniques were certainly part of the web of ideas Joyce was attempting to verbalize.

> Shadows by the film folk, masses by the good people. Promptings by Elanio Vitale. Longshots, upcloses, outblacks and stagetolets by Hexenschuss, Coachmaher, Incubone and Rocknarrag.[41]

And he was very conscious of how films – 'those fickers which are returnally reprodictive of themselves'[42] – can, like imaginary rivers, loop back and rerun, and so replay through endless time.

The November *transition* included the 'Fourth Watch of Shaun', Joyce's final contribution for the time being. With the pressure of deadlines lifted, he told Harriet, he felt 'a sudden drop' and collapsed into a kind of stupor; he was sleeping sixteen hours a day and was 'incapable of thinking, writing, reading or speaking'.[43] Finally he was in more of a listening mood.

In this stuporous frame of mind following the completion of 'Shaun', he attended a centenary performance of *William Tell* at the Paris Opera with O'Sullivan in the leading role, and his friendship with the singer suddenly became an obsession. As Gilbert wrote, 'J.J. is now all Sullivan.' (Joyce persuaded him to drop the 'O'.) Visiting Square Robiac, Gilbert was drawn into a game in which Joyce (with Giorgio's help) listed the high notes hit by the tenor in the Rossini opera, statistics he intended using to impress his friends. Every visitor would be regaled with sad tales of Sullivan's persecution in England and America by orchestras and fellow artists, including McCormack. Even in Paris where he had been engaged to sing *Tell* and Raoul in Meyerbeer's *The Huguenots* he was not being given a fair outing. However, Joyce had persuaded John Pollack of the London *Morning Post* to write an article in praise of his singing, at which Gilbert commented, 'What wirepulling!'[44] He also managed to get similar pieces into the *Daily Telegraph*, *Daily News*, *Manchester Guardian*, and several Irish, French and American papers.

On 10 December Harry Crosby committed suicide (or was murdered) with his mistress in a Manhattan hotel room. Crosby's demise was just one of the events prompting Jim the Penman to pen yet another of his querulous letters to Harriet complaining about his shaky finances. Apart from the consequent loss of the Crosbys' Black Sun press as an immediate outlet for future publications,[45] a 25,000-franc deal with the Fountain Press in New York had fallen through thanks to the Crash, and he had received a tax demand for 24,000 francs. So, while money would be coming from the second French edition of *Ulysses*, due out on Christmas

Eve, and from an illustrated de luxe edition of *Circe* in the New Year, he needed an immediate £150 – 'dynamite', he said, to dispel 'the cloud-bank'.[46]

That month, Joyce and Paul Morand presided at a PEN Club dinner for Ford Madox Ford and Aldous Huxley. Huxley, whose sight was also impaired, sat next to Joyce and recalled how they discussed the *Odyssey*. To Huxley's surprise, Joyce seemed primarily concerned with the etymology of the name. 'It really comes from the words Udyce, meaning nobody,' he said, 'and Zeus, meaning God; the Odysseus is really a symbol of creation of God out of nothing.' He reminded Huxley of a medieval philosopher fixated by terminology, a man unaware of the limitation of words. 'Joyce seemed to think that words were omnipotent. They are *not* omnipotent.'[47]

As part of his campaign to promote Sullivan, Joyce recruited supporters to attend the tenor's performances and applaud wildly. There was no shortage of acolytes eager to join the ranks. The twenty-two-year-old Leon Edel found himself drawn into the conspiracy when Miss Beach informed him that 'Odysseus wants all hands on deck' to join his claque for a performance of *The Huguenots*. Edel managed to get a seat from which he could observe the chief claqueur in action, and just before curtain-up he spotted Joyce, with Giorgio at his side, immaculate in evening dress topped off with his 'Latin Quarter' hat, being guided to an aisle seat a dozen rows from the front. As soon as Sullivan appeared, Joyce began to applaud. The claque followed suit and stopped the show. Edel decided that Sullivan had a fine voice which had 'sung better days', but to his worshipful admirer he was beyond reproach. As soon as his aria ended Joyce's voice rang out – 'clear, bell-like, high', shouting 'Bravo! Bravo!'[48] Philippe Soupault recalled Joyce and his wildly cheering claqueurs provoking two encores for the great *William Tell* aria. It was probably in appropriately self-mocking mood that he referred in *Finnegans Wake* to the 'leader of a band of twelve mercenaries, the Sullivani'.[49] Beckett remembered a similar occasion where Joyce cried 'Bravo! Up Cork!', and the Sullivani were treated afterwards to champagne and chicken at the Café de la Paix.[50]

Joyce realized that he was cutting an absurd figure, writing later that 'the spectacle of the immensely illustrious author of *Ulysses* endeavouring to hustle crowds of journalists and protesting admirers into that old fashioned playhouse to hear antiquated music sung by old-timer Sullivan' only made him look ridiculous. But he did not much care, because Sullivan's was 'the greatest human voice I have ever heard'; it made Chaliapin seem like a windbag and McCormack seem trivial.[51]

Following the Crash and the exodus of American expatriates, Joyce lost some good friends, including McAlmon and the Nuttings. At Beach's shop there were fewer would-be Fitzgeralds and Hemingways. But there were compensations. Christmas was celebrated with the arrival of the German *Ulysses* and the second French edition from Gallimard.

28

'Always something new on the Robiac front'
(1930)

'It is and it is not the voice of God.' Alexander Pope, *Imitations of Horace*

New Year at Square Robiac was the usual jolly affair. According to Stuart Gilbert, there had been tension between Joyce and Eugene Jolas over an offensive article in *transition*, but they achieved an alcoholic reconciliation as midnight welcomed in 1930. By two thirty, Joyce, decked in his hunting waistcoat as usual, was merrily dancing a jig to 'Auld Lang Syne', and Nora, indignant that he was making a fool of himself, asked everyone to leave. But Gilbert thought Joyce's cavorting revealed a rather noble side to him. 'He is a nimble dancer. If Joyce had not been a writer he'd have been a meistersinger; if not a singer, a ballerino.'[1]

Helen Fleischman later described the progress of a typical Square Robiac party. Guests would arrive intermittently, greeted at the door by a nervous Nora and given a drink. No attempt was ever made to break the ice and the atmosphere was uneasy, marked by painful silences until Joyce came in. His entrance was always carefully staged – the humble author moving blindly around, unable to recognize his friends until prompted by Nora. As the wine, whiskey and cognac began to flow, the climate warmed. Maria Jolas would play and sing, in a powerful contralto, songs of her native south. Then there would be calls for Joyce to perform and he was soon regaling the company with 'Molly Brannigan' or 'The Old Ale and the New'. Lucia would sing Italian folk-songs and Giorgio operatic arias. The evening would reach a climax with everyone dancing and Joyce performing his rhythmic contortions and capering high-kicks, egged on by the applauding onlookers. Nora would end the proceedings by telling Mrs Jolas to stop playing and Joyce would collapse exhausted and breathless, eyes sparkling wickedly. Finally, after a burst of 'For He's a Jolly Good Fellow' and 'Good Night Ladies', Nora would start ushering the guests on their way. Next day came the post-mortem at which Nora and Giorgio would indulge in an orgy of backbiting, mercilessly mocking the previous night's guests for their behaviour or appearance. Although Lucia and her father always remained aloof from this, Joyce was barely able to conceal his amusement. It struck Helen Fleischman that here very probably was a source of the washerwomen's gossiping in *Anna Livia Plurabelle*.[2]

Gilbert, having sneered in private about Joyce's Sullivan campaign, wrote about it more tactfully in letters to Harriet explaining what was afoot. It was quite exciting visiting the Joyces and hearing the latest news. 'There is always something new on the Robiac front,' he said. But he was concerned that Joyce's work was suffering. 'I hope Mr Joyce will soon have launched his singer at Covent Garden or the Metropolitan and returned to *HCE* and "Messrs (or Mrs) Liffi"!'[3] In his diary he wrote, 'J.J. still absorbed in Sullivan; he has got in touch with Lady Cunard, said to be the mistress of [Sir Thomas] Beecham, and she may get his hero launched. His interest in *Work in Progress* seems quite dormant, if not dead.' Joyce's main activity was wining and dining journalists and editors who might help lift 'his idol' onto the pedestal he deserved. Eugene Jolas also took a jaundiced view of this, complaining that he was 'acting like a wire-pulling, intriguing American politician'. Gilbert put this diversion from writing down to Joyce's guaranteed income. 'Miss Weaver did him a bad turn when she gave him all that money; he can follow caprice instead of sticking to his work.'[4]

Joyce had avoided another eye operation, but, as Gilbert told Harriet, his sight was actually improving and the doctor thought that in time he would be able to read well enough.[5] But Lucia's behaviour and increasing obsession with her physical imperfections were beginning to worry him. Gilbert recorded that out walking with him one day, 'Joyce became quite human and complained of his daughter not being "normal", and her incapacity to stick to anything!' In his usual sardonic fashion, he found Joyce's 'quest of normality in his family' 'comic'.[6] Lucia's eye operation was performed by Collinson on 29 January. As Joyce later told Harriet, it took a mere twenty minutes, was fairly painless, and within a week her eyes were perfectly normal.[7]

Adrienne Monnier had her own theory about the Sullivan affair. To her, it was Joyce's way of keeping himself in the limelight as he knew that only by courting publicity was he likely to put his *Work in Progress* across. Publicity sold better than largely incomprehensible prose. Whatever the truth, he managed, through Lady Cunard, to secure Beecham's promise to introduce Sullivan to Covent Garden. However, having swallowed the singer's tale of woe completely, he now got involved in sending letters to the press accusing various parties of persecuting the man – good publicity but bordering on libel. Beach and Monnier were mystified that he should make such efforts on behalf of a relatively unknown singer. To this Joyce replied, 'I know little about literature, less about music, nothing about painting and less than nothing about sculpture; but I do know something about singing, I think.'[8] Sullivan was the tenor *he* might have been and it was that dream of an unfulfilled ambition he was reliving.

To Gilbert's satisfaction, Joyce had resumed work, and by mid-March he had completed 'Haveth Childers Everywhere', the chapter in which he had included names from Harriet's book on cities. The number had grown to forty-one, many culled from the *Encyclopaedia Britannica*. Gilbert thought his method was becoming more mechanical, as he noted. 'For the "town references", he scoured all the capital towns in the Encyclopaedia and recorded in his black notebook all the "punnable" names of streets, buildings, city-founders. Copenhagen, Budapest, Oslo, Rio . . . On the last day he inserted punnishly the names of 60 Mayors of Dublin (taken from the Dublin Postal directory of 1904).' Now Joyce was suffering bouts of depression, but was, Gilbert concluded, gradually recovering from his 'Sullivanitis'.[9]

Having completed 'Haveth Childers Everywhere', he launched into a long account of his woes for Harriet, with a request for money attached. From what he called his 'pool of despond', he reported on tension between himself and Miss Beach over his overdrawn royalty account and rumours being spread about him, Sullivan and Nora. Furthermore, his New York lawyer had sent him a bill for £600 which he had no intention of paying, and there were 14,000 francs owed in taxes. Less despondently, he could report that *Exiles* was being produced in Berlin and Milan, Stuart Gilbert's book and *Haveth Childers Everywhere* as a separate volume were due out in April, as were Polish, Czech and German editions of *Ulysses*.[10]

Despite his victory over Samuel Roth, piracy still threatened. One of Gilbert's despised '*marchands des mots*', Jacob Schwartz, a London bookdealer, had obtained a copy of Joyce's student paper on James Clarence Mangan and his *Fortnightly Review* article, 'Ibsen's New Drama'. On 7 March he had published them together in a finely bound edition of forty copies under his Ulysses Bookshop colophon. Challenged by Joyce, he claimed they were never intended for sale, but shortly afterwards the London bookdealers Davis and Orioli were advertising copies at 10 guineas each. When later that year James R. Wells, now with the Fountain Press (who had just published *Haveth Childers Everywhere* in New York), wanted to bring out 'The Day of the Rabblement' and the Mangan essay in a single volume, he first agreed a deal with Joyce, then, having heard about Schwartz's edition, cancelled it. Joyce had to repay the advance.

The reception of Gilbert's book on *Ulysses* was mixed. In the *Cambridge Review*, Herbert Read declared it 'wholly admirable and immensely illuminating'.[11] The longest notice came in the *New Statesman* from Dubliner Conal O'Riordan. If Joyce's book was 'queer', he wrote, Gilbert's exposition of it 'has his original beaten to a frazzle'. To him it seemed 'an elaborate hoax'. Anyone looking for a simplification of Joyce's work there, he wrote, 'may as well go hang himself'.[12] Gilbert himself referred to it as 'my futile book',[13] and years later Joyce told Vladimir Nabokov that it had been 'a terrible mistake, an advertisement for [*Ulysses*]. I regret it very much.'[14]

Another source of Sylvia Beach's displeasure was her feeling that Joyce's new book should have gone to her rather than bit by bit to other publishers. But, he told Harriet, he had to pay due attention to where the power and wealth lay – in America. As it happened, *Haveth Childers Everywhere* would first be published in Paris by Henry Babou and Jack Kahane, for an advance of 25,000 francs, but much of their stock was bought by Wells for the Fountain Press. At the same time, in June, thanks to Eliot, a cheap English edition of *Anna Livia Plurabelle* would come from what was now Faber and Faber in a Criterion Miscellany edition. Reviewing both books in the *New Statesman*, G. W. Stonier called Joyce 'one of the very few great writers of our time' who deserved 'not a little admiration'. *Haveth Childers Everywhere* he thought 'a collector's piece, beautifully printed and bound, but, to me at least, almost completely unintelligible'. Nevertheless, occasional passages in *Work in Progress* amazed by 'their beauty and complete originality', and only improved as they were read and re-read.[15]

Nora, who was forty-six on 21 March, was recovering well from her hysterectomy and taking daily walks in the Bois de Boulogne. But she still felt she had to get back to prepare teas for what she called 'the troops of men', helpers who visited the flat daily.[16] One of those visitors was Paul Léon, a lanky, talkative, improvident man whose wife was a well-paid fashion-guide for American tourists. Léon's second name was Leopold and his wife was called Lucie. Such coincidences were significant to Joyce, and it was not long before the two men became close. When Joyce decided to go to Switzerland that April he left his affairs and correspondence in the capable hands of his new friend.

Léon was a refugee from Bolshevik Russia, a one-time student of philosophy and law at Moscow University. In Paris he worked for a French law journal and had edited a collection of letters. He recalled how, with Joyce, one was soon drawn into what he called 'a fine network of half-expressed thoughts and feelings that created an atmosphere of such suavity that it was difficult to resist, all the more so since it contained no element of restraint'. And he appreciated 'his exquisite gentleness, together with his infinite power of comprehension'.[17] Joyce in turn was attracted to Léon's levity and devotion. That summer the Russian told his brother that he was working for 'the greatest writer of our time'. 'He is writing in a way that nobody understands or can understand . . . I've found it wonderfully amusing to translate simple ideas into incomprehensible formulas and to feel it may be a masterpiece.'[18] Seeing them together – the stoop-shouldered Léon and the blindly fumbling Joyce – Philippe Soupault nicknamed them 'the halt and the blind'.[19]

The trip to Switzerland was probably precipitated by a shock. Dr Edward Hartmann, to whom Dr Fontaine had referred Joyce, suggested that the most likely cause of his eye trouble was congenital syphilis, and Joyce noticed a sudden aloofness in Fontaine's manner. He quickly sought a second opinion from Collinson who assured him that he and Borsch had discounted this utterly because of the nature of his attacks and the way his eyes had responded to treatment. It so happened that two months earlier, an article about him in the *Neue Zürcher Zeitung* had produced a surprise letter from Marthe Fleischmann, the woman who had so aroused his lust and stirred his imagination in Zurich twelve years earlier. She reminded him of their earlier acquaintance, and, having heard of his eye trouble, recommended that he consult Professor Alfred Vogt of Zurich.[20] When his old Zurich friend Georges Borach also wrote urging him to see Vogt, Joyce quickly decided to do so. Having left Giorgio in charge of the flat, by 12 April he, Nora and Lucia were settled in Zurich's St Gotthard Hotel, just off Bahnhofstrasse.

Vogt, who saw Joyce right away, detected an advanced secondary cataract in his good right eye which had gone undetected in Paris. To reassure him, it was arranged for him to have a second opinion from Dr Hermann Pagenstecher in Wiesbaden where he went immediately. As a result he asked Harriet to postpone a planned visit to Paris on the 15th and, on the 18th, Lucia informed her that both Vogt and Pagenstecher had discounted Hartmann's diagnosis.

Still not quite sure whom to believe, Joyce returned to Paris to seek yet another opinion from Dr Félix Lapersonne, author of an important manual of neuro-ophthalmic pathology. He also planned to extend his lease on the Square Robiac flat for a further six months, and finally to meet Harriet to talk about his money and eye problems. When Lapersonne concurred with Vogt and Pagenstecher, he knew what to do. Before returning to Zurich, however, Joyce insisted on taking Miss Beach and her father to hear Sullivan once more. He could now boast that his efforts had resulted in engagements for the singer in Dublin and a recording contract with Columbia Records. His appearance in Dublin was a success but unfortunately the Columbia recording was considered too poor to release.[21]

The Joyces were back in Zurich by mid-May, this time with Giorgio, while Lucia remained with Helen Fleischman in Paris. At her father's suggestion, she had been studying art with Alexander Calder, the designer of mobiles, but without her dancing she had become anxious and insecure. Her passion for Beckett prompted her to press him into some kind of declaration. She invited him to dinner and there declared herself to him. But according to her biographer, Beckett was only too aware of the strong unfulfilled erotic bond between Lucia and her father and her consequent compulsion to find a genius father-substitute. Also, if his depiction of her as Syra-Cusa is any guide, he became alarmed because of her predilection for unprotected sex.[22] He told her plainly that he came to Square Robiac to see her father and not her. Lucia was devastated and at Nora's insistence Joyce told Beckett that he was no longer welcome at the apartment. Beckett was crushed and for a time the two were estranged. Thereafter Lucia sought male affection wherever she could find it. Joyce even hinted at a liaison with the rakish McAlmon, resulting in a proposal.[23] But none ever replaced the young Irish poet. In later years she would say, 'My love was Samuel Beckett. I wasn't able to marry him.'[24] She transferred her attentions to the bohemian Calder, whose abandoned lifestyle some think precipitated her later mental breakdown.

On Joyce's mother's birthday, 15 May, Vogt operated on him for tertiary cataract in the left eye. It was his ninth eye operation. Eight days later, Helen arrived at the St Gotthard, and, while Joyce was still at Vogt's *Augenklinik*, she quickly took on the role of amanuensis, bringing Harriet up to date with events in Zurich.[25] The operation, she reported, had been halted halfway through when the back part of Joyce's eyes threatened to collapse after being left in a viscous state due to scopolamine poisoning following his previous two operations. The surgeon did, however, manage to create an opening in the lens. Then, after ten days convalescence he suffered a sharp attack of iritis which Vogt managed to suppress, but the outcome would only be revealed when his bandages were removed.[26]

Thirteen days after the operation Joyce was still unable to see anything but light, and a week later Vogt found that blood had leaked into the incision and had to be removed from the frontal chamber of the eye. However, blood had entered further, into the vitreous part, and would take several months to disperse. The back of the lens had also clouded over, almost like a secondary cataract. To deal with this, Vogt thought a tenth operation was necessary. Furthermore, Joyce's right eye also presented a complicated cataract for which more surgery would be required. The tenth operation was deferred till mid-September, but Vogt believed that if the two operations were carried out at the right time and with special instruments, there was every chance that he would recover a fair measure of clear and practical vision.[27]

By the end of May, Joyce was allowed out of bed and permitted to walk in the clinic gardens. A few Zurich friends came to visit him, including the architect Siegfried Giedion-Welcker and his wife Carola, an art critic who had written an article on *Ulysses* and whom he had met previously in Paris. Since then she had written about Joyce's 'Linguistic Experiment' and had become a devoted admirer.[28] She recalled how delighted Joyce was when he first 'saw' her green outfit and the red rose Helen had pinned to her dress when she visited. She also noted his superstitious habit of chewing garlic – to fend off journalists and debt collectors, no doubt. As Carola got to know the family, Nora confided in her that she had difficulty sleeping. Asked why, she said, 'I go to bed and then that man sits in the next room and continues laughing about his own writing. And then I knock at the door, and I say, now Jim, stop writing or stop laughing.'[29]

At the beginning of June, Joyce was still at the clinic having leeches attached to his eyes. On being discharged (on the 5th) he received a celebrity send-off. As he left the clinic the nurses and students presented him with flowers and refused to accept tips. Even Vogt declined to accept fees. The doctor wanted him to spend two weeks more in recovery but Joyce, who had other plans, persuaded him to prescribe temporary spectacles and discharge him. On the 17th, poised to return to Paris, he wired Miss Beach asking her to reserve seats for a Sullivan performance.

Helen and Giorgio had returned to Paris early. His son, clearly besotted, was determined to marry, and the bride-to-be had raised the matter of Joyce and Nora's marital status, which rendered Giorgio illegitimate and therefore not his legal heir. Joyce was persuaded to write to Monro Saw asking the easiest way of ensuring Giorgio's inheritance. It meant providing details of his son's stated nationality at birth and on all subsequent passports, and so he found himself being propelled in a direction not of his own choosing.

To Joyce's delight, a booking for Sullivan to sing Romeo at Covent Garden on the 20th was confirmed, his campaign's ultimate achievement. He asked Harriett to reserve tickets. However, at the last minute the performance was cancelled and Joyce put it down to the Irishman's quarrelsome character and anti-Semitism which upset directors. Despite this setback, Joyce was preparing two of his most successful but equally embarrassing stunts. On the 23rd he helped Sullivan compose a letter to be sent to the *New York Herald Tribune* and circulated to the French press, challenging the tenor Giacomo Lauri-Volpi to a singing contest – the latter singing his version of Arnold's aria from *William Tell* followed by Sullivan's rendering. A week later at the Paris Opera, while Sullivan was singing the role, a bizarre happening at the end of the first act provided him with a marvellous piece of contrived publicity. As one newspaper reported, as the applause faded 'a man in one of the boxes whom many recognized as James Joyce ... dramatically leaned forward, raised a pair of heavy dark glasses from his eyes, and exclaimed: *"Merci, mon Dieu, pour ce miracle ... Après vingt ans, je revois la lumière."'* ('Thank God for this miracle. After twenty years I can again see the light.') Vogt had given his permission for him to remove his dark glasses for the occasion.

Shakespeare and Company were now selling the tenth edition of *Ulysses* and suddenly Joyce found himself credited with 22,500 francs in royalties – encouraging news and a boost for his flagging self-confidence. With storms in Paris, he was anxious to escape to England, hoping to stay for a week at Llandudno in North Wales – a country with cultural links to Brittany and, according to local legend, also to St Patrick.[30] Joyce, Nora and Lucia crossed the Channel on 2 July. Giorgio was left to the kind ministrations of the eager Helen Fleischman at her summer villa at Saint-Jean-de-Luz.

Again they stayed for a few days at the Euston Hotel while Nora indulged herself in the pleasures of shopping in her favourite city. Joyce was invited to Gerald Griffin's Bloomsbury flat where they were joined by Herbert Hughes, now music critic of the *Daily Telegraph*. There Joyce entertained them with Irish ballads and comic songs of which he had built a sizeable repertoire – from Mr Dooley to his Bloomesque version of Molly Brannigan. He told Griffin that he could never return to Dublin. 'I would get an iron welcome there – to put it mildly – for my attitude towards the Catholic Church and especially towards the Jesuits!' But, as Griffin noted, whatever his argument with Irish Catholicism and the Jesuits, his obsession with the faith he had renounced endured. On one occasion they went together to High Mass at Westminster Cathedral where Joyce listened 'with wrapt attention' to the singing of Taverner's Plainsong. Afterwards he analysed the performance meticulously, having found the 'Ite, Missa Est' tedious and lacking in spirit. 'It should have rung out more like a triumphal chant,' he declared, swinging his ashplant dramatically to emphasize the point.[31]

While in London Joyce met Eglinton, now in exile from the new Ireland, who had once prophesied that he would return to Dublin begging, and Herbert Gorman whom finally he had approved as his biographer and to whom he gave a list of people to contact. Harriet, when they met, was pleased to find her protégé in comparatively good form. 'I thought he seemed a good deal better ... than he had been in Paris in the spring,' she told Sylvia Beach. 'No doubt the cheering results of the operation had something to do with this. But he got rather tired running about London – Mrs Joyce too.'[32]

After a brief visit to Llandudno (where Beckett and Judge Michael Lennon were supposed to join them but failed to appear) and a short trip to Oxford to pay homage to the shade of Walter Pater, they were back in London by 4 August. Though troubled with lumbago, Joyce wanted to meet people he hoped would assist with the Sullivan campaign, notably the wealthy Richard Guinness and Lady Ottoline Morrell. There was dinner at Scott's in Soho with Herbert and Suzanne Hughes, John Dulanty, the Irish High Commissioner, and Colum's friend Robert Lynd, literary editor of the *Daily Chronicle*, whom he had met in Belfast in 1912. In her autobiography, Lynd's wife Sylvia recalled Joyce drinking white wine but eating nothing except a banana and speaking exclusively to Lucia in Italian. Afterwards, at Hughes's house, he spoke English and cheerfully sang and played the piano. On another occasion they dined at the Trocadero in Piccadilly where his favourite wine, Fendant de Sion, was served. They had been warned not to mention the name 'Sullivan', but someone did inadvertently and that prompted a long monologue from Joyce during which he produced a manuscript in praise of the tenor which he wanted Hughes to get published in the *Telegraph*. Sylvia noticed how he smoked interminably and remained impassive, whatever happened or was said throughout the meal.

Before returning to France Joyce told Harriet that he and Nora intended getting married and she was left wondering whether they planned a double wedding with Giorgio and Helen. In the event, Harriet acted as a conduit in the preparation of the necessary documents with Monro Saw while continuing to supply Joyce with books and papers. In August she sent him the *Saturday Review* carrying Stuart Gilbert's essay 'The Growth of a Titan', ghosted by Joyce. In September she sent the current number of *Music and Letters*, containing an article, 'The Tenor Voice of Europe', by his friend (and Giorgio's singing teacher) the composer Edgardo Carducci which paid fulsome tribute to Sullivan and to Joyce's championing him.

> I owe it to Mr James Joyce if I have been able to understand a voice like that of Mr Sullivan, the most remarkable tenor of our generation and perhaps the only one which can be called a genuine survivor of those golden ages ... we have been glancing at.[33]

Joyce can hardly have wished for a better acknowledgement of his Sullivan campaign, especially as it concluded with Joyce's table of high notes required for singing *William Tell* compared to *I Puritani*, *Tannhäuser* and *Bohème*. A knowing reader might have detected a familiar hand guiding Carducci's pen.

En route to the ferry they stopped at the grand Lord Warden Hotel in Dover (a favourite of Thackeray and Dickens) where Joyce found that the manager, a Mr McGee, and his secretary, Guiney, an odd couple of bookish fellow Irishmen, were fans of his work. This pair happily escorted their distinguished guests to the ferry. By mid-August they were back in France, enjoying the sea at Arcachon. When finally they returned to Paris they found it stifling, with thunderstorms threatening, and quickly retreated to the coast, this time to Etretat on the Normandy coast.[34] Here they had unbroken sunlight and, within sight and sound of the healing sea, Joyce's lumbago slowly cleared up.

Back in Paris, his portrait was still in demand – the iconic, lean, unsmiling figure with piratical eyepatch always attracted artists. His last portraitist, Patrick Tuohy, overcome by depression, had committed suicide in New York; this time his pursuer was Augustus John, commissioned to draw a frontispiece for *The Joyce Book*, a collection of settings for his poems being edited by Herbert Hughes. Composers engaged for the project included Arnold Bax, Vaughan Williams, Eugene Goossens and George Antheil. Joyce tried to conscript Antheil also to compose a symphony for *Anna Livia Plurabelle*, and an opera based on Byron's *Cain* as a vehicle for Sullivan, suggesting that he use the loudspeaker from Rouen's railway station for the voice of the Angel of the Lord.

In late September, through Nancy Cunard, Beecham was finally prevailed upon to attend a Sullivan concert with Joyce and her mother Lady Cunard in attendance. Afterwards, the conductor announced his verdict – 'It is certainly an amazing voice,' he said, and promised to do what he could to get the tenor to London.[35] Joyce told Antheil that Beecham had declared Sullivan's 'the most amazing tenor voice he ever heard'. The singer did eventually perform in London under Beecham's baton in Berlioz's *Damnation of Faust* at the Philharmonia Hall, but not until April 1936 when *The Times* commented, 'Mr John Sullivan's voice is too throaty a quality to suit the texture of Berlioz's music and too tight in production to turn the phrases and draw the vocal line with the clear definition they require.'[36] Clearly, he needed Joyce there with his twelve Sullivani to lead the cheering.

Shortly afterwards Joyce was involved in an accident when his taxi, crossing the Esplanade des Invalides, was struck by another car. He was flung about violently but fortunately managed to avoid getting glass in his eyes. He emerged with a large bump on the forehead and back pain, but the doctor who saw him found no sign of internal injury. However, for days afterwards he felt 'very listless', he told Harriet. Perhaps in the circumstances it was as well that Sullivan had decided to leave the Paris Opera in October – to the relief of his friends, he said.[37]

Joyce's typist was now Paul Léon. Gilbert regarded this new arrangement with characteristic cynicism: 'I am no longer useful, as he has a permanently attached slave in Léon. On the whole, a relief.'[38] Léon was asked to read a preface to Gilbert's book commissioned from Jung (Joyce's Tweedledum) by Daniel Brody of Rhein-Verlag, and, having done so, said he would be proud to have such a preface.[39] However, it ridiculed *Ulysses*, saying that it could just as well be read backwards as forwards. Joyce was puzzled, and asked Brody why Jung was so rude to someone he had never met and who had nothing to do with psychoanalysis. Brody said there could be only one explanation, 'Translate your name into German' (where 'Joy' translates as 'Freude'). Joyce, scornful of this piece of typical central European small-mindedness, cabled telling him to include it, saying simply, 'Niedrigerhängen', meaning 'Ridicule it by making it public.'[40] But Goll and Larbaud prevailed on Brody to spike it.

Joyce was amused to be told that there were plans afoot for the *NRF* to boost what he called 'Lawrence's ... *Lady Chatterbox's Lover*', and could not imagine anyone spending 100 francs on such a book when genuine pornography was so much cheaper in the Paris backstreets. Ironically, both *Lady Chatterley* and *Ulysses* were listed in *The Secret Guide to Places and Houses of Pleasure in Paris*, beside Maupassant, Radclyffe Hall, and such enticing literary morsels as *The Vices of Love*, *The Flagellation of Suzette*, *Lady Bumtickler's Revels*, and *The Sweet Games of Love*. *Ulysses* was styled 'Erotic literature at its best'.[41]

For Giorgio, intent on marrying in December, validating his legitimacy was a matter of urgency, so Joyce proposed to move to England to establish residence there, regularize his marriage and so ensure his son's inheritance. At the end of September he gave notice on his flat. He felt his sight had improved, but temporized about leaving, not wanting to risk his eyes on a windy autumn crossing. He did not plan to retire from Paris, he assured friends, merely to change his mode of living for one favoured by Nora – a summer home in London to escape the Paris heat and the costly hotels Jim so enjoyed.

Augustus John had arrived at Square Robiac and made several sketches,[42] one of which, 'an excellent sanguine one', according to Joyce, would go into Herbert Hughes's book. The two 'great men' were photographed for the *Sunday Dispatch*, a picture destined for London's National Portrait Gallery. One of John's drawings joined the Square Robiac collection, now so crowded that he had to refuse one portrait of him painted by Budgen in Zurich.[43]

When Eliot heard that Joyce intended going to Zurich on 23 November, he wrote saying, 'I trust that everything will pass satisfactorily – I shall mention you meanwhile in my prayers, if you do not consider that an impertinence.' Joyce sent this to Miss Beach, asking her to show it to no one as it would only provoke laughter, but added that he needed all the prayers that were ever uttered.[44]

He had not dispensed altogether with Gilbert who in mid-November met him and Nora for dinner at Prunier's. There Joyce told him that he had only managed to write a painful eight pages since the spring. He asked his friend to go through a few children's songs for him – he especially liked 'Looby Light', sung as children danced in a circle.[45] 'Here we dance looby, looby,/Here we dance looby light,/Here we dance looby, looby,/all on a summer's night.' This went, via his notebook, into the draft of Book II, Chapter 1 of *Finnegans Wake* (now called 'The Games Chapter') which he said was coming out 'like drops of blood', but was the 'gayest and lightest' thing he had ever done.[46]

The bane of Nora's life was the forthcoming union of Giorgio and Helen. She was so deeply pessimistic about it that Joyce felt that he had to proceed around the flat 'like an aged old rat walking over broken bottles'. The engaged couple were now living together but Nora was not on speaking terms with the bride-to-be.[47] There was an eleven-year age gap between Helen and Giorgio, she was divorced with a son from her previous marriage, and, according to Stuart Gilbert, Nora took exception to her son marrying into a Jewish family. Lucia may have shared her mother's antipathy towards Helen but Joyce never expressed anti-Semitic sentiments; he found Jewish history and culture fascinating and he valued his friendships with Jews such as Schmitz and the Sinclair brothers.

On 23 November the Joyces arrived in Zurich accompanied by the Gormans, and booked into the Carlton Elite on Bahnhofstrasse. When he saw Vogt on 24th he was told that the condition of his right eye and the prevailing weather in Zurich made it advisable to postpone surgery until the spring. By and large, said Vogt, Joyce had made good progress, and an operation to remove the cataract in the right eye and the post-cataract membrane in the left could be considered at a later date. He was fitted with new glasses and found his eyesight improved. He lingered in Zurich briefly for the pleasure of hearing a lecture about himself on Swiss radio, and to meet Daniel Brody, who travelled from Munich personally to hand him a copy of the third German edition of *Ulysses*, handsomely printed on India paper in two volumes.

Back at Square Robiac on the 27th, Joyce was ready to enjoy a night of drunken merriment among friends. Gilbert, on the point of leaving for England, joined the family and a few others for an evening's entertainment.

> On Friday a dinner chez J.J. at which, on ... little more than a bottle [of Fendant] J.J. managed to get blind drunk before midnight. Fell off his chair on to the floor, talked unintelligibly. McGreevy and I helped him to bed – I said goodnight and held out my hand; he pressed his lips

against it! The family still hostile to Mrs Fleischman and Jews in general. Anyhow Mrs F is marrying George Joyce on Wednesday (the 11th) and can snap her fingers. I foresee a swift reconciliation. Mrs F's presents are worth to the Joyces at least 200 pounds a year. They cannot do without ... someone like her.[48]

Joyce had sobered up sufficiently on 9 December to sign over the rest of the world rights of *Ulysses* to Miss Beach. That, he hoped, would safeguard him against further piracy. He would continue to receive a 25 per cent royalty, and she would be able to set her own price if she ever gave up her rights to another publisher.[49]

The unwelcome marriage duly took place on 10 December at the Mairie of the 6th arrondissement with McGreevy as a witness, and Gilbert's prophecy proved uncannily accurate. On the 22nd Joyce told Harriet that Nora and Helen were 'on the most affectionate terms'. Now, he added, by French law Giorgio was 'the monarch of all he surveys'.[50] Gilbert recorded his own sardonic satisfaction in his journal on Christmas Day. 'The reconciliation is achieved. Despite Joyce's predilection for the family Christmas dinner under his own roof, Mrs Joyce has had her own way and the dinner (to which we are not invited) will take place at her daughter-in-law's. But the general meeting of the Faithful will take place as usual at his place.'[51] Man Ray was commissioned to photograph the happy couple, an intense-looking Giorgio staring, as if mesmerized, into the knowing eyes of the smiling bride. Following Christmas celebrations, the newly-weds departed on honeymoon to Germany in their new Buick – a wedding present from the bride's father, Adolph Kastor. Joyce's present was an American typewriter, a Remington, his 'new toy', he called it.

It was just after the wedding, at a party, that Lucia shocked William Bird. 'I was attending a celebration of some sort at the Joyces', he recalled, 'and she was there. I sat down in a corner beside her. After a few banalities, she said, "Mr Bird, I know what's the matter with me – I'm sex-starved." I said, "That's rot, Lucia – what have you been reading?" Norah bounded over from across the room. "Don't talk to her, Mr Bird. Any kind of conversation only makes her worse."'[52]

At that time, Lucia was bereft. Her 'love', Alexander Calder, had ditched her and returned to America to get married. She never knew why he went away as he simply disappeared and never wrote.[53] Then, at a party thrown by bohemian friends of Calder, she met the twenty-three-year-old Albert Hubbell, a married man separated from his wife. Hubbell was surprised at her eagerness and ardour. They soon became lovers, and according to Hubbell she was a virgin when they first made love. When he asked her what her parents would think of her being out late with him, she replied, 'Oh, don't worry about *them*.'[54] Although he felt he could love her, he was also alarmed because she spurned any form of birth control and he began to fear the consequences of their love-making. In time Hubbell and his wife were reconciled and he gradually abandoned Lucia. She later hinted at some unpleasant sexual experience involving Hubbell's friends the Trautmans and an American called Waldo Peirce. According to Cary F. Baynes, who was close to her later in Zurich, she admitted to her father having done 'terrible' things in her life, acting in 'ways that women should not'.[55]

After these traumas of abandonment and guilt, Lucia is reported to have been 'on the sexual prowl', having assignations with sailors, staying out at night and being more and more harangued by her mother for not behaving like other girls. 'My mother,' she told her cousin, Bozena Schaurek, 'doesn't approve of me.'[56] If the mother–daughter relationship was becoming increasingly strained, her father, however concerned he felt, remained detached, inscrutable, and tolerant.

Just before Christmas, Joyce informed Harriet that Gorman was writing his biography and that he was supplying him with relevant information. He also mentioned having helped Padraic Colum with his essay 'Joyce as Poet' for *The Joyce Book*. Wherever he could, as with *Our Exagmination*, he would edit and control what was written about him. He was also eager to oversee translations of his work, and joined the séances among the various translators of *Anna Livia Plurabelle*. Samuel Beckett and Alfred Péron began the French translation late in 1930. When Beckett returned to Ireland in May the following year, others would pick up where he left off.

While Joyce may have been approaching the New Year in merrily bibulous mood after the usual Christmas binge, a sobering letter from Fred Monro, forwarded by Harriet, must have given him pause. 'You may quite well say that it is no business of mine,' wrote the lawyer, 'but it occurs to me that Mr Joyce should make an effort to keep within his means. He has now realized £2,000 of capital of the investments in his name.' However much she had indulged him in the past Harriet now added a stern note of her own. 'Now that's a nice new year's thought to send you, isn't it? ... Anyway I suppose that now that your son is as you put it, monarch of all he surveys, your expenses will be somewhat lessened. Now it's your turn to ask most suavely what business that is of mine. So here we leave it.'[57]

There are two versions of what happened that New Year's Eve. Padraic Colum told of a dinner attended by the Jolases, the Gilberts and the Colums, where, at Joyce's request, Maria Jolas sang an operatic aria and

Colum recited Blake's 'Hear the Voice of the Bard'. 'That,' he recalled, 'was an evening of good food, good wine, good companionship, good talk, music, and poetry.'[58] Joyce told Harriet that he had had a bad New Year – because he was broke.

Looking nonchalant and relaxed: that 'faraway look' had just won his patron Harriet Weaver to an understanding of 'Work in Progress' (*Finnegans Wake*), a book on which she had earlier told him he was wasting his genius.

TOP LEFT With John Drinkwater in Salzburg in 1928. Joyce first encountered the playwright at a meeting of the PEN Club in London and found him an enthusiastic fan of both *Ulysses* and *Finnegans Wake*.

TOP RIGHT Stuart Gilbert, seen here with Joyce and Nora on holiday in Torquay in 1929, kept a diary of sharp and cynical comments on the activities and attitudes of the great author. He also wrote a book about *Ulysses* and helped translate it into French.

The dancing fish: in the costume she made herself, Lucia danced to Schubert's *March Militaire* in a competition at Paris's Bal Bullier to the applause of all except the judges.

Joyce decided that the Irish singer John Sullivan was the greatest tenor of his generation and went to great lengths to promote him, even persuading friends and admirers to form a claque to cheer him on during performances. Here he is out walking in Paris with Sullivan and the diminutive Irish poet James Stephens.

This wedding photograph of Giorgio and Helen Joyce reveals just how besotted Joyce's son was with the American divorcée.

Joyce placed great importance on the family portraits he inherited. This portrait of his father, painted by Patrick Tuohy, was widely admired in both Dublin and Paris.

When her parents went to London to get married in June 1931, Lucia had to give up plans to set up a dance studio in Paris in order to accompany them. This picture shows her at the back of their Kensington flat looking duly miserable. The following year she prevented her parents from returning to London by throwing a *cris de nerfs* at the Gare du Nord.

To ensure his children's inheritance, Joyce reluctantly agreed to marry Nora to legalize their union. When the London press got wind of it, they were door-stepped and pursued all the way to the Kensington Register Office and back.

TOP LEFT Paul Léon, Joyce's devoted secretary, took over where Samuel Beckett left off after he returned to Ireland in 1931. He considered Joyce a great genius and thought that his unrelenting search for a cure for Lucia's madness unreasonably interfered with his great project, *Work in Progress*.

TOP RIGHT The wealthy Harriet Shaw Weaver settled a substantial amount of money on Joyce to allow him to devote himself entirely to writing. But she had failed to anticipate that his extravagance would siphon off much of her settlement, and his demands for money would be unabated.

Maria Jolas, with her husband Eugene, published excerpts from *Work in Progress* in their magazine *transition*. It was her husband who guessed the title *Finnegans Wake*, at which Joyce said, 'Ah Jolas, you've taken something out of me.'

By 1939 *Work in Progress* was ready for publication, but Joyce had difficulty reading the proofs because of his poor eyesight. When Faber republished the book in 1945, they issued a 16-page booklet listing 628 corrections to the text; a 2011 edition incorporates 9,000 corrections.

Pictured with his back to the camera at the confluence of the Rivers Sihl and Limmat in Zürich, this was Joyce's favourite photograph. 'At last a view of myself which I can look at with some pleasure,' he wrote.

Paul Ruggiero, a Zürich bank clerk, had been a student of Joyce's, and when he fled to Switzerland from France in 1940 he helped him and his family find a home. Later, when Joyce was dying, he got him to sign a power of attorney permitting Nora to draw funds from his Swiss account.

Getting permission from the Vichy authorities in the Unoccupied Zone of Southern France to leave for Switzerland was, for Joyce, a bureaucratic nightmare from which he and his family did finally emerge, but, to his deep disappointment, Lucia had to be left behind in German-occupied territory.

The day of Joyce's funeral was cold and the lions were roaring in the zoo beyond Fluntern Cemetery. The suggestion that Joyce be given a religious funeral was declined by Nora, who said, 'I couldn't do that to him.'

On Joyce's deathbed, Nora agreed that Mrs Giedion, their Swiss friend, could have a death mask made of her husband. Afterwards she offered it to Nora but expected her to pay for it, which, in her impoverished condition, she was unable to do. The mask, and copies of it, ended up in various museums and libraries.

After the Irish government refused to have his body repatriated to Ireland, Nora was first buried separately from James, but they were later interred together in this *Ehrengrab*, a grave of honour, donated by the city of Zürich.

29

A Very English Wedding

(1931)

'If the prisoner is happy, why lock him in? If he is not, why pretend
that he is?' George Bernard Shaw, *Man and Superman* (1903)

The New Year began inauspiciously. Joyce had very reluctantly come to
admit that the Sullivan campaign had proved useless. Then Antheil told
him he was not interested in composing an opera based on Byron's *Cain*,
unless Joyce himself wrote the libretto. But Joyce replied that for him to
rewrite the text of a great English poet would be bad manners, and if
Antheil could not do the job 'with enthusiasm and with spiritual profit'
to himself or his art, he would find someone else to do it.[1] He later said
that he thought Pound, who was reported to be madder than ever, was
behind Antheil's change of heart.

Joyce was in poor health. His eyesight had deteriorated and he was
unable to sleep. However, Miss Beach persuaded him to attend a reading
by Edith Sitwell at the bookshop. There he was approached by a tall
bearded figure who introduced himself as Louis Gillet. The Frenchman
apologized to Joyce for his earlier critical essay, and said he had rethought
his position. He had now read the book several times, he said, and was
working on another article about it and about his *Work in Progress*.[2]
Astonished at his lack of animosity, Gillet invited Joyce to dinner. Letters
and signed copies of books were then exchanged (one from Gillet expressed 'humility and devotion'). Shortly afterwards, he wrote to Joyce
saying what a privilege it was to have met him and to know his great
Ulysses. He complimented him on his new work which he regarded as
'poetry' – Joyce's attempt to recast the mind was creating a new music on
a cosmic scale – and asked if he could read a few pages of *Work in
Progress* with him.[3] In February he organized a formal dinner for Joyce
and Soupault, for which Beach and Monnier (who considered the honour
'*extraordinaire!*') raised a subscription.

John Joyce, in nostalgic mood, wrote at the end of January 1931
wishing him a happy birthday, and asking if he recalled 'the old days in
Brighton Square, when you were Baby Tuckoo, and I used to take you out

in the Square and tell you all about the moo-cow that used to come down from the mountain and take little boys across'. Having noticed from a photograph that Giorgio now wore glasses, he said he hoped Lucia's sight was not similarly impaired.[4] John himself had had eye trouble and Charlie now required glasses. The Joyces, it seems, had inherited a weakness.

Joyce was still keeping open his lifeline to James Stephens, his chosen replacement should he be unable to continue his novel, updating him about his health and inviting him to a celebration of their joint birthday on 2 February. However, there are differing versions of *that* occasion. Padraic Colum claimed that, wanting to 'frame' Joyce on the brink of his fiftieth year, he chose this occasion for the pen portrait he published the following year in the *Dublin Magazine*.

> Slender, well-made, he holds himself very upright; he is tastefully dressed, and wears a ring in which is a large stone. The pupils of his eyes are enlarged because of successive operations, but his gaze is attentive and steady. There is a small tuft of beard on his chin. The flesh of his face has softness and colour – the glow that a child's face has ... His hands have now the softness, the sensitivity, of a man who has to depend a good deal on touch. All the lines of his face are fine; indeed his appearance is not only distinguished but winning. This appearance and his courtesy give him great dignity ... But head and forehead curve upward and outward, giving a sense of fullness and resonance ... One can easily think of this head as having correspondence with a musical instrument ... The abundant hair, brushed backward, has lines in it that are like strings, like iron-grey strings.[5]

That evening, Colum wrote, Joyce received guests lying on his sofa, decked out with a bright necktie and his colourful waistcoat. The party then moved to Les Trianons, with the Colums, the Stephenses, Miss Beach and John Sullivan. There they drank Clos St Patrice, 'the only saint', according to Joyce, 'who a man can get drunk in honour of', and he was persuaded to sing his Molly Bloom parody of 'Molly Brannigan' and 'Oh the Brown and Yellow Ale', about a man selling his wife to a sinister stranger.[6]

The other version came from Joyce, in a long two-part letter to Harriet two weeks later, complaining that he had had 'the worst birthday in history' and been unable to afford 'the usual reunion' with his friends. 'I sat in the corner of the drawing room sulking and waiting for the arrival of camel loads of presents and volleys of telegrams but that was the good it did me.' He was only rescued, he said, when Helen and Giorgio returned from their honeymoon and led him off to Les Trianons.[7] No mention of a shared birthday with Stephens or any of the others, recalled by Colum. Joyce was of course pleading, against Fred Monro's wise advice, for more of his stock to be cashed and needing to pile on the agony for Harriet. He was owed 21,000 francs, he said, but couldn't get his hands on a franc of it. He also had the £20 advance from James Wells to repay. Gilbert took a purely cynical line, seeing this poverty-pleading as an expression of dissatisfaction with his interminable book. 'He is obviously bored with the whole business, but they seem to be passing through a financial crisis and he needs the money, or thinks he does.'[8]

Preparing now to leave Square Robiac, Joyce put his books into storage and left the piano and family portraits with Giorgio. In Paris, he said, everyone he knew appeared to be either sick, wrecked, mad, or all of these together – Larbaud very ill, deep in melancholy and locked in his flat; Fargue gone mad, wanting to fight imaginary duels. However, with the aid of Léon and Soupault, the French *Anna Livia Plurabelle* had been completed – another 'committee' job, this time with seven translators to credit – Beckett, Alfred Péron, Goll, Jolas, Léon, Monnier and Soupault as well as himself. Joyce declared it 'one of the masterpieces of translation',[9] and announced that it would soon appear in the *NRF* thanks to Miss Monnier who was also arranging a séance to launch it. She and an actress would read both his original English version and the 'committee's' translation – followed, he joked, by him dancing the Highland fling.

He was also helping sift through papers and rake through memories for his biography. Gorman, his biographer, was already in touch with the Austrian poet Felix Beran, Gerald Griffin and Judge Michael Lennon, who had replied at length. Livia Svevo and Pound were unforthcoming, and Gogarty wrote saying that doctors never gave away anecdotes about their friends. (Six years later, in his first book of memoirs, however, he had seemingly changed his mind.) Gorman said he had met lots of opposition, with people calling him 'a hack' among other things. Joyce defended his choice, pointing out to his friends that Gorman had been the first to write a book about him and had written biographies of Hawthorne, Dumas and Longfellow. His main interest, he said, was 'to see that the facts and dates are correct'.[10] Gorman was no hack but was in danger of becoming Joyce's autobiographical amanuensis.

In his reply to Gorman, His Honour Judge Lennon said, 'I know little or nothing about him [Joyce], except what I heard from an old relative of his & this you can have *sans payer*.'[11] After offering a few basic (incorrect) facts about place of birth and education, and repeating a few half-truths about John Joyce, Lennon referred Gorman to his old College friends Curran and Fallon for further information. He later wrote mentioning an article he had written for the New York *Catholic World*, telling Gorman to use it as he wished, but not to mention it to Joyce who might find it offensive. He was less fortunate elsewhere. Fallon refused to help and Stanislaus was unprepared to copy documents or pay anyone else to do so.

Stannie's reluctance to co-operate with Gorman seemed to Joyce yet another act of betrayal, especially after he had written from Trieste damning him and all his latest works.

> With the best will in the world I cannot read your work in progress. The vague support you get from certain French and American critics, I set down to pure snobbery. What is the meaning of that rout of drunken words? It seems to me pose, the characteristic you have in common with Wilde, Shaw, Yeats, and Moore. You want to show that you are a superclever superman with a superstyle. It riles my blood to see you competing with Miss Stein for the position of Master Boomster. But whereas she never had anything to lose, you have – … breadth, sanity, and a real style, which was a registering instrument of rare delicacy and strength.[12]

There can have been no plainer expression of Shaun abusing Shem in the Third Book of *Finnegan*, Joyce's own family post-mortem. He replied sadly that he was sorry his brother took the same line as a madman from Trieste who had recently written to threaten him.

Lennon's *Catholic World* article seemed well calculated to inflame the hostility of already suspicious Dubliners. Here, it said, was a writer of no great merit who had traduced those who were destined to liberate Ireland from British oppression, abandoned his Catholic faith and morals and eloped with a waitress to live in sin in a far country where he worked for the British at a time when brave patriots were dying for Ireland. It cast aspersions on James's father and ended with the unpleasant innuendo that his loss of sight was some sort of punishment for his loss of faith.[13] This farrago of mistruths was grist to the gossip mill, and could only reinforce the intense prejudice against him which already existed. Having read the article, Padraic and Mary Colum, who were keen for Joyce to visit Ireland, kept it from him for several months. When he did finally see it, rather than share their fury, Joyce was simply perplexed that someone he had entertained to dinner, given a signed copy of *Ulysses* and sat up talking with till after midnight, could have written about him in such a fashion. He wanted Eugene Jolas to print some of Lennon's insulting remarks in *transition* alongside equally offensive comments about him from Jung. Jolas declined the suggestion but Joyce thought that such attacks contributed to his controversial image. The whole affair merely strengthened his belief that he could only expect betrayal in Dublin and had better stay away. Stephens told him he was too princely by nature and not angry enough, and Joyce admitted that he had been 'a sap'. This sense of vulnerability probably explains his readiness to litigate.

Joyce worried when Harriet failed to reply to his letters for a while, until it emerged that she had been ill. However, the weight of gloom descended further when he suddenly felt deserted by his helpers. He sent her a catalogue of his woes. Most of his friends were either ill or out of town and the only person available, apart from Léon, was his daughter-in-law Helen who was helping to copy his almost illegible notes. Then three banks in the city had just crashed, Nora had had a series of colds, and he worried that Monnier's séance might mark the end of his Paris career just as the one with Larbaud had launched it. On top of that he had no idea what his book was about, his hair was thinning, his false teeth were troubling him and he could not afford the dentist.[14]

The women in the family were also feeling edgy though for different reasons. Nora was unhappy about going to London to face possible public revelations about her marital status; Lucia, when she discovered that she was illegitimate, was shocked and mortified and her attitude towards her mother, already strained, became openly hostile. Once, when Nora lost patience with her and shouted 'You bastard!' she yelled back, 'If I am a bastard, who made me one?'

Joyce was disturbed. His 'bella bambina', his sainted Angel of Light, was beginning to worry him. She had now given up dancing and begun to attend drawing classes, astonishing her teacher with her designs. But she had given that up to begin a novel, then, abandoning that, had started attending fashion shows. She was full of determination to do something, he admitted, but the problem was how to direct her energy, and the men who hovered around him were unworthy of her. For herself, Lucia was deeply unhappy about leaving Paris because she and Kitten Neel had planned to launch a physical-culture class together, and moving to London would wreck their dream.

Although Joyce had now decided to establish British residence, regularize his marriage and secure his children's inheritance, marrying in London risked exciting press attention and gaining a dubious reputation there. His past, he told Harriet, was catching up with him and he probably deserved all he got on account of what he called his 'many iniquities'. However, the plan was to take a small furnished flat in London, then move to Zurich to see Vogt before returning to Paris. Without asking directly for more money, he wrote simply, 'I have just sufficient funds to enable me to exist for about three days more.'[15] However low the state of his finances and state of his mind, he still managed to host a St Patrick's

Day celebration which he christened 'the last supper'.[16]

Livia Svevo's 'lunatic' brother, Bruno Veneziani, had suddenly appeared at the flat asking for letters of introduction to various artistic personages, including Milhaud and Gide, which Joyce agreed to provide, probably to get rid of him. Gide later wrote telling Adrienne Monnier that he had received an exquisite letter from Joyce but thought so highly of him that he dared not reply. However, changing his mind, on the same day he wrote to Joyce, beginning, 'What a pleasure to receive a letter from the great Joyce!' and looking forward to the pleasure of making his acquaintance.[17] Monnier told him that such a letter from Gide was 'a rarity', and Beach declared it 'a marvel'.

Although short of money, Harriet, concerned by Joyce's tales of woe, sold some shares of her own in order to get over to Paris for Monnier's séance which was held at La Maison des Amis des Livres on 26 March. Leon Edel, who also attended, recalled the scene. Tables had been cleared back, and around a hundred chairs set out. Edel found himself sitting just opposite Joyce, noticing his sad face and clipped moustache – a distant, melancholy and aloof figure, wrapped in deep gloom. Soupault spoke 'with charm and liveliness' about translating *Anna Livia*, and Adrienne Monnier, dressed in her long robes with a white shawl, read from it 'in the accents of the Comédie Française, singsong, in her high musical voice, up and down, up and down, no low tones'. She then wound up a gramophone and played the recording of Joyce reading from his book. Edel had arrived at the meeting a sceptic, but found himself deeply affected. 'I had wondered again and again why Joyce was "wasting" his unique gifts in fashioning an entire book out of portmanteau words, the kind Lewis Carroll put together in "Jabberwocky." But from the moment I heard Joyce's recording of this section of *Anna Livia Plurabelle* I became a convert. I felt that there was method in the madness.'[18] The solemnity of the event was enlivened when McAlmon, who refused to take the occasion seriously, raised his hands mockingly in prayer during the readings. This prompted Edouard Dujardin to rush over and slap his face, thinking he was pretending to be shocked at the size of his wife's ankles about which she was highly sensitive. Before Harriet left Paris Joyce tapped her for £160.

Despite his professed poverty, when the family left Square Robiac they were booked into the exclusive Hotel Powers just off the Champs-Elysées. The move took four days between the feast day of St Isidore (mentioned in the 'Cyclops' episode) and that of St Julie (referred to in *Finnegans Wake*). The trauma of removal brought on another of Joyce's nervous breakdowns, leaving him in a state of collapse, and the London trip was postponed till he recovered properly.

Even before Joyce left Paris the English newspapers were reporting his coming, without, it seems, any inkling of his true intention. Two weeks after leaving Square Robiac the Joyces checked into the Terminus Hotel in Calais where storms held them up briefly before they braved the Channel. They arrived in London on the evening of 26 April, taking rooms at the Hotel Belgravia, close to the boat-train terminus at Victoria. Lucia began attending the Grosvenor School of Modern Art in nearby Warwick Square, which her parents hoped she would find diverting.

Joyce's priority was to get *Ulysses* published in America and England. But everywhere the after-effects of the Wall Street Crash were being felt. There was less money around, book sales were suffering and publishers were favouring shorter books. Eliot, fearing that publishing the whole book would invite prosecution, was interested in bringing out extracts as '*Criterion Miscellanies*' (a series of monographs published by Faber between 1929 and 1936 as an offshoot of the *Criterion* magazine).

To qualify for British residence Joyce needed to convince the British authorities that he was in England to stay, and taking an unfurnished flat would strengthen his claim. Finally he took a five-month lease on a first-floor flat, 28b Campden Grove, off Kensington Church Street. To Miss Beach he described it as a 'tiny place at a low rent'. It was a short walk from the Albert Hall and a short taxi-ride from the cinemas and theatres of the West End. There were good restaurants nearby – Slater's on Kensington High Street became a favourite – and, since Nora hated cooking in the tiny kitchen, there was always cooked chicken to be had from Barkers' emporium. In fact their nickname for the flat became 'Barkers' Chicken'. Harriet, who had found the flat, arranged subscriptions for Joyce to the W. H. Smith Lending Library and the Times Book Club. With the gloom of the Great Depression hanging over London, Joyce dubbed the street 'Campden Grave', a street full of mummies.

Babou and Kahane's edition of *Haveth Childers Everywhere* appeared in Paris, quickly followed by Eliot's *Criterion Miscellany* edition from Faber in London. Eliot told Joyce that by publication day they had received 4,700 orders for it. Sylvia Beach declared it 'a good-looking little book' which contained 'some of the funniest things in *Work in Progress*', and early English reviews she thought 'sporting'.[19] The 'sporting' G. W. Stonier in the *New Statesman*, declared that 'It is possible to regard this book as a proof that Mr Joyce, recoiling further and further from the underworld of Mr Bloom and Dublin, has at last really shut himself up in his own snail's-house, leaving for the exasperated reader only a track.'[20] 'Anon' in the *TLS* commented that 'Read aloud, as Mr Joyce's work should be, the prose of this fragment has a stateliness appropriate to its matter, in ponderous, masculine contrast to the streamlike melodies of *Anna Livia Plurabelle*.'[21]

In the *Dublin Magazine*, Colum called it 'more like a piece of mythology than a novel'.[22]

The news that Joyce was in England was enough to prompt his Dublin enemies to mobilize. John Cusack, son of Michael, whom he had caricatured in the 'Cyclops' episode, told William D'Arcy that in the event of him coming to Ireland libel notices were waiting to be served on him by Major Owen Tweedy, Mr J. C. Doyle, Mr James Daly, Miss A. Tracy, a Mr William Puretoy and Reuben J. Dodd.[23] It was just another reason for Joyce to steer clear of the Island of Saints and Sages.

Relations on the Beach-Monnier front were coming under strain. Joyce was contemplating a US edition of *Ulysses*, but Beach, who owned the American rights, was frustrating his plan. She was exasperated by his continual borrowing on his royalty account which also offended the austere and high-minded Monnier. In his letter to her, Gide had expressed admiration at Joyce's willingness to experiment to the limit without concern for worldly success or money. She and Beach, however, knew differently. When Joyce rejected Kahane's offer for another fragment, saying that he must always 'go to the limit' in what he could get for his work, the dam of resentment burst, and Monnier penned him a letter of barely concealed disgust. Gide's admiration, she told him, was misplaced: what he did not know was that quite to the contrary Joyce was very much concerned about money and success.

> You wish others also to go the limit; you lead them by rough stages to some Dublingrad or other which they're not interested in, or rather, you try to lead them./In Paris rumour has it that you are spoiled, that we have ruined you with overwhelming praise and that you no longer know what you are doing ... /My personal opinion is that you know perfectly well what you are doing, *in literature* ... but it's folly to wish to make money at any cost with your new work. I won't say you can't make any ... but it is most unlikely. The three pamphlets ... have scarcely sold more than two-thirds or at most three-fourths ... /Times are hard, and the worst isn't over. We're travelling now third class and soon we'll be riding the rods.

Despite this stern reprimand he could, said Monnier, be assured of her 'great and faithful admiration'.[24] Léon was outraged and called the letter 'an impertinence', but Joyce was probably well aware that his profligacy and continual demands for funds was stretching the loyalty of the once-worshipful Beach and her parsimonious lover. As usual he barely reacted to this reprimand, and, as if to cock a snook at rue de l'Odéon, wrote asking Beach for a 1,000-franc note to be sent by registered post, and enquiring the price of a case of Clos St Patrice. Then, when Colum suggested she would get $10,000 for the US rights of *Ulysses*, as if to show him that she too could play for high stakes, Beach asked $25,000.

Joyce and Nora were by no means isolated in 'Campden Grave'. They dined with Eliot, Herbert Hughes, John Dulanty, and the Lynds, and had visits from Colum, Giorgio and Helen. Lucia mentioned a Sunday trip to Canterbury to watch an historical pageant, an Albert Hall concert which included Schubert's *Unfinished Symphony*, and a cinema visit to see Lillian Gish in *Orphans of the Storm*. On 10 May, inscribed copies of the Faber *Anna Livia Plurabelle* and *Haveth Childers Everywhere* were sent to Beckett, who, later that summer, passing through London, took Lucia out to dinner and was shocked by how ill she looked – 'knackered', he said.[25]

When Padraic Colum visited Campden Grove, he had what he called 'one of the friendliest sessions I ever had with Joyce', and remembered Nora's admiration at his work being widely published in magazines. Why couldn't Jim do the same thing, she asked, instead of writing for obscure periodicals like *transition* which hardly anybody read? 'It is better to have one good trick than a dozen poor ones,' Colum told her, but she was unimpressed. Later Joyce remarked to him, 'Isn't it extraordinary that none of my family read anything I write?' Nora's indifference was probably something of an act; she told Colum that she 'often read and liked the *Anna Livia* episode in *Work in Progress*'.[26] Power also got the impression that she had read more of *Ulysses* than she pretended, and certainly knew the 'Penelope' episode well enough, sometimes quoting passages from memory. Beckett could only recall her quoting poetry.[27]

Huebsch was once again interested in *Ulysses* but was faced with Beach's excessive demand for US rights. She told Joyce that business was poor and only *Haveth Childers* and *Anna Livia*, the cheapest and slimmest volumes of his, were selling at all well. Consequently, he had no more than 1,000 francs in his account – roughly £8. He did receive some £25 from Rhein-Verlag for the sale of his German *Ulysses*, but there were bills to pay: 1,000 francs to Collinson, and 260 francs to Les Trianons and around 100 francs to his florist.

In June came word that Helen was pregnant. The idea of continuing his line meant a great deal to Joyce, as the family portraits attest. When Arthur Power came visiting, they drove out of London to dine at a restaurant along the Portsmouth road. On the return journey he announced in 'a low intimate voice' that he had just received important news. 'What?' asked Power. When Joyce told him he replied, 'Is that all?'

'It is the most important thing there is,' said Joyce, meaning 'Another Joyce is born,' and Power decided that sometimes his limitless egoism came close to madness. They drove back to Campden Grove in silence and their goodbyes were 'distant'. Power had challenged something at the heart of Joyce's sense of self-worth and their once close relationship never quite recovered.[28]

On Bloomsday, 16 June, Joyce wired Miss Beach who marked the occasion by entertaining Helen and Giorgio. Shortly afterwards he discovered that his brother Charlie was in a London hospital suffering from tuberculosis. Having visited him a few times, he, Nora and Lucia were now nervous about the possibility of being infected. After his discharge Joyce visited Charlie at his home, offering his typewriter so that his unemployed nephew George could learn typing, and a pound a week for copying his notes. Hearing of this, Sylvia Beach wrote saying, 'It is not very gay for any of you there, I am afraid.'[29]

On 29 June, Joyce was handed the lease on 28b Campden Grove, thus becoming a UK resident, a voter and liable for jury duty. The following day, on Monro's advice, he applied for a special marriage licence, arranging the ceremony for 4 July (his father's and brother George's birthdays). To shield his identity he wrote down all his Christian names (James Augustine Aloysius Joyce) and omitted his place of birth. He was also keen to keep the truth behind the wedding secret, telling Helen and Giorgio not to betray the fact that they were just about to be 'made honest'. To confuse the newshounds, he joked, the bride would be dressed as a lifeguard while the groom would wear green satin, a white veil and carry an orange-coloured umbrella. But a few hours after registering his intention to marry, Joyce was buttonholed in Campden Grove by an Associated Press reporter whom he only shook off finally by referring him for answers to Fred Monro who happened to be out of town. But the Joyces' front door-bell rang all that day, and at midnight, when they returned from dining out, there was a reporter camped on the front steps.

The day before the wedding, 3 July, Joyce was at Monro's home by 8.30 a.m. When the lawyer suggested he confess all, Joyce said he had nothing to confess. The line they finally agreed was that he and Nora underwent a form of marriage in Austria in 1904 which was invalid because Nora had given a false name (Gretta Greene) and it was not registered with the British Consulate. They were marrying now 'for testamentary reasons'.

The wedding was scheduled for 11.15 a.m. at Kensington Register Office in Marloes Road, a short walk from Campden Grove. That morning, London was greeted with the headlines Joyce had been so anxious to avoid. The *Daily Express* carried news of the notice to marry, complete with photograph of Joyce in hat and bow-tie, and informed its readers that he lived in Campden Grove, had a flat in Paris, had undergone several operations for failing eyesight and had refused to comment on the story. But the *Daily Mirror* was quick to sniff a scandal, saying

> The bride's name is given as Nora Joseph Barnacle, aged 47, of the same address./Mr Joyce is the author of *Ulysses*. According to *Who's Who* he was married in 1904 to Miss Nora Barnacle of Galway.[30]

The *Telegraph* had a longer piece tucked away on page twelve which mentioned the couple's having lived for many years in Trieste and having two children. It would need more than an orange umbrella or fake uniform to prevent them from being waylaid by prowling hacks on the way to the altar.

Not only was Campden Grove swarming with journalists, Joyce told Harriet, but the street outside the Registry Office was occupied by a squad of cameramen. Having run the press gauntlet, inside the Office there was a delay while the Registrar's clerk argued that the couple should be divorced from an irregular marriage before they could marry in accordance with regular English law. Fred Monro, who had accompanied them, convinced the clerk otherwise and the ceremony proceeded, witnessed by Monro and a Mr Clark, borrowed from the Registrar's Office. On the marriage certificate Joyce was entered as a forty-nine-year-old bachelor of independent means and Nora as a spinster aged forty-seven. An official cloak was thereby drawn over twenty-seven years of 'sinful living'. Joyce found a reason to joke about it. With the King then signing into law a bill extending the right to marry within the family, nicknamed the 'Marry-Your-Aunt Bill', now, he said, he should sign a 'Marry-Your-Wife Bill'.[31]

On the way back from the Registry Office along Marloes Road, a photographer snapped the newly-weds, Nora wearing a smart coat with a high fur collar, despite the summer heat, and hiding her face coyly beneath the brim of a fashionable cloche hat. Beside her, Fred Monro conceals his lower face with his left hand, and close behind, ashplant in hand, is Joyce, sporting that bow-tie, and staring grumpily ahead from under a broad-brimmed hat tilted back above a furrowed brow. This picture appeared on page three of the *Evening Standard*, together with the story of the 1904 'marriage' to Miss Barnacle. Later Joyce was door-stepped by a *Sunday Express* reporter wanting to know the story behind 'Nora Barnacle, Spinster'. He was handed a letter from the *Express* editor offering him half the middle page for an article, with the implied threat of a hostile story if he refused. Joyce declined the offer, saying that he neither read newspapers nor wrote for them. But of course he read newspapers avidly, and next day made sure he bought the *Sunday Express* to see if the editor's threat had been carried out. It had not.

A week after the wedding, the Lynds threw a great literary party at their Hampstead home in Keats Grove, where the garden was festooned with fairy lights and nightlights in coloured jars. Just after midnight everyone moved indoors to the drawing room where Joyce went to the piano and sang 'Phil the Fluther's Ball' and the sadly poignant 'Shule Aroon'. For the first time Joyce found himself among leading lights of English letters, including Goronwy Rees, J. B. Priestley, Victor Gollancz, Norman Collins, Max Beerbohm, Arthur Ransome, Humbert Wolfe and Isaiah Berlin, some of whom performed their own party pieces. But Joyce stole the show, as the Lynds' daughter recalled. 'Against his own low accompaniment he recited ... *Anna Livia Plurabelle*. He neither spoke it nor sang it: he used something like the *sprechstimme*, or pitch-controlled speech, familiar from *Moses and Aaron*, and other works by Schoenberg. And the sound of it was lovely beyond description.'[32] Priestley also recalled the evening, comparing Joyce's easy presence in Hampstead with the 'heroic' Joyce he had found among his American idolators in Paris. 'He was all amiability, and sang, in a pleasant light tenor, many comic songs. Probably it is too difficult to sing comic songs to pilgrims from American Eng. Lit. departments.'[33]

The story in the London papers had filtered through to Joyce's relatives. There was a violent reaction from Nora's family in Galway, and in London, Charlie's zealously Catholic wife forbade him her house and her son any further contact with his immoral uncle. She threw Charlie's copy of *An Exagmination* onto the fire and later destroyed all his brother's letters and signed copies of his various books. Dublin, Joyce predicted, would soon follow suit, with Irish associates like McGreevy not far behind. In Paris, according to Giorgio, the rumour was that the London marriage was just another publicity stunt.

Joyce had hoped finally to travel to Cornwall in search of legends, but got no further than Stonehenge in Wiltshire. Nora refused to go, but her sister Kathleen, who was visiting them, did, and later recalled what happened. 'It was a very dreary day, and we could see nothing to amuse us but the wide open space of grass, and once in a while a soldier would come along on a motor-cycle. I said, "Where are we going? This is a terrible place!" And he said, "Kathleen, I am fourteen years trying to get here."'[34] To Frank Budgen he referred to the voice of John Sullivan as 'the voice of Stonehenge', implying an awesome inexplicable mystery.[35] He noticed that Kathleen was not wearing the watch he had given her in Bognor and asked about it. Much embarrassed, she admitted that she had pawned it, at which Joyce let out his famous guffaw and said, 'That's just what I'd do.'

Ralph Pinker, who now ran the Pinker agency, informed him that his agreement with Sylvia Beach gave her exclusive rights to *Ulysses* but the $25,000 (£5,000) she was asking for US rights was absurd. Maria Jolas claimed that the hand of Adrienne Monnier was behind this demand. When Bennett Cerf of Random House showed interest in the book Beach told him that an American edition would kill her business which depended heavily on American sales. Cerf denied this and said the best he could offer was £1,000, an offer she rejected. The feeling on Beach's part was that she had devoted ten years to Joyce for little in return despite his having given her manuscripts, the future value of which it was impossible to calculate.

Meanwhile Joyce had been sent a bill for £600 by his American lawyers for establishing his US copyright of *Work in Progress* which he refused to pay, believing that the US publisher should pay. As a gesture, he offered Beach a first option on *Work in Progress* for which Harcourt Brace and Viking Press in America and Faber in England had now made decent offers. He said he needed a quick response from her because the currently high interest in the work could decline.[36] She said that while she would love to publish *Work in Progress* more than anything in the world, she did not have the capital and he would need an immediate advance which she could not afford.[37]

In mid-July another 'worry' presented itself when Daniel Brody wired to say that the *Frankfurter Zeitung* had published a story, '*Vielleicht ein Traum*' ('Perchance to Dream'), purporting to be by 'James Joyce, the author of the great English novel *Ulysses*', and he suspected forgery. Joyce, his sense of persecution instantly inflamed, quickly alerted his friends; his sight, he told them, was too poor for him to be able read it easily. He wondered whether Miss Beach had shown, lent or sold one of his early manuscripts to someone, a suggestion which did nothing to lessen the strain between them. She denied having parted with a single paper but, from then on, it was Léon to whom he would send his manuscripts for safe-keeping.

When Joyce protested to the newspaper, the editor apologized, saying that the story was by an English writer, Michael Joyce, whose name had been misread by the translator, Irene Kafka. Kafka in turn blamed her secretary. However, this failed to soothe the author's injured feelings, and he consulted widely over whether to sue the paper, suspecting that Michael Joyce was an invention. But as Harriet (doing research for him at the British Museum) found out, 'Perchance to Dream' by Michael Joyce had first appeared in the *London Mercury* the previous December.

When both Kafka and Michael Joyce wrote regretting what had happened, egged on by Giorgio, Miss Beach, Padraic Colum and Harold Nicolson, Joyce demanded a more fulsome apology in the *Zeitung* itself. When that was unforthcoming, he instructed Fred Monro to hire a German lawyer who warned Joyce that he could damage his reputation by appearing petty and spiteful. Grudgingly, the offended author climbed down, but then found himself facing sizeable legal costs.

The August issue of the *Revue des Deux Mondes* carried Louis Gillet's long-awaited essay examining *Work in Progress* in the context of Joyce's existing oeuvre. Gillet began by comparing Proust's use of Bergson's theory of time with Joyce's use of Vico's theory on the circularity of history. Within that compass, he said, Joyce recycled the great myths – the thunderous and fearsome birth of religion, Adam and Eve, Noah's Ark – all were there. Great literary themes and forms were there too. It was not a novel as we normally think of it. 'Despite the very humble status of the heroes, it is rather a Divine Comedy, a new Paradise Lost.' The daemon driving Joyce to create his 'new language' had grown to monstrous proportions and anyone approaching the book needed to bear in mind its 'several superimposed meanings', recognizing that its author's genius lay in his creation of unities and universes and in his 'melomania' – an inclination towards music, for which he had created 'an instrument of countless strings'. Gillet's tone was far more reverential than in his previous review and concluded by quoting from Rabelais, 'Mr Chatterbox, God bless you, you have so fresh a tongue.'[38]

Reading this article George Moore quickly sent his congratulations. It was 'as well considered as an article by Sainte-Beuve,' he said. He admired Gillet's attempt to 'disentangle Joyce's metaphysics' and the way he dealt with Joyce's newly 'invented' language. However, art was concerned with what the eye could see and not with the thinking mind, for which life was just 'the dreaming of a shade'. With Joyce there were no appearances, only 'syllogism'. Moore described their meeting and their discussion of *Ulysses*. 'I concluded that one of us had a blind patch in his mind somewhere. Which of us it is it would be an affectation for me to decide.'[39] Sylvia Beach wrote declaring Gillet's article on Joyce the most important about him since Larbaud's, and Adrienne Monnier said it was having a great effect in France.

On 5 August Joyce made out a new will, naming Nora Joseph Joyce his sole executor and trustee, and giving Harriet Weaver responsibility for his literary work. His portraits were willed to Giorgio. The only family name omitted was Lucia's. She, who had been in a highly nervous state throughout their time in London, had decided to return to France to stay with Helen and Giorgio at Montigny-sur-Loing near Fontainebleau. Joyce decided she needed escorting down to Dover – a good excuse to revisit the Lord Warden Hotel.

Bad weather delayed Lucia's departure for a week. Joyce's friend McGee, the hotel manager, offered to accompany her across the Channel and see her safely through Customs, and his daughter, Joan, was rewarded with a signed copy of *Pomes Penyeach*. Back in France with Helen and Giorgio, Lucia found that a frequent visitor was their friend Alex Ponisovsky, Léon's brother-in-law, on whom she had once had a crush. Now they began to spend time together, sometimes staying late at her brother's apartment in rue Huysmans.

To celebrate Harriet's birthday, James and Nora took her to dine at Kettner's in Soho, a restaurant founded by Napoleon III's chef and once a haunt of Oscar Wilde, Edward VII and Edward's mistress Lily Langtry. There was also news from Miss Beach to drink to. In spite of the hard times, young American students were busily buying Joyce's books, she reported, and now Gillet's article was bringing in French buyers. He was, she wrote, one of the few authors whose sales seemed unaffected by the Crash.

Gorman had been tempted away from Joyce's biography to write one of Mary Queen of Scots. But when Sylvia Beach challenged him about this, he assured her that he was concentrating full time on Joyce; to Eliot, who had commissioned the book for Faber, he gave the same assurance, saying it would be ready by January. Joyce now agreed to allow him access to his correspondence with Monro Saw, and asked Harriet to show Gorman any letters of his she might have kept, except those referring to his marriage.[40]

A contract with Faber to publish *Work in Progress* was signed, and Joyce, delighted, told Eliot that he thought the type would need to be large and clear so that no letter or word could be mistaken. But then, to sour his mood, came the lawyers' bills for his pursuit of the *Frankfurter Zeitung* for misusing his name. Shortly afterwards he collapsed with intestinal pains and what he called 'heaviness in eyes'.[41]

With so much happening, and anxious to have Lucia back within the family, Joyce felt it was time to return to Paris. Hoping to sub-let the flat in Campden Grove for six months, he and Nora left for Dover where the hotel manager McGee escorted them on board the ferry through a side-gate, bypassing passport and Customs checks, to reserved places in the observation saloon. By the end of September they were settled temporarily at 'La Résidence', at 41 Avenue Pierre 1er de Serbie, just off the Champs-Elysées, and began searching for a new apartment. But Joyce was faced with an impending devaluation and a corresponding decrease in income. At its best the pound had been worth 128 francs; now he anticipated a miserly 60. All he could hope to afford was a small furnished flat for a few months rather than a long-term lease. Ralph Pinker had asked him to find out whether Beach would accept an offer of £1,600 for the US rights of *Ulysses*. But, as he might come to depend more on income from royalties in the future, and she would pay him in francs, he felt he had to treat the matter with circumspection.

When Joyce finally managed to see the elusive Beach she told him that Samuel Roth had produced an edition of 10,000 copies of *Ulysses*, and suggested that Hemingway's US lawyer should be put on to the case. But for once Joyce had had his fill of lawyers. He told her that Pinker believed the best way to stop Roth was to bring out an authentic US edition, to which she repeated that such an edition would wreck her business and reduce her to farming chickens. While he had done well from her editions since 1922, she had earned nothing until recently and the rest of her business had suffered – hence her high price for American rights. She resisted all attempts at compromise, asking Joyce what he would live on if his income from her dried up? When Mary Colum heard about Beach's obstructionism she swore. She and Padraic were convinced that a US edition would bring him the Nobel Prize and pave the way for an English edition.[42]

After a month the Joyces took a furnished flat on a four-month lease at 2 rue St-Philibert in Passy, not, in Colum's view, the cheeriest home they had had in Paris.[43] But despite the gloomy district, the gloomy flat, the gloom over an unlet London flat and a lawyer's bill of £48, Joyce continued working. He was helped by house rules discouraging visitors and requesting residents to be in bed by 10.15 p.m. However, no pianos were permitted, so he could not easily escape his isolation through song.

As if to remind him where he had left off, Ogden's Basic English version of *Anna Livia Plurabelle* appeared in the journal *Psyche*. The article declared that this had been achieved with the aid of Joyce and his gramophone recording, and claimed that 'the reader will see that it has generally been possible to keep all the same rhythms'.[44] To H. G. Wells, the irony of this unlikely co-operation was too great to overlook. In *The Shape of Things to Come*, his 'history of the future', Dr Philip Raven notes that, 'While Ogden sought scientific simplification, Joyce worked aesthetically for elaboration and rich suggestion, and vanished at last from the pursuit of his dwindling pack of readers in a tangled prose almost indistinguishable from the gibbering of a lunatic. Nevertheless he added about twenty-five words to the language which are still in use.'[45]

Harriet finally got Beach to admit that her excessive demand for the US rights in *Ulysses* had a hidden goal, namely to teach the male-dominated New York publishers that a woman could stand up against them and therefore needed to be respected. 'These men,' she told her, quoting Adrienne Monnier, 'are very primitive, but they must be resisted.' However, the two women now seemed in a more conciliatory mood.[46]

As it deepened, the Great Depression changed the economic landscape in odd ways. In late October Harriet wrote saying that autumn was a lean time of year for her, with no dividends coming in between October and February, so could Joyce send her £37 of the £287 she had lent him over the past year? It was a strange reversal of roles for benefactress and beneficiary. Joyce took over a week to reply that he had quite forgotten borrowing money from her in Paris before she left for England.

Harold Nicolson, who had dubbed Joyce 'the Einstein of English fiction', was scheduled to give a broadcast talk about him in a series called *The New Spirit in Literature* on the BBC on 24 November. Miss Monnier, having made her point about male publishers, arranged a dinner to mark Nicolson's broadcast. A radio was set up in her dining-room and tuned to London in time for the eight-thirty talk. Nicolson came on and announced immediately that under pressure he had been forced to abandon it. According to Joyce, the absurdity of a dinner arranged in order to listen to two sentences produced gales of laughter. 'The company expressed itself volubly in French about the BBC directors etc after which we all went in to table and had a merry meal.'[47] The story, as Nicolson explained, was that he was called in to see Sir John Reith, the BBC's Director General, and told not to mention Joyce in his talk. Nicolson was outraged, threatening to write to *The Times*, and a compromise was reached. He was allowed to give the talk provided he did not refer to *Ulysses*. Later, Nicolson had to admit that Reith had been right because it was forbidden to name on 'the wireless' any book prohibited by the Home Office.[48] The talk which he was finally allowed to give on 6 December was an oddity. He discussed Joyce's life, the influences behind his work (Homer, Rabelais, Dujardin etc.), his recording from *Anna Livia Plurabelle*, and even quoted from *Ulysses*, without once mentioning the banned title. It was a small victory for the censors, but also a clever piece of manoeuvring by Nicolson, and Joyce cabled his congratulations. It prompted him to offer a strange, *Wake*-like effusion in the form of a letter in defence of the persecuted Sullivan – called 'From a Banned Writer to a Banned Singer',[49] later published in the *New Statesman* and distributed to all his friends by Harriet.

Meanwhile the Albatross Press in Hamburg, newly founded by John Holroyd-Reece and Kurt Enoch, was planning to launch its 'Modern Continental Library' paperback series with *Dubliners*. But Herbert Hughes's *The Joyce Book* was delayed by Philipp Jarnach's reluctance to admit that he found the verse too uninspiring for him to set to music, and the elaborate capitals (*lettrines*) which Lucia had painted for the various poems were too late for inclusion. Joyce therefore began searching for a publisher who could and would use them. He was ready, if necessary, to pay for the work secretly so that Lucia would think that someone really wanted to publish her work.

The truce between him and the rue de l'Odéon booksellers did not last. When Benjamin Conner, Joyce's Paris-based American lawyer, sent Joyce a further bill for $2,000 for work on the case against Roth, Joyce referred it to Beach, arguing that when the affair blew up she and not he owned the US rights in *Ulysses* and was therefore responsible for payment. When he read to her over the phone a letter he had written to the lawyer referring to the signed agreement between them as 'a mere formalization or expression in writing of a state of fact and an understanding existing previously', implying that it might not after all be a legal contract, she called him a 'liar' and a 'cheat'. She then launched into what he called 'a violent tirade' and he told her not to get one of her headaches. He later told Harriet that he was concerned for Beach because she was the daughter of a suicide and part of an 'unnatural' relationship with Monnier. Later he reported that his photograph had been removed from her bookshop, and although he owed her a lot and she had been kind to him over the years, he now thought she was behaving like Monnier's puppet and he feared for her sanity.

News came on 23 December, from John Joyce's landlord, that John was seriously ill in Drumcondra Hospital, and unlikely to last long. He urged James to write to his father before it was too late. Joyce immediately cancelled his usual Christmas celebrations, but any thought of hurrying to his father's bedside was countered by a powerful instinct against ever returning to Ireland. It was a mixture of fear, distrust, and dread of bursting the bubble of illusion which enabled him to continue living in the now-mythical Dublin of his youth. He cabled the doctor brother of an old Dublin friend, Kenneth Reddin, asking him to ensure that his father received the best attention available and to send all bills to him. He later told Harriet, 'I spent the four days after Xmas sending messages to my father by wire and letter and by telephone to the hospital every evening.'[50] John died on 29 December, surrounded by mementos of his favourite son – photographs, press-cuttings and signed copies of his books.[51] The cause of his death was given as 'Senile decay and Endocarditis'. Joyce was consumed with remorse at not visiting his dying father, but as he told Pound, 'In spite of my own deep feeling for him I never dared to trust myself into the power of my enemies.'[52]

Only the son of John Stanislaus Joyce could have written *Finnegans Wake* in collaboration with the husband of Nora, the father of Lucia and

Giorgio and the brother of Stanislaus. Only through his presence and significance in his life was Joyce able to conceive and deliver Humphrey Chimpden Earwicker, Anna Livia, Issy, Shem and Shaun. But John's presence and significance was crucial. Gillet thought that the 'peculiar rapport' between this father and son was 'the central factor in Joyce's life, the basis, the axis of his work'.[53]

30

Death, Birth and Madness

(1932–1933)

'A great work of art is like a dream: for all its apparent obviousness
it does not explain itself and is always ambiguous.'

Carl Jung, *Collected Works*

Still conscience-stricken at not having visited his father for some twenty
years, on New Year's Day 1932, the day of his funeral, Joyce unburdened
himself to Eliot and Pound. 'A poor heart', always loyal to him, was gone,
he wrote, and he was broken by it.[1] His guilt was only intensified by the
knowledge that he had deliberately fostered the illusion that he would
visit the old man. When he asked Con Curran and Michael Healy whether
his father had said anything about him towards the end, they both
reported the same words, 'Jim never forgets me.' It hardly eased the pain.
To Harriet, he wrote saying that his father 'had an extraordinary affection
for me', but was 'the silliest man I ever knew', albeit cruelly ruthless
and cunning. Even on his deathbed he was thinking and speaking of
his favourite son, and, as a fellow sinner, he said, he still liked the old
man despite his faults. From him he had inherited not just the family
portraits, his colourful waistcoat and 'a good tenor voice', but also 'an
extravagant licentious disposition' from which what talents he had
probably sprang.[2] Unable to afford a proper suit of mourning, he told
Harriet, he was reduced to wearing a dyed green jacket, striped trousers
and tan shoes.

However, his feelings of remorse did not move him to attend his father's
funeral, and he had to depend on accounts of the occasion from Curran
and Michael Healy who followed the cortège to Glasnevin Cemetery. He
sent a wreath (inscribed, 'With Sorrow and Love') asking Harriet to sell
£100 of his stock to cover all funeral costs. Afterwards Niall Sheridan, the
young Irish poet and literary commentator, told him that his father was
buried by none other than Corny Kelleher, the undertaker who had
'buried' Dignam in *Ulysses*. John received obituaries in the Irish press and
the *Chicago Premier*, which pronounced him 'a master of vernacular and
a fine storyteller'. 'His versatility enabled him to adapt his style to all
surroundings, whether that of a drawing room or a saloon. He was full of

reminiscences of Irish life of the last half century, and his stories were usually embellished with rare artistry.'[3]

Although Stuart Gilbert reported that *Work in Progress* was 'advancing rapidly', its grieving author told Harriet that he was somehow paralysed and felt like abandoning it. 'Why go on writing about a place I did not dare to go to at such a moment, where not three persons know me or understand me?', adding that he had heard that the editor of the Dublin *Independent* had objected to an allusion to him in his father's obituary. The mental image of a hostile Dublin was being continually reinforced. To escape this confusion of fear and wretchedness he began taking pills in search of the healing oblivion of a decent night's sleep.

By 5 January Joyce had emerged from his state of mourning sufficiently to begin wondering what had happened to books and letters he had sent his father, and asked John's old friend Alf Bergan, the executor of his will, to find out. Bergan reported that Eileen had taken away a valise containing letters, documents and signed copies of his books. She handed back the valise but kept the books inscribed to his father, except an unsigned copy of *Exiles*.[4] When John's will was granted probate his estate was valued at £665 0s 9d, a goodly sum for 1931, but when all debts were paid, James, his sole legatee, received £36 12s 1d, around £1,300 ($2,100) in today's money.

Although Sylvia Beach was keenly excited about celebrating Joyce's Jubilee, he said there was nowhere to hold such a celebration – not his tiny flat, nor Giorgio's place, where Helen was heavily pregnant. However, after sending Sylvia ten branches of lilac (a symbol of peace and tranquillity) tied with a blue bow to mark the tenth anniversary of *Ulysses*, his fiftieth birthday party was held (without Beach) at the Jolases' flat in the rue de Sévigné where the Gilberts, the Sullivans and the Colums turned up to celebrate. But, discovering that Beckett had been invited, Lucia, feeling betrayed, suffered her first serious violent brainstorm. The outburst culminated in a chair being thrown at her mother. Joyce, as usual, looked on helplessly, and Giorgio had to call a taxi and take her to a *maison de santé* where she remained for a week. After this, Nora was always fearful of her daughter, and Lucia never again trusted Giorgio. The incident was only the opening scene of a family tragedy on which the curtain would not fall during Joyce's lifetime.

The evening somehow stumbled along, first with dinner chez Jolas and then at Giorgio and Helen's place in the rue Huysmans. There was a cake with fifty candles, and a sugar replica of *Ulysses* with ten birthday candles. Georg Goyert, his German translator, sent flowers. As her birthday present, Harriet cancelled Joyce's debts to her and offered to find him a tenant for his London flat. But her timing was out, and in the wake of his father's death and Lucia's breakdown Joyce sent her a furious reply, rejecting her offer of help, a letter so angry that later she destroyed it. In reply she wrote him a humble letter apologizing for her 'too officious interference' and reciting her many faults, failings and sins. She had become almost as dependent on him as he was on her.

If Joyce was angry with Harriet, Lucia was angry with *him*. The Colums were afforded an insight into the internal dynamics of the Joyce family, as Padraic recalled:

> [Lucia] came to see us sometimes that spring, and we were surprised at the violence with which she spoke against Joyce. Once when we suggested she come some place with us she said, 'If anyone talks of my father I'll leave.' When I mentioned to her some of the hardships Joyce had endured she said, 'I saw him crying when he found he couldn't see to write.' But she said it without any sympathy.[5]

This display of callous disdain and barely suppressed violence, and Joyce's refusal to acknowledge it, would soon come to a head, and things would never be the same again for him and his family. He tried desperately to understand what had happened to his beautiful daughter. 'Whatever spark or gift I possess has been transmitted to Lucia and it has kindled a fire in her brain,' he told Harriet, a suitably incandescent image for an Angel of Light.[6]

His friends were increasingly concerned about his rift with Beach. Colum undertook to try to persuade her to annul the contract granting her US rights to *Ulysses*, stressing to her how damaging it would be for Joyce's career to have no American edition of the book. Finally she agreed to hand back the rights and a new agreement was reached whereby she would retain publication and marketing rights to her Paris edition. But as to her reissuing the book she would, she said, need 60,000 francs to cover her expenses. From that time onwards, Joyce turned to Paul Léon for help with negotiations previously undertaken by Beach.

The plight of Lucia, lonely and distracted, aroused the sympathies of Léon and his wife Lucie. They persuaded Alex Ponisovsky to take an interest in her, even pushing him into proposing marriage, telling him 'You can't treat this girl like an American; she has been brought up very properly and your frequent meetings with her can only have one meaning for her family.'[7] Neither Joyce nor Nora were unhappy about this. Nora had long thought her daughter should marry and Alex was a charming and attractive young man. However, when Giorgio heard of the engagement, he was dismayed. As far as he was concerned his sister was mad and not in a fit state to contemplate matrimony. The engagement party was held at the Restaurant Drouand in the Place Gaillon. Afterwards, however, at the Léons' flat in rue Casimir-Périer Lucia collapsed. 'It was,' recalled Lucie, 'more like a funeral than a party.'[8]

According to her biographer, this was the moment at which Lucia became psychotic. Her immediate condition was described as 'catatonic'. To Ponisovsky, this can hardly have been encouraging. He had long been in love with Peggy Guggenheim's sister Hazel, and although he proposed to Lucia to oblige the Léons, he soon came to regret it. Lucia probably also realized that the engagement was a mistake. They were both on the rebound: her obsession remained for Beckett, his for Hazel Guggenheim.[9]

In February, offers for *Ulysses* and *Work in Progress* came from both America and England. Jonathan Cape wanted to publish an edited version of *Ulysses* but Joyce was not interested. However, with prosecutions for obscenity making news in England, Cape's nervousness was understandable. Eliot, too, feared prosecution over *Ulysses*, and his cautious offer to publish selected episodes in *Criterion Miscellany* editions was also rejected by Joyce who categorically refused to make concessions to censors. If Eliot wanted to print an expensive limited edition, that would be another matter; the censors would ignore it. Of the four American offers received he preferred that from Random House's Bennett Cerf, a friend of Helen's brother, which included immediate publication of the unabridged unaltered text, without a preface, and with Random taking all the risks and prepared to fight the ban.

On 15 February Helen gave birth to a son. He was named Stephen James Joyce and his delighted grandfather now became 'Nonno' as well as 'Babbo'. The event lifted Joyce out of the slough of his despond and inspired the poem 'Ecce Puer', his first serious verse for eight years, marking the birth of a grandchild – 'Of the dark past/A boy is born ...' and the death of a father – 'O, father forsaken,/Forgive your son!' The imagery of the dark past and the final Christ-like confession of guilt are loaded with allusion and ambiguity. However, against his wishes, the child was secretly baptized, revealing that others in the family were capable of rebelling.

The emotional turmoil of the past weeks finally overtook Joyce, and on the last day of February Léon reported him suffering from eye trouble, insomnia and intestinal grippe. More happily, there were now six or seven books about him either already published or about to appear, including the one by Frank Budgen. Furthermore, Roth's pirated *Ulysses* had been seized and destroyed and Miss Beach was at last prepared to talk to Léon about a European edition, though not one she herself would be publishing.

When Harriet visited Paris in early March, she found Joyce still suffering from biliousness and undertook to deliver all the completed pages of *Work in Progress* to Frank Morley, Eliot's colleague at Faber. She also agreed to see Fred Monro to explain his financial situation and his continual demands on his capital. When he heard that Monro understood his position, Joyce immediately wrote asking for £150 for a quarter's rent.

Ashamed of his earlier anger towards her, and replying to Harriet's confession of faults, Joyce listed his own failings. He was unworthy of her munificence, of Nora's unswerving devotion, of his father's lifelong and sometimes pathetic pride in him. But he felt perfectly worthy of the friendship and attentions of the ladies of the rue de l'Odéon, having never betrayed their friendship or offended them in anything he had written. He signed off with his usual plea of poverty. But Gilbert noted that while there was no end to the protestations of penury, there was no halt either to expensive taxi-rides and dinners at Les Trianons.[10]

By 25 March, Léon and Holroyd-Reece were corresponding about a possible European edition of *Ulysses* from the Albatross Press, and Robert Kastor, acting for Joyce in New York, had accepted the contract agreed with Cerf at Random House for a US edition. A week later, Joyce sent Cerf an account of the history of the book's publication, which the publisher decided to use as a preface. In it he expressed his gratitude to Sylvia Beach for bravely undertaking to produce a work which, at the time, no publisher in the English-speaking world would touch.

Planning to return to London, Joyce relinquished his Passy apartment, bought train and ferry tickets, and did the rounds of their friends bidding them farewell. Going to London always excited Nora and getting away would help Joyce put behind him his long, exhausting struggle with Beach and Monnier. Only Lucia was unhappy – still shattered by rejections in love and her artistic frustrations. She wanted to remain in Paris, but was too nervous to stay in a hotel alone and there was no room at Giorgio's, what with the new baby, his nurse and Helen's son David from her previous marriage. It was in that state of mind that, after much discussion, she trailed along with her parents to the Gare du Nord on 17 April.

As the Joyces were about to board the boat train for Calais Lucia had her second *crise de nerfs*, a fit of hysteria accompanied by much howling and weeping, this time so public, so loud, so disturbing and so prolonged (an *allegro con brio* performance, Joyce called it) that it had the desired effect. The family would not be leaving for London. The whole incident lasted forty-five minutes. Gilbert, who was there to say his farewells, concluded that in reality none of them wanted to go and they all repaired for lunch to Les Mariniers. After that they took rooms at the Hotel Belmont, Harriet's favourite Paris hotel. The only comfort Joyce could draw from the whole affair was that he had remained calm throughout and that he could probably get a refund on their tickets. He took Lucia to see Fontaine who referred her to Dr Henri Codet, a psychiatrist with an office in the rue de l'Odéon. Now Joyce would have to pay more attention to her. She was really a child, he decided, and the one hope for rehabilitation came from her *lettrines* which he thought exquisite.[11]

The lease on his London flat still had eighteen months to run, but with the Depression and little money about, Joyce knew he was bound to lose income. Added to that, having established his English residence, he was now being pursued by the UK Inland Revenue for back taxes.[12] However, at last a tenant was found for the Campden Grove flat, a Monsieur Taillifer, acting chef at the US Embassy. Joyce never returned to England, but hoped that he had now done enough to ensure his children's inheritance.

When Codet saw Lucia he prescribed several weeks' isolation, lying beside an open window, reading as much as possible while taking veronal, valerian and phosphate of lime. Gilbert thought that all Lucia needed was 'a good smacking'. Joyce too was acting strangely, refusing to eat at the hotel, dining out every evening and ending up 'half seas over', while Nora was 'nearly as jumpy as her daughter', blaming everything on Jim – their homelessness, and Lucia's illness especially. Gilbert decided that the problem with the Joyces was that they lived empty lives, forming only fleeting attachments to things and making few real friends. That was why Joyce filled his life with pointless campaigns, such as the one to boost John Sullivan, the one against Miss Beach, and the one to portray himself as the victim of endless persecution. He was, thought Gilbert, deeply cynical about human intentions, and other people's troubles left him unmoved, except for those of close family members.[13]

Matters between Joyce and Nora came to a head one day in May when she, fed up with his nightly drunkenness, threatened to leave him. She refused to go to a matinee with him and he asked Gilbert to accompany him instead, pouring out his fears about being deserted. After the play they repaired to a bistro opposite the Belmont and phoned reception only to be told 'Mrs Joyce left five minutes ago.' Back in his room they saw that her slippers were still there and he took Gilbert off to have tea at Le Berry on the Champs-Elysées. On their return they found Nora back again but saying that it was all over between them and she would be moving out. She began to pack while Joyce curled up in a chair looking dejected, saying he couldn't do without her and couldn't they go away, just the pair of them together. Gilbert captured the scene:

> She tells him she wishes he would drown himself. Says he gives her and
> Lucia an unbearable life, is responsible for everything. Then goes and sits
> on an armchair looking out the window. Talks of the money he has

wasted on Sullivan and on tips; that is why they can't afford to have a decent flat now. Joyce has just received some 20,000 Francs (advance from America on *Ulysses*). Offers to pay a year in advance. She insists on going, says she will pass the hat round to her friends.

At that point Gilbert had to leave, but, on calling back at seven forty-five that evening, Nora told him she'd 'given in again'. The drama, he concluded, had played itself out.[14]

If the drama was played out, Nora had now gained the upper hand and was determined to ensure that her capricious husband did not relapse into dissolution. Thomas McGreevy soon noticed the effects of Nora's new puritanical regimen. On 10 May he wrote to Yeats:

> Joyce in the sober day time ... says things that may be brooded over for weeks. After one glass of wine in the evening he begins to talk in the real sense of the word but after the second Mrs Joyce says he has had enough and carries him off and though she's right from the point of view of his sight and his work one is none the less inclined to curse matrimony a little more vigorously even than usual.[15]

In London, a prosecution for obscenity ending in imprisonment had put the wind up Eliot. He approached the Home Office about publishing *Ulysses*, but they were adamant that legal action would follow. For Faber that ended the matter, but if they had now lost interest others had not, and on 11 May Pinker informed Joyce that Allen Lane of the Bodley Head[16] was enquiring after the book. Lane, a resourceful and determined character, decided to work on the authorities through a Home Office contact and a police solicitor. In the meantime, *Work in Progress* had stopped progressing; the bubble inside which Joyce worked had burst and other things were now occupying his mind – the campaign to get *Ulysses* legalized in the US and, above all, the urgent need to save Lucia's sanity.

Sometime during the week of 15 May, the Joyces returned to the gloomy Avenue St Philibert flat in Passy. Since her *crise de nerfs* at the Gare du Nord, Lucia had had three more collapses at intervals of ten days, her most violent, according to Joyce, on 21 May. Finally, she left the apartment where things were very tense between her and Nora and moved in briefly with the Léons. Then, after a confrontation with Lucie about Alex Ponisovsky, she was taken in by Padraic and Mary Colum. They were convinced that a job was what she needed and since a friend of theirs, a distinguished American entomologist, needed someone to transcribe notes, they induced him to take Lucia on. But she lasted only a few hours, returning after lunch, flopping down on a sofa and complaining, 'Why

do I, an artist, have to waste myself on that kind of work?' Fearing
she might harm herself, that night Mary slept with her, pinning their
nightdresses together to prevent her escape. On Sunday, while Lucia was
attending mass with Colum, Joyce rang, and learning where she was said,
'Now I know she's mad.' Gilbert thought that what others saw as madness
was normal for Lucia. Asking the Colums' maid, 'Do you have a lover?'
which others thought 'somewhat insane', he thought 'typically Joycean –
shocking for the pleasure of shocking, a favourite way of attracting attention with both Lucia and her father.'[17]

By a ruse, the Colums brought a psychiatrist to see her, Mary posing as
the patient and answering in Lucia's stead with her sitting by. The psychiatrist declared that there was nothing wrong with her, and Mary, who
had studied the subject a little, believed that the girl's illness was due to
her home circumstances. She needed a warm and loving environment
where she was valued, she decided. But Mary herself was ill, awaiting a
serious operation, and a long stay with them was impossible. They wanted
Lucia to meet her friends again, and Ponisovsky came to visit. Lucia
cooked a meal and afterwards appeared at the door saying that she and
Alex were going to the theatre. When Alex demurred she said she would
go alone. The Colums tried to stop her and only succeeded in doing so at
the foot of the steps leading down from their apartment. When they
returned Ponisovsky had escaped over the roof.

Dr Fontaine examined Lucia and found that her only trouble was
'nerves'. However, it was decided that she should spend time at the *maison
de santé* at L'Hay-les-Roses. Her father, Giorgio and Mary took her there
in a taxi without telling her where they were going, a deception about
which Mary felt particularly guilty. 'We entered the office of the director
of the sanitarium,' she remembered, 'and as he began to talk to me, Lucia
threw me a look of bewildered appeal which I can never forget.'[18] She
was admitted by the chief psychiatrist Dr Gaston Maillard who said he
feared it was 'hebephrenic psychosis' with a poor prognosis. She was
forbidden letters and phone-calls, and prescribed two or three weeks of
peace and quiet. But as she was free to leave, Joyce expected her back at
any time. Determined to deflect responsibility from himself, he told
Harriet that to his relief her outbursts were not against him (although the
Colums remembered otherwise). However, he was deeply moved by her
plight and hoped the publication of her book would brighten her
outlook.[19]

Gilbert did not share the liberal view of Lucia as the lovely, gifted, sadly
disturbed child needing the ministrations of psychiatrists, a new interest
or change of environment; he saw her as selfish, conceited, idle and the
author of her own misfortunes. 'She cultivates her father's imperious airs

and spells of silence. And few young men in these times of free and facile conjugation would put up with that.' Although she professed 'the feminist desire "to work"' she had, he said, a feminine aversion to any work that did not require her to embellish her body and sparkle. She was without glamour yet expected everyone to amuse, feed and clothe her. But now she had collided with reality, except that she still had people like the Colums to dance attention upon her. As for Ponisovsky, he was too naturally dignified for Joyce whose own air of superiority was cultivated. '"Silence, exile and cunning" are his specialty, for (as he knows) silence is the most telling sort of exhibitionism and "exile" in France the supreme luxury for a writer; the land where they say "cher maître" to any *littérateur* whatsoever.'[20]

Of her own accord Lucia left the *maison de santé* on 5 June, arriving home in what Joyce described as 'a distressed state', but she was finally persuaded to return. There was a glimmer of hope for him when Louis Gillet, to whom he had shown Lucia's *lettrines*, expressed admiration for them in the *Review des Deux Mondes* – 'a wonder of atavism', he called them, like 'whims of an old Irish illuminator'. Her hand, he suggested, 'was guided by St Patrick or Holy Colomban'.[21] These intricately painted initial letters illustrating *Pomes Penyeach* were due to be published in August and, Joyce was proud to announce, nineteen copies had already been sold.

By the end of June the first of a long series of medical bills for Lucia had arrived – Dr Fontaine: 800 francs, Dr Codet: 2,900 francs, Dr Maillard: 7,432 francs – Total 11,132 francs. These were sent to Harriet to explain why he needed an immediate £200 of his next month's stipend. The bills would keep coming for the rest of his life and hers. But for the moment things looked promising at the *maison de santé*. Lucia had been given a young companion-nurse, had asked for her paints and had already completed seven letters of the alphabet intended as a present for this new friend.

Quarrels had now erupted between Giorgio and Ponisovsky, Giorgio and Léon, Nora and Helen, Lucie Léon and an impassive Joyce. Mrs Léon, he reported, became hysterical, blaming him for wrecking her brother Alex's matrimonial prospects, even though he saw the young man daily and tried to hold the ring between contending parties. Nor did the doctors make things easier. Much to Lucia's annoyance, on 21 June Doctors Fontaine and Codet paid an unannounced visit to her at the clinic. Doctors made her fearful, especially Fontaine, and she refused to speak – her father's way of coping. Deciding that she was in a bad way, they proposed a period of total isolation which was said to work well in extreme cases.

Joyce, horrified at this suggestion, arranged for his daughter to join the Jolases, accompanied by a nurse-companion, in Feldkirch, a small town high in the mountains on the Swiss-Austrian border, through which they had passed en route to Switzerland in 1915. To make it easier for Lucia to accept, they would pretend that the nurse, Mathilde Wönecke, was not being paid but just joining her on holiday. Gilbert recorded a charade in which Joyce handed the nurse the money for her fare privately and she then handed it back to Joyce in front of Lucia saying it was for her ticket. The plan was that he and Nora would move to Zurich to be close to her, taking the address of a good Swiss neurologist to be consulted if necessary. This arrangement he knew would make it impossible for him to write. *Work in Progress* would again have to mark time.

Lucia came home briefly with her nurse, looking weak and wan, but far less jumpy. Joyce was pleased that Nora, out shopping, was not there to upset her. There was nothing wrong with her mind, he decided, and she seemed to be working well at her *lettrines* since seeing Gillet's encouraging notice. If Nora and Giorgio wrote her off as a hopeless case from the start, Joyce continued to believe that her talent would restore her to health. On 3 July he smuggled her out of Maillard's clinic, and sent her off, with Nurse Mathilde, to the Jolases at Feldkirch. He felt bad about 'double-crossing' the three doctors who had seen her, but would probably be blamed anyway – if all turned out well, for having put her into the clinic, and if it failed, for having obstructed the doctors.[22]

The lease of the Avenue Philibert flat having expired, Joyce returned his possessions to storage. After a final drunken night out with William Bird, he and Nora left for Zurich where once again they booked into the Carlton Elite. Three days later, on 10 July, Mrs Jolas reported from Feldkirch that Lucia seemed to have settled down happily and she was very optimistic about her staying with them. However, Joyce did wonder whether these 'good reports' were 'rigged' for his benefit.[23]

Vogt, whom he saw on the 19th, thought Joyce had delayed seeing him for too long. The cataract in his right eye, which had been operable on his last visit, was now, he judged, total and complicated by glaucoma. The retina was also atrophied and in Paris he had been wrongly prescribed atropine which was poisonous. Furthermore, the retina and optic nerve, which were well enough previously, were no longer normal. He would have to deliberate for a few days, he said, before deciding whether to allow blindness to ensue or perform two difficult operations in succession. If that happened, Joyce would have to take up residence in Switzerland for several months, meaning that work on his novel would have to be suspended.[24] He told Harriet that if he had to write now it would be nothing but writing for money, and the only writing for money he did was in writing to her and Monro. When he informed Faber about the situation offering to refund their advance, the sympathetic Eliot suggested that he postpone delivery for six months. Meanwhile Joyce worried about his work, his eyes, and whether to tell Lucia about the risky operations Vogt had suggested. The Jolases believed she should be left alone to enjoy some tranquillity; Joyce thought she needed him to remain within call.

Bennett Cerf requested that the most favourable reviews of *Ulysses* be pasted into a copy of the book and mailed to him at Random House. Léon did so, and on 18 July Cerf wrote to say that US Customs had seized the copy, and the case would come to court in the fall. This meant that the authorities had not only the book, but the literary assessment of it, to enter as evidence.[25] Random House had retained the attorney Morris Ernst, who waived his fee in return for a percentage of the profits should the case succeed. The great climactic battle over the banning of the book was about to be joined.

Strangely enough, Lucia was still engaged to Ponisovsky. She wanted to break it off but refused to do so in a letter, vowing that, as he had made her wait, she would keep him on the hook for another four years. She planned to remain in Feldkirch with her nurse and Joyce decided to set them up in a small flat there. So far she was costing him 4,000 francs a month and that could increase if ever she needed medical attention. In view of this, he asked Harriet to arrange for a large sum to be raised from the sale of his war loan stock. However, the Public Trustee, who had control of the money, required a detailed request direct from Joyce which, for some reason, he felt unable to supply. It was just another worry to add to those already heaped on to him by those around him – Miss Beach, Lucie Léon, the Colums, the Jolases all advising what he should do about Lucia; and Helen, Giorgio, and Doctors Collinson and Hartmann, urging him not to undergo another operation by Vogt. He was, he told Harriet, beset by a circle of hysterics just as he faced a period of crippling expenses.

Mrs Jolas had hinted to Lucia that her father might need further eye operations and she was becoming anxious, wanting to leave Feldkirch and join him in Zurich, news of which only made *him* anxious. To complicate matters even more, Collinson had told him categorically that he did not have glaucoma, while Vogt said he had, and was angry with him for not having gone to him earlier. However, he had also said that he would not see Joyce again until he had achieved 'psychic tranquillity'. That was not easy. Lucia continued to haunt him. While she might have done some idiotic and even bad things which had come to haunt her and threaten her sanity, it was mainly his misguided attempt to set himself up in England that had brought destruction upon his family, he decided.[26]

It was these worries he now blamed for keeping him from seeing Vogt and so losing the sight in his left eye.

Lucia's biographer suggests that she was trying to reconcile the memory of the dancer she had been with what she had become, while those around her were faced with the question of whether she had a psychiatric condition or was just a rebellious spirit in exile from a counter-culture of avant-garde dancers and artists to which she felt she belonged. She told her companion that she had lost her soul and hoped it had gone to a better place. When Mathilde suggested she lower her sights, and rein in her vaulting ambition, Lucia told her that she preferred abundance and had 'seen the mountain peaks and the ocean' with her own eyes.[27]

The Jolases turned up during the first week of August with a letter Lucia had written to her companion which Joyce found 'disquieting' because of the disconnection of thought it revealed – an odd reaction perhaps from an author who created art from verbalizing disjunctions of consciousness and whose prose she might have been mimicking. Despite his apprehension, he convinced himself that her mind must be untroubled because she had gained weight. He did not show the letter to Nora but sent it to Harriet to read. And although Lucia had also written him 'a perfectly normal' letter saying she would come to see them both in Zurich, Nora now insisted on visiting her in Feldkirch, even though it meant going alone.

Left by himself, Joyce moved to a single room in the hotel but was unable to sleep. When Nora called suggesting he go to Feldkirch to resume his work with Eugene Jolas he said he could not afford to go there until money arrived from Monro. But he later admitted to Lucia that he feared that Feldkirch, being high in the mountains, would be plagued by thunderstorms. He tried working at the hotel, but found it difficult without his notebooks. To escape boredom he entertained a few Zurich friends – Edmund Brauchbar, Paul Suter and Felix Beran, the Austrian poet. But finding Borach and Ruggiero out of town, he took to walking the Bahnhofstrasse till midnight then pacing his room till 3 a.m.

He did, however, manage to meet Daniel Brody, his German-Swiss publisher, who passed on a letter from Carl Jung. He had revised his earlier article on *Ulysses*, he wrote, having been urged to do so because it 'presented the world such an upsetting psychological problem'. It had proved to be 'a very hard nut', forcing his mind to 'the most unusual efforts' and 'rather extravagant peregrinations' for a scientist. But after three years of brooding he had, he thought, managed to put himself into it and was deeply grateful to Joyce and his great opus for teaching him so much, even though 'it meant too much grinding of nerves and of grey matter'. He wasn't sure that Joyce would enjoy what he had written about the book because he had been unable to disguise how much he was bored by it and cursed what he admired. 'The 40 pages of non stop run in the end is a string of veritable psychological peaches. I suppose the devil's grandmother knows so much about the real psychology of a woman. I didn't.'[28]

According to Samuel Beckett, Joyce was proud of this letter, especially the last remark, but Nora would say witheringly, 'He knows nothing at all about women,' and to Harriet he called the letter 'imbecile'. To Goyert he wrote, 'He seems to have read *Ulysses* from first to last without one smile. The only thing to do in such a case is to change one's drink!'[29] Nevertheless he had copies sent without comment to all his friends.

By 15 August he was ensconced in the Hotel Löwen at Feldkirch – 'a nice old town', he said, and the people 'old-fashioned and polite'.[30] There was something to celebrate apart from the family reunion because on that day also the facsimile handwritten *Pomes Penyeach*, with Lucia's illustrations, was published in Paris by Kahane and Desmond Harmsworth would reissue it later in London. Joyce asked Miss Beach to boost the book at her bookshop and informed all his friends that Lucia had almost completed an alphabet of *lettrines* for an illustrated edition of Chaucer's poetic *ABC* (his translation of Guillaume de Deguileville's 'Hymn to the Holy Virgin'). Having achieved something of her own probably gave her the strength finally to write to Ponisovsky breaking off their stormy and fragile engagement. Joyce thought this was a sign that she was at last recovering, but noted that sending the letter had left her anxious, awaiting a reply.

Finally at Feldkirch he settled back to work, busily preparing for Eugene Jolas the episode he called 'The Children's Hour' (later published as *The Mime of Mick, Nick and the Maggies*). But it was hard going with his troublesome eyes, and he felt lucky to have Jolas there to help. However, he was again suffering violent attacks of stomach pain which a Dr Von Microskoff put down to nervousness caused by thunderstorms. Nora blamed it on overwork in Paris and Léon thought anxiety over Harriet's commitment to him had brought it on.

Miss Beach had also caused him pain in recent years and, aware of this, Léon now pushed her to say whether or not she was prepared to publish a further edition of *Ulysses*. It depended on which way the US court case went, she said, and sent him a statement of Joyce's account which showed that since publication the book had earned him in the region of 120,000 francs. She also sent what Joyce considered a long, disconnected letter seeming to blame him for her ill-health, an accusation he could well have turned back on her. However, her attitude towards republication had softened, and shortly afterwards she agreed that Albatross Press do a

European edition as they had of *Dubliners*, a proposal Joyce had already discussed with Holroyd-Reece.

In early September he received an invitation to join an Academy of Irish Letters which Yeats and Shaw were setting up. It was to consist of twenty-five Academicians who had done creative work with Ireland as its subject and ten Associates thought worthy of election for other reasons. 'If you go out of our list it is an empty sack indeed,' Yeats told Joyce. 'I would think it a great thing if you would trust us so far as to give your assent when this letter reaches you ... and I am alarmed lest your name does not reach me in time.'[31] Colum, Gogarty, Eglinton, O'Flaherty and O'Faolain were among those who accepted. Joyce declined, saying simply that he had no right to nominate himself to membership of such an academy. But it irked him when newspapers listed him among their number, telling Frank Budgen, that what an Englishman wrote about him in the press was as unbelievable as what an Irishman might say in a bar.[32]

A week later he was back at the Carlton Elite, while Lucia took Mathilde, her companion, to Vence where Lois Hutton, her old dance teacher, ran a theatre. Joyce had decided that his daughter was no longer facing possible incarceration but would need gentle handling. Nora was anxious to keep an eye on her, and so, he grumbled, he was to be 'dragged' after her to Nice. Before leaving, he saw Vogt who had decided that it was too difficult to operate on his right eye without causing collateral damage. He prescribed new glasses and wanted to see him every three months for a year before making a final assessment.

By the 20th, he and Nora were in Nice at the Hotel Métropole. When Lucia and Mathilde visited them two days later they found Joyce working on his fragment for *transition*. After they left he was struck down by an upset stomach, and it didn't help his sense of well-being, he said, that his loose upper plate kept falling out in the street, leaving his shrunken gums too sore for him to utter witticisms. Furthermore, the Albatross Press's Holroyd-Reece was phoning and cabling, wanting to fly down from Hamburg to see him.[33] After some negotiations, Léon got Reece to agree to an advance of 15,000 francs down (12,000 for Joyce, 3,000 for Miss Beach) and a proportionate division of royalties. Seeing the proposal, Beach was very pleased until she realized that her royalties were limited to just five years. When she complained that it should be for life and that the same should go for the US edition of *Ulysses*, she was told that she had no right to any money from a book she had refused to publish. Told that what she would receive was coming from Joyce personally, she quickly agreed to the terms, expressing her gratitude for the arrangement.

Quite suddenly Lucia decided that she must return to Paris so they followed her – in such a hurry that Joyce had to postpone the final fitting of his new upper plate. On 20 October they moved into the Hotel Lord Byron on the Champs-Elysées. The first priority was to find a flat and look after Lucia. Nurse Mathilde, having upset all the women in Joyce's circle by expressing strong views about what was best for Lucia, was dismissed. She was replaced part-time by the gossipy Myrsine Moschos, who had been banished from the Beach-Monnier presence, ostensibly for dishonesty but possibly for knowing and saying too much about her employers. Joyce commented that if she and Fargue cared to pool their recollections they could make a million. Moschos slept overnight with Lucia and kept her company until lunchtime, while a French girl stayed with her during the afternoons. (Lucia's biographer believes that she had engaged in a lesbian affair with Mathilde and Myrsine had picked up where she had left off.)

Lucia once again became the subject of controversy between those who, like Helen, Maria Jolas and Dr Fontaine, believed her to be disturbed and in need of medical help and those, like Mary Colum, Kay Boyle and Joyce, who considered her strangeness a mark of untapped genius. Giorgio thought she was incurable. The hiring of Miss Moschos caused a further problem for Joyce. When Sylvia Beach heard that the Joyces had employed her, she told them sharply that she was not to be sent with messages to rue de l'Odéon on any account.

To his irritation, Joyce found that Beach, having listed *Pomes Penyeach* as out of print, was selling off copies at five times the usual price. And Kahane and Harmsworth, he thought, had made a hash of their editions – he had given them 1,000 francs to be paid to Lucia, but they seemed incapable of getting money from those who had subscribed to it. Nevertheless, he was enormously proud of his daughter's illustrations, sending his friends copies of whatever notices there were. In the *Revue des Deux Mondes*, both Louis Gillet and Fritz Vanderpyl had commended her for resurrecting an ancient form, and in interviews with *Mercure de France*, *Paris Midi*, the *New York Herald Tribune* and the London *Daily Telegraph*, she had spoken of dance, flowing calligraphy, and the *Book of Kells* as sources of her inspiration. Her biographer saw in this a sense of how powerfully the dance had shaped her mind and how she took from her philosophy of human movement and gesture the vision that guided her art and hand.[34] Now, too, her illustrations of alphabetical *lettrines* for *A Chaucer ABC*, compiled over several months, were finished.

Dr Fontaine told Joyce that Codet, the psychiatrist, was annoyed that he had removed Lucia from the clinic and from his control, and that if anything went wrong with her he would have to bear the responsibility. Now the debate turned on whether she should be allowed a place of her own or put away. Fontaine wanted her kept under observation by Codet.

Joyce was reluctant, Giorgio enthusiastic. Maria Jolas suggested she be examined by Jung. Joyce sent to Shakespeare and Company for a copy of *Pomes Penyeach* to be reserved for Codet, who it was agreed, Lucia would again consult. But Gilbert thought he smelt a witch-hunt:

> The neurotic Lucia seems to have quite recovered and is interested, above all, in her publicity. She has, I think, some talent, and if she worked for the glory of God, not her own, would make a little name in the world of missals, evangelaries and the like ... however, there seems to be a conspiracy on foot to send her back to 'observation,' i.e. a half madhouse. Her charming sister-in-law is in the movement, also the woman doctor Fontaine. The Jolases, always on the scent of neuroses, hallucination and the like, adorers – like all good Americans – of the medicine-man, concur ... people who themselves are 'touched' are quickest to see insanity in others. I wonder if the heretic-hunters in the past were not themselves half-sceptics.[35]

When in November the Jolases took Joyce and Lucia to a music-hall to see the French comic parodist Bétove, sitting directly behind Lucia was Codet, 'a dreadful-looking man who must have been through the hoop several times himself', thought Joyce. But he liked him and considered him 'honest and disinterested'. And a man who could laugh at the likes of Bétove could not be so bad. Joyce was not utterly dismissive of Codet, who had diagnosed Lucia's condition as schizophrenia which might have a physical source (Joyce's own diagnosis).[36] Lucia, he reported, viewed the psychiatrist calmly. It never crossed his mind that the music-hall situation had been engineered by the Jolases to allow Codet to observe the patient. Shortly afterwards, Joyce gave her 4,000 francs to buy a fur coat, far better for her inferiority complex than visiting a psychoanalyst, he thought. He was encouraged to see her encounter Ponisovsky in the street and show no reaction to him.

After much delay, on 1 November, Herbert Hughes's *The Joyce Book* was published. Hughes contributed the preface, there was a poem by Stephens, an introductory essay by Colum, and 'an appreciation' by Arthur Symons who still enthused over Joyce's verse as he had some thirty years earlier. 'There is in these poems a rare lyrical quality, with touches of pure magic, and some give me the effect of a warm wind wafting the scent of heather over me ...'[37] The book also included the Augustus John drawing which Joyce called 'sanguine' and he wrote to the artist, praising his drawing and wishing he could make out the lines better.[38] He also congratulated the various composers. To Arnold Bax, who had contributed a setting for 'Watching the Needleboats at San Sabba', he wrote saying how much he admired the 'very evocative' and 'very singable' and 'slightly Norwegian strain' which ran through it.[39] Now wishing that his *Pomes Penyeach* was more widely available, he suggested to Beach that if she was reluctant to reissue the collection he would find another publisher.

By 17 November, the Joyces had left the Hôtel Lord Byron and returned briefly to 9 rue de l'Université. A lease had been taken from the end of November on a flat at 42 rue de Galilée close to the Champs-Elysées, which had set Joyce back 2,000 francs for a month's rent and charges. He justified this to Harriet, saying that recently Lucia had been 'a stiff problem', and the new Paris flat was exactly the comfortable home sweet home he had yearned for. When Harold Nicolson visited them there he recalled it as 'a little furnished flat and stuffy and prim as a hotel bedroom. The sitting-room was like a small salon at a provincial hotel, and the unreal effect was increased by there being florists' baskets about with arranged flowers.'[40]

Since returning from the south, Joyce had managed to keep Lucia away from doctors and clinics, but she was antagonizing people, including members of her own family, by her brutal outspokenness, and Joyce had to warn Harriet that she had talked about visiting her in London. Then, hinting at the poisonous atmosphere which he felt surrounded him, he added that he sometimes felt like a sightless man groping through fog. 'I wonder what kind of people you encounter for wherever I walk I tread on thistles of envy, suspicion, jealousy, hatred and so on.'[41]

In December Faber published Joyce's *Two Tales of Shem and Shaun* alongside Eliot's *Sweeney Agonistes* – both selling at half-a-crown. In the *New Statesman*, under the headline 'Crazy Week', G. W. Stonier struck a suitably jocular note, treating the authors as music-hall performers – 'Eliot the white-faced coon with his jazz marionettes, and that foine bold Oirish tenor, James Joyce.' Joyce's *Two Tales*, he said, was less successful than Eliot's fragments because it was part of a larger unavailable whole while *Sweeney* was on its own and going nowhere. With *Work in Progress* Joyce was wasting his time, but in it he had found 'a genuine new folk humour and fresh orchestration which will be found nowhere else in literature'. However, said Stonier, if he had a choice between Joyce and a popular music-hall comedian like Bud Flanagan, he preferred Flanagan.[42]

The *Daily News* compared him unfavourably to Lewis Carroll, suspecting a 'leg-pull'. The humour of the book was largely philological and the music of the prose best appreciated by listening to the gramophone recording of Joyce reading *Anna Livia Plurabelle*. '[Read in] Mr Joyce's beautiful voice the nonsense becomes strangely musical and even poetic and at times moving.' But, 'It can be no more than one of the greatest curiosities of literature to which a serious writer ever devoted his time.'[43]

A review by D. G. Bridson in *New English Weekly* in January pleased Joyce in two ways – it showed a reviewer in the process of retuning his understanding to this new form of literature, and showed how it could appeal to a wider audience. By approaching it through its music rather than its sense, said the review, the meaning would arise from within the sound itself.

The Albatross edition of *Ulysses* (from 'the Odyssey Press') was also published that December. Royalties would soon start being paid, Léon told Harriet, but in the meantime Joyce would like another £100. 'The reason why Mr Joyce does not write to you himself,' he added, 'is that the state of his personal affairs at home have brought upon him a strain which has made him come very near to collapse. The only strength he draws on is his work which he continues through thick and thin every afternoon.' The strains at home centred around Lucia again, and those who were badgering him to have her committed. He thought she was best kept at home and kept occupied in order to get her through a difficult time. 'He has assumed therefore an attitude of rather rough aloofness and tries to ignore outbursts and storms, but he suffers from it very deeply and last week he had two [tearful] collapses.' That was why he was investing so much in Lucia's art work and working for its success.[44]

The strain of Lucia's illness was now so acute that the slightest setback could plunge Joyce into a depression. When 28b Campden Grove was left vacant for a short time over the New Year the small loss of income seemed to leave him paralysed with misery. It gave Léon another excuse to ask Harriet for yet more financial help, explaining how a lack of funds only intensified Joyce's gloom. He was 'exhausted ... both physically and mentally' and seemed 'sometimes at the end of his forces'.[45] Harriet sent the required money to him almost by return. Then luckily, early in January, a Mrs Green took the London flat for three guineas a week.

However, on Saturday the 14th, Joyce's fragile psyche finally broke down on a trip to Rouen to hear John Sullivan sing. Nora remained behind with Lucia and he took as his companion a young Cambodian prince, a fan who had changed his name to René-Ulysse in 1922. In Rouen, an outbreak of grippe had turned the theatre into what Joyce called a 'coughing booth'. Even the cast were affected, except Sullivan who was in great form. On the train journey home Joyce collapsed. Fortunately his royal companion was a medical student and saw him safely home.

Although no flu symptoms were found, the Rouen trip triggered what he called 'a night of mild horrors including sleeplessness, hallucinations of the ear ... and sometimes of the eye too'. According to Miss Moschos, he had emitted 'sounds of woe and affright', but fortunately, he told Harriet, he was sleeping in a room alone. However, next morning, he had suddenly panicked and fled out into the snow-covered streets, followed by a frozen Miss Moschos, 'the only at that hour fully clad female of my household'. Ten minutes later he was back in the flat with Léon, attempting to explain that he was in danger. He was taken to a Dr Debray who diagnosed an abuse of sleeping pills – on occasion he had been taking up to six at once. In Rouen he had dispensed with them and the collapse was put down to this sudden withdrawal. Debray prescribed three consecutive days of sleep which left him exhausted, but not too exhausted to ask Harriet for another £150. The one good outcome of these events, Joyce told her, were the prolonged expressions of concern from 'that *subtile et barbare* person', Lucia.[46]

Nino Frank encountered that concerned, subtle and barbarous daughter one morning in the Champs-Elysées:

> I had never seen her so pretty, so gay, so strangely tranquil. We exchanged a few joking words, then I watched her move off with a lithe, startlingly light step ... She was on the threshold of madness.[47]

Her father's efforts to bring her success were still being frustrated. Annoyed that Cape had refused *Pomes Penyeach*, he asked Pinker to find another publisher for all his books for which Cape had rights. To Colum he bemoaned the fact that few of his wealthy admirers had bought copies.

When George Moore died in London on 21 January, Joyce sent a wreath, and was offended to see no mention of it in press reports of the funeral. He made sure that, with Alf Bergan's help, his tribute to his parents was properly delivered, and in February a headstone bearing both their names was erected at Glasnevin Cemetery. A plan to dedicate a bench to his father close to his last address, however, came to nothing.

On 30 January the future of Europe was sealed when Hitler was elected Chancellor of the German Reich, and Jews and Liberals began to leave the country in large numbers. Joyce was viscerally anti-authoritarian. He had a poor opinion of Italy under Mussolini and now, he thought, the Germans were going 'daft'. He advised Frank Budgen to avoid German publishers with his book about the writing of *Ulysses*.[48]

Harriet, concerned about Joyce's recent breakdown, decided to see him for herself. Léon, who was worried that he had missed his December appointment with Vogt, hoped she would help persuade him to return to Zurich. But her visit was a complete disaster. Nora had booked her into the nearby Hôtel Galilée, but when she arrived on 14 February, she found Joyce still recovering from his collapse – forbidden to work by Debray and anxious to resist those urging him to hand Lucia over to Tweedledums and Tweedledees. Harriet enquired among his friends as to just what was wrong with him, but, on hearing that she had been discussing him with Miss Beach, he retreated into his protective silence and refused to see her. After two weeks she returned to London, saying that she felt powerless to help him because he had been 'so elusive' and left her 'in a false position' vis-à-vis the rue de l'Odéon. But before departing she told Léon that she would willingly return to Paris to look after Lucia, who seemed to like her, so as to leave Joyce and Nora free to go to Zurich.

In March, 'Campden Grave' lived up to its nickname when Mrs Green, Joyce's tenant, died there. With little hope of re-letting it, he gave instructions for the lease to be sold and the place cleared of its contents, which Harriet arranged. She was worried, however, that Joyce had stopped work and was procrastinating over the trip to Zurich. The capital she had given him, she told Léon, was meant to leave him free to write and if that meant going to Zurich it seemed reasonable to use the funds for that purpose. But he was complaining that living there would cost them 4,000 francs a week each, which, she pointed out, was more than double per head what she had paid in Paris.

Perhaps to soothe her feelings, Léon sent news that Joyce was sleeping better and, while still very nervous, had started work again. However, in mid-March he reported a second breakdown. This he put down in part to his disappointment over her last visit to Paris. But what prevented him leaving for Zurich was inertia and the inability to reconcile conflicting emotions. Georges Borach had even suggested kidnapping him and getting him there by any means possible. It did not help that people were constantly wanting help, which he was unable to refuse. Ivan Goll, for example, needed help translating *Anna Livia Plurabelle* into German, and Budgen came to read his manuscript to Joyce and note his suggested changes. According to Léon, he practically dictated every sentence his friends wrote about him. That, of course, was the way he liked it, especially after Michael Lennon's scurrilous article.

Nevertheless, the inevitable misrepresentations persisted. Louis Golding had published a slim volume about Joyce that year, and John Eglinton contributed an article on him to *Life and Letters*, placing his work in a biographical context. Neither, he thought, was accurate.[49] He enquired through Pinker whether Gorman was still working on his biography, and suggested putting him in touch with Budgen. But Gorman, after confirming that the book was making progress, said he had no intention of giving material to Budgen whose own work would only steal his thunder.[50]

As well as encouraging Lucia with her art work, Joyce tried various alternative cures for her, hoping to keep her away from psychiatrists. In March he had found a Dr Henri Vignes, a noted French obstetrician, whose special treatment was, according to Léon, 'absorption of sea-water for the time being by the mouth but later by injection'. After a month of this Lucia had lost 2,000 grammes which, the doctor confidently informed Joyce, showed that she was responding well. She had in fact suffered a relapse but this time had pulled through by herself – another good sign, thought the doctor, who prescribed a further month's treatment. But the gossips were saying that Joyce was making himself ill over his daughter, while one of his devotees told him that his eyes were definitely now beyond repair. This comment, Léon told Harriet, precipitated 'a complete breakdown', causing sleeplessness and headaches which Joyce immediately thought must be meningitis. Debray examined him and found nothing wrong. However, he advised Joyce to leave Paris for a week or two, and Zurich seemed the obvious place to go. Finally, said Léon, as they were anxious to leave as soon as possible, could she please tell Monro to sell more capital shares to cover all costs.[51]

Asked by the lawyer to specify the expenses he anticipated for the sum in question, his list included: tailor 1,000 francs, dressmaker (Mrs Joyce) 800 francs; dressmaker (Miss Joyce) 1,000 francs; shoemaker 300 francs; three tickets for Zurich 3,000 francs; seven days in a Zurich hotel etc. 4,000 francs.[52] At the beginning of April, Monro Saw told Joyce just how much his capital had suffered from the falling interest rate and his own depredations: his future monthly income would be reduced by a third. The news brought Harriet another long letter from Léon. Joyce had reacted badly, he said, and had given up hope of going to Zurich or even continuing with his book. It was the effect that a lower standard of living might have on his daughter that worried him most. On the other hand Lucia was much improved of late and there were good prospects of income from the Albatross edition of *Ulysses* and from the American edition, once it was un-banned. His home circumstances were not tranquil, he was suffering a loss of confidence, and until he had Vogt's opinion on his eyes he could not continue writing. The unspoken request was for yet more funds.[53] One note of cheer came when the Servire Press in The Hague agreed to bring out a de luxe edition of *A Chaucer ABC*.

Miss Moschos had moved on and Lucia was now feeling much better. She had given up bookbinding, abandoned painting classes and was studying engraving. The Jolases and Philippe Soupault told Léon that they were impressed by Joyce's success at treating a nervous disease, even though it was at the expense of his own health. As if to confirm that opinion he had suffered a painful attack of colitis, stopped work and now sat at home brooding. In spite of painful stomach spasms which left him writhing, Dr Fontaine found nothing wrong, diagnosing 'a disequilibrium of the system of the sympathetic nerve with the focus of the dislocation in the epigastric part of his stomach provoking the terrible pains'. No particular diet was necessary, she said, and 'the state of his intestines was infinitely better than they were when she last saw them ... 3 or 4 years ago'.[54] Her prescription was rest and tranquillity. When it came to Joyce's stomach ailments, his nervous state would continue to offer a convenient pretext for slipshod diagnoses.

Léon was greatly concerned that Joyce was so depressed over the state of his family life and had now resigned himself to the inevitable encroachment of incurable blindness. He himself felt powerless to assist, he told Harriet, and no longer felt welcome at the Joyces because Nora blamed him for encouraging Ponisovsky to pursue Lucia. Only if Joyce insisted was he admitted to the flat and this caused him some embarrassment. His letter ended with a prayer – that Joyce would get himself to Zurich before it was too late.[55] It was cleverly designed to work on her sense of guilt about not having helped him enough. Harriet immediately sent £200 for the trip, £100 of which came from her own already-depleted funds.

It was up to her, she now decided, to see Joyce in person and see that he got away to Zurich. She was careful to conceal her true reason for visiting Paris from Miss Beach, pretending it was primarily to see her and to bring her a Limerick shawl for her sister. This time, however, things went better. Joyce was more amenable and they had plenty to discuss.[56] When Harriet reassured him of her continuing support, he at last felt able to start work again, though not as yet to see Vogt.

Léon had difficulty understanding how Joyce's income could have shrunk by a third, so Harriet sat down and made an audit of his various investments and income from them. It was not as bad as Monro had suggested. On his Pacific, Johannesburg and Canadian investments plus a modest income from his £5,000 war stock, his annual income amounted to £703 10s 0d.[57] But the cost of maintaining his air of affluent respectability was prodigious. His pocket was an ever-open drain down which poured the benefaction of his long-suffering patron. His capital was seeping away and never did seem to buy him the peace and quiet in which he could work; his wife was unhappy and his daughter increasingly hostile and contemptuous towards him.

While Joyce was unable to decide about going to see Vogt, the architect Siegfried Giedion-Welcker and his wife Carola, an art critic, arrived in Paris and suggested they accompany the Joyces to Zurich. The offer was accepted, and on 22 May finally they all set off. Based this time at the Hôtel Habis Royal, Joyce paid two visits to Vogt, and on 30 May Harriet, Giorgio and Stanislaus were sent a summary of the doctor's report.

At his first consultation, Vogt judged that the left eye (the better one) had improved slightly since September 1932. Progress had been slow but there had been 'no exudate or precipitation in gape'. His reconstructed pupil was slowly opening upwards and would continue to do so for between three and four years until it had reached 4 millimetres. An operation might hasten the process but would be dangerous. In around three years' time a tiny operation to remove the outer film would be possible and advisable. At the second consultation Vogt decided that Joyce's right eye had 'disimproved', the cataract nearly all calcified so that he had no vision. The retina was invisible, insensitive to light and partly atrophied. Tests had not shown positively that there was glaucoma, so, though difficult and dangerous, an operation was still on the cards. Without it that eye would be blind, though sight could also be lost during an operation. When Joyce asked what he could gain from such an operation, Vogt replied, 'Two eyes better than one.' When he asked if it might imperil the left eye he was told, that 'if there was a traumatic iritis in the right eye after the operation it would probably extend to the left and undo all the good'. Vogt refused to decide for him but said that were he in Joyce's place and in the hands of a surgeon like himself, he would take a chance. He gave him a few days to think it over and said he would be prepared to operate straight away or in September, which was when he next wished to see him anyway.[58]

The dreaded operation was postponed, his next appointment was fixed for September and the family returned to Paris. Kahane (now publishing alone) had agreed to produce an Obelisk Press edition of *A Chaucer ABC* for 20,000 francs, and to Joyce's delight, proofs including Lucia's illustrations and Louis Gillet's preface arrived. Gillet asked for a fee of between 1,000 and 1,200 francs and said he would try to get the book reviewed in *Nouvelles Littéraires* when it appeared.[59] For such a distinguished name, Joyce was more than happy to pay.

John Francis Byrne, his old friend from college days, came for a short stay and suggested that Nora and Lucia might revisit Ireland. Joyce was appalled. Rather than risk losing his womenfolk, he decided to spirit them off to Evian-les-Bains, the spa on the Swiss-French border, and take the water-cure in the hope of bringing some relief to his troubled intestines. In early July the family arrived in Evian with just 1,300 francs and took rooms at the Grand Hotel costing 300 francs a day. Unsurprisingly it wasn't long before Joyce was running short of funds, and telling Léon, 'I must have money at hand not in bobs and scraps.' But he was also trying out a new regime. 'I have begun a cure here of abstinence,' he wrote, so now spa water had replaced the Swiss white wine he so loved. His plan was to remain in Evian throughout July, then take a house offered by the Giedion-Welckers for August, and finally to see Vogt again in September before returning to Paris.

Two problems now threatened his well-laid plan. First, Harriet expressed concern that, while pleading poverty, he was living lavishly at a grand hotel in a fashionable Alpine spa, and having to draw on so much of his capital. And second, the Joyce women were getting restless, as he told Léon. 'The wife says the place is boring for Lucia, too boring, that she is becoming neurasthenic again. So off we go. Where, I have no idea.'[60] Meanwhile, he continued his healthy programme. On 7 July he wrote, 'I am meeting a very strict diet, r[ye] bread, ice, juices, w[ater?] etc. and yet I had six continual hours of pain last night.'[61]

An unfortunate scene ensued when Lucia found and read the Jolases' and Soupault's letters to Léon which attributed her cure to her father. She exploded with anger and demanded that he write letters immediately to these sadly deluded individuals, explaining to them that her father was a failure and a physical wreck who could neither write nor sleep on account of a ruined constitution. What was more, she claimed, he was seriously broken down and his life was now devoted to squandering her inheritance. She wrecked an arrangement to visit Edmond Jaloux, who lived across Lake Geneva in Lausanne, by accusing her father of simply looking for admiration. Unsettled by this attack, he wrote telling Jaloux not to expect them after all.

Lucia's complaints failed to curb Joyce's continued spending. He wrote at length to Léon about money – money for hotels, money for doctors, money for Gillet, money for long-distance phone calls, money for his Paris concierge, money for Budgen, and money for Léon, who was expected to sort out this chaos of debt. Amid this financial and emotional confusion, he was determined to continue the water treatment – starving, abstaining, walking for three and a half hours a day. But his stomach cramps persisted and he began to think that taking the waters was after all a fake cure. 'I came away to rest, Lord help me. Please wire 2,000 francs tomorrow without fail,' he wrote, adding, 'Keep these news all to yourself.' Appearances, at all costs, had to be maintained.[62]

Learning that Harriet disapproved of his choice of Evian as a holiday destination, on 12 July, after just nine days, Joyce decided to abandon the treatment. A week later, when she learned that he was there for a cure and not merely for pleasure, she felt guilty that he had stopped it on her account and told him that if he wanted any more of his shares sold she would arrange for it immediately through Monro. But by now Joyce had left Evian for what he called 'the city of S.S. Felix and Regula (= Prosperity and Order)'.[63]

At the Zurich Bahnhof, Lucia repeated her Gare du Nord performance –

a screaming, shrieking collapse. Somehow they got her to the St Gotthard Hotel where they were to stay, and arranged for her to be seen by Professor Hans Maier, who specialized in schizophrenia at the University of Zurich psychiatric hospital, the Burghölzli. Maier concluded that she was 'not lunatic but markedly neurotic'.[64] He recommended she be seen by Dr Oscar Florel at Les Rives de Prangins Sanatorium, at Nyon just outside Geneva.

After five days in Zurich, their planned stay at the Giedion-Welcker villa fell through when Nora and Lucia suddenly objected to it. On the 23rd Joyce suffered a night of absolute agony lasting over eight hours, after which they moved hotels. Although some money had arrived, he wrote urgently to Léon, 'I want more.'[65] To compound his misery they were visited by a thunderstorm. Léon found the frequent moves puzzling, but Harriet sent the money unquestioningly.

The long-postponed trial of *Ulysses* in America was scheduled for 22 August before Judge John M. Woolsey. Informing Joyce of this, Bennett Cerf asked if he might reproduce the schematic chart which Gorman had been given, thinking it would make the book more accessible to the general reader. Joyce was appalled that Cerf even knew about the chart and told him that it was literary criticism and not part of the text of the novel. A version of it had already appeared in Gilbert's book, but seeing it as a prologue to *Ulysses* would make the American reader feel that the novel was not worth reading. Denied the use of the chart in the book itself, Cerf prepared a leaflet entitled 'How to Enjoy Joyce's Great Novel' which included a map of Dublin, a list of characters and a breakdown of the chapters, drawing heavily on the schema.

On 30 July the family left for Geneva where their new address was the Richemond, one of the city's most exclusive hotels, overlooking the lake. It was, Joyce told Stanislaus, 'the finest city for its size that I have ever seen and beautifully situated on the banks of the Rhone'.[66] The following day, Lucia was taken for observation to Florel's clinic at Prangins. She arrived in what has been described as 'a dreamlike state' and 'obsessed with fear about the supposed conflicts between her parents, although in their presence she was expansive and loquacious'.[67] Shortly after they left, she became panic-stricken and on 4 August they brought her back to Zurich. Florel's diagnosis was 'schizophrenia with pithiatism', a form of hysteria amenable to suggestion. Joyce wrote a seven-page letter to Giorgio in Italian, so concealing the grim details from Helen and justifying his next move. Feeling that he now had good cause to ask the Public Trustee for permission to realize some of his war stock, he immediately asked Harriet to make the necessary approach. She told him that he needed to specify exactly how the money would be spent for Lucia's benefit and would have to fill in a number of forms. She would not be in London to help out, but if he needed more of his money he could arrange that directly through Monro.

On the 23rd, Joyce suffered a bad nervous collapse, but recovered sufficiently to organize the family's return to Paris. Almost immediately on arrival at rue de Galilée, he was again struck down with stomach pains so excruciating that he took to his bed. Debray ascribed his condition to 'nerves' and prescribed laudanum compresses. Léon told Harriet that over the summer Joyce had lost seven kilos, and that his collapse was 'a culmination of continuous worry in the last four or five years', and 'the hell' he had gone through recently.[68] Again, with the diagnosis of 'nerves' no further investigations were carried out. With her father recuperating in bed and still trying to recover from her mental upheavals and near-incarceration in a Swiss asylum, Lucia wrote to Stanislaus saying that they had just returned from 'a very nice time' in Geneva.[69]

One of the moral problems consuming Joyce, Léon told Harriet, was that he had jettisoned his religious beliefs but not the religion-inspired sense of guilt that powered his genius. His children, who he was proud to think had grown up without religion, however, were abandoned in a wilderness of conflicting demands with no clear way of navigating through them. Now that Lucia seemed so lost and confused, he told Budgen, he had been reproached for having denied his children a religious upbringing. 'But what do they expect me to do?' he asked. 'There are a hundred and twenty religions in the world. They can take their choice. I should never try to hinder or dissuade them.' As Budgen commented, 'This was certainly true, for Joyce would never have denied to others the freedom he claimed for himself.'[70] Nor did he question the action of the cunning DeWitt Eldredge, who smuggled a copy of *Ulysses* into the Vatican that summer and held it under his coat while the Pope blessed him. It was an occasion for him to intone, '*Quaecumque benedixerunt, benedicantur*' ('Whatsoever things they have blessed are blessed.')[71] Joyce hoped the book might be placed on the Vatican Index. Sadly for him it never was.

The situation at 42 rue Galilée was unpredictable and varied from hour to hour, Léon told Harriet, and he couldn't give her a correct picture because of Joyce's distrustful attitude. Now, instead of getting back to his novel he was helping Gilbert with a translation of Dujardin's *Les Lauriers sont coupés*. And there had been scenes with Lucia which left Joyce nervous, adding to his worries about the declining value of the pound. Ignoring the financial panic following events in Germany, Joyce seemed determined to find an unfurnished flat in which to finish his book. What he needed were 'some conditions of comfort and ease surrounded by his books which at present are scattered in some three or four different places in two countries'.[72]

He was again under pressure from his Parisian 'admirers' to send Lucia to a sanatorium, but, after Prangins, he was adamantly against that and engaged another 'nurse-companion', Pauline Bloire, to keep her company. She was back in the care of Vignes, and another theory had been floated – that she had 'ruined her nervous system by five years dancing'. Now, every time Léon met Joyce he was presented with another explanation of Lucia's condition; the only thing that did not vary was the fact that *he*, the father, was 'the culprit'.[73] Overcome by nerves and worry he cancelled his September appointment with Vogt.

Gorman was now under suspicion. Thinking that it was his copy of the *Ulysses* chart which had been shown to Random House, through Pinker Joyce withdrew his authorization for the biography. Within days, however, Gorman wrote to Léon from London saying that his book would be finished by January and he would send him the script – delayed, he claimed, by circumstances beyond his control. He had had no contact with Random House for years. 'If they say that I gave it to them or authorized them to get, or agreed to their publishing it,' he wrote, 'they are barefaced liars.' He had been sent the chart to help him revise his 1924 book, *James Joyce: The First Forty Years*. 'It was not communicated to me confidentially. There was never anything said about showing or not showing it.' Some friends, he admitted, had been shown it in the privacy of his study and one of them might have copied it. He had written to Cerf asking from whom he had obtained the copy. If Joyce wished to withdraw his backing for the biography, said Gorman, he would like to hear it from Joyce personally.[74]

The publication of *Ulysses* in America and Britain was now a priority for Joyce. Léon wrote to Frank Morley at Faber suggesting that prevailing Home Office attitudes towards the book could be easily tested, as Cerf had tested the US authorities, by importing a copy openly and seeing what followed. The outcome of the trial in America was, of course, crucial and a victory was bound to affect the climate in England.[75] Prompted by Léon's letter, Eliot and Morley travelled to Paris to discuss the questions of copyright and possible censorship with him and Joyce. Their discussion took place in a restaurant and lasted six hours, before the men from Faber departed, leaving Joyce and Léon to drink the night away, explaining the novel to the lady *patronne*. Back in London, Eliot and his colleagues continued to dither. Meantime, however, they did earn Joyce's approval by publishing *Pomes Penyeach* in a pale green wrapper at 2 guineas. 'Not too bad,' he told Harriet, 'for a book which E.P. told me to put in the family bible.'[76]

The case for lifting the ban on *Ulysses* in the USA was presented to Judge Woolsey on 25 November by Morris Ernst who had prepared carefully edited extracts from supportive letters from sympathetic liberals, including John Dos Passos, Rebecca West, Arnold Bennett, and Edmund Wilson – many of whom had reviewed the book favourably.[77] Ernst also brought Stuart Gilbert's book to the judge's attention and he was said to have been impressed by 'his scholarly analysis of "indecency" in *Ulysses*'.[78] On 6 December 1933, Woolsey handed down his ruling on *Ulysses*. He found the book not to be obscene and corrupting of public morals. As the London *Times* reported, the judge declared it 'a most disturbing book', but not so disturbing as to justify a continuation of the ban. It was 'sincere and honest' and more inclined to be 'emetic' than 'aphrodisiac'. According to law, he said, the court must concern itself only with the effect of the book on 'a person with average sex instincts – what the French would call l'homme moyen sensuel'.[79]

The *New Republic* noted that 'The engaging feature of Judge Woolsey's decision however and the quality which distinguishes it from his previous censorship rulings largely dealing with semi-medical works, is the care he devoted to such critical problems as the literary merits of the novel and the amount of consideration to which it is entitled, if it possesses the merit, the responsibility of an author to his chosen technique, and similar insufficiently considered matters.'[80] The Woolsey judgement confirmed the ascendancy of the aesthetic justification for obscenity over the hitherto prevailing moral view.[81]

Cerf wasted no time. On the same day he cabled to Léon, 'ULYSSES CLEARED TODAY WILL PUBLISH IN JANUARY.'[82] And there were congratulations and celebrations all round, in Paris, New York and London. Thanks were despatched from Paris – to Cerf, Robert Kastor and Morris Ernst – and the message was passed around the world by the newspapers. The following day, the *New York American* carried the headline '*Ulysses* Gets Right of Entry.' Cerf would print an edition of 10,200 and *Ulysses* was destined for the best-seller list.

When Stanislaus wired his congratulations, he was invited to Paris for Christmas. With *Ulysses* due out in America in January, all things were possible. 'Broken-backed England next,' Joyce told him. Stannie should come to Paris and meet his great-nephew Stevie, and Lucia, who was 'much better, in excellent health', lively as a March hare and as full of pride as ever. But that was in spite of the ten doctors who had 'treated' her. He was warned, however, to say nothing to her about dancing or illness as she was beginning to forget them both. He had, said Joyce, got her singing, and her candle was burning for St Lucia's Day in the next room, but that saint had had her work cut out looking after his eyes.[83] What was not mentioned was how his daughter's brutal outspokenness discomfited visitors to the apartment. The pious McGreevy was offended and frightened off after she had persuaded her credulous father that all his male visitors had succeeded in seducing her.[84] On her saint's day, Nora found her at 11 a.m. already wearing full evening dress. And when the phone at 42 rue Galilée grew red hot with calls from friends and admirers congratulating Joyce about the un-banning of *Ulysses*, she cut the phone wires – twice.

Eliot wrote from London, 'I am delighted to hear that the censorship of ULYSSES in America appears to have lifted. I do not suppose that this will have any direct influence on the situation here, nevertheless it is a useful parallel to be able to draw.' He was still awaiting Fred Monro's report on the history of the book.[85] Joyce replied somewhat indignantly; the ban on *Ulysses* in America did not *appear* to have been lifted; it *was* lifted. He could not understand what Eliot wanted to know from Monro. He referred him to the lengthy account of Woolsey's ruling in the *New York Herald Tribune* and urged him to lose no more time in getting the book into print. The American half of the English-speaking world had surrendered. The English half would soon follow, after a few fearful roars from the British lion.[86] It soon stirred. On 12 December Pinker reported that he was already negotiating with Allen Lane while Faber had merely expressed interest.

Cerf at last replied to Gorman's enquiry about the chart, apologizing that he had been dragged into the dispute between him and Joyce about it. It had been shown to him by someone (unnamed) who had done so in good faith, he said. He had written to Léon making it clear that he (Gorman) was not implicated. Furthermore, he said, Random House were interested in his biography which they could publish 'hand in hand with' the novel to sell them as a twin pair.[87] With Gorman off the hook, the way was clear for him to continue the biography unimpeded.

Joyce sent press clippings about the Woolsey judgement to Alf Bergan, following it up with a Christmas card designed by Lucia and a gift of money, hoping that Alf would drink a Christmas toast to Judge Woolsey. Doubtless with similar Dublin celebrations in mind, he ordered a dozen bottles of Clos St Patrice, 1920, from Avignon for Curran, and promised him a copy of the US edition of *Ulysses* and the judge's full ruling in due course.[88] Michael Healy also received a case of St Patrick's best with an injunction to toast not only the judge who had liberated his book but also the Pope who had blessed it.

Celebrations did not stop there. A great New Year's Eve party was planned, what Eugene Jolas called 'Joyce's Bal de la Purée'. Despite a bout of flu and laryngitis, he was happily spending the money he now anticipated would come flooding from across the Atlantic. He summed up 1933 as only 'James Job Joyce', the poet of despair, could: 'What a year! Fog, illness, disaster, madness.'[89]

31

Ulysses Unbound

(1934–1936)

'Everything mankind does, their hope, fear, rage, pleasure, joy, business, are the hotch-potch of my little book.' Juvenal, *Satires*

On 11 January, the London *Daily Sketch*'s 'Mr Gossip' came up with a literary scoop. 'A London firm of publishers has just signed a contract with James Joyce for the publication in England of *Ulysses*,' he announced, adding that unlike in America the propriety of the novel had not been tested in the British courts, even though some 8,000 copies had been already imported from Paris and one was 'sold at a Bond Street auction when the library of a famous law lord was disposed of'.[1] The following day the story moved on to the front page. Allen Lane, it seems, had followed Cerf's lead and forced the issue.

COMEDY OF STORY BANNED IN ENGLAND
'This parcel contains a copy of *Ulysses* by James Joyce'. With these words on the outside, a parcel was recently delivered by registered post to Mr Allen Lane of the Bodley Head publishing office in London. 'I had posted it myself overnight in Paris,' Mr Lane told the *Daily Sketch* yesterday referring to the exclusive announcement of 'Mr Gossip' in yesterday's *Daily Sketch* that the most famous banned book of our time might soon be published openly in London. 'The registration stamp was close to the letter I had printed and these must have been seen by at least six officials whose duty presumably it would have been to stop the entry of a prohibited book. I did it deliberately to show it is the easiest thing in the world to send a copy into England though the book may not be published here./As you know a decision has now been given in America that *Ulysses* is fit for publication there. As soon as I saw that I flew over to Paris with the purpose of arranging a contract for its publication in London./I am now in communication with the Home Office and Scotland Yard and also taking up the matter with the Society of Authors. For that purpose I am collecting all the evidence I can to submit to the Home Office or to the Director of Public Prosecutions.[2]

January the 25th saw the long-awaited launch of the American *Ulysses*, carrying a foreword by Morris Ernst, Joyce's letter to Cerf about his trials in getting the book published, and the text of Judge Woolsey's decision. Another distinctive feature was a full-page 'S' on the first page of the text. Priced at $3.50 in an attractive Art Deco black and red wrapper, the book could expect substantial sales. Cerf sent six copies to Joyce which arrived on the 30th in good time for his fifty-second birthday and the twelfth anniversary of the Paris publication of *Ulysses* – 2 February 1934, also the official publication date of Cerf's edition. He returned two signed copies for the lawyer who had conducted the case for Random House, Morris Ernst, and for Cerf and his partner, Donald Klopfer.

The American reviewers, many of whom had reviewed *Ulysses* in 1922, were paying homage to what was now considered a classic. Horace Gregory, in the *New York Herald Tribune*, wrote, 'Bloom will outlive us all and will remain (as Uncle Toby has survived) as the arch symbol of humanity in a transient world.'[3] And in the *Evening Journal*, Gilbert Seldes greeted its US debut as 'the publishing event of the year'. Citing his earlier review he declared, 'I felt it to be a great affirmation to everything in life – the good and the evil. I still feel so.'[4]

On the author's birthday, the 'subtile and barbare' Lucia reacted to the celebrations by slapping Nora's face and was immediately removed in the care of Nurse Bloire to the Château de Suresne, a sanatorium at Suresnes – no longer Joyce's 'much better girl in excellent health', and her St Lucia's Day candle had been long extinguished. (Her biographer claims that records show Lucia having already spent seven days at the Château in January, and speculates that it was possibly to have an abortion.)

Harriet came to Paris for a week, concerned by Léon's accounts of Joyce's worries and distractions, but found him incommunicado and missed whatever muted birthday celebration he was able to arrange.[5] Léon told her later that he was shielding her from Lucia who had declared that she (Harriet) had placed a curse upon her for preventing Joyce returning to London by her performance at the Gare du Nord. At Suresnes, she was examined by Maillard, who decided that she should be placed in a nursing home under supervision – forcefully if necessary. A return to Prangins was agreed and a colleague of Florel's, Dr Frédéric Humbert, travelled to Paris and escorted her back to Nyon.[6] According to Helen, with the onset of Lucia's illness Joyce was transformed from the open, hospitable social being he had previously been. There would be no more wild parties at the flat. Birthdays and Bloomsdays would be celebrated in restaurants and other people's houses. The ghost at the banquet was always Lucia.

If Harriet had been denied an audience with Joyce, Harold Nicolson was more successful. Despite the recent upheavals, with Giorgio in attendance, he put on a brave performance.

> Joyce glided in ... He was very spruce and nervous and natty. Great rings upon little twitching fingers. Huge concave glasses which flicked reflections of lights as he moved his head like a bird, turning it with that definite insistence to the speaker as blind people do who turn to the sound of the voice ... He was very courteous, as shy people are. He told me how the ban had been removed from *Ulysses* (Oolissays, he calls it) in America. He had hopes of having it removed in London also and was in negotiation with John Lane [The Bodley Head]. He seemed rather helpless and ignorant about it all, and anxious to talk to me.

The unreality of Joyce's life must have been especially heightened for Nicolson, who had just been discussing with the Romanian Foreign Minister Hitler's war intentions and plans for bombing British cities. As he wrote in his diary:

> One has the feeling that [Joyce] is surrounded with a group of worshippers and that he has little contact with reality. This impression of something unreal was increased by the atmosphere of the room, the mimosa with its ribbon, the bird-like twitchings of Joyce, the glint of his glasses, and the feeling that they [Joyce and his son] were both listening for something in the house – a shriek of maniac laughter from the daughter along the passage ... My impression was ... of a very nervous and refined animal – a gazelle in a drawing room. His blindness increases that impression. I suppose he is a real person somewhere, but I feel that I have never spent half-an-hour with anyone and been left with an impression of such brittle and vulnerable strangeness.[7]

Anti-government riots in Paris on 6 February, left Joyce traumatized. The prospect of an extreme left- or extreme right-wing dictatorship horrified him and intensified his sense of insecurity. When someone suggested he could always move to England, Léon told Harriet that he would do so only 'metaphorically-speaking at the point of the bayonet'.[8]

In view of Joyce's fragile state of mind, Léon was annoyed (he said) to be approached by the secretary of the young artists' movement called Les Amis de 1914, informing him that its patron, the Honourable Mrs Reginald (Daisy) Fellowes, the wealthy socialite and Paris editor of *Harper's Bazaar*, had planned an evening in honour of Joyce and was anxious to meet him. Dujardin, Gillet and Fargue had agreed to speak, and the actress

Rachel Berendt would read from a fragment of *Work in Progress*. Léon said that Joyce was extremely unlikely to want to be disturbed.

To Léon's surprise, Joyce was happy to attend. However, he declined to speak, saying that speaking about oneself was impolite. The meeting, for which most of his 'circle' turned out, took place in a large wooden hall beside the Brasserie Coupole in Montparnasse. Presiding at the meeting, the beauteous Mrs Fellowes offered her studied literary opinion of his work. When on board her yacht in the Aegean, she declared, 'I never lie in my deck chair without a copy of *Ulysses* by my side.' True to his word, Joyce sat silent throughout, eyes modestly downcast. To him, thought Léon, it must have seemed like a visit to the zoo. But in fact Joyce saw things quite differently. The reading by Rachel Berendt, whom he had coached, went so well that he proposed that the BBC do a programme of her reading from his work. Nor, like Léon, did he think badly of Mrs Fellowes, sending her an inscribed copy of *The Mime of Mick, Nick and the Maggies* when it appeared and receiving in return a charming thank-you letter penned personally from her luxurious villa at Cap Martin.

Still wanting to keep Harriet primed to help him, Léon wrote her another long letter explaining in detail Joyce's desperate circumstances and distressed state of mind. The 'emptiness' of the apartment following Lucia's departure had left him feeling anguished and isolated. Now that she was to be permanently confined, the costs for him were likely to be very high. More important was the effect her illness had had on his writing. 'Three years of unceasing worry about Miss Joyce which have caused him almost to abandon his work – it is remarkable that he was even able to accomplish what he did.'[9] He needed the right atmosphere to complete his *Work in Progress* – that unfurnished flat, his desk and his books around him. Added to this he had had another eye attack and again postponed his visit to Vogt. Finally he got to the point of his letter. The way out of 'his present irritable and almost hypochondriac state', Léon thought, would be if Harriet wrote reassuring him that she had not forgotten him and would always assist him. She could also help by having books he had stored in England sent to Paris, and by persuading Miss Monnier to bring out that cheap French edition of *Ulysses*. Lastly, he invited her to the readings Joyce was trying to organize for May.[10]

Harriet responded to Léon's call for help within a week, choosing her moment carefully. On St Patrick's Day she wrote directly to Joyce, somewhat apologetically, thinking that he might still harbour a grudge over her earlier unannounced visit. She urged him to find the flat he wanted, try to finish *Work in Progress* before interest evaporated, and keep his long-delayed appointment with Vogt. Finally she gave him the assurance requested. 'Will you please understand that I am, as far as may be, there somewhere in the background in case of need?'[11]

The publication of Budgen's *James Joyce and the Making of 'Ulysses'* in March added impetus to the launching of *Ulysses* in America. Joyce was surprised at how the book had turned out, telling Budgen, 'I never knew you could write so well. It must be due to your association with me.'[12] Reviewing it in the *Herald Tribune*, Lewis Gannett wrote that while enjoying the literary interpretations of sections of the book, far more fascinating was 'the picture of the conscientious, eternally exploring artist, always picking up new meanings of life, always pulling out of his waistcoat pocket, in a café, train or street, little writing blocks and scribbling notes – fragments of song and parody, a phrase overheard, a note on caning ships' boys – and going home to attempt, with the aid of his eyeglass, to decipher them, to file them in big orange envelopes someday to bring them out transformed into one of those strange phantom word adventures.'[13]

Joyce was still undecided about seeing Vogt, but on 24 March, he and Nora were 'kidnapped' by their friends, the businessman René Bailly and his Galway wife, for a car trip to Marseilles. En route, at Bailly's sudden suggestion, the Marseilles trip turned into a trip to Zurich by way of Monte Carlo, Grenoble and Neuchâtel, a journey of 2,500 kilometres – his first ever real motor trip, said Joyce. He kept Léon informed of their progress by telephone and Giorgio and Helen by letter. He might after all, he told Harriet, get to see Vogt. But he also told her that news had reached him that on Friday 30 March his friend Georges Borach had been killed in a car accident on the very road along which they were travelling. As they were to pass the exact spot where Borach was killed he kept this from Nora until they arrived in Zurich. Then, he said, she immediately wanted to leave, finding the city haunted by the dead man.

From 10 April Joyce was under observation by Vogt. Meanwhile he visited Borach's parents, an elderly couple he found 'pitiable' in their grief, and reflected on how little he knew of his friend. He then met Budgen's acquaintance, Bernhard Fehr, Professor of English at Zurich University, who introduced him to the composer Othmar Schoeck. Joyce was impressed enough by Schoeck's music to suggest he compose that opera of Byron's *Cain*, the idea Antheil had declined. But Schoeck was not interested either. At the end of a week Vogt informed Joyce that his right eye was so calcified that it required at least two operations with unpredictable outcomes. Joyce decided against the knife, settled for a new pair of spectacles and made another appointment for September.

The following day he and Nora were on the train for Paris. En route, he composed a poem inspired by a performance of Ibsen's *Ghosts* he had seen in Paris earlier. It was both a homage to his old master and a reflection on the mysteries of inherited madness – something which must have been preying on his mind ever since Lucia's insanity began to manifest itself. Dwelling on the thought of one sound child and one child 'blighted', he continued,

> Blame all and none and take to task
> The harlot's lure, the swain's desire.
> Heal by all means but hardly ask
> Did this man sin or did his sire.[14]

Diplomatically, Harriet saw nothing in the rhyme relating to Joyce but referred to it as alluding to the demise of Borach.

In March an appeal against Woolsey's judgement had been approved by the US Attorney General, which meant another six months of uncertainty for Joyce's fragile nerves to withstand. But publishers were not much deterred. George Macy of the New York Limited Editions Club wanted to bring out a de luxe edition of *Ulysses*, illustrated by Matisse. Cerf raised no objections and, eager to meet his new author, announced a forth-coming visit to Paris, as did Allen Lane. When Cerf arrived, Joyce was still away, so Helen entertained him for lunch. He told her that up to 15 April 33,000 copies of *Ulysses* had been sold. The Catholics were up in arms about the judgement, he said, and it was they who had pressurized the government to lodge an appeal.

Helen had persuaded Giorgio to visit the United States, to meet her family and see if he could further his singing career over there. He could also deal directly with US companies interested in film rights of his father's novels. Nora was opposed to the idea, thinking they would not return if the dollar continued to depreciate against the franc. Before they left, Joyce promised Giorgio that Lucia would remain at Prangins until his return. The couple sold their Rolls-Royce and on 19 April sailed with their two-year-old son for New York on board the German liner SS *Bremen*. Reporters would be awaiting their arrival: the son of James Joyce was news. Her brother's departure would be kept from Lucia for fear of upsetting her.

The appearance of *The Mime of Mick, Nick and the Maggies* (with Lucia's cover, initial letter and tailpiece) seemed to bear out Harriet's warning that interest in Joyce's new work was likely to fade. The *New York Evening Sun* offered the melancholy opinion that it 'does not appear to have set the local Thames on fire to judge by the virtual absence of comment or even interest'.[15] Even the usually enthusiastic G. W. Stonier, in the *New Statesman*, seemed to have grown impatient, saying, 'Reading the fifty pages of this new "fragment" ... we are reminded, with awe and almost with horror, of the parent work, that vast snowball trundling down some hidden slope, of which this is merely a chip thrown into the sky. How many thousand Micks and Anna Livias has it gathered up in its course? And when will it reach the bottom?'[16] An unsigned review in the *Morning Post* complained that it was necessary to learn a new language to understand Joyce's 'revolutionary vocabulary' and asked whether it was worth the effort.

With rumblings of revolution in France and a new war looming, people were warning Joyce not to settle in Paris, but on Friday 13 July, after four months of searching, he finally signed the lease of an elegant apartment just off the Avenue Bosquet at 7 rue Edmond-Valentin at an annual rent of 11,500 francs. It was a well-heated fourth-floor flat, with five rooms, and a lift, in a quiet street with little traffic. However, workmen would be getting it into shape during August ready for their moving in on 1 September.[17] It would be Joyce's last settled home and his penultimate flat in Paris. It stood close to the Pont d'Alma with the Eiffel Tower dominating one end of the street. Arranging everything had left Nora exhausted, so it was decided they would leave for the coast, possibly for Belgium.

Through Léon and Dr Florel, Joyce arranged for someone in Geneva to send flowers to Lucia for her birthday. The deception that Giorgio and Helen were in Paris and he and Nora were in Geneva was part of an elaborate charade intended to avoid anything that might disturb the delicate balance of her mind. By another deception, Max Pulver, a graphology expert at the University of Zurich, was sent Lucia's letters to examine and told they were written by someone else, but Pulver claimed that pressure of work prevented him forming an opinion about them. Joyce thought that probably he resented being approached in an underhand way or had found his reading too unpleasant to write down.[18] He also decided that the doctors at Prangins knew little more about cases like Lucia's than he did.

Having found their future home, on 19 July he and Nora left for Belgium, stopping briefly at Liège before moving on to the Grand Hotel Britannique at Spa – one of the most charming places he ever knew, he said – to take the waters. The weather was not so charming, which meant he spent lots of time indoors working and writing letters. On arrival, he wrote asking Léon his opinion of the Spa 'cure' – iron water to drink and carbonic water for bathing – and for copies of the *Irish Times*. He soon became fascinated with the Walloon language spoken around Spa – a sure sign that he was back at work again.

World events again began to intrude as news of the assassination by

Nazis of the Austrian Chancellor, Engelbert Dollfus, was loudly announced by newsboys in the streets. Nora was so panicked that Joyce decided they would soon have to move. 'I am afraid poor Mr Hitler-Missler will soon have few admirers in Europe apart from ... my nephews, Masters W. Lewis and E. Pound,' he told Harriet – though such expressions of political sentiment rarely filtered into his work.[19] If the two 'nephews' had expressed pro-Fascist sympathies, Joyce was now political only insofar as he hated and feared dictatorships of any colour.

Since 16 May the US Court of Appeal had begun considering the case for and against the Woolsey judgement on *Ulysses*. On 7 August, the book was finally given a green light in America when, by two to one, the Court upheld Woolsey's opinion that *Ulysses* was neither lewd nor immoral. The view that prevailed was that while the book might have a harmful effect on some people, 'art certainly cannot advance under compulsion to traditional forms'. This judgement confirmed a new judicial and public climate of greater tolerance of works judged to be of literary merit.[20] Joyce thought that the dissenting judge's quoting of 'obscene' passages from the book, with page numbers, would only provide excellent publicity for the book. He had newspaper reports of the case distributed among friends, critics and publishers. The judgement was a particular relief for Allen Lane who now pressed ahead with his plans to bring out *Ulysses*, leaving Joyce greatly impressed that a British publisher had sufficient courage to act, and was ready for a fight.

He was less impressed by happenings at Prangins where Lucia had got herself into emotional difficulties, having 'fallen', he wrote, for 'some undesirable gent' in Nyon. Although the doctors were keeping them apart, Lucia had become upset.[21] Joyce, however, thought that this sort of thing was not uncommon in women; it was not especially 'crazy' and would soon pass. The following day he received a more worrying report from Florel, and decided to visit the clinic to discover exactly what was going on. He was not prepared to continue paying 7,000 francs a month when the results after six months' treatment were so poor.[22] Again he wrote to reassure Giorgio that Lucia would remain there until his return from America, as promised.

The world beyond Joyce's immediate circle was continuing to change at an ever-increasing pace. His letters to Giorgio and Helen began to contain references to people leaving Germany or avoiding it. And he advised his brother not at any price to spend his holidays in Austria where Nazi anti-government terrorism was on the increase.[23] News from Ireland was hardly more encouraging. The Guinness brewery was leaving Dublin – another bit of Joyce's old Dublin about to vanish. He asked his friend Thomas Pugh who had photographs of the old city to send them. They would allow him to retain images of the Dublin in which his imagination still lingered.

To give Nora a rest before their visit to Prangins, on 16 August they began a fortnight's stay at the Grand Hotel Brasseur in Luxembourg – amid tranquil rose-gardens,[24] where Joyce could sit and reflect on the prospective un-banning of *Ulysses* in England. Then, after an indecipherable eight-page letter from Lucia, Joyce felt he must get to her as soon as possible. They travelled to Montreux, a short journey from Nyon, and from there Joyce phoned Florel asking him to prepare Lucia for their visit. Florel insisted that they meet first and Lucia would join them later. But when they arrived at Florel's villa on the afternoon of Sunday 26 August, Nora caught sight of her daughter on the lawn and, although she slipped into the house unobserved, Lucia spotted her father and ran to him shouting 'Babbo! Babbo!' Unprepared for this, as she smothered him with hugs and kisses he cursed her doctors who, it seemed, had told her the exact time of their arrival. Florel now admitted that after some seven months they were unable to diagnose Lucia's condition. His nurses were at a loss what to do with her. She had been kept under restraint behind barred windows and under constant observation. Joyce was profoundly shocked at the state she was in. If she remained there, he told Carola Giedion, he felt she would 'simply fade out'.[25]

After a couple of days in Geneva they sat down to contemplate their next move. Having tried Vignes' salt-water treatment, Pulver's graphology, and Florel's psychiatry, Joyce now remembered Budgen talking about a young woman being treated for an excess of white blood cells. Lucia, he had been told, had four times the normal number, a condition called leucocytosis. The wife of Fritz Fleiner, Rector of Zurich University (a friend of Budgen), suggested a Zurich haematologist, Professor Doctor Otto Naegeli. A thorough examination by Naegeli would, they hoped, establish or eliminate any physical condition underlying her mental disorder.

On Wednesday 12 September there was another 'scene' with Lucia who was in the mood to abuse her parents over what had happened to her. Joyce told Léon that while Nora was distraught, he simply remained calm, just repeatedly asking her pardon. A week later she set fire to her room, and the following day Joyce removed her from Prangins to Maier's private clinic at the Burghölzli – 'Zurich's Bedlam', he called it. A week later she was moved again, this time to the private sanatorium of Dr Theodor Brunner at Küsnacht, where one of the staff was Carl Gustav Jung.

The moving from doctor to doctor and clinic to clinic, and the consuming sense of guilt evident in Joyce's repeated apologies to his afflicted daughter, reflected the confusion and loss of control he now felt over the fortunes of his family. The search for the shaman with the miracle cure absorbed a great deal of his time. It would be some years before he accepted that his lovely 'wonder wild' daughter was incurably lost to him. Like his Bird-Girl on Dollymount Strand she had been there one moment and gone the next, but the memory would haunt him to the grave.

For Joyce, returning to Zurich's Carlton Elite meant another chance to hand out large tips to obsequious porters, and to eat well at the Kronen-halle. When Pugh wrote saying he had enjoyed the *Mime* fragment, Joyce replied that 'unkind people' had told him that it sounded 'just as well if read backwards'[26] – exactly what Jung had said about *Ulysses*. He and his daughter were about to come under the professional gaze of that particular 'unkind person'. Now, he thought, a great deal would depend on what this famous analyst could do for her.

When Jung interviewed Lucia, Joyce went along too. At their first meeting, each must have regarded the other with extreme caution. When he saw Joyce, said Jung, it was impossible not to see and feel his resistance and their conversation was correspondingly uneventful and futile. 'As we talked, by some effect of glasses and the position of the light behind him, the enlarged pupils suggested that full-eyed concentration of a wild animal' in which he saw 'the cold shadow side of life'. Lucia, on the other hand, he regarded as 'far more lively, but unfortunately ... already too far gone'.[27] He would see her for a month before offering Joyce his conclusions.

Naegeli had found Lucia not to be anaemic, tubercular or syphilitic, but he did find 'a blood anomaly'. His 'poor child', Joyce told Harriet, was not 'a raving lunatic', and he had another new diagnosis of his own. She was one who overreached herself attempting to do and understand too much. Her dependence on him, he realized, was now absolute and her affection, repressed over the years, was finally being unleashed on the parents she blamed for her troubles.[28] It must have helped to have the sympathetic but clear-headed Léon as their guest in Zurich for three days. Afterwards he wrote telling Joyce that it was not only Lucia's life he must fight for but also his own. Harriet echoed the sentiment, urging him to return to Paris for the sake of his work and for Lucia's benefit. Being alone in Küsnacht would strengthen her. Jung was of the same opinion, telling him that if he and Nora did not leave Zurich he would be unable to continue treating his daughter. But Joyce refused, saying that he had left her once and it had been a disaster. In any case Nora had now decided she wanted to make a home in the city.

Léon was acutely aware of the enormous drain of Lucia's treatment on Joyce's available resources. Harriet warned him that unless he approached the Public Trustee, she could only help him by selling some of her own stock, thus reducing her income and making it more difficult for her to help him in the future.[29] She was in danger of becoming the financial victim of a man who was now paying for an expensive Paris apartment, an expensive Zurich hotel room, and an expensive clinic for his daughter.

On 8 October, at the Kronenhalle with the Giedions, James and Nora celebrated their thirtieth 'wedding' anniversary. But he was missing Giorgio and growing fearful that his son and his family would never return to France. Meanwhile, Helen's German relatives were getting out of the country; Europe was no longer a healthy place in which to be Jewish.

After a month, Jung had come to a conclusion about Lucia. Recalling the case twenty years later, he said:

> If you know anything of my Anima theory, Joyce and his daughter are a classical example for it. She was definitely his 'femme inspiratrice' [a spiritual companion sharing his fantasies and inspiring his greatest work], which explains his obstinate reluctance to have her certified. His own Anima, i.e., unconscious psyche was so solidly identified with her, that to have her certified would have been as much an admission that he himself had a latent psychosis. It is therefore understandable, that he could not give in. His 'psychological' style is definitely schizophrenic, with the difference, however, that the ordinary patient cannot help himself talking and thinking in such a way, while Joyce willed it and moreover developed it by all his creative forces. Which, incidentally explains, why he himself did not go over the border. But his daughter did, because she was no genius like her father, but merely a victim of the disease. In any other time of the past Joyce's work would never have reached the printers, but in our blessed XXth century it is a message, though not yet understood.[30]

He did not tell Joyce this, but said that he was undecided what action to take; that psychoanalysis was possible but the outcome was uncertain and might cause a deterioration.

Reporting to Giorgio, Joyce said that although Jung had made a good impression on him, and he believed he had had many successes, what he had said about Lucia and psychoanalysis he had known himself all along. Jung's opinion that he too was touched by madness would have pleased him, had he known of it. He told Power, 'Hamlet was mad, hence the great drama; some of the characters in the Greek plays were mad; Gogol was mad; Van Gogh was mad; but I prefer the word exaltation, exaltation which can merge into madness, perhaps. In fact all great men have had that vein in them; it was the source of their greatness; the reasonable man achieves nothing.'[31] Jung's September bill for Lucia's treatment was 3,600 francs. Added to a monthly fee of 7,000 for her living expenses at Küsnacht and his Paris rent (around £400 altogether), any money he was earning did not stay with him for long. He told Budgen that if the road ahead did not lead to ruin he hoped someone would inform him.[32]

Fortunately Lucia seemed to have become much calmer, and Dr Brunner reported her taking automobile trips and playing billiards. Joyce was pleased too that when Léon saw her on his visit to Zurich she was calm. In this calmer state, she was, he said, acutely intuitive, even clairvoyant. Those who had warped her gentle kindly nature were themselves failures. To help her write more clearly he bought her a fountain pen, and she had written him a strange letter saying that she was spoiled, was costing him a fortune and he should return to Paris. She had met hysterical women artists at Prangins and she hoped she would not become like them. A quiet garden and a dog was what she would like. It was a shame he disliked Ireland which seemed very beautiful from pictures she'd seen and from what she'd heard. If she went to any other country it would have to belong in a way to him.[33] 'Sometimes', he told Giorgio, 'she has the wisdom of the serpent and the innocence of the dove.'[34]

Joyce was loath to leave Lucia but she seemed to have settled at last and was asking for plastic surgery to cover a scar on her face, which was taken to be a good sign. Satisfied that he could safely leave Zurich for a while, he and Nora decided to return to Paris, move into their new apartment, and then return to spend Christmas with their daughter. When he told Lucia their plan, she said nothing, but the next day she again set fire to her room, and a day later blacked her face with ink. Any idea of leaving Switzerland was postponed. There seemed no way out of the labyrinth inside which they had all become trapped.

Despite his immediate worries, Joyce was trying to work, sending progress reports and requests for books to Léon. But Léon was so frustrated by his indecision about leaving Lucia at Küsnacht that he told him bluntly what he thought. His writing career was languishing, he said, the public's memory was short and he could easily fall into oblivion. He should get back to Paris and his work rather than allow Lucia and her doctors to play expensive games with him.[35] Although these pleas would eventually have their desired effect, Joyce's spirits were hardly raised by the arrival of the *foehn*, an attack of nervous exhaustion, a bout of tracheitis and the onset of colitis. He was, he told Léon, too tired even to speak.

To add to his wretchedness Lucia was again behaving strangely, drafting telegrams to a variety of people, some of them dead. The doctors were unable to make a diagnosis. On 17 December she finally kept her appointment with the plastic surgeon, accompanied to the clinic by Mrs Giedion and a nurse. But once there she refused the operation.[36] Her father excused this by saying that she probably did not want to appear in bandages at Christmas-time. But the prospect of merry celebrations was bleak. Most of their Zurich friends would be out of town and Nora felt herself pushed to the edge of sanity. Joyce sent word to Harriet to ask Eliot to have an Anglo-Catholic mass said for the three Joyces.

Lucia joined them at the Carlton Elite for Christmas lunch at which Joyce even allowed himself a daytime drink of champagne. She made her own impression – 'all dressed up ... powdered and perfumed'. Everyone present, said Joyce, seemed taken by her grace and charm. She came again on Boxing Day, and parents and daughter retired to the hotel's music room where she sang all her father's favourite Irish songs to his accompaniment.[37] One she sang was 'A Ballynure Ballad', a somewhat suggestive country song ending:

> Says this wee lad to this wee lass
> 'It's will you let me kiss ye
> For it's you have got the cordial eye
> That far exceeds the whiskey'
> With a my ring-doo-a-day
> With a my ring-a-doo-a daddy o

> 'This cordial that you talk about
> There's very few o' them gets it
> For it's only them with muslin gowns
> And crooked combs that catch it'
> With a my ring-doo-a-day
> With a my ring-a-doo-a daddy o

Echoes of that intense father-daughter symbiosis appeared to linger as if to remind Joyce that Lucia was a haunting presence in his *Work in Progress*. As a New Year's present he sent her tickets for *The Magic Flute*; she sent him some Virginia cigars. To her mother she sent lilies.

At the end of 1933 Lucia's medical expenses had amounted to little more than 1,000 francs; by the end of 1934 the figure had mushroomed into many thousands more. The sad irony of the situation was that earlier she had complained that her father was squandering her inheritance; now a large portion of it was being spent on her.

Despite his great victory of 1934, the New Year was hardly the bright shining dawn Joyce might have hoped for. The cloud of Lucia's madness loured over him. Surrounded by those urging her incarceration, his own instinct was to keep her out of the hands of clinical psychopomps whose manifold diagnoses invariably included himself – a distaste duly reflected in the great work. As one of the interrogators says of Earwicker, in Book III, Chapter 3 of *Finnegans Wake*, 'He does not believe in our psychous of the Real Absence, neither miracle wheat nor soulsurgery of P. P. Quemby' – a reference to a then fashionable spiritual healer.[38]

The second week of January, he told Léon, was his worst for months. A friend, the lawyer Wladimir Rosenbaum, came to inform the Joyces that Lucia had been to see him and told him she had decided not to sue Ponisovsky but would leave him her jewellery. Her one idea, he told them, was suicide. When he left, Nora had stormed for two hours, accusing Joyce of messing up their children by failing to educate them, wasting their inheritance, driving one to America and another to contemplate suicide. He had, he told Léon, remained silent throughout this onslaught. However, two days later, on 14 January, he paid off Brunner and Naegeli, removed Lucia from Küsnacht (out of the orbit of Jung) and took her to the Carlton Elite where she was lodged in a hotel annex together with a hired companion. That day Brunner recorded, 'Against our advice Joyce took daughter with him to private pension in Zurich with a nurse.' The following morning he took a taxi to the composer Othmar Schoeck's villa outside Zurich, but no sooner had he arrived than Nora phoned to say that Lucia was causing another of her scenes at the hotel, refusing to stay with the nurse and calling for her Aunt Eileen. Joyce hurried back to the Elite, and that afternoon cabled to ask Eileen to join them from Ireland. Following that, he was unable to work for four days.

Bad as this was, another worry was bearing down on him. Harriet's endowment was greatly diminished, and unless he wrote to the Public Trustee requesting the release of his government stock his other remaining shares would have to be sold. He was, he said, prostrated by the news that all his available money was gone.[39] Even so, in the comparative tranquillity of the hotel, he did manage somehow to get back to *Work in Progress*. It helped to hear that Lane was planning to publish *Ulysses* in the autumn and that Cape wanted to reprint *Exiles*. There was also a film contract for *Ulysses* on offer which Léon advised him against.[40]

Giorgio had now given two broadcast concerts in New York, and had sung at several tea parties, including one given by the President's wife. All this had aroused some interest in the press there. The *New Yorker* sent their best man, James Thurber, to interview him for its 'Talk of the Town' column. Although Thurber focused briefly on the young singer, it was clearly his father who interested him. His questions ranged over Joyce's sight, his manner of writing and his literary interests. He was blind in one eye, said Giorgio, but had now replaced writing with blue crayons on large sheets of white paper with writing in pen or pencil. He typed but with just one finger, and hating professional typists, got friends to do his typewriting. Because of his eyesight, friends also read to him from dictionaries, encyclopaedias and other reference books. He found *Ulysses* and his earlier works boring, and only read to himself and his friends from his *Work in Progress*, chuckling from time to time as he did so and re-reading those bits he enjoyed the most. Giorgio then offered a rare glimpse into his father's working day. '[He] gets up around nine, writes a little, but spends most of the morning telephoning. He actually likes talking on the phone, and chins with his friends by the hour. Before lunch he plays and sings, and afterwards works until five o'clock ... After five [he] walks, alone ... He likes the opera, the theatre (never misses a Thursday matinee), song recitals, and even movies.' 'He has,' reported Thurber, 'been at his new book for years; nobody knows when it will be finished, but Giorgio thinks it's about half done.'[41] Later Joyce commented, 'The interview in *New Yorker* is the usual thing. They will get tired of me soon and move on to Giorgio himself.'[42]

On 16 January, another Lucia scene was triggered when Nora visited her at the Villa Elite and found herself unwelcome. Lucia then did the round of her doctors, demanding to know whether there was a cure for her short of murder. When Joyce got back to the hotel at 6 p.m. he found Nora and the nurse in the restaurant in hot dispute while Lucia prowled around drinking black coffee. On his arrival she suddenly left. The women wanted to chase after her but Joyce restrained them, sparking another argument in which he was again blamed for his daughter's plight. When she returned, mumbling, the nurse resigned. Another, older nurse was hired but Lucia refused to sleep in the Villa, so Mrs Giedion gave them a room for the night. Nora wanted to send her back to Küsnacht, but Joyce was sceptical – she had a different idea every week, he said, usually after receiving a letter from Galway. It worried him that his wife and daughter were so bitterly at odds. He felt incapable of helping and was unable to work.

They finally decided to take Lucia back to Paris where Eileen had agreed to join them. They arrived on 31 January and again checked into La Résidence, in the Avenue Pierre 1er de Serbie. Lucia seemed to have been calmed by the move and the prospect of meeting Eileen. On Joyce's birthday, there was a muted celebration at Fouquet's on the Champs-Elysées – 'a miserable meal', he said, costing 'a poor 1,000 francs or so', with the Jolases, Gilberts and Léons, but without his usual high-kicking dances or singing or candle-decked cake or people telling him how handsome he looked while he sat on the floor in a corner, clutching bottles of wine, puffing on cigars – 'nodding at all the men and winking at all the women'.[43] Everyone at the table that night declared that Lucia was so much better, he said. The crisis was past, but that was nothing to do with the doctors.[44]

Around 10 February the Joyces moved into the renovated apartment at 7 rue Edmond Valentin. It was, recalled Nino Frank, similar to their place at Square Robiac, 'substantial and anonymous' with 'a vast drawing room, where Mrs Joyce's portrait occupied the place of honour'.[45] Jacques Mercanton, who later befriended Joyce, noted its 'sober and elegant furniture, a big reproduction of a Vermeer, photographs, fine editions of *Ulysses* in the glazed bookcase'.[46] A few weeks later they hosted a Sunday tea party where the portraits were made the centre of attention by a proud and revivified Joyce. From there, Joyce and Léon would sometimes stroll down to the Seine together and sit watching the river flow between the Pont d'Alma and Pont Royale. In his imagination, thought Léon, it was the 'riverrun' of the Liffey flowing through his *Work in Progress*.[47]

Harriet invited Lucia to stay with her in London. She would travel to England with Eileen, then join her later for a holiday in Bray. According to Eileen, '[Jim] couldn't take Lucia himself because she had turned against Nora so much that he couldn't have that. Much as he loved Lucia, he always put Nora first.'[48] But Lucia insisted that she and Eileen travel to England separately, so she was alone when on 14 February Harriet met her off the boat-train at Victoria and took her to her flat in Gloucester Place. 'I was favourably impressed with Lucia the first moment I saw her,' she told Joyce, 'and the favourable impression has deepened since.' The girl was depressed and lacked concentration, she thought, but it was absurd to call her insane. On meeting Eileen in London, Lucia announced that she planned to buy a pistol. When her aunt suggested she buy two in case the first one did not work, she slapped her on the back and laughed.[49] Her intended target was never disclosed but Joyce said she went to London hoping to see Samuel Beckett. In fact, when they did meet, she did not produce a pistol but went to a concert with him.

Harriet was sending regular reports about Lucia to Joyce through Léon to keep them from Nora. For the first ten days, she reported, the 'patient' was 'tractable' and she felt confident that she could be managed. But when Eileen had to return to Dublin for a week, Lucia became depressed – overcome by tiredness, throwing up and becoming feverish. When Harriet took her to see a Harley Street psychiatrist she introduced herself as a one-time lunatic. When Harriet demurred, Lucia regarded her with what she called 'a dark and ambiguous expression'. 'I did not at the time know,' she said, 'that she liked to pose as having been insane.'[50] Twice she ran away,[51] and once Harriet called Scotland Yard to report her missing before phoning Joyce in Paris.[52] There were *crises de nerfs* and Harriet brought in a nurse friend, Edith Walker, to help manage her.[53] Eileen rejoined them, but on announcing that she had to return again to Dublin, Lucia declared that she too wanted to go to Ireland. Joyce sent money for her stay, while Nora sent a word of warning: she had best avoid Galway as there could be trouble when people found out that she did not attend High Mass or Holy Communion. On the other hand, Irish air and Irish eggs would be good for her. Harriet paid for their ferry tickets and first few days in Dublin. 'I do hope,' she told Joyce, 'that there will be less cause for worry now that Lucia is at last in the land of her heart's desire. May it retain its glamour for her.'[54] For Joyce, however, the glamour of Ireland had faded. When trying to renew his British passport that April he was offered an Irish one but refused. He had no interest in belonging to the 'Irish Free Fight'.

The economic depression had badly affected Sylvia Beach's business and she decided to sell some of her manuscript collection, including many items by Joyce. Adrienne Monnier wrote on 15 March asking if he minded the proposed sale and, incidentally, included an article announcing it in the *New Yorker*. Beach's archive contained proofs of *Ulysses*, 1,500 pages of *Stephen Hero*, a partial manuscript of *Dubliners*, manuscripts of *Chamber Music*, *Pomes Penyeach*, and his lecture on Defoe. There were copies of 'The Day of the Rabblement', 'The Holy Office', his *Ulysses* schema and the letter protesting about the pirating of *Ulysses* bearing all the famous signatures. But most painful for Joyce was that her sales catalogue also included personal gifts including his signed first edition of *Ulysses* and the poem written to her to mark its publication. Beach probably thought she was merely recouping some of the money Joyce had borrowed so recklessly on account over the years. But he was unhappy because he considered it mostly 'rubbish' given to her in the hope of keeping her happy. Now he saw himself being inveigled into agreeing through clever publicity, telling Giorgio, 'The rumour is ... that she, by generously sacrificing all her rights in my favour, has reduced herself to starvation.'[55] Harriet dubbed it 'a wretched affair',[56] and although Joyce felt he could not object he was deeply hurt.

For Joyce, poverty remained a nightmare prospect. He told Harriet that when Nora read her letters aloud to him and money was mentioned he put his fingers in his ears. Furthermore, he refused to approach the Public Trustee who would want to know exactly how any money realized from his government stock would benefit his children. His own mental state, he confessed, was sliding downhill. He was exasperated and exhausted, he said, after 'presiding over mothers' meetings' for a year. As to him and his work, 'Perhaps I shall survive and perhaps the raving madness I write will survive and perhaps it is very funny. One thing is sure, however. *Je suis bien triste.'*[57] But Harriet proved herself a loyal friend. When he complained about unpaid royalties and his depreciating investments, she advanced him £100, and, when unexpectedly she had £300 of capital repaid to her in April, she gave him £250 to cover his immediate debts. A month later he returned her generosity by gifting her the original Matisse illustrations for *Ulysses*,[58] which later the *Telegraph* critic called 'amazing' and 'vibrating with movement'.[59]

By 17 March Lucia, the young pilgrim, was in Dublin, lodged with her Aunt Eva. But it wasn't long before she became restless, suspecting the Dublin Joyces of conspiring with the Paris Joyces to control her, and wanting to move out. Eileen booked her rooms at two top Dublin hotels, the Gresham and Buswells. She left both saying she wanted to be nearer the College of Art in Thomas Street. After ignoring Nora's birthday on 21 March, she wrote her a letter which, according to her father, 'drove her half mad' as it was probably intended to do. When she asked her father what he was writing, he said something for *transition* which he would send her when published, adding, 'The devil knows what it means.'[60] If she was unhappy, he said, he would come and rescue her, but Michael Healy had promised to take her to Galway if that was what she wanted. When Eileen wrote of the trouble Lucia was causing he told her that the 'scenes' that had frightened her and Harriet were nothing compared to what her mother had withstood for four years.[61]

Eileen considered her brother pathetically wrong in believing that Lucia would eventually recover. But he was more realistic than she supposed, telling Harriet he was only too aware that Lucia had no prospects but he could still distinguish the 'beautiful and shapely' from the 'ugly and shapeless.' Believing in Lucia, he said, left him as usual in a minority of one. Eileen, he thought, was not being straight with him; like the rest of his family she was no longer to be trusted.[62] Yet, when Harriet suggested that his daughter might return home she found Joyce reluctant to have her – probably because of Nora. He wrote asking his old friend Curran to look out for Lucia in Dublin, admitting that in the past his eyes had been veiled where she was concerned. However, she was, he said, worth any number of his own family.

Meantime Lucia had decided to escape Dublin and left for Bray where her cousins, Bozena and Nora, provided her with a comfortable bungalow next to theirs. On the four pounds a week she received from her indulgent father she lived in luxury while her hard-working cousins struggled along on what little they could earn. But she caused a scandal by her loose behaviour and wild ways, once painting her room at the bungalow black in imitation of Isadora Duncan's black-furnished apartment in Paris – her so-called 'domain of Circe'.[63] Seeing Giorgio's interview in the *New Yorker* which made no mention of her, she twice attempted suicide. Her behaviour was not appreciated by the pious and conservative locals. The Ireland she had yearned for, where she had been welcomed with lavish affection as a five-year-old and a teenager, had gone, and she was no longer an innocent young girl. Now she was a strangely behaved misfit in a small mid-thirties Irish town, and her unpredictability made people extremely nervous.[64] After a while she abandoned Bray for Dublin, where she went on a drugs binge and was found wandering the streets – lost, vulnerable and hungry.[65] The city of *Dubliners* and *Ulysses* she had hoped to find was no more than a ghost town of the imagination. It was, according to her father's latest fragment for *transition*, 'a phantom city, phaked of philim pholk'.[66]

Joyce, uneasy about her silence and the absence of letters from Eileen, asked Michael Healy and Con Curran to check on his daughter. Their reports were so disturbing that he dispatched Maria Jolas to investigate, but Lucia refused to meet her and disappeared. Curran, however, found her and got her into a nursing home in Finglas. From there, to pre-empt any attempt to return her to Paris, she wrote to Harriet saying she was tired of Bray and wanted to live in Sussex. Joyce was torn between playing the permissive parent and wanting to prevent his daughter doing damage to herself. But now she was in Ireland he felt he had lost control of her and was filled with 'a blind man's rage and despair'. On all sides he heard that he was an evil influence on his children, but he was more like Paris, he told Harriet, 'a haughty ruin ... a decayed reveller'.[67] And now, Lucia, like a *young* haughty ruin, had ended up in a Dublin nursing home.

She was not alone in failing to find the land of her dreams. Giorgio was becoming fed up with America where his singing career was floundering. People there wanted crooners, not Irish tenors singing classical arias. All he had earned from singing after a year in the US, he said, was $35 and the country 'made him vomit', but his father told him it was 'a passing phase'. He should not expect much from his 'curious circle of friends' there. In time he would come to love it.[68] That summer, Giorgio developed an overactive thyroid brought on by stress, and his doctor recommended a partial thyroidectomy. To cheer him up Joyce told him about a jolly evening at Les Trianons with the Jolases and Léons when he was prevailed upon to recite poems by Yeats, a recital which lasted two hours. 'Everybody congratulated me on my extraordinary memory, my clear diction and my charming voice. Someone added: What a pity he is such a fool!'[69] But he worried that, having lost Lucia to madness, he might now be losing his son to America. 'Our six lives,' he lamented, 'are in such a broth not to say dishwater.'[70]

Mrs Jolas returned from Dublin with a far worse tale to tell than Curran or Healy. Her story so shocked Joyce that his sleep was plagued by nightmares and horrific imaginings, and *Work in Progress* stalled yet again. He felt certain now that Eileen and Harriet had conspired to keep bad news from him. He was always informed, he told Giorgio sarcastically, that Lucia was 'getting on fine' and the 'blue-eyed and prim-mouthed' Harriet had walked straight into Eileen's 'booby-trap'. Knowing that his son and daughter-in-law thought Lucia should simply be locked away, he told them not to jump to any such conclusion. This was the result of her being separated completely from her parents for the second time.[71]

Nora thought Lucia should be left in Finglas from where she was writing sensible letters, and had even written a pleasant one to her. But when Harriet informed him that she had expressed a wish to live in Sussex, Joyce hoped that something of that kind could be arranged. He approved the idea of England because it suited his latest theory about Lucia's illness. A Paris specialist, Naum Ischlondsky, who had developed a bovine serum for treating mental cases, had recommended the London physician W. G. MacDonald, who regarded such an illness as essentially a glandular disorder. Joyce was still nurturing the idea that his daughter's problem was physical, stemming from what Naegeli in Zurich had found – a 'blood anomaly'. The prospect of more doctors' fees did not deter him, even though a third of his earnings from *Ulysses* had drained away and his holdings were depleted. 'I will go on selling; it's not my fault that the stock has fallen in price,' he told Léon. 'When it is exhausted I will give lessons.'[72] But he was desperate and saw no immediate way to raise the funds needed. To Curran he confessed that 'the medical faculty of half Europe has very considerately and very considerably lightened my bag of marbles to the extent of about £5,000 in the last $4\frac{1}{2}$ years'.[73]

Lucia left Dublin on 26 July, escorted across to England by Curran and his wife, and was met at Holyhead by Harriet. She and Edith Walker had prepared the London flat and Edith had agreed to wear ordinary clothes rather than her nurse's uniform. After violent initial resistance from the patient, MacDonald administered the first injection of Ischlondsky's bovine serum. He then ordered that the reluctant patient be confined to bed. Early reports suggested good results from the new treatment, and Joyce felt that his own ideas about his daughter's illness were vindicated. For more than a year, he told Curran, he had been 'harping on the subject of a glandular disturbance', but none of the 'so-called mind doctors' would listen to him.[74] Writing to Lucia, he apologized for his own slowness in understanding her. Then, reflecting on his 'isolation method' of composition, added, 'O yes 8 years to write a book and 18 for its successor. But I will understand, in the end.'[75] Privately he hoped that MacDonald with his injections would do what the Paris and Zurich mind-plumbers had failed to do, and was encouraged enough to feel able to return to his usual demanding work-programme.

Believing that Lucia was now on the way to recovery Joyce was anxious that all traces of her illness be expunged as far as possible. When Eileen wrote offering to return the personal possessions Lucia had left at the bungalow, Léon told Harriet to sever all contact with her but to keep this from Lucia who still thought fondly of her aunt. He also asked her not to mention his daughter's Irish visit or mental condition to anyone. But Joyce still had to contend with Giorgio's insistence that his sister be locked away permanently, telling him that if he had seen her after seven months' confinement at Prangins he would see things differently. Under the new treatment she seemed to be improving, even taking up drawing again, he said.

Sadly for Joyce, the apparent improvement in Lucia was not maintained. She became violent and an extra nurse was required to restrain her. Then, to Harriet's relief, MacDonald agreed that she could convalesce in the country. In mid-September they moved to a bungalow at Reigate in Surrey – Loveland's Cottage – where Lucia could sit out in the garden sunning herself and feeling less constrained. There she became calmer, and her father even wrote to her about her future.

In September, on a trip to Fontainebleau with Herbert Gorman and his wife, the Joyces heard that Giorgio and Helen were sailing from New York on the 25th. They quickly returned to Paris where Joyce celebrated by having a new set of teeth made. When the young couple arrived they moved into a large garden flat at the Villa Scheffer, just off the Avenue Henri Martin, where Joyce and Nora became frequent visitors. They had much to talk about. Reports from Harriet were still optimistic, but in early October Lucia had sent letters to her father which concerned him. It appeared that all her clothes had been lost in Ireland, including her fur coat, which depressed her. He asked whether MacDonald would agree to him sending Mrs Jolas over to see her. However, a few days later, Harriet wrote to say that she was so improved that the second nurse had been dismissed.

A photograph of Lucia lolling in a hammock in the garden of Loveland's Cottage clutching a book gave him some reassurance, and in the hope of enticing her back to 'normality' he told her that the next stage of her convalescence should be 'a nice fur coat'. 'How does that strike you?' he asked. Sounding more like a Madison Avenue ad-man than the author of *Ulysses*, he signed off with, 'Buy yourself a fine fur and give poverty a kick.'[76] He had great faith in the therapeutic value of fur coats for women. Meanwhile he was sending out desperate messages about his own perilously tottering financial position.

Lucia's period of 'good progress' in England, it transpired, was only the calm before the storm. She became too unwell to contemplate shopping for that fur coat. When word of this reached Paris, Maria Jolas was dispatched on another mission to check on her and again the report she brought back was disturbing. Not helped by MacDonald's ban on sedatives, Lucia had reverted to unpredictable outbursts – childish rages, hysterics, tantrums, hunger strikes, throwing things and suicide attempts. The doctor finally conceded that his prediction of recovery within six months of his injections was premature. Just as troubling to Joyce was the news from Harriet that his daughter was 'hankering to go to church'.

MacDonald visited Paris to discuss Lucia's case with the Joyces. He had decided to take her for blood tests to St Andrew's Hospital in Northampton, where he was Head Physician.[77] He was full of optimism and left a good impression on the worried parents. On 14 October he returned to Loveland's Cottage and arranged for Harriet and Edith to escort Lucia to Northampton where he continued his serum treatment.

One welcome break from his anxieties for Joyce was an approach from a young French-Swiss writer, Jacques Mercanton, a student at the Collège de France, who was planning to write something about *Work in Progress*. Invited to the apartment, Mercanton found Joyce in a relaxed mood, in slippers, tight trousers, smoking-jacket and blue woollen shirt, stretched out on the floor searching for a station on the radio through a magnifying glass. After assuring himself that his visitor was not a journalist, Joyce moved from talking about Switzerland, music and singing to speaking openly about his work. Like others before him – Budgen, Gilbert, Gorman and Beckett, and a new young acolyte, Armand Petitjean – Joyce appeared to regard Mercanton as someone through whom he could explain his work to puzzled readers, so achieving publicity while himself remaining aloof and enigmatic. He explained to his visitor how he was trying to reproduce the immediacy of the nocturnal world through the accumulation of languages and trying to project the reality of an 'eternal present', proceeding, he said, 'as the Demiurge goes about the business of creation, starting from a mental outline that never varies. The only difference is that I obey laws I have not chosen.'[78]

Although Allen Lane already had Francis Meynell's book design, he was suddenly being annoyingly cautious over the launching of *Ulysses*, telling Pinker that the Director of Public Prosecutions had been 'particularly vigilant recently'. He did not want to prejudice matters by acting prematurely. But America was now a free market for Joyce and on 22 October 1935 the New York Limited Editions Club published *Ulysses* with its six etchings and twenty sketches by Matisse – an edition of 1,500 copies plus 250 copies signed by both Joyce and the artist.

Joyce was quite unaware that his Canadian stock had yielded nothing for the past three years and that Harriet had paid out 'fictional' dividends to him from her own pocket. With Joyce's capital depleting fast, his high rate of spending showing no signs of abating, and with MacDonald charging exorbitant fees, Harriet worried more and more that he would be unable to continue without additional help from her. She asked Léon whether someone could 'pull strings' to get him the Nobel Prize – Maria Jolas's suggestion.[79] However, she asked him to keep her financial concerns from Joyce. Oblivious to all this, that Christmas Joyce sent a telegram of thanks to Harriet, and to everyone he sent Christmas cards designed by Lucia, wishing them 'a happy and tranquil 1936'.

At the end of January, Harriet and Edith visited Lucia at St Andrew's Hospital in Northampton. Left in a room alone with her medical notes, Edith glanced at them and noticed the word 'carcinoma'. Having suspected that Lucia might have cancer, she immediately told Harriet, who, thinking that Joyce should know, wrote to Maria Jolas suggesting she inform him gently of what was feared. But the note in Lucia's medical record had been dangerously misconstrued. Cancer was merely one of several ailments for which Lucia was being investigated.

Unfortunately, on receiving Harriet's letter, Mrs Jolas went straight to Joyce and announced a doctor's hypothesis as an actual diagnosis. The effect on Joyce and Nora was devastating, and Joyce suffered another eye-attack. MacDonald was invited urgently to Paris where he quickly explained the medical situation. Joyce was furious with Harriet for the pain she had caused them and the resulting disruption to his work. MacDonald told them that the progress he had predicted for Lucia had all along been thwarted by two well-meaning but incompetent do-gooders. Again feeling betrayed, Joyce wrote Harriet an angry letter breaking off all communication with her. MacDonald followed this up with a strongly worded note forbidding her and Edith any further access to his patient. Edith wrote back indignantly to say that it was *her* mistake and not Harriet's. But the damage was done. Maria Jolas, however, realizing that she had handled the matter ineptly, offered to provide a home for Lucia when she left Northampton.

Harriet's blunder had made it doubly difficult for her to tackle Joyce on the question of money. She was distressed at how rapidly he had gone through the funds she had given him. Short of winning the Nobel Prize or selling the film rights of *Ulysses*, she told Léon, 'the only other way I can see of tackling the very serious financial situation is for Mr Joyce, though against the grain, to economize in every possible direction.' Finally she had realized her big mistake. 'I am blaming myself now for not having made the capital more inaccessible to Mr Joyce, accessible for needs but not for luxuries ... From the rapidity with which the royalties of the first edition of *Ulysses* melted away I ought to have taken warning and had the imagination, foresight and firmness to protect Mr Joyce against himself.' But, she acknowledged, the harm was done and she suggested that his Canadian Pacific shares, not yielding interest, be transferred to her for £800.[80]

By 12 February Harriet had recovered sufficiently from the shock of Joyce's explosion of wrath to write him a conciliatory letter, trying to explain her rash behaviour.

> In my alarm I lost my head. I shall be unhappy till I know whether you can forgive me for the pain and trouble I have caused you ... Since I am forbidden to visit Lucia any more ... perhaps you will allow me to write to her now and then. Hope Mrs Jolas's kind offer to take Lucia into her new house can soon be accepted.[81]

A week later, Joyce heard that Lucia was asking to leave St Andrew's. MacDonald said he could not prevent her discharging herself unless she was committed. But Joyce told Mrs Jolas that he would never agree to his daughter being incarcerated among the English. She was despatched to Northampton to bring Lucia back to her home at Neuilly where she now ran a bi-lingual school.

When he learned that the transfer of his Canadian Pacific stock would adversely affect Harriet, Joyce refused to proceed with the transaction, and asked Monro to compensate her from his own stock. He also refused her request that she come to Paris to resolve their misunderstandings, and matters between them did not improve. Lucia was unable to return to France because her passport had been left behind in the London flat. Joyce cabled Harriet to ask whether she had sent the passport to Northampton and whether the long-unpaid bill of MacDonald's had been settled. Her reply was brief and to the point. 'PASSPORT REACHED NORTHAMPTON BILL PAID REGARDS.'[82] For some reason Joyce took offence, calling her cable '*désagréable*', 'curt' and 'a snub'.

After three weeks with Mrs Jolas in Neuilly, Lucia's behaviour worsened and she was removed to another clinic. According to Maria, she went 'completely mad' and had to be taken away in a straitjacket. This led to a break with the Jolases. With Joyce in a state of nervous paralysis over his daughter, he was flinging blame in all directions except towards himself. Lucia was briefly at the Maison de Santé Velpeau in Neuilly, then from 23 March spent a month at the Clinic Villa les Payes in Vésinet, west of Paris. There, after assaulting her nurses, she was isolated by the chief physician, who considered her a danger to his staff and inmates.[83]

On the advice of Karol Agadjanian, a Polish friend of Léon who specialized in the psychology of hallucinations, on 26 May Lucia was moved to the *maison de santé* of Dr François Achille Delmas at Ivry, at the end of the Paris métro. The clinic was a pleasant house in large grounds with equally large fees. Delmas was sceptical about Lucia having 'dementia praecox', as previously thought. He favoured Joyce's view that it was hormonal imbalance that caused her violent mood swings, a condition called cyclothymia. He wrote requesting reports from all the institutions to which she had been admitted – from Nyon, Zurich, Dublin and Northampton as well as Paris.

Harriet again expressed her readiness to come to Paris to settle their misunderstandings face to face, but, to her distress, Joyce replied that he did not care if they were cleared up or not. She immediately suggested that he might prefer to give the US edition of *Ulysses* with the Matisse drawings which she had ordered through him, to someone else. If so, she would return it to him. When Léon passed on the message that she would not be coming he remarked sourly that she would not be missing much. Her proposal that she return the book she had ordered from him, however, clearly shocked him. He quickly wrote to her apologizing for his ill-tempered message, saying that he had been much upset by her disagreeable telegram, stung by what he saw as an unfriendly snub, and could only imagine that she had requested the book only in order to fling it back at him.[84] But, he added, if the book was being offered in friendship, then he would be happy to have it back.

In May, Léon estimated that around half a million francs had been spent attempting to find a cure for Lucia. But the need for further funds continued. Pride kept Joyce from applying to the Public Trustee and having to explain why he, a known 'wholesale squanderer', now needed money 'for the education of Giorgio aged 31 and father of a son aged $4\frac{1}{2}$ and Lucia aged 29'.[85] Consequently his letters to Monro continued – requests for a hundred or two hundred pounds, and bundles of bills for Lucia's upkeep and treatment for settlement. In late May he asked for money from his Canadian Pacific shares to pay for Giorgio's thyroid operation, which, in view of his and Helen's wealth, Harriet thought extraordinary. Later, to protect the investment, she bought £2,330 of this stock, secretly, intending to sell it if it rose in value and make over the balance to him.

Hitler's reoccupation of the Rhineland in March had heightened political tension, and Joyce felt ever more beleaguered in Paris. On 5 June, writing to Mary Colum, who was moving with Padraic to America, he spoke of his family woes, his growing sense of isolation and what he called 'the disturbed conditions now abroad in the world' creating a nerve-racking atmosphere in which to work. 'It has been almost impossible for me to continue writing with such terrible anxiety night and day. Still I am doing what I can.'[86]

His next bills for Monro he sent via Harriet, cataloguing his various tribulations – son confined to bed, daughter in the madhouse, seven doctors to pay. Some close to him had criticized him for paying for expensive treatment when he might simply have had Lucia locked away cheaply. But, he said, he would never do that while there was the slightest hope of her recovery, nor would he condemn or punish her for 'the great crime' of falling victim to 'one of the most elusive diseases known to man' about which medicine was completely ignorant. No money would compensate her if, through neglect masquerading as prudence, he allowed her 'to fall into the abyss of insanity'. 'If you have ruined yourself for me as seems highly probable,' he told Harriet, 'why will you blame me if I ruin myself for my daughter?'[87]

32

The ABC of Blind Love and Ruination

(1936–1938)

Demoniac frenzy, moping melancholy,
And moon-struck madness.

Milton, *Paradise Lost*

Caresse Crosby had plans for a book of Joyce's collected poems and in early July Léon began negotiating with her. The upshot was a Black Sun Press limited edition of 800 published in December. Huebsch's *Collected Poems of James Joyce*, appeared as a Viking Press edition the following year. The few reviewers who took notice saw them as evidence that beneath the dark satirist lurked a lyrical sentimentalist. The *New York Times* review, for example, headlined, 'James Joyce's Poetry does not Suggest *Ulysses*', argued that 'These lyrics, which are sometimes little more than an exquisite sigh, are to James Joyce what Swift's "little language" was to the author of Gulliver, a sort of baby-talk intended to please women.' The poet, it suggested, was Joyce's 'alter ego'.[1]

That July, when James Stephens came to ask him to 'take up the mantle' as Ireland's foremost writer and join Yeats's Academy of Irish Letters, he had no difficulty refusing. More enticingly, Lord George Carlow, heir to an Irish earldom, owner of the Corvinus Press, dedicated to producing books 'beautiful beyond all those yet produced', wanted to bring out a fragment of *Work in Progress*. Joyce was happy to agree, provided it included *lettrines* by Lucia. Carlow loved both the artwork and the offered fragment (taken from *transition 23*) which he would publish as *Storiella As She Is Syung*. Then came news that Lane had finally found a printer for *Ulysses* and he sent Joyce a copy of the cover with Eric Gill's design for the binding. All this spurred him on with his work, and in July Lucie Léon took proofs of Parts I and III of *Work in Progress* to England for Harriet to correct, while Joyce ploughed on with Part II.

The sound of warplanes exercising over Paris was an intimation of the change which was slowly transforming European consciousness. On 19 July civil war erupted in Spain and the approaching Berlin Olympics would show to the world the assertive face of the dictatorial right. The young were engaged in war and words of war, and their literary interests were reflecting that change of mood and commitment. Joyce, on the other hand, felt he had more personal enemies with whom to contend, and talk of war simply did not interest him.

Lucia's copy of *A Chaucer ABC* (for which Harriet shared the cost) duly arrived in time for her twenty-ninth birthday on 26 July and, after presenting it to her, Joyce made plans to escape from the heat of Paris. He and Nora headed at long last for Denmark, travelling via Hamburg. At Villier-sur-Mer near Deauville where Lucia had once attended summer camp, Nora bought presents to send to Ivry. Her doctor, Delmas, was asked to ensure that the Deauville label was removed from the parcel and that it be left at the porter's lodge for Lucia to collect as if it had been delivered by hand. By 21 August they were in Hamburg where Joyce visited the Albatross Press. From there he informed Giorgio and Helen that his feet were dancing towards Denmark and he was headed for Copenhagen in the morning.

His visit to Denmark was a pilgrimage to the home of Hamlet, Ibsen and Earwicker. It was also the homeland of those who had raped, pillaged and populated Ireland, and whose bodies, like that of the giant Finn MacCool, lay beneath its soil. Viking blood, he thought, flowed in his own veins. This concatenation of associations was woven into *Work in Progress*. 'Be ownkind. Be kithkinish. Be bloodysibby. Be irish. Be inish. Be offalia. Be hamlet. Be the property plot. Be Yorick; and Lankystare. Be cool.'[2] At the Turist Hotel in Hamlet's city, Joyce's arrival was quickly noticed. Before long the newspapers were requesting interviews, which as ever he declined.

Having successfully repelled all journalists he was tricked into talking to one – Ole Vinding, who ingratiated himself by masquerading as an artist and for three days showed the Joyces around Copenhagen. He noted their conversations and later sent a transcript to Joyce asking for his approval. The answer was 'No', but after Joyce's death he did publish it. Vinding found the frail, restless, talkative Joyce exhausting and saw Nora as the silent passive shadow accompanying him. He enjoyed speaking his old-fashioned Ibsenite Danish, was endlessly curious about words new to him, preferred walking to taking cars or trams, and was intent on behaving 'thriftily' – denying Nora an Icelandic sweater and once even a cup of tea. Everything centred around himself. 'He was,' wrote Vinding 'like a spoiled boy with his quiet, eternally permissive mother,' and spoke about his new novel which he said was three-quarters finished.

I haven't lived a normal life since 1922, when I began *Work in Progress*. It demands an enormous amount of concentration. I want to describe the night itself. *Ulysses* is related to this book as the day is to the night. Otherwise there is no connection between the two books ... Since 1922 my book has become more real to me than reality, and everything has led to it; all other things have been insurmountable difficulties, even the smallest realities such as, for instance, to shave in the morning. There are, so to say, no individual people in the book – it is as in a dream, the style gliding and unreal as is the way in dreams.[3]

The appearance of the book in fragments, Joyce said, corresponded with the nature of the book itself and the nature of the book also determined the way he wrote it. 'I can only write alone, more and more alone. It has developed that way, like my style, which has developed and changed so that what I write simply cannot be expressed in any other way than like dream talk. With day-time talk such as I used in my youth, I would not achieve anything.' One observation of Vinding's is revealing. 'He sucked energy from his surroundings,' he wrote.[4] That feeling of a strangely vampiric presence might explain what lay at the heart of a family whose members felt they had to flee – abroad like Giorgio, into an ironic silence like Nora, or into an alternative reality like Lucia.

In London, the Director of Public Prosecutions was informed that Foyles bookshop was planning to put on sale an 'indecent book', namely *Ulysses*. This could have threatened Allen Lane's plans, but Foyles' circular announcing the book was cleverly vague about a publication date and gave no indication of the publisher. The *Morning Post*, however, reported that the book had been published a week earlier by the Bodley Head and that Lane had previously consulted the Home Office. Responding to this, a puzzled Home Office official noted in a memo that there was no record of any such consultation. Although previous seizures of the book had been lawful and correct, he said, the book had been declared not to be obscene in the United States, and was now being lectured on at Cambridge. The Home Office's uncertainty about maintaining the ban could not have been better for Joyce and for Lane.[5]

Lane's de luxe edition of *Ulysses* was finally published in England on 3 October 1936. Prominent advertisements appeared in the *TLS*, *Times* and *New Statesman*, because Lane wanted to demonstrate that the book was not being published furtively. Joyce asked Harriet to distribute copies of the *TLS* to thirty different people. On publication day he cabled his thanks for her loyal support and generosity over the years. The olive green cover, Eric Gill binding and jacket design were simple and fresh. The signed edition was priced at 6 guineas and the trade edition at 3 guineas. The errata slip which had appeared in the US edition had gone. But it was found later that Lane's printer had introduced his own errors, the price Joyce had to pay, it seems, for his neologistic compulsions.

Visions of the future began to appear. Djuna Barnes now revealed herself to be an apt Joycean disciple. In the same issue of the *New Statesman* carrying Lane's advertisement for *Ulysses*, Peter Quennell declared that her *Nightwood*, 'for bitterness and crazy violence, leaves the darkest chapters of *Ulysses* far behind'.[6] Other young writers, such as William Faulkner and Malcolm Lowry, were also knocking at Joyce's door. On 12 November, Eugene O'Neill, a writer much influenced by *Ulysses*, was awarded the Nobel Prize.

Barely had Joyce returned from Copenhagen than he collapsed with stomach pains – 'in terrible anguish', said Léon. His puzzled doctors again put it all down to nerves. Harriet wondered whether the attack had been brought on by something she had written. On 5 November Léon told her that since his return Joyce had been nowhere and seen no one but had just been sitting listlessly within his own four walls. However, although clearly in bad shape, within the last five days he had started to prepare a new fragment for *transition*.[7]

Reviewing Lane's edition of *Ulysses*, G. W. Stonier, the *New Statesman's* resident Joycean, recognized its importance in the history of literary censorship. The Woolsey judgement, he wrote, was 'the rare case of a book condemned for its obscenity being afterwards reclaimed by the weight of literary opinion'. He expressed scepticism about Joyce enthusiasts acclaiming *Ulysses* 'a classic'. However, he acknowledged that the book, was 'the repository of a whole corpus of unwritten poetry, doggerel as it bobs to the surface of the mind, soliloquies of a modern Hamlet, phrases and fag-ends of lines, the brooding commentary of Stephen Dedalus and the Bouvard-like reveries of Bloom', which, together with its brilliant pastiches, made *Ulysses* 'a bonfire of literature, a glowing revenge'.[8] Like Stonier, Alan Clutton-Brock in the *TLS* noted the lyrical qualities of the text. 'Passages that are genuine poetry alternate with the harshest and most deliberately contemptuous parodies, uproarious burlesque with subtle indications of character ... it is above all the profusion and fertility of language that will fascinate the reader.'[9] When shortly afterwards, in the same paper, the same reviewer (Clutton-Brock) reviewed Lucia's *Chaucer ABC* and found it 'a genuinely original work' of 'great elegance and delicacy'[10] the proud father ordered eight copies.

Léon sent Harriet a long letter concerning the state of Joyce's mind. 'Mr Joyce says his situation is so black that nobody would want to see him,' he wrote. 'Ill luck is pursuing his children and the lack of success of his daughter's book has disgusted him.' The comparative critical silence following the British publication of *Ulysses* had only intensified his sense of alienation. However, he would now welcome a visit from her. 'I am sure that he wants to see you and the more so that all he wants to tell you is hardly expressible otherwise than orally and because I am sure he would like to see you in his practically total estrangement from people.'[11]

Two days later, Harriet arrived in Paris, planning to stay for a fortnight. Because Joyce was so preoccupied with writing, she spent a good deal of time with Sylvia Beach. When they did meet, she and Joyce ironed out their misunderstandings and, as was his wont, he immediately asked her to run errands for him in London – including sending a copy of the English *Ulysses* to Judge Woolsey with as many reviews as possible. He discussed with her his latest fragment with its mention of Buckley and the General, and she wished them both a smooth debut. After this visit, however, Harriet never saw Joyce again and the confidential tone in which he had unburdened himself to her faded from his letters.

As the New Year of 1937 dawned, news came that Lane's Bodley Head had failed and he had set up a new company, Penguin Books. The sense that some malign power was stalking him was difficult for Joyce to resist. 'John Lane, The Bodley Head' under new management would mean his having to renegotiate the *Ulysses* contract. It meant more delay for that cheap English edition he so badly wanted. He asked that errors introduced to the limited edition be corrected, and the Albatross edition taken as a guide. But he foresaw what he called 'the usual programme of incompetence, pusillanimity and tergiversation' if Ralph Pinker got involved,[12] and left matters to Léon and Monro who were told to resist all attempts to reduce his royalties. Léon only dissuaded Joyce from dismissing Pinker by stressing his efficiency at collecting royalties and holding useful records of all his past literary transactions.

Nino Frank chanced across Joyce one day in the Champs-Elysées – 'a familiar silhouette' all alone, switching his cane and 'whistling under his breath, the brim of his felt hat turned up ... looking even more jaunty, more youthful than usual'.[13] Inviting Frank to the apartment, Joyce suggested they translate *Anna Livia Plurabelle* into Italian together. Thinking the work would mostly fall on himself, Frank protested at the difficulties it would pose. But Joyce spoke with urgency, telling him, 'We must begin work before it's too late. For the moment there is still one person in the world, myself, who can understand what I have written. I can't guarantee that in two or three years I will still be able to.'[14] It took two afternoons a week over three months to complete the translation. Frank was shocked at Joyce's playful approach to the task and his readiness to stray from the sense of the original if the sound or rhythm of certain words appealed to him. He even added in a few extra rivers.

Herbert Gorman, Joyce's biographer, was back in town, and Joyce wanted him to visit places in Ireland that mattered to him – Chapelizod, and Howth, especially when the rhododendrons were out. The rhododendrons on Howth Head are a recurrent motif in *Ulysses* and it is lying amid them that Molly Bloom recalls awaiting her moment to say 'Yes' at the end of *Ulysses*. In *Work in Progress* the Head was also the head of the giant Finn. The trusty Curran was again recruited to see that Joyce's 'Boswell' got to wherever he needed to go. But not wanting Gorman to know about Lucia's visit to Ireland, he pretended not to know Eileen's whereabouts. It was a subject he preferred to avoid, he told Curran. Those who had made up their minds about Lucia were either mystified or bored with the subject; the rest seemed 'more pleased than sorry'. But whatever malady had struck her down had not yet 'laid her out', and she had escaped Ireland alive, therefore he continued to hope.[15]

The truth was carefully kept from others, too. The artist Myron Nutting and his wife Helen reappeared after some nine years, and in bringing them up to date about Lucia, Joyce wrote that she was hopeful and seemed finally 'on the road to recovery'.[16] And in mid-July even Curran was receiving the same optimistic message: 'Some doctors and people who saw Lucia lately agree that she is much better than $2\frac{1}{2}$ years ago. What a dreadful trial to be laid on any girl's shoulders! . . . The 26th is her birthday. Will you please send her a message (not a present, it's too complicated with the customs).'[17]

Joyce's old adversary, Gogarty, had recently published an autobiography, *As I Was Going Down Sackville Street*, of which the *TLS* said that the author 'has stepped forth from the pages of *Ulysses* intent on refashioning existence in his own terms'.[18] If Joyce might have been upset by it, others were even more angered. Joyce's old acquaintance and Beckett's cousin, Harry Sinclair, believed that he, his brother and father had been libelled by the author's anti-Semitic jibes. The case they brought against Gogarty was a local sensation and would captivate Dublin for five months before the court found against him. Beckett, back in Dublin and living at home, was the chief witness and his appearance in court caused a serious breach with his highly respectable if somewhat neurotic mother. The case cost Gogarty £900 and drove Beckett back to France.

Although downcast about Lucia and reluctant to show himself in public, Joyce did make exceptions to the rule. That May, Louis Gillet gave a lecture on him at the Paris Italian Club, followed by a dinner in his honour. Then, in June, Joyce agreed to speak at the Fifteenth Congress of International PEN in Paris, but only to air his continuing grievance about international copyright piracy. If PEN stood, as it claimed, for 'the art of literature and for its free and open diffusion from country to country', that, he thought, should be conditional on authors' rights being protected and their being adequately compensated for their labours.

He entitled his address 'The Moral Right of Writers', but, because of his poor eyesight, it was read for him while he looked on. In it he outlined the history of *Ulysses* in the USA, its pirating by the unscrupulous Roth, the protest signed by 167 writers, and the outcome of court proceedings against the pirate. A pirated or prohibited work, Joyce concluded, belongs to its author by natural right and only the court can protect it from mutilation or illegal publication and the misuse of the author's name. This was greeted with loud applause.[19] But the mood of the moment was too political for Joyce. Finding no one interested in following up his argument, he left. Unsurprisingly perhaps, that summer, a predominantly communist Writers' Congress in Republican-held Madrid declared Joyce, along with Kafka, Proust, Eliot, Yeats and Lawrence, politically incorrect. Marxist criticism bewildered him. 'I don't know why they attack me,' he told Eugene Jolas. 'Nobody in any of my books is worth more than a thousand pounds.'[20] He refused to answer Nancy Cunard's famous questionnaire about authors' attitudes towards the Spanish Civil War, sending her instead his PEN conference speech, saying 'Print that, Miss Cunard!'[21] Beckett replied simply 'UPTHEREPUBLIC!'

Not long afterwards, he was invited to Shakespeare and Company for a reading by Hemingway and Stephen Spender (who earlier, in Oxford, had argued that in an age of ideology, writers like Joyce and Virginia Woolf were passé). Joyce turned up with Jolas, but, although he admired Hemingway, his reading from his new book about Spain (*For Whom the Bell Tolls*) began to bore him and he started yawning loudly, much to his companion's discomfort. Spender then read one of his poems about revolution in Spain and, as Jolas told it, 'After a few sentences, Joyce pulled my sleeve. "Let's go ... " I tried to persuade him to stay a little longer, but he would have none of it. To my great embarrassment he rose, and after stumbling over our neighbours' feet, we left. Joyce was certainly allergic to any suggestion of politics.'[22] Spender later recalled the evening and Joyce's presence, but failed to remember the walk-out. The poet's biographer merely records that 'Joyce slipped away before Stephen had a chance to be introduced.'[23]

Lucia's illness induced Joyce to read about mental illness and left him eager to correspond with others whose children had been similarly stricken – Mrs Giedion, Mrs Sullivan and Adolph Kastor. He was fascinated by the case of Nijinsky, the ballet dancer, whose dementia praecox was reported to have been cured by insulin treatment, and wondered whether this might be the cure for Lucia.

Delmas reported that her condition was 'stationary'. To Joyce, that seemed good news for once. Pound was told she was 'much improved' and Harriet that she had undergone 'a wonderful improvement'. According to Helen, Joyce visited Lucia regularly. They would meet in a private room with a piano where they would play and sing, and usually end up dancing together.[24] He encouraged others to visit her and send presents. When Mrs Giedion planned to call on Lucia, she was told through Léon not to sound too enthusiastic about her recent holiday but to give the girl hope of a future holiday together when she was better.[25] Giorgio visited her once but he was so shocked by her aggression that he never returned. Nora just stayed away.

On 8 August Joyce wrote to Harriet saying that he aimed to finish *Work in Progress* by his next birthday and was putting in long hours to meet that deadline. When Curran wrote encouraging him to visit Ireland, he said that until he had completed his book he was 'taking no chances' with his fellow-countrymen, even though in his heart he was walking the streets of Dublin and along the strand and voices were whispering, 'Never say never.'[26]

He was again being assailed by painful stomach cramps and advised by the doctor to leave Paris and to seek relief in Switzerland, ordered to refrain from drinking and smoking and to eat rump-steak and vegetables. After two nights in Basel, he and Nora travelled the few kilometres to Rheinfeld along the Rhine. Unfortunately, they found the place noisy with trains running through the town from 4.30 a.m. But the riverrun of his book was still flowing and rivers were continuing to charm him. 'Anna Rhenana runs under my window all night complaining in guttural Schwyz-Duitsch of being pressed into service by me with 500 odd otters [?] as train bearers to a drunken draggletail Dublin drab. Lord help me if I ever come near that warrior-girl Anna Amazonia!'[27]

Contacted by the Giedions, they moved on to Zurich for a short stay at the Carlton Elite. There they were greeted by thunderstorms and, to Joyce's horror, two people were killed by lightning just outside the Giedions' house. To escape the Alpine storms, in early September they journeyed westwards to Dieppe on their favourite sea-coast. With the end of the long and winding road of *Work in Progress* in sight, Joyce could enjoy the sound of the sea and reflect on the novel he was about to bring to birth. He told Frank Budgen that his father's encounter with a tramp in Phoenix Park was the basis for his book.[28] To Helen, he said that what was intended as a slim book had suddenly fallen over a crag and become a waterfall.[29] It amounted to a dark essay in self-analysis with conflict within families, incestuous ruminations, essays into Irish history, fable, myth and legend, the thunderous doom awaiting Earwicker in punishment for unspoken crimes and unspeakable sins and a final awakening from the tumult of nightmare and guilt. And yet, all this was swept along in a river of brilliant, erudite, and witty word-play. The waterfall was a confusion of tongues, a rare musical extravaganza.

And a plot of sorts can be discerned within the 'plotless plot' of the *Wake*. There is the form of a dream which in turn is the form of a river taking its course and returning to its source; it is also a stream of unconsciousness, and a series of cabaret acts, of episodes or vignettes. Within these moving forms protean characters come and go, form and transform themselves, representing at various times the family of Humphrey Chimpden Earwicker (Anna Livia, Shem, Shaun and Issy), Mutt and Jeff (based on the cartoon characters), the Mookse and the Gripes (based on the fable of the Fox and the Grapes), and the Ondt and the Gracehoper (the Ant and the Grasshopper). The action takes off with the fall of Finnegan, the hod carrier, who dies and is resurrected at his wake by the smell of whiskey. The fall of Finnegan parallels the fall of Adam and Eve, Humpty Dumpty, Parnell, and ultimately the fall of Earwicker. The story ends with a sign of new beginning as Anna Liffey finally flows out into the sea and merges with the oceanic human element, the stuff of life, but returns again to its old riverrun on the opening page of the never-ending story.

The approaching publication of the cheaply available trade edition of *Ulysses* in England began to make Joyce fearful that the authorities might act against it. Back in Paris, he asked the publisher to ensure that it was as widely distributed as possible in an effort to prevent this occurring. On 1 October it was duly advertised in *The Times* as 'The complete text of Mr Joyce's great novel, for the first time made available at a price within the reach of the serious student of fiction [25 shillings] as distinguished from the collector of rare books.'[30]

That autumn the publication of *Storiella As She Is Syung* was delayed when the printers had problems setting Joyce's text. However, there was a cheering surprise. Someone sent him the 22 October issue of the *Osservatore Romano*, the official Vatican weekly. It contained an essay on Irish literature referring to 'the famous European iconoclast and rebel, James Joyce, who after having sought to renovate the old naturalism, attempted in *Ulysses*, to translate plastically the inner reality, and, who, in *Work in Progress*, in an experiment, both oneiric and linguistic, is seeking to open up new paths for the expression of human sentiments'.[31] Joyce told Mercanton, '[The essayist] must have written that under the influence of some skeptical old cardinal who wanted to amuse and mystify everybody a little. Even me.'[32]

Lucia had another set-back in November, and finally Joyce came to accept that her illness was cyclical. In December, Beckett, now returned to Paris and back in favour, was invited round and enlisted to work with Giorgio on the galleys of *Work in Progress*. He remembered Joyce giving him a copy of the last chapter to read on a trip away from Paris, and his delighted reaction when he phoned from St Lazare Station to tell him how much it had moved him. 'He was very fond of the ending of the book, which was full of premonitions of death – he was overcome by the writing of it.'[33]

Eliot at Faber was anxious to see the completed manuscript. By mid-December Parts I and III were in proof form and Part II was now mostly in his hands, followed by pages of corrections and enlargements forwarded by Léon. Even at this late stage it was a work in progress being fed to the publisher straight off the typewriter. Joyce had had to withdraw into creative isolation in order to push his experiment to a conclusion for his self-imposed deadline of February the 2nd. Even so, he needed assistance from an army of friends to prepare it for submission. As Léon told Harriet, 'It takes some five or six people to check the corrections, verify the additions and read the proofs. Himself, he does the composing part quite alone and . . . works daily to about five in the morning.'[34]

At Christmas 1937, Joyce sent 'a small offering' to Alf Bergan asking him to drink everyone's health. But in sending £2 to Eileen he asked Léon to add a less than seasonal message saying, 'Mr Joyce asked me to add that whenever letters come from his family in Dublin it causes trouble here.'[35] That Christmas afternoon he spent with Lucia and, in his ever-optimistic way, thought her somewhat better though still not stable. That evening, Beckett was invited to dinner by the Joyces, where he met and began an affair with Peggy Guggenheim.

Yet again Joyce was about to lose the son who had become his closest confidant within the family. Helen's father was gravely ill and she and Giorgio decided to leave for New York at short notice. 'We passed a bad Xmas,' he wrote, 'and it looks as if we are going to have a worse S. Sylvester Night!'[36] The penultimate year of *Work in Progress* would not end with the bang of Tim Finnegan's wake but with the whimper of James Joyce's own sense of impending loss.

*

Joyce was now slaving to complete *Work in Progress* by his fifty-sixth birthday. Just one final fragment would appear in *transition*. Beyond that, Joyce was determined that his new novel would appear in the summer of 1938 and so was decidedly unhappy when Huebsch mentioned postponing the Viking edition till autumn. He asked Eliot to stress to him the importance of the agreed publication date, 4 July, his father's birthday. Eliot was surprised to hear how close to completion the book was. The final decision about its publication date, he said, would be made by Huebsch and Frank Morley who would meet in New York shortly. Joyce was unimpressed. Huebsch had once thought that *Ulysses* could never be published in the USA and Morley that it would be unpublishable in England. Eliot was anxious to know the title, even if in confidence, but Joyce was not yet ready to divulge it.

Joyce continued to make new friends. George Pelorson, a friend of Beckett from Trinity College, asked permission to translate *Pomes Penyeach*. And James Johnson Sweeney, an Irish-American art critic on the editorial board of *transition*, came to discuss passages of his book. When Joyce quizzed him on his grasp of the meanings concealed within the neologisms and convoluted phraseology, he demonstrated how any reading of it could yield multiple interpretations.

Just as Helen and Giorgio were about to depart for New York, catastrophe struck Beckett. On the night of 6 January, returning along the Avenue d'Orléans with Alan and Belinda Duncan from an evening out, he was accosted by a trampish pimp and, when pushed away, the man attacked and stabbed him just above the heart, perforating the pleura. The attacker fled and Beckett was taken to the Hôpital Broussais, where, at one point, he lay close to death. Joyce was summoned and quickly brought in Dr Fontaine and had Beckett moved from the Salle Commune to a private room at his expense.

Nino Frank went with Joyce to visit the patient, recalling the encounter between the two Irishmen as marvellously absurd. In the gloomy hospital room, he wrote, they 'marinated in intolerable silences', communicating only intermittently. 'I have never felt so close to Ireland, to its sentimental isolation, to the very air of *Ulysses*, as I did that day, sitting between those two brothers, in their shape and their keenness like twin knifeblades. The elder and the younger were united by a profound bond, to find the explanation of which one need go no further than Swift or simply any postcard showing a Dublin pub, some shops, and the passers-by.' After Beckett was interrogated by the police, Joyce told Frank, 'He is truly Irish. He doesn't hold it against the tramp at all, but do you know what he's mad about? The knife made a hole in his overcoat. He wants the judge to make it up to him and buy him another one.'[37] Beckett in fact dropped all charges. His family flew from Dublin to be with him, and Joyce visited him twice before he was discharged on 22 January. The assailant was thought to be unbalanced rather than delinquent, and Beckett, according to Frank and Pelorson, inclined to be violent when drunk.

Joyce had decided that if Viking and Faber could not guarantee publication of his book on 4 July, he would leave for a much-needed holiday in Switzerland, and resume work in the autumn. On 26 January, Geoffrey Faber wrote personally to Joyce saying that Faber could publish in July only if they received the complete manuscript before the middle of February.[38] Huebsch wrote simply to say that July was unsuitable for Viking. And even Carlow's *Storiella*, it transpired, would not appear in time for his birthday.

Long hours of work had affected his eyes, and when Collinson told him that he had a retinal congestion, should stop work and go straight to see Vogt in Zurich,[39] this gave Joyce the excuse to escape from what he called his 'prodigious solitary labours' and the private world in which he had long imprisoned himself. But before leaving Paris he had his birthday to celebrate. Frank remembered the party taking place at Giorgio and Helen's Villa Scheffer flat. Evidently a sense of abandonment prevailed.

> We sang, we laughed, Joyce blew out the candles on his birthday cake, we also drank a lot. Someone put an inviting dance tune on the record player, and suddenly, while I was confessing my ignorance of the most elementary steps, Joyce took me by the arms and compelled me to whirl about with him. In vain the others and I tried to stop him; he was enjoying the joke . . . he dragged me along with a child's joyful giddiness – and I will never forget the agonizing sensation of trying to hold up this man, fragile as a statuette, while all present looked on in consternation. Fortunately the step was only a bourrée style applied to the waltz. In any case the party was soon brought to an end.[40]

His birthday did not go entirely unnoticed in the wider world. Con Curran reported a Radio Éireann broadcast marking the occasion, with contributions from himself and Gorman. The Vatican paper's kind words about him had encouraged the broadcasters. Joyce was delighted and commented ironically though incorrectly, 'It is the first time in more than thirty years they have mentioned my name there.'[41]

A few days later, the Joyces were at the Hôtel de la Paix in Lausanne. The weather was foggy and so were Joyce's eyes. Jacques Mercanton, who lived nearby, was invited to meet him that afternoon. He was greeted in the hotel lounge by Nora who told him that Jim had been working hard and intended to enjoy a few lazy days. Finally, he appeared at the top of the stairs and made an entrance – large hat on back of head, swathed in a long scarf and carrying a cane, feeling his way down step by step. He took the visitor's arm and led him out of the hotel to be taken for a walk. He expressed amusement over the Irish radio broadcast and the *Osservatore Romano*'s words of praise, and mentioned Eliot's wanting to know the title of his book. 'I have kept it to myself for sixteen years,' he said. 'I will supply it at the last minute, when I please. To be so exacting about a book like mine is absurd.'[42] Over dinner he ate little, drank white wine and talked about everything but literature.

Joyce's hospitality had a price that day. As they parted, he handed Mercanton a bundle of proofs, saying, 'We will have a look at that abracadabra together tomorrow. But don't put yourself out.' 'Lazy days' were forgotten. Next day he spoke self-deprecatingly of the hostile criticism of *Work in Progress*, saying, 'It is I who could draw up the best indictment against my work. Isn't it arbitrary to pretend to express the nocturnal life by means of conscious work, or through children's games?' And as for the time and labour involved, 'A book like that has no ending. It could go on forever. But I must finish. It will be impossible after more than fifteen years of work on it to avoid repeating myself.'[43] He admitted to using forty languages he didn't know to express what he called 'the dream state'.

As they read through a page of text Joyce indicated how he thought this song, that phrase or that allusion would appeal across cultures, his eyes lighting up with 'secret and melancholy gaiety' at the idea. But then, his mood changed and he said, as if answering an unasked question, 'Why should I regret my talent? I haven't any ... Chance furnishes me what I need. I am like a man who stumbles along; my foot strikes something, I bend over, and it is exactly what I want.' At the end of the evening he grew sad and brought up the painful subject of Lucia, saying, 'Sometimes I tell myself that when I leave this dark night, she too will be cured.'[44]

Wearying of Lausanne, they moved to Zurich, back to the Carlton Elite where Joyce planned to rest for a week before seeing Vogt. Léon, in Paris, was kept busy sending out messages, issuing instructions, passing on mail and ringing Delmas to check on Lucia. To Joyce, Harriet was now (and secretly perhaps always had been) a figure of fun from whom to extract money by laying it on as thickly as possible. He told Léon to write to her exaggerating his situation, using the sort of gobbledegook her class and sort liked to read, and ask her if she had heard the Irish broadcast – that was, if she had not been busily parading along Oxford Street calling for the Sunday closure of brothels.

Zurich was raked with wind, rain and blizzards and buzzing with rumours of Hitler. Mrs Giedion told Joyce that her husband Siegfried had beaten Thomas Mann to the Eliot Norton Professorship at Harvard, and for eight lectures would receive $10,000 or 300,000 francs. She also brought news that Dr Berman, the endocrinologist he had recommended, appeared to have saved their ailing daughter from either death or insanity.

After ten days in Zurich without seeing Vogt, Joyce was running short of money and had to send urgently to Monro for £100. When, finally, he did see Vogt he was assured that he would lose no more of what little sight he had. But shortly afterwards he suffered another eye-attack, this time in his better right eye. Even so, they entertained Wilhelm and Greta Herz, relatives of Helen, saw the composer Othmar Schoeck again, and at a concert at the Tonhalle met Joyce's old friend Paul Suter, who had worked for twenty years as publicity manager for a soup company. Suter's boss, it transpired, was a great fan of *Ulysses* and invited them to his factory, sending a limousine and treating them to a grand lunch followed by tea at a country club served by liveried flunkeys. A new soup, it was announced, would be named after his book.[45]

He had a less congenial meeting with the cashier of the Carlton Elite, who refused to cash a Lloyds cheque drawn on a Swiss bank until it was cleared, leaving Joyce broke over the weekend. He was outraged, after so many years as a patron there and entertaining and tipping so lavishly.[46] His love affair with the hotel ended abruptly, and he never returned. Fortunately, on the day he left, again broke, Carola Giedion came to the hotel personally and lent him 300 francs to see him through his journey back to Paris.

Joyce could no longer ignore the growing political crisis in Europe, especially following the *Anschluss* when German troops marched into Austria. If Switzerland was next, he told Mrs Giedion, 'All I can say about the future in Z'ch is I hope whoever has it will respect Villa Giedion, Othmar Schoeck, Vogt's clinic and the Kronenhalle.' But 'he can hang all the staff of the Elite Hotel in comfortable sacks out of their own windows for all I care and meanwhile Heaven help the poor jews who fall into the hands of [the hotel's] cashier'. Before he left, Carola took some photographs. One of Joyce, gazing out over the Limmat with his back to the camera, he called his favourite photograph. 'At last a view of myself which I can look at with some pleasure,' he wrote,[47] and ordered several copies for friends.

When Mercanton phoned to say he was in Paris, Joyce invited him over for Good Friday afternoon. What he found was a scene from an absurdist play. 'I found him installed in his bedroom, half-reclining in a chaise-longue, Stuart Gilbert seated near him at a little table. They were going over a passage that, according to Joyce, was "still not obscure enough," and inserting Samoyed words into it. "Dog tongue," said Stuart Gilbert. "Bitch of a tongue," replied Joyce.' Over tea, he announced that they were happily 'sinning against all the rules of the church' – no prayers or fasting for him, though he did, as always on such occasions, attend church later that day for the liturgies.[48] As for his daughter, he told Helen later, he had spent Easter Day with her, 'teaching her some Latin, eating *panettoni di Milano* and fooling generally'.[49]

Meanwhile, Helen's father having recovered, and with Stephen wanting to return to Paris, Giorgio had booked passages on the *Queen Mary*. By the end of April, they were back in Paris. Although in New York Giorgio had twice sung on the CBS, his American career had gone nowhere. However, in Paris, Joyce had Nino Frank trying to get him a contract with Radio Luxembourg and Lord Carlow in London putting out feelers to friends at the BBC, including the musical scholar George Rogers. But while Giorgio was hoping to resume his singing career in Europe, Helen was becoming depressed. Joyce's response was to bombard her with flowers and cheer-up cards.

Although he mostly avoided Shakespeare and Company, he was never one to shy away from publicity. When Gisele Freund planned a photo-shoot at the bookshop, Joyce agreed to be pictured with Beach and Monnier. Freund was invited to photograph Giorgio, Helen and Stephen at the apartment, producing the iconic picture of him (looking vague), his son (looking gloomy) and grandson (trying to cheer him up) posed before Patrick Tuohy's portrait of his father – the Joyce family portrait gallery updated in one frame. Joyce also posed for solo portraits – looking pensive, playing the piano and, in a close-up, displaying his beringed fingers clutching his latest walking-stick. With an eye to publicizing his new book he was captured correcting proofs of *Work in Progress*, nose-to-page, peering through a magnifying glass. These pictures, and some of Joyce with Eugene Jolas, appeared in various illustrated magazines the following spring, notably in *Time* and in *Picture Post* accompanied by reviews of the new book.[50]

Despite his preoccupation with work and his family, another matter was beginning to concern him. In March he had received an appeal from Jewish acquaintances, to whose friendship and rich culture he owed so much, to help friends and fellow-Jews evade the clutches of the rampaging Nazis. Now, in June, at the prompting of Daniel Brody and through a friend at the French Foreign Office, he helped Hermann Broch, the Austrian novelist (and author of a book about Joyce),[51] escape from Vienna to Paris. In May, Edmund Brauchbar and Gustav Zumsteg (whose mother owned Zurich's Kronenhalle) asked him to assist friends and family members escape to Ireland or England. In October, having sought the assistance of Benjamin Huebsch in New York, he helped the family of Paul Pèrles, son of a Viennese bookseller, who was Brauchbar's cousin, get to America via London. The following year he would assist the son of Charlotte Sauermann, a soprano at the Zurich Opera, to escape to the West. In all he helped some fifteen or sixteen Jews escape to safety. To Jacques Mercanton he said pityingly, 'Those poor Jews!' Here was a man finally awake and ready to help, faced with the barbarism that negated art and human kindness. Léon was impressed. It showed him a side of Joyce he had never suspected. Zumsteg would not forget his help and would later be able to help him in return, when he, too, needed to escape the Germans.

Acknowledging the arrival of copies of *Storiella*, Joyce told Carlow that he was still working night and day without knowing exactly when his work would end, and still gathering material from wherever he could. But with *Work in Progress* nearing the end of its fifteen-year journey, the effort to discover the mystery title intensified. Over dinner at Fouquet's with the Jolases one evening in July, after several bottles of Riesling, the challenge was repeated. Suddenly, recalled Eugene Jolas, Nora began to sing a song about Mr Flannigan and Mr Shannigan. At this, Joyce looked startled and told her to stop. Then he mouthed F and W at which Maria guessed 'Fairy's Wake'. Astonished, Joyce cried, 'Brava. But something is missing.' A few days later, Jolas believed he had guessed the title. That evening, on 2 August, dining again at Fouquet's with the Joyces, he casually dropped the words '*Finnegans Wake*'. Joyce, he remembered, 'blanched', set down his wineglass and said sadly, 'Ah Jolas, you've taken something out of me.' Thereafter he lightened up, became quite jolly and ended the evening by hugging him, dancing a few steps and saying, 'How would you like to have the money?', to which Jolas replied, 'In sous.' Next morning he turned up at the Jolases' house with a bagful of ten-franc pieces, telling Jolas's daughters to serve them up to their father for lunch with the hors d'oeuvres. The couple were, however, sworn to secrecy until publication day.[52]

Giorgio had taken the still-depressed Helen off to a sanatorium in Montreux, and, although reluctant to leave his work and desert Lucia, on 19 August Joyce left with Nora for Switzerland. Léon was instructed to forward mail to Lucia so that she did not know they were out of town, and to call Delmas from time to time to check on her well-being. After visiting Giorgio and Helen in Montreux, Joyce reflected sadly how his daughter-in-law's illness seemed only to confirm that he and his family were dogged by ill fortune.

He spent 1 September with Mercanton in Fribourg where he talked about Ruskin, Newman and Mallarmé, and refuted the suggestion of Gerard Manley Hopkins as any serious influence on *Work in Progress*. On a walk by the lake he questioned Mercanton closely about the names of mountains and wines of the vicinity, toying with the words, their sounds and vocal parallels. He asked Mercanton to get him two books he needed, *Le Rime* of Petrarch and Spenser's *Epithalamion*, so he could enrich the pages of *Anna Livia Plurabelle* and the last pages of *Work in Progress*, with further river allusions. 'You will see,' he said, 'those last pages are simple, banal. The mystery is gone. It is daylight again.' He also revealed the strange spell the work ('that monster') had cast over him. 'Yet,' wrote Mercanton, 'that monster was his only pleasure, and his face brightened as he explained the meanings of words in the passage he had proposed I should study.'[53]

On 11 September Joyce asked Léon to send more money and announced that they were planning to visit Dijon.[54] There was a brief stopover in Zurich where he again suffered stomach cramps. This time he consulted a specialist who advised X-rays, but the advice was ignored and he headed back to France. Returning to Paris briefly, Joyce penned another urgent note about Brauchbar's refugees to Huebsch. He and Nora then travelled to the coast and were soon back at a favourite old-fashioned hotel, the Hôtel du Rhin & de Newhaven at Dieppe. Lucie Léon, in need of convalescence, accompanied them.

Now Joyce was growing concerned about the fate of his daughter in case of war. Delmas had informed him that should hostilities break out, the Ivry sanatorium (all 105 patients and 60 staff) would relocate to the 70-room Hôtel Edelweiss at La Baule, close to Saint-Nazaire on the Normandy coast, where the Delmas family had a home. But Joyce said he thought that years among lunatics for a girl said not to be deranged was 'a very poor solution'.[55] For Lucia to believe that her parents were in Switzerland, postcards addressed to her were sent to Mercanton to be mailed from Lausanne. After a rainy week in Dieppe, Lucie Léon returned home, and on 28 September the Joyces decided to go south to La Baule to see where their daughter would end up if Delmas transferred his hospital there. Lucia's case, he still thought, was misunderstood. She was very ill, he told Georg Goyert, but he and Nora believed the illness would pass.[56]

The Munich Agreement of 30 September 1938 meant that for the time being the European crisis was past. Hitler was left free to occupy the Sudetenland and the prospect of war receded. Delmas' plans were for the moment suspended and the Joyces returned to Paris. The city was still tense, Joyce told Brody – hardly an atmosphere conducive to his putting the last fine touches to *Work in Progress*.[57] He was furious that politics in the form of Hitler had been allowed to disturb his creative tranquillity and told Colum, 'Let him have Europe!'[58]

On 14 November, although Joyce cabled Harriet that *Work in Progress* was finished, there was still the postscript (Book IV of *Finnegans Wake*), commonly referred to as the 'Recorso', where night gives way to daylight and the winding thread of the narrative leads the reader back to the beginning. This postscript, Léon thought, had probably been held in its final form in Joyce's formidable mind for years – one in which, having subverted the Church, mindless nationalism, sacred aspects of the family, the formalities of language, the traditions and canons of literature, finally and simultaneously he defends and then indicts the novel itself, and thereby subverts himself too.

On Thanksgiving Day, 24 November, at a dinner given in his honour at Fouquet's, Helen read the two pages he had written for the 'Recorso' chapter. Léon recalled Joyce's evident delight at the sound of his own words:

> This occasion, when to an orchestral accompaniment of clattering dishes and clinking glasses, his own words created harmony in the surrounding discordance, was one of the rare times when I sensed that he was either satisfied or proud of himself.[59]

As a result of that reading, Joyce rewrote the chapter and thus began a process of revision and expansion which was to occupy him night and day for up to six weeks. Over that period the two initial pages grew to thirty-five, and Joyce's army of volunteers were galvanized into helping him over the last lap of the marathon.

> All Joyce's friends were pressed into helping with the typing. Mrs Jolas was typing in Neuilly, Mr Gilbert was typing in his rue Jean-du-Bellay apartment, and I was dictating in our flat in the rue Casimir-Périer. Around seven in the evening, the different fragments were assembled at the headquarters of the master-brain in the Rue Edmond-Valentin.

At one point Léon, dashing to 'headquarters', found he had left the envelope of proofs he was carrying in a taxi. There followed an agonizing two hours before the honest cabbie returned them. Joyce, he recalled, was the only one among them who remained cool and unflustered.[60]

Throughout that period of frenetic revision Joyce was being pressed by the printers who had promised him a copy for his fifty-seventh birthday on 2 February 1939. The formal publication would follow in due course. By the end of November Faber knew the title and Richard de la Mare, who was handling the manuscript for the firm, asked if he had permission to let Huebsch into the secret. But Léon told him that 'Mr Joyce wishes to keep the title secret because he is afraid of attack by American-Irish elements who used their influence against *Ulysses*; the title is a form of a song of a comic Irish music-hall type and would give opportunity for advance attack.'[61] The haunting fear of betrayal remained as powerful as ever.

In early December Joyce collapsed in the Bois de Boulogne. The doctor warned him that it was due to overwork, but he kept going. By the middle of that month Léon recorded that 355 pages had been finally revised, and he wondered at Joyce's powers of concentration at a time when tragedy threatened Europe and his financial problems continued to oppress him. Yet old loyalties persisted, and those oppressive fears did not prevent him paying a subscription to the Parnell Grave Memorial Fund in Dublin.

Léon, ever faithful though ever sceptical, passed on his opinion of the great work to Harriet:

> I can easily understand how any person who is concerned with the grave social, political and economic problems of this oppressive period will be painfully affected by its colossal triviality, its accumulation of words, meaningless, I suppose for the ordinary intelligent reader of today ... But it is impossible to deny that he has acted according to his conscience and that he has actually consumed almost all his substance, physical and spiritual, moral and material in the writing of a book likely to be received with derision by his ill-wishers and with pained pleasure by his friends. And in this attitude he has remained true to himself.

The final section, Léon told her, 'deals with the mixing of the fresh water of the Liffey and the salt water of the Irish sea at the Dublin estuary!'[62]

On 1 January 1939, Joyce wrote to Livia Svevo to say that, after so many years of 'combing and recombing the locks of Anna Livia' he had 'finished finishing' his book.[63] But it had not finished with him. There were still last-minute confusions with editors and printers having difficulty grasping what he and his book were about. As with *Ulysses*, his neologisms and experiments with page layout presented problems to typesetters used to setting standard books in mostly standard English. After many letters to and fro, Richard de la Mare wrote saying that 'the printers are reaching the end of their tether'.[64] Nevertheless, he promised Joyce that he would get a copy of *Finnegans Wake* to him in time for his birthday.

Following the passing of Moore and George Russell, the death of Yeats aged seventy-three on 28 January at Roquebrune-Cap-Martin removed the third great early personal influence on Joyce's writing career. Unlike the others, Yeats had always seen in him the light of genius and the shape of Ireland's literary future. As with Moore, Joyce sent a wreath but it arrived late and was unacknowledged. When, through Mary Colum, the news reached Mrs Yeats she immediately wrote to thank him, but not before he had had time to feel slighted yet again.

33
A Puzzle for a Puzzled World
(1939)

'The devil knows whether you will be able to understand what the
story means or what this entire wordspiderweb is about.'

Joyce to Ferdinand Prior

By now for Joyce, receiving his book by 2 February was not a mere whim
but a deep superstition. And after a period of extreme nervous expectation
Faber managed to get a copy to him by 30 January. Formal publication,
however, was now set for 4 May, so Joyce had time to send in yet more
corrections, which he did.

At her Paris home, Helen had something special planned for this special
birthday. The table was decked with a silver tray standing for the English
Channel, flanked on either side by Dublin (with a glass bottle representing
Nelson's Pillar) and Paris (symbolized by a church-shaped lamp and a
windmill) with strips of silver paper for the rivers Liffey and Seine. The
occasion was attended by the usual crowd – and a new friend, Dr Daniel
O'Brien of the Rockefeller Foundation. Nino Frank recalled the climax of
the evening:

> At dessert there appeared another superb edifice [of cake] which
> represented James Joyce's books with their titles. Only one was missing
> ... 'Finnegans Wake,' pronounced James Joyce. And so Finnegans Wake
> made its solemn entry into the world.[1]

The most elaborate cake (appropriately enough for the most confected of
his prose fictions) was now set in pride of place. White wine, of course,
was drunk (Giorgio preferred cognac). After dinner, Joyce talked about
how the idea for his book first came to him in Nice. He did not feel up to
performing his usual high-kicking dance, but he and Giorgio sang a duet,
with Mrs Jolas at the piano, and Helen read the 'final' final fragment of
the no-longer-anonymous great work.

With celebrations over, Joyce took Huebsch to task over a report that
the Viking edition of *Finnegans Wake* had been delayed. He got Léon to
send an angry telegram accusing Huebsch of holding back the book and

damaging his interests. He followed this with a threat to take the book elsewhere if Viking were not interested in bringing it out right away.[2] Huebsch protested that Joyce and Léon failed to understand that so far he had received only 128 pages of text from Faber, and the delay there was due to the endless list of corrections Joyce was sending in. Maria Jolas said that Huebsch almost lost his mind over the book. Joyce as usual put the worst construction on the delay, convinced that it would give his American-Irish enemies a chance to mount a campaign against him. The malice of Michael Lennon still cast a long baleful shadow. As Léon told Harriet, 'Mr Joyce believes that great harm has been done to his work before its appearance on the American market; this situation is a complete anticlimax for [him] after his seventeen years work, he does not like to talk about it, today he is ill in bed and running a temperature.'[3]

Huebsch felt insulted by the threatening tone of Léon's letters and refused to answer them. But he told Joyce that 6,000 copies of the trade edition of *Finnegans Wake* would be ready by the end of March[4] and no publication date could be set until the sheets from England were cleared by Customs. There were further hiccoughs. A Faber title-page reading 'Finnegans Wake James Joyce' he dismissed as a malevolent joke. And, when Viking Press published a doltish blurb stating 'The scene of the book is laid in Dublin and Paris', he told Eliot that many would be disappointed they had not added 'the Riviera and St Moritz'.[5]

That spring the Léons gave a dinner for their friends the Joyces, the Jolases and the Nabokovs. Two years earlier Joyce had attended a lecture on Pushkin by Nabokov (a Cambridge University contemporary of Ponisovsky), but they had never met. Léon was especially interested to see how Joyce and the Russian would interact, expecting a dazzling exhibition of word-play between them. They were disappointed. Lucie Léon thought Nabokov was intimidated by the presence of the Irish genius, but thirty years later Nabokov, reading this comment, expressed amusement, saying that far from being the bashful and worshipful youngster she had depicted, he had been a man of forty, well aware of the contribution he had already made to Russian literature. 'Had Mrs Léon and I met more often at parties, she might have realized that I am always a disappointing guest, neither inclined nor able to shine socially.'[6] Nabokov claimed in interviews that he was not influenced by Joyce and called *Finnegans Wake* 'a cancerous growth of word-tissue' to which he was indifferent, as he was to all regional dialect, even if it was 'the dialect of genius'. But he thought highly of *Ulysses* which he had first encountered at Cambridge in 1922 and his novel *The Gift* is said to do for Berlin what Joyce in *Ulysses* did for Dublin while 'Nausicaa' is thought to have inspired *Lolita*.

Now preparing to relinquish the rue Edmond-Valentin flat, Joyce gave away most of his books and furniture, while Léon sorted through his discarded papers, and his manuscripts and proofs were sent to Harriet for safe keeping.[7] He also decided finally to jettison Pinker after learning that his brother, Eric, who ran the agency's New York bureau, had been found guilty of purloining $20,637 of royalties belonging to the British novelist E. Phillips Oppenheim, and was sentenced to two and a half to five years in Sing Sing Prison. With Léon no longer objecting, and at the end of March, Monro was instructed to revoke Joyce's agreement with Pinker and ask his publishers to pay all future royalties to him. The Joyces' new home would be at 34 rue des Vignes in Passy.

When the Nazis occupied the whole of Czechoslovakia on 15 March, Joyce had cause to worry more than ever about the fate of his daughter. He continued his Sunday visits to Ivry and Beckett began visiting regularly, too. But Lucia was not the only lost mind in his family. Helen was succumbing in similar fashion. Never having fully recovered from her first breakdown, she seemed to have fallen into the same downward spiral as her sister-in-law. According to Lucie Léon, Giorgio, terrified of mental illness after what had happened to Lucia, was as unsympathetic towards his wife's condition as he had been to that of his sister, and in April he had their son Stephen forcibly removed from her.

Meanwhile, Jacques Mercanton had offered an essay on *Finnegans Wake* to Jean Paulhan, editor of the *NRF*, and had also written an article on '*Ulysses* and *Don Quixote*'. He had also procured a copy of Francini Bruni's pamphlet on Joyce (based on his 'riff-raffish' lecture in Trieste in 1924) and wanted to pass it on to Joyce. They met in the half-empty apartment and Mercanton found him uneasy on several counts – about Lucia's likely fate, the plight of his Jewish friends, the delayed publication of his book, and its coincidence with the approaching war, which he saw only from a personal point of view. 'Let us leave the Czechs in peace,' said Joyce, 'and occupy ourselves with *Finnegans Wake*.' They took a walk along the Seine and a taxi-ride to the new apartment. Taking shelter in a bar, Joyce recited from memory passages from the last part of the *Wake*. The style and sense of his words, as often was the case, seemed to reflect and capture his own haunted state of mind. 'And it's old and old it's sad and old it's sad and weary I go back to you, my cold father, my cold mad father, my cold mad feary father, till the near sight of the mere size of him, the moyles and moyles of it, moananoaning, makes me seasilt saltsick and I rush, my only, into your arms.'[8] And as Anna Livia at the sea's edge says, 'I only hope whole the heavens sees us. For I feel I could near to faint away. Into the deeps. Annamores leep . . .'[9] It was as if he had written a strange and haunting obituary to his own work. Something had passed out of his life.

They moved to the rue des Vignes on 15 April. When Maria Jolas called on them, Nora told her, 'I've just spent the most awful day – tearing up his letters to me.' Joyce, she reported, didn't budge or pay any attention. 'Why did you do that?' she asked. 'Oh they were nobody's business,' said Nora. 'There weren't many anyway – we've never separated.'[10] But enough of them have survived to give a flavour of their likely contents.

In his own strange way, Joyce came to terms with the publication day of *Finnegans Wake*, noting that 4 May was the Feast of St Monica, a saint whose virtues were much extolled by his namesake, St Augustine. But in his mind he was still uncertain about what he had produced. On 1 May he told Livia Svevo that he was probably an idiot to have spent eighteen years of his life on such a 'monster'. He had been fated to do so and could not have done otherwise. But now he was glad to be rid of it.[11] The sense that he might have written himself out left friends like Eliot wondering what he could possibly write after the *Wake* without altering his whole cast of mind. *Time* magazine reported on 8 May. 'At present Joyce is not writing. His wife is trying to get him started on something, because when he is not working he is hard to live with.'

Despite his fears, both the Faber and Viking editions of *Finnegans Wake* appeared promptly on 4 May, as promised.[12] If there were misprints, few readers would have known or probably cared. In fact, they were plentiful. 'Every time Mr Joyce looks at *Finnegans Wake*,' Léon told Richard de la Mare, 'he finds misprints. He would like to start making corrections for the second edition.'[13] However, because of the war, it was not reprinted until 1945 when Faber issued a sixteen-page booklet listing 628 misprints notified to them by Joyce when it was too late to make corrections.

He wrote to Harriet in appropriately tradesman-like language as her 'obedient servant' saying that he had now fulfilled the commission she had given him in September 1926 on sending him a photograph of the Giant's Grave, that the goods had been duly delivered and her patronage was greatly appreciated. He added a suitably satirical note suggesting that her order had been faithfully discharged by one James Crapper, an allusion to the celebrated supplier of water-closets 'by appointment' to the House of Windsor.[14]

Con Curran and Kenneth Reddin sent congratulations and Sean O'Casey wrote saying that the *Wake*, though 'very high over my head', had given him and a painter friend 'many a laugh' reading it aloud. 'It is an amazing book; and hardly to be understood in a year, much less in a day.'[15] But the Dublin gossips had already formed opinions. Joseph Holloway recorded that on 5 May a friend had offered to lend him an advance copy, of which he could make no sense. 'I declined with thanks. Such sort of gibbering talk as the book was composed of wasn't worthwhile bothering about.'[16] And when the book was advertised in the *Irish Times* as '*Finnegans Wake* by Sean O'Casey' Joyce was convinced that his enemies were wreaking a peculiarly Irish form of vengeance on him. O'Casey, equally outraged, wrote saying it was no misprint but deliberate. 'I know many of Dublin's Literary Clique dislike me, and they hate you (why, God only knows), so that "misprint" was a bit of a joke.'[17] Faber complained to the editor, who wrote to Joyce apologizing personally for the mistake, but since no apology appeared in the paper, both writers continued to believe it was intentional. Joyce cleverly used the gaffe to get the book properly advertised in the *Irish Times*, by courtesy of Faber – one in the eye for his Dublin critics, he felt.

In America, his celebrity was confirmed when on 6 May one of Gisele Freund's colour photographs of him graced the cover of *Time* magazine, even though the review inside, by Clifton Fadiman, was largely an expression of bewilderment. 'A god, talking in his sleep, might have written it ... Can any reader who, like myself, is neither linguist nor polyhistorian get anything out of such a book except a feeling of savage frustration? Not much, I think.'[18] But Joyce received the usual intelligently engaged response from Padraic Colum writing in the *New York Times*: 'Even if [the reader] does not understand all that is on any one page he will find sentences lovely in their freshness and their beauty and sentences that one can chuckle over for months ... here is a narrative that gives a new dimension.'[19]

In England, the *Sunday Times* had declared its intention to ignore the book as 'irrelevant to literature', which Joyce took as a mark of honour to be mentioned at every opportunity. And there was a *Daily Express* review amusing enough for him to relish repeating – 'An Irish stew of verbiage by the author of *Ulysses* with unexpected beauty emerging now and then from the peculiar mixture.'[20] Harold Nicolson, who had championed *Ulysses* in 1931, reviewing *Finnegans Wake* for the *Daily Telegraph*, admitted having 'failed to penetrate the meaning of this enormous allegory'.[21] In his diary he wrote, 'I truly believe that Joyce has this time gone too far in breaking all communication between himself and his reader. It is a very selfish book.'[22] It caught the mood of many of the reviewers faced with close to seven hundred pages of labyrinthine prose.

In the *New Statesman*, the always sympathetic G. W. Stonier compared reading it to learning Chinese, but added that a patient reading carried its own lucidity, 'and where the meaning fades music tides us over'.[23] There was an appreciative review in the *Irish Times*, but in the *Observer*, Gogarty took the opportunity to mockingly subvert Dublin's Dante and his less than divine comedy. He began by expressing astonishment at

Joyce's achievement. 'The immense erudition employed, and the various languages ransacked for pun and word-associations is almost incredible to anyone unaware of the superhuman knowledge the author had when a mere stripling.' But he was only building him up for a knock-down. 'In some places the reading sounds like the chatter during the lunch interval in a Berlitz school ... This is the most colossal leg-pull in literature since McPherson's Ossian. Mr Joyce has had his revenge.'[24]

The review which upset him most, recalled Beckett, was Richard Aldington's in the *Atlantic Monthly*. The sting was in the tail, which read, 'The boredom endured in the penance of reading this book is something one would not inflict on any human being, but far be it from me to discourage any reader who prefers to use a perfectly good five-dollar bill to buy *Finnegans Wake* rather than to light a cigarette with it. (The latter course will give more lasting satisfaction.) Translated into native Tasmanian, this book should have a well-deserved sale.'[25] Beckett recalled that, as each review was read to him, Joyce sighed deeply. It may have been from exhaustion as much as disappointment. The *Wake*, he told Budgen, received over four hundred notices (including a letter of appreciation from Ford Madox Ford – 'possibly the last public act of his life', said Joyce on hearing of his death in June that year). However critical he was of the publicity and distribution, the book caught the attention of the literary world and created some excitement. Huebsch reported that by the end of June, 4,000 copies of the American edition had already been sold.

Herbert Gorman now wrote to say that his Joyce biography was finished and would be published in July. He sent him the proofs of four chapters to be checked for errors. Joyce was horrified. He immediately cabled Gorman's publishers, Farrar & Rinehart, demanding to see the complete manuscript and final proofs before authorizing the book. On 6 June Léon wrote to Gorman repeating the request and threatening to withdraw authorization. Joyce's earlier comments and amendments had been ignored, he said; too much was based on Michael Lennon's scurrilous *Catholic World* article. What most concerned him were passages about his 'wastrel' father, and about himself 'living in sin' till his London marriage. There must be no such references to his father or any mention of his 1931 marriage, said Léon. Gorman should also delete a piece of gossip about Shaw's reaction to *Ulysses* which Shaw himself had refuted. Many of these errors, Léon concluded, were to be found in Gorman's previous book on Joyce from fifteen years earlier.[26] When after that Gorman fell silent, Joyce was left worrying about the sort of biography he would publish, perhaps fearing Earwicker's fate: '(his biografiend, in fact, kills him very soon, if yet not, after)'.[27]

The BBC let him down again. A programme on *Finnegans Wake*, featuring Beckett and Pelorson, was 'bungled', he complained, and now, after an audition, it had turned down Giorgio for being 'not up to BBC standard'. If so, Joyce commented sourly, he didn't think much of their standard. He wrote asking George Rogers, who had attended the audition, whether there had been something in the atmosphere – some hostility towards his son, some stage-fright, haste, or lack of preparation on his part which could explain this negative judgement.[28] Rogers replied, assuring him that Giorgio had sung well, so the mystery remained. (However, a BBC report on later audition-recordings by Giorgio casts serious doubts on the quality of his singing.)[29]

Fleeing the heat of Paris, the Joyces spent four or five days with Giorgio at Etretat where Stephen was at summer school, then headed for Lausanne, leaving Léon to keep in touch with Lucia. In Berne, seeing no sign of the *Wake* in Swiss bookshops, Joyce grew depressed, telling Léon that it was a 'washout' in Europe, and 'a fiasco' in America. England was even worse, he said.[30] Short of money yet again, Monro Saw were instructed to sell £50 more of his dwindling stock.

Hoping to meet Mercanton, they moved on to Montreux. As it happened the young writer was passing through the city en route for Florence and they came across him on the terrace of the restaurant where he and Joyce had last dined. 'Suddenly I saw his tall form standing there before me, and I heard Mrs Joyce cry out in delighted surprise.' With Hitler making threats against Poland, it was a breathless moment before the expected war engulfed Europe, an 'enchanted, suspended pause', he recalled.

> Joyce told amusing anecdotes about the publication of *Finnegans Wake*, about the stupefaction of some readers ... When I alluded to the possibility of another project in a still distant future, he answered: 'For the moment I am taking a rest. Now it is time for the others to do a bit of work.'[31]

His fears about Lucia led him back to Ivry where he saw Delmas, who assured him that arrangements were in place to move his patients to La Baule in a fleet of cars as soon as the French mobilized. Joyce could, if he wished, travel down there and await their arrival, he said. Taking Delmas at his word, he and Nora returned again to La Baule where he managed to get a close look at the deserted Hôtel Edelweiss, a handsome old building standing in its own grounds. Speaking to the janitor he was disturbed to learn that no such visitors were expected. Uncertain what to do, he saw his daughter now trapped in a city that might at any time come under attack.

They settled into the Hôtel St Christophe. Three days later, on 1 September, Hitler's Wehrmacht invaded Poland. War throughout Europe was inevitable. On the 3rd, both Britain and France declared war on Germany. In desperation, Joyce cabled Giorgio and Léon, still in Paris, asking them to find out what was happening at Ivry. Rumours had filtered through – there had been air-raid alarms there; Delmas thought the experience was good for his patients; all the female inmates had been evacuated.

But finally, on the 11th, Delmas, his staff and patients arrived and established themselves in a large chateau, Charmettes, at Pornichet, just three kilometres outside La Baule. To his relief, Joyce found that Lucia had survived the journey in good shape. The only ones to have suffered were himself and Nora. Suddenly all was back to normal and his letters reverted to requests to Léon for newspapers, more money, reviews to be despatched to Harriet, papers to be set aside for him and a change of clothes. Giorgio and Helen had invited them to stay at their country villa, but Joyce wanted them all to be together, including Lucia. If a *maison de santé* could be found within an hour of Giorgio's place, he thought that would be the next best arrangement.

Much to his frustration, proofs of the rest of Gorman's biography arrived when he had no help at hand to read them. Most of his friends had left Paris and even Léon was talking about emigrating. When John Farrar of Farrar & Rinehart wrote asking if they could proceed with the book, Joyce cabled an immediate 'No', not until he had had time to revise the proofs to his own satisfaction.[32] Some of the changes he was anxious to make concerned his motivations. For example, his reason for not setting foot in Ireland since 1912 was mainly the quicklime attack on Parnell at Castlecomer which had seared itself in his memory and (for the sake of the books he was trying to finish) his wish not to suffer a similar fate. He asked Gorman not to reveal the source of this information.[33] After so much censoring – no mention of Lucia, the marriage in 1931 or his father's lifestyle – the biographer felt that it was being used by Joyce simply to project his preferred self-image. The many facets of his personality were therefore never properly illuminated. Gorman, it is reported, never forgave Joyce for butchering his book, and never produced another biography.

At the outset of her stay at La Baule, the prospects for Lucia seemed discouraging. Within the first week she had suffered what Joyce called 'a series of crises', so noisy and disturbed that he was not allowed to see her. He was again tempted to move in with Helen and Giorgio if a place for Lucia could be found close by. Léon was instructed to ask Delmas for his bill and enquire about relocating her.[34] Still feeling somewhat helpless, he was pleased to run into another refugee from Paris, Daniel O'Brien. Visiting a restaurant together one night, they found it crowded with British and French soldiers. When they broke into 'La Marseillaise', Joyce joined in and his voice stood out so clearly that he was lifted onto a table for a solo performance. O'Brien was greatly impressed, saying, 'You never saw such an exhibition of one man dominating and thrilling a whole audience ... if a whole German regiment had attacked at that moment, they would never have got through.'[35]

The plan to move in with Helen and Giorgio collapsed when Helen had another breakdown and doctors decided that their presence would be inadvisable. Giorgio, who was also facing possible conscription, had taken refuge with his friend Ponisovsky in Paris and was hitting the bottle hard while Helen had sought sanctuary at the Ritz Hotel. Peggy Guggenheim claimed that there she began having reckless affairs and Giorgio wanted her sent home to New York. Léon, however, thought her more hysterical than mad, telling Joyce that his son's attitude was 'incomprehensible', and all he needed to do was make love to her – advice which Joyce found distasteful. He told Léon that Helen's letters to him (which he sent to Dr Fontaine for an opinion) showed, in the doctor's words, 'an exalted state', and Stephen's future now began to concern him. But Fontaine thought Joyce's letters to Helen (in which he chastised her for neglecting his son) were unhelpful. Nora must have thought the same about letters written to *him*, and began to intercept them, destroying those she considered 'rubbish'. One of Harriet's letters met this fate, Joyce discovered, and he warned Léon not to forward any mail.

Paris had been militarized and a pass was needed to enter the city. It seemed that, like Lucia, they were stranded in La Baule for the foreseeable future, so Joyce asked Léon to start forwarding his *Irish Times* and have Nora's fur coat sent down. However, there were moments of levity. On 8 October Daniel O'Brien threw a surprise party to celebrate the Joyces' thirty-fifth 'wedding anniversary'. As the wine flowed, Joyce was in his element laughing and capering in his best party style.

Helen's behaviour had become more and more unrestrained. According to Peggy Guggenheim and Beckett, she dragged young Stephen around Paris making a spectacle of herself with men and spending money like confetti. After a violent outburst when she caught Giorgio and Guggenheim together at the Hotel Lutétia, she was confined to the *maison de santé* at Suresnes. Stephen was left in the care of his father, and Helen's brother embarked for France, intending to escort her back home.[36] By mid-October the Joyces had got themselves back to Paris. Finding the apartment building deserted and the heating off, they moved into the Hotel Lutétia, taking Stephen with them. Eugene Jolas had returned to

America and Maria planned to evacuate her school to the Château de la Chapelle at Saint-Gérand-le-Puy, a small village near Vichy, where it was agreed that Stephen would join them. Joyce returned briefly to the freezing rue des Vignes apartment to collect some books and there, according to Beckett who accompanied him, cursed the war as pointless and 'jumped to the piano and sang at the top of his voice for half an hour'.[37]

Since Léon had sided with Helen against Giorgio, relations between him and Joyce had cooled. However, the Russian was Joyce's main channel of communication with his publishers, lawyers and many others. Breaking with him would not make life any easier, but to Joyce his children were above reproach, and he asked Ponisovsky to instruct Léon to return all his important personal papers and documents. Léon was so surprised that he phoned for confirmation of this instruction and was shocked to hear Joyce repeat the request in person. On 19 November he left a package for Ponisovsky to pass to Joyce. It contained his various contracts, an envelope of reviews, Pinker's royalty statements, and copies of papers prepared for the US revenue authorities – giving a complete picture of Joyce's earnings from the beginning. Léon's covering letter carried no greeting and no final salutation. Their relationship, it seemed, was over.

Gorman's carefully edited life of Joyce was published on 10 November. The worst designs and wiles of the 'biografiend' had been thwarted, and this became the version of his life which would remain largely unchallenged for twenty years; it would also help determine the direction from which Joyce's work was approached and read. Neither the publisher nor Gorman bothered to inform Joyce of its publication or send him a copy; he had to order one from Brentano's, which took three months to reach him. He found the oversight hurtful and annoying, but the equally offended biographer never contacted him again.

Just before Christmas Joyce heard from Carola Giedion-Welcker, recently returned from America, where her husband was still at Harvard, finishing a book and attempting to procure for him the Eliot Norton Chair currently held by Stravinsky. It was reassuring to know that friends were anxious to help him escape the dangers of war, but even if a generous offer did arrive he could not uproot himself at short notice. To desert Lucia, Helen, Giorgio and Stephen was unthinkable. The best plan, it seemed, was to remain in France but move to a safer place than Paris. Beckett, who now spent more time with Joyce following his break with Léon, found him in a constant state of indecision, a poor dinner companion prone to expensive drinking sprees.

When Maria Jolas suggested that Joyce join her at Saint-Gérand to celebrate Christmas in the company of what remained of his family, he accepted gladly. On 23 December Beckett saw Joyce, Nora and Giorgio on to the train for the south. By Christmas Eve they had checked into the Hôtel de la Paix at Saint-Gérand, where Maria had reserved rooms for them. The hotel, overlooking the village square, was a very ordinary country *auberge* – café downstairs, simply furnished bedrooms on the first floor, and in no way comparable to the grand establishments to which they were accustomed. Not long after they arrived Joyce collapsed with stomach cramps and over the festive season ate little and drank only white wine. But if his health was shaky, so were his finances. He had managed well enough while he could call on funds from Monro, but new wartime regulations restricted the movement of capital from England. With Lucia's fees to pay he would have to economize, an adjustment he found difficult and painful.

There was a Christmas party at the Château de la Chapelle at which Joyce appeared looking fairly subdued and rather blank after his earlier seizure. Then Maria began playing the piano and an evening of music and jollity ensued. Roused from his torpor, Joyce joined her in singing 'Ye Banks and Braes' and, suddenly caught up in the moment, he too began to play and sing, inviting the company to join in. By the end of the evening he was jolly and tipsy, waltzing by himself before asking Maria to dance with him. As he put his arm around her he said, 'Come on, let's dance a little. You know very well that it's the last Christmas' – almost exactly his father's words of thirty years earlier. Afterwards he was in such high spirits that he had to be calmed down to bring the evening to a close.

34

'Going downhill fast'

(1940)

War's annals will cloud into night
Ere their story die.

> Thomas Hardy, 'In Time of
> "The Breaking of Nations"'

According to Beckett, before leaving Paris Joyce had said – 'with something like satisfaction' – 'We're going downhill fast.'[1] It was a sentiment he did not hesitate to share with his various friends. Budgen, Mercanton, Larbaud, Carola Giedion, Curran and Brody all received news of his gloom over the reception of his work and his disastrous family circumstances. When he later complained to Harriet that his personal affairs 'seem to be public knowledge', he had only himself to blame.

Deep in the heart of the enchanting Auvergne, little happened at Saint-Gérand, and Giorgio soon became bored. Early in the New Year he returned to Paris, moving in with Ponisovsky at the Lutétia.[2] Meanwhile, Joyce, remote from both his daughter and his workplace, felt trapped in an emotional and intellectual limbo. Despite the worldwide coverage of the *Wake*, no one in Saint-Gérand seemed to have heard of it or him. As Louis Gillet noted when he visited him later, the village was remote and Joyce was a stranger.

> The simple folk, full of consideration, did not suspect at all the quality of the extraordinary guest they had among them: a prince of the mind, an artist of world-wide renown, a man whose books were famous from Moscow to New York and from Berlin to Tokyo, and who had received among the heaps of telegrams for his fiftieth birthday one from Prague, addressed 'to the first of all living poets'.[3]

Joyce grew depressed, had little or nothing to say to Nora, and only livened up when one of Maria's Parisian 'refugees' talked with him about opera or when a conversation with Maria turned to religion. When he attacked Catholic education and she pointed out that her children were being raised as Catholics, he said, 'Oh, it's different in France. In Ireland Catholicism is black magic.'[4]

With both his daughter and daughter-in-law in asylums and his son without a home, Joyce now took over responsibility for Stephen. He saw him regularly at the Chateau, entertaining him with stories from Homer, and had him to stay at the hotel at weekends. There was a heavy snowfall that winter and navigating the local lanes became hazardous. Saint-Gérand had more than its fair share of dogs and, as he made his way slowly around, feeling his way forward with his stick, his fear of being attacked returned. He filled his pockets with pebbles to throw at any dog foolish enough to approach him. The sight of this stranger in long black coat with a walking-stick and dark glasses seemed bizarre to the locals – 'that poor old man', they called him.

Joyce's thoughts were ever with Lucia, but, unable to visit La Baule, he enquired about her directly from Delmas who replied, 'She walks in the garden in the afternoon and reads a book ... She has somehow accepted your absence and doesn't seem to be greatly affected by it.'[5] He sent the letter to Giorgio in Paris with a note asking him to phone the doctor occasionally to check on his sister while he explored the possibility of finding her a *maison de santé* near Saint-Gérand.

He was pleased to hear that his and Nino Frank's translation of *Anna Livia Plurabelle* had caused 'a great uproar' in Rome when it appeared in *Prospettive*, and asked Daniel Brody, now in Holland, whether he couldn't publish a German translation there. 'After all,' he wrote, 'it is only about rivers and washerwomen.'[6] But it was the fate of the whole *Wake* that concerned Joyce most. Although he felt pessimistic about its reception, some reviews he admitted were very good – such as Harry Levin's in the *Kenyon Review*, and one in the *Nieuwe Rotterdamsche Courant*, referring to him as 'a juggler'.[7] On receiving a review from Helsinki, he was taken with the idea that his book had proved prophetic. The Finns were fiercely resisting the Russians and a Finn won the Nobel Prize that year, so 'the Finn again wakes'. However, his prevailing mood was one of dejection – the book's reception in Europe had, he complained, been 'a complete fiasco'.[8] The wide appreciation he had expected had not materialized.

At the end of January, on a visit to Paris, he called on Paul Léon. Lack of money had compelled him to end their feud. They were quickly back on their old terms and Léon began by sorting out his problem with the French tax authorities. He wrote immediately to Fred Monro asking – more in hope than in expectation – for £100, and to Huebsch at Viking and Bennett Cerf at Random House requesting that royalties for the *Wake* and for *Ulysses* be paid directly to Joyce for the duration of hostilities.[9] Huebsch replied by sea-mail – a letter which did not reach Joyce till 11 March, containing a cheque for $45. But the London overseas branch of his bank, Lloyds & National Provincial, he learned, had managed to transfer £24 1s 9d (4,391 francs) into his Paris account.[10] And thanks to help from James Johnson Sweeney of *transition*, now in New York, money from Cerf also got to him through the Crédit Lyonnais in Paris. With his financial affairs back in familiar hands, life became a little less stressful. In mid-February, Giorgio came to celebrate Stephen's birthday bringing Beckett with him; and as a birthday present, Joyce made a French translation of his poem 'Ecce Puer' which his grandson had inspired. Giorgio's movements were now a mystery to his father and for two months afterwards he had no idea where he was – seemingly not always staying with Ponisovsky.

Reviews of Gorman's biography were beginning to appear. The *New Yorker* called it 'a book about a hero' and the *New York Times Book Review* made it a front-page spread illustrated by one of Augustus John's sketches. By March it was on sale in Europe, but not, according to Giorgio, in Paris. Joyce was certainly happier with it than was its author, and told Gillet he was anxious that it should be republished with additional pages devoted to *Finnegans Wake*.

Maria invited the Joyces to stay at the Château de la Chapelle over the Easter holidays and Giorgio and Beckett came visiting again on St Patrick's Day. Beckett later recalled how ill Joyce looked, and how, unhappy with some of the negative reviews of the *Wake*, he even considered simplifying the punctuation to make it easier for the general reader.[11] Maria also found him depressed by the book's reception, saying, 'Why should I write anything else – nobody reads this one.'[12] Feeling guilty about not seeing Lucia that Easter, he asked Beckett to attend the services at Moulins Cathedral with him, and asked Maria to accompany him to inspect an asylum he thought might be suitable for her.

When the school term began, the Joyces moved to Vichy where they had heard that Valery Larbaud was living, paralysed and unable to speak, and quickly arranged to visit him. They were still in Vichy when on 2 May, another sad chapter of the Joyce family saga ended and Helen finally left with her brother for New York, accompanied by two doctors and two nurses.[13] She escaped just in time. A week later the tide of the war suddenly turned. The so-called 'Phoney War' in the west, where neither side made a move, ended when Hitler launched his blitzkrieg through Belgium and Holland. Three weeks later he invaded France.

Having seen the way the fortunes of war were moving, on 10 June Mussolini threw in his lot with the Germans and declared war on England and France. However, the Battle for France was drawing to a close. By 4 June the last British troops were evacuated from Dunkirk and on the 14th Paris fell to the Germans. On the 16th, Joyce's last Bloomsday, Beckett arrived in Vichy with Suzanne Dumesnil, the young woman he would later marry. They were broke, but Beckett had a cheque which no one would cash. Joyce asked Larbaud to help and he lent them 20,000 francs to see them on their way. After taking their leave, Beckett and Suzanne headed on foot for Toulouse hoping to escape the country. However, events overtook them and Beckett remained in France to do dangerous work for the Resistance, narrowly avoiding capture and execution.

With the Germans poised for victory and French Fascists moving into Vichy with the expectation of assuming power in the country, the Joyces retreated to Saint-Gérand and sought sanctuary with Maria in the château until they found a flat in the village. On the 12th Léon turned up in a donkey cart, joking that Christ had entered Jerusalem on such a creature. Lucie joined him a few days later. Giorgio, having avoided conscription, also arrived hoping to lie low. With the enemy expected any day, Maria, if asked, would say he was an Italian teacher.

The French surrender came on 20 June, and now there was no easy way out of the country. On 1 July Maria moved her school to the Hôtel du Commerce where the Joyces joined her. There, every afternoon, Nora served tea, somehow acquiring extra cakes from the local *confiserie*, and every evening at seven thirty, Maria and the Léons joined them for a meal in the hotel's private dining-room. Maria always thought Joyce looked somewhat the worse for wear on these occasions, and Nora would say with some distaste, 'Look at the man – look at him – he can't stand a glass of wine.' It turned out that before dinner Joyce was in the habit of slipping out of the back door of the hotel to the downstairs café and knocking back a few Pernods, to help deaden the intermittent stomach cramps.

Joyce and Léon now took time to go through *Finnegans Wake*, noting down errors and misspellings. But such diversions only partially alleviated his state of anxiety. He was missing Lucia more than ever and was especially worried because La Baule was now in a newly designated military area close to the naval base at Saint-Nazare and likely to be bombed. Every time he wrote to friends he would mention her situation. Added to that he was now completely cut off from any money in England and had no idea what had happened to his books and papers left behind in Passy. When Lucie Léon returned to her job with the *New York Herald Tribune* in Paris in July, she promised to visit the flat and report back to them.

The Irish legation had moved to Vichy where the Minister was Sean Murphy whom Joyce had once met through the René Baillys. At various times over the following months Murphy offered him and Giorgio Irish passports, giving them the right to leave occupied France whenever they wished, but both declined. Joyce could never quite bring himself to draw the curtain on the old Ireland in which his imagination still dwelt, and he clung doggedly to his British passport. In any case his mind was focused on finding another way out of France. At the end of July, a letter arrived from Carola Giedion inviting the family to her home in Zurich. Joyce was delighted and asked her to find out whether a private hospital he knew at nearby Kilchberg would be prepared to take Lucia at minimal cost. In anticipation of a positive answer, he wrote immediately to the Swiss legation in Lyon enquiring about entry visas. He would also need permits from both the French and Germans and Lucia would need nurses to escort her to the Swiss border.

On 4 August, German troops entered Saint-Gérand, and by coincidence on the same day permission came from the occupying authorities for Lucia to leave France. Immediately Joyce wrote to his former student Paul Ruggiero announcing their plans to head for Zurich, asking if the city was crowded and how easy it would be to get a flat there. 'As you see,' he added, 'history repeats itself.'[14]

Robert Murphy, chargé d'affaires at the American legation in Vichy, which had assumed responsibility for protecting British citizens in the area, advised Joyce to get Huebsch to cable royalties directly to the Embassy through the US State Department. If he were to get all his family to Switzerland he would need every penny he could muster. Joyce passed on Murphy's advice to Huebsch and wrote asking Cerf for an advance on royalties.

To Mercanton he wrote enquiring about suitable schools for Stephen in Lausanne, where Giorgio hoped to settle. He detailed his main outgoings – 1,500 francs monthly for the boy's schooling, 2,700 francs monthly for Lucia whose condition he explained. 'Her case is cyclothymia [extreme mood swings] dating from the age of seven and a half. She is about thirty-three, speaks French fluently. Her character is gay, sweet and ironic, but she has sudden bursts of anger over nothing when she has to be confined in a straitjacket.'[15] If Lucia had shown signs of this disturbed condition as far back as 1912 he had never mentioned it previously.

By the end of August the Germans had withdrawn and France was divided into two: the Occupied Zone administered directly by the Germans and the Unoccupied Zone administered by French Fascists under Marshal Pétain and Pierre Laval. By now Maria (feeling sad at deserting the confused and helpless Joyces) had closed her school, intending to return with her daughters to America. Before she left, in the hope of stirring Huebsch and Cerf into action, Joyce gave her power of attorney to act for him in the USA.

The rumour came that the landlord of the rue des Vignes flat, to whom Joyce owed arrears of rent, wanted it cleared and Léon decided to go to Paris to keep an eye on things and, once a sale was announced, to salvage what he could of Joyce's property. Both the Léons were taking a chance;

the situation was growing more and more dangerous for Jews and for them living in Paris was a highly risky business.

Joyce was increasingly nervous about the situation in France and eager to leave. Fortunately he had influential friends who were willing to help, out of gratitude for helping their friends and family escape the Nazis, such as Brauchbar and Gustav Zumsteg who offered valuable advice on obtaining Swiss entry visas. As referees Joyce gave Giedion, Vogt, Schoeck, Moses Prager of the Carlton Elite and Mentona Moser, a colleague of Florel. Brauchbar's father offered himself as financial guarantor. The guarantee for the whole family would amount to 50,000 Swiss francs, or around 750,000 French francs, plus an extra 3,000 in legal expenses ('an impossible sum for any one man,' said Ruggiero). Joyce approached the French Red Cross about getting Lucia to Switzerland but his letters went unanswered. By mid-September he was growing desperate. He wrote a long letter to Sweeney in New York, stressing his financial plight, and asking him to phone Mrs Jolas on her arrival and read it to her.

One concerned friend, Louis Gillet, took the time to travel to Saint-Gérand, causing quite a stir in a village unused to visits from distinguished *Académiciens*. Gillet saw Joyce as a strange, helpless creature trapped again by nets he was unable to fly.

> That day I found him agitated by a deadly anxiety; he was all impatience to flee elsewhere ... During our meal he could not sit down and circled around the table, stopping at last, exhausted by torment, to take only a draught of wine. He dreamed of going to Switzerland where he had spent a few happy years during the last war, believing that there he would rediscover his youth. He was irritated by the delays and the formalities ... fluttering like a sylph, like a furious bee limed by the crepe of its wings. One would fancy he had received ... a summons from fate commanding him to leave; he was longing to get away and fly ... to the country where once his genius had hatched. Once there, he said to himself, all would be rest, deliverance. What he took for a call of happiness, was a flap of wings from the beyond ... Death gave him an enigmatic sign from there, inviting him to this last journey, the only one made today without passport.[16]

Gillet returned to Vichy to do what he could to help, promising to send Joyce a copy of an article he had written on *Finnegans Wake* for the *Revue des Deux Mondes*.

Giorgio was in favour of moving to Switzerland but Nora feared that it might be Hitler's next target and could not bear the thought of air-raid warnings. Gillet wrote urging them to take the chance. He had visited Sean Murphy at the Irish legation and arranged for Joyce's English money to be sent to France through Dublin. Meanwhile, he said, the U K government had deposited money with the American Ambassador at Vichy so that British subjects in need could draw up to £15 a month.[17] If Joyce could not get to Zurich, Gillet recommended Nice where he would find helpful friends such as Gide and Martin du Gard.

But Joyce had set his heart on Switzerland even if it meant for once living modestly. The *maison de santé* at Kilchberg wanted 15 francs a day to take Lucia, and the Zurich Burghölzli asked 25 francs, both beyond his means. Then he found an asylum charging 8 francs 50 at Corcelles-sur-Chavornay, just outside Lausanne. The days of expensive sessions with Jung were long gone. He knew he would have to move fast but having had no news of his daughter for weeks he had no idea how to get her safely out of France. He would need to get her a German exit visa and settle a three-months bill with Delmas.

The Swiss entry permit had still not arrived, so Zumsteg referred Joyce to the Geneva lawyer Georges Haldenwang. On 15 October he asked Ruggiero if it was a matter of money or because there were already too many foreigners in Zurich? Haldenwang seemed to provide the answer two days later. For 200 Swiss francs, or 3,000 French francs, he said, he could get visas issued within a month rather than the usual four to nine months. But Brauchbar senior was now dragging his feet over the guarantee.

The plan was to get to Lausanne, then arrange for Lucia's exit, settle her at her private hospital and place Stephen in a suitable boarding school before proceeding to Zurich. On 25 October Joyce told Ruggiero they had French exit visas and were ready to leave as soon as the Swiss entry permits arrived. The reason behind the latest hold-up became clear when, on 29 October, he learned from Mrs Giedion, who had visited the offices of the Police Fédérale des Etrangers (Aliens Police) in Zurich, that they thought that Joyce was a Jew – a problem for them apparently. 'I am thunderstruck!' he wrote, 'There's a remarkable discovery!'[18] Mercanton wrote to the police on his behalf, affirming that Joyce was in fact Aryan, not Jewish. They had, he said, confused him with Leopold Bloom, a character in his book.[19]

All Joyce's papers on the French side were now in order. The US legation in Berne had assured him that once he reached Switzerland, money from New York would be available to him through them. Maria Jolas sent news from New York that she had raised a fund on his behalf, some $6,000 (around 25,000 Swiss francs). And a letter from Harriet informed him that it was just possible to get a monthly sum through Ireland as long as it did not exceed £30. But his application for those Swiss entry visas seemed to have hit a brick wall and nobody quite knew why.

At this moment of confusion, and at short notice, the guests of the Hôtel du Commerce were asked to leave, and the Joyces moved to a flat at the Maison Ponthenier. The state of their nerves was hardly improved when they received visits from the Mayor and police wanting to know why the family had not left after being given exit visas. The problem lay at the Swiss end, Joyce explained. On 1 November, having been told that his case was 'still pending with the Swiss Federal Police', he told Mrs Giedion, 'They are raising one difficulty after another. We are aliens, then Jews, then beggars. What next. Burglars, lepers?' The behaviour of the Swiss, he said, contrasted oddly with the 'courteous and favourable' treatment he had received from the French and Germans.[20] Amid all this anxious uncertainty, Nora heard that her mother had died in Galway and she wept inconsolably.

Tiring of Haldenwang's foot-dragging, Ruggiero took over the case and approached the police directly. It transpired that the forms, declarations, references, and guarantees of funds Joyce had so far submitted were insufficient and a declaration of his own financial position was required urgently. This, said Ruggiero, should be submitted to the Swiss legation in Vichy, or, to save time, directly to the Police Chief in Zurich.

Things seemed to look up when Carola Giedion wrote saying that her husband Siegfried had settled his financial guarantee in consultation with Brauchbar and the money had been deposited at Ruggiero's bank, the Crédit Suisse. (In fact, Ruggiero had persuaded the authorities to lower the required guarantee to 20,000 Swiss francs.) Matters were moving slowly because so many were applying to enter Switzerland that the police had their work cut out coping with the paperwork. The Joyces should be patient and try not to upset the French authorities too much by their continuing presence there.

At long last, on 11 November Joyce heard from Lucia and, to his relief, she sounded in good spirits. He had paid 23,500 francs of the eventual 32,000 (from Mrs Jolas's fund) for her annual upkeep, he told Mrs Giedion, so he hoped he could get her out without much trouble once in Switzerland. However, the family's French exit visas were due to expire at the end of November and their renewal was by no means guaranteed. Good documentation would have to be provided for both the French and Germans to justify an extension and Giorgio would have to cycle into Vichy to collect the visas when they eventually came through.

The personal declaration Joyce prepared for the Swiss revealed that the money gifted to him by Harriet, which in 1928 had yielded £900 a year, now brought him in only £300 – a measure of his profligacy over the past twelve years. He declared deposits totalling 194,320 French francs in London and Zurich and an income totalling 172,300 francs including 52,800 francs (£300) from British war stock, 52,500 francs in royalties due from American publishers and 26,000 from British publishers, plus some income for Stephen from his grandfather Adolph Kastor. Property he declared included some furniture, books and papers at his Paris apartment. His wife, son and daughter, he added, had no goods to their name.[21] This he had stamped and dated at the Mayor's office in Saint-Gérand, and sealed in an envelope ready to be mailed to Zurich.

The following morning he was visited unexpectedly by Gia Augsburg, the male nurse designated by the *maison de santé* at Corcelles to escort Lucia from La Baule to Lausanne. He spent several hours talking about her with Joyce and stayed for lunch. As he was returning to Lausanne through Vichy, Joyce asked him to post his financial declaration express from the town, to explain the position to Sean Murphy at the Irish legation and to Walter Stucki, the Swiss Ambassador, and to visit the Ministry of the Interior to see if their exit permits could be extended. Augsburg drove off on his mission, saying that he was returning to Lausanne immediately and would do what he could for Joyce there. A couple of days later he wrote from Lyon saying that he had visited the Ministry of the Interior and that a M. Georges Demay would write to him about his exit permits the following day. But no letter arrived and on enquiring he was told that Augsburg had not been to the Ministry.

Joyce wrote to his old acquaintance Armand Petitjean, now working with the Vichy government, seeking his assistance with the exit permits. Anticipating Petitjean's question as to why he wanted to leave France, he wrote, 'You will ask why I persist in wishing to penetrate that country which is so hermetically helvetic. Simply because, living here, I am cut off from my resources and the Embassy of the USA has let us know that we will not be able to count for long on the monthly aid which it is giving us.'[22] It is clear that in his mind the net was closing.

To his horror, on the 26th he heard from Ruggiero that the declaration entrusted to Augsburg had still not arrived. Instead of mailing it in Vichy the courier had decided to deliver it in person once he got to Lausanne, but he had been in no hurry and the delay caused Joyce much further agonizing and much trouble. The following morning he dispatched another financial deposition by express post, and at 5 p.m. a telegram from Ruggiero announced that permits had finally been granted. Now all he needed was Vichy's agreement to an extension to their exit visas which had expired on the 30th. On the same day he heard that the Germans had revoked Lucia's permission to leave the country, and so to all intents and purposes his daughter was trapped behind enemy lines. He contacted the League of Nations, Count Gerald O'Kelly, Irish chargé d'affaires in Paris and the Rockefeller Foundation's Patrick O'Brien, in the hope that they could help extricate Lucia from France. But for the time being all that was possible was for Giorgio to cycle to Vichy, pick up their Swiss entry visas and get their exit permits extended. Joyce wrote ahead to book rooms at the Hôtel de la Paix in Lausanne.

Pedalling into Vichy on 2 December, Giorgio met Petitjean and urged him to act. Petitjean told him that he hoped to be able to send him a wire about the permits by the 5th. But Giorgio had learned that the question had again been raised of his 'mobilisability' (a word not even found in *Finnegans Wake*, said Joyce). How could they be sure he was not conscripted by the British? Joyce wrote to Petitjean on the 3rd to try to resolve the matter, 'This mobilisability exists neither in fact nor in law,' he said. 'Born in Italy, Irish, son of parents both from southern Ireland, never having lived and not living either in Great Britain or in Northern Ireland he is not touched by any law about British military service.' His multinational family, like his multinational work, did not exactly fit conventional expectations. He asked Petitjean to try to avoid a 'misfortune' being made into a 'misdirection'.[23]

On 4 December a law was introduced restricting the movement of foreigners, so the family was trapped in Saint-Gérand until visas and permits arrived enabling them to leave for good. On the 5th Joyce received a telegram from Demay informing him that exit visas had been granted to all except Giorgio whose case was still being considered by the *sous-préfet* at Lapalisse. Defying the law, Giorgio cycled the ten kilometres to the town where he presented the four passports and the three exit permits to an official who, seeing the problem, winked at Giorgio and passed on just the passports to the *sous-préfet* who promptly stamped them.

Timing was now crucial as the Joyces' Swiss entry permits were due to expire on the 15th. But even at that late stage, there was yet another hitch. Both his and Nora's British passports needed renewing, and there was no British embassy or legation where this could readily be done. Giorgio again cycled into Vichy, and after some wrangling persuaded a reluctant Robert Murphy at the American legation to renew them.[24]

On the 12th Joyce sent a last communication to Sylvia Beach and the following day a telegram to Ruggiero announcing their imminent departure. The whole Joyce caravan, luggage and all, would require some sort of conveyance. Giorgio found a chauffeur-driven car but no petrol. Once more he pedalled into Vichy, this time to hunt for fuel. The US Embassy turned him away but eventually he found a bank clerk who, after much haggling, sold him a gallon of petrol. Finally, at a few minutes past midnight on 14 December the Joyces were driven to the railway station at nearby Saint-Germain-des-Fosses to catch the 3 a.m. train heading for the Swiss border. At 10 p.m. the family disembarked at Geneva.

35

Death in Exile

(1940–)

'One by one they were all becoming shades.' Joyce, 'The Dead'

After a night in Geneva, the Joyces proceeded to Lausanne where they were met by Jacques Mercanton.

> I can still see his slender silhouette on the railway platform, in the shadow of a wintry twilight, his face very pale, aged, marked by fatigue [he recalled]. He advanced through the crowd, which his tall figure dominated, holding onto his wife's arm like a blind man. His hat was turned down over his eyes, his cane hooked over his wrist. He seemed to have come from very much farther away than neighbouring ... France ... much farther even than his native Ireland, at the frontier of the sea ... He had entered into eternal exile.[1]

The Hôtel de la Paix was expecting them. Distracted and exhausted as he was, once settled Joyce took Stephen for a walk and treated him to marzipan and a bar of Swiss chocolate. After lunch he visited the *maison de santé* at Corcelles where he hoped to settle Lucia. Mercanton noted how frail he seemed, how his hair was greying and thin, and recalled Nora expressing concerns over his health. He was eating less and less and some days was so fatigued, she said, she thought he would just slip away. She, too, was showing signs of age, her hair now more white than auburn, and she was suffering the onset of arthritis.

Next day, 17 December, they moved on and at 8 p.m. arrived in Zurich where Mrs Giedion and Ruggiero made up the welcoming party. Ruggiero remembered Joyce's first words: 'We can never repay what you have done for us.' Aware of the stressful uncertainty of the previous few months, the young banker had booked them into two well-furnished rooms at the restful Pension Delphin, set in a large park.[2] The first thing Joyce did was to write thanking Fred Monro for the £50 he had found awaiting him at the US Embassy. Two days later he followed up with urgent telegrams requesting £300 to cover the cost of maintaining his family and getting Lucia out of occupied France.

Mrs Giedion pictured him the day after his arrival, venturing out with Stephen into a city blanketed in snow, to buy his grandson a French edition of the Greek epics.

> It was a memorable sight to see him ... hand in hand with the lively little child, to whom this radiantly white element was an exciting novelty. Joyce followed slowly, his posture and gestures seeming more tired than before. Or was it only the strong, blinding effect of the wintry blanket that delayed his step?[3]

He took the boy to see the confluence of the Limmat and the Sihl, where his favourite photograph had been taken with his back to the camera.

He wrote to thank Sweeney for help with American royalties, and, being told that help over their entry visas had come from the Mayor of Zurich, he quickly wrote to thank him, too.[4] History was, as he had foreseen, repeating itself. He was back where exile had begun for a young runaway writer and his runaway 'wife'.

After their arrival, Ruggiero called each morning at the Pension Delphin to ensure that all was well. He, too, had a prophetic moment with Joyce. 'On entering his room where he awaited me, I had the bad habit of placing my hat on their bed, and each time he said to me, "Ruggiero, take that hat off the bed. I am superstitious and they say that means someone will die."'[5]

When they joined the Giedions for Christmas dinner, Joyce turned up wearing his father's colourful waistcoat, bearing a bunch of red poinsettias for Carola and an ashtray in Cretan colours for Siegfried. That evening he sat at table proudly, the head of three generations of Joyces. Mistletoe was produced and games were played, with Stephen hiding under the table. Good fellowship prevailed. Christmas hymns and secular songs were sung, some in Irish, some in Latin, Joyce's fine tenor complementing Giorgio's rich bass. An old acoustic recording was played, of John McCormack singing 'Ah, Moon of My Delight', from Liza Lehmann's *In a Persian Garden*, a song he loved, a haunting echo from his lyrical youth:

> Ah, moon of my delight, that knows no wane,
> The moon of Heav'n is rising once again:
> How oft hereafter rising shall she look
> Through this same garden after me – in vain!

And when thyself with shining foot shall pass
Among the guests star-scatter'd on the grass,
And in your joyous errand reach the spot
Where I made one – turn down an empty Glass![6]

Not quite ready yet to turn down an empty glass, Joyce declined to stay the night, saying, 'The Pope does not leave the Vatican.'

On Boxing Day, St Stephen's Day, Ruggiero invited the Joyces to tea and entertained them with two pieces on the cello, accompanied at the piano by his son. Then Giorgio sang '*O vulnera doloris*' by Giacomo Carissimi, and Ruggiero undertook to approach the Zurich Aliens' Police on his behalf seeking permission for him to sing at concerts in Switzerland. The Joyces left, promising to return soon for a fish and white wine supper, a Joyce favourite.

That evening at an old Kreuzplatz restaurant, against a background of antiquated wood-panelling and with his carafe of Fendant at hand, Joyce seemed, recalled Carola, 'to inhale the stability from the locale and climate, while outside was the chaos of world events'. After the treadmill of bureaucratic evasion, obstruction and bungling, he had at last found sanctuary. 'Here one still knows where he stands, here life has remained constant,' he told her. But the Swiss obsession with hygiene and modernity seemed to him to ooze complacency. He preferred the medieval world which the rustic ambience of the old restaurant evoked for him. As they parted outside, to go their separate ways into the cold night and the blackout, he told them, 'You have no idea how wonderful dirt is.' It was, thought the Giedions later, a strangely portentous remark.[7]

As 1941 dawned, he made a few more friends. Heinrich Straumann had succeeded Bernhard Fehr as Professor of English at Zurich University, and Ernst Howald was its new Rector. Joining them for dinner, Joyce ordered Vienna roast and drank the inevitable Fendant, conversing happily in German. He spoke about his attachment to Dublin, but warned them that local knowledge was no aid to understanding the *Wake* – the reader should just allow the language to have its effect. And, as he had told others, reading Vico on the social dimension of cultures would also help, he said.

Hearing that Stanislaus had been moved to Florence, he sent him the names of various people to contact – Pound in Rapallo, Linati in Rome, Francini in Florence; and a Triestine friend had put him in touch with the 'refined' Miss Vera Esposito, Signora Dockrell, who was also in Florence. When Stannie called on the Dockrells it was an uncomfortable encounter. His strong anti-Fascist opinions did not sit well with them, nor his hostility towards the Irish cultural nationalism which Vera had embraced so passionately in her youth. And her low opinion of brother Jim had never changed.[8]

On 7 January, the Joyces dined with the Zumstegs. Two days later, after visiting an exhibition of French nineteenth-century paintings, they joined Ruggiero to celebrate his birthday at the Kronenhalle. Despite all efforts to tempt him with the choicest dishes, Joyce refused to eat, simply drinking Fendant and smoking long Virginia cigarettes. The talk that evening was mostly about Zurich during the previous war, when by day he was so absorbed in composing *Ulysses* and at night discovering the delights of Swiss white wine. As they left the restaurant at around 1.30 a.m. Nora nearly slipped on the steps and said to Joyce, 'Why do you make me go out at night in such terrible weather?' Ruggiero saw them back to the Pension Delphin and said his final goodnights.

Next morning, the 10th, at 4.30 a.m., Joyce woke with agonizing stomach pains. Two doctors saw him – the local doctor, Dr Heinz Wehrli, and a consultant surgeon, Dr Heinrich Freysz, who administered morphine and decided he should be moved to the Red Cross Hospital on Gloriastrasse. On the morning of Saturday the 11th, after Freysz had him X-rayed it was evident that he had a perforated ulcer, complicated by haemorrhage, and required immediate surgery. Joyce was reluctant to agree, fearing he had cancer, like his mother, and dreading the loss of consciousness under anaesthetic. His son assured him that he did not have cancer, but he then worried about how they would pay his medical bills. Ruggiero, alerted by Giorgio, visited him that morning, and, seeing Joyce so weak and worried about money, had what he called 'an inspiration'. If he did not survive the operation, Ruggiero knew that neither Nora nor Giorgio would have access to Joyce's account at the Crédit Suisse where he worked. In the hospital office he made out a power of attorney in Giorgio's name which, he explained to Joyce, it would be a good precaution for him to sign. Without even reading it Joyce signed, saying 'Ruggiero, do everything for the best,' which, said Ruggiero, left him feeling 'distressed and sad'.[9] Freysz operated on him the following morning.

Afterwards Joyce was weak but able to see his family. 'I didn't think I would survive,' he told Nora. But that afternoon his condition deteriorated and he lost consciousness, waking only to ask that Nora's bed be placed next to his as his had been close to hers in hospital once. ('He might die before his mother came,' thought young Stephen Dedalus.) Professor William Loeffler from Zurich University, a friend of Joyce's, was consulted and ordered a blood transfusion. Although the transfusion went well enough, Joyce was now in a semi-conscious state – 'apart', as Loeffler put it.

Nora and Giorgio kept vigil at his bedside but in the evening they were encouraged to return to the hotel for the night, assured that they would be phoned if his condition changed. At 1 a.m. Joyce regained consciousness and asked the nurses to call them before again lapsing into a coma. But an hour passed before they were summoned and by the time they arrived, Joyce was dead. (The *New York Times* kindly stated, 'His wife and son were at the hospital when he died.') The great Joycean caravan had finally come to a halt. He was just three weeks short of his fifty-ninth birthday. Giorgio called Ruggiero and told him simply, 'Papa is dead.' As Nora left the hospital in a taxi in tears, the taxi-driver, attempting to comfort her, said, 'Never mind, Madame, there are always others.'

It was the 13th of the month, the date he feared, the date on which his mother had died. Ironically it was also thirteen years to the day that he had written to Frank Budgen to say, 'I have been and am painfully ill – inflammation of intestines – caused by overwork and worry,'[10] and some nineteen years since, by way of conversation, at their famous meeting, he had mentioned his stomach pains to the none-too-healthy Marcel Proust.

That day the cold was intense. According to Carola Giedion, the Zürichsee was frozen over and the snow so heavy that the confluence of the Limmat and the Sihl which Joyce had loved so much was obscured from view. As he lay on his deathbed, with Nora's permission Mrs Giedion arranged for a death-mask to be made by the sculptor Paul Speck. Two impressions were taken and, claimed Maria Jolas, two months later Nora received the bill for them. Since she was unable to pay, Mrs Giedion hung on to the masks. One of these is now at the Joyce Foundation in Zurich and the other at the Joyce Museum in the Martello Tower at Sandycove. It is said that Speck made a third mask, copies of which can be found at the universities of Basle and Lausanne and the Zentralbibliothek in Zurich. Joyce's reflection on Mangan's last impression not only captures his own perfectly but speaks also of the sorrowful clown sitting behind the satirical motley. 'The death mask that is left to us shows a refined, almost aristocratic face, in whose delicate lines it is impossible to discover anything but melancholy and great weariness.'[11]

An autopsy found two ulcers, one of which had bled extensively, and badly damaged intestines. 'On opening the abdomen,' read the report, 'there were enormously dilated loops of small bowel as large as a thigh, coloured purple exhibiting easily removed fibrous deposits,' and, 'the abdominal aorta's intima is extensively destroyed or calcified, sparse thrombitis deposits.'[12] The diagnosis of Dr Fontaine and other Parisian physicians of 'stomach cramp due to nerves' was clearly ill-informed and fatal guesswork. Freysz signed the death certificate on which the Joyces' wedding-day was given as '8 October 1904' followed, appropriately enough, by a question mark, later crossed out by some hand unknown. His brother George had died similarly, in agony from a perforated bowel, but there was no one at the end to play and sing Jim's favourite songs or compose a dirge for him, as he had done for George.

The news soon spread. Lucia is said to have read about her father's death by accident in a newspaper. Harriet heard it on the radio, as did Joseph Holloway whose diary merely records, 'James Joyce died this morning early after operation.' McGreevy, who also heard it over the air, wrote more graciously, 'It seems to me that it marks the end of nineteenth-century individualism in literature in the sense that he was its last great genius.'[13] The Joyces' friend Greta Herz informed Robert Kastor who passed the news to Helen. Léon learned of his death from the owner of a café where he and Joyce took coffee. Stanislaus was phoned the day after his brother's death by the 'refined' Vera Dockrell who had been asked to pass on the news by Francini. Budgen was on air-raid watch in a dugout during the London Blitz when someone showed him a copy of the *Evening Standard* announcing Joyce's passing. Hearing later about his visit to that art exhibition the afternoon before he fell ill, he wrote, 'Somehow there seems to me to be an affinity there, I mean between French nineteenth-century painters and Joyce, in the sense that all the work of his imagination and intellect was rooted, as was theirs, in a natural sensibility.'[14]

In the *Neue Zürcher Zeitung* on the 14th, an advertisement placed by Nora announced the death and invited those wishing to offer condolences to the funeral at the Fluntern Cemetery at 2 p.m. on the 15th. Offered a Catholic burial, Nora refused, saying, 'I couldn't do that to him.' Nor would it be a Dignam-style cortège of carriages winding through the streets bearing friends and old cronies with tall tales to tell about the dear departed. The day was icy and the light subdued. Carola Giedion recalled that 'a mysterious sun, milky and round like the moon, seemed to hide behind a misty glass'. There was sleet as well as snow in the air. With a petrol shortage, most mourners got to the cemetery by tram, a slow winding climb up the hill to Fluntern at the northern edge of the city. The silence of the necropolis was punctuated from time to time by the roar of animals from the nearby zoo.

There being no priest, those gathered around the coffin in the Fried-hofkapelle that day felt awkward, not knowing quite what to do. Apart from the Joyce family, those present included Ruggiero, Mercanton, the Giedions, Dr Vogt, and August Suter. Lord George Harcourt Johnstone, the 3rd Baron Derwent, British attaché in Berne, turned out for the Empire and he was joined by Max Geilinger, the poet, for the Swiss Society of Authors, and Professor Heinrich Straumann for the University of Zurich. Max Meili, the tenor, from the Schola Cantorum Basiliensis, sang '*Addio terra, addio cielo'* from Monteverdi's *L'Orfeo*. Joyce's grave, no. 1449, stood at the far end of a wall. There, Nora bent forward several times to catch a last glimpse of him through the glass window in the coffin, murmuring 'Jim, how beautiful you are!'[15] Then, as it was being lowered into the grave, she made a sad gesture of farewell with open arms, a 'birdlike swooping gesture', as if to call him back,[16] and Suter threw a rose after him for his friend Frank Budgen. The grave was decked with a green wreath shaped like an Irish harp, entwined with grass-green ribbons. However, it was the British Lord Derwent who led the eulogies, saying that although Joyce had never abandoned his own culture, it was appropriate that he had died in Zurich because he had chosen to belong to Europe.[17]

This was no 'funfaral', and although there would be no boisterous wake for Finnegan's wakener (just a quiet one given by Mrs Giedion), there was a suitably comic aspect to the affair which might have been dreamt up by the creator of Dedalus, Bloom and Dignam himself. A deaf old man, who had apparently followed the coffin from the Pension Delphin (or who might have been an ancient haunter of graveyards), was spellbound enough by the dignity of the occasion to keep asking in a loud voice, 'Who is to be buried here?' and, when told, asked, 'But who is James Joyce?' The answer he received was not recorded.

Nora did not attend the wake but returned directly to the pension to mourn alone. All money due to her husband now went to Joyce's estate in London to await the processing of his will, so Nora was quite suddenly reduced to comparative penury. Without money from England or the US, and having to care for Giorgio and Stephen as well as herself and Lucia, she was forced to find ever more Spartan accommodation. And although Stephen received a generous settlement from his grandfather Adolph Kastor, Giorgio, who might have earned a little from singing, was refused permission to do so. Nora's financial plight was alleviated somewhat when Harriet Weaver sent £250 to cover the costs of the funeral. But the thriving circle of friends and acquaintances she had enjoyed as the wife of a celebrated author was widely scattered, and for her the good living, lavish parties and luxury shopping expeditions had gone for ever.

Carola Giedion now requested the return of the 15,000 Swiss francs she and Siegfried had lodged in Joyce's account as a guarantee, but that, too, was frozen until the will had been proved. Harriet had been designated Joyce's literary executor and Nora had inherited his estate. However, Fred Monro somehow failed to impress on Nora the urgency of applying for probate, and because she did not have her husband's papers to hand and mail between Switzerland and England had slowed to a crawl, she was unable to prove the will within the three months required. The role of executor therefore passed to the Public Trustee in London. The British court would take eighteen months to decide that Joyce had died a British domicile, but by that time the two countries were cut off and Nora received nothing from the estate until after the war.

According to Giorgio, Nora spent a great deal of her time visiting the grave at Fluntern. A few Zurich friends stood by her. Evelyn Cotton, who had acted with the English Players, remained close, Ruggiero's wife would often take tea with her, and she was always welcome to dine free at the Kronenhalle. With Joyce's American publisher, Ben Huebsch, Maria Jolas set up a committee to raise funds for the remaining Joyces. And from England, Harriet managed to get a little money to Nora from time to time.

Three days after his brother's death, Stanislaus wrote to her, saying, 'I am so stunned by the blow myself that I can well imagine what a terrible shock it is for you and Georgie and I sympathize with you deeply and so does Nelly. She writes to me that she does nothing but cry. She liked James as she calls him, very much, although she had met him only twice.'[18] He was unable to leave Florence for the duration of the war, he said, but urged Giorgio to safeguard any papers his father might have left behind. The posthumous business of accumulating and securing Joyce's manuscripts and memorabilia had begun.

*

Grave no. 1449 was meant to be temporary, until Nora could get him repatriated to Ireland, and she asked Harriet to look into this. Harriet approached Count O'Kelly, the Irish chargé d'affaires in Paris, but the hostility to Joyce among Catholic clergy, scholars and politicians was so intense that the request was refused. Unlike Parnell and Yeats, for James Augustine Joyce there would be no triumphant return of remains to the Isle of Saints and Sages. Even in death the notorious apostate remained an outcast. Nora never forgave this refusal and rejected Eliot's suggestion that manuscripts of *Finnegans Wake* (in Harriet's care) be lodged at the National Library in Dublin. They went instead to the British Museum where his benefactress had spent time helping to research the book.

While Catholic opinion was antagonistic, and at his old schools, Clongowes and Belvedere, Joyce's death went unacknowledged, there was no hostility from the leading Irish papers. Arthur Power was phoned by the *Irish Times* requesting an obituary. 'The news came as a thunderbolt to me,' he wrote, 'and I turned away from the telephone with remorse and dismay. So much of my life in Paris had been bound up with him and Mrs Joyce, both of whom had given me a steady friendship as close as if I had been a member of the family,' and although their friendship had lessened over time he still recalled 'the memory of the fire which once warmed us both ...'[19]

Two days later, two more of his friends, Con Curran and Kenneth Reddin, published obituaries in the *Irish Times*. For Curran, Joyce was a towering figure both in Ireland and beyond. 'His later life belongs to world literature, where his influence has been as widespread, as profound and as disruptive as that of Picasso in painting. He was as great a master of English prose as Yeats was of English verse – that is to say, he was one of the two greatest figures in contemporary English literature.'[20] Reddin wanted to disabuse those who considered him a traitor to their island, arguing that, 'Joyce was worth half a dozen Irish legations in any country he had chosen to live in. All European writers knew of him, and he took care to let them know that he was Irish. In making Dublin famous he made Ireland famous in European letters.'[21] In *The Bell*, the Dublin-born Elizabeth Bowen made the case for repatriating Ireland's great literary exile. 'Let us strip from Joyce the exaggerations of foolish intellectual worship he got abroad, and the notoriety he got at home, and take him back to ourselves as a writer out of the Irish people, who received much from our tradition and was to hand on more.'[22]

The *Irish Press* interviewed Joyce's two closest sisters. Eileen said, 'They say he was anti-Catholic, but he never missed a service during all the Holy Weeks he spent with me in Trieste.' And Eva added that 'He always expressed his love of Dublin and of the Dublin people, and often said that he would love to live here again. However some people may criticize what he wrote, he was our eldest brother and our idol, and to us, at least, his writings had the stamp of genius. He had the kindest disposition . . .'[23]

In France he was eulogized as a great figure of European literature. The loftiest tribute came from André Gide, who wrote, 'Courage is finest when shown at the end of life. I admire it in Joyce as I admired it in Mallarmé, in Beethoven, and in a few rare artists, whose work ends as at the summit of a cliff, exposing the sheerest aspect of their genius to the future, without revealing the imperceptible steps by which they have attained this amazing light.'[24]

Not surprisingly, perhaps, a more censorious note was struck in puritanical England. The *TLS* obituarist came close to damning him with faint praise:

Ulysses may not be – we think it is not – the marvellous manifestation of genius acclaimed by the devotees, for occasional flashes of lightning, even such strange new flashes, are not sufficient reward for the weary reader's plod through acres of boredom and brain-sick words. But one thing these works established was that Joyce knew all about the art of writing. If one clear impression comes from the mass of obscurities in *Ulysses* it is that its author had read vastly and forgotten nothing.[25]

The Times began by citing 'extreme' opinions of Joyce's work – dismissive comments from Gosse, Arnold Bennett and Russell. It repeated the canard about him saying to Yeats, 'You are too old to be influenced by me,' and Yeats's comment, 'Never have I encountered so much pretension with so little to show for it.' While admitting grudgingly that *Ulysses* was 'intensely alive, fundamentally Irish, full of Rabelaisian "humour", with its highly developed sense of time and a fantastic imaginative facility', it also mentioned his 'failure to appreciate "the eternal and serene beauty of nature"', and the 'scabrous' nature of passages in the novel, and its 'many repellent or merely boring passages'.[26]

Both McGreevy and Eliot sent letters to *The Times* objecting to this obituary. Neither was printed. However, a revision of Eliot's letter was published by Cyril Connolly in the March number of *Horizon*. He began bluntly, 'I have read with stupefaction your obituary notice on the greatest man of letters of my generation.' He dismissed the view of older men such as Gosse as unimportant. 'To some of Joyce's younger contemporaries, like myself, *Ulysses* still seems the most considerable work of imagination in English in our time, comparable in importance (though in little else) with the work of Marcel Proust. I do not believe that posterity will be able to controvert this judgment, though it may be able to demonstrate the relative insignificance of the literary achievement of the whole period.' He objected to the contention that 'Joyce failed to appreciate "the eternal and serene beauty of nature"' which could, he argued, be disputed by reference to several passages in *A Portrait of the Artist*, *Ulysses* and *Finnegans Wake*. There were numerous passages in the obituary which were false, snobbish and misleading. 'I do not believe that your notice will much affect the world's opinion of Joyce,' he ended, 'but I fear lest it may be used as evidence by those who choose to believe that England has lost respect for that one of the arts for which it has been chiefly renowned.'[27]

American opinion was also mixed. Van Wyck Brooks, in *The Opinions of Oliver Allston*, saw him as 'James Joyce, the sick Irish Jesuit, whom Eliot described as orthodox, and who had done more than Eliot to destroy tradition'. The *New York Times* was more detached, sketching his life story and only hinting at an opinion by calling *Ulysses* 'his greatest work' and *Finnegans Wake* 'distinguished'. In *Poetry*, Thornton Wilder saw Joyce's greatest contribution being his use of the interior monologue. 'He alone has been able to suggest the apparent incoherence and triviality of this incessant woolgathering, and yet to impose upon it a coordination beyond itself, in art.'[28]

Any hope of Lucia getting out of Occupied France died with her father. Neither Nora nor Giorgio had that empathy or concern for her that her father nurtured. Four days after his death, on 17 January, Giorgio wrote to Maria Jolas, 'I hope Dr Delmas has not put Lucia in the street as needless to say I cannot pay him nor can I communicate with him.'[29] The abandonment of the girl by her mother and brother can perhaps be understood in the light of Giorgio's telling Richard Ellmann, 'My father spent all his money on Lucia.'[30] Nora's attitude towards her daughter is difficult to fathom. To Brenda Maddox, her biographer, it was one of enduring maternal concern; to Lucia's biographer, Shloss, it was enduring indifference. Maddox saw Giorgio as the villain who resented the money spent on his sister and influenced his mother against her; Shloss laid the neglect of Joyce's 'wonder wild' at the feet of them both.

Lucia herself, it seems, failed to come to terms with her father's death for a long time. When Nino Frank visited her at Pornichet, he recalled her saying of him, '*Cet imbécile, qu'est-ce qu'il fait sous la terre? Quand est-ce qu'il se décide à sortir? Il vous regarde tout le temps.*' ('That imbecile, what is he doing under the ground? When will he decided to leave? He's watching us all the time.') She was, as Frank remarked, Joyce's most Joycean offspring.[31]

The death of Joyce was followed shortly afterwards by that of his brother Charlie, who died of 'chronic fibroid tuberculosis' in hospital at St Albans on 18 January. Virginia Woolf (who had written so disapprovingly of *Ulysses* yet herself adopted the interior monologue Joyce had rediscovered), drowned herself on 31 March. Sir Horace Rumbold, cast as a hangman in *Ulysses*, died at the age of seventy-two quietly at his Wiltshire home on 24 May 1941, and Joyce's old Zurich adversary, Percy Bennett, died in Brighton in November 1943, aged seventy-seven. Henry Carr outlived them all, succumbing to a heart attack on a visit to London in 1962. He was seventy-four.

Nora, who became increasingly debilitated with arthritis, died in Zurich on 10 April 1951 of uraemic poisoning. As there was no room beside her husband in grave no. 1449, she was buried in a new grave some fifty yards away, according to the rites of the Catholic Church. In 1966, the Joyces were re-interred together in an *Ehrengrab*, a grave of honour, donated by the City of Zurich. It is marked by a statue of Joyce[32] – seated, spindly legs crossed, gazing sightlessly through pebble glasses into the 'far away'.

Following his divorce from Helen, Giorgio married Dr Asta Jahnke-Osterwalder, a Munich eye surgeon. He died aged seventy-one in Konstanz, West Germany, in 1976, and Asta followed in 1993. Both joined James and Nora in the family tomb. The 1981 Nobel Prize winner Elias Canetti is buried right next to him. That prize always was just out of Joyce's reach.

Lucia survived the war, during which Dr Delmas died, and returned to Ivry. In 1951 she was moved to St Andrew's hospital in Northampton where she had been a patient briefly in 1936. Over the following years she received visits from Beckett, Sylvia Beach, the Gilberts, Frank Budgen, Maria Jolas, Stanislaus's wife and son, Giorgio's adopted son and his second wife, and Harriet Weaver. Giorgio visited her once but chose not to return; his only communications thereafter were via birthday and Christmas cards.[33] As her condition was improved by modern drugs, she wrote poignant, if childlike, letters to friends such as Stuart Gilbert's wife Moune, in which she yearned for the life she had once enjoyed with her parents in France and said how desperately she missed them. Harriet acted as her guardian and, with the help of Fred Monro, administered Joyce's estate until her own death in 1961. Jane Lidderdale, Harriet's niece, succeeded her aunt as Lucia's guardian. Following a stroke, Lucia died at St Andrew's on 12 December 1982, aged seventy-four.

Stephen Joyce went to America in 1946 to live with the Kastors, returning to France later to marry and eventually take over as joint trustee of his grandfather's literary estate. After the war Stanislaus resumed his professorship in Trieste and continued living there until his death on 16 June 1955, the fifty-first anniversary of Bloomsday. He wrote and broadcast about his brother, and a book about their early days together, *My Brother's Keeper*, appeared after his death. A diary he had kept as a young man in Dublin, much of it about brother Jim, also appeared posthumously; his *Book of Days*, concerning their time together in Trieste, remains unpublished, as are two memoirs of the Joyces by Helen Fleischman Joyce, who recovered from her illness and died in 1964 aged seventy.

Paul Léon's destiny was perhaps the most tragic. Hearing that Joyce's landlord at the rue des Vignes was at last intending to auction the contents of his flat to recoup the unpaid rent, Léon alerted his brother-in-law Ponisovsky who had access to funds, and they succeeded in buying up all of Joyce's books and papers. At great risk to himself, a Jew in a Nazi-occupied city, Léon trundled the material through Paris in a pushcart to his own flat. He parcelled up the papers and delivered some to Count O'Kelly at the Irish Embassy for lodgement in the National Library of Ireland, with an injunction that they be left sealed for fifty years; the rest were stored with a Paris lawyer, Maître Charles Gervais. One day in August Beckett ran into Léon in the street, and was alarmed to see him walking openly in Paris when a new Nazi round-up of Jews was in progress. Léon said he would be leaving the next day, after his son had taken the baccalaureate. But that day, 21 August 1941, the Gestapo picked him up, and the following year he was shot as a Jew.

Of the other players in the cast, Joyce's sister 'Poppie' died aged eighty in 1964, Gogarty, his Dark Angel, died in 1957 aged seventy-nine, Adrienne Monnier committed suicide in 1955, aged sixty-three and Sylvia Beach died aged seventy-five in 1962. Stuart Gilbert reached eighty-two before dying in 1969, and Maria Jolas lived to be ninety-four, passing away in 1987. Ezra Pound, fully dedicated to Mussolini's Fascist Italy, began his 'treacherous' broadcasts on 23 January 1941, three of which dealt with Joyce and most appreciatively with *Ulysses*. He just avoided being tried and executed for treason in 1945. Instead he was declared legally insane and spent twelve years in a mental asylum in America before returning to Italy and dying there on 1 November 1972, aged eighty-seven.

Joyce in his many facets was as polymorphic and mercurial as any of his characters in *Finnegans Wake*. He passed through phases of Jesuitical piety, Parnellite nationalism, anti-bourgeois and anticlerical rebellion, socialism, intellectual aloofness and Ibsenite devotion. He was altar boy, classroom joker, young know-all, great operatic tenor manqué, a carousing 'medics' pal', a patron of brothels, *poète maudit*, exile, prurient lover, writer of licentious letters, 'undiscovered genius', fond father, failed businessman, temporary bank clerk, original language teacher, eccentric dancer, blind Dante, fighter against censorship and literary piracy, lyrical poet, opera buff, brave experimental writer of prodigious virtuosity and, finally, 'acclaimed genius'. But he was other things, too. He was brutally honest but highly manipulative, a social rebel who preferred the bourgeois life, a Catholic apostate who retained a strong affinity for the Church and its liturgy, an exile who never left Dublin, a maker of the future who lived in the past, a shy man who loved his fame. He took offence easily and rushed to litigate, heedless of consequences. Above all, he was extremely egocentric; others hardly existed for him, except to be used to serve his various needs, keep him in funds or provide material for his fiction. He could be heartless but also caring, as he was with his wife, daughter and dying father, and he was moved to help those who were threatened with Nazi persecution.

He was a man of extremes, capable of swinging from cultivated reserve to wild exuberance. When he wrote, all boundaries fell before the force and sweep of his imagination, but he could sink into solitary depression – becoming despairing and withdrawn. His mind was poised between excesses and gripped by a creative tension which gave him his impetus to write. From early childhood he was regarded as extraordinarily gifted, and as the precocious youth developed into the brilliant writer, he was soon acclaimed 'a genius' by those who admired him and a 'diabolical pornographer' by those who felt threatened by him. Beyond everything else, he had a gift and a passion for languages, and he turned an abundance of words into forms beyond poetry. Not only did he demonstrate a command of a wide range of literary styles, from Chaucer to modern slang, but was able also to create his own style, a style which has been immensely influential, emulated but never matched.

Notes

Abbreviations and short titles

Correspondents

AE = George Russell
CGJ = Carl Gustav Jung
EP = Ezra Pound
FB = Frank Budgen
GBS = George Bernard Shaw
GJ = Giorgio Joyce
GR = Grant Richards
HG = Herbert Gorman
HJ = Helen Joyce
HSW = Harriet Shaw Weaver
JJ = James Joyce
JQ = John Quinn
JSJ = John Stanislaus Joyce
LJ = Lucia Joyce
MC = Mary Colum
NB = Nora Barnacle
NJ = Nora Joyce
PC = Padraic Colum
PH = Patricia Hutchins
PL = Paul Léon
RM = Robert McAlmon
SB = Sylvia Beach
SG = Stuart Gilbert
SJ = Stanislaus Joyce
TSE = T. S. Eliot
WBY = William Butler Yeats

Joyce's Works

CM = *Chamber Music*
SH = *Stephen Hero*
Portrait = *A Portrait of the Artist as a Young Man*
FW = *Finnegans Wake*
PP = *Pomes Penyeach*
CW = *Critical Writings*
P & SW = *Poems and Shorter Writings*, ed. Richard Ellmann, A. Walton Litz and John Whittier-Fergusson (1991)

Other Books Consulted

Beach = Beach, Sylvia, *Shakespeare and Company* (1957)
Budgen = Budgen, Frank, *James Joyce and the Making of 'Ulysses'* (1972)
Byrne = Byrne, J. F., *Silent Years* (1953)
Colums = Colum, Mary and Padraic, *Our Friend James Joyce* (1958)
Costello = Costello, Peter, *James Joyce: The Years of Growth 1882–1915* (1994)
Curran = Curran, Constantine P., *Joyce Remembered* (1968)
Ellmann = Ellmann, Richard, *James Joyce* (1982)
Ferris = Ferris, Kathleen, *James Joyce and the Burden of Disease* (1995)
Gilbert, Paris Journal = Gilbert, Stuart, *Reflections on James Joyce: Stuart Gilbert's Paris Journal* (1993)
Gorman = Gorman, Herbert, *James Joyce* (1941)
Jackson and Costello = Jackson, John Wyse, and Peter, Costello, *John Stanislaus Joyce* (1999)
Maddox = Maddox, Brenda, *Nora* (1988)
MBK = Joyce, Stanislaus, *My Brother's Keeper* (1958)
McCourt = McCourt, John, *The Years of Bloom* (2000)
Mikhail = Mikhail, E. H., *James Joyce: Interviews and Recollections* (1990)
NLI Book = *James Joyce–Paul Léon Papers*, National Library of Ireland, Dublin (1992)
O'Connor = O'Connor, Ulick, *The Joyce We Knew* (2004)
Potts = Potts, Willard (ed.), *Portraits of the Artist in Exile* (1979)

Power = Power, Arthur, *Conversations with James Joyce* (1974)

Rodgers = Rodgers, W. R. (ed.) *Irish Literary Portraits* (1972)

SB Letters = Banta, Melissa, and Oscar Silverman (eds), *James Joyce's Letters to Sylvia Beach 1921–1940* (1992)

Sheehy = Sheehy, Eugene, *May it Please the Court* (1951)

Shloss = Shloss, Carol Loeb, *Lucia* (2003)

Sullivan = Sullivan, Kevin, *Joyce Among the Jesuits* (1967)

Library and Archive Sources

BL = British Library, London (Weaver Collection)

Cornell = Cornell University, Ithaca, NY.

HRC = Harry Ransom Research Center, Austin, Texas.

National Archives = National Archives, Kew, England

NLI = National Library of Ireland, Dublin.

NYPL = New York Public Library

SIU = Southern Illinois University, Carbondale

TCDL = Trinity College Dublin Library

Tulsa = University of Tulsa, Oklahoma

Preface

1. 'Odysseus' is the Greek original of the Latin 'Ulysses'.
2. Jackson and Costello, *John Stanislaus Joyce*; Maddox, *Nora*; Shloss, *Lucia*.
3. He did in an early undergraduate essay describing a painting write about 'a well clad Jew' with 'that horrible cast of countenance, so common among the sweaters of modern Israel' with bared teeth and 'snarl of malice'. But this perception of Jews hardly survived for long.

1: Past Imperfect (1800–1882)

1. Jackson and Costello: 4.
2. To J. B. Pinker, 29 July 1918, *Letters I*: 115.
3. Costello: 36.

4. Jackson and Costello: 28.
5. *MBK*: 23.
6. Jackson and Costello: 39.
7. *Ibid.*: 40.
8. *Ibid.*: 379.
9. *Ibid.*: 265.
10. 'Interview with Mr John Stanislaus Joyce [Joyce's father]', in Maria Jolas (ed.), *A James Joyce Yearbook*, Transition Books, Paris, 1949: 159–69.
11. *Ulysses*: 107.
12. Ferris: 125.
13. Jackson and Costello: 101 and *Who Was Who*.
14. Gilbert, *James Joyce's 'Ulysses'*: 211–12. This passage, Gilbert admitted, was dictated to him by Joyce.
15. Costello: 48.
16. Beckett to Ellmann 1953, Tulsa.
17. *Dubliners*: 187.
18. *A James Joyce Yearbook*, ed. Maria Jolas: 162.
19. Costello: 28–9.
20. *Dubliners*: 175–225; *Ulysses*: 205, 781.
21. Alf Bergan to Ellmann, Tulsa.
22. *Ulysses*: 540.
23. *Portrait*: 32.

2: The Dawn of Consciousness (1882–1888)

1. *Portrait*: 7.
2. From JSJ, 16 May 1909, *Letters II*: 228.
3. *Portrait*: 7.
4. To NB, 23 December 1909, *Letters II*: 279.
5. *Portrait*: 347.
6. Eva Joyce in Rodgers: 35.
7. *SH*: 126.
8. *FW*: 468.
9. *Ibid.*: 361.
10. 'Ireland at the Bar', *CW*: 198; *Ulysses*: 691.
11. *Portrait*: 184.
12. *Ibid.*: 24.
13. Probably the Joyce children's version of 'Auntie'.

14. *Portrait*: 7.
15. Jackson and Costello: 131; 422.
16. *MBK*: 7.
17. *Portrait*: 7.
18. *Ibid.*: 10.
19. *MBK*: 7.
20. One of Danby's best-known paintings is *The Departure of Ulysses from Ithaca*.
21. *MBK*: 18.
22. *FW*: 62.
23. Jackson and Costello: 130.
24. The Dublin City Public Library was opened in 1884.
25. *Ulysses*: 82.
26. *MBK*: 44–5.
27. E.g. the Ugly Duckling in 'Grace', Humpty-Dumpty in *Ulysses* and *FW*.
28. *MBK*: 23.
29. Bergan to Ellmann, Tulsa.
30. *MBK*: 23.
31. *Portrait*: 7–8.
32. *ibid*.
33. Eileen Vance to Ellmann, 28 December 1953, Tulsa.

3: Willingly to School (1888–1893)

1. *Portrait*: 9.
2. *Ibid.*: 21.
3. Lieut. Col. P. R. Butler to Ellmann, September 1953, Tulsa.
4. *Portrait*: 8.
5. Sullivan: 14.
6. *Ulysses*: 149.
7. *Portrait*: 12.
8. *SH*: 209.
9. *Portrait*: 43.
10. *Ibid.*: 49.
11. *Ibid.*: 24.
12. *Ibid.*: 42.
13. *MBK*: 35–6.
14. Jackson and Costello: 308.
15. *MBK*: 36.
16. *Portrait*: 15.
17. *Ibid.*: 64.
18. *Ibid.*: 22.
19. *Ibid.*: 31.
20. Jackson and Costello: 158–9.
21. Costello: 104.
22. *Portrait*: 65.
23. *MBK*: 45.
24. *Portrait*: 48.
25. Bradley, *James Joyce's Schooldays*: 74.
26. *FW*: 226.
27. To Mrs William Murray, 22 December 1922, *SL*: 199.
28. *FW*: 201.
29. Costello: 117.
30. *Ulysses*: 325.
31. Ulick O'Connor, *Oliver St John Gogarty*: 38.
32. *Ulysses*: 871.
33. *P & SW*: 165.
34. *Portrait*: 66.
35. Conmee eventually became Principal of the Jesuit Order in Ireland.
36. Rodgers: 56.

4: Belvedere: In the Arms of the Jesuits (1893–1898)

1. *MBK*: 17.
2. To HSW, 17 January 1932, *Letters I*: 312.
3. *Ulysses*: 286.
4. Sullivan: 23–8.
5. *SH*: 28.
6. Sheehy: 3.
7. 'Trust Not Appearances,' *CW*: 15.
8. *SH*: 28.
9. *Portrait*: 83.
10. *MBK*: 29.
11. *Ulysses*: 617 (The implication in this quotation and other parts of *Ulysses* that Dodd was a Jew is false. In the Irish Census of 1911, he and his family are all listed as Catholics.)
12. *Ibid.*: 232. (Even more intense is Bloom's mind dwelling on the odours of women's bodies following his 'climactic' fantasy over Gerty MacDowell in the 'Nausicca' episode)

13. Power, *Conversations*: 93.
14. William Fallon in O'Connor: 47. Fallon claims to have seen Joyce arrive late at the fête.
15. Ellmann: 41.
16. *SH*: 65; *Ulysses*: 782.
17. Ellmann: 45–6.
18. Eileen Schaureck to Ellmann, 27 June 1953, Tulsa.
19. Fallon in O'Connor, *The Joyce We Knew*: 43.
20. *MBK*: 70.
21. SJ, *Dublin Diary*: 106.
22. *MBK*: 74–5.
23. *Portrait*: 125.
24. Patrick Butler to Ellmann, September 1953, Tulsa.
25. *MBK*: 82, Elizabeth J. Boyd, 'James Joyce's Hell-Fire Sermons', *Modern Language Notes*, vol. 75 (Nov. 1960): 561–71.
26. *MBK*: 75.
27. *Portrait*: 154; Ellmann: 42.
28. Gorman: 46.
29. *MBK*: 90. Arthur Symons published a book of poems called *Silhouettes* in 1892.
30. *Ibid.*: 124–5.
31. *Ibid.*: 21.
32. *Ibid.*: 56.
33. Colums: 49.
34. Byrne in Mikhail: 3.
35. In 1954 Dodd sued the BBC for broadcasting a reading of *Ulysses* which included references to him. He won an award of £950 plus costs of £1,746 1s 4d.
36. Eugene Sheehy in O'Connor: 15.
37. Eugene Sheehy to Ellmann, 25 June 1953, Tulsa.
38. *MBK*: 59.
39. *Portrait*: 69–70.
40. Sheehy: 8.
41. Ellmann: 56; Felix Hackett to Ellmann, Tulsa.
42. *Portrait*: 155–6.
43. *Ulysses*: 658.
44. To HSW, 17 January 1932, *Letters I*: 312.
45. To Alf Bergan, 25 May 1937, NYPL.

5: Cultivating 'the Enigma of a Manner' (1898–1899)

1. Gogarty in Rodgers: 33.
2. *Ulysses*: 263.
3. To Henrik Ibsen, 8 March 1901, *Letters I*: 52.
4. *SH*: 42.
5. *Ibid.*: 30.
6. *Ibid.*: 32.
7. *MBK*: 17.
8. J. F. Byrne: 43–4.
9. Sheehy: 23.
10. Ellmann: 52.
11. Colums: 67.
12. Mary Sheehy to Ellmann, Tulsa.
13. *SH*: 131.
14. Colums: 13.
15. 'Force', *CW*: 17.
16. *Ibid.*: 23–4.
17. SJ, 'Early James Joyce', *Listener*, 26 May 1949: 897.
18. *Ulysses*: 266–7.
19. *MBK*: 238.
20. May Joyce Monaghan in Mikhail: 183.
21. *Portrait*: 159.
22. *MBK*: 238.
23. To NB, 29 August 1904, *Letters II*: 48.
24. Eileen Schaurek in Rodgers: 35.
25. *Ibid.*
26. *MBK*: 87.
27. To NB, 29 August 1904, *Letters II*: 48.
28. Hutchins, *James Joyce's World*: 47.
29. 'Interview with Mr John Stanislaus Joyce', *A James Joyce Yearbook*: 169.
30. Ellmann says 11 February.
31. *Daily Express*, 16 May 1902.
32. WBY, 'Who Goes With Fergus?', *Countess Cathleen*, Act 2.
33. Sheehy in O'Connor: 18.
34. Curran: 3–4.
35. *Ibid.*: 4.
36. *Ibid.*: 34–5.

6: Making a Reputation (1900–1902)

1. 'Drama and Life', *CW*: 38–45.
2. *SH*: 38.
3. 'Drama and Life', *CW*: 45.
4. To Henrik Ibsen, 8 March 1901, *Letters I*: 51–2.
5. Quoted in Colums: 26.
6. *MBK*: 128–9.
7. Parandowsky in Potts: 147.
8. Scholes, *The Cornell Joyce Collection*.
9. Byrne: 63.
10. *SH*: 29.
11. Colums: 24.
12. *MBK*: 97.
13. *Ibid.*
14. Power: 64.
15. 'Ireland: Island of Saints and Sages', *CW*: 165.
16. *The Times*, 5 April 1900: 10.
17. *MBK*: 96.
18. *Ibid.*: 115.
19. From William Archer, 23 April 1900, *Letters II*: 7.
20. To William Archer, 28 April 1900, *Letters II*: 7.
21. The only D'Annunzio play in which Duse appeared that season at the Lyceum was *La Gioconda*, not *La Città Morta*, as some have claimed.
22. *Portrait*: 159.
23. *SH*: 177–8. In the last chapter of *A Portrait*, in Stephen's diary entry for 15 April, he encounters a girl, who might be Emma, with whom he has a friendly conversation about his future plans and she wishes him well. If this *was* Emma, it raises the possibility that the street encounter and his propositioning of her was more fantasy than reality.
24. From William Archer, 15 September 1900, *Letters II*: 8.
25. Curran: 15.
26. *Ibid.*: 41.
27. *Freeman's Journal*, 9 January 1901.
28. *The Times*, 19 January 1899.
29. Ellmann: 63.
30. Colums: 38.
31. Gogarty in Mikhail: 22.
32. From William Archer, c.15 September 1901, *Letters I*: 10–11.
33. *P & SW*: 77; *MBK*: 119.
34. To Henrik Ibsen, 8 March 1901, *Letters I*: 52.
35. 'The Holy Office', *CW*: 152.
36. *Ulysses*: 545.
37. *Portrait*: 224.
38. *MBK*: 215.
39. *Dubliners*: 103.
40. Padraic Colum in Colums: 19; O'Connor: 65.
41. 'The Day of the Rabblement', *CW*: 70.
42. *Ulysses*: 179–83.
43. *SH*: 135.
44. *FW*: 180.
45. Power: 42.
46. Colums: 26.
47. *MBK*: 163.
48. *Freeman's Journal*, 2 February 1902. Quoted in Meenan, *Centenary History of the Literary and Historical Society of University College, Dublin 1855–1955* (1957): 85.
49. William D'Arcy to Ellmann, 5 December 1959, Tulsa.
50. *P & SW*: 180.
51. *MBK*: 136.
52. Byrne: 87.
53. *SH*: 124.
54. Costello: 177.
55. D'Arcy to Ellmann, 16 June 1964, Tulsa.
56. *SH*: 62.
57. Soupault to Ellmann, July 1953, Tulsa.
58. Sheehy: 18–19. Sheehy is wrong. Hamlet's words on killing Polonius are 'Thou wretched, rash, intruding fool, farewell!' On dragging away his body he says: ' . . . this counsellor/Is now most still, most secret and most grave,/Who was in life a foolish prating knave./Come, sir, to draw toward an end with you' (*Hamlet*, Act III, Sc IV). In Act II, Sc II, as Polonius leaves him he does comment, 'these tedious old fools.'

59. Thomas Kettle, review of *Chamber Music*, *Freeman's Journal*, 1 June 1907.

60. Gerald Griffin, *The Wild Geese* (London, Jerrolds, 1938): 24.

7: An Uncertain future (1902)

1. To Mrs John Stanislaus Joyce, 20 March 1903, *Letters II*: 38, *SL*: 20.

2. AE To WBY, [?11 August 1902], *Letters II*: 11–12.

3. AE to Sarah Purser, 15 August 1902, *Letters II*: 12.

4. Ellmann: 100.

5. *Ulysses*: 178.

6. *Letters from AE*, ed. Alan Denison (New York: Abelard Schumann, 1961): 50.

7. Ellmann: 98.

8. From AE, [early October 1902], *Letters II*: 13.

9. WBY, quoted by Ellmann in *Eminent Domain* (Oxford University Press, 1967), simply says 'in the street'.

10. AE to WBY, [early October] 1902, 'Some Characters of the Irish Literary Movement', quoted by Ellmann: 100.

11. WBY quoted by Ellmann, *The Identity of Yeats*: 86.

12. Ellmann: 101, n. discusses this story.

13. From WBY, 18 December 1902, and [October? 1902], *Letters II*: 24, 13.

14. Ellmann, *The Identity of Yeats*: 86.

15. *CW*: 71, n. 1.

16. *Ulysses*: 277.

17. *MBK*: 174.

18. Colums: 13–14.

19. D'Arcy to Ellmann, 20 February 1960.

20. Bergan interview with Niall Sheridan.

21. SJ, *Dublin Diary*, [29 September 1904]: 105.

22. Gogarty in Rodgers: 34.

23. *MBK*: 114.

24. Colums: 64.

25. To Lady Gregory, [November 1902],

Letters I: 53, *SL*: 8.

26. From WBY, 3 November 1902, *Letters II*: 14.

27. Gonne's marriage was stormy and soon ended.

28. From Lady Gregory, [?23 November 1902], *Letters II*: 15.

29. From T. C. Harrington, 29 November 1902, *Letters II*: 17–18.

8: 'Sinister genius' (1902–1903)

1. *FW*: 192.

2. Herbert Hughes (ed.), *Joyce Book* (London, The Sylvan Press, 1932): 79.

3. From W. B. Yeats to Lady Gregory, [4 December 1902], *Letters II*: 17, n.1.

4. To his family in Dublin, [6 December 1902], *Letters II*: 19.

5. Joyce calls him Eugene Routh. Probably Harold Victor Routh (1878–1951), educated at Cambridge University (Classics) and the Sorbonne (French); later Reader in English at London University.

6. Gorman: 100.

7. *MBK*: 200.

8. Gorman: 104.

9. *P & SW*: 193.

10. SJ to Ellmann, 1954, Tulsa.

11. To Mrs JSJ, [15 December 1903], *Letters II*: 21; Ellmann 1959: 118.

12. *Dubliners*: 72.

13. From Mrs JSJ, [?18 December 1902], *Letters II*: 22.

14. From WBY, 18 December 1902, *Letters II*: 23.

15. To Lady Gregory, 21 December 1902, *Letters II*: 22.

16. Stanislaus had Joyce's first meeting with Gogarty at the National Library. Gogarty insisted they had met earlier on a Dublin tram.

17. From Mrs JSJ, 2 March 1903, *Letters II*: 32.

18. Gogarty in Rodgers: 26.

19. Gogarty, *As I Was Going Down Sackville Street*: 299.

20. *Portrait*: 97.
21. Sheehy: 30–1.
22. *Ulysses*: 30.
23. *Portrait*: 160.
24. From JSJ, 31 January 1903, *Letters II*: 27.
25. *The Times*, 11 February 1903.
26. From Maud Gonne, February 1903 (Cornell), quoted in *MBK*: 199.
27. The marriage lasted barely three months. McBride, a violent man, later met a violent death – shot in Dublin's Kilmainham Jail after the 1916 Easter Uprising.
28. From Gogarty, [21 February 1903], quoted in Lyons, *James Joyce and Medicine*: 56–7.
29. To SJ, 8 February 1903, *Letters II*: 28, *SL*: 14; Ellmann 1959: 125.
30. To JSJ, 26 February 1903, *Letters II*: 30–1, *SL*: 15.
31. From Mrs SJS, 2 March 1903, *Letters II*: 32.
32. To SJ, 9 March 1903, *Letters II*: 35, *SL*: 17; Ellmann 1959: 129.
33. Gorman: 102.
34. Power: 33.
35. *Ulysses*: 784.
36. To SJ, 9 March 1903, *Letters II*: 35; Ellmann 1959: 125.
37. From Mrs JSJ, 19 March 1903, *Letters II*: 36–7.
38. To Mrs JSJ, 20 March 1903, *Letters II*: 37, *SL*: 18.
39. Quoted in Ulick O'Connor, *Oliver St John Gogarty*, 1981 edn: 30.
40. *Ulysses*: 8.
41. To Mrs JSJ, 20 March 1903, *Letters II*: 38; *SL*: 18–20; Ellmann 1959: 125.
42. Ben Jonson, 'As bright as is the Sun her Sire', Ben Jonson, *Dramatic Works and Lyrics*, Selected by John Addington Symonds (Walter Scott, London, 1886).
43. J. M. Synge to Lady Gregory, 26 March 1903, quoted in Ellmann: 125.
44. To Mrs JSJ, 20 March 1903, *Letters II*: 38.
45. From JSJ, 10 April 1903, *Letters II*: 41 n. 1.
46. *Ulysses*: 265.
47. *P & SW*: 194.

9: A Death in the Family (1903–1904)

1. Cirrhosis may lead to cancer of the liver, and Joyce even states this in a letter he later wrote to Nora Barnacle, but that is not evident from her death certificate.
2. *Ulysses*: 265.
3. From 'May' Joyce, 1 September 1916, *Letters II*: 383.
4. Ellmann: 129.
5. WBY to Lady Gregory, late April 1903, *Letters of W. B. Yeats*, ed. Allan Wade: 399.
6. Colums: 36.
7. W. J. Lawrence, quoted by Jorn Barger on Internet Timeline of Joyce's life, September 2000 (updated May 2001).
8. Francini Bruni in Potts: 33, Maria Jolas to Ellmann, 23 July, 1953, Tulsa.
9. *MBK*: 231.
10. *Ibid.*: 233.
11. *Ibid.*: 151.
12. Poem XII in *Chamber Music*.
13. *Ulysses*: 4.
14. *MBK*: 233.
15. *Ulysses*: 8.
16. To NB, 29 August 1904, *Letters II*: 48; Ellmann: 129.
17. *MBK*: 240.
18. *Ibid.*: 238.
19. *Ibid.*: 235.
20. *Ibid.*: 236–7.
21. *Ibid.*: 236.
22. *Ibid.*: 238.
23. *Ibid.*: 248.
24. *Ibid.*: 245.
25. SJ, *Dublin Diary*, [1903]: 1.
26. From Gogarty, 22 May 1904, quoted in Lyons, *James Joyce and Medicine*: 60–1.
27. In his *Mourning Becomes Mrs*

Spendlove, Oxford University Press, 1948, Gogarty claims that Joyce got the title from Jenny kicking her chamber-pot while changing behind a screen into some purloined undies of the sort that fascinated Joyce: 55.

28. Ellmann: 131.
29. *MBK*: 3–4.
30. *Ibid.*: 247–8.
31. *Ibid.*: 120.
32. SJ, *Dublin Diary*, [2 February 1904]: 12.
33. From Gogarty, early 1904, Cornell Catalogue: 528.
34. SJ's *Dublin Diary*, 29 February 1904: 13.
35. *Ibid.*: 14.
36. *Ibid.*: 15.
37. From Gogarty, [10 March 1904], quoted in J. B. Lyons, *Joyce and Medicine*: 59–60.
38. From Gogarty, 23 March 1904, quoted in *ibid.*: 61.
39. *Chamber Music*, VII.
40. Eglinton in Rodgers: 32.
41. To NB, [late July? 1904], *SL*: 44.
42. SJ, *Dublin Diary*, 29 March 1904: 21.

10: Nora (1904)

1. Colums: 36.
2. Griffin, *The Wild Geese*: 26.
3. Curran in Rodgers: 30.
4. Gorman: 122.
5. It seems likely that Joyce retrieved it and left it in Trieste with all the other material which Stanislaus still held at his brother's death. It was sold at Sotheby's on 8 July 2004 for £12,000.
6. From Curran, 17 May 1904, *Cornell Catalogue*: 470.
7. *Joseph Holloway's Abbey Theatre*, ed. Robert Hogan and Michael J. O'Neill (SIU Press, 1967): 40.
8. Maddox: 36.
9. *FW*: 139.
10. Jacques Mercanton in Potts: 238.

11. To NB, 15 June 1904, *Letters II*: 42; Ellmann 1959, 162.
12. *Ulysses*: 93.
13. The question of which of these inspired the story is discussed in Maddox: 28.
14. To NB, 7 August 1909, *Letters II*: 232.
15. To NB, 8 July 1904, *Letters II*: 43; Ellmann 1959: 165.
16. *Ulysses*: 279.
17. Vera Esposito Dockrell to Ellmann, 3 May 1955, Tulsa.
18. To Curran, 23 June 1904, *Letters I*: 55.
19. To SJ, 18 [September] 1905, *Letters II*: 108.
20. Scholes, *The Workshop of Daedalus*: 93.
21. D'Arcy to Ellmann, 26 March 1960, Tulsa. Some consider D'Arcy unreliable. The Irish Census shows Alfred H. and Marion Hunter living in Lower Mount Street in 1901, and in Great Charles Street in 1911. The 1904 Thorn's Directory of Dublin has an Albert (Hugh) Hunter at 28 Ballybough Road and an Alfred H. Hunter living at 'Glenvar', Howth Road, Clontarf.
22. To Constantine Curran, 23 June 1904, *Letters I*: 55.
23. Curran: 49–50.
24. To Curran, 3 July 1904, *Letters I*: 55.
25. Jackson and Costello: 269.
26. SJ, *Dublin Diary*, [18 July 1904]: 169.
27. *Ibid.*, [31 July 1904]: 46.
28. *Ibid.*, [6 August 1904]: 60.
29. *Chamber Music*, XVII.
30. 'The Holy Office', *CW*: 149.
31. SJ, *Dublin Diary*, [13 August 1904]: 51.
32. *Ulysses*: 115.
33. Holloway Diary, 27 August 1904, NLI.
34. To NB, 29 August 1904, *Letters II*: 48; Ellmann 1959: 174.
35. *Ibid.*
36. SJ, *Dublin Diary*, [13 August 1904]: 56.

37. *Ibid.*, [13 August 1904]: 55.
38. Gogarty in Mikhail: 25.
39. Quoted by Ellmann: 172–3.
40. From NB, 16 September 1904, *Letters II*: 54.
41. Byrne: 148.
42. In March 1905, Joyce returned Skeffington 'his two guineas', *Letters II*: 85.
43. To James Starkey, [8 October 1904], *Letters II*: 49.
44. Costello: 235.
45. *Portrait*: 223 (Ellmann points out that Stephen's famous commitment to 'silence, exile and cunning' is his interpretation of the Carthusian motto of the protagonist in Balzac's *The Country Doctor*: 'Fuge ... Late ... Tace.')
46. *Portrait*: 229.
47. Griffin, *The Wild Geese*: 24.

11: Birds of Passage (1904–1905)

1. Maddox: 79.
2. To NB, 3 December 1909, *SL*: 182.
3. To SJ, 11 October 1904, *Letters II*: 65, *SL*: 40.
4. Franz K. Stanzel, 'Austria's Surveillance of Joyce in Pola, Trieste and Zurich', *James Joyce Quarterly*, Vol. 38, 3/4, Spring/Summer, 2001: 361–71.
5. McCourt: 9.
6. To HSW, 11 March 1931, quoted by Alessandro Francini Bruni in Potts: 3.
7. Alessandro Francini Bruni in Potts: 11.
8. SJ, 'Memories of James Joyce', *Listener*, 26 May 1949: 896.
9. To SJ, 3 December 1904, *Letters II*: 73.
10. To Mrs William Murray, New Year's Eve 1904, *Letters I*: 57.
11. Francini Bruni says Horthy came to be taught French; Amalija Globočnik, a fellow Berlitz teacher, said he did not attend the Berlitz but that she taught him Croatian privately.
12. *Ulysses*: 777–8.
13. To SJ, 19 November 1904, *Letters II*: 71; To JSJ, 10 November 1904, *Letters II*: 69, *SL*: 42–3.
14. *Chamber Music*, XII and XVI.
15. To SJ, 19 November 1904, *Letters II*: 71.
16. To SJ, 28 December 1904, *Letters II*: 75.
17. To Mrs William Murray, New Year's Eve 1904, *Letters I*: 57.
18. To SJ, 28 December 1904, *Letters II*: 76.
19. To SJ, 7 February 1905, *Letters I*: 79.
20. To SJ, [?2 or 3 May 1905], *Letters II*: 89, *SL*: 60.
21. To Mrs Josephine Murray, New Year's Eve 1904, *Letters I*: 58, *SL*: 49.
22. *SH*: 27.
23. To SJ, 28 February 1905, *Letters II*: 84, *SL*: 56.
24. To SJ, 13 January 1905, *Letters II*: 76, *SL*: 50.

12: At a Crossroads (1905–1906)

1. Ibsen, speech in Copenhagen, 1898.
2. To NB, 7 September 1909, *Letters II*: 249, *SL*: 170.
3. To SJ, 15 March 1905, *Letters II*: 85, *SL*: 58.
4. To SJ, 4 April 1905, *Letters II*: 87, *SL*: 59.
5. To SJ, pmk 11 June 1905, *Letters II*: 91, *SL*: 63.
6. To SJ, [?2 or 3 May 1905], *Letters II*: 89, *SL*: 61.
7. To SJ, 12 July 1905, *Letters II*: 94, *SL*: 63.
8. From SJ, 31 July 1905, *Letters II*: 103.
9. To SJ, 12 July 1905, *Letters II*: 95, *SL*: 66.
10. *Chamber Music*, XVIII.
11. To SJ, 12 July 1905, *Letters II*: 96, *SL*: 67.
12. To SJ, 19 July 1905, *Letters II*: 99.

13. From SH, 29 July 1905, *Letters II*: 102.
14. SJ, Trieste Diary, 19 April 1908 (quoted in McCourt: 240).
15. To SJ, 18 [September] 1905, *Letters II*: 107.
16. To William Heinemann, 23 September 1905, *Letters II*: 109.
17. To SJ, 18 [September] 1905, *Letters II*: 107.
18. Ellmann: 215.
19. Maddox: 94; McCourt: 63.
20. To GR, 26 April 1906, *Letters I*: 60–1.
21. To GR, 5 May 1906, *Letters II*: 134, *SL*: 83.
22. From GR, 10 May 1906, *Letters II*: 139n.
23. To GR, 13 May 1906, *Letters II*: 137.
24. To GR, 20 May 1906, *Letters I*: 62–3, *SL*: 88.
25. To GR, 23 June 1906, *Letters I*: 64, *SL*: 89.
26. McCourt: 41.

13: The Conception of *Ulysses* (1906–1907)

1. To SJ, 31 July 1906, *Letters II*: 145.
2. To SJ, 2 August 1906, *Letters II*: 145.
3. To SJ, 7 August 1906, *Letters II*: 146.
4. To SJ, 6 September 1906, *Letters II*: 157.
5. To SJ, c. 12 August 1906, *Letters II*: 148.
6. To SJ, 19 August 1906, *Letters II*: 151.
7. To SJ, 16 August 1906, *Letters II*: 150.
8. Notes to *Exiles*, Tulsa.
9. To SJ, 31 August 1906, *Letters II*: 154. (*Orco Dio* translates as 'God is an ogre'.)
10. From GR, 24 September 1906, *Letters II*: 168, n. 1.
11. From GR, 26 October 1906, *Letters II*: 185, n. 1.
12. To SJ, 6 November 1906, *Letters II*: 187.
13. *Exiles*: 125.
14. To SJ, 13 November 1906, *Letters II*: 189–94.
15. Symons to Mathews, 8 October 1906, *James Joyce Quarterly*, vol. 23, no. 1 (Fall, 1985): 12–13.
16. To SJ, 7 December 1906, *Letters II*: 202.
17. To SJ, 13 November 1906, *Letters II*: 190.
18. *Ibid.*: 191–2.
19. To SJ, 3 December 1906, *Letters II*: 200.
20. *Ibid.*: 198.
21. To SJ, pmk 10 January 1907, *Letters II*: 206.
22. SJ, Trieste Diary, 16 January 1907, unpublished, Ellmann papers, Tulsa.
23. Georges Borach, 'Conversations with James Joyce', *College English*, 1954, 15: 326.
24. See Danis Rose, *A Reader's Ulysses* (London: Picador 1998), 1997: xxxi.
25. To SJ, 12 February 1907, *Letters II*: 212.
26. To SJ, 11 February 1907, *Letters II*: 213.
27. To SJ, 16 February 1907, *Letters II*: 215.
28. *Letters II*: 183, n. 8.
29. To SJ, [?1 March 1907], *Letters II*: 217.
30. SJ, Trieste Diary, 3 March 1907 (quoted in McCourt).

14: Going Freelance in Trieste (1907–1909)

1. SJ, Trieste Diary 7 March 1907 (quoted in McCourt).
2. SJ, Trieste Diary, 6 April 1907.
3. *Ibid.*
4. *Ibid.*
5. *Ibid.*: 17 and 19 April 1907.
6. From JSJ, 24 April 1907, *Letters II*: 221.
7. Arthur Symons, review, 'A Book of Songs,' *Nation* I, no.17 (22 June 1907): 639.
8. Thomas Kettle, review, *Freeman's Journal* (11 June 1907): n. p.

9. McCourt: 123.
10. SJ, Trieste Diary: 26 August 1907.
11. From Mrs William Murray, 29 July 1907, Cornell.
12. Colums: 227; SJ, Trieste Diary, 26 August 1907.
13. SJ, Trieste Diary, 16 August 1907. Ellmann says December, McCourt gives 16 August.
14. SJ to Ellmann, 1954, Tulsa.
15. SJ, Trieste Diary, 20 September 1907.
16. To GR, 15 October 1905, *Letters II*: 123.
17. Power: 98.
18. *Dubliners*: 225. See Brett Hart's description of a snowfall in the Californian Sierras in *Gabriel Conroy*, which gave Joyce the name of its sad protagonist.
19. SJ, Introduction to Svevo, *As a Man Grows Older*, trans. Beryl de Zoete. (Schmitz, although born and brought up Jewish, converted to Catholicism when he married his cousin, Livia Veneziani.)
20. SJ, Trieste Diary, 21 September 1907.
21. *Ibid.*: 10 November 1907.
22. *Ibid.*: 15 December 1907.
23. *Ibid.*: 2 January 1908.
24. *Ibid.*: 12 October 1908.
25. *Ibid.*: 18 November 1908.
26. To Margaret Joyce, 8 December 1908, *Letters II*: 227.
27. SJ, 'The Meeting of Svevo and Joyce', *Joyce in Svevo's Garden*: 73.
28. SJ, Intro to Svevo, *As a Man Grows Older*: v.
29. From Ettore Schmitz, 8 February 1909, *Letters II*: 227.
30. 'Oscar Wilde: The Poet of *"Salomé"*', *CW*: 201–5.
31. Quoted in McCourt: 155; see also G. K. Chesterton, 'The Futurist'.
32. From JSJ, 16 May 1909, *Letters II*: 228.

15: The Exile's Return (1909–1910)

1. Gogarty in Mikhail: 31.
2. To SJ, 4 August 1909, *Letters II*: 230–1.
3. Byrne: 156–7.
4. To SJ, 16 August 1909, *Letters II*: 234.
5. To NB, 19 August 1909, *Letters II*: 235.
6. To NB, 22 August 1909, *Letters II*: 239.
7. Holloway Diary, 8 September 1909, NLI.
8. *CW*: 208.
9. To NB, 31 August 1909, *Letters II*: 242.
10. To NB, 2 September 1909, *Letters II*: 243.
11. To NB, 3 September 1909, *Letters II*: 246.
12. To NB, 5 September 1909, *Letters II*: 248.
13. To NB, 7 September 1909, *Letters II*: 249.
14. To SJ, 7 September 1909, *Letters II*: 250–1.
15. To Carlo Linati, 10 December 1919, *Letters II*: 272.
16. To NB, [?25 October 1909], *Letters II*: 254.
17. To NB, 27 October 1909, *Letters II*: 255.
18. To NB, [?25 October 1909], *Letters II*: 254.
19. *Ibid.*
20. *Ibid.*
21. To N.B., 27 October 1909, *Letters II*: 255.
22. Richard Best interview with Ellmann, 16 April 1953, Tulsa.
23. To NB, 1 November 1909, *Letters II*: 258.
24. To NB, 18 November 1909, *Letters II*: 265–6.
25. To NB, 22 November 1909, *Letters II*: 269.
26. To NB, 9 December 1909 and 20 December 1909, *SL*: 105 and 191–2.
27. Whether he meant he was contemplating future profits or

trying mitigate his guilt for how he had depicted them in his book is not clear.

28. To N B, 23 December 1909, *Letters II*: 278–9.

29. To N B, 24 December 1909, *Letters II*: 281.

30. Mabel Joyce to S J, 28 December 1909, Cornell.

16: Portrait of the Artist in Retrospect (1910–1912)

1. Shloss: 62.
2. Eileen Schaurek in Mikhail: 63.
3. Ellmann: 308.
4. Eileen Schaurek in Rodgers: 41.
5. *Dubliners*: 128.
6. From Ettore Schmitz, 15 June 1910, *Letters II*: 286.
7. Francini Bruni in Potts: 18.
8. Silvio Benco in Potts: 52.
9. Maurice Furlan to Ellmann, 23 November 1953, Tulsa.
10. Francini Bruni, quoted in McCourt: 31.
11. From George Roberts, 9 February 1911, Cornell.
12. From George Roberts, 10 June 1911, Cornell.
13. From George V, King of Great Britain, 11 August 1911, Cornell.
14. To The Editor, *Northern Whig*, 17 August 1911, *Letters II*: 291–4.
15. Eileen Schaurek to Ellmann, 1953, Tulsa.
16. Eva Joyce to S J, 8 July 1911, Cornell.
17. May Joyce to S J, 25 July 1911, Cornell.
18. To Maria Kirn, 30 August 1911, *Letters II*: 293. See also *Thomas F. Staley*, in 'James Joyce in Trieste,' *Georgia Review*, 16 (Winter 1962): 446.
19. As has been well-noted, Joyce's Everyman figures Bloom and Finnegan emerged from the same mould as Blake's Albion and Defoe's Robinson Crusoe. *CW*: 214.

20. *CW*: 217–18.
21. James Joyce, 'Daniel Defoe' translated from Italian Ms and edited by Joseph Prescott, *Buffalo Studies*, 1 (1964): 24–5.
22. *MBK*: 61.
23. *Giacomo Joyce*: 3.
24. Eva Joyce to S J, 12 May 1912, Cornell.
25. 'The Shade of Parnell', *CW*, 226–7.
26. To Eileen Joyce, 30 May 1912, *Letters II*: 296.
27. *Notizie Scolastiche*, Civico Sculoa Popolare, Cornell.
28. To N B, ?12 July 1912, *Letters II*: 297.
29. *Ulysses*: 117–18.
30. From George Roberts, 9 August 1912, Cornell.
31. To S J, 17 July 1912, *Letters II*: 298.
32. *Finnegans Wake*: 407.
33. To Ettore Schmitz, postcard held at Martello Tower Museum, Sandycove.
34. From George Lidwell, quoted in letter to S J, [20 August 1912], *Letters II*: 306, n. 2.
35. To George Roberts, 21 August 1912, *Letters II*: 309.
36. To S J, [21 August 1912], *Letters II*: 307.
37. To N B, [22 August 1912], *Letters II*: 311.
38. To S J, 23 August 1912, *Letters II*: 312.
39. To G R, 4 March 1914, *Letters I*: 74.
40. *Ulysses*: 694.
41. 'Gas from a Burner,' *CW*: 243–5.
42. To S J, [21 August 1912], *Letters II*: 307.
43. To Carlo Linati, 19 December 1919, *Letters I*: 132.

17: A Portrait Completed; A Masterpiece Begun (1912–1915)

1. *Giacomo Joyce*: 9.
2. *FW*: 465.
3. To Mrs William Murray, 9 December 1912, *Letters I*: 72.
4. Leone Dario de Tuoni, quoted by McCourt: 210.

5. *Ulysses*: 391.

6. *Exiles*: 114.

7. To SJ, 9 September 1913, *Letters II*: 324.

8. *Pomes Penyeach*: 14.

9. *Ibid.*: 15.

10. *Exiles*: Note 13, November 1913.

11. *Pomes Penyeach*: 16.

12. Foster, *W. B. Yeats*, vol. I: 439.

13. Douglas Goldring, *South Lodge* (London: Constable, 1943): 48.

14. From EP, 15 December 1913, *Pound–Joyce Letters*, ed. Forrest Read: 17; *Letters II*: 326.

15. *Chamber Music*: 44.

16. From JSJ, 5 May 1914 *Letters II*: 331.

17. *Blast*, I, 20 June 1914: 28.

18. To GR, 16 May 1914, *Letters II*: 334.

19. From Arthur Symons, 29 June 1914, *James Joyce Quarterly*, iv, no. 2 (Winter 1967): 98.

20. 'Studies in the Dismal', *The Times*, 16 June 1914: 6.

21. *Athenaeum*, 20 June 1914: 875.

22. *Irish Book Lover*, Unsigned review, vi, no. 4, (November 1914): 60–1.

23. Gerald Gould, *New Statesman*, iii (27 June 1914): 374–5.

24. *Everyman*, unsigned review, xc, (3 July 1914): 380.

25. EP, '"Dubliners" and Mr James Joyce', *The Egoist*, i, no. 14 (15 July 1914): 267.

26. To EP, 17 March 1915, *Letters III*: 508.

27. From H. L. Mencken, 20 April 1915, *Letters I*: 79.

28. From EP, c. June 1915, *Pound–Joyce Letters*: 34–5.

29. To SJ, 16 June 1914, *SL*: 209.

30. Paola Cuzzi to Ellmann, July 1954, Tulsa.

31. Ellmann: 339–40.

32. Franz K. Stanzel, 'Austria's Surveillance of Joyce in Pola, Trieste and Zurich', *James Joyce Quarterly*, vol. 38, 3/4 (Spring/Summer 2001): 365.

33. Jackson and Costello: 300; *FW*: 301.

34. Joyce quoted by Gorman: 144.

18: The Exile in Exile (1915–1917)

1. Stefan Zweig, *The World of Yesterday* (Cassell, London, 1943): 274.

2. Ottocaro Weiss to Ellmann, 16 June 1954, Tulsa.

3. WBY to Gosse, [24 July1915], *Letters of W. B. Yeats*: 597.

4. To H. G. Wells, 8 July 1925, *Letters II*: 351.

5. Pound to the Royal Literary Fund, 3 August 1915, *Letters*: 359–60.

6. WBY to Edmund Gosse, [28 August 1915], *Letters II*: 362.

7. Georges Borach, 'Conversations with James Joyce', *College English*, 1954, 15: 325 (entry dated 1 August 1917), Zurich.

8. Ellmann: 359.

9. From EP, c. 7 September 1915, *Letters II*: 364.

10. She would later publish Eliot's *The Lovesong of J. Alfred Prufrock*, Lewis's *Tarr*, and volumes of poetry by Aldington and Pound.

11. Claud Sykes interview with Ellmann, June 1954, Tulsa.

12. To Michael Healy, 2 November 1915, *Letters I*: 84–6.

13. Ellmann: 436ff.

14. Edward Garnett's report was enclosed in letter from Jonathan Cape to Pinker, 26 January 1915, *Letters II*: 371–2.

15. Shaw to SB, 22 January 1950, Texas. Quoted in Ellmann: 443 n.

16. Deming (ed.), *James Joyce: The Critical Heritage*, vol 1: 131. One committee member, Frederick Whalen wrote, 'This play we certainly ought to accept at once.' Sturge Moore commented: 'This seems to me the only kind of good play which the S.S. would be false to its best traditions in not producing.' Lee Mathews wrote,

'I don't want the S.S. to play this but it has interest. Circulate it & find out if Mr Joyce has written any more,' and R. C. Herz said, 'Reminiscent of Strindberg at his worst. Putrid!'

17. *Ibid.*: 131.
18. *Ibid.*: 133.
19. To Carlo Linati, 19 December 1919, *Letters I*: 133.
20. From Sir Cecil Hertslet, British Consul General, 1 March 1916, Cornell.
21. HSW to Edward Marsh, 11 September 1917, Berg Collection, NYPL.
22. Huebsch to Weaver, 16 June 1916, *Letters I*: 91.
23. George Moore to Edward Marsh, 3 August 1916, *Letters II*: 380–1.
24. Edward Marsh to Herbert Asquith, 18 August 1916, National Archives.
25. To Sir Otto Niemeyer, Secretary to the Treasury, 28 August 1916, National Archives.
26. From JSJ, 11 September 1916, Cornell.
27. To The Rt. Hon. Herbert Asquith, National Archives.
28. To WBY, 14 September 1916, *Letters I*: 95.
29. To HSW, 8 November 1916, *Letters I*: 98–9.
30. To Mrs Thomas Kettle, 26 September 1916, *Letters I*: 96.
31. From EP, 20 December 1916, *Pound–Joyce Letters*: 85.
32. WBY to EP, 11 February 1917, *Letters II*: 388.
33. EP, 'At last the Novel Appears', *The Egoist*, iv, no. 2, [February 1917]: 21–2.
34. WBY to EP, 11 February 1917, *Letters II*: 388.
35. EP 'At last the Novel Appears,' *The Egoist*, iv, no. 2, [February 1917]: 21–2.
36. 'A Dyspeptic Portrait,' unsigned review, *Freeman's Journal*, 7 April 1917, n. p.

37. *Irish Book Lover*, April–May 1917, viii, nos. 9–10: 113.
38. A. Clutton-Brock, 'Wild Youth', *TLS*, no. 789 (1 March 1917): 103–4.
39. J. C. Squire, *New Statesman*, ix, 14 April 1917: 40.
40. H. G. Wells, *Nation*, xx, 24 February 1917: 710, 712.
41. H. L. Mencken, *The Smart Set* (August 1917): n. p.
42. John Macy, *The Dial*, lxii, no. 744 (14 June 1917): 525–7.
43. Philipp Jarnach interview with Dr Hans-Joachim Lang, 9 February 1959, Ellmann Papers, Tulsa.
44. To his anonymous admirer, 6 March 1917, *SL*: 224.
45. May Joyce Monaghan in Mikhail: 183.
46. From John Quinn, 13 March 1917, NYPL.
47. From C. P. Curran, 26 February 1917, Cornell.
48. Jane Heap, 'James Joyce,' *Little Review*, iii, no.10 (April 1917): 8–9.
49. Margaret Anderson, *Little Review*, iii, no.10 (April, 1917): 9–10.

19: The Coming Forth by Day of Leopold Bloom (1917–1918)

1. Budgen: 69.
2. To EP, 9 April 1917, *Letters I*: 101.
3. *Ibid.*: 102.
4. From Monro Saw, 14 April 1917, BL.
5. Hughes (ed.), *The Joyce Book*: 79.
6. Paul Suter to Dr Alfred Dutli, 1956, Ellmann Papers, Tulsa.
7. To HSW, 18 July 1917, *Letters I*: 106.
8. Maddox: 199.
9. Georges Borach, 'Conversations with James Joyce', *College English* 1954, 15: 325–7.
10. From NB, [about 4 August 1917], *Letters II*: 401–2.
11. To J. B. Pinker, 8 August 1917, *Letters II*: 402.
12. From NB, [11: August 1917], quoted

in Maddox: 202; Scholes, *The Cornell Collection*: 758.

13. Quoted from a letter from NB seen by Ellmann, but now lost.

14. From NB, [11: August 1917], quoted in Maddox: 202.

15. From NB, [about 12 August 1917], *Letters II*: 403.

16. To EP, 20 August 1917, *SL*: 226–7.

17. From HSW, 6 September 1917, *Letters II*: 406.

18. From WBY, 26 August [1917], Cornell.

19. Sykes to Ellmann, June 1954, Ellmann Papers, Tulsa.

20. This is a point well discussed by Ellmann: 408.

21. Danis Rose and John O'Hanlon, *James Joyce: The Lost Notebook* (Split Pea, Edinburgh, 1989).

22. Wim Van Mierlo, 'The Subject Notebook', *Genetic Joyce Studies*, 7 (Spring 2007).

23. To Edouard Dujardin, 10 November 1917, *Letters II*: 410.

24. Maddox: 205–6.

25. Ellmann: 419.

26. *Ulysses*: 28.

27. From EP, 17 December 1917, *Letters II*: 414.

28. EP, 'Paris Letter', *The Dial*, vii, no. 4, January 1922: 73–8.

29. Ezra Pound, *Guide to Kulchur* (Faber, London, 1938), Chapter 13: 96 n.

30. EP to Margaret Anderson, n.d., *Pound–Joyce Letters*: 130.

31. McCourt: 248.

32. From 10th Anniversary greetings from Margaret Anderson to the James Joyce Society, February 1957.

20: Earthly Trials (1918)

1. From HSW, 8 March 1918, *Letters II*: 418.

2. From EP, Good Friday [29 March] 1918, *Pound–Joyce Letters*: 131.

3. EP to John Quinn, 3 April 1918, *Pound–Joyce Letters*: 132.

4. *Ulysses*: 134.

5. Virginia Woolf, 'Modern Novels', *TLS*, no. 899, 10 April 1919: 189–90.

6. Leonard Woolf, *Beginning Again: An Autobiography of the Years 1911 to 1918* (Hogarth Press, London, 1964): 246.

7. *Ibid.*: 246–7.

8. Virginia Woolf to HW, 17 May 1918, BL.

9. Philip Howard, 'Sir John French Disclosed Battle Plans in Love Letters' *The Times*, 29 November 1975: 3.

10. Gorman: 254.

11. 'Dooleysprudence', *CW*: 246–8.

12. 'JGW', *Freeman's Journal*, 15 June 1918: 4.

13. Desmond MacCarthy, *New Statesman*, xi, 21 September 1918: 492–3.

14. Arthur Clutton-Brock, 'The Mind to Suffer', *TLS*, 25 July 1918: 346.

15. To Forrest Reid, 1 August 1918, *Letters I*: 118.

16. To HSW, 18 May 1918, *Letters I*: 113–14.

17. Budgen: 11.

18. *Ibid.*: 12.

19. *Ibid.*: 16.

20. *Ibid.*: 20.

21. Zweig, *The World of Yesterday*: 275.

22. Philipp Jarnach to Dr Dutli, 1953, Ellmann Papers, Tulsa.

23. Paul Suter to Dr Alfred Dutli, 1956, Ellmann Papers, Tulsa.

24. Budgen, *Myselves When Young*: 186.

25. Paul Suter to Dr Alfred Dutli, 1956, Ellmann Papers, Tulsa.

26. To J. B. Pinker, 9 June 1918, *Letters I*: 114.

27. Horace Rumbold to Foreign Office, 18 July 1918, National Archives.

28. Internal memoranda, Foreign Office, National Archives.

29. Stephen Gaselee to Sir Horace Rumbold, 24–29 July 1918, FO file, National Archives.

30. To Sir Horace Rumbold, 30 November 1918, *Letters II*: 426.
31. Stoppard, *Travesties*: ix–xi.
32. Conrad L. Rushing, 'The English Players Incident. What Really Happened?' *James Joyce Quarterly*, vol. 57 (Spring/Summer 2000): 371–88.
33. To Sir Horace Rumbold, 11 March 1919, HRC.
34. SJ, Trieste Diary, 8 May 1908.
35. Georges Borach, 'Conversations with James Joyce,' entry for 21 October 1918.

21: Settling Scores and Moving On (1918–1920)

1. Budgen: 36.
2. *Ibid.*: 188.
3. *Ulysses*: 205.
4. Budgen: 21.
5. Budgen in Rogers: 64; Ellmann: 438.
6. Budgen: 355.
7. *Ulysses*: 861. See also Ronan Crowley, 'Dressing Up Mr Bloom for "Circe"' *James Joyce Broadsheet*, 17 (October 2010): 3.
8. From EP, 22 November 1918, *Letters II*: 423.
9. Vela Pulitzer to Ellmann, n.d., Ellmann Papers, Tulsa.
10. Budgen, *Myselves When Young*: 188.
11. Lucia Joyce, 'My Life,' HRC (see David, 'Shadow of His Mind: The Papers of Lucia Joyce', *Joyce at Texas: Essays on the James Joyce Materials at the Humanities Research Center*: 69).
12. TSE to Scofield Thayer, 30 June 1918, *Letters of T. S. Eliot, Vol. 1: 1898–1922*, London, Faber, 1988: p/b 236; h/b 268.
13. WBY to JQ, 23 July 1918, *Letters of W. B. Yeats*: 651.
14. S. J. Brown, *Ireland in Fiction* (Dublin: Maunsel, 1916): 140.
15. Budgen, *Myselves When Young*: 199.
16. Frau Walter Bollmann to Ellmann, Ellmann Papers, July 1954, Tulsa.
17. To Marthe Fleischmann, [?early December 1918], *Letters II*: 433.
18. Budgen, *Myselves When Young*: 194.
19. To Marthe Fleischmann, [2 February 1919], *Letters II*: 436.
20. Quoted in Budgen: xvi.
21. *Ibid.*: 190.
22. *Ibid.*
23. Ottocaro Weiss to Ellmann, 16 June 1954, Ellmann Papers, Tulsa.
24. To FB [? end] 1919, *Letters I*: 131.
25. Quoted by Paul Vanderham, *James Joyce and Censorship* (Basingstoke: Macmillan, 1998): 28.
26. *Ibid.*: 32.
27. To HSW, 25 February 1920, *Letters I*: 137.
28. *Ulysses*: 595.
29. To Marthe Fleischmann, [9 December 1918], *Letters II*: 436.
30. To FB, 17 July 1933, *Letters I*: 336.
31. From Monro Saw, 24 June 1919. (On an equivalent earnings basis today's value would be in the region of £800,000.)
32. From Huebsch to HSW, 31 October 1918, *Letters I*: 121–2.
33. To Monro Saw, 20 May 1919, quoted by Ellmann: 457.
34. From SJ, 25 May 1919, *Letters II*: 443.
35. To FB, 19 June 1919, *SL*: 238–9.
36. Heinrich Straumann, 'Four Letters to Marthe Fleischmann', *Letters II*: 428.
37. Luening, Otto, *Odyssey of an American Composer* (New York: Scribner's, 1980): 185–200.
38. *Ulysses*: 328–9. Joyce may have been influenced in creating this sound poetry by hearing Marinetti recite experiments of this kind or by hearing Hugo Bali at the Cabaret Voltaire, where Dadaist poets strutted their stuff.
39. To HSW, 20 July 1919, *SL*: 240.
40. From HSW, 6 July 1919, *Letters II*: 445.
41. To HSW, 6 August 1919, *SL*: 241.
42. To FB, 19 June 1919, *Letters I*: 126.
43. To HSW, 2 July 1919, *Letters I*: 126.

44. To JQ, 3 August 1919, NYPL.

45. From HSW, 6 July 1919, *Letters II*: 445.

46. *Pomes Penyeach*: 24.

47. To SJ, 8 September 1919, *Letters II*: 450.

48. Vivien Eliot to Mary Hutchinson, 26 September 1919, *Letters of T. S. Eliot*: p/b 334; h/b 399.

49. Ottacaro Weiss to Ellmann, 13–14 June 1954, Ellmann Papers, Tulsa.

50. From Edith McCormick, 13 October 1919, quoted by Ellmann: 467.

51. Gorman: 262.

52. *Ulysses*: 499–500.

53. To FB, 20 March 1920, *Letters I*: 139, *SL*: 251–2.

54. EP to JQ, 25 October 1919, *Pound–Joyce Letters*: 161. But Joyce owed as much to George Saintsbury's *A History of English Prose Rhythm* and William Peacock's *English Prose from Mandeville to Ruskin* as he might have done to Rabelais.

55. Power: 71.

56. Lidderdale and Nicholson, *Dear Miss Weaver*: 56. From HSW, 30 June 1920, Ellmann Notes, Tulsa.

57. To J. B. Pinker, 13 March 1920, *Letters II*: 462.

58. To HSW, 16 August 1920, *Letters II*: 15–16.

59. From HSW, 7 January 1922, Ellmann Notes, Tulsa.

60. Lidderdale and Nicholson, *Dear Miss Weaver*: 174.

61. To HSW, 29 August 1920, BL.

62. To FB [? end] 1919, *Letters I*: 130.

63. To FB, 7 November 1919, *Letters I*: 131.

64. Maurice Furlan to Ellmann, 22 November 1953, Ellmann Papers, Tulsa.

65. Benco in Potts: 57.

66. This question is thoroughly explored in Carol Loeb Shloss's *Lucia*.

67. To FB, 3 January 1920, *Letters I*: 134, *SL*: 245.

68. *Ibid.*: 134, *SL*: 245.

69. From JSJ, 17 [January?] 1920, *Letters II*: 457.

70. To HSW, 25 February 1920, *Letters I*: 137.

71. To Mrs William Murray, 15 January 1920, *Letters I*: 135.

72. To Mrs William Murray, [? early] 1920, *Letters I*: 136.

73. From HSW, 16 March 1920, Ellmann Notes, Tulsa.

74. To JQ, 11 March 1920, *Letters II*: 460.

75. To FB, 23 March 1920, *Letters I*: 139–40; *SL*: 250 dated 15 March 1920.

76. From Mrs William Murray, 27 March 1920, Cornell, quoted by Maddox: 259.

77. To FB, 18 May 1920, *Letters II*: 465.

78. T. S. Eliot, *Athenaeum*, July 1919; Deming (ed.), *James Joyce: The Critical Heritage*: 17.

79. From EP, 2 June 1920, *Pound–Joyce Letters*: 174.

80. To HSW, 12 July 1920, *Letters I*: 142.

81. To HSW, 1 February 1927, *SL*: 318–19.

82. EP to JQ, 19 June 1920, *Pound–Joyce Letters*: 178–9.

83. To JQ, 24 June 1920, NYPL.

84. Vanderham, *James Joyce and Censorship*: 42.

22: *Ulysses*: Inside the Dismal Labyrinth (1920–1921)

1. McAlmon and Boyle, *Being Geniuses Together, 1920–1930*.

2. TSE to EP, 3 July 1920, *Letters of T. S. Eliot 1898–1922*: p/b 388; h/b 472.

3. Beach: 114.

4. *Ibid.*: 35.

5. To HSW, 16 August 1920, *Letters III*: 15.

6. Beach: 35–6.

7. *FW*: 167.

8. Pound to Serruys, pmk 20 July 1920, *Pound–Joyce Letters*: 181.

9. To FB, 27 July 1920, *Letters I*: 143–4.

10. Lewis only mentions the boots but

a letter from Joyce to Pound indicates that there were clothes in the parcel, too.

11. Lewis, *Blasting and Bombadiering*: 265–70.
12. TSE to his mother, 24 August 1920, *Letters of T. S. Eliot 1898–1922*: p/b 404; h/b 495.
13. TSE to JQ, 9 May 1921, from *ibid*.: p/b/452; h/b 543.
14. C.C.M., 'Some Recent Books', *Dublin Review*, lxvi, no. 382, January–February–March 1920): 135–8.
15. Lewis to Ellmann, 1950, Ellmann Papers, Tulsa; Power: 101.
16. To HSW, 16 August 1920, *Letters III*: 15.
17. To Carlo Linati, 6 September 1920, *Letters I*: 146.
18. To SJ, 14 September 1920, *Letters III*: 22.
19. *Ulysses*: 698.
20. To Francini Bruni, [?8 September 1920], *Letters III*: 20.
21. To Carlo Linati, 21 September 1920, *Letters I*: 146–7.
22. To HSW, 17 April 1921, *Letters I*: 163.
23. To JQ, 17 October 1920, NYPL. Huebsch later denied ever having mentioned a possible pirated edition, so this may be Joyce's reading of what he saw as an implied threat. (I am grateful to Professor Robert Spoo for making this point.)
24. To HSW, 10 November 1920, BL.
25. From HSW, 12 November 1920, Ellmann Notes, Tulsa.
26. To FB, Michaelmas 1920, *Letters I*: 147; *SL*: 271.
27. To FB, 24 October 1920, *Letters I*: 148–9.
28. Vanderham: 42.
29. To JQ, 24 November 1920, NYPL.
30. To JQ, 17 November 1920, NYPL, quoted in Maddox: 238.
31. To EP, 12 December 1920, *Letters III*: 32–3.
32. To John McCormack, 8 December 1920, *Letters III*: 32.

33. To FB, 10 December 1920, *Letters I*: 151–2.
34. To EP, 20 December 1920, *Letters III*: 34.
35. To JQ, 7 January 1921, *Letters I*: 156.
36. Beach: 64.
37. To JQ, 7 January 1921, NYPL, passage omitted from *Letters I*: 155–6; To HSW, 4 February 1921, *Letters I*: 156.
38. Vanderham: 45–53.
39. An observation picked up from a commentary on later *Little Review* episodes from a University of Buffalo exhibition catalogue.
40. To FB, end February 1921, *Letters I*: 159–60.
41. To HSW, 1 March 1921, BL.
42. To HSW, 3 April 1921, *Letters I*: 161.
43. Nutting to Ellmann, 1952, Ellmann Papers, Tulsa.
44. F. Scott Fitzgerald to Max Perkins, [c. 15 November 1929], *Letters of F. Scott Fitzgerald*, ed. Andrew Turnbull (New York: Scribner's, 1963): 235.
45. Samuel Putnam, *Paris Was Our Mistress* (Tulsa: SIU Press, 1970): 138.
46. Beach: 47.

23: An Eventful Labour (1921–1922)

1. Beach: 32.
2. To JQ, 19 April 1921, *Letters III*: 40.
3. Beach: 65.
4. From JQ, 5 June 1921, NYPL.
5. Richard Aldington, *English Review*, xxxii (April 1921): 331.
6. TSE to RM, 2 May 1921, *The Letters of T. S. Eliot 1898–1922*: p/b 45; h/b 563–4.
7. TSE to JQ, 9 May 1921, *ibid*.: 452.
8. To HSW, 2 May 1921, *Letters I*: 165.
9. To FB, [31 May 1921], *Letters III*: 42.
10. RM to Ellmann, 13 October 1953, Ellmann Papers, Tulsa.
11. McAlmon and Boyle, *Being Geniuses Together*: 23.
12. To Claud Sykes, 6 June 1921, *Letters III*: 44.

13. To Francini Bruni, 7 June 1921, *Letters III*: 45.

14. SB accounts, University at Buffalo, NY.

15. To Valery Larbaud, 5 June 1921, *Letters III*: 43.

16. To Francini Bruni, 7 June 1921, *Letters III*: 46.

17. To HSW, 24 June 1921, *Letters I*: 165–7, *SL*: 283–4.

18. *Ibid.*, *SL*: 281–4.

19. To HSW, 7 August 1921, *Letters I*: 168.

20. To Valery Larbaud, [Summer 1921], *Letters I*: 168–9. Joyce is said to have used 'Yes' after he overheard Lillian Wallace use it repeatedly in a conversation with a house painter.

21. To FB, 16 August, 1921, *SL*: 285.

22. *Ibid.*: 285.

23. To FB, 6 September 1921, *Letters I*: 172.

24. To RM, 27 August 1921, *Letters I*: 170.

25. To HSW, 30 August 1921, *Letters I*: 171.

26. GBS to SB, 10 October 1921, reprinted in Beach: 32.

27. Shaw to Pound, 8 March 1922, Lilly Library.

28. To RM, 10 October 1921, *Letters I*: 173–4.

29. To Josephine Murray, 14 October 1921, *Letters I*: 174.

30. To HSW, 1 November 1921, BL.

31. Maddox: 253. Maddox calculates 40,565 francs as £2,000, but the exchange rate was around 50 francs to the pound.

32. Beach: 74.

33. To Valery Larbaud, [about 14 December 1921], *Letters III*: 55.

34. Vivien Eliot to Mary Hutchinson, [20 December 1921], *Letters of T. S. Eliot 1898–1922*: p/b 497; h/b 618.

35. Joseph Hone, 'A Letter from Ireland,' *London Mercury*, January 1922: 308.

36. Djuna Barnes, 'James Joyce,' *Vanity Fair*, xviii (April 1922): 65.

37. Man Ray to Patricia Hutchins, 23 May 1948, TCDL.

38. Burton Rascoe, *A Bookman's Daybook* (New York: Horace Liveright, 1929): 27.

24: *Ulysses*: Birth and Afterbirth (1922–1924)

1. Helen Nutting, Paris Diary, 22 February 1922, Northwestern University, Evanston, Illinois.

2. To HSW, 8 February 1922, *Letters I*: 180, *SL*: 288–9.

3. McAlmon and Boyle, *Being Geniuses Together*: 167–8.

4. From SJ, 26 February 1922, *Letters III*: 58–9.

5. To SJ, 20 March 1922, *Letters III*: 61.

6. Sisley Huddleston. '*Ulysses*', *Observer*, 5 March 1922: 4.

7. George Slocombe, *Daily Herald*, 17 March 1922: 4.

8. Carola Giedion-Welcker to Ellmann, 13 July 1954, Ellmann Papers, Tulsa.

9. WBY to Olivia Shakespeare, 8 March (1922), *The Letters of W. B. Yeats*: 679.

10. S. P. B. Mais, 'An Irish Revel: And Some Flappers', *Daily Express*, 25 March 1922: n.p.

11. 'Aramis,' 'The Scandal of *Ulysses*', *Sporting Times*, no. 34, 1 April 1922: 4.

12. Valery Larbaud, 'James Joyce,' *Nouvelle Revue Française*, xviii (April 1922): 385–405.

13. Pound on *Ulysses*, *Mercure de France*, 15 April 1922.

14. From a letter from a relative in Dublin, 29 March 1922, enclosed in Joyce's letter to HSW, 10 April 1922, copy in University College London Joyce Collection.

15. Holloway Diary, 14 June 1938, NLI.

16. Ulick O'Connor, 'James Joyce and Oliver St John Gogarty: A Famous Friendship', *Texas Quarterly*, iii (Summer 1960): 191.

17. *Register of Prohibited Publications for Ireland*, TCDL.
18. Ernest Boyd, 'The Expressionism of James Joyce', *New York Tribune*, 28 May 1922.
19. Mary Colum, *Freeman's Journal*, 19 July 1922: 450–2.
20. Shane Leslie, 'Ulysses', *Quarterly Review*, ccxxxviii (October 1922): 219–34.
21. John Eglinton, 'Dublin Letter', *The Dial*, I, xxii (October 1922).
22. To HSW, 22 October 1922, *Letters I*: 188.
23. John Middleton Murry, *Nation and Athenaeum*, xxxvi, 22 April 1922: 124–5.
24. Katherine Mansfield to Violet Schiff, 1 April? 1922, Cornell; Violet Schiff to Wyndham Lewis, 31 April 1922, Cornell.
25. Arnold Bennett, 'James Joyce's Ulysses', *Outlook* (London) (29 April 1922): 339.
26. To HSW, 16 May 1922, *Letters I*: 184–5.
27. T. S. Eliot, '*Ulysses*, Order and Myth', *The Dial*, 1, xxv (November 1923): 480–3; Deming (ed.), *James Joyce: The Critical Heritage*: 26.
28. Hart Crane to an unknown recipient, 27 July 1922, from *The Letters of Hart Crane 1916–1932*, ed. Brom Weber (New York: Hermitage House, 1952): 94–5.
29. Compton MacKenzie, *My Life and Times*, Octave V: 1915–1925 (London: Chatto & Windus, 1966).
30. Virginia Woolf, *Diary*, 16 August 1922, in *The Diary of Virginia Woolf, vol. 2: 1920–1924*, ed. Anne Olivier Bell (New York: Mariner Books, 1980).
31. Hemingway to Sherwood Anderson, 9 March 1922, Ms Newberry Library, Chicago; Ellmann: 529.
32. Joseph Collins, 'James Joyce's Amazing Chronicle', *NYT Book Review*, 28 May 1922: 6, 17.
33. Edmund Wilson, '*Ulysses*', *New Republic*, xxxi, no. 396 (5 July 1922): 64–6.
34. To RM, 11 February 1922, *Letters I*: 181.
35. To SB, 11 February 1922, *SB Letters*: 11.
36. To NB, [April] 1922, *Letters III*: 63.
37. McAlmon in Mikhail: 107.
38. To Mrs William Murray, 23 October 1922, *Letters I*: 189, *SL*: 290.
39. To Curran, 6 August 1937, *Letters I*: 395.
40. To Mrs William Murray, 23 October 1922, *Letters I*: 191.
41. Richard Davenport-Hines, *A Night at the Majestic* (London: Faber, 2006): Chapter 1.
42. Ellmann: 535–6.
43. Beach: 67.
44. JQ to HSW, 27 July 1922, NYPL.
45. *FW*: 245.
46. HSW to Ellmann, 1956, Ellmann Papers, Tulsa.
47. To SB, 29 August 1922, *SB Letters*: 12.
48. Hutchins, *James Joyce's World*: 139.
49. To HSW, 4 October 1922, *Letters III*: 67.
50. JQ to HSW, 2 October 1922, NYPL.
51. John Rodker to Ellmann, Ellmann Papers, Tulsa.
52. *Tristram and Isolde* in French becomes *Tristan et Iseult*. Joyce seems to use them indiscriminately: Tristan usually but Tristram in *Finnegans Wake*.
53. Helen Nutting Diary, 9 October 1922, Northwestern University, Evanston, Illinois.
54. Power: 91.
55. To HSW, 27 October 1922, *Letters III*: 68.
56. Valery Larbaud, 'The *Ulysses* of James Joyce', *Criterion*, no. 1, October 1922: 103.
57. To Mrs William Murray, 10 November 1922, *Letters I*: 193.
58. *Ibid.*: 194.

59. 'Rottenness in Literature', *Sunday Chronicle* (29 October 1922): 2.
60. Internal Memo, Home Office, 29 November 1922, National Archives.
61. Power in O'Connor: 99.
62. Power: 30–1.
63. *Ibid.*: 32.
64. To Mrs William Murray, 21 December 1922, *Letters I*. 198.
65. To HSW, 6 February 1923, *Letters I*: 200.
66. Rodker informed Ellmann that only 400 had been seized and the rest had got through.
67. To HSW, 11 March 1923, *Letters I*: 201.
68. *FW*. 380.
69. To SB, 25 April 1924, *SB Letters*: 37.
70. To HSW, 18 March 1923, BL.
71. HSW to SB, 23 March 1923, BL.
72. Stephen Gwynn, 'Modern Irish Literature', *Manchester Guardian*, 15 March 1923: 38–9.
73. S. W. Harris to Chief Constables, 24 May 1923, National Archives.
74. To HSW, 22 May 1923, BL.
75. Kathleen Barnacle Griffin to Ellmann, 1953, Ellmann Papers, Tulsa.
76. Lidderdale and Nicholson, *Dear Miss Weaver*: 222.
77. From T. S. Eliot, Friday, [?29] June 1923, Eliot, Valerie (ed.), *The Letters of T.S. Eliot*, vol. 2: 1923–1925 (London: Faber, 2009): 172.
78. To HSW, 5 July 1923, *Letters III*: 203.
79. *Ulysses*: 466.
80. From HSW, 4 July 1923, BL.
81. To HSW, 5 July 1923, *Letters III*: 202–3.
82. Budgen: 347.
83. Power: 95.
84. Kathleen Barnacle Griffin to Ellmann, 1953, Ellmann Papers, Tulsa.
85. To SB, 12 July 1923, *SB Letters*: 17–18.
86. To HSW, 10 September 1923, BL.
87. McAlmon and Boyle, *Being Geniuses Together*: 106.
88. To HSW, 9 October 1923, *Letters I*: 204.
89. *Ibid.*
90. Power: 48.
91. To HSW, 17 December 1923, *Letters I*: 207.
92. *FW*: 305. For James Townsend Saward see Dilnot, George, *The Trial of Jim the Penman* (London: 1930).
93. William Empson disagreed with Hugh Kenner that *A Portrait* was itself an elaborate lie. 'Joyce's Intention', in Empson, *Using Biography* (London: Chatto & Windus, 1984): 203.
94. Shloss: 114.
95. *Ibid.*: 113.
96. Kay Boyle to Ellmann, 6 January 1983, Ellmann Papers, Tulsa.
97. To RM, [early 1924], *Letters I*: 209.
98. To RM, [?18 February 1924], *Letters III*: 88.
99. To HSW, 17 February 1924, BL.
100. To Italo Svevo (Ettore Schmitz), 20 February 1924, *Letters I*: 211–12.
101. To Ettore Schmitz, 21 November 1925, *Letters III*: 133.
102. The term 'pubescent delinquent' is borrowed from Shloss: 75.
103. To HSW, 7 March 1924, *Letters I*: 212–13.
104. The manuscript today resides in the Rosenbach Museum in Philadelphia.
105. To HSW, 24 March 1934, *Letters I*: 213.

25: A Conspiracy of Concealment (1924–1926)

1. Ford Madox Ford, 'Literary Causeries: vii. So She Went Into The Garden', *Chicago Tribune Sunday Magazine*, 6 April 1924: 3, 7.
2. To HSW, 6 April 1924, *Letters III*: 93.
3. To SB, 12 April 1924, *SB Letters*: 35.
4. To HSW, 19 April 1924, BL.
5. To HSW, 7 May 1924, BL.
6. To HSW, 25 May 1924, *Letters I*: 214.

7. To HSW, 4 June 1924, BL.
8. Edmund Gosse to Louis Gillet, 7 June 1924, Gillet, *Claybook For James Joyce*: 31–2.
9. To Valery Larbaud, 6 June 1924, *Letters III*: 97–8.
10. From Ettore Schmitz, 10 June 1924, *Letters III*: 98.
11. To HSW, 8 June 1924, BL.
12. From SB, 12 June 1924, Joyce Foundation, Zurich.
13. Ellmann: 566.
14. LJ to HSW, 15 June, 1924, BL; LJ to HSW, 23 June 1924, BL.
15. Sylvia Beach claimed that 'Bloomsday' was her invention, but its earliest use was probably by Valery Larbaud in his April 1922 review of *Ulysses* in the *NRF*, and by Pound in an essay ('Paris Letter') in *The Dial*, lxxii, 6 (January 1922): 623–9.
16. To HSW, 27 June 1924, *Letters I*: 216.
17. Beach and Monnier to Ellmann, 5 August 1953, Ellmann Papers, Tulsa.
18. To SB, 23 July 1924, *SB Letters*: 42–3.
19. Lloyd Morris, *A Threshold in the Sun* (London: Allen & Unwin, 1948): 243.
20. From SB, 22 July 1924, Ellmann Notes, Tulsa.
21. From SJ, 7 August 1924, *Letters III*: 102–4.
22. To HSW, 16 August 1924, *Letters I*: 220.
23. *Ibid.*
24. To HSW, 30 August 1924, BL.
25. To HSW, 9 November 1924, *Letters II*: 110, *SL*: 303–4.
26. To HSW, 7 September 1924, BL.
27. *Ibid.*
28. To HSW, 31 October 1924, BL.
29. Lidderdale and Nicholson, *Dear Miss Weaver*: 250.
30. To SB, 16 October 1924, *SB Letters*: 50.
31. Lidderdale and Nicholson, *Dear Miss Weaver*: 249–50.
32. To Mrs William Murray, 2 November 1924, *Letters I*: 221–2.
33. *FW*: 406.
34. *FW*: 488.
35. *FW*: 594. Joyce also parodied *The Waste Land* in a letter to Harriet Weaver and also in *Finnegans Wake* (see Ellmann: 528, 572).
36. To HSW 9 November 1924, *Letters III:* 110.
37. To HSW, 16 November 1924, *Letters I*: 222.
38. Statement of Joyce's tax-free Investments, June 1924.
39. To HSW, 23 December 1924, *Letters III*: 111.
40. HSW to SB, 12 March 1925, Princeton University, NJ.
41. To HSW, 22 December 1924, Ellmann Notes, Tulsa.
42. From HSW, 30 December 1924, Ellmann Notes, Tulsa.
43. *FW*: 532.
44. *FW*: 580.
45. HSW to SB, 11 April 1925, Princeton University, NJ.
46. To HSW, 7 March 1925, *Letters III*: 115.
47. To Ernest Walsh, 13 March 1925, *Letters III*: 117.
48. To HSW, 25 March 1925, *Letters III*: 117–18.
49. Helen Nutting Diary, 22 April 1925, Northwestern University, Evanston, Illinois.
50. To HSW, 25 April 1925, *Letters I*: 227.
51. *FW*: 533n.
52. *FW*: 116–17.
53. *FW*: 450.
54. First quoted in Herbert Gorman, *James Joyce*: 280 n., and turned into direct speech in Ellmann: 549.
55. Gillet, *Claybook for James Joyce*: 26.
56. To HSW, 17 June 1925, BL.
57. *The Contact Collection of Contemporary Writers* (Paris: Three Mountains Press, 1925).
58. Edwin Muir, 'James Joyce: The Meaning of Ulysses', *Calendar of*

Modern Letters (London), 15 (July 1925): 347–55.

59. EP to the Editor of the *Chicago Tribune*, 3 September 1925.

60. To SB, 5 July 1925, *SB Letters*: 54.

61. To SB, [probably July 1925], *SB Letters*: 55.

62. To SB, [31 July] 1925, *SB Letters*: 60.

63. To HSW, 8 July 1925, BL.

64. To SB, 25 July 1925, *Letters I*: 229.

65. To HSW, 29 August 1925, *Letters I*: 232.

66. From SJ, 13 February 1926, Ellmann Papers, Tulsa.

67. Louis Gillet, 'Du côté de chez Joyce', *Revue des Deux Mondes*, xxviii (August 1925): 686–97. Reproduced in translation in *Claybook for James Joyce*: 48.

68. To HG, [about 4 September 1925], *Letters III*: 126–7.

69. *FW*: 355.

70. Edgell Rickward to SB, 3 October 1925, BL.

71. To HSW, 10 October 1925, *Letters I*: 234–5.

72. To HSW, 22 October 1925, *Letters I*: 235.

73. *This Quarter* (Milan), 2 (Autumn–Winter 1925–6).

74. HSW to SB, November 1925, BL.

75. From HG, 25 November 1933, in M. Magalaner (ed.), *A James Joyce Miscellany II*, 1959: 9–14.

76. To HSW, 11 November 1925, *Letters I*: 237.

77. To GBS, 26 November 1925, *Letters III*: 146, where dated 1926.

78. LJ to HSW, 6 December 1925, BL.

79. LJ to HSW, 17 December 1925, *Letters III*: 135.

80. Philippe Soupault to Ellmann, July 1953, Ellmann Papers, Tulsa.

81. Helen Nutting Diary, Christmas 1925, Northwestern University, Evanston, Illinois

82. To HSW, 20 January 1926, *Letters I*: 239.

83. From HSW, 15 February 1926, Ellmann Notes. Ironically, the play was produced by William Fay who in 1904 had helped throw a drunken Joyce out of the Camden Street rehearsal rooms for upsetting the 'refined' Miss Vera Esposito.

84. From Ettore Schmitz, 15 February 1926, *Letters III*: 137–8.

85. From Claud Sykes, 18 February 1926, BL.

86. 'Stage Society. *Exiles*', *The Times*, 16 February 1926: 12.

87. *Daily News*, 'A Drama of the Mind,' 16 February 1926: 4.

88. *Exiles*, *Morning Post*, 16 February 1926.

89. To HSW, 28 February 1926, BL.

90. To HSW, 5 March 1926, BL.

91. *FW*: 556.

92. To HSW, 5 March 1926, *Letters III*: 138.

93. Mary Colum in Mikhail: 163. Despite Joyce's attraction to women, his misogyny did sometimes resurface. He told Gilbert that 'La femme c'est mien,' and Power that he found all women 'cold' and Jolas that all talk of love made him feel like 'puking'.

94. Frank O'Connor in Rodgers: 51–2.

95. Colums: 169.

96. To HSW, 18 March 1926, *Letters I*: 240.

97. To HSW, 23 March 1926, BL.

98. *FW*: 466.

99. To HSW, 21 May 1926, *Letters I*: 241.

100. *Ibid.*

101. Jacques Mercanton in Potts: 207.

102. McGreevy Papers, Trinity College Dublin.

103. To HSW, 7 June 1926, *Letters I*: 241.

104. From HSW, 10 June 1926, Ellmann Notes.

105. To HSW, 15 July 1926, *Letters I*: 242.

106. From SB, 9 September 1926, Zurich Foundation.

107. Daniel Brody to Ellmann, Ellmann Papers, Tulsa.

108. To HSW, 24 September 1926, *Letters I*: 245.

109. To HSW, 18 August 1926, *Letters I*: 244 n.
110. *Ibid.*: 244.
111. To SB, 24 August 1926, *Letters I*: 244.
112. *FW*: 4.
113. To SJ, 5 November 1926, *Letters III*: 145.
114. *900: Cahiers d'Italie et d'Europe*, Rome-Florence, 1 (Automne 1926): 107–31.
115. Nino Frank in Potts: 79.
116. *FW*: 8.
117. Thomas Wolfe to Aline Bernstein, 22 September 1926, from *The Letters of Thomas Wolfe*, ed. Elizabeth Nowell, 1956: 114–15.
118. To SB, 11 September 1926, *SB Letters*: 71.
119. To HSW, 26 September 1926, *Letters III*: 142.
120. From SB, 29 September 1926, Joyce Foundation, Zurich. For the third quarter of 1926 *Ulysses* had sold 2,400 copies earning for Joyce the net sum of 61,627.50 francs.
121. From EP, 15 November 1926, *Letters III*: 146.
122. From HSW, 1 October 1926, Ellmann Notes, Tulsa.
123. From Eileen Joyce, 7 November 1926, SIU (translated).
124. But a letter Joyce sent to Beach was written on the back of a statement from the Lloyds and National Provincial Bank, Paris, dated 5 November 1926.
125. To HSW, 18 February 1927, *Letters III*: 165, *SL*: 320.
126. To SJ, 8 January 1927, *Letters III*: 149.
127. From HSW, 20 November 1926, Ellmann Notes, Tulsa.
128. From EP, 19 November 1926, *Pound–Joyce Letters*: 225–6.
129. To Helen Nutting, 17 December 1926, *Letters III*: 148–9.
130. Jolas, *The Man from Babel*: 89.

26: Fending off the Pirates and Envisioning the Invisible (1927–1928)

1. GBS to SB, 18 December 1926, quoted in a footnote to Joyce's letter to HSW, 16 January 1927, *Letters III*: 150.
2. To SB, [probably late January 1927], *SB Letters*: 115.
3. Arnold Bennett, 26 March 1927, *Journals*, ed. Newman Flosser (London: Cassell, 1932–33): 531.
4. WBY to Olivia Shakespeare, 24 March 1927, *Letters of W. B. Yeats*: 724.
5. *FW*: 414–19.
6. To HSW, 22 January 1927, BL.
7. From HSW, 28 January 1927, Ellmann Notes, Tulsa.
8. To HSW, 1 February 1927, *Letters I*: 249.
9. From HSW, 4 February 1927, Ellmann Notes, Tulsa.
10. To HSW, 8 [or 10] February 1927, BL.
11. From HSW, 11 February 1927, Ellmann Notes, Tulsa.
12. From HSW, 19 February 1927, Ellmann Notes, Tulsa.
13. From Archibald MacLeish, [c. 10 March 1927], BL.
14. Shloss: 136.
15. To HSW, 16 April 1927, *Letters I*: 251.
16. From HSW, 26 April 1927, Ellmann Notes, Tulsa.
17. *Ulysses*: 631 and 822.
18. From SB, 29 April 1927, Ellmann Notes, Tulsa.
19. From SG, 9 May 1927, *Letters III*: 158.
20. In fact Stephens was illegitimate and his surname and date of birth were invented.
21. To SB, 27 May 1927, *SB Letters*: 121–2.
22. To HSW, 8 July 1927 [more likely 3 July], *Letters I*: 257.
23. To HSW, 10 July 1927, *Letters III*: 162.

24. To HSW, 23 August 1927, Ellmann Notes, Tulsa.
25. To HSW, 14 September 1927, *Letters I*: 259.
26. To HSW, 29 October 1927, *Letters I*: 260.
27. To HSW, 14 September 1927, *Letters I*: 259.
28. To Valery Larbaud, [?18 October 1927], *Letters III*: 164.
29. To HSW, 28 October 1927, *Letters I*: 259.
30. McAlmon and Boyle, *Being Geniuses Together*: 278.
31. To HSW, 4 November 1927, *Letters I*: 260.
32. To HSW, 9 November 1927, *Letters I*: 261.
33. SB to HSW, 14 November 1927, BL.
34. HSW to SB, 20 November 1927, Princeton University, NJ.
35. To SB, 1 January 1928, *SB Letters*: 132–3.
36. To HSW, 1 January 1928, BL.
37. From Monro Saw, 2 January 1928, BL.
38. Helen Nutting Diary, February 1928, Northwestern University, Evanston, Illinois.
39. To HSW, 15 February 1928, *Letters III*: 171.
40. Nino Frank in Potts: 82.
41. *Ibid.*: 82–3.
42. From HSW, 23 March 1928, Ellmann Notes, Tulsa.
43. To HSW, pmk 26 March 1928, *SL*: 329–31.
44. His knowing of Tweedledum and Tweedledee makes his previous claim never to have read Carroll's Alice books questionable.
45. *FW*: 270.
46. To HSW, 8 April 1928, *Letters III*: 175.
47. To HSW, 16 April 1928, *Letters III*: 176.
48. 'The *Work in Progress* of James Joyce and Old Norse Poetry', *transition 13* (Summer 1928): 209–13.
49. To F. Scott Fitzgerald, 11 July 1928, *Letters III*: 180.
50. F. Scott Fitzgerald to Max Perkins, [c. 21 July 1928], *The Letters of F. Scott Fitzgerald*: 230.
51. According to Mathew Broccoli's biography of Fitzgerald, Herbert Gorman told of a dinner at Beach's with the Joyces and Fitzgeralds at which he and his wife were present, where a drunken Fitzgerald threatened to jump from the window unless Nora declared her love for him. He adds that Gorman was an unreliable witness.
52. McAlmon and Boyle, *Being Geniuses Together*: 314–15.
53. To SB, 17 July1928, *SB Letters*: 141.
54. Lucia Joyce, 'The Real Life of James Joyce Told by Lucia Joyce', unpublished MS, copy in Joyce Collection, University College London.
55. To HSW, 12 August 1928, BL.
56. West, *The Strange Necessity*: 15.
57. Sean O'Faolain, 'Style and the Limitations of Speech', *Criterion*, viii, no. 30 (September 1928): 67–87.
58. From HSW to SB, 1 October 1928, Princeton University, NJ.
59. To HSW, 2 October 1928, BL.
60. Jack Yeats to Thomas McGreevy, 4 April 1929, TCDL.
61. Eugene Sheehy, in O'Connor: 35.
62. Virginia Woolf to Christobel McLaren, 2 December 1928, *The Virginia Woolf Bulletin*, no. 15, January 2004: 29.
63. From John Drinkwater, 3 December 1928, BL.
64. To HSW, 23 October 1928, *Letters I*: 270.
65. Cyril Connolly, 'The Position of Joyce', *Life and Letters*, ii, no. 11 (April 1929): 273–90; also in *The Condemned Playground* (London: Hogarth Press, 1985): 1–15.

66. To HSW, 23 October 1928, *Letters I*: 273.

67. *Ibid.*: 271.

68. From H. G. Wells, 23 November 1928, *Letters I*: 274–5.

69. To HSW, *Letters I*: 278.

70. To HSW, 15 December 1928, BL.

71. To HSW, 2 December 1928, *Letters I*: 277.

72. Helen Nutting Diary, Christmas Eve 1928, Northwestern University, Evanston, Illinois.

73. NY Supreme Court Adjudication in the Case of Joyce vs. Samuel Roth and the Two Worlds Publishing Company, 27 December 1928.

27: A French Connection (1929)

1. Gilbert, *Paris Journal*, 1 January 1929.

2. Nino Frank in Potts: 89.

3. HSW To SB, 14 January 1929, Princeton University, NJ.

4. Gilbert, *Paris Journal*, 24 January 1929.

5. To SJ, 26 January 1929, *Letters III*: 187.

6. Gilbert, *Paris Journal*, 16 February 1929.

7. Gilbert, *Paris Journal*, 5 March 1929.

8. Gilbert, *Paris Journal*, 5 and 15 March 1929.

9. Nino Frank in Potts: 87.

10. Quoted by Stephen Spender, *New York Times*, 26 May 1957.

11. Charles de St-Cyr, *La Semaine à Paris*, 1928, Rondelle Collection of the Performing Arts, 6; quoted in Shloss: 5.

12. Beckett, *Dream of Fair to Middling Women* (London: Calder, 1993): 121.

13. Quoted in Bernard McGinley, *Joyce's Lives: Uses and Abuses of a Biografiend* (London: University of North London Press, 1996).

14. Maria Jolas to Ellmann, 1953, Ellmann Papers, Tulsa.

15. To Valery Larbaud, 29 July 1929, *Letters I*: 283.

16. Nino Frank in Potts: 86.

17. Colums: 199.

18. Beckett to Ellmann, 28 July 1953, Ellmann Papers, Tulsa.

19. Beach in Mikhail: 179.

20. To HSW, 16 July 1929, *Letters I*: 281–2.

21. Gilbert, *Paris Journal*, 1 June 1929.

22. Gilbert, *Paris Journal*, 20 August 1929.

23. To Valery Larbaud, 30 July 1929, *Letters I*: 284.

24. *Ibid.*

25. *Daily Dispatch*, 4 September 1930.

26. Hamish Miles, *Criterion*, October 1930, x, no. 38: 188.

27. *New York Times*, 23 August 1929: 20.

28. D. G. Bridson, *New English Weekly*, 5 January 1933: 281–2.

29. *FW*: 25.

30. Gilbert, *Paris Journal*, 20 August 1929.

31. *Thom's 1850 Dublin Directory* gives the date as 1173 and states that Henry, having defeated Roderick O'Connor King of Ireland, granted to Dublin all the rights enjoyed by the men of Bristol.

32. Nigel Nicolson (ed.), *Harold Nicolson: Diaries and Letters 1909–1963* (Weidenfeld & Nicolson, 2004), entry for 4 February 1924.

33. George Moore to Louis Gillet, 20 August 1931, quoted in Gillet, *Claybook for James Joyce*: 32.

34. Arnold Bennett, *Evening Standard*, 19 September 1929: 7.

35. To Valery Larbaud, [?late September 1929], [Paris], *Letters III*: 194.

36. To HSW, 19 October 1929, *Letters I*: 285.

37. Shloss: 196–7.

38. To HSW, 19 October 1929, *Letters I*: 286 (unpublished passages in original letter in Weaver Collection at BL).

39. Hans Richter to Ellmann 1958, Ellmann Papers, Tulsa.

40. Sergei Eisenstein, *Immoral Memories* (Boston: Houghton Mifflin, 1983): 214.

41. *FW*: 221.

42. *FW*: 298.

43. To HSW, 22 November 1929, *Letters I*: 286.

44. Gilbert, *Paris Journal*, 29 December 1929.

45. The Black Sun Press would continue under Caresse Crosby, publishing Hemingway and William Faulkner, among others.

46. To HSW, 12 December 1929, BL.

47. From 'James Joyce in Paris', in Mikhail: 118.

48. Edel, *Stuff of Sleep and Dreams*: 69.

49. *FW*: 573.

50. Samuel Beckett to Ellmann, 21 June 1954, Ellmann Papers, Tulsa.

51. To HSW, 18 March 1930, *Letters I*: 291.

28: 'Always something new on the Robiac front' (1930)

1. Gilbert, *Paris Journal*, 2 January 1930.

2. Helen Fleischman Memoir, HRC.

3. SG to HSW, 27 January 1930, BL.

4. Gilbert, *Paris Journal*, 29 January 1930.

5. SG to HSW, 27 January 1930, BL.

6. Gilbert, *Paris Journal*, 29 January 1920.

7. To HSW, 18 March 1930, *Letters I*: 280.

8. To HSW, 18 March 1930, *Letters I*: 292.

9. Gilbert, *Paris Journal*, 28 April 1930.

10. To HSW, 18 March 1930, *Letters I*: 289–92.

11. Herbert Read, 'James Joyce: Romantic or Classic', *Cambridge Review*, li (13 June 1930): 488–9; Deming (ed.), *James Joyce: The Critical Heritage*: 518.

12. Conal O'Riordan, *New Statesman*, 31 May 1930: 247.

13. Gilbert, *Paris Journal*, 28 April 1930.

14. Ellmann: 616n.

15. G. W. Stonier, 'Mr James Joyce in Progress', *New Statesman*, xxxv, no. 896 (28 June 1930): 372, 374.

16. NJ to HSW, 28 March 1930, BL.

17. PL to Jean Paulhan, c. 29 January 1941, *A James Joyce Yearbook*: 116–17.

18. PL to Alexander Léon, June 1930, quoted by Ellmann: 630.

19. PL to Jean Paulhan, c. 29 January 1941, *A James Joyce Yearbook*: 120.

20. From Marthe Fleischmann, 14 February 1930, Ellmann Notes, Tulsa.

21. Later Sullivan did record most of his arias and numbers of Irish ballads, both acoustically and electronically.

22. Shloss: 194.

23. To HSW, 24 April 1934, *Letters I*: 340 (unpublished passages in original letter in Weaver Collection at BL).

24. Shloss: 188, no. 16; Dominique Maroger, 'Dernière rencontre avec Lucia', in *James Joyce*, ed. Jacques Aubert and Fritz Senn (Paris: Editions de l'Herne, 1985): 77.

25. Helen Fleischmann to HSW, 23 May 1930, BL.

26. Helen Fleischmann to HSW, 28 May 1930, BL.

27. Report of Dr Alfred Vogt, 30 May 1930, *Letters III*: 197–8.

28. *Neue Schweizer Rundschau*, xxii, Heft 9, September 1929.

29. 'An Interview with Carola Giedion-Welcker and Maria Jolas', ed. Richard M. Kain, *James Joyce Quarterly*, 2 (Winter 1974): 96.

30. Colums: 183.

31. Griffin, *The Wild Geese*: 31.

32. HSW to SB, 29 July 1930, Princeton University, NJ.

33. Edgardo Carducci, 'The Tenor Voice of Europe', *Music and Letters*, September 1929: 318–24.

34. To HSW, 6 September 1930, *Letters III*: 202.
35. From Sir Thomas Beecham, 22 September 1930, Ellmann Notes, Tulsa.
36. *The Times*, 4 April 1936.
37. To HSW, 27 September 1930, *Letters I*: 294.
38. Gilbert, *Paris Journal*, 25 October 1930.
39. From PL, 25 September 1930, Ellmann Notes, Tulsa.
40. Daniel Brody to Ellmann, n.d. Ellmann Papers, Tulsa.
41. Léon Collection, NLI. *Letters III*: 254, n2.
42. To HG, 30 October 1930, *Letters III*: 206.
43. To FB, 16 November 1930, HRC.
44. To SB, n.d. [probably October–November 1930], *SB Letters*: 167.
45. Gilbert, *Paris Journal*, 14 November 1930.
46. To HSW, 22 November 1930, *Letters I*: 295.
47. *Ibid.*
48. Gilbert, *Paris Journal*, 8 December 1930.
49. From SB, 9 December 1930, Joyce Foundation, Zurich.
50. To HSW, 22 December 1930, *Letters III*: 208.
51. Gilbert, *Paris Journal*, 25 December 1930.
52. William Bird to Ellmann, 24 October 1953, Ellmann Papers, Tulsa.
53. Shloss 202; Lucia Joyce, 'My Life'. (See David Hayman, 'Shadow of His Mind: The Papers of Lucia Joyce', *Joyce at Texas: Essays on the James Joyce Materials at the Humanities Research Center*: 69.)
54. Albert Hubbell to Ellmann, August 1981, Ellmann Papers, Tulsa.
55. Cary F. Baynes, 'Notes on Lucia', quoted in Shloss: 205.
56. Bozena Delimata to Richard Ellmann, 27 June 1953, Ellmann Papers, Tulsa.
57. Fred Monro to HSW; HSW to JJ, 30 December 1930, Ellmann Notes, Tulsa.
58. Colums: 186–7.

29: A Very English Wedding (1931)

1. To George Antheil, 3 January 1931, *Letters I*: 297–8.
2. To HSW, 18 February 1931, *Letters I*: 301.
3. From Louis Gillet, 7 January 1931, *Letters III*: 211.
4. JSJ, 31 January 1931, *Letters III*: 212.
5. Colums: 179–80.
6. *Ibid.*: 179ff.
7. To HSW, 16 February 1931, *Letters I*: 299–300.
8. Gilbert, *Paris Journal*, 1 March 1931.
9. To HSW, 4 March 1931, *Letters I*: 302.
10. To HSW, 16 February 1931, *Letters I*: 300.
11. Michael Lennon to HG, [after 9 February 1931], Gorman Papers.
12. From SJ, 14 April 1931, *Letters III*: 216, n. 4.
13. Michael Lennon, 'James Joyce', *Catholic World*, cxxxii, March 1931.
14. To HSW, 11 March 1931, *Letters I*: 303.
15. *Ibid.*: 302–3.
16. To HG, [?19 March 1931], *Letters III*: 214.
17. From André Gide, 30 April 1931, *Letters III*: 218.
18. Edel, *Stuff of Sleep and Dreams*: 77.
19. From SB, 9 May 1931, Joyce Foundation, Zurich.
20. G. W. Stonier, *New Statesman*, xxxv, no. 896 (28 June 1930): 372, 374.
21. *TLS*, October 1930: 147.
22. *Dublin Magazine*, vi, no. 3 (July–September 1931): 33.
23. D'Arcy interview with Ellmann, 27 April 1960.
24. From Adrienne Monnier, 19 May 1931, Ellmann, Tulsa Notes, translation from Ellmann: 652–3.

25. Knowlson, *The Life of Samuel Beckett*: 134, quoted by Shloss: 195.
26. Colums: 198.
27. Beckett to Ellmann, 28 July 1953, Ellmann Papers, Tulsa.
28. Power: 110. Power wrongly placed this happening a year later when Joyce was no longer living in Campden Grove.
29. From SB, 1 July 1932, Joyce Foundation, Zurich.
30. *Daily Mirror*, 4 July 1931: 2.
31. To Colums, 18 July 1931, *Letters III*: 221.
32. Sylvia Lynd's *Autobiography*, reprinted in Norrie (ed.), *Writers and Hampstead* (London: High Hills 1987): 106.
33. J. B. Priestley, *Margin Released* (London: Heinemann 1962): 157–8.
34. Kathleen Barnacle Griffin in Rodgers: 61.
35. Budgen in Rodgers: 61.
36. To SB, 13 July 1931, *SB Letters*: 173.
37. SB, 15 July 1931, Ellmann Notes, Tulsa.
38. Louis Gillet, 'James Joyce and his new Novel', *Revue des Deux Mondes*, August 1931.
39. Moore to Gillet, 29 August 1931, quoted in Gillet, *Claybook for James Joyce*: 32–4.
40. To HSW, 16 August 1931, BL.
41. To SB, [mid-September 1931], *SB Letters*: 178.
42. To HSW, 1 October 1931, *Letters III*: 230.
43. Colums: 208.
44. 'Anna Livia Plurabelle', *Psyche*, London, 12, 2 (October 1931) 92–5.
45. H. G. Wells, *The Shape of Things to Come* (London: Hutchinson. 1933): 416.
46. From HSW, 20 October 1931, Ellmann Notes.
47. To HSW, 27 November 1931, *Letters III*: 235.
48. Harold Nicolson to Patricia Hutchins, TCDL. (Ironically, Nicolson later became a governor of the BBC.)
49. 'From a Banned Writer to a Banned Singer', *CW*: 258–68.
50. To HSW, 17 December 1932, *Letters I*: 312.
51. Bozena Delimata to Ellmann, n.d., Elmann Papers, Tulsa.
52. To EP, 1 January 1932, *Letters III*: 239.
53. Gillet in Potts: 189.

30: Death, Birth and Madness (1932–1933)

1. To TSE, 1 January 1932, *Letters I*: 311.
2. To HSW, 17 January 1931, *Letters I*: 312.
3. *Chicago Premier*, 2 January 1932.
4. PL to Alfred Bergan, 4 February 1932, *NLI Book*: 74.
5. Colums: 211.
6. Quoted in Shloss: 7.
7. Lucie Léon to Ellmann, 31 August 1953, Ellmann Papers, Tulsa.
8. *Ibid.*
9. Shloss: 218–19.
10. Gilbert, *Paris Journal*, 26 April 1932.
11. To HSW, 20 April 1932, BL.
12. *Ibid.*
13. Gilbert, *Paris Journal*, 6 May 1932.
14. *Ibid.*
15. McGreevy to WBY, 10 May 1932, TCDL.
16. The company was named 'John Lane, The Bodley Head' after its founder.
17. Gilbert, *Paris Journal*, 9 July 1932.
18. Colums: 216.
19. To HSW, 22 May 1932, BL.
20. Gilbert, *Paris Journal*, 24 May 1932.
21. From Louis Gillet, [c. 1932], Cornell.
22. To HSW, 10 July 1932, *Letters I*: 321.
23. From Maria Jolas, 10 July 1932, BL.
24. To PL, 12 July 1932, *NLI Book*.
25. Cerf to PL, 18 July 1932, NYPL.
26. To HSW, 21 July 1932, BL.
27. Shloss: 239.
28. From C. G. J., c. August 1932, *Letters III: 253.*

29. To Georg Goyert, 22 October 1932, *Letters III*: 262.
30. *Ibid.*
31. From WBY, 2 September 1932, *Letters III*: 258–9.
32. To FB, 9 October 1932, *Letters III*: 260.
33. To PL, 25 September 1932, *NLI Book*.
34. Shloss: 245.
35. Gilbert, *Paris Journal*, 5 November 1932.
36. To HSW, 11 November 1932, *Letters I*: 328; Shloss: 242.
37. Arthur Symons, Preface to Hughes (ed.), *The Joyce Book*.
38. To Augustus John, quoted in part in Sotheby's principal catalogue for a sale on 17 December 1979, 102. Reproduced by Ellmann: 627.
39. To Arnold Bax, 29 March 1933, *Letters III*: 276.
40. Nicolson, *Diaries*, 4 February 1934.
41. To HSW, 25 November 1932, *Letters I*: 328.
42. G. W. Stonier, 'Crazy Week', *New Statesman*, 3 December 1932.
43. London *Daily News*, 12 December 1932, NLI.
44. PL to HSW, 14 December 1932, BL.
45. PL to HSW, 4 January 1933, BL.
46. To HSW, 18 January 1933, *Letters I*: 332. Maria Jolas told Ellmann that she and Eugene had accompanied Joyce to Rouen, but there is no mention of them in this letter about that visit.
47. Nino Frank in Potts: 90.
48. LJ to FB, 3 September 1933, *Letters III*: 283–4.
49. To W. K. Magee, 21 March 1933, *Letters I*: 336.
50. HG to PL, 1 April 1933, *NLI Book*: 97.
51. PL to HSW, 23 March 1933, *NLI Book*.
52. PL to HSW, 31 March 1933, *NLI Book*.
53. PL to HSW, 2 April 1933, *NLI Book*: 42.
54. PL to HSW, 25 April 1933, *Letters III*: 276–7.
55. *Ibid.*: 278.
56. Lidderdale and Nicholson, *Dear Miss Weaver*: 326.
57. Statement of JJ's annual receipts and payments, noted by Harriet Weaver, 5 May 1933, *NLI Book*.
58. Vogt's report on Joyce, Zurich, 30 May 1933 (Joyce Foundation, Zurich).
59. From Louis Gillet, 3 June 1933, *NLI Book*: 96.
60. To PL, 6 July 1933, *NLI Book*: 9.
61. To PL, 7 July 1933, *NLI Book*: 10.
62. To PL, 9 July 1933, *NLI Book*.
63. To FB, 17 July 1933, *Letters I*: 336.
64. Ellmann: 677.
65. To PL, 23 July 1933, *NLI Book*.
66. To SJ, 13 August 1933, *Letters III*: 282.
67. Ellmann: 665.
68. PL to HSW, 23 September 1933, *Letters III*: 285.
69. LJ to SJ, 5 September 1933, *Cornell Catalogue*.
70. Budgen: 353.
71. To SJ, 18 October 1933, *Letters III*: 288n.
72. PL to HSW, 23 September 1933, *Letters III*: 286.
73. *Ibid.*: 287.
74. From HG, 25 November 1933, reprinted in *A James Joyce Miscellany II*, 1959, ed. M. Magalaner: 9–14.
75. PL to HSW, 23 September 1933, *Letters III*: 288.
76. To HSW, 30 November 1933, quoted in Ellmann: 610.
77. A detailed account of the strategy employed by Cerf, Ernst and his team in presenting a highly selective literary case to the court is to be found in Joseph Kelly, *Our Joyce: From Outcast to Icon* (Austin: University of Texas Press, 1998): 129–32.
78. Vanderham, *James Joyce and Censorship*: 128.
79. *The Times*, 8 December 1933.
80. *New Republic*, 13 December 1933.

81. Vanderham, *James Joyce and Censorship*: 131.

82. Bennett Cerf to PL, 6 December 1933, NLI.

83. To SJ, [about 8 December 1933], *Letters III*: 293–4.

84. Ellmann: 667.

85. From TSE, 11 December 1933, *Letters III*: 294.

86. To TSE, 18 December 1933, *Letters III*: 295.

87. Bennett Cerf to HG, 12 December 1933, from *A James Joyce Miscellany II*, 1959.

88. To Constantine Curran, 20 December 1933, *Letters I*: 338.

89. To FB, 30 December 1933, *Letters III*: 296.

31: Ulysses Unbound (1934–1936)

1. *Daily Sketch*, 11 January 1934 (Lord Birkenhead had been an official censor during the war and Attorney General and Lord Chancellor afterwards). When Alfred Noyes alerted the police to the book's inclusion in the auctioneer's catalogue it was withdrawn from sale.

2. *Daily Sketch*, 12 January 1934.

3. Horace Gregory, *New York Herald Tribune*, 21 January 1934, book section: 1–2.

4. Gilbert Seldes, *New York Evening Journal*, 27 January 1934.

5. From HSW, 17 March 1934, Ellmann Notes, Tulsa.

6. Medical bills of Lucia Joyce, *NLI Book*.

7. Nicolson, *Diaries*, 4 February 1934: 110–11.

8. PL to HSW, 11 March 1934, BL.

9. *Ibid.*

10. *Ibid.*

11. From HSW, 17 March 1934, Ellmann Notes, Tulsa.

12. Budgen: 353.

13. *New York Herald Tribune*, 14 March 1934.

14. 'Epilogue to Ibsen's *Ghosts*,' *CW*: 273.

15. *New York Evening Sun*, [?April] 1934.

16. G. W. Stonier, *New Statesman*, viii, 22 September 1934: 364.

17. To GJ and HJ, 13 July 1934, *Letters III*: 309.

18. To Carola Giedion-Welcker, 22 July 1934, *Letters III*: 310.

19. To HSW, 28 July 1934, *Letters III*: 311.

20. The best discussion of the hearing may be found in Vanderham: 132–49.

21. To HJ, 9 August 1934, *Letters III*: 316.

22. To PL, 22 August 1934, *NLI Book*: 14.

23. To SJ, [mid-August 1934], *Letters III*: 319.

24. To GJ and HJ, 21 August 1934, *Letters III*: 321.

25. To Carola Giedion-Welcker, 2 September 1934, *Letters III*: 323.

26. To T. W. Pugh, 22 September 1934, *Letters III*: 326.

27. CGJ, 2 March 1954; interview with PH.

28. To HSW, 22 September 1934, *Letters I*: 346.

29. HSW to PL, 5 October 1934, Ellmann Notes, Tulsa.

30. CGJ to PH, 29 January 1955, interview quoted by Ellmann: 680.

31. Power: 60.

32. To FB, 18 December 1934, *Letters III*: 332.

33. To HSW, 21 October 1934, *Letters I*: 349–51.

34. To GJ, 21 November 1934, *Letters III*: 332.

35. From PL, 14 December 1934, Ellmann Notes, Tulsa.

36. She later told Harriet that she did not like the way the doctor looked, dressed in white like a cook with other nurses and Mrs Giedion there too.

37. To GJ and HJ, 28 December 1934, *Letters I*: 354–5.
38. *FW*: 536.
39. To PL, 10 January 1935, *NLI Book*.
40. Joyce had always considered the novel unfilmable, but did once toy with the idea, even discussing a suitable actor for Bloom – Charles Laughton, George Arliss and even Charlie Chaplin were mentioned.
41. James Thurber, 'The Talk of the Town', *New Yorker*, 12 January, 1935: 11.
42. To GJ and HJ, 5 February 1935, *Letters I*: 358.
43. *Ibid.*
44. *Ibid.*: 357.
45. Nino Frank in Potts: 91.
46. Mercanton in Potts: 208.
47. PL to Jean Paulhan, *A James Joyce Yearbook*: 121–2.
48. Eileen Schaurek in Mikhail: 67.
49. From HSW, 17 February 1935, Ellmann Notes, Tulsa.
50. From HSW, 18 March 1935, Ellmann Notes, Tulsa.
51. From HSW, 4 March, 1935, *NLI Book*.
52. From HSW, 27 February 1935, *NLI Book*.
53. From HSW, 18 March 1935, Ellmann Notes, Tulsa.
54. *Ibid.*
55. To GJ and HJ, 19 March 1935, *Letters III*: 351.
56. From HSW, 18 March 1935, Ellmann Notes, Tulsa.
57. To HSW, 7 April 1935, *Letters I*: 362.
58. To HSW, 1 May 1935, *Letters I*: 365.
59. *Daily Telegraph*, 8 February 1936.
60. To LJ, 28 March 1935, *Letters I*: 359.
61. To Eileen Schaurek, [16 March 1935], *Letters III*: 350.
62. To HSW, 1 May 1935, *Letters I*: 365.
63. Shloss: 344.
64. *Ibid.*: 343.
65. Bozena Delimata to Ellmann, Ellmann Papers, Tulsa.
66. *FW*: 264.
67. To HSW, 1 May 1935, *Letters I*: 366.
68. To GJ and HJ, 1 April 1935, *Letters I*: 360–1.
69. To GJ, 25 June 1935, *Letters I*: 371.
70. To GJ, 10 July 1935, *Letters III*: 367.
71. To GJ and HJ, 16 July 1935, *Letters III*: 369.
72. PL to HSW, 19 July 1935, quoted in Ellmann: 687.
73. To Constantine Curran, 10 August 1935, *Letters I*: 379.
74. To Mr and Mrs Constantine Curran, 31 July 1935, *Letters I*: 378.
75. To LJ, n.d. [?July 1935], *Letters I*: 377.
76. To LJ, 17 October 1935, *Letters III*: 377. Joyce told Budgen that he was not interested in women's bodies, only their clothes.
77. From HSW, 25 November 1935, Ellmann, Tulsa Notes.
78. Mercanton in Potts: 209.
79. HSW to PL, 29 January 1936, *NLI Book*.
80. HSW to PL, 7 February 1936, *NLI Book*.
81. From HSW, 12 February 1936, Ellmann Notes, Tulsa.
82. HSW to PL, 22 February 1936, *NLI Book*: 60.
83. PL to HSW, Ellmann Papers, Tulsa.
84. To HSW, 5 April 1936, Ellmann Notes.
85. To HSW, 9 June 1936, *SL*: 381.
86. To Mary Colum, 5 June 1936, *Letters III*: 385.
87. To HSW, 9 June 1936, *SL*: 381.

32: The ABC of Blind Love and Ruination (1936–1938)

1. 'James Joyce's poetry does not suggest *Ulysses*', *New York Times Book Review* (10 October 1937): 4. Ellmann thought that Joyce tended to treat women like dolls.
2. *FW*: 465.
3. Ole Vinding in Potts: 149.
4. *Ibid.*: 140.

5. Home Office memo, 29 October 1936, DPP to HM Attorney General, National Archives.
6. *New Statesman*, 13 October 1936: 592.
7. PL to HSW, 7 November 1936, *NLI Book*: 67.
8. G. W. Stonier, 'Leviathan', *New Statesman*, 10 October 1936: 551–2.
9. Alan Clutton-Brock, 'Interpretations of "Ulysses"', *TLS*, 23 January 1937: 56.
10. Alan Clutton-Brock, *TLS*, 21 November 1936: 954.
11. PL to HSW, 18 November 1936, *NLI Book*.
12. To Fred Monro, 2 May 1937, *NLI Book*: 136.
13. Nino Frank in Potts: 90.
14. *Ibid.*: 96.
15. To Constantine Curran, 19 May 1937, *Letters III*: 338–9.
16. To Mr and Mrs Myron Nutting, 30 June 1937, *Letters III*: 400.
17. To Constantine Curran, 14 July 1937, *Letters I*: 394.
18. *TLS*, 10 April 1937.
19. *CW*: 275.
20. Quoted in Ellmann: 5.
21. To Nancy Cunard, [1937], quoted in Ellmann: 704.
22. Jolas, *The Man from Babel*: 169–70.
23. John Sutherland, *Stephen Spender: The Authorized Biography* (London: Viking, 2002): 222.
24. Helen Fleischman, Memoir, HRC.
25. To PL, 14 August 1937, *NLI Book*: 26.
26. To Constantine Curran, 6 August 1937, *Letters I*: 395. (My translation of *Non dico giammai ma non ancora*.)
27. To Constantine Curran, 19 August 1937, *Letters I*: 396.
28. To FB, 9 September 1937, *Letters I*: 396.
29. To HJ, 11 September 1937, Joyce Foundation, Zurich.
30. *The Times*, 1 October 1937: 8.
31. Quoted in Jolas, *The Man from Babel*: 171, and Griffin, *The Wild Geese*: 29.
32. Mercanton in Potts: 211.
33. Beckett to Ellmann, 28 July 1953, Ellmann Papers, Tulsa.
34. PL to HSW, 18 December 1937, *Letters III*: 409.
35. PL to Eileen Schaurek, 21 December 1937, *NLI Book*: 116.
36. To Carola Giedion-Welcker, 31 December 1937, *Letters III*: 410.
37. Nino Frank in Potts: 96.
38. From Geoffrey Faber, 26 January 1938, *NLI Book*: 182.
39. PL to HSW, 2 February 1938, *NLI Book*: 70–1.
40. Nino Frank in Potts: 94.
41. Mercanton in Potts: 211.
42. *Ibid.*: 211.
43. *Ibid.*: 213.
44. *Ibid.*: 214.
45. To GJ and HJ, 8 March 1938, *Letters I*: 399.
46. PL to Carola Giedion-Welcker, 9 March 1938, *Letters III*: 407.
47. To Carola Giedion-Welcker, 28 March 1938, *Letters III*: 418.
48. Mercanton in Potts: 214.
49. To IIJ, 20 April 1938, *Letters III*: 420.
50. Geoffrey Grigson, 'James Joyce', *Picture Post*, 13 May 1939, and *Time Magazine* review, 8 May 1939.
51. Hermann Broch, *James Joyce und die Gegenwart* (*James Joyce and the Present*) (Frankfurt: Suhrkamp, 1972).
52. Eugene Jolas, 'My Friend James Joyce', in Givens (ed.), *James Joyce: Two Decades of Criticism*: 16–17.
53. Mercanton in Potts: 218.
54. To PL, 11 September 1938, *NLI Book*.
55. To PL, 21 September 1938, *NLI Book*: 30.
56. To George Goyert, 11 October 1938, *Letters III*: 433.
57. To Daniel Brody, 5 October 1938, *Letters III*: 432.
58. Colums: 230.
59. PL to Jean Paulhan, c. 29 January 1941. 'In Memory of James Joyce',

reprinted in *A James Joyce Yearbook*: 124.

60. *Ibid.*: 124–5.

61. PL to Richard de la Mare, 22 December 1938, *NLI Book*: 184.

62. PL to HSW, 10 December 1938, quoted in Lidderdale and Nicholson, *Dear Miss Weaver*: 373.

63. To Livia Svevo, [1 January 1939], *Letters III*: 435.

64. Richard de la Mare to PL, 17 January 1939, *NLI Book*: 184.

33: A Puzzle for a Puzzled World (1939)

1. Frank in Potts: 98 n.

2. PL to Huebsch, 7 February 1939, *NLI Book*: 217.

3. PL to HSW, 14 February 1939, *NLI Book*.

4. Huebsch to PL, 22 March 1939, *NLI Book*.

5. To TSE, [?April 1939], *Letters III*: 404.

6. Brian Boyd, *Vladimir Nabokov* (London: Chatto & Windus, 1990), vol. II: 504.

7. PL to HSW, 10 March 1939, *NLI Book*.

8. *FW*: 627.

9. *Ibid.*: 625–6.

10. Maria Jolas to Ellmann, 22 July 1953, Ellmann Papers, Tulsa.

11. To Livia Svevo, [1 May 1939], *Letters III*: 439.

12. The limited Faber edition was priced at 5 guineas, the cheaper one at 25s – an exorbitant and 'imbecilic' price, Joyce thought.

13. PL to Richard de la Mare, 22 July 1939, BL. Danis Rose and John O'Hanlon are reported to have found and corrected some 9,000 errors in the 1939 edition of *Finnegans Wake*. See Steven Carroll, '9,000 changes in amended "Finnegans Wake"', *Irish Times*, 5 March 2010.

14. To HSW, 4 May 1939, BL.

15. From Sean O'Casey, 30 May 1939, *Letters III*: 442.

16. Holloway Diary, 5 April 1939, NLI.

17. From Sean O'Casey, 30 May 1939, *Letters III*: 442.

18. Clifton Fadiman, *Time*, 6 May 1939.

19. Padraic Colum, *New York Times Book Review*, 7 May 1939.

20. 'The Beachcomber', *Daily Express*, 11 May 1939.

21. Harold Nicolson, 'The Indecipherable Mystery of Mr Joyce's Allegory', *Daily Telegraph*, 5 May 1939.

22. Nicolson *Diaries*, 29 April 1939: 187–8.

23. G. W. Stonier, *New Statesman*, xvii, 20 May 1939: 788, 790.

24. Oliver St John Gogarty, *Observer*, 7 May 1939: 4.

25. Richard Aldington, *Atlantic Monthly*, clxiii, June 1939.

26. PL to HG, 6 June 1939, *Letters III*: 443–4.

27. *FW*: 55.

28. To George Rogers, 3 August 1939, *Letters III*: 451.

29. In March 1950, two records of Giorgio singing 'Adieu to Girlish Days', words and tune by James Joyce, and 'Within This Hallowed Dwelling', from Mozart's *The Magic Flute*, were considered by the BBC Music Department. The producer Maurice Brown, who specialized in Irish folk song, reported that 'Personally, I think it is obviously a voice, but [with] very little training or even brain behind it.' (Memo: Maurice Brown to E. Lochspeiser, Music Dept, BBC Written Archives, 2 March 1950.)

30. To PL, Friday ?1 August 1939, *NLI Book*: 32.

31. Mercanton in Potts: 249.

32. To John Farrar, 21 September 1939, *Letters III*: 456–7.

33. To HG, 2 October 1939, SIU.

34. To PL, 25 September 1939, *NLI Book*: 34.

35. O'Brien quoted in Ellmann: 727–8.
36. Edmund Brauchbar, 30 July 1940, Letters III: 479.
37. Beckett to Ellmann, 28 July 1953, Ellmann Papers, Tulsa.

34: 'Going downhill fast' (1940)

1. Beckett to Ellmann, 28 July 1953, Ellmann Papers, Tulsa.
2. Peggy Guggenheim, *Out of This Century* (New York: André Deutsch, 1980): 207.
3. Gillet, *A Claybook for James Joyce*: 164.
4. Ellmann: 731.
5. From Dr. F. A. Delmas, 27 February 1940, Joyce Foundation, Zurich.
6. To Daniel Brody, 10 January 1939, *Letters III*: 464.
7. To Daniel Brody, 3 March 1940, *Letters I*: 409.
8. To Jacques Mercanton, 9 January 1940, *Letters III*: 463.
9. PL to Bennett Cerf, 1 February 1940, *NLI Book*: 220.
10. From Lloyds and National Provincial Bank Ltd., 7 March 1940, Joyce Foundation, Zurich.
11. Samuel Beckett to Ellmann, 28 July 1953, Ellmann Papers, Tulsa.
12. Maria Jolas to Ellmann, 22 July 1953, Ellmann Papers, Tulsa.
13. Shloss notes how many of the young women of that Parisian literary circle ended up in asylums – Lucia, Helen Fleischman, Yva Fernandez, Kay Boyle, Zelda Fitzgerald, and Nancy Cunard.
14. To Paul Ruggiero, 4 August 1940, *Letters I*: 414.
15. To Jacques Mercanton, pmk 13 August 1940, *Letters III*: 482.
16. Gillet, *A Claybook for James Joyce*: 165.
17. From Louis Gillet, 11 September 1940, Ellmann Papers, Tulsa.
18. To Jacques Mercanton, 29 October 1940, *Letters III*: 492.

19. Mercanton in Potts: 251.
20. To Carola Giedion-Welcker, 1 November 1940, *Letters III*: 494.
21. Declaration to the Zurich Kantonale Fremdenpolizei, 19 November 1940.
22. To Armand Petitjean, 23 November 1940, *Letters III*: 500.
23. To Armand Petitjean, 3 December 1940, *Letters III*: 503.
24. Ellmann: 738.

35: Death in Exile (1940–)

1. Mercanton in Potts: 251.
2. Ruggiero in Potts: 284.
3. Carola Giedion-Welcker, Potts: 276.
4. To the Mayor of Zurich, 20 December 1940, *Letters I*: 427.
5. Ruggiero in Potts: 284.
6. The words are from Edward Fitzgerald's *The Rubaiyat of Omar Khayyam*.
7. Carola Giedion-Welcker in Potts: 277.
8. Vera Esposito Dockrell to Ellmann, 14 April 1955, Ellmann Papers, Tulsa.
9. Ruggiero in Potts: 285.
10. To FB, 13 January 1928, *Letters III*: 168.
11. 'James Clarence Mangan', *CW*: 178.
12. Post-mortem no. 55/12 F. Obd., Dr Zollinger Clinic, Red Cross, quoted in Ellmann: 741.
13. McGreevy, 13 January 1941, Notebooks, TCDL.
14. Budgen: 365, clxiii.
15. Carola Giedion-Welcker, 'The Last Months of the Life of James Joyce' ('Les derniers Mois de la Vie de James Joyce', *Le Figaro Littéraire* (28 May 1949): 6.
16. John and Vera Russell, 'The Last Days of James Joyce: Death in Zurich', *Sunday Times*, 17 January 1965: 50.
17. 'James Joyce: Hail and Farewell', in

Carola Giedion-Welcker (ed.), *In Memoriam James Joyce* (Zurich: Fretz & Wasmuth Verlag, 1941): 13–15.

18. SJ to NJ, 16 January 1941, James Joyce Foundation, Zurich.

19. Power: 111.

20. Constantine Curran, *Irish Times*, 14 January 1941.

21. Kenneth Reddin, *Irish Times*, 14 January 1941.

22. Elizabeth Bowen, 'James Joyce', *The Bell*, I, no. 6 (March 1941): 49.

23. *The Irish Press*, 14 January 1941: 6, quoted in Mikhail: 171.

24. George Markow-Totevy, 'Gide et Joyce', *Mercure de France*, 1960: 338.

25. Unsigned notice, *TLS*, 25 January 1942.

26. *The Times*, 14 January 1941: 7.

27. T. S. Eliot, 'A Message to the Fish', *Horizon*, iii (March 1941): 173–5.

28. Van Wyck Brooks, *The Opinions of Oliver Allston* (London: J.M. Dent, 1941): 199; *New York Times*, 13 January 1941; Thornton Wilder, 'James Joyce, 1882–1941', *Poetry*, lvii (1940–1).

29. GJ to Maria Jolas, 17 January 1941, Jolas Collection, Beinecke Library, New Haven, CT.

30. GJ to Ellmann, 8 August 1953, Ellmann Papers, Tulsa.

31. Nino Frank to Ellmann, Ellmann Papers, Tulsa.

32. By American sculptor, Milton Hebald.

33. Shloss: 415; LJ to Kathleen and John Griffin, 26 February 1962, HRC.

Select Bibliography

Works of James Joyce

1. *Chamber Music* (1907), Jonathan Cape, London, 1980
2. *Dubliners* (1914), Jonathan Cape, London, 1947
3. *A Portrait of the Artist as a Young Man* (1916), Penguin, London, 1993
4. *Exiles* (1918), Panther, London, 1982
5. *Ulysses: The Corrected Text* (1922), Bodley Head, London, 1986; *Ulysses*, Penguin Books, London, 2000
6. *Pomes Penyeach*, Faber, London, 1971
7. *Anna Livia Plurabelle*, Faber (Criterion Miscellany no. 15), 1930
8. *Haveth Childers Everywhere*, Faber (Criterion Miscellany no. 26), 1931
9. *Two Tales of Shem and Shaun* (1936), Faber, London, 1932
10. *Collected Poems*, Black Sun Press, New York, 1936
11. *Finnegans Wake* (1939), Faber, London 1939; Penguin, London, 1992
12. *Stephen Hero*, Grafton, London, 1977
13. *Giacomo* Joyce (1968), Faber, London, 1983
14. *Letters of James Joyce*, Vol. I, ed. Stuart Gilbert, Viking, New York, 1952
15. *Letters of James Joyce*, Vol. II, ed. Richard Ellmann, Viking, New York, 1966
16. *Letters of James Joyce*, Vol. III, ed. Richard Ellmann, Viking, New York, 1966
17. *Selected Letters of James Joyce*, ed. Richard Ellmann, Faber, London, 1975
18. *The Critical Writings of James Joyce*, ed. Ellsworth Mason and Richard Ellmann, Cornell University Press, Ithaca, NY, 1989
19. *Poems and Shorter Writings*, ed. Richard Ellmann, A. Walton Litz and John Whittier-Fergusson, Faber, London, 1991
20. *The Essential James Joyce*, ed. Harry Levin, Triad Panther, St Albans, 1977
21. *The Portable James Joyce*, ed. Harry Levin, Penguin, Harmondsworth, 1979
22. *The Joyce Book*, ed. Herbert Hughes, Sylvan Press, London, 1932

Other published Joyce letters, notes and manuscripts

1. Banta, Melissa, and Oscar A. Silverman, (eds), *James Joyce's Letters to Sylvia Beach, 1921–1940*, Plantin, Cardiff, 1992
2. Connolly, Thomas E., *James Joyce's Books, Portraits, Manuscripts, Typescripts, Notebooks, Page Proofs*, Edwin Mellen Press, Lampeter, 1997
3. Groden, Michael (ed.), *The James Joyce Archive*, 63 vols, Garland, New York, 1977–9
4. Herring, Philip F., *Joyce's* Ulysses *Notebooks*, University Press of Virginia, Charlottesville, 1972
5. Scholes, Robert E., *The Cornell Joyce Collection*, Cornell University Press, Ithaca, NY, 1961
6. Scholes, Robert, E., and Richard M. Kain, *The Workshop of Daedalus*, Northwestern University Press, Evanston, IL, 1965

7. Spielberg, Peter, *James Joyce Manuscripts and Notebooks at Buffalo*, University of Buffalo, 1962

Biographies and Letters

Beja, Morris, *James Joyce: A Literary Life*, Gill & Macmillan, Dublin, 1992

Bradley, Bruce, S. J., *James Joyce's Schooldays*, Gill & Macmillan, Dublin, 1982

Budgen, Frank, *The Making Of 'Ulysses' And Other Writings*, Intro. Clive Hart, Oxford University Press, 1972

Byrne, J. F., *Silent Years*, Farrar, Straus & Young, NY, 1953

Costello, Peter, *James Joyce: The Years of Growth 1882–1915*, Kyle Cathy, London, 1992

Davies, Stan Gebler, *James Joyce: A Portrait of the Artist*, Abacus, London, 1977

Ellmann, Richard, *James Joyce*, Oxford University Press, 1959/1982

Eliot, Valerie (ed.), *The Letters of T. S. Eliot, Vol. 1: 1898–1922*, Faber, London, 1988 (p/b and h/b)

Gilbert, Stuart, *Reflections on James Joyce: Stuart Gilbert's Paris Journal* (ed. T. Staley and R. Lewis), University of Texas Press, 1993

Gorman, Herbert S., *James Joyce: His First Forty Years*, Huebsch, NY, 1924.

Gorman, Herbert S., *James Joyce: A Definitive Biography*, John Lane The Bodley Head, London, 1941

Jackson, John Wyse, and Peter Costello, *John Stanislaus Joyce*, Fourth Estate, London, 1997

James Joyce–Paul Léon Papers, National Library of Ireland, Dublin, 1992

Joyce, Stanislaus, *My Brother's Keeper*, Faber, London, 1958

Joyce, Stanislaus, *The Complete Dublin Diary*, Cornell University Press, Ithaca and London, 1971

Joyce, Stanislaus, *Joyce in Svevo's Garden*, MGS Press, Trieste, 1995

Laoi, Padraic, *Nora Barnacle Joyce*, Kennys Bookshop, Galway, 1982

Lidderdale, Jane, and Mary Nicholson, *Dear Miss Weaver*, Viking Press, NY, 1970

Maddox, Brenda, *Nora*, Hamish Hamilton, 1998

McCourt, John, *The Years of Bloom*, Lilliput Press, Dublin, 2000

O'Brien, Edna, *James Joyce*, Weidenfeld & Nicolson, 1999

Pindar, Ian, *Joyce*, Haus Publishing, London, 2004

Read, Forrest (ed.), *Pound–Joyce: The Letters of Ezra Pound to James Joyce*, Faber, London, 1968

Sullivan, Kevin, *Joyce Among the Jesuits*, Columbia University Press, NY, 1967

Memoirs

Anderson, Margaret, *My Thirty Years' War*, Horizon Press, NY, 1969

Beach, Sylvia, *Shakespeare and Company*, Plantin, London, 1987

Budgen, Frank, *Myselves When Young*, Oxford University Press, London, 1970

Byrne, J.F., *Silent Years*, Farrar, Straus & Young, NY, 1953

Colum, Mary, *Life and the Dream*, Doubleday, NY, 1947

Colum, Mary and Padraic, *Our Friend James Joyce*, Doubleday, NY, 1958

Curran, Constantine P., *Joyce Remembered*, Oxford University Press, 1968

Freund, Giselle, *Three Days with James Joyce*, Persea Books, NY, 1985

Gillet, Louis, *Claybook for James Joyce*, Abelard-Schuman, London/NY, 1958

Gogarty, Oliver St John, *As I Was Going Down Sackville Street*, Penguin, Harmondsworth, 1954

Gogarty, Oliver St John, *Intimations*, Sphere, London, 1986

Gogarty, Oliver St John, *Mourning Became Mrs Spendlove*, Creative Age Press, NY, 1948

Gogarty, Oliver St John, *Tumbling in the Hay*, Sphere Books, London, 1982

Huddleston, Sisley, *Back to Montparnasse*, Lippincott, Philadelphia, 1931

Jolas, Eugene, *Man from Babel*, Yale University Press, New Haven and London, 1998

Jolas, Maria (ed.), *A James Joyce Yearbook*, Transition Press, Paris, 1949

Léon, Lucie, *James Joyce and Paul L. Léon: The Story of a Friendship*, Gotham Book Mart, NY, 1950

Lewis, Wyndham, *Blasting and Bombardiering*, Calder & Boyars, London, 1967

Lewis, Wyndham, *Rude Assignment*, Black Sparrow Press, Santa Barbara, 1984

Luening, Otto, *Odyssey of an American Composer*, Scribner & Sons, NY, 1980

Mikhail, E. H. (ed.), *James Joyce: Interviews and Recollections*, Macmillan, London, 1990

Nicolson, Harold, *The Harold Nicolson Diaries: 1907–1963*, Weidenfeld & Nicolson, London, 2004

O'Connor, Ulick (ed.), *The Joyce We Knew*, Mercier Press, Cork, 1967

Potts, Willard (ed.), *Portraits of the Artist in Exile*, Wolfhound Press, Dublin, 1979

Power, Arthur, *Conversations with James Joyce*, Millington, Dublin, 1974

Power, Arthur, *From the Old Waterford House*, Ballylough Books, Waterford, 2003

Rodgers, W. R. (ed.), *Irish Literary Portraits*, BBC, London, 1972

Ryan, John (ed.), *A Bash in the Tunnel: James Joyce by the Irish*, Clifton Books, Brighton, 1970

Sheehy, Eugene, *May it Please the Court*, Fallon, Dublin, 1951

Svevo, Italo, *James Joyce* (trans. Stanislaus Joyce), New Directions, 1950, City Lights Books, San Francisco, 1968

Williams, William Carlos, *The Autobiography of William Carlos Williams*, New Directions, 1967

Books about Joyce, his Contemporaries and his World

Bair, Deidre, *Samuel Beckett: A Biography*, Vintage, London, 1990.

Caws, Mary Ann (ed.), *Maria Jolas: Woman of Action*, University of Southern Carolina Press, 2004

Crivelli, Renzo S., *James Joyce: Triestine Itineraries*, MGS Press, Trieste, 2005

Delaney, Frank, *James Joyce's Odyssey: A Guide to the Dublin of Ulysses*, Hodder, London, 1981

Edel, Leon, *Stuff of Sleep and Dreams*, Chatto & Windus, London, 1982

Ellmann, Richard, *The Consciousness of Joyce*, Faber, London, 1977, Oxford University Press, NY, 1981

Ellmann, Richard, *Four Dubliners*, Penguin, London, 1986

Fitch, Noel Riley, *Sylvia Beach and the Lost Generation*, Norton, NY, 1983

Flanner, Janet, *Paris Was Yesterday*, Virago, London, 1973

Foster, Roy, *Modern Ireland 1600–1972*, Penguin, Harmondsworth, 1990

Gunn, Ian, and Clive Hart, *James Joyce's Dublin*, Thames & Hudson, London, 2004

Hartshorn, Peter, *James Joyce and Trieste*, Greenwood Press, Westport, London, CT., 1997

Hutchins, Patricia, *James Joyce's Dublin*, Grey Walls Press, London, 1950

Hutchins, Patricia, *James Joyce's World*, Methuen, London, 1957

Igoe, Vivien, *James Joyce's Dublin Houses and Nora Barnacle's Galway*, Wolfhound Press, Dublin, 1997

Kenner, Hugh, *Dublin's Joyce*, Chatto & Windus, London, 1955

Knowlson, James, *The Life of Samuel Beckett*, Bloomsbury, London, 1996

McAlmon, Robert, and Kay Boyle, *Being Geniuses Together, 1920–1930*, North Point Press, San Francisco, 1984.

McCourt, John, *James Joyce: A Passionate Exile*, Orion, London, 2000

O'Connor, Ulick, *Oliver St John Gogarty*, New English Library, London, 1967

Yeats, W. B., *Autobiographies*, Bracken Books, London, 1995

Notes and Commentaries

Arnold, Bruce, *The Scandal of Ulysses*, Sinclair-Stevenson, London, 1991

Attridge, Derek (ed.), *Cambridge Companion to James Joyce*, Cambridge University Press, 1990

Beckett, S., W. C. Williams et al., *Our Exagmination Round His Factification . . .* New Directions, New York, 1979

Beja, Morris (ed.), *James Joyce's 'Dubliners' and 'A Portrait of the Artist as a Young Man'*, A Case Book, Macmillan, London, 1973

Bulson, Eric, *The Cambridge Introduction to James Joyce*, Cambridge University Press, 2004

Burgess, Anthony, *Re Joyce*, Norton, NY and London, 1968

Campbell, Joseph, and Henry Morton Robinson, *A Skeleton Key to Finnegans Wake*, Faber, London, 1947

Connolly, Thomas E. (ed.), *Joyce's Portrait: Criticisms and Critiques*, Appleton-Century-Crofts, NY, 1962

Deming, Robert H. (ed,), *James Joyce: The Critical Heritage*, vols. I and II, Routledge & Kegan Paul, London 1970; Barnes & Noble, NY, 1970

Ellmann, Richard, Recorded Discussion about James Joyce's Works, Sussex Tapes. [n.d.]

Ellmann, Richard, *Ulysses on the Liffey*, Faber, 1972; Oxford University Press, NY, 1972

Fargnoli, A. N., and Michael P. Gillespie, *James Joyce A to Z*, Oxford University Press, 1995

Ferris, Kathleen, *James Joyce and the Burden of Disease*, University Press of Kentucky, Lexington, 1995

Gibson, Andrew, *Joyce's Revenge: History, Politics and Aesthetics in Ulysses*, Oxford University Press, 2002

Gifford, Don, *Joyce Annotated (Dubliners and Portrait)*, 2nd ed., University of California Press, Berkeley, 1982

Gifford, Don, *Ulysses Annotated*, University of California Press, 1989

Gilbert, Stuart, *James Joyce's 'Ulysses'* (1930, rev. 1952), Penguin, Harmondsworth, 1969

Givens, Seon (ed.), *James Joyce: Two Decades of Criticism*, Vanguard Press, NY, 1946

Kenner, Hugh, *Joyce's Voices*, Faber, London, 1978

Kenner, Hugh, *Ulysses*, Allen & Unwin, London, 1980

Levin, Harry, *James Joyce: A Critical Introduction*, Faber, 1960

Lyons, J. B., *James Joyce and Medicine*, Humanities Press, NY, 1974

McHugh, Roland, *Annotations to Finnegans Wake*, Johns Hopkins University Press, 1982

Magalaner, Marvin, and Richard M. Kain, *Joyce: The Man, the Work, the Reputation*, Calder, 1957; Collier, NY, 1962

Parrinder, Patrick, *James Joyce*, Cambridge University Press, 1984

Startup, Frank, *James Joyce: A Beginner's Guide*, Hodder & Stoughton, 2001

Tindall, William York, *A Reader's Guide to Finnegan Wake*, Thames & Hudson, 1969

Tindall, William York, *A Reader's Guide to James Joyce*, Thames & Hudson, 1959

West, Rebecca, *The Strange Necessity* (1928), Virago, London, 1987

Other Relevant Reading

Antheil, George, *Bad Boy of Music*, Samuel French, Hollywood, 1990

Blast (1), Black Sparrow Press, 1992

Book of Kells, Thames & Hudson, London, 1994

D'Annunzio, Gabriele, *The Triumph of Death*, The Modern Library, NY, 1923

Dujardin, Edouard, *The Bays Are Sere*, Libris, London, 1991

Flaubert, Gustave, *Bouvard and Pécuchet*, Penguin, Harmondsworth, 1976

Foster, R. F., *W. B. Yeats: A Life*, 2 vols., Oxford University Press, 1998/2005

Gatt-Rutter, John, *Italo Svevo: A Double Life*, Clarendon Press, Oxford University Press, 1988

Ibsen, Henrik, *When We Dead Awaken*, Ivan Dee, Chicago, 1992

Lamb, Charles, *Adventures of Ulysses*, Edward Arnold, 1890

Le Fanu, Sheridan, *The House by the Churchyard*, Anthony Blond, London, 1968

Lermontov, Mikhail, *A Hero of Our Time*, Penguin, London, 2003

Mahaffy, J. P., *Conversation*, Penn Publishing Co., Philadelphia, 1908

Meenan, James (ed.), *Centenary History of the Literary and Historical Society of University College, Dublin 1855–1955*, Kerryman, Tralee, 1957

Meyers, Jeffrey, *The Enemy: A Biography of Wyndham Lewis*, Routledge & Kegan Paul, London, 1908

Moody, A. David, *Ezra Pound: Poet*, vol. 1, Oxford University Press, 2007

Noyes, Alfred, *Two Worlds for Memory*, Sheed & Ward, London, 1953

Ovid, *Metamorphoses*, Penguin, London, 2004

Sacher-Masoch, Leopold Von, *Venus in Furs*, Penguin, London, 2000

Stoppard, Tom, *Travesties*, Faber, London, 1975

Svevo, Italo, *A Life*, Penguin Modern Classics, London, 1982

Svevo, Italo, *As a Man Grows Older*, trans. Beryl de Zoete, Putnam, London, 1980

Svevo, Italo, *Confessions of Zeno*, Putnam, London, 1948

Svevo, Livia, *Memoir of Italo Svevo*, Libris, London, 1989

Turnbull, Andrew (ed.), *The Letters of F. Scott Fitzgerald*, Penguin, Harmondsworth, 1968

Wade, Allan (ed.), *The Letters of W. B. Yeats*, Rupert Hart-Davis, London, 1954

Yeats, W. B., *A Vision*, Macmillan, London, Papermac, 1981

Yeats, W. B., *Collected Poems* (1933), Macmillan, London, 1985

Yeats, W. B., *The Countess Cathleen*, Kessinger Publishing [n.d.]

Journals

1. *Genetic Joyce Studies*. electronic Journal for the Study of James Joyce's *Works in Progress*
2. *In Between: Essays and Studies in Literary Criticism*, vol. 12, 2003 (special issue on James Joyce, University of Delhi)
3. *James Joyce Literary Supplement*, University of Miami
4. *James Joyce Broadsheet*, University of Leeds
5. *James Joyce Journal*, James Joyce Research Centre in Association with the National Library of Dublin
6. *James Joyce Quarterly*, University of Tulsa, Oklahoma
7. *Joyce Studies Annual*, Harry Ransom Research Center (HRC), Austin, Texas. There are James Joyce Centres in Dublin, Zurich, Antwerp and Trieste and a James Joyce Society in New York

University collections

There are major Joyce collections at the following:

1. British Library: Harriet Shaw Weaver Collection
2. State University of NY at Buffalo: Lockwood Memorial Library
3. Cornell University: James Joyce Collection
4. Harry Ransom Research Center, Austin, Texas: Stuart Gilbert and Helen Fleischman Papers
5. Harvard University: Houghton Library
6. The James Joyce Centre, Zurich:

Jahnke Bequest, Giedion-Welcker
Papers, Sylvia Beach Letters

7. National Library of Ireland, Dublin:
Paul Léon Collection

8. New York Public Library: John Quinn
Collection

9. University of Southern Illinois:
Croessmann Collection

10. University of Tulsa: Richard Ellmann
Papers

11. Yale University Library: Slocum
Collection

Other university and library holdings are
listed in the James Joyce Calendar, HRC,
Austin, Texas

Index of Poems and Songs

General Index